Readings
in
Managerial
Economics

Readings in Managerial Economics

Edited by
KRISTIAN S. PALDA

Queen's University
Kingston, Ontario

Prentice-Hall, Inc., *Englewood Cliffs, New Jersey*

Library of Congress Cataloging in Publication Data

PALDA, KRISTIAN S   comp.
  Readings in managerial economics.

  1. Industrial management—Mathematical models—Ad-
dresses, essays, lectures. 1. Title.
HD20.4.P35   658.1   72-6298
ISBN 0-13-759951-X

© 1973 by PRENTICE-HALL, INC.
Englewood Cliffs, New Jersey

10 9 8 7 6 5 4 3 2 1

Prentice-Hall International, Inc., *London*
Prentice-Hall of Australia, Pty. Ltd., *Sydney*
Prentice-Hall of Canada, Ltd., *Toronto*
Prentice-Hall of India Private Limited, *New Delhi*
Prentice-Hall of Japan, Inc., *Tokyo*

Printed in the United States of America

Contents

Preface   ix

Part 1
THE GOALS OF THE FIRM

1 The Objective of the Firm   3
James C. Van Horne

2 Managerial Pay and Corporate Performance   5
Wilbur G. Lewellen and Blaine Huntsman

3 The Firm and Its Objectives   15
William J. Baumol

4 The Theory of Multidimensional Utility   16
Analysis in Relation to Multiple-Goal
Business Behavior: A Synthesis
C. E. Ferguson

5 Profits, Learning, and the Convergence of   23
Satisficing to Marginalism
Richard H. Day

v

Part 2
THE PRODUCTION SUBMODEL OF THE FIRM

6 Production Functions and Performance Evaluation   34

Kristian S. Palda

7 The Sources of Measured Productivity Growth: United States Fertilizer Mineral Industries, 1936–1960   43

G. S. Sahota

8 A Study of Production and Factor Shares in the Halibut Fishing Industry   58

Salvatore Comitini and David S. Huang

9 Diminishing Returns and the Cost Function: A Reconsideration   64

Sven Danø

10 The Firm's Cost Function: A Successful Reconstruction?   70

Jack Hirschleifer

11 Multiple Regression Analysis of Cost Behavior   84

George J. Benston

12 Linear Programming and Theory of Production   98

William J. Baumol

13 Internal Economies   108

Alec Nove

Part 3
THE R & D SUBMODEL
OF THE FIRM

14 Research and Development, Production   117
Functions, and Rates of Return

Jora R. Minasian

15 The Determinants of Industrial Research and   122
Development : A Study

Henry G. Grabowski

16 The R&D Factor in International Trade and   132
International Investment of United States
Industries

William Gruber, Dileep Mehta, and Raymond Vernon

Part 4
THE MARKETING SUBMODEL
OF THE FIRM

17 Marginal Cost Pricing of Airport Runway   151
Capacity

Alan Carlin and R. E. Park

18 Marketing Mix Decisions for New Products   160

Philip Kotler

19 A Simultaneous Equation Regression Study of   169
Advertising and Sales of Cigarettes

Frank M. Bass

20 Economic Analysis for Marketing Decisions   180

Kristian S. Palda

Part 5
THE FINANCIAL SUBMODEL
OF THE FIRM

21 A Comparison of Alternative Theories of   188
Corporate Investment Behavior
Dale W. Jorgenson and Calvin D. Siebert

22 Risk Analysis in Capital Investment   209
David B. Hertz

23 A Portfolio Analysis of Conglomerate Diversification   222
Keith V. Smith and John C. Schreiner

24 Investment Decision under Uncertainty: 234
Theory and Practice
James C. T. Mao and John F. Helliwell

25 Some Surrogate Evidence in Support of the   246
Concept of Optimal Financial Structure
Eli Schwartz and J. Richard Aronson

26 Rates of Return on Common Stock   254
Eugene F. Brigham and James L. Pappas

Part 6
THE OVERALL MODEL
OF THE FIRM

27 The Firm Decision Process: An Econometric   271
Investigation
Dennis C. Mueller

28 An Econometric Model of a Japanese   290
Pharmaceutical Company
Hiroki Tsurumi and Yoshi Tsurumi

29 Agfa-Gevaert: Merger or Partnership?   316
The Economist

Preface

The readings chosen for this book are designed to meet the needs of students taking a course in managerial or business economics. They might also prove useful in supplementing a course in the theory of the firm.

Typically, such courses are offered in the senior year of the undergraduate curriculum and at the M.B.A. level. At that stage the student will have already been exposed to microeconomic theory, elementary calculus and least-squares regression. He will also have acquired a working knowledge in such functional fields of management as finance, marketing, and production. Such a background will equip the reader for the selections in this volume; if certain rough stretches are encountered, they are usually not central to the main theme of the selection and can be safely avoided.

Traditionally, managerial economics deals with these broad topics: profits, demand and forecasting, competition (or market structure), cost, pricing, and capital budgeting. All of these topics are covered in this volume. However, there are other possible and useful perspectives on the firm and its problems. The organization of these readings is based on the concept of "partial" and "overall" models of the firm.

The firm's decisions are viewed from the point of view of top management, the executives responsible for the main functional activities of the enterprise: production and cost, research and development, marketing, and finance.

Accordingly, the first five readings are devoted to the subject of the *goals* of the firm as a whole. This topic is not substantially different from that which is often designated "profit" or "profit management" in managerial economics texts. The three last readings, building in part upon the "partial equilibrium" analyses of preceding selections, attempt to present an integrated view of the total enterprise, and thus go beyond the profit topic itself. In a sense they furnish material for the building of the *overall* model of the firm.

The second group of readings (6-13) has been chosen with the aim of presenting various aspects of the production submodel of the firm. Topics discussed include production and cost functions, linear programming, internal and external economies, and other related subjects.

The third group of readings (14-16) addresses itself to R & D decisions. Readings 17-20, the fourth group, take the marketing perspective, which views such important topics as pricing, advertising, and demand estimation.

The financial submodels of the firm, and the capital budgeting and portfolio selection techniques—developed by the financial people and peculiarly suited to overall firm decisions—are sampled in the fifth group (21-26). As already mentioned, the last group (27-29) is chiefly concerned with the overall model of the firm.

For the convenience of the reader, each group of readings is preceded by a brief introduction by the editor pinpointing the highlights of each selection.

The correspondence of this framework for managerial economics with that of the more traditional concepts is explained in the accompanying chart. This table also shows the primary emphasis of each selection and the secondary areas it touches on. Thus Selection 7, an article by Sahota, is chiefly devoted to the estimation of production functions, but it also contains interesting findings with regard to questions of cost, R & D, and market structure. Indeed, whenever possible, the editor has selected readings that deal with more than one subject.

The general tenor of this book is shaped above all by the editor's conviction that managerial economics should be concerned with normative prescriptions and, in equal measure, with the possibility of their operational application. There is thus a heavy weighting toward contributions which stress theory (i.e., build models) and, at the same time, attempt to verify it empirically (i.e., estimate the models' parameters). As a consequence, a certain dose of econometrics is present in many of the selections.

Two subsidiary themes echo through many of the readings: emphasis on multiperiod—as opposed to single-period—optimization and stress on the importance of the multiproduct (or conglomerate) firm.

One deliberate omission is of selections dealing primarily with what might be called "techniques" or "methodology." Thus, with one exception, programming is not discussed; missing also are selections, again with one exception, dealing with decision theory. Despite this omission, in part dictated by the ever-present submarine problem (what to take aboard and what to jettison when space is restricted), the editor hopes that these readings—most of which have been tested in his own classroom discussions—will enhance the reader's insight into one of the most fascinating creations of modern man—the firm.

The editor of this volume wishes to acknowledge gratefully the helpful suggestions he received from the three reviewers who lent a helping hand in the preparation of this reader. They are Professor Edwin S. Mills, Princeton University; Professor Irvin Brossack, Indiana University; and Professor Richard B. Hoffman, University of Missouri—Saint Louis. Where their suggestions were not heeded, the editor assumes his responsibility.

Kristian S. Palda

No.	Author(s)	Topics as Arranged in this Volume — Goals of Firm (Profits)	Production (Production)	Cost (Cost)	R & D	Marketing (Pricing, Advertising)	Finance	Overall	Topics Stressed in Traditional Managerial Economics Texts† — (Demand)	(Market Structure)	(Capital Budgeting)	Topics Stressed in Microeconomic Texts — Resource Allocation
1	Van Horne	X*					✓**	✓				
2	Lewellen & Huntsman	X					✓	✓				
3	Baumol	X		✓		✓		✓		✓		✓
4	Ferguson	X		✓				✓	✓			✓
5	Day	X		✓		✓				✓		✓
6	Palda		X		✓							
7	Sahota		X									
8	Comitini & Huang		X					✓				
9	Danø		✓	X								X
10	Hirshleifer		✓	X			✓	✓				X
11	Benston			X								✓
12	Baumol		X	✓				✓				
13	Nove		✓	✓								
14	Minasian				X				✓			✓
15	Grabowski		✓		X				✓			✓
16	Gruber, Mehta, Vernon				X	X			✓	✓		✓
17	Carlin & Park		✓	✓		X						
18	Kotler					X						
19	Bass					X				✓		
20	Palda						✓	✓			✓	
21	Jorgenson & Siebert						X	✓			✓	✓
22	Hertz						X	✓			✓	✓
23	Smith & Schreiner	✓					X	✓				✓
24	Mao & Helliwell						X				✓	
25	Schwartz & Aronson						X					
26	Brigham & Pappas						✓	✓				
27	Mueller	✓				✓	✓	X				
28	Tsurumi & Tsurumi	✓	✓	✓	✓	✓		X	✓		✓	✓
29	The Economist	✓	✓	✓	✓	✓		X	✓		✓	✓

† Applies also to topics in parentheses in first block of rows.
* X designates the topic given primary emphasis in a reading.
** ✓ designates topics given secondary emphasis in a reading.

Readings
in
Managerial
Economics

part 1

The Goals
of the Firm

Profit maximization is the central assumption in managerial economics.
As one student of this field put it, "profits are the one pervasive objective
running through *all* business situations; other objectives are more a matter
of personal taste or of social conditioning and are variable from firm to firm,
society to society and time to time" (W.W. Haynes, *Managerial Economics*
[Austin, Tex.: Business Publications, Inc., 1969], p. 9). Yet a precise definition of the term *profit maximization by the firm* is by no means widely agreed
upon and depends, in the last analysis, upon ethical assumptions. A clear
and rigorous definition of this term is taken by Van Horne, the author of the
first reading, to be the maximization of the market price of the firm's common
stock over a reasonably long run.

In the second selection, Lewellen and Huntsman build a powerful empirical case for the assumption that management maximizes the market value
of equity, even in large industrial corporations in which ownership is widely
diffused. The evidence presented by Lewellen and Huntsman is the strongest
refutation of the so-called managerial theories of the firm available to date.
However, the topic of what corporate management maximizes is by no means
closed and continues to stimulate further research.

And many economists are dissatisfied with the assumption that profits
are the only goal of a firm. Perhaps the best-known objector is Baumol,
author of the third selection. In this excerpt from one of his books, he argues
cogently that the entrepreneur has, typically, a multiplicity of objectives
rather than a single goal.

Now a theory of the firm—and of its applied branch, managerial economics—does not find it easy, in the construction of its models, to incorporate
more than one goal into the objective function which is to be optimized.
Ferguson, author of the fourth reading, offers an algorithm designed to make
at least a start toward the reconciliation of the multiple—and sometimes
conflicting—objectives.

The fifth selection's author, Day, addresses himself to a slightly different
problem. He shows that an entrepreneur, despite the absence of much crucial information and without a fully defined profit motive, will—provided
he acts as a normal person who prefers rewards and avoids penalties—

succeed in reaching a profit goal *as if* he followed the simple rule of equating marginal revenue with marginal cost. Here, admittedly in the setting of the simplest neoclassical model of the firm, is another reconciliation—this time between the psychological learning model of man and the economic model of man.

1

The Objective of the Firm

JAMES C. VAN HORNE

· · ·

In this book, we assume that the objective of the firm is to maximize its value to its shareholders. Value is represented by the market price of the company's common stock over the long run, which, in turn, is a reflection of the firm's investment, financing, and dividend decisions. By the long run, we mean a period long enough so that we are able to work with an average, or normalized, market price. Management cannot make decisions on the basis of day-to-day fluctuations in market price of the firm's stock. Moreover, it should not make decisions that will raise the market price of the firm's stock over the short run at the expense of market price over the long run. For example, a company might cut its research and development expenditures significantly in order to increase current earnings. In turn, this action may result in an increase in market price per share, particularly if the market is fooled by the increase in earnings. However, the market-price increase is likely to be only a temporary phenomenon. Without sufficient research and development, future profits are likely to suffer, and the result will be a drop in the market price of the firm's stock. The adage "penny wise and pound foolish" is particularly applicable in this case; our perspective, in maximizing shareholder wealth, must extend beyond the immediate future.

From James C. Van Horne, Financial Management and Policy, © *1968. Reprinted by permission of Prentice-Hall, Inc., Englewood Cliffs, New Jersey.*

PROFIT MAXIMIZATION VERSUS WEALTH MAXIMIZATION

Frequently, maximization of profits is regarded as the proper objective of the firm, but it is not as inclusive a goal as that of maximizing shareholder wealth. For one thing, total profits are not as important as earnings per share. A firm could always raise total profits by issuing stock and using the proceeds to invest in Treasury bills. Even maximization of earnings per share, however, is not a fully appropriate objective, partly because it does not specify the timing of expected returns. Is the investment project that will produce a $100,000 return five years from now more valuable than the project that will produce annual returns of $15,000 in each of the next five years? An answer to this question depends upon the time value of money to the firm and to investors at the margin. Few existing stockholders would think favorably of a project that promised its first return in 100 years, no matter how large this return. We must take into account the time pattern of returns in our analysis.

Another shortcoming of the objective of maximizing earnings per share is that it does not consider the risk or uncertainty of the prospective earnings stream. Some investment projects are far more risky than others. As a result, the prospective stream of earnings per share would be more uncertain if these projects were undertaken. In addition, a company will be more or less risky depending upon the amount of debt in relation to equity in its capital structure. This risk is known as financial risk; and it, too, contributes to the uncertainty of the prospective stream of earnings per share. Two companies may have the same expected future earnings per share, but if the earnings stream of one is subject to considerably more uncertainty than the earnings stream of the other, the market price per share of its stock may be less.

Finally, this objective does not allow for the effect of dividend policy on the market price of the stock. If the objective were only to maximize earnings per share, the firm would never pay a dividend. At the very least, it always could improve earnings per share by retaining earnings and investing them in Treasury bills. To the extent that the payment of dividends can affect the value of the stock, the maximization of earnings per share will not be a satisfactory objective by itself.

For the reasons given above, an objective of maximizing earnings per share may not be the same as maximizing market price per share. The market price of a firm's stock represents the focal judgment of all market participants as to what the value is of the particular firm. It takes into account present and prospective future earnings per share, the timing and risk of these earnings, the dividend policy of the firm, and any other factors that bear upon the market price of the stock. The market price serves as a performance index or report card of the firm's progress; it indicates how well management is doing in behalf of its stockholders. Management is under continuous review. If a stockholder is dissatisfied with management's performance, he may sell his stock and invest in another company. This action, if taken by other dissatisfied stockholders, will put downward pressure on market price per share. In this case, the market price of the stock would be an index of stockholder discontent. . . .

2

Managerial Pay and Corporate Performance

WILBUR G. LEWELLEN AND BLAINE HUNTSMAN*

At the core of most economic analyses of industrial behavior is the proposition that the managers of an enterprise guide its activities

From American Economic Review (*September 1970*), *pp. 710–20. Reprinted with permission of authors and publisher.*

* The authors are, respectively, associate professor of industrial management at Purdue University and associate professor of finance at the University of Utah. The research was supported with funds supplied by the National Bureau of Economic Research, the Purdue Research Foundation, and the Ford Foundation's grant for research in business finance to the Sloan School of Management at the Massachusetts

in such a way as to maximize the monetary well-being of its owners. The theory of the firm in its conventional form depends heavily

Institute of Technology. The advice and counsel of Professors Frank Bass, George Horwich, Robert Johnson, and Edgar Pessemier of Purdue, Professor John Lintner of Harvard, and Professor Bruce Baird of Utah are gratefully acknowledged. The computations were performed at the computer centers of Purdue University and the Massachusetts Institute of Technology. Of course, the opinions and conclusions presented are solely the authors'.

on this presumption, and the alleged alloca-tive efficiency of the private enterprise system is founded on its implications. Corporations can, of course, simultaneously pursue a vari-ety of goals, with different top management groups placing differing degrees of impor-tance on a range of alternative objectives. If, however, it should turn out that profit-related goals are consistently subordinated, the relevance of much of our received eco-nomic doctrine would become suspect.

That doctrine notwithstanding, the possi-bility has been raised in recent years that goals other than maximization of profits or share prices may well govern managerial behavior. The dissenting point of view can be traced to the descriptive arguments advanced by Adolph A. Berle and Gardiner C. Means nearly forty years ago. They asserted, in substance, that the rise of the giant corpora-tion was increasingly serving to separate con-trol from ownership. The natural corollary of this contention is that management is not necessarily constrained to act with the own-ers' welfare in mind, but can be expected instead to serve primarily its own economic self-interest. More recently, William J. Baumol (1958, 1962, 1967) has suggested that management can—and, in fact, does—cater to such self-interest by maximizing the total sales revenues of the enterprise, with profit increases being but a secondary issue. Baumol's argument is based at least in part, on the observation that executive salaries appear to be ". . . far more closely correlated with the scale of operations of the firm than with its profitability" (1967, p. 46). How-ever, it is not clear a priori that the economic self-interests of ownership and management *can* be neatly separated. For example, most top executives have substantial stock hold-ings in their own firms and receive a size-able fraction of their total compensation in the form of stock options and other stock-related pay arrangements (see Wilbur G. Lewellen 1968, 1969a).

The intent of the present paper is to ex-amine empirically the question of whether the financial rewards reaped by high level corpo-rate executives are more strongly influenced by company performance as measured by total corporate revenues or—alternatively—as measured by either of two standards of shareholder welfare. The results should provide a basis for drawing at least some tentative conclusions as to the expected nature of managerial behavior in the con-temporary industrial environment.

We are aware that several previous em-pirical studies have been conducted with the same stated objective. Typically, the meth-odology has been to compare the respective degrees of correlation between executive compensation and firm sales on the one hand, and executive compensation and firm profits on the other. Perhaps the most thor-ough of these studies is that by Joseph W. McGuire, John S. Y. Chiu, and Alvar O. Elbing[1] who concluded that sales and com-pensation were more highly correlated than were profits and compensation, and inter-preted those results as supportive of the Baumol hypothesis. The findings presented in the current paper lead to interpretations that run counter to those of McGuire, et al., and are based on tests of a multivariate regres-sion model which is designed to reduce the effects of various statistical and measure-ment biases. Our findings also reflect the use here of more comprehensive indices both of executive remuneration and shareholder welfare than have been characteristic of earlier investigations.

I. THE SAMPLE

The very large firm is obviously the one in which the phenomenon of the separation of ownership from control—and its possible con-sequences in terms of managerial behavior—is likely to be most severe. For that reason, the sample examined consists of 50 firms drawn from the top of the *Fortune* magazine list of the nation's 500 largest industrials. Virtually all the firms involved would be regarded as "blue chips" in the language of the investment community, all enjoy a very wide public distribution of their common

[1] Others include those of Arch Patton. David R. Roberts, and Oliver E. Williamson.

stock, and a broad spectrum of industry categories is represented.

While data on such items as company sales and profits are readily accessible in published financial statements, certain other information which is essential to the proper execution of a study of the sort undertaken here is not so easily obtained. In particular, a truly comprehensive measure of managerial remuneration requires that the worth of *all* the major constituents of the relevant pay packages be recognized, including, in addition to cash salaries and bonuses, the full range of indirect, deferred, and contingent compensation arrangements that executives enjoy. The raw material for an evaluation of these devices for senior management is publicly available only in the proxy statements which corporations must submit in conjunction with their annual shareholders' meetings. Because of variations in the manner in which firms present these data, however, and because of changes in the SEC's reporting rules over the years, it is not always possible to put together an adequate record of top executive rewards for every large company one might care to inspect.[2] As a result, it became necessary to dip down as far as the corporation ranked 94th on *Fortune*'s most recent tabulation[3] in order to assemble a sample of 50 whose executives' earnings histories could be compiled accurately for any length of time. Those 50 firms currently account for approximately one-fourth of the total sales and profits of the entire manufacturing sector. They are listed in the Appendix.

The study examines the cross-sectional relationships between executive compensation and company performance at three-year intervals, beginning with 1942 and ending with 1963. This period was chosen because the requisite figures were available on total executive remuneration from an earlier investigation of the components of managerial

---

[2] A discussion of the methods of compiling the data is contained in Section III.

[3] The 1968 list was the latest one available at the time the analysis here was initiated.

pay by one of the authors (Lewellen 1968). Since similar information would have been exceedingly expensive to duplicate for other periods, as shown in Section III, its existence seemed a compelling argument in favor of exploiting that resource for our present purposes. The entire time span was analyzed in order to detect any inter-temporal evolution in the underlying relationships which might have arisen from phenomena such as continuing corporate growth. The years examined also encompass an era of significant structural change in the economy, especially in the tax environment, and include the pervasive influence of several business cycles and two wars.

II. THE MODEL

The major hypotheses which have been advanced to explain observed levels of senior executive compensation can be summarized in their simplest forms as follows: (i) A firm's top management is rewarded primarily on the basis of its ability to increase the profits of the enterprise; or (ii) The compensation of top executives depends upon the volume of sales generated by the corporation whose affairs they administer. Given the widely accepted proposition that the market value of a firm's equity at any point in time is approximately equal to the discounted worth of the future returns anticipated by actual and potential owners, (i) can be interpreted as the analogue of the share price maximization precept.

Of these hypotheses, (i) conforms with the behavioral assumptions underlying the conventional theory of the firm, while previous empirical findings (McGuire, Chiu, and Elbing, Patton, Roberts) appear to support (ii). Other possible viewpoints include the propositions that executives are rewarded according to *both* profit and sales performance, or, at the opposite extreme, that neither item is relevant. The model developed here is designed to test this range of alternatives.

The Basic Model

Abstracting, for the moment, from potential statistical and measurement problems, and in the absence of theoretical reasons to specify an alternative form of functional relationship, we may begin by postulating that a top executive's compensation is related in linear fashion to both the profits and sales of the firm he manages. The structural form of the relationship can be written:

$$C_{i_t} = a_0 + a_1 \pi_{i_t} + a_2 S_{i_t} + u_{i_t} \qquad (1)$$

where C, π, and S represent executive compensation, corporate profits, and corporate sales, respectively, and u is a random disturbance term. Subscript i denotes the firm and subscript t the period to which the measure applies.

By supplying a basis for observing the magnitude of the cofficients a_1 and a_2 and the levels of statistical significance attaching thereto, the above specification provides a natural vehicle for inferring the relative influence of the two independent variables upon compensation, and thereby testing the alternative hypotheses. The emergence of a positive value for the constant term a_0 would imply, in effect, that executive rewards rise less than in proportion to company sales and/or profits. Thus, it seems probable that a $50 thousand difference in annual profits between two firms in the $100 million profit range would result in a smaller difference in the pay of their respective chief executives than would the same dollar profit difference in the case of two firms whose yearly earnings were in the $100 thousand range. Represented graphically, the compensation vs. profits or compensation vs. sales relationship would therefore be expected to be concave downward for a sample of enterprises differing widely in size, and the linear approximation to any segment of such an underlying relationship would necessarily include a positive intercept value. It follows, then, that a_1 and a_2 must be interpreted in marginal—although constant for the sample range—terms throughout.

Statistical Problems

Unfortunately, direct application of equation (1) to any generalized sample of cross-sectional data can be expected to encounter several possible sources of statistical bias. For one thing, the efficiency of least square estimates depends upon the variances of the disturbance terms being constant. Examination of scatter diagrams of pilot regression runs using equation (1) revealed, as anticipated, that the error terms were *not* constant but were approximately in proportion to the dependent variable. Moreover, and as one might also suspect, those firms relatively large by virtually any scale criterion were also characterized by relatively high sales and profits levels. This scale-associated linkage between the independent variables poses the threat of serious collinearity,[4] with resultant difficulties in estimating the separate influences of those variables. The regression coefficients produced by fitting data to (1) were characterized by inordinately large standard errors, suggesting that the correlation between the independent variables was indeed too high to permit the generation of reliable estimates.

An approach which attacks both these problems is the weighted regression technique.[5] Since scatter diagrams of equation (1) indicated that the error terms (u_{i_t} for all i) tended to vary directly with the dependent

---

[4] The high degrees of correlation between the independent variables in their natural form were indicated by the presence of simple correlation coefficients which, in most cases, exceeded .9. This high degree of observed correlation is consistent with the results of a prior study by Bevars D. Mabry and David L. Siders, which employed correlation analysis to investigate the relationship between profits and sales.

[5] An alternate approach commonly used to ameliorate scale-related problems, given that there are no a priori grounds for specifying a linear vis-à-vis a multiplicative relationship, is to convert the natural values of the variables into logarithms. Results of the tests of the *log* transform of (1) were in fact characterized by somewhat lower simple correlation coefficients between *log* π_{i_t} and *log* S_{i_t}, but the scatter diagrams still suggested the presence of excessive heteroscedasticity. The *log* transform was therefore rejected as a device for testing the hypothesis.

variable, an appropriate weighting procedure is to divide each variable in (1) by any one of several scale-related deflators, provided there are acceptable grounds for expecting that the variances of the deflators bear a proportionate relationship to those of the u_{i_t}. Moreover, by creating ratios in which both numerator and denominator are associated with the firm's size, the weighted regression approach eliminates the basic reason for expecting high degrees of correlation between the variables as a consequence of a common scale factor. Following the Miller and Modigliani precedent, book value of total assets was the weighting factor chosen because the resulting deflated variables have ". . . natural and useful economic interpretations in their own right" (Merton H. Miller and Franco Modigliani 1966, p. 350).[6] Deflating (1) by total book assets, denoted by A, yields the following form:

$$\frac{C_{i_t}}{A_{i_t}} = a_0\left(\frac{1}{A_{i_t}}\right) + a_1\left(\frac{\pi_{i_t}}{A_{i_t}}\right) \qquad (2)$$
$$+ a_2\left(\frac{S_{i_t}}{A_{i_t}}\right) + u_{i_t}^*$$

Since the variances of the deflator selected are hypothesized to be roughly proportional to those of the u_{i_t}, the error terms in the original equation, we would expect the variances of the new error terms $(u_{i_t}^* + u_{i_t}/A_{i_t})$ to be approximately constant over the sample range. Examination of scatter diagrams indicated that the requisite least squares assumption of homoscedasticity was in fact met by (2). As to the collinearity problem tests of the model evinced materially smaller standard errors of the coefficient estimates in addition to producing consistently high t-values in conjunction with tests of significance. Both these phenomena suggest that

the deflated variables are not sufficiently collinear as to interfere with the formation of reliable coefficient estimates.[7]

III. MEASUREMENT

An empirical test of the model necessitates that meaningful measures of the separate variables be obtained. This section defines the measures chosen and discusses the rationale underlying their selction.

Executive Compensation

Previous studies seeking to determine the influence of corporate performance on executive compensation merit some skepticism in the sense that only *partial* indices of compensation, typically, cash salary plus bonus payments alone were employed (McGuire, Chiu, and Elbing, Patton, Roberts). Other forms of remuneration such as pension benefits, deferred pay, qualified profit-sharing plans, and stock options have been ignored entirely. These latter items, however, frequently result in annual after-tax increments to executives' wealth that are of magnitudes many times the concurrent salary and bonus awards.

The proper treatment of deferred and contingent elements represents a task of major proportions. Lewellen's 1968 study embodies the relevant analysis and provides comprehensive measures of total executive earnings within the sample companies. The approach employed in appraising the worth of the noncash components of managerial remuneration was to calculate, for each individual senior executive and for each year in which he appeared in his firm's proxy statements, what might be termed the "current income equivalent" of his various deferred and con-

---

[6] That "natural and useful interpretation" in the present context relates to the fact that equation (2) now implicitly describes a process whereby management is viewed as maximizing company sales or profits per dollar of resources employed, i.e., maximizing subject to the available resource constraint.

[7] It might be noted that the model (2) is now linear homogeneous. Accordingly, consistency in interpretation requires that it be tested with the constant term suppressed. In order to check this specification, we first ran the regression with a constant term added and found it in no case to be significantly different from zero.

tingent pay schemes. This consisted of the amount of additional direct cash income he would have required from his company to be as well rewarded after taxes as he was by all the supplemental compensation arrangements he actually enjoyed. In the case of a pension plan, for example, the procedure was to determine the additional salary or bonus the executive would have needed if he were to be enabled, with those additions, to purchase for himself an individual retirement annuity from an insurance company similar in form and equal in value to the benefits promised him under his employers' retirement plan. Similar calculations were made for other fringe benefits and the aggregate worth of his entire compensation package established. The total remuneration figures used in the present study therefore represent the sum of all such estimated current income equivalents plus salary and bonus.[8]

As a matter of both convenience and efficiency, the compensation of the single highest-paid executive in each firm for each year is taken into account here as the dependent variable measuring the size of the firm's managerial pay package. While it may seem more appropriate that the remuneration of *all* the senior policy-making individuals in a corporation be tested for a relationship to company performance, it happens that the pay of a firm's top man is a suitable surrogate for the pay of his closest subordinates in terms of their relative standing vis-à-vis corresponding officials in other firms.[9]

For comparability with prior empirical work, the model was initially tested using only the salary and bonus receipts of the senior officer of each company as the dependent variable, and then tested again using the more comprehensive total compensation measure instead. The symbol C_{i_t} is employed below to denote the salary plus bonus, and $C_{i_t}^*$ to denote the total remuneration, of the top executive of firm i in year t.

Measurement of Profitability

The model was also subjected to two different sets of tests, each using a separate index of shareholder welfare as an independent variable. The first set incorporated a direct measure of book profits while the second employed an equity market value measure. The book profit choice is perhaps the more conventional, and provides a basis for comparing our findings with those of earlier writers. Nevertheless, some caution must be exercised in interpreting regression results which depend on such a measure.

There are statistical drawbacks associated with the use of reported profit which stem from both its determination and behavior as contrasted with the same features of the other hypothesized performance criterion— namely, corporate sales revenues. While relatively uniform bases exist for recording revenues,[10] profit measurement is conditioned by a range of accounting options which are much less uniform. The areas of depreciation policy and inventory valuation offer prominent examples. Additionally, an examination of the year-to-year changes in reported corporate profits vis-à-vis sales changes indicates that the former measure is much more sensitive to short-run economic influences than is the latter, and consequently is more volatile. Profits therefore are more apt to depart from their "true" or "normal" values when observed in any given year than are sales giving rise to the likelihood that the

---

[8] The relevant computations were made by matching throughout the after-tax present value of the actual compensation arrangement being considered on the one hand, and its contrived current income equivalent on the other. For the details, see Lewellen (1968, ch. 2–6). A similar computational approach can be found in a study by Leonard R. Burgess.

[9] When the sample corporations were ranked in selected years, first according to the total compensation of their top executive alone, then the total for their top three executives combined, and finally the total for their top five executives combined, the Spearman rank correlation coefficients between the three schedules were consistently on the order of .95 and were significant at the .0001 level in all instances (see Lewellen 1968, pp. 227–28).

[10] The definition employed here is the standard one of gross sales less discounts, returns, and allowances.

profits coefficients in regression equations of the form being tested here will tend to be biased downward.[11] But, because in our tests profits proved consistently to be a more powerful explanatory variable than did sales, steps either to adjust the profit measure for accounting disparities among firms or to remove some of the random noise by various normalization procedures were not taken. If they had been, the only likely effect would be to increase further the size and, presumably, the significance of the profits coefficients. Such an effect would in no way alter the interpretation of our results.

Besides these statistical problems, the use of reported profits for any particular year as the index of corporate achievement implies that no conflict exists between short- and long-run maximization strategies by management, i.e., that there is no real trade-off between increasing the current year's net income and increasing the current value of future income. There are, however, a variety of circumstances which could lead to such a conflict. For example, a cutback in expenditures for the proper maintenance of plant and equipment can produce very favorable current profit results, but at the sacrifice of subsequent earnings because of the deterioration of physical assets. Conversely, expensed outlays for research into new product opportunities will reduce immediate reported profits but can provide the foundation for sizeable future earnings. Growth-oriented decisions, depending on the market expectations they generate, may furnish substantive current benefits to shareholders by increasing the market value of their holdings. The recent literature of business finance is, of course, rich in its emphasis on the maximization of share prices as the correct managerial

goal (see David Durand, Myron J. Gordon, Lewellen (1969 b), John Lintner, Modigliani and Miller (1958), Alexander A. Robichek and Stewart C. Myers). It was for this reason that the retests using equity market value (denoted below by V_{i_t}) in place of profits were conducted.

Measurement of Assets

As will be recalled, a measure of total book assets was introduced into the final version of the model (2) as a deflator. The asset measure used, denoted A_{i_t}, is defined net of depreciation for firm i as of the beginning of year t.

Summary of the Variable Definitions

The notation adopted, then, is as follows:

C_{i_t} = Salary plus bonus payments received by the chief executive of firm i during year t;

$C_{i_t}^*$ = Total after-tax compensation of that executive, including the equivalent value of all major deferred and contingent compensation arrangements;

π_{i_t} = Reported total after-tax profits of firm i during year t;

S_{i_t} = Total sales revenues of the firm, net of discounts, returns, and allowances;

V_{i_t} = Total market value of the firm's outstanding common stock as of the beginning of year t;

A_{i_t} = Total book value of the assets of the firm, net of depreciation, at the beginning of year t.

These measures, as formulated from the data gathered from the 50 corporations in the sample, were fitted to the model developed in the preceding section.

IV. THE EMPIRICAL RESULTS

Table 1 shows the results of the initial tests which were conducted using profits and

---

[11] A well-publicized single-equation model which is characterized by two independent variables, one subject to both measurement errors and random fluctuations, is that commonly used to test the relative influence of dividends and retained earnings on share prices. For a detailed discussion of the procedures for dealing with these phenomena in the context of the dividend policy equation, see Irwin Friend and Marshall Puckett.

TABLE 1   Regression Results: Profits, Sales, and Compensation

Year	Regression Equation:$\frac{C_{i_t}}{A_{i_t}} = a_0\left(\frac{1}{A_{i_t}}\right) + a_1\left(\frac{\pi_{i_t}}{A_{i_t}}\right) + a_2\left(\frac{S_{i_t}}{A_{i_t}}\right) + u^*_{i_t}$							Regression Equation:$\frac{C^*_{i_t}}{A_{i_t}} = a_0\left(\frac{1}{A_{i_t}}\right) + a_1\left(\frac{\pi_{i_t}}{A_{i_t}}\right) + a_2\left(\frac{S_{i_t}}{A_{i_t}}\right) + u^*_{i_t}$						
	a_0	t	a_1	t	a_2	t	R^2	a_0	t	a_1	t	a_2	t	R^2
1942	95.3[a]	8.86	5039.5	2.35	−86.6	1.20	.806	40.1[a]	13.99	1928.1	3.37	−28.6	1.49	.912
1945	101.0	6.52	3307.2	1.98	−50.8	.81	.744	41.9	7.52	1610.8	2.68	−27.6	1.21	.798
1948	86.7	8.38	1413.9	2.48	12.6	.30	.833	73.0	9.63	447.7	1.07	6.6	.20	.830
1951	109.9	12.89	1397.0	3.04	− 5.6	.20	.927	68.1	9.58	1202.9	3.14	−14.6	.65	.880
1954	129.3	9.68	1192.5	3.27	−23.1	.97	.910	85.8	4.55	1188.7	2.13	− 8.7	.26	.751
1957	112.9	7.59	963.5	3.89	6.6	.40	.929	146.6	1.96	461.6	.37	30.6	.37	.439
1960	121.3	6.65	660.7	3.12	15.1	.88	.919	130.5	3.40	1181.2	2.65	1.8	.00	.761
1963	155.3	9.24	677.5	3.91	−15.6	1.08	.932	71.8	2.35	875.8	2.77	17.4	.66	.737

[a] Times 10^3. For purposes of the regression runs, executive compensation was measured in actual dollars and all other variables were measured in millions of dollars. The economic interpretation of the profit coefficient (a_1) listed for 1963—to take an example—therefore is as follows: For corporations in the size range encompassed by the sample, every \$1 million differential in reported company profit was, on the average, accompanied by a \$677.50 differential in the annual pre-tax salary and bonus earnings of the firm's chief executive.

TABLE 2   Regression Results: Market Values, Sales, and Compensation

Year	Regression Equation:$\frac{C_{i_t}}{A_{i_t}} = a_0\left(\frac{1}{A_{i_t}}\right) + a_1\left(\frac{V_{i_t}}{A_{i_t}}\right) + a_2\left(\frac{S_{i_t}}{A_{i_t}}\right) + u^*_{i_t}$							Regression Equation:$\frac{C^*_{i_t}}{A_{i_t}} = a_0\left(\frac{1}{A_{i_t}}\right) + a_1\left(\frac{V_{i_t}}{A_{i_t}}\right) + a_2\left(\frac{S_{i_t}}{A_{i_t}}\right) + u^*_{i_t}$						
	a_0	t	a_1	t	a_2	t	R^2	a_0	t	a_1	t	a_2	t	R^2
1942	98.0[a]	9.72	339.2	2.82	−25.3	.48	.815	41.5[a]	15.08	109.9	3.35	− 1.5	.10	.912
1945	98.9	6.63	263.9	2.78	−33.5	.63	.762	41.8	7.61	103.3	2.95	−13.6	.70	.803
1948	86.9	8.75	239.9	3.25	9.0	.24	.846	73.3	9.66	51.9	.92	12.9	.45	.829
1951	111.1	12.81	105.3	2.73	14.1	.58	.925	69.1	9.35	78.1	2.37	6.8	.33	.870
1954	128.6	9.78	101.0	3.55	− 4.3	.22	.913	85.2	4.49	88.6	2.16	13.6	.47	.748
1957	118.8	7.63	39.8	3.13	19.4	1.20	.922	148.7	2.01	26.6	.44	33.5	.44	.440
1960	126.7	6.99	23.5	3.07	17.7	1.05	.919	138.1	3.93	59.7	4.03	− 4.4	.14	.796
1963	160.1	9.68	28.9	4.12	−10.1	.74	.934	78.3	2.72	45.6	3.73	19.1	.81	.766

[a] Times 10^3. Again for these runs, compensation was measured in dollars, and all other variables in millions of dollars. As indicated in connection with Table 1, the economic interpretation of the market value coefficient for, say, 1963 in the left-hand panel would take the following form: For companies in the relevant size range, a differential of \$1 million in the firm's total equity market value was accompanied by a \$28.90 differential in the annual pre-tax salary plus bonus enjoyed by its top executive.

sales as the measures of corporate performance. Table 2 displays the results of the retests in which equity market value was substituted for profits. Both tables are divided into two panels. The left-hand panel records the findings when salary plus bonus payments alone are adopted as the measure of chief executive compensation, while the right-hand side indicates the results when total executive pay is the dependent variable.

Profits, Sales, and Compensation

The evidence in Table 1 provides strong support for the hypothesis that top management's remuneration is heavily dependent upon the generation of profits. In particular, the signs of the coefficients of the profit measure are positive for each cross-section regardless of the compensation measure employed. Moreover, the profit variable proves highly significant for all runs in which the dependent variable consists of executive salary plus bonus payments, and for six of the eight years in the case of total compensation as the dependent variable. By contrast, the sales measure is in no instance statistically significant, and the sales coefficients are approximately equally divided among years with respect to sign.

In view of the previously cited findings of earlier studies (see McGuire, Chiu, and Elbing, Roberts) in which the compensation measure adopted was essentially the same as our C_{i_t} (top executive salary plus bonus), we were more than mildly surprised at the apparent strong influence of π_{i_t} on C_{i_t} here, as well as at the accompanying lack of any statistically significant relationship between C_{i_t} and S_{i_t} (the left-hand panel of Table 1).[12] Those earlier studies had led us to anticipate an initially weak relationship between profits and remuneration—or perhaps none at all—and, in addition, to expect that corporate sales would show up as the variable more strongly influencing managerial rewards. In other words, we were prepared to find that our first attempts would at best provide a basis for comparing the results of subsequent runs using more highly developed measures of the relevant variables, and that any major insights would stem from the introduction of such improved measures.

It is not likely that differences in either the sample bases tested or the time periods examined can account for the substantive differences between the findings presented here and those of Roberts and of McGuire, Chiu, and Elbing. All three samples were drawn from the nation's largest industrial firms, and the time span covered in the current study encompasses the years tested in both of the previous investigations. A more plausible explanation lies in the fact that the tests here were conducted with the framework

of a more completely developed multivariate model designed to cope with the serious statistical problems discussed in Section II.

A second unexpected feature of the test results was the lack of improvement in fit upon substitution of total executive compensation for salary plus bonus as the dependent variable (right-hand panel of Table 1). Rather, both the levels of statistical significance associated with profits and the coefficients of multiple correlation *diminished* slightly for most years when C_{i_t} was replaced by $C_{i_t}^*$. There are at least two possible explanations for this phenomenon: (i) The performance of the model using the partial compensation measure, C_{i_t}, was substantially better than anticipated, leaving relatively little room for improvement; (ii) A sizeable proportion of $C_{i_t}^*$, especially in the later years tested, is attributable to compensation arrangements whose values depend importantly on short-term fluctuations in employer-company share prices—stock options, for example. Because these short-term fluctuations reflect a host of random influences, the total compensation figures embody a considerable "noise" component.[13]

The general pattern of changes in both sets of results over time highlights an additional point. Looking again at the left-hand panel of Table 1, it can be seen that the *size* of the profit coefficients shows a marked year-to-year decrease for seven of the eight periods tested (a_1 shows a very slight increase between 1960 and 1963). Similarly, in the right-hand panel, excluding the only two runs for which the profit variable is not statistically significant (1948 and 1957), a corresponding secular decline is evident. Since the com-

---

[12] We were also surprised—especially in the light of the scaled nature of our model—at the rather high degree of explanatory power it displayed. The coefficients of multiple correlation exceeded .9 for the five most recent years tested, and were nowhere lower than .737.

[13] In the early years shown, the bulk of senior executive compensation consisted of salary and bonus payments. Consequently, for these early years the results of the tests employing $C_{i_t}^*$ do not differ materially from those in which C_{i_t} is the dependent variable. However, as the disparity between the partial and total compensation measures widens over time, i.e., as rewards other than salary and bonus become progressively more important in the total pay package, the regression results also diverge. For a discussion of the indicated shift in emphasis within the managerial compensation package, see Lewellen (1968).

panies in the sample have grown over time, the simultaneously decreasing size of the profit coefficients supports our earlier expectation that the compensation vs. profits relationship is concave downward. The increasing values of a_0 displayed in the Table reflect the same phenomenon.

To summarize: the results shown in Table 1 indicate that equations utilizing salary plus bonus payments alone as a measure of executive remuneration yield slightly better regression fits than do those employing total compensation. But regardless of which compensation measure is adopted, reported company profits appear to have a strong and persistent influence on executive rewards, whereas sales seem to have little, if any, such impact.

Market Values, Sales, and Compensation

Because of the possible conceptual and measurement difficulties that are associated with annual book profit as a direct index of shareholder welfare, the model was retested using the alternative measure discussed in Section III, the total market value of the firm's outstanding common stock. This measure was chosen because it presumably incorporates the investing public's evaluation of future as well as current returns to owners, and also avoids the potential statistical problems that arise from differences in accounting procedures among firms.

The results of the retests are set forth in Table 2 and parallel those of the initial tests in virtually all relevant respects, with market value now appearing to be a major factor in the determination of compensation levels. Specifically, the coefficients of the market value variable have positive signs for all cross-sections no matter which measure of compensation serves as the dependent variable. In addition, the market value measure proves highly significant for all eight years when salary plus bonus is the dependent variable, and for six of the eight years when the performance measures are regressed

against total compensation. Again, the sales variable is statistically insignificant in all cases and the sales coefficients vary in sign.

The total explanatory power of the equations containing equity market value as a control variable roughly matched that of the corresponding equations in which book profit was employed. The historical pattern of the retest results is also similar to that of the initial tests in that the secularly declining size of the market value coefficients and the secularly increasing a_0 values suggest downward concavity in the underlying relationship. Thus, the substitution of equity market value for profits in the equations has no material impact on either the nature or the interpretation of the findings.

V. SUMMARY AND CONCLUSIONS

The question of whether a corporation's profitability or its sales revenue has the stronger influence on the rewards of its senior officers has been examined here by means of a multivariate analysis. The underlying issue is that of the personal payoff to the professional manager for pursuing operating objectives that enhance the monetary well-being of shareholders. Because the results of the study persistently indicate that both reported profits and equity market values are substantially more important in the determination of executive compensation than are sales—indeed, sales seem to be quite irrelevant—the clear inference is that there is a greater incentive for management to shape its decision rules in a manner consonant with shareholder interests than to seek the alternative goal of revenue maximization. The evidence presented therefore can be interpreted as support for the notion that a highly industrialized economy characterized by a diverse set of suppliers of capital, sizeable aggregations of productive resources, and a professional managerial class can in large measure still be analyzed by models which are based on the assumption of profit-seeking behavior.

APPENDIX

Companies in the Sample

Allied Chemical	International
American Can	Harvester
American Cyanamid	International Paper
American Metal	IT&T
Climax	Jones and Laughlin
American Tobacco	Steel
Anaconda	Lockheed Aircraft
Bendix	National Dairy
Bethlehem Steel	Products
Boeing	North American
Borden	Aviation
Caterpillar Tractor	Phillips Petroleum
Cities Service	Procter & Gamble
Continental Can	RCA
Continental Oil	Republic Steel
Douglas Aircraft	Reynolds Tobacco
Dow Chemical	Shell Oil
DuPont	Sinclair Oil
Eastman Kodak	Standard Oil
Firestone Tire	(Indiana)
General Electric	Swift
General Foods	Texaco
General Motors	Tidewater Oil
General Tire	United Aircraft
B.F. Goodrich	U.S. Rubber
Goodyear Tire	U.S. Steel
Gulf Oil	Westinghouse
Inland Steel	Electric
IBM	

REFERENCES

W. J. BAUMOL, "On the Theory of Oligopoly," *Economica*, Aug. 1958, *25*, 187–98.
——, "On the Theory of Expansion of the Firm," *Amer. Econ. Rev.*, Dec. 1962, *52*, 1078–87.
——, *Business Behavior, Value, and Growth*, rev. ed., New York 1967.

A. A. BERLE AND G. C. MEANS, *The Modern Corporation and Private Property*, New York 1934.
L. R. BURGESS, *Top Executive Pay Package*, New York 1963.
D. DURAND, "Costs of Debt and Equity Funds for Business: Trends and Problems of Measurement," *Conference on Research in Business Finance*, New York 1952, 215–47.
I. FRIEND and M. PUCKETT, "Dividends and Stock Prices," *Amer. Econ. Rev.*, Sept. 1964, *54*, 656–82.
M. J. GORDON, *The Investment, Financing, and Valuation of the Corporation*, Homewood, Ill. 1962.
W. G. LEWELLEN, *Executive Compensation in Large Industrial Corporations*, New York 1968.
——, 1969a, *The Cost of Capital*, Belmont, Calif. 1969.
——, 1969b, "Management and Ownership in the Large Firm," *J. Finance*, May 1969, *24*, 299–322.
J. LINTNER, "The Valuation of Risk Assets and the Selection of Risky Investments in Stock Portfolios and Capital Budgets," *Rev. Econ. Statist.*, Feb. 1965, *47*, 13–37.
B. D. MABRY AND D. L. SIDERS, "An Empirical Test of the Sales Maximization Hypothesis," *Southern Econ. J.*, Jan. 1967, *33*, 367–77.
J. W. McGUIRE, J. S. Y. CHIU, and A. O. ELBING, "Executive Incomes, Sales, and Profits," *Amer. Econ. Rev.*, Sept. 1962, *52*, 753–61.
M. H. MILLER AND F. MODIGLIANI, "Some Estimates of the Cost of Capital to the Electric Utility Industry," *Amer. Econ. Rev.*, June 1966, *56*, 333–91.
F. MODIGLIANI and M. H. MILLER, "The Cost of Capital, Corporation Finance, and the Theory of Investment," *Amer. Econ. Rev.*, June 1958, *48*, 261–97.
A. PATTON, *Men, Money, and Motivation*, New York 1961.
D. R. ROBERTS, *Executive Compensation*, Glencoe, Ill., 1959.
A. A. ROBICHEK and S. C. MYERS, *Optimal Financing Decisions*, Englewood Cliffs, N. J. 1965.
O. E. WILLIAMSON, *The Economics of Discretionary Behavior*, Englewood Cliffs, N. J. 1964.
Fortune, "The Fortune Directory of the 500 Largest U.S. Industrial Corporations," June 1968, *77*, 186–204.

3

The Firm and Its Objectives

WILLIAM J. BAUMOL

We have now discussed the data which the firm needs for its decision-making—the demand for its products and the cost of supplying them. But, even with this information, in order to determine what decisions are optimal it is still necessary to find out the businessman's aims. The decision which best serves one set of goals will not usually be appropriate for some other set of aims.

ALTERNATIVE OBJECTIVES OF THE FIRM

There is no simple method for determining the goals of the firm (or of its executives). One thing, however, is clear. Very often the last person to ask about any individual's motivation is the person himself (as the psychoanalysts have so clearly shown). In fact, it is common experience when interviewing executives to find that they will agree to every plausible goal about which they are asked. They say they want to maximize sales and also to maximize profits; that they wish, in the bargain, to minimize costs; and so on. Unfortunately, it is normally impossible to serve all of such a multiplicity of goals at once.

For example, suppose an advertising outlay of half a million dollars minimizes unit costs, an outlay of 1.2 million maximizes total profits, whereas an outlay of 1.8 million maximizes the firm's sales volume. We cannot have all three decisions at once. The firm must settle on one of the three objectives or some compromise among them.

From William J. Baumol, Economic Theory and Operations Analysis, *Second Edition*, © *1965*, pp. 255–97. *Reprinted by permission of Prentice-Hall, Inc., Englewood Cliffs, New Jersey.*

Of course, the businessman is not the only one who suffers from the desire to pursue a number of incompatible objectives. It is all too easy to try to embrace at one time all of the attractive-sounding goals one can muster and difficult to reject any one of them. Even the most learned have suffered from this difficulty. It is precisely on these grounds that one great economist was led to remark that the much-discussed objective of the greatest good for the greatest number contains one "greatest" too many.

It is most frequently assumed in economic analysis that the firm is trying to maximize its total profits. However, there is no reason to believe that all businessmen pursue the same objectives. For example, a small firm which is run by its owner may seek to maximize the proprietor's free time subject to the constraint that his earnings exceed some minimum level, and, indeed, there have been cases of overworked businessmen who, on medical advice, have turned down profitable business opportunities.

It has also been suggested, on the basis of some observation, that firms often seek to maximize the money value of their sales (their total revenue) subject to a constraint that their profits do not fall short of some minimum level which is just on the borderline of acceptability. That is, so long as profits are at a satisfactory level, management will devote the bulk of its energy and resources to the expansion of sales. Such a goal may, perhaps, be explained by the businessman's desire to maintain his competitive position, which is partly dependent on the sheer size of his enterprise, or it may be a matter of the interests of management (as distinguished from shareholders), since management's salaries may be related more closely to the size of the firm's operations than to its profits, or it may simply be a matter of prestige.

In any event, though they may help him to formulate his own aims and sometimes be able to show him that more ambitious goals are possible and relevant, it is not the job of the operations researcher or the economist to tell the businessman what his goals should be. Management's aims must be taken to be whatever they are, and the job of the analyst is to find the conclusions which follow from these objectives—that is, to describe what businessmen do to achieve these goals, and perhaps to prescribe methods for pursuing them more efficiently.

The major point, both in economic analysis and in operations-research investigation of business problems, is that the nature of the firm's objectives cannot be assumed in advance. It is important to determine the nature of the firm's objectives before proceeding to the formal model-building and the computations based on it. As is obviously to be expected, many of the conclusions of the analysis will vary with the choice of objective function. However, as some of the later discussion in this chapter will show, a change in objectives can, sometimes surprisingly, leave some significant relationships invariant. Where this is true, it is very convenient to find it out in advance before embarking on the investigation of a specific problem. For if there are some problems for which the optimum decision will be the same, no matter which of a number of objectives the firm happens to adopt, it is legitimate to avoid altogether the difficult job of determining company goals before undertaking an analysis. . . .

4

The Theory of Multidimensional Utility Analysis in Relation to Multiple-Goal Business Behavior: A Synthesis*

C. E. FERGUSON

I. INTRODUCTION

The theory of multidimensional vector ordering, or what is now more generally called lexicographic ordering, has received some attention in economic literature, especially in extensions of the von Neumann-Morgenstern theory of cardinal utility analysis.[1] In the utility context, "multidimensional" or "lexicographic" ordering has the following meaning. Consider two alternatives, which may be bundles of commodities, combinations of

From Southern Economic Journal (*October 1965*), *pp. 169–75. Reprinted with permission of author and publisher.*

* [C. E. Ferguson taught at Duke University.] The work embodied in this paper was supported by an Auxiliary Research Award granted by the Social Science Research Council.

[1] See, for example, Nicholas Georgescu-Roegen, "Choice, Expectations, and Measurability," *Quarterly Journal of Economics*, LXVIII (1954), pp. 503–34; C. E. Ferguson, "An Essay on Cardinal Utility," *Southern Economic Journal*, XXV (1958), pp. 11–23; and John S. Chipman, "The Foundations of Utility," *Econometrica*, XXVIII (1960), pp. 193–224.

lottery tickets, business objectives, etc.: x^0 = $(x_1^0, x_2^0, \ldots, x_n^0)$ and x^1 = $(x_1^1, x_2^1, \ldots, x_n^1)$. Let u be a preference index function. A regular ordering ranks $u(x^0) > u(x^1)$ if, and only if, $x_i^0 \geqq x_i^1$ for all i and the strict inequality holds for at least one component.

In a lexicographic ordering a hierarchy of wants is recognized; the components of the vector x are not regarded as equally important. For convenience, let the elements of each vector be numbered so that x_1 is "more important" than x_2, x_2 is "more important" than x_3, etc. Then $u(x^0) > u(x^1)$ if $x_1^0 > x_1^1$, irrespective of the relationships between x_i^0 and x_i^1 ($i = 2, 3, \ldots, n$). If $x_1^0 = x_1^1$, comparison is based upon the second component. Thus $u(x^0) > u(x^1)$ if $x_1^0 = x_1^1$ and $x_2^0 > x_2^1$, etc. Proceeding in this manner, vector elements associated with variables lower in the hierarchy of wants are considered only after the higher order wants are satisfied.[2]

The point of immediate interest is the applicability of multidimensional utility theory to a certain class of microeconomic problems. In the past few years, multiple-goal or "satisficing" models of business behavior have become very popular.[3] But these models are relatively so new that unifying analytical techniques have not been widely developed. The purpose of this paper is to extend the works of Encarnacion and myself to show that multidimensional utility analysis provides a unifying analytical technique

and that it also provides a simple and convenient expository device.[4]

II. A DIGRESSION ON HISTORY

Since their inception, profit-maximizing models of business behavior have certainly not been without their critics. But for the most part the critics were merely critical, failing to propose substantive alternatives for theoretical use. It is only within fairly recent years that specific alternative hypotheses have been advanced. Among the first of these was the famous Hall and Hitch "average-cost pricing" thesis, together with its subsequent echoes in the writings of Harrod, Edwards, Rothchild, etc.[5] The average-cost pricing thesis is very questionable on theoretical grounds,[6] and it is devoid of empirical content. Consequently, this particular alternative attracted only passing notice.

A second approach not directly involving simple profit maximization was suggested by Scitovsky.[7] In particular, he showed that if an entrepreneur attempts to maximize satisfaction, he will expend the same amount of "effort" as if he were attempting to maximize profit *only* in the special case in which the marginal rate of substitution between entrepreneurial activity and money income

[2] For a more thorough discussion, see Melvin Hausner, "Multidimensional Utilities," and R. M. Thrall, "Applications of Multidimensional Utility Theory," both in R. M. Thrall, Clyde Coombs, and R. Davis, eds., *Decision Processes* (New York: John Wiley, 1954), pp. 167–80 and pp. 181–86 respectively. Also see Jose Encarnacion, Jr., "A Note on Lexicographical Preferences," *Econometrica*, XXXII (1964), pp. 215–17.

[3] In addition to the citations in Section II, see Dale K. Osborne, "The Role of Entry in Oligopoly Theory," *Journal of Political Economy*, LXXII (1964), pp. 396–402; *idem.*, "On the Goals of the Firm," *Quarterly Journal of Economics*, LXXVIII (1964), pp. 592–603; and C. E. Ferguson, *A Macroeconomic Theory of Workable Competition* (Durham, N.C.: Duke University Press, 1964).

[4] Jose Encarnacion, Jr., "Constraints and the Firm's Utility Function," *Review of Economic Studies*, XXXI (1964), pp. 113–19; and C. E. Ferguson, "An Essay on Cardinal Utility," *loc. cit.*

[5] R. L. Hall and C. J. Hitch, "Price Theory and Business Behavior," *Oxford Economic Papers*, May 1939, pp. 12–45; R. F. Harrod, "Theory of Imperfect Competition Revised," in *Economic Essays* (New York: Harcourt, Brace, 1952), pp. 139–87; H. R. Edwards, "Price Formation in Manufacturing Industry and Excess Capacity," *Oxford Economic Papers*, N. S. VII (1955), pp. 94–118, K. W. Rothchild, "Price Theory and Oligopoly," *Economic Journal*, LVII (1947), pp. 299–320.

[6] See J. R. Hicks, "The Process of Imperfect Competition," *Oxford Economic Papers*, N. S. VI (1954), pp. 41–54; and C. E. Ferguson, "Static Models of Average-Cost Pricing," *Southern Economic Journal*, XXIII (1957), pp. 272–84.

[7] Tibor de Scitovsky, "A Note on Profit Maximization and Its Implications," *Review of Economic Studies*, II (1943), pp. 57–60.

is independent of the level of money income. Somewhat later I proposed a utility model in which an entrepreneur's level of satisfaction is a function of profit and the deterrence of entry.[8] In both cases utility functions were employed in the analysis of business behavior; but in neither case was multidimensional utility analysis required.

It would seem that the first constrained, multiple-goal model of business behavior was advanced by Reder, who proposed to "... maximize the present value of a firm's net worth subject to the condition that he [the current entrepreneur] retains control of the firm."[9] Reder was quickly followed by Cooper, who suggested that corporate control is a paramount consideration and, indeed, that a model of business behavior must necessarily encompass liquidity and corporate control, as well as profit.[10]

Subsequent to the pioneering models of Reder and Cooper, many writers have proposed constrained, multiple-goal theories of business behavior. Only a few of these can be noted here, and they are mentioned without regard to chronological order. The term "satisficing behavior" was presumably introduced by Simon to describe models in which the entrepreneur is assumed to strive for "satisfactory," but not necessarily maximum, levels of many variables.[11] Simon himself, however, was not as much interested in the

models *per se* as in using the assumption of satisficing behavior to explain the statistical equilibria of adaptive organisms rather than the statical equilibria of profit-maximizing mechanisms.

Lintner, Meyer and Kuh, and Carter and Williams all constructed models of investment behavior which essentially involve a dividend pay-out constraint.[12] Kaplan, Dirlam, and Lanzillotti suggested that business pricing policies are based upon a number of different objectives and that "... the pricing policies are in almost every case equivalent to a company policy that represents an order of priorities and choice from among competing objectives rather than policies tested by any simple concept to profit maximization."[13]

Finally, one of the most noted proponents of constrained, multiple-goal models is William Baumol. In a static situation, Baumol suggests that many firms set their price and output policies so as to maximize sales (total revenue) provided a "satisfactory" level of profit is attained.[14] In a dynamic context, according to Baumol, the firm's objective is to maximize its rate of growth of sales, subject to maintaining a "satisfactory" rate of profit and a "satisfactory" dividend policy.[15] Both of Baumol's models are used

[8] "Static Models of Average-Cost Pricing," *loc. cit.*, pp. 275–80.

[9] M. W. Reder, "A Reconsideration of the Marginal Productivity Theory," *Journal of Political Economy*, LV (1947), pp. 450–58, citation from p. 455.

[10] W. W. Cooper, "The Theory of the Firm: Some Suggestions for Revision," *American Economic Review*, XXXIX (1949), pp. 1204–22.

[11] H. A. Simon, "Theories of Decision-Making in Economics and Behavioral Science," *American Economic Review*, XLIX (1959), pp. 253–83; H. A. Simon and C. P. Bonini, "The Size Distribution of Business Firms," *American Economic Review*, XLVIII (1958), pp. 607–17. For related studies, see Irma G. Adelman, "A Stochastic Analysis of the Size Distribution of Firms," *Journal of the American Statistical Association*, LIII (1958), pp. 893–904; Lee E. Preston and Earl J. Bell, "The Statistical Analysis of Industry Structure: An Application to Food Industries," *Journal of the American Statistical Association*, LVI (1961), pp. 925–32; and P. E. Hart and S. J. Prais, "The Analysis of Business Concentration: A Statistical

Approach," *Journal of the Royal Statistical Society*, Series A, CXIX (1956), pp. 150–91.

[12] J. Lintner, "Distributions of Incomes of Corporations among Dividends, Retained Earnings, and Taxes," *American Economic Review*, XLVI (1956), pp. 97–113; John R. Meyer and Edwin Kuh, *The Investment Decision* (Cambridge, Mass.: Harvard University Press, 1957); and C. F. Carter and B. R. Williams, *Investment in Innovation* (London: Oxford University Press, 1958).

[13] A. D. H. Kaplan, Joel Dirlam, and Robert Lanzillotti, *Pricing in Big Business* (Washington, D. C.: The Brookings Institution, 1958); and Robert F. Lanzillotti, "Pricing Objectives in Large Companies," *American Economic Review*, XLVIII (1958), pp. 921–40, citation from p. 939 of the latter.

[14] William J. Baumol, "Price Behavior, Stability, and Growth," in *The Relationship of Prices to Economic Stability and Growth: Compendium of Papers Submitted by Panelists* (Washington, D. C.: U. S. Government Printing Office, 1957), pp. 49–59; and *Business Behavior, Value and Growth* (New York: Macmillan, 1959).

[15] William J. Baumol, "On the Theory of Expansion of the Firm," *American Economic Review*, LII (1962), pp. 1078–87.

in the next section to establish the link between constrained, multiple-goal business behavior and the theory of multidimensional utility analysis.

III. MULTIPLE GOALS AND MULTIDIMENSIONAL UTILITY ANALYSIS

A. Establishing the Relationship

Let us begin by considering Baumol's static model, in which it is assumed that an entrepreneur attempts to maximize sales subject to maintaining a satisfactory level of profit. This model actually has two possible outcomes. First, if earned or expected profit is equal to or less than the satisfactory level, the entrepreneur disregards the sales goal and behaves as though he were purely a profit maximizer. Second, if the satisfactory level of profit is achieved, the price-output policy is determined so as to maximize sales revenue. In the terminology of multidimensional utility analysis, profit is the dominant component and sales the subordinate one.

Denote profit by x_1 and sales revenue by x_2. Thus any situation is represented by the vector $x = (x_1, x_2)$. Suppose the satisfactory level of profit is $x_1{}^*$.[16] According to the description of the model, further profit does not enhance the utility or satisfaction of the entrepreneur. In other words, if $u(x)$ is the utility function,

$$\left.\frac{\partial u}{\partial x_1}\right]_{x_1 > x_1{}^*} = 0.$$

Thus the optimum vector x^* is found by selecting the price-output policy that maximizes x_2 (sales) subject to $x_1 \geq x_1{}^*$. In particular, let us compare two situations: $x^0 = (x_1^0, x_2^0)$ and $x^1 = (x_1^1, x_2^1)$. The former is preferred to the latter if, and only if, $x_1^i \geq x_1{}^*$ for $i = 0, 1$ and $x_2^0 > x_2^1$. If this problem is not feasible, i.e., $x_1^i < x_1{}^*$ for $i = 0, 1$, the

optimum vector x^* is the one whose first component is greater $(x_1^i > x_1^j$ for all $j \neq i)$.

This simple two-variable model can easily be generalized. Suppose there are m goals $x_1, x_2, \ldots, x_m$ arranged in order of descending importance. Further, let each goal be defined so that

$$\left.\frac{\partial u}{\partial x_i}\right]_{x_i \leq x_i{}^*} > 0 \text{ and } \left.\frac{\partial u}{\partial x_i}\right]_{x_i > x_i{}^*} = 0.[17]$$

Every possible situation is described by a vector $x = (x_1, x_2, \ldots, x_m)$; and the optimal vector x^* is found by selecting the set of policies which solves the following constrained maximization problem: maximize x_m subject to $x_i \geq x_i^*$ for $i = 1, 2, \ldots, m - 1$. If this problem is not feasible the least important goal (x_m) is dropped from consideration. The new problem accordingly becomes: maximize x_{m-1} subject to $x_i \geq x_i^*$ for $i = 1, 2, \ldots, m - 2$. One thus works in sequence until a feasible problem is determined, all lower-ordered goals being discarded in route. If goal $k(<m)$ is the least important objective for which a feasible problem exists, the vector x^0 is the optimal vector x^* if, and only if, $x_i^0 \geq x_i^*$ for $i = 1, 2, \ldots, k - 1$ and $x_k^0 > x_k^j$ for all $j \neq 0$.

To recapitulate: each possible situation is represented by a vector $x = (x_1, x_2, \ldots, x_m)$. The set of alternatives is $X = \{x\}$; and the task of the entrepreneur is to choose x in X according to the rules of vector ordering. If goal $k < m$ is the least important goal for which a feasible solution exists, the entrepreneur's attention is restricted to the subset

$$\bar{X} = \{\bar{x} \mid x_i \geq x_i^* \text{ for}$$
$$i = 1, 2, \cdots, k - 1\} \subset X,$$

where $\bar{x}$ is a vector such as

$$\bar{x} = (x_1^*, x_2^*, \ldots, x_{k-1}^*, x_k;$$
$$x_k + 1, \ldots, x_m).$$

---

[16] The actual task of determining the satisfactory level is quite complicated, if not impossible. For a critique, see Osborne, *op. cit.* [Footnote 3].

[17] That is, let each goal be defined *positively* in the sense that an increase in the value of the variable increases utility up to the "satisficing" or "saturation" point. Thus if the *j-th* goal is "prevent entry," a suitable measure for x_j might be the reciprocal of the number of entrants.

In this case, as in the former more general situation, the entrepreneur's problem is to select a set of policies leading to the optimal $\bar{x}$ in $\bar{X}$.[18]

B. Graphical Approaches to Multiple-Goal Behavior

Two different graphical devices have been developed to illustrate constrained, multiple-goal models of business behavior. The first of these was presented in my 1958 essay, the second more recently by Encarnacion.[19] Each of these graphical techniques is now explained by means of suggestive problems.

First, let us use Baumol's static, constrained sales-maximization model to explain the graphical device I suggested. Using notation already introduced, any particular situation is represented by the vector $x = (x_1, x_2)$, where x_1 represents profits and is the dominant component. At the outset it is convenient to normalize the vector components so that $0 \leq x_i \leq 1$. To that end, set the "satisfactory" level of profit $x_1^* = 1$ and define $x_1 = 1$ for any $x_1 \geq x_1^*$. Thus if $x_1 < x_1^*, x_1 < 1$. Actually no difficulty is encountered if there is negative profit; however, it is easier to restrict our analysis to cases in which $x_1 \geq 0$. As a consequence, x_1 is restricted to the unit interval.

Next, let p represent market price and $q = f(p)$ quantity sold. Accordingly, $x_2 = pq = pf(p)$. Solving $f(p) + pf'(p) = 0$ for the sales-maximizing price p^* and substituting in the demand function to obtain $q^* = f(p^*)$, one can determine the maximum attainable sales x_2^*. Define $x_2^* = 1$; thus, since sales cannot be negative, $0 \leq x_2 \leq 1$.

In Figure 1 profit (x_1) is plotted on the abscissa and sales (x_2) on the ordinate. Every alternative situation can be represented by a point $x^i = (x_1^i, x_2^i)$ on the graph. The point

[18] For a more extended discussion of the method of determining the optimal vector in a multidimensional vector ordering, see C. E. Ferguson, *A Macroeconomic Theory of Workable Competition*, pp. 83–87.

[19] Ferguson, "An Essay on Cardinal Utility," *loc. cit.*, [Footnote 1] pp. 19–21; Encarnacion, "Constraints and the Firm's Utility Function," *loc. cit.*, [Fn. 4] pp. 116–18.

FIG. 1

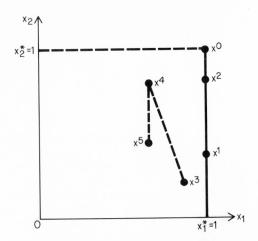

$x^0 = (1, 1)$ would certainly be optimal if it were feasible; however, the likelihood of its being a feasible alternative is negligible. In the event x^0 does not exist, one first determines whether there are points on the line $x_1^* x^0$. Suppose there are two such situations, x^1 and x^2. In this case, x^2 is the optimal feasible solution because $x_1^2 = x_1^1 = x_1^*$ and $x_2^2 > x_2^1$.

In general, however, there is no reason to suppose that positions satisfying the profit constraint exist. To this end, assume there are no situations which lead to a point on the line $x_1^* x^0$. This is equivalent to saying that the problem "maximize x_2 subject to $x_1 \geq x_1^*$" is not feasible. In this case, the subordinate component is usually ignored; the entrepreneur normally behaves as though he were purely a profit maximizer. Other things equal, consequently, he selects the point lying closest to the line $x_1^* x^0$ without regard to the height of the point. Thus the vector x^3 is preferred to the vector x^4 because $x_1^3 > x_1^4$, the fact that $x_2^4 > x_2^3$ being immaterial. The second component (sales) only affects choice when two situations have identical first components. For example, suppose vectors x^4 and x^5 are the only attainable ones. In neither situation is a satisfactory level of profit forthcoming; but x^4 is preferred to x^5 because $x_1^4 = x_1^5$ and $x_2^4 > x_2^5$. This should make the basis of choice quite clear. Any two alternatives are first compared with respect to their dominant components (x_1^i). If these are different, the alternative with the greater dominant component is immediately selected because the associated $u(x)$ is greater. Lower-ordered objectives are considered only when higher-ordered ones are satisfied. Thus total revenue becomes the relevant decision variable only when the entrepreneur can choose among alternatives involving identical profit levels.[20]

Second, Baumol's dynamic model can be used to illustrate Encarnacion's graphical technique which is generally superior to the one I developed. The most important objective is the current ratio, denoted x_1. Second in importance is the profit rate x_2, third is the amount of investment funds forthcoming in the next period as a percentage of capital x_3,[21] and fourth is the rate of growth of sales x_4. Thus any particular situation is depicted by the four-dimensional vector $x = (x_1, x_2, x_3, x_4)$.

The investment funds forthcoming in the next period (x_3) may generally be considered a function of the profit rate (x_2) and the rate of growth of sales (x_4). The former determines retained earnings, given a fixed dividend pay-out rate. The latter helps determine investors' expectations regarding the firm's future and thereby influences the amount of outside funds available to the firm. Consequently, we set $x_3 = g(x_2, x_4)$.

During any period of time, and perhaps over time as well, the current ratio, the profit rate, and the rate of growth of sales are closely related. For example, a decrease in promotional expenditures will augment the current ratio but will also probably cause a decrease in the rate of growth of sales. Similarly, the immediate profit rate might be increased by refusing to introduce new commodities into the firm's product line; again, the rate of growth of sales would probably be affected adversely. Generally, it is impossible to augment one of these variables without causing a decrease in one or

both of the others. Therefore, we write this relationship formally as

$$h(x_1, x_2, x_3 \mid t) = 0.$$

In this expression t is a parameter representing the state of the market at time period t; the expression itself is merely a transformation function among the three variables for each stipulated set of market conditions.

Now consider Figure 2. First assume a

FIG. 2

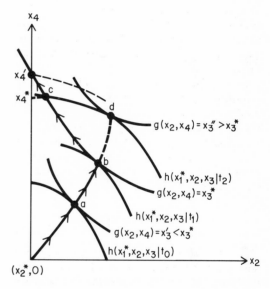

satisfactory level of the current ratio is attainable and, in fact, attained. If this were not so, all situations would be ranked according to be first component only. The figure thus represents a contour map of a four-dimensional surface intersected by a plane at the level $x_1 = x_1^*$. It is further assumed that at least a satisfactory profit rate is attained. The origin of coordinates is thus the point $(x_2^*, 0)$.[22] The curve $h(x_1^*, x_2, x_3 \mid t_0)$ represents the transformation function for the set of market conditions in time period t_0. The graph is reduced to two dimensions by

[20] With the *caveat* that profit in excess of the satisfactory level is not material.

[21] That is, the sum of retained earnings of the current period and outside funds made available to the firm.

[22] If the two highest objectives are not attained, the problem essentially reduces to a two-dimensional one and can be be analyzed by my graphical device.

constructing "indifference" curves for various x_3 levels from the relation $x_3 = g(x_2, x_4)$. That is, solving $g(x_2, x_4) = \bar{x}_3 = $ a constant, one determines various combinations of x_2 and x_4 values giving rise to a stipulated x_3 value.

Initial equilibrium is attained at point a; the situation is represented by the vector

$$x^a = (x_1^*, \quad x_2 > x_2^*, x_3' < x_3^*, x_4 < x_4^*).$$

The first two objectives are attained, the second two are not. But given the transformation relation $h(x_1^*, x_2, x_3 \mid t_0)$, the highest attainable value of x_3 is realized; and at this equilibrium point, the marginal rate of transformation between x_2 and x_4 equals the marginal rate of substitution between them for the given x_3 level.

Now suppose in time period t_1 market conditions improve so that the transformation curve shifts outward to $h(x_1^*, x_2, x_3 \mid t_1)$. Further, suppose this is just consistent with attaining the target value x_3^* for forthcoming investment funds. The equilibrium position shifts from a to b, the latter being a situation represented by

$$x^b = (x_1^*, x_2 > x_2^*, x_3^*, x_4 < x_4^*).$$

The sales growth objective is the only one not satisfied; but at the equilibrium point, the marginal rate of transformation between profits and sales equals the marginal rate of substitution between them with respect to the "satisficing" level x_3^* of x_3. An improved position cannot be achieved, given the existing market conditions.

But let the market again improve in time period t_2, so that the transformation curve shifts outward to $h(x_1^*, x_2, x_3 \mid t_2)$. The equilibrium adjustments are now vastly different than in the two previous situations. The firm does not move from b to d, where it would attain a greater rate of profit and a greater level of forthcoming investment funds (and also the tangency conditions). Instead, the firm moves along the curve $g(x_2, x_4) = x_3^*$ to the point c, where the sales growth objective is attained. Writing

out the vectors corresponding to points c and d makes this clear:

$$x^d = (x_1^*, x_2^d > x_2^*, x_3'' > x_3^*, x_4 < x_4^*)$$

and

$$x^c = (x_1^*, x_2^c > x_2^*, x_3^*, x_4^*).$$

In keeping with the general assumption, previously expressed,

$$\left. \frac{\partial u}{\partial x_i} \right]_{x_i > x_i^*} = 0.$$

The facts that x_2^d exceeds x_2^c and x_3^d exceeds x_3^* are immaterial because values in excess of the "satisficing" level do not augment utility. But an increase in the rate of growth of sales does until $x_4 = x_4^*$ because, again by previous hypothesis,

$$\left. \frac{\partial u}{\partial x_i} \right]_{x_i < x_i^*} > 0.$$

Clearly, $u(x^c) > u(x^d)$ because $u(x_i^c) = u(x_i^d)$ for $i = 1, 2, 3$ and $u(x_4^c) > u(x_4^d)$. Thus in the equilibrium adjustment from b to c the firm ignores the "tangency" condition because x_3 is no longer an effective constraint variable.

Finally, let us suppose that x_4' rather than x_4^* represents the target value of the sales growth variable. The firm would still move from b to c, rather than from b to d, because it leads to a greater increase in utility:

$$\left(\frac{\partial u}{\partial x_4} > 0 \text{ while } \frac{\partial u}{\partial x_2} = \frac{\partial u}{\partial x_3} = 0 \right).$$

If the transformation curve shifts outward permissively to the position shown by the dashed line, the firm would attain equilibrium at point x_4'. In this case, all targets would be precisely attained, i.e., the position is $x^* = (x_1^*, x_2^*, x_3^*, x_4')$. However, target rates of sales growth in excess of x_4' would never be attained because such rates are not compatible with the realization of a more important objective, $x_2 \geq x_2^*$.

IV. CONCLUSION

It is interesting to observe that constrained, multiple-goal business behavior and the theory of multidimensional utility analysis can be placed in one-to-one correspondence. That it should have taken so long to establish the connection is really somewhat unusual, because the connection is such a valuable one, at least from a pedagogical standpoint. It permits one to use simple geometrical devices to analyze and explain a large class of important economic models. It also places the theory of entrepreneurial behavior firmly on the ground of utility analysis, as Scitovsky suggested in 1943.[23] Furthermore, the utility analysis is purely ordinal, thereby not requiring one of the more heroic assumptions of cardinal analysis.[24] Finally, it is also interesting to observe that the theory of multidimensional utility analysis, originally developed in the context of and for use in problems associated with cardinal utility analysis, can be adapted for use in an ordinal setting.

[23] Scitovsky, op. cit. [Footnote 7].

[24] This point was not emphasized in the text. However, it should be clear that if $u(x)$ is one utility function possessing the required sign conditions, then $F(u(x))$ also possesses the required sign conditions if $F(u)$ is a monotonically increasing transformation, i.e., $F'(u) > 0$ for all values of u. One should also note that the normalization of components in the exposition of my graphical device does not imply cardinality of the utility function.

5

Profits, Learning and the Convergence of Satisficing to Marginalism*

RICHARD H. DAY

In his recent address before the American Economic Association, Kenneth Boulding suggested that economists had underemphasized information and had overlooked the role of the market as a teacher.[1] The purpose of the present paper is to help rectify this imbalance by presenting a model of economic learning in a situation of extreme ignorance.

A firm that produces a single homogeneous commodity is considered. Its choice is simply to increase or decrease production, and the information on which this choice is based is limited to a knowledge of the past two period's outputs and profits. Neither the demand function for output nor the cost function is known to the firm. It is the last assumption —ignorance of cost—that distinguishes the present subject most sharply from the classical models.

A strategy is constructed that uses only the information postulated and—if the unknown

From The Quarterly Journal of Economics (May 1967), pp. 302–11. Reprinted with permission of author and publisher.
* [Richard Day is a professor at the University of Wisconsin.] The work on this paper was supported by a grant from the National Science Foundation.

[1] The Richard T. Ely Address at the American Economic Association, December 28, 1965, "The Economics of Knowledge and the Knowledge of Economics," American Economic Review, Papers and Proceedings, LVI (May 1966).

demand and cost environment is stable—approximates maximum profit for the industry. The accuracy of the approximation depends upon the degree to which the decisionmaker is a "satisficer" or a "maximizer" where these attributes are well defined in terms of certain behavioral parameters. In the present case the difference between these two attributes is literally one of degree rather than one of kind as some authors have argued.[2] A simple learning process with limited information approaches the classical rule of optimality: marginal revenue equals marginal cost. It would appear that because its profit reward is so effective at inducing the correct response from its pupils the market is indeed a good teacher.[3]

It may come as something of a surprise to those familiar with advanced theories of learning and information[4] that a principle of such profound importance can be illustrated with a model of such meager proportions. Such a feat is not really unusual in economics. The concepts of supply and demand equilibrium, comparative advantage, and the theories of rent, monopolistic pricing, and the cobweb cycle are all examples of equally simple analyses. But it is fair to note that, like these conventional principles, the present contribution is not a full blown, operational theory. It is instead a theoretical cartoon: it simplifies the problem to make its point, leaving it to the "editorial" to develop the argument in more realistic detail.

A notable recent development in microeconomics is the rise of behavioral and organizational theories.[5] In a recent review article I considered a major contribution to this new field, *A Behavioral Theory of the Firm* by Cyert and March, *et al.*[6] That review suggested, contrary to the opinion expressed in the book, that there is a profound underlying unity existing between the competing viewpoints of rational choice and behavioral principles.

That such an intimate connection should have escaped the notice or been minimized by the proponents of the new approach is quite understandable. They have surely broadened by a considerable margin the operational understanding of the business concern and have contributed a substantial number of useful concepts and operational methods for analyzing its behavior. On the other hand, in its present state behavioral theory fails to answer important questions formulated in optimizing theory and creates confusion in the theory of the firm in a wholly unnecessary way.

In this paper the unity between the behavioral and rational approaches is illustrated. Our learning model is constructed along purely "behavioral" lines and then shown to converge to the traditional "rational" result under "perfect" knowledge.

THE LEARNING MODEL

Our decisionmaker considers a single decision variable, output x, and a single goal, satisfactory profits π. The information available for a rational choice is low. Indeed, we assume that the decisionmaker does not know his profit function, neither its form nor its parameters. He does, however, know his past two decisions x_t, x_{t-1} and their consequence in profits π_t, π_{t-1}.

An unknown objective function cannot be

---

[2] Simon, for example, writes "administrative theory is peculiarly the theory of intended and bounded rationality—of the behavior of human beings who *satisfice* because they have not the wits to maximize." Herbert Simon, *Administrative Behavior* (2d ed.; New York: Macmillan, 1965), p. xxiv. However, I show in this paper a situation where wits enough to learn and a modicum of patience lead to a close approximation of the rewards received by the *homo economicus* of Cournot, Marshall, Robinson and Chamberlin.

[3] Boulding has no doubt overstated his case. Many authors at least as early as Walras have tried to deal with the market as a kind of learning process. A beautifully cogent statement of the information content of profits is in Robert Dorfman, *The Price System* (Englewood Cliffs, N.J.: Prentice-Hall, 1964).

[4] I have particularly in mind theories of sequential statistical decisions, and, more generally, Bayesian statistics.

[5] For example see Simon, *op. cit.*, and Richard M. Cyert and James G. March, *et. al., A Behavioral Theory of the Firm* (Englewood Cliffs, N.J.: Prentice-Hall, 1963).

[6] Richard H. Day, "A Behavioral Theory of the Firm by Richard M. Cyert and James G. March," *Econometrica*, Vol. 32 (July 1964), pp. 461–64.

maximized. In the absence of information sufficient to do so the rational procedure would be to adopt a learning process that improves goal fulfillment. Such a process can be based on two simple principles: (1) successful behavior should be repeated and unsuccessful behavior avoided;[7] (2) unsuccessful behavior should be restrained by greater caution if a repetition of it seems desirable again at some future time.

As there are two possible choices with two possible outcomes, contingencies may arise and a strategy is adopted for each. The strategies are summarized in Table 1.

TABLE 1

Past Behavior	Known Consequence of Past Behavior	
	Increase in Profits	Decrease in Profits
Expanded output	Expanded output again.	Contract output. Be more cautious in next expansion.
Contracted output	Contract output again.	Expand output. Be more cautious in next contraction.

Beyond these principles the decisionmaker must have a criterion of goal fulfillment. Under the information state assumed here a criterion consistent with the learning process is that when a past change of action leads to only a "small" change in reward, the last output may be repeated, for insufficient payoff is expected from further changes. The definition of what is a "small" change is a behavioral property and may be called— after Simon—the *satisficing parameter*. With this introduction we may specify the behavioral model as follows:[8]

Goal:
Satisfactory profit rate.

[7] One can find analogies of the present use of this principle in experimental psychology. For example see B. F. Skinner, "The Experimental Analysis of Behavior," *American Scientist*, Vol. 45 (Sept. 1957), pp. 343–71.

[8] In order to dramatize our convergence to neoclassical principles, I have described the model in terms as closely patterned as possible after the work of the behavioral school.

Criterion:
Profit rate is satisfactory when change in output leads to sufficiently small change in profit, say ϵ.

Decision Variable:
Output in the next period, x_{t+1}.

Information:

1. Outputs of past two periods x_t, x_{t-1} (past behavior).
2. Profits received in past two periods π_t, π_{t-1} (consequence of past behavior).
3. Change in profit per unit change in output.

$$\rho_t = \frac{\pi_t - \pi_{t-1}}{x_t - x_{t-1}}.$$

Behavioral Parameters:

1. Rate of expansion in output allowed at time t: $\alpha_t^+ > 0$.
2. Rate of contraction in output allowed at time t: $\alpha_t^- > 0$.
3. Reduction factor on rates of change in output if greater caution is desired: $0 < \theta < 1$.
4. "Satisficing parameter": $\epsilon > 0$.

Learning Strategies or Behavioral Rules:

1. If output was unchanged, determine if environment has shifted in rule 2. Otherwise consider the effect of past behavior on profits in rule 3.
2. If profits are unchanged, the environment was stable. Exercise rule 9. If profits have changed a new exploration of the environment should begin. Use rule 2.1.
   2.1 Set expansion and contraction parameters to their initial values. Go to rule 8.
3. Compute rate of change of profit per unit change in output. A small rate suggests further experiments will have a low payoff. Profits are taken as satisfactory. Exercise rule 9. A high rate suggests further experiments may bring rewards. Assume profits are unsatisfactory and consider rule 4.
4. If profits increased, then last decision was successful. Go to rule 6. If profits decreased, then last decision was unsuccessful and greater caution is desired. Go to rule 5.
5. Be more cautious. If output was expanded, exercise rule 5.1. Otherwise follow rule 5.2.
   5.1 Reduce expansion coefficient and go to rule 7.

5.2 Reduce contraction coefficient and go to rule 8.

6. Past action was successful. Leave expansion and contraction coefficients unchanged. If output was increased, go to 8. If output was decreased, go to 7.

7. Contract output. Step 10 happens.

8. Expand output. Step 10 happens.

9. Leave output unchanged. Step 10 happens.

Environmental (Information) Feedback:

10. Realized profit is some function of output unknown to decisionmaker but determining his profit or payoff which becomes new information for the next decision.

* * *

The model just outlined may be formulated as a flow chart as shown in Figure 1. It explicitly incorporates several prominent behavioral principles: (1) satisficing, as indicated by the parameter ϵ; (2) imperfect, local information; (3) information feedback; and (4) simple behavioral rules or standard operating procedures.[9] The list of learning strategies and the model in flow chart form are slightly complicated by the necessity to account for all special cases. For example, if the decisionmaker is in equilibrium, i.e., if $x_t = x_{t-1}$ but profits have changed, then the external environment (profit function) has shifted and the learning process should begin anew. This possibility is treated in rule 2.1, and rules 1 and 2 involve tests to determine if this strategy should be invoked.

DEMAND, COST, AND ENVIRONMENTAL FEEDBACK

In standard theory the firm possesses a cost function say $C = C(x)$. If the firm is the single producer of the commodity in question, then it possesses a demand function say $x = D(p)$ where p is the price charged. Under the assumption that D has an inverse D^{-1} we have $\pi = f(x) = xD^{-1}(x) - C(x)$. The function f defined by the conditions of

demand and cost, determines the payoff resulting from the production decision. Thus $\pi_t = f(x_t) = x_t D^{-1}(x_t) - C(x_t)$. But while the demand and cost conditions determine the payoff from decision, their knowledge cannot be exploited by the decisionmaker. For this reason the profit function f determines environmental feedback, and it is through this feedback that demand and cost conditions influence behavior.

If the environment as represented by C and D^{-1} is stable, then the procedure should lead to satisfactory, or at least improving performance; otherwise, we should not denote the behavioral rules as a learning process. Consequently, we are led to examine the dynamic properties of the model; the existence of an equilibrium, its stability, and efficiency in terms of goal fulfillment.

Before turning to these issues the model is summarized to facilitate comparison with other approaches. Let ψ stand for the sequence of behavioral rules or learning strategies that transform information x_t, x_{t-1}, π_t, π_{t-1} into decisions—or action—x_{t+1}. We may call this sequence the "decision operator" that transforms "information-" or "state-space" into "decision-" or "control-space." Let Ω stand for the environmental feedback function f relating decisions to consequences. We may refer to it as the environmental operator transforming decision or "control space" back into state or information space. With these terms the model is summarized in Figure 2 below.[10]

SATISFICING'S CONVERGENCE TO MARGINALISM

In taking up dynamic questions let us first observe that the process has an infinite number of unstable equilibria. Suppose that demand and cost conditions are stationary, that is that D and C do not shift. Then for arbitrary $\bar{x} > 0$ (we outlaw negative produc-

---

[9] See Cyert and March, *op. cit.*, especially Chaps. 5 and 6.

[10] For a more detailed treatment of decisionmaking theory using this terminology, see Day, "Recursive Programming," Systems Formulation, Methodology and Policy Workshop Paper 6519, Social Systems Research Institute, University of Wisconsin, Dec. 1965.

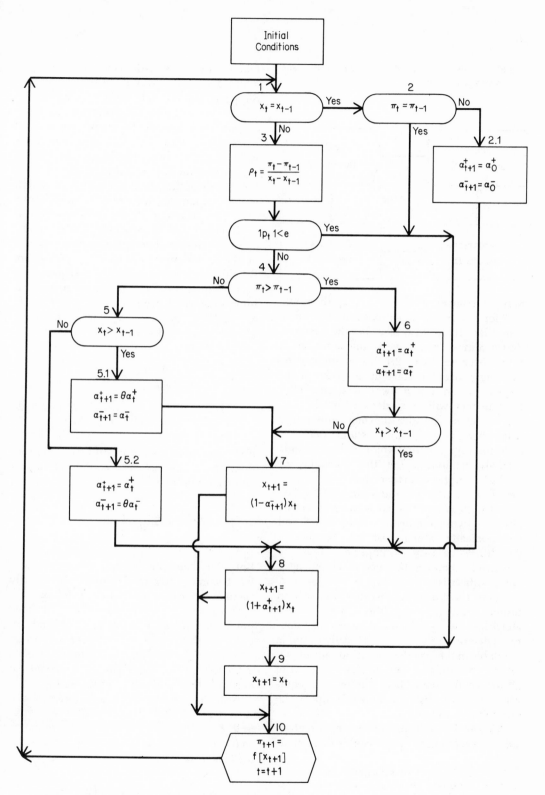

FIG. 1 The learning model with environmental feedback

27

FIG. 2 The model as a loop of operations on state and decision spaces

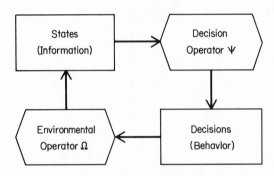

tion, of course) if $x_0 = x_{-1} = \bar{x}$, then $x_{t+1} = \bar{x}$ for $t = 0, 1, \ldots$, so that $\bar{x}$ is an equilibrium. But it is unstable, for the slightest shift in x away from $\bar{x}$, will cause a change in π. But because of rule 2.1 this will induce the learning process to start up and except for the case when $\bar{x}$ is a local maximum of f, the tendency will be to depart from it.

Now let us consider the more interesting case where $x_0 \neq x_{-1}$ and assume that f is continuously differentiable with a single (global) maximum. Let this point be $\pi^* = f(x^*)$. Suppose further that $f(x_1) < f(x_2)$ for all $x_1 < x_2 < x^*$ and that $f(x_3) > f(x_4)$ for all $x_3 > x_4 > x^*$. That is, we assume the function is monotonically rising to π^* and monotonically falling past π^*. Because of the differentiability assumption f must be concave in the neighborhood of x^* but need not be otherwise.[11]

Under these assumptions there are still an infinite number of equilibria, but they are all within a well-defined distance of the maximum decision x^* and though locally unstable are stable in the broader sense that output will return to within a well-defined distance of x^* for *any* departure from the original equilibrium. This distance depends upon the satisficing parameter ϵ.

Without introducing too much formalism we may sketch in the proof of this theorem as

follows. Let x_0, x_{-1}, the consequent π_0, π_{-1}, θ and α_0^+, α_0^- be given as initial conditions. Suppose $|\rho_1| > \epsilon$ and $\pi_0 > \pi_{-1}$ so that the action is repeated (increase or decrease output as the case may be). It will continue to be repeated until $\pi_t < \pi_{t-1}$ and the decision is unsuccessful. This must happen because of the monotonicity assumption coupled with the global optimum. If the course of action was an expansion, we will refer to this time period as t_1^+ and if it was a contraction as t_1^-. In either case the action is avoided and its opposite chosen. Eventually either $|\rho_t| < \epsilon$ or the action turns unsuccessful and so on. By this process we generate a sequence of periods t_1^+, t_2^+, ... and t_1^-, t_2^-, ... so that at some time say t_e we shall have (a) $\alpha_{t_e}^+ = \theta^e \alpha_0^+$ and (b) $\alpha_{t_e}^+ = \theta^{e-1} \alpha_0^-$, or alternatively $\alpha_{t_e}^+ = \theta^{e-1} \alpha_{t_e}^+$ and $\alpha_{t_e}^- = \theta^e \alpha_0^-$. Consequently

$$\rho_{t_e} = \frac{\pi_{t_e} - \pi_{t_e-1}}{x_{t_e} - x_{t_e-1}}$$

$$= \frac{f(x_{t_e-1} + \theta^{e-1} \alpha_0^+ + x_{t_e-1}) - f(x_{t_e-1})}{\theta^{e-1} \alpha_0^+ + x_{t_e-1}}$$

if the last unsuccessful action was a contraction. Or, if the last unsuccessful action was an expansion, then

$$\rho_{t_e} = \frac{f(x_{t_e-1} - \theta^{e-1} \alpha_0^- x_{t_e-1}) - f(x_{t_e-1})}{\theta^{e-1} \alpha_0^- x_{t_e-1}}.$$

But after the oscillation occurs long enough, θ^{e-1} becomes a *very* small number—arbitrarily small as t increases indefinitely. Consequently ρ_t must also get arbitrarily small. At some point, say t_e, $|\rho_{t_e}| < \epsilon$ where t_e depends on ϵ. When this occurs the process comes to an end $x_{t+1} = x_t$, and an equilibrium has been achieved. This argument is sufficient to establish the validity of the theorem.

Now for each ϵ there will correspond a t_e and a θ^{e-1}. Let us write $\delta_\epsilon^+ = \theta^{e-1} \alpha_0^+ x_t$ and $\delta_\epsilon^- = \theta^{e-1} \alpha_0^- x_{t_e}$. Then we have shown that for all $\epsilon > 0$ there exists either a δ_ϵ^+ or a δ_ϵ^- such that

$$f_+' \cong \left| \frac{f[x_{t_e} + \delta_\epsilon^+] - f[x_{t_e}]}{\delta_\epsilon^+} \right| < \epsilon.$$

[11] It must however be sufficiently sloping away from x^*. More precisely $|f'(x)| > \epsilon$ for all x except those in a neighborhood of x^* where ϵ is the satisficing parameter.

or that

$$f'_- \cong \left| \frac{f[x_{t_e} + \delta^-_\epsilon] - f[x_{t_e}]}{\delta^+_\epsilon} \right| < \epsilon.$$

We now come to the central result of this paper. If we let the "satisficing parameter" ϵ get arbitrarily small, then the first of these expressions, is the "right-hand derivative" and the second the "left-hand derivative" of the function f both evaluated at the point x_{t_e}. But because f is differentiable these both approach f' as ϵ gets very small. That is to say $\rho_{t_e} \longrightarrow 0$ as $\epsilon \longrightarrow 0$ and therefore the decision equilibria of the learning behavior approach arbitrarily close the point of maximum profit $\pi^* = f(x^*)$. At this point of course $\rho_{t_e} = MR - MC = 0$. *Thus we may say that satisficing—in this model—converges to the monopoly profit solution for the firm* as given by the rule that marginal revenue equals marginal cost when these are derived from perfectly known demand and cost functions.

A SIMPLE EXAMPLE

A simple example can be used to illustrate the analysis. Assume the demand function $D^{-1}(x) = 10 - x$ and cost function $C(x) = 1 + 2x$, so that $x^* = 4$ and $\pi^* = 15$. Let $\theta = .5$, $\alpha_0 = 1.0$, $\alpha_0^- = 1.0$, let $\epsilon = .05$ and finally, set the initial conditions $x_0 = 8$, $x_{-1} = 9$ with $\pi_0 = -1$, $\pi_{-1} = -10$. With this situation $x_4 = x^*$ but $\rho_4 = 1.0$ so that the decisionmaker expects to receive a further payoff by reducing output still one more unit, even though he is already unwittingly at the optimum. Instead, of course, he receives

a profit reduction of one unit, so that we have $x_5 = 14$, and $\rho_5 = -1.0$. Now because of the unsuccessful decision $\alpha_6^+ = \theta\alpha_0^+ = .5$ and output is contracted. The contraction brings output back again to the optimum, $x_6 = x^*$. As $\rho_6 = 1.0$, however, a further contraction is pursued. This time it leads to a profit reduction so that $\alpha_8^- = \theta\alpha_0^- = .5$. Oscillations about x^* continue until $\rho_t < .05$.[12]

The probability of drawing initial conditions at random such that the global optimum is reached after a finite number of steps is zero. Given the complete ignorance of demand and given the prior unlikelihood of ever stumbling onto the global optimum, our decisionmaker is not so foolish as this extreme example might have made him seem if we had forgot for a moment the premises on which his behavior is predicted. These are entirely different from the standard theory of monopoly. Still our market finds an apt pupil in our decisionmaker. Given a sufficiently small satisficing parameter, and a stable environment for a sufficient period of time, he achieves most if not all the rewards of his monopolistic, infinitely wise counterpart.

---

[12] The model, like the typical behavioral study, can be readily simulated by hand or by computer. Simulations for widely varying cost and demand conditions including Monte Carlo studies for cases when the environmental operator contains stochastic shocks would yield useful insights. Some work of this kind has been done by John Quinn, programmer, Social Systems Research Institute, University of Wisconsin. His results, however, are not extensive and merely illustrate the points already developed in the paper.

part 2

The Production Submodel
of the Firm

Right at the outset it should be pointed out that cost, a basic topic in managerial economics, is usually discussed in terms of "production cost," and cost functions are derived from production functions. Thus, selections dealing with cost are included under the heading of the production submodel of the firm.

In Selection 6, Palda reviews some of the basic concepts of economic production theory, and stresses its guidance to performance evaluation and control. He then discusses the price and technical efficiency components which together contribute to the selection of the optimal input mix. Finally, with the help of an actual empirical example of production function estimation, he shows how the best production factor mix can be chosen and in what way accountants can contribute to such a selection.

In Reading 7 Sahota uses the powerful concept of the production function to uncover econometrically the sources of productivity growth in two important American industries over a quarter of a century. He examines three components which could account for the 89 percent productivity increase in the potassium industry and for the 75 percent productivity growth in the sulfur industry over this period: (1) technical change within the individual firms, (2) technical change caused by the more rapid growth of the successful, i.e., efficient firms, and (3) technical change accounted for by economies of scale, i.e., by the overall growth of the size of operations of these firms. Only the first component is judged as having been responsible for the efficiency increase in the production of the two industries. Almost half of the overall productivity increase is attributed to technical improvement in the quality of labor which, in turn, flowed about equally from additional schooling and from on-the-job training. Only about a third of the productivity increase could be traced to improvements in capital equipment. As similar findings emerge from several other productivity studies, the importance to firms of the education of employees and management—both of the "school-diploma" and on-the-job training kind—cannot be underestimated in the modern economy.

Comitini and Huang (Reading 8) undertake a study of the halibut fishing industry in the same production function framework. They first pay careful attention to the *type* of the function which they shall fit; then they concentrate on the nature of technical progress in that particular industry. What they find, is the importance of the *managerial* input in this industry. Theirs is one of the rare studies of the quantitative impact of managerial skills on the success of the firm; such studies are now largely confined to farming, fishing, and similar "simple" activities, but hopefully they will be forthcoming in more complex situations.

A simple theoretical bridge between production and cost functions is built by Danø in Reading 9. His standard treatment of the subject soon expands into an ingenious explanation which accounts for one of the most bothersome empirical findings in modern microeconomics: the observed constancy of marginal cost in literally dozens of studies. Idle capacity, or the variable utilization of capital, is seen as the underlying answer to this problem. The reader's understanding of the nature of cost functions will be much deepened by reading Danø's article; this will make him ready for the one important development in cost theory in the last three decades, which is explained in the next selection.

Hirschleifer (Selection 10) also takes as his starting point the constant marginal cost phenomenon, but he shows how it can be explained with the help of a new cost theory postulated by Alchian. Alchian suggested that cost can be regarded as a function of the quantity of output in two different dimensions: *rate* of output and scheduled *volume* of output. The value of Hirschleifer's exposition is twofold: his detailed discussion of those business situations in which the volume of output is a crucial variable and his reconciliation of the traditional rate-of-output theory with Alchian's rate-volume hypothesis. Hirschleifer also briefly discusses the learning curve, an important cost topic for which no space could be found in this volume.

A lucid explanation of how a complex cost function can be estimated with the help of multiple least-squares regression is detailed in Benston's article (Selection 11). The reader can adopt this perspective on Benston's presentation: How do we estimate unit cost (be it total, variable, or marginal) as a function of output, given that there are so many other variables (such as size of order, other products in the line, and seasonal influences)which enter the picture? Holding these other variables at their average level is the task of regression analysis. The particular merit of Benston's exposition is his careful examination of all the assumptions underlying the least-squares estimation method and the implications of such assumptions in the collection of the statistical raw material. In the course of this exposition, the reader is offered a brief introduction to the econometric framework within which the least-squares method—the estimation procedure most widely used nowadays in economics—can be applied.

There is a wealth of readings available on linear programming and its applications to the production problems of the firm. Nonetheless, and despite our stated intention of excluding purely "technique" topics, the other excerpt from Baumol's book (Reading 12) merits inclusion on two important grounds. First, it is one of the most felicitously written short expositions of linear programming, and secondly, it lucidly shows the affinities of the linear programming and neoclassical approaches to the production theory of the firm.

The reading which concludes this part is an excerpt from an article by the English economist Nove. This writer takes more of a bird's-eye view of the cost problems of the firm than the previous selections did. He addresses himself to questions of contemporary relevance: Under what circumstances may large firms (including state enterprises) be more efficient than smaller units? What are the limits of efficient size? What are the implications of the multiproduct character of the typical modern enterprise? Can marginal analysis be usefully applied in the divisionalized firm? etc.

6

Production Functions and Performance Evaluation

KRISTIAN S. PALDA

I THE ANALYTICAL FRAMEWORK FOR PERFORMANCE EVALUATION

The analytical framework for the evaluation of economic performance of a firm is simple and follows directly from the optimization rules discussed in preceding chapters (and, in particular, in Chapter 1). As usual, the difficulty is in getting satisfactory estimates of the numerical values of the variables involved.

Of the two sets of rules for profit maximization—the Brems-Verdoorn and the classical—we find the latter to be more convenient to use in a scheme for performance evaluation. This scheme can be represented diagrammatically as in Figure 1.

FIG. 1

(a) $MR \overset{\frown}{=} MC$

(b) $MR \overset{\frown}{=} p\left(1 + \dfrac{1}{\eta}\right)$

(c) $\eta \overset{\frown}{=} \dfrac{p\delta q}{\delta a} \overset{\frown}{=} \dfrac{p}{c}\,\eta_q$

(d) $MC \overset{\frown}{=} \dfrac{MFC_1}{MPP_1} \overset{\frown}{=} \cdots \overset{\frown}{=} \dfrac{MFC_n}{MPP_n} \overset{\frown}{=} MR$

In this scheme we ask the following questions in turn:

1. Does the marginal revenue generated by the product's sales tend to approximate the marginal cost of the product's manufacturing and marketing activities?
2. On the *marketing* side, is marginal revenue in line with the price elasticity of demand for the product, η?

From Kristian S. Palda, Economic Analysis for Marketing Decisions, © *1969. Reprinted by permission of Prentice-Hall, Inc., Englewood Cliffs, New Jersey.*

3. Still on the marketing side, does η in turn tend to be in line, according to the Dorfman-Steiner theorem, with the marginal sales effect of advertising ($p\,\delta q/\delta a$) and with the product of markup over cost (p/c) and quality elasticity of demand (η_q)?
4. On the *production* side, are the ratios of all marginal factor costs to their respective marginal products (MFC/MPP) equal to each other *and* to marginal cost?

In the unlikely event that all these indicators could be estimated with considerable accuracy and that affirmative answers could be given to the four questions, the happy conclusion of the performance evaluation process could be that the firm is in profit-maximizing equilibrium at least in the short run and that no corrective measures appear necessary.[1]

The process of performance evaluation can, at least conceptually and for a start, be split into three categories: marketing, production, and financial. . . .

·   ·   ·

2. Production Performance

Equality (d) as shown in Figure 1 indicates the optimal balance in the employment of productive resources and the optimal level of the output. As was mentioned, capital limitations may preclude activities from being carried to optimal levels (to where the MFC/MRP ratios attain equality with the MC/MR ratio. [and are, themselves, equal to unity]) Nevertheless, the "relative activity levels" rule still holds, and for our purposes it can

---

[1] A qualification must be entered: The firm may not be operating on the most efficient production function available to it.

be considered to be the focal point of this chapter. It may be restated in several equivalent verbal forms, of which two of the most widely used are: (1) A dollar's worth of any input should add as much product as a dollar's worth of any other input; or (2) the principle of equimarginal returns means that all activities should be carried to levels where they all yield the same marginal returns per unit of cost.

Thus the basic question to be asked for the purposes of performance evaluation is whether equimarginal returns on inputs are being obtained or, to put it differently, whether productive resources are being employed in the right proportions. An answer to it is quite as difficult to obtain as it is to determine whether Dorfman-Steiner conditions prevail on the demand side.

Before we proceed we must enter a qualification about the title of this section. We separated the treatment of performance evaluation into "marketing" and "production" categories somewhat artificially. What we labeled as "marketing performance evaluation" really amounts to problems dealing with the determination of optimal output and optimal division of effort between price, advertising, and quality. What we label as "production performance evaluation" is meant to be *any* appraisal of input mixes, be they of a production *or* of a marketing character.

Theoretically, as we so tiresomely repeat, fully efficient (that is, profit-maximizing) operations throughout the firm prevail when at the predetermined volume of output a tangency of the isoquant hyperplane with the isocost hyperplane obtains. In diagrammatic form and with only two inputs, this occurs at point Q' in Figure 2. (Competitive resource markets—a straight isocost line—are assumed.) We may, however, expect the firm to be less than fully efficient. Farrell has proposed the decomposition of economic efficiency into a *technical efficiency component* and a *price efficiency component*.[2] This points

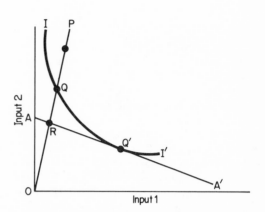

FIG. 2 (Redrawn from M. J. Farrell, "The Measurement of Productive Efficiency," *Journal of the Royal Statistical Society* (Series A, 1957), diagram 1)

the way to estimation procedures and, ultimately, to improved means of performance evaluation.

If there are two inputs (traditionally, capital and labor) and one output, then the isoquant II' describes a production function. Isocost line AA' describes the relationship between the prices of the two inputs. Suppose we observe the firm producing output II' with a combination and quantity of resources described by point P. The point Q represents an efficient firm using the two inputs in the same proportion as P but using only a fraction OQ/OP as much of each input. The distance OQ relative to OP indicates the degree to which the same amount of output could be produced with a smaller quantity of inputs, still combined in the same proportion. Thus OQ/OP can be termed "technical efficiency." This is the measure with which we shall be primarily concerned.

"Price efficiency" is defined as the distance OR relative to OQ. It measures the fraction of costs for which the output could be produced and marketed if the relative proportions were to be changed in view of their prices. If the firm were fully efficient on both technical and price accounts, its costs for a unit of output would be a fraction OR/OP of what they actually are. Farrell designates this fraction as "overall efficiency" and it

[2] M. J. Farrell, "The Measurement of Productive Efficiency," *Journal of the Royal Statistical Society* (Series A, 1957), pp. 253–281.

can be defined as

$$\frac{OR}{OP} = \frac{OQ}{OP}\frac{OR}{OQ} \qquad (1)$$

where the first term on the right side measures technical and the second price efficiency. Were the firm to conduct its activity at point Q rather than P, its technical efficiency would be at its maximum value of 1; were it at point Q', its overall efficiency would reach the maximum value of unity.

The decomposition of overall efficiency is important, because although we may expect all firms in an industry to have equal access to a production technology (and we mean to include marketing activities under the word "production" as well), not all firms will be faced by the same environmental conditions leading to same factor input prices. Thus, if we wish to compare the performance of one firm to the rest of the industry, we may legitimately ask only whether its *technical* efficiency is as good as that of its rivals; the answer about *price* efficiency cannot be had from comparisons.

But how can we estimate the efficient production function(s) open to the industry? In principle, this can be attempted by fitting an envelope to a scatter of points in the input plane, as in Figure 3. The points are based on a sample of firms in the industry and rep-

resent various input combinations for a unit of output. The envelope represents then the observed standard of technical efficiency in the industry.[3]

Industry, wholesale, and retail trade associations usually provide a fair amount of productivity data (output per man, sales per clerk, sales per square foot of floor space); media provide a wealth of information about their productivity in reaching audiences; salesmen's organizations and the Dartnell Institute offer some data about outside salesmen's productivity. From such information some notion about the most efficient output per input possibilities can be gained, and management can then attempt to evaluate the performance of the company. It can gauge, at least roughly, the distance PQ at which the firm performs and compares it to the most efficient possibility OQ. In short, it can try to answer the question: Are we getting maximum output for a given set (combination) of inputs?[4]

The second question, Are we choosing an optimum set (combination) of inputs? can only be answered in the context of the

[3] If constant returns are not assumed, the procedure tends to break down. The reason for this is that the linear distances along the ray $ORQP$ in Figure 2 are no longer appropriate measures of efficiency differences. For a critique of Farrell's approach and copious suggestions about improving on it theoretically as well as statistically, see Marc Nerlove, *Estimation and Identification of Cobb-Douglas Production Functions* (Chicago: Rand McNally & Co., 1965), chap. 5. Space considerations preclude the development of Nerlove's chief points here.

[4] Three studies of immediate relevance to the problem discussed above are, for manufacturing, George H. Hildebrand and Ta-Chung Liu, *Manufacturing Production Functions in the United States, 1957* (Ithaca, N.Y.: Cornell University Press, 1965); for distribution, Margaret Hall, John Knapp, and Christopher Winsten, *Distribution in Great Britain and North America: A Study in Structure and Productivity* (London: Oxford University Press, 1961); and for the individual firm, John W. Kendrick and Daniel Creamer, *Measuring Company Productivity* (New York: National Industrial Conference Board, 1965). For a sample of the detailed data we can expect to come in increasing amounts from the National Bureau of Economic Research, see Victor R. Fuchs, "A Statistical Analysis of Productivity in Selected Service Industries in the United States, 1939–1963," *Review of Income and Wealth* (September, 1966), pp. 211–244.

FIG. 3 (Redrawn from M. J. Farrell, "The Measurement of Productive Efficiency," Journal of the Royal Statistical Society (Series A, 1957), diagram 2)

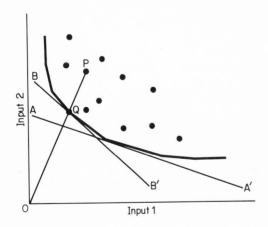

input prices with which the firm is faced. Thus if the price ratio of the inputs is represented by the slope of AA', the optimum set will be different from a situation in which price line BB' prevails.

Put in economic terms (we shall turn to more "business-like" language in the second part), we wish to ascertain the firm's production function and derive several isoquants from it. We then want to ascertain if the firm's resource combination corresponds to the tangency of the hyperplanes of the relevant isoquant and the isocost, the latter being defined by prices prevailing in the factor markets.

Given a Cobb-Douglas production function of the form

$$Y = aX_1^{b1}X_i^{bi} \qquad (i = 2, 3, \ldots, n) \quad (2)$$

which it is necessary to estimate, the isoquants are derived by expressing one input as a function of the other inputs

$$X_1 = \left(\frac{\bar{Y}}{aX^{bi}}\right)^{1/b1} \qquad (3)$$

where $\bar{Y}$ is a specified level of output. By substituting various amounts of inputs into the isoquant relation, various amounts of X_1 are found and the isoquant Y in Figure 4

FIG. 4

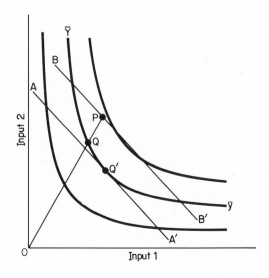

can be mapped.[5] (Repeating the procedure for several realistic outputs, an isoquant *map* can be graphed.) We can, for purposes of illustration, imagine the output as the number of magazine readers in the "above $10,000 yearly" income class exposed to a given ad over a three-month period. The inputs can be thought of as various amounts of space over the same period in magazines A and B.

Performance evaluation then consists of finding (a) whether output $\bar{Y}$ is being attained with the means of the most efficient production function (that is, is there a substantial distance between Q and P), and (b) if production appears to be carried on efficiently, are inputs combined optimally, given their respective prices?

We turn to agriculture for an illustration of the experimental approach to production function estimation.[6] In the early 1950s a group of swine-nutrition experts and agricultural economists at Iowa State University conducted a series of experiments designed to estimate pork production functions and the related equations of isoquants, isoclines (constant rate of substitution contours), and marginal substitution rates.[7] The chief problem to which an answer was sought was which combination of corn and protein (in the form of soybean oilmeal) should be used in producing 100 pounds of pork.

We refer here only to results pooled from experiments 536 and 551 in which aureomycin was used as a feed supplement. These experiments included treatments with six levels of protein. Treatments were applied to lots of four hogs each, at three levels of initial weight: 34, 75, and 150 pounds.

[5] The graph obviously represents only 2, rather than i, inputs.

[6] The marketing experiment that appears to come closest to being useful for production function estimation is reported in J. Sterling Livingston and Robert T. Davis, *Cases in Sales Management* (Homewood, Ill.: Richard D. Irwin, 1962), pp. 291–300 (Superior Electronics case). The report, however, does not permit convincing elaboration.

[7] Earl O. Heady and John L. Dillon, *Agricultural Production Functions* (Ames, Iowa: Iowa State University Press, 1961), chap. 8. Also Heady et al., "An Experiment to Derive Productivity and Substitution Coefficients in Pork Production," *Journal of Farm Economics* (1953), pp. 341–355.

Weight readings were then taken over a 40-, 75-, and 50-pound range, respectively, for each initial weight. A Cobb-Douglas function was fitted to the results. The statistical analysis is summarized in the four equations in Table 1. Y is gain in pounds per pig, C is pounds of corn, and P is pounds of soybean meal (protein) fed.

Pork isoquants corresponding to each equation are shown in Figure 5. Marginal

isocosts that vary in slope as the prices of corn and protein-feed fluctuate. Table 2 shows how this step is accomplished.

It shows that (for example) with a price of 4.6 cents per pound of oilmeal and a price of 2 cents per pound of corn (that is, with a price ratio of 2.3) the least-cost combination of feed to produce a gain of 100 lb for a 110-lb pig is 24.7 lb of oilmeal and 306.8 lb of corn. At that point

FIG. 5 Pork isoquants showing the combination of corn and soybean meal which will produce 100 pounds of gain for pigs of 60, 110, and 175 pounds (Reproduced from Earl O. Heady and John L. Dillon, Agricultural Production Functions (Ames Ia.: Iowa State University Press, 1961), p. 288, fig. 8.8)

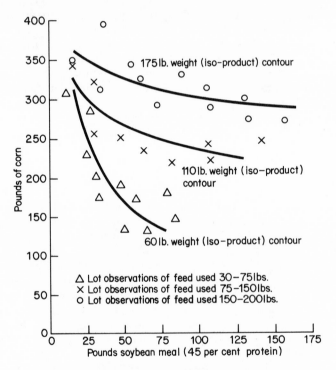

physical products of corn and soybean meal from the *overall* function are, respectively,

$$\frac{\delta Y}{\delta C} = 0.871 P^{0.200} C^{-0.364} \qquad (4)$$

$$\frac{\delta Y}{\delta P} = 0.274 C^{0.636} P^{-0.800} \qquad (5)$$

These data were then used to calculate tangencies of the relevant isoquants with

$$\frac{MFC_P}{MFC_C} = \frac{4.6}{2.0} = \frac{MPP_P}{MPP_C} = \frac{\delta Y/\delta P}{\delta Y/\delta C} = \frac{\delta C}{\delta P} = 2.3$$

(We recall that the marginal rate of technical substitution is the slope of the isoquant: $\delta C/\delta P = f_P/f_C$.)

To sum up: The relative technical efficiency of the firm must be ascertained. If the firm seems to perform well on this count compared to its competitors, these questions are then raised: (1) are the ratios of marginal

TABLE 1 Cobb-Douglas Regression Equations and Corresponding Pork Isoquants from Hog-Feeding Experiments

34–75 lb	$Y = 1.600P^{0.297}C^{0.533}$	$C = \left(\dfrac{Y}{1.600P^{0.297}}\right)^{1/0.533}$
	$N* = 76 \quad t_p^* = 14 \quad t_c = 19$	
75–150 lb	$Y = 0.714P^{0.142}C^{0.767}.$	$C = \left(\dfrac{Y}{0.714P^{0.142}}\right)^{1/0.767}$
	$N = 112 \quad t_p = 9 \quad t_c = 31$	
150–200 lb	$Y = 0.439P^{0.092}C^{0.856}$	$C = \left(\dfrac{Y}{0.439P^{0.092}}\right)^{1/0.856}$
	$N = 111 \quad t_p = 5 \quad t_c = 27$	
Overall (34–200 lb)	$Y = 1.369P^{0.200}C^{0.636}$	$C = \left(\dfrac{Y}{1.369P^{0.200}}\right)^{1/0.636}$
	$N = 299 \quad t_p = 21 \quad t_c = 52$	

* N is sample size and t's are ratios of regression coefficients to their own standard errors.

Source: Earl O. Heady and John L. Dillon, *Agricultural Production Functions* (Ames, Iowa: Iowa State University Press, 1961), pp. 272–275.

TABLE 2 Least-Cost Feed Combinations to Produce 100 Pounds of Gain for Pigs of 110 Pounds (Midpoint of 75-to 150-lb Range)

Feed quantities to produce 100 lb gain*		Marginal Rates of Substitution of Oilmeal for Corn $\delta C/\delta P$; lbs Corn Replaced by 1 lb Oilmeal	Price per Pound SBOM	Least-Cost Combination	
Pounds SBOM	Pounds Corn		Price per Pound Corn	Pounds SBOM	Pounds Corn
20	319	2.95	3.0	19.7	319.8
25	306	2.27	2.3	24.7	306.8
30	295	1.83	1.8	30.4	295.1
35	287	1.52	1.5	35.4	286.9
40	281	1.30	1.3	40.0	280.5
45	275	1.13	1.1	46.0	273.3
50	269	1.00	1.0	49.9	269.3

* Check against middle isoquant in Figure 5.

Source: Based on Earl O. Heady and John L. Dillon, *Agricultural Production Functions* (Ames, Iowa: Iowa State University Press, 1961), pp. 289 and 291, tables 8.9 and 8.10.

revenue products ($MPP_i \times MR$) to marginal factor costs approaching the value of 1, and (2) are these ratios approaching equality between themselves?

Question (1) goes directly back to equality (d). If the MFC/MRP ratios are approaching unity, the firm is both operating at the right level of output ($MR = MC$) and maximizing profit from the use of each factor of production, for then the marginal profit from factor employment is zero ($MRP = MFC$). We have already pointed out that limited capital may not allow the firm to operate at an optimum overall level and that in such an instance the performance of the financial function may be called into question. In any case, for such assessment to be possible, management must estimate the marginal products of its various inputs. In the most usual case the firm will buy its inputs in competitive markets and so marginal factor cost will equal the price of the factor; it will sell its product during a given period at a fixed price. Estimation difficulties will thus center on the production function.

No further estimation is, of course, required to answer question (2). An affirmative answer to this question is probably the single most crucial imperative for optimal operations under any condition, including that of capital shortage. The equality guarantees that the last dollar invested in each activity (input) brings the same return.[8]

. . .

[8] The greatest wealth of theoretical discussion, of

II SOME SUGGESTIONS FOR PERFORMANCE EVALUATION

How can the analytical framework for performance evaluation be translated into operational language meaningful to the controller of the enterprise? Some tentative thoughts follow.

The deviation of actual from desired performance is usually called by accountants a *variance* and *variance analysis* designates the examination of such variance for control purposes.[9] Accepting this terminology, a moment's reflection will show that performance evaluation implies:

1. A voice in the setting up of budgets.
2. Detection of significant variances from budget.
3. Analysis of such variances.

We shall take up these steps in turn.

1. The overall budget of the enterprise is ideally set, for a given period, at a level that will enable the firm to sell such a volume of output that its marginal cost (properly discounted over the planning horizon) will equal marginal revenue (equally so discounted). More realistically, a given sum of money will be available (including loans) and is to be spent optimally. This implies— we assume the firm will fall *short* of optimal

output—that output is to be maximized, given the monetary constraint. The optimum is achieved when there is equality between all MRP/MFC ratios.

We can envisage a cascading process of budget allocation decisions. At the highest rung the decision is to allocate resources between the three basic functions: finance, marketing and production. It would be idle to pretend that more than very rough guessing can be employed to estimate marginal productivities (in terms of either unit or dollar sales) at this level.

The next rung is the allocation of the functional budgets among subfunction activities. Examples are manufacturing, engineering, quality control, and R & D on the production side; personal selling, advertising, sales promotion, and warehousing on the marketing side. And so on, down to more and more specialized activities.

Typically at these more disaggregated levels of activities the budgets are translated into standards, physical or pecuniary, the latter being called standard costs. Such standards, especially on the manufacturing side (the dwindling exception is R & D), are set up not only on the basis of past performance, but also by comparison to competitors or firms using similar processes. Although the physical portion of the standards can be derived from the "most efficient" production functions, the actual recommended combinations of inputs resulting in (monetary) standard costs per unit of some sub-output (such as units of intermediate products or a call on a customer) must take isocosts into account. The controller or the executive in charge of performance evaluation should thus draw the attention of the budgeting committees to any changes in relevant productivity indices in the industry or to changes in input prices. As has been suggested in accounting literature, the firm could develop, within relevant price ranges of both inputs and finished product, input-mix solutions for various price ratios of the substitutable inputs and store them in a computer information system. When prices change, the appropriate stored input-mix solutions are

---

applied normative prescriptions, and of actual empirical examples of the marginal productivity approach is to be found in farm economics literature. Earl O. Heady of Iowa State is the author and coauthor of numerous books and articles on farm management economics from which industrial management could greatly profit. Particularly useful in our present context is Earl O. Heady and John L. Dillon, *op. cit.* On a less technical level Earl O. Heady and Harald R. Jensen, *Farm Management Economics* (Englewood Cliffs, N.J.: Prentice-Hall, 1954) is recommended.

[9] The budgeting procedure consists of (1) setting a standard or budgeted amount for each cost classification for the coming period; (2) comparing actual performance with the budget or standard; (3) reporting and analyzing the variances of the actual performance from the budgeted performance...." H. Bierman, Jr., L. E. Fouraker, and R. K. Jaedicke, "A Use of Probability and Statistics in Performance Evaluation," *Accounting Review* (July, 1961), pp. 409–417.

FIG. 6 (Reproduced from Earl O. Heady and John L. Dillon. Agricultural Production Functions (Ames, Ia.: Iowa State University Press, 1961), p. 301)

found and budget standards adjusted accordingly.[10, 11].

Such a computer program, in very simple form, has been developed years ago for U.S. farmers. Its inventors baptized it the "pork costulator." It is reproduced above as Figure 6. It is derived directly from the marginal productivity data of the hog-feed experiments described previously and from corn-protein price ratios. Commenting upon the pork costulator, its inventors utter words not only of explanation but also of relevance to all businessmen, be they farmers or not:

It is known, of course, that few hog farmers understand calculus or the application of basic economic principles. They cannot go out to the pig pen and equate the appropriate partial derivatives and price ratios, to specify the optimum ration or marketing weight. How-

ever, it is possible to develop mechanical aids to let a farmer make calculations and decisions as if he understood the basic mathematical and economic principles. To illustrate this point, the pork costulator developed by the authors is illustrated.

The costulator is a mechanical device constructed from three sheets of heavy metal. The center or square sheet is about 12 inches square. Disks of a slightly smaller diameter were cut from the other two sheets, with one riveted to each side of the square piece. Prices of corn were printed at the edge of each disk. A slit, through which is read the least-cost and least-time ration for particular price ratios, was cut in the disk on one side for 35–75 pound and 75–150 pound hogs. A similar slit was provided for 150–225 pound hogs on the disk on the other side. The ration data is printed on the center square. By matching the current protein price printed on the edge of the disk with the current corn price printed on the center square, the appropriate price ratio is specified. By glancing through the slit for hogs of a particular weight, the producer can read off the ration which minimizes feed costs per pound of gain, or the ration which minimizes time required for marketing at 225 pounds. Certain auxiliary information also is indicated

[10] Zenon S. Zannetos, "Standard Costs as a First Step to Probabilistic Control," *Accounting Review* (April, 1964), pp. 296–304.

[11] For thinking about a more profound revision of the budgetary process see N. Dopuch, J. G. Birnberg, and J. Demski, "An Extension of Standard Cost Variance Analysis," *Accounting Review* (July, 1967), pp. 526–536.

and includes the components of these rations, the range of price ratios over which it would be profitable to provide self-feeding and free choice of rations by hogs, rates of gain and time to marketing. In effect, the farmer can use the costulator as his "mathematical brain." In matching up the feed prices and reading off the appropriate information, he is accomplishing the equivalent of (a) equating partial derivatives with price ratios and (b) simultaneously solving a set of equations for magnitude of feed variables for attaining least-cost or least-time rations. He need not know mathematics to apply and use the principle.[12]

2. If budgetary standards are set taking account of economic theory, analysis of variance can contribute to optimal control procedures. Before the variance is analyzed it must, however, be detected and adjudged significant. It is here that statistical quality control thinking can significantly reduce decision costs.

There are two main elements to statistical quality control: sampling, and the assessment of the significance of deviations (is process out of control). The idea of sampling implies not only that but a small proportion of actual costs generated over time will be examined and matched against standard costs; it implies also that but a fraction of costs will be recorded in the first place.[13] Although such procedures are advocated by many accountants, it is probable that under prevailing practice most firms still record all actual costs, no matter how standardized the production (or selling) process is. The cost of information for control purposes tends in such cases to be unnecessarily inflated.

Once a sample of unit costs had been taken and a deviation from standard observed, it must be decided whether this deviation represents a statistically significant tendency of the process to get "out of control." (For example, is the mean of the observed sample more than two standard deviations away from the mean of the "population" that has been set as the standard?) Accounting variances acquire thus a probabilistic significance

and are not reported in meaningless absolute figures. Readings on variances can be taken from the highest plausible aggregated activity down. This not only serves the various management rungs of control, but makes—in the case of large statistical populations—the application of the central limit theorem more plausible at the more aggregate levels.[14] Each class of variances can also be observed over time to see if they converge to zero over the longer run.

The last step in reporting variances is the joining of economic with statistical considerations. The "significance" of the reportable variance must not only be established in statistical terms but must also take into account the *costs* that will ensue if it is studied and acted upon (such as the time value of the executives concerned, the costs of corrective action, and the revenue consequences).[15]

3. Accountants have honed the analysis of variance to a fine art, breaking it down into "volume," "price," "mix," and other component variances from budget. The analysis is now technically very sophisticated, as the reading of almost any issue of the *Accounting Review* will document.[16] Despite this sophistication, the connection between the economic analytical framework that we outlined and the accounting analysis is rather tenuous. The present writer does not therefore feel competent to offer practical suggestions here extending beyond those already advanced or implied in the first section of this chapter and in the first part of the second section.

[12] Heady and Dillon, *op. cit.*, p. 300.

[13] Zenon S. Zannetos, "Mathematics as a Tool of Accounting Instruction and Research," *Accounting Review* (April, 1963), pp. 326–335.

[14] Zannetos, *Accounting Review* (April, 1966), *op. cit.*, p. 300.

[15] The deviation of actual from forecast sales may obviously be handled as a variance from budget in terms of the foregoing analysis. The vast literature that is available about *forecasting*, however, is concerned with the performance of forecasters rather than salesmen or advertising. In this sense it is not relevant to our theme. See, for instance, Henri Theil, *Applied Economic Forecasting* (Amsterdam: North-Holland Publishing Co., 1966).

[16] The interested reader may wish to start with Ching-Wen Kwang and Albert Slavin, "The Simple Mathematics of Variance Analysis," in the July, 1962 issue and work his way through successive articles to C. R. Hasseldine, "Mix and Yield Variances," *Accounting Review* (July, 1967).

7

The Sources of Measured Productivity Growth: United States Fertilizer Mineral Industries, 1936–1960*

G. S. SAHOTA

In this study, intrafirm technical progress, or improvements in the state of the arts, are separated from scale economies and productivity changes due to interfirm shifts of resources, by fitting production functions and employing covariance analysis. With a view toward determining the sources of the resulting series of intrafirm technical change, several hypotheses are formulated and tested by using the distributed lag models and other relations.

The Covariance Matrix method employed in this study (which has not been used extensively, partly because the equations are non-linear in the coefficients) has a number of theoretical and statistical advantages over the traditional methods of measuring productivity, such as the single equation least squares method and the factor shares method. First, it permits the separation of technical advance from the contributions of physical factors without building into the empirical model the twin restrictive assumptions of constant returns to scale and competi-

From The Review of Economics and Statistics *(May 1966), pp. 193–204. Reprinted with permission of author and publisher. Copyright © 1966 by the President and Fellows of Harvard College.*

* The author is an associate professor of economics at Vanderbilt University. He wishes to thank Professors T. W. Schultz, H. G. Johnson, L. G. Telser, and Zvi Griliches under whose able supervision he completed his Ph.D. thesis. The present paper is a summary of a chapter of this thesis. He is also indebted to the members of the Agricultural Economics Workshop of the University of Chicago for helpful suggestions. Whatever errors remain are the sole responsibility of the author.

There are three major minerals that are used in making fertilizer, viz., potassium, sulfur, and phosphate rock. Due to lack of data regarding the last-mentioned mineral, only the potassium and the sulfur industries are studied in this paper.

tive factor-pricing—both being necessary conditions in the factor shares method[1] as used by Solow,[2] Kendrick,[3] and others. Second, it enables us to dispense with the necessity of (artificially) imposing the condition of constancy (linear or log-linear) on the rate of technical change, as is commonly done in fitting production functions to time-series data.[4] Third, it is supposed to reduce the simultaneous equation bias of single

[1] These two assumptions underlie the productivity estimates made both by those who use the arithmetic scheme of weighting the inputs for aggregation, thereby assuming an infinite elasticity of substitution among the inputs, and by those who use the geometric weighting scheme, thereby assuming the underlying production function to be of the Cobb-Douglas type. In the first group may be mentioned studies by John W. Kendrick, *Productivity Trends in the United States* (Princeton: National Bureau of Economic Research, Princeton University Press, 1961); Moses Abramovitz, "Resources and Output Trends in the United States Since 1870," *American Economic Review*, XLVI, No. 2 (1956), 5–23; and several others in different countries. Among the studies of particular interest in the second group may be mentioned those by Robert M. Solow, "Technical Change and the Aggregate Production Function," *Review of Economics and Statistics*, XXXIX (Aug. 1957), 312–320; and Benton F. Massel, "Determinants of Productivity Change in United States Manufacturing," *Yale Economic Essays*, Vol. II, No. 2 (1962), 303–351. Neither of these assumptions is, however, essential if the weights being used are the estimated coefficients of the fitted production function (instead of the market shares) as employed, for instance, by Zvi Griliches in "The Sources of Measured Productivity Growth: United States Agriculture, 1940–1960," *Journal of Political Economy*, LXXI, No. 4 (1963), especially 344–345.

[2] R. Solow, *op. cit.*

[3] J. W. Kendrick, *op. cit.*

[4] See, for example, Jan Tinbergen, "On the Theory of Trend Movements," in L. H. Klaassen et al., eds., *Collected Papers*, (Amsterdam: North-Holland, 1959); and O. Aukrust, and J. Bjerke, "Real Capital and Economic Growth in Norway 1900–56," *Income and Wealth*, Series VIII (1959).

equation least squares regressions[5] and weaken the tendency towards indeterminacy of the production function coefficients due to multicollinearity in aggregate time-series data.[6] Last, being computed rather than obtained as a residual, the technical change series is net of random errors which, in the traditional residual methods, are collected in the productivity index.

ELASTICITY OF SUBSTITUTION

Before estimating the production function, its form must be specified. For this purpose, the elasticity of substitution between at least the two major factors of production, labor and capital, must be determined.

The estimates of the elasticity of substitution between labor and capital, σ_{lk}, are made by imposing a constant-elasticity-of-substitution (CES) production function[7] on the data, that is to say, assuming the σ_{lk} to remain constant during the period for which it is being estimated, but allowing it to take any values, viz., $\sigma_{lk} \gtreqless 1$. A particular test will be to find out whether σ_{lk} is significantly different from unity in which case the Arrow, *et al.* method[8] of estimating the production function will be used. If it is not significantly different from unity, the Cobb-Douglas production function will be employed.

The following log-linear relation is estimated:

$$\frac{V}{L} = b_0 w^{b_1} \qquad (1)$$

where V is value added in 1954 prices, L denotes man-hours, and w stands for average hourly earnings in 1954 prices.

Given the assumption of a CES production function, neutral technical change, and the exogenous nature of the wage rate, the slope coefficient, b_1, in this equation is an estimate of σ_{lk}.

The results of fitting such a relationship to various combinations of data and different forms of the relation for the periods 1936–1947, 1947–1960, and 1936–1960, separately for the sulfur and the potassium industries, are noted in Table 1.

Four types of estimates are made: (a) direct estimates as in method used by Arrow, *et al.* (Regressions 1–6); (b) estimates taking labor quality into consideration by introducing a measure of education per man, since differences in the price of labor over time may not otherwise reveal true differences in labor cost, as more highly paid labor may also be more efficient (Regressions 7–12); (c) those based on the Koyck-Nerlove type of distributed lag model,[9] to allow for lagged adjustment to changes in wage rates whereas the previous two types of estimates assume instantaneous adjustments (Regressions 13–18); and (d) those based on first differences of the variables of Regressions (1), (2), (3), and (4), with a view toward testing autocorrelation among the residuals.

The coefficients of almost all the regressions are significant at conventional levels. The first differences in Regressions 19-22 reduce the serial correlation of the residuals somewhat as shown by the increased values of the Durbin-Watson test statistics (not reported in Table 1). However, the coefficients of these regressions do not provide any different

[5] A proof of the reduction of simultaneous equations bias when cross-sectional and time-series data are pooled and the covariance analysis is carried out (as is done in the present study) is given by Irving Hoch in "Estimation of Production Function Parameters Combining Time-Series and Cross-Section Data," *Econometrica*, XXX, No. 1 (1962), 34–53.

[6] See Lawrence R. Klein, *An Introduction to Econometrics* (Englewood Cliffs, N.J.: Prentice-Hall, 1962), 62–64; also Yair Mundlak, "Empirical Production Function Free of Management Bias," *Journal of Farm Economics*, XLIII, No. 1 (1961), 44–57; and J. Kmenta, "Some Properties of Alternative Estimates of the Cobb-Douglas Production Function," *Econometrica*, XXXII, Nos. 1 and 2 (1964), 183–189.

[7] Constant-elasticity-of-substitution production function as first used by K. J. Arrow, H. B. Chenery, B. S. Minhas, and R. M. Solow, "Capital-Labor Substitution and Economic Efficiency," *Review of Economics and Statistics*, XLIII (Aug. 1961), 225–250.

[8] Arrow, et al., *op. cit.*

[9] L. M. Koyck, *Distributed Lags and Investment Analysis* (Amsterdam: North-Holland, 1954); and Marc Nerlove, *Distributed Lags and Demand Analysis for Agricultural and Other Commodities*, U.S. Department of Agriculture, Agricultural Handbook No. 141 (Washington, D.C., 1958).

TABLE 1 Estimates of Elasticity of Substitution, σ_{lk}, in the Sulfur and Potassium Industries, United States, 1936–1960[a]

Regression Number (1)	Industry and Period (2)	Wage Rate (3)	Wage Rate Deflated by Education Index (4)	Lagged Value of "Value Added" (5)	σ_{lk} (6)	R^2 (7)	Standard Error of Estimate (8)	Degrees of Freedom (9)
Sulfur								
1)	1936–1947	1.05 (2.14)	...	...	1.05	0.61	0.103	46
2)	1947–1960	1.14 (2.53)	...	...	1.14	.78	.087	54
3)	1936–1960	1.11 (2.44)	...	...	1.11	.75	.089	98
Potassium								
4)	1936–1947	0.85 (1.71)	...	...	0.85	.58	.112	48
5)	1947–1960	1.08 (2.89)	...	...	1.08	.80	.087	68
6)	1936–1960	0.97 (2.29)	...	...	0.97	.72	.093	112
Sulfur								
7)	1936–1947	...	1.08 (1.91)	...	1.08	.62	.093	46
8)	1947–1960	...	1.19 (2.60)	...	1.19	.77	.088	54
9)	1936–1960	...	1.13 (2.39)	...	1.13	.75	.089	98
Potassium								
10)	1936–1947	...	0.90 (1.42)	...	0.90	.59	.108	46
11)	1947–1960	...	1.13 (2.72)	...	1.13	.79	.086	68
12)	1936–1960	...	1.01 (2.53)	...	1.01	.69	.095	112
Sulfur								
13)	1936–1947	0.519 (1.21)	...	0.510 (2.60)	1.06	.72	.097	45
14)	1947–1960	0.455 (2.12)	...	0.602 (4.52)	1.14	.86	.077	53
15)	1936–1960	0.48 (2.00)	...	0.57 (3.19)	1.11	.83	.069	97
Potassium								
16)	1936–1947	0.385 (1.40)	...	0.490 (2.21)	0.77	.65	.101	45
17)	1947–1960	0.380 (2.50)	...	0.575 (2.32)	0.90	.87	.071	67
18)	1936–1960	.40 (1.85)	...	.59 (2.25)	1.02	.84	.078	111
First differences:								
Sulfur								
19)	1936–1947	1.01 (1.75)	...	...	1.01	.65	.092	46
20)	1947–1960	1.09 (2.15)	...	...	1.09	.80	.081	54
Potassium								
21)	1936–1947	.88 (1.63)	...	...	.88	.61	.096	46
22)	1947–1960	1.05 (2.25)	...	...	1.05	.77	.083	68

[a] The numbers in parentheses are the t values of the corresponding coefficients. The ten, five, and one percentage points with 46 degrees of freedom of the regression coefficients are 1.680, 2.012, and 2.690, respectively, for a two-tailed test. R^2 stands for the correlation of multiple determination. The relation used for regressions 13 to 18 is,

$$(1b) \qquad \frac{V_t}{L_t} = b_0 w^{b_2}\left(\frac{V_{t-1}}{L_{t-1}}\right)^{b_3},$$

whence $\sigma_{lk} = b_2/(1 - b_3)$. For instance, the estimate of the σ_{lk} in Regression 13 is $.52/(1 - .51) = 1.06$.

Sources: The data were compiled mainly from annual balance sheets and other statistics as reported in Moody's *Industrial Manual* for all the four sulfur firms and all the five potassium firms investigated in this study. These data were supplemented from divers sources. Special attention was paid to the preparation of capital series. Corrections were made to allow for idle capacity, the book values were deflated by a Creamer-Stigler type of deflator. See for example, George J. Stigler, *Capital and Rate of Return in Manufacturing Industries* (Princeton: Princeton University Press, 1963, p. 122), and the accountants' depreciation charges were corrected in accordance with the life-spans of different machines and equipment as given in United States Treasury Department, IRS, *Income Tax, Depreciation and Obsolescence, Estimated Useful Lives, and Depreciation Rates,* Bulletin "F", (Jan. 1942); and *Depreciation Guidelines and Rules,* Publication No. 456 (Washington: United States Government Printing Office, 1962).

results. None of the σ_{lk} coefficients are significantly different from unity even at the 20 per cent level. A reasonable inference from these estimates, therefore, is that there is no strong evidence against the application of the Cobb-Douglas production function which, therefore, will be used in this study.

THE COVARIANCE MATRIX METHOD OF ESTIMATING A PRODUCTION FUNCTION

Having found no evidence against the assumption of the underlying production function being of the Cobb-Douglas type, the theoretical form of the model for pooled time-series and cross-sectional data may be stated as follows:

$$\ln Q_{it} = B + \alpha_1 \ln L_{it} + \alpha_2 \ln K_{it}$$
$$+ \sum_{i=1}^{I-1} \beta_i D_i^{(F)} + \sum_{t=2}^{T} \gamma_t D_t^{(Y)} + e_{it}, \quad (2a)$$

or,

$$\ln Q_{it} = \alpha_1 \ln L_{it} + \alpha_2 \ln K_{it}$$
$$+ \sum_{i=1}^{I} \beta_i D_i^{(F)} + \sum_{t=2}^{T} \gamma_t D_t^{(Y)} + e_{it}, \quad (2b)$$

where $i = 1, \ldots, I$; and $t = 1, \ldots, T$, for L_{it}, K_{it}, and Q_{it}. Q_i, L_i, and K_i stand for physical output, man-hours, and gross capital stock in 1954 prices, respectively, in the ith firm, and the absence of subscript i denotes the aggregate for the industry. The subscript t denotes a time period of one year. The $D_i^{(F)}$'s are the firm dummy variables and the $D_i^{(Y)}$'s are the year dummy variables. In other words, the $D_i^{(F)}$'s are variables that take the value of unity in the ith firm, zero in all others, and the $D_t^{(Y)}$'s are the variables that take the value of unity in the tth year and zero in all other years. Symbolically,

$$D_1^{(F)} = 1 \text{ for all } \ln Q_{it} \text{ with } i = 1,$$
$$\text{and } = 0 \text{ for all other } \ln Q_{it},$$
$$D_2^{(F)} = 1 \text{ for all } \ln Q_{it} \text{ with } i = 2,$$
$$\text{and } = 0 \text{ for all other } \ln Q_{it},$$

and so on, and

$$D_2^{(Y)} = 1 \text{ for all } \ln Q_{it} \text{ with } t = 2,$$
$$\text{and } = 0 \text{ for all other } \ln Q_{it},$$
$$D_3^{(Y)} = 1 \text{ for all } \ln Q_{it} \text{ with } t = 3,$$
$$\text{and } = 0 \text{ for all other } \ln Q_{it}$$

and so on.

In (2a), the dummy for the base year and for one firm in terms of which γ_t's and β_i's, respectively, are to be measured, are omitted (i.e., they take zero values). Thus the necessary number of $D_t^{(Y)}$'s is one less than the number of cross-sections that are being estimated together, and the number of $D_i^{(F)}$'s is one less than the number of firms in the sample. In (2b), instead of omitting the dummy for one of the firms, the general constant term, B, is suppressed. For if both are retained in the same regression, the matrix will become singular.[10] The e_{it}'s are random terms, and are supposed to be independently and identically distributed, with zero mean and constant variance. It may be seen that (2a) and (2b) contain a standard analysis of covariance model.

The coefficients β_i may be interpreted as indices of interfirm technical efficiency levels,

[10] Either a dummy from each of the sets of the dummy variables used in a regression must be omitted or the general constant must necessarily be suppressed. Otherwise, we shall get singularity. This will occur for the simple reason that the vector of the constant terms becomes a linear multiple of the sum of the vectors of the dummies of a set which, by definition, are always equal to one. On the other hand, if both the constant and a variable of a set of dummies are suppressed, the regression coefficients may become biased as, for those observations for which there is neither a dummy nor a constant in the regression, the regression line will be forced to pass through the origin. Whether a dummy or the general intercept is suppressed, in the absence of computational mistakes, the results ought to be exactly the same except that in the former case the coefficients of the dummy variables included in the regression are measured from the value of the general constant while in the latter case they are measured from the origin. In the present regressions, the base-year-dummy variable was suppressed once and for all. As regards the firm dummies, alternative regressions were run. In one set of regressions, the intercept was suppressed using the Noconstant-linear-regression (NCLR) Program of IBM 7090 (Department of Business Economics, the University of Chicago, 1963). In the other set of regressions, the constant was also computed and counter-checks were carried out by using the BIMD 29 Program (Bailey-Thornber modification) on the same computer, *ibid.*

which will reflect mainly the quality of management and/or geological conditions of the mines of the respective firms. They may also reflect quality of other inputs, e.g., labor and capital, if superior quality inputs have a tendency to be positively associated with superior quality management and mines.[11] The coefficients γ_t are the estimates of technical change between the base year and the tth year.

MAIN RESULTS OF THE FITTED PRODUCTION FUNCTION

Regressions of (2a) and (2b) were run for the data for four firms of the sulfur industry and five firms of the potassium industry, separately, for the periods 1936–1947 and 1947–1960.[12] The results are presented in Table 2.[13] The major findings are as follows:

1) All the firm dummy coefficients are significantly different from zero, but none is significantly different from any other. Therefore, the null hypothesis of identical interfirm efficiency levels cannot be rejected.

[11] It may be noted that these interfirm-technical-efficiency differences do not affect the intrafirm regression coefficients since, if the firms are found on their particular production function, the estimates of the slope given by the a's will be the same regardless of the changing position of the firm constants.

[12] The separation of the overall reference period into two sub-periods (1936–1947 and 1947–1960) was necessitated mainly by the limitations of the computer programs. The IBM programs referred to in footnote 10 did not allow the inclusion of variables in excess of 30 in one multiple regression. Accordingly, I could not use all the 24 year dummies of the period 1936–1960 along with the five firm dummies and the three real variables in the same multiple regression. However, this sub-division of the reference period does not seem to conflict with the general impression that the stability of the production function might have been disturbed around the year 1947 (even though in the present case the regression coefficients of the second sub-period hardly seem to fall outside the tolerance limits set by the regression results of the former sub-period).

[13] Since both types of regressions give identical results (with the exception, as explained in footnote 10, that the values of the coefficients of the firm dummies have to be interpreted somewhat differently in the two types of regressions), only the coefficients obtained from the regression of (2b) are reported here.

One of the important advantages of estimating a production function by the Covariance Matrix method instead of the traditional least-squares method lies in the removal of the firm or management effect which might otherwise bias the production coefficients. Since the coefficients of the firm dummy variables are not statisically significant, that advantage is nonexistent in the present regressions. However, the non-existence of such effects is in itself a finding of meaningful significance. We have sustained a null hypothesis instead of merely assuming it to be so.

2) The coefficients of year-dummy variables are, in general, statistically significant at the conventional levels. Those that are not significant fall mainly in the World War II period and the early years of the reference period. Considering the fact that the year-dummy coefficients denote pure technical change, i.e., productivity growth net of scale economies and the effects, if any, of interfirm shifts of resources, their values are quite high. For example, the coefficient of the year-1960 dummy, with 1936 as the base, rises to 189 in potassium and to 175 in sulfur.

3) The sum of coefficients of labor and capital exceeds unity in all the regressions. If the production function is well-specified, constant returns to scale would be expected to prevail in the long run. The existence of the oligopolistic market structure and the collusive agreements in these industries may, however, hinder the firms from pushing their output to the constant-returns point. Nevertheless, since there would be a persistent tendency for the most dominant economic behavior—that of profit maximizing—to prevail, the sum of elasticities is tested for significant differences from unity.

As may be observed from Table 2, the sum of coefficients in the sulfur industry is higher than one at the two per cent one-tailed level during 1936-1947 and at the ten per cent one-tailed level during 1947–1960. In the potassium industry, however, the sum of elasticities is not significantly larger than unity even at the 20 per cent one-tailed level of significance. Accordingly, increasing returns to scale are suggested in the sulfur industry,

TABLE 2 Estimates of the Production Functions in the Potassium and the Sulfur Industries, United States, 1936–1947 and 1947–1960[a]

Coefficient of	Potassium		Sulfur	
	Regression (1) 1936–1947	Regression (2) 1947–1960	Regression (3) 1936–1947	Regression (4) 1947–1960
Labor	0.41 (3.51)	0.50 (4.11)	0.23 (5.86)	0.26 (6.35)
Capital	.76 (4.66)	.55 (5.02)	.95 (14.29)	.86 (12.39)
Firm dummies				
D_1	−4.47 (−4.50)	−2.63 (−2.96)	−3.21 (−7.99)	−2.90 (−5.30)
	(−.47)	(.74)	(.13)	(−.25)
D_2	−3.52 (−3.99)	−2.58 (−1.84)	−3.58 (−6.75)	−2.20 (−4.20)
	(.55)	(.22)	(−.60)	(1.12)
D_3	−3.93 (−4.28)	−2.92 (−2.05)	−3.14 (−8.57)	−2.95 (−5.40)
	(.08)	(−.18)	(.33)	(−.35)
D_4	−3.97 (−3.52)	−2.76 (−1.75)	−3.11 (−5.50)	−3.10 (−4.40)
	(.03)	(.00)	(.27)	(−.45)
D_5	n.a.	−2.94 (−2.05)		
		(−.20)		
Year dummies				
D_{1936}	0.00 …		0.00 …	
D_{1937}	−.006 (−.61)		−.138 (−1.41)	
D_{1938}	+.004 (+.38)		.213 (2.05)	
D_{1939}	−.026 (−2.56)		.069 (.64)	
D_{1940}	−.017 (−.76)		.094 (.85)	
D_{1941}	−.013 (−1.32)		.040 (.37)	
D_{1942}	−.010 (−.69)		.119 (.11)	
D_{1943}	+.006 (+.38)		.031 (.29)	
D_{1944}	.073 (.43)		.130 (1.17)	
D_{1945}	.081 (.53)		.231 (2.44)	
D_{1946}	.058 (.35)		.253 (2.26)	
D_{1947}	.104 (.59)	0.00 …	.400 (3.67)	0.00 …
D_{1948}		.056 (0.48)		.035 (0.40)
D_{1949}		.119 (1.03)		.059 (.68)
D_{1950}		.136 (1.18)		.103 (1.19)
D_{1951}		.028 (0.23)		.194 (2.10)
D_{1952}		.287 (2.37)		.065 (.69)
D_{1953}		.376 (3.21)		.073 (.70)
D_{1954}		.384 (3.30)		.200 (1.89)
D_{1955}		.329 (2.74)		.196 (2.00)
D_{1956}		.393 (3.11)		.201 (1.88)
D_{1957}		.601 (4.98)		.236 (3.49)
D_{1958}		.560 (4.73)		.320 (4.11)
D_{1959}		.722 (6.05)		.275 (3.44)
D_{1960}		.720 (6.01)		.247 (2.34)
R^{2b}	.995	.997	.996	.998
$\bar{R}^{2c}$	.993	.996	.994	.997

Residual variance	.018	.033	.018	.014
Sum of coefficients	1.17 (0.92)	1.05 (0.30)	1.18 (2.12)	1.12 (1.90)
Durbin-Watson statistic	1.79	1.93	2.56	2.32
Degrees of freedom	31	50	31	37
Mean output of[d]				
Firm 1	9	36	4	13
Firm 2	8	19	24	55
Firm 3	6	33	3	9
Firm 4	5	18	48	80
Firm 5	n.a.	1.5	...	...

[a] The dummy variables, D's, are to be interpreted as follows:

$D_1 = 1$ in the case of Firm 1, $= 0$ for all other firms,
$D_2 = 1$ in the case of Firm 2, $= 0$ for all other firms,

and so on;

$D_{1937} = 1$ in the year 1937, $= 0$ in other years,
$D_{1938} = 1$ in the year 1938, $= 0$ in other years,

and so on;

$D_{1948} = 1$ in the year 1948, $= 0$ in other years,
$D_{1949} = 1$ in the year 1949, $= 0$ in other years,

and

$D_{1960} = 1$ in the year 1960; $= 0$ in other years, and so on.

Logarithms of output, man-hours, and capital were taken to the base e. The coefficients $\beta_i (i = 1, \ldots, I)$, if multiplied by 100, measure the percentage superiority (in the case of the coefficient being above average) or inferiority (in the case of the coefficient being below average) of the technology of the respective (ith) firm as compared with the average firm. The coefficients $\gamma_t (t = 1, \ldots, T)$, if multiplied by 100, measure the percentage increase of output due to (neutral) technical change in the tth year over the base year. For example, in case the coefficients of the potassium firms in period 1936–1947 were significantly different from the overall constant term (in the present regressions they are not), firm 1 would be eight per cent less efficient and firm 3 would be five per cent more efficient than the weighted average technical efficiency of industry. Similarly, technical change between the years 1947 and 1960 in the potassium industry is 72 per cent.

The period 1936–1960 was broken into two sub-periods, 1936–1947 and 1947–1960, mainly for the reason that the IBM programs used did not permit more than 30 variables to be included in a multiple regression. In order to calculate technical change for the entire period from 1936 to 1960, therefore, the 1947–1960 indices have to be converted to the base 1936. In the case of potassium, for example, it is 189 $[= (110.4/100) \times 172]$. The estimated technical change between any two years is obtained by taking the difference between the respective coefficients. Thus technical change between 1949 and 1950 in the potassium industry is 0.017 $(= .136 - .119)$. The numbers in parentheses are the computed t-values. Except for the two cases mentioned below, they are computed for the two-tailed tests against "zero." That is, they are just the ratios between coefficients and their respective standard errors. The numbers in the second set of parentheses against the firm dummies are the t-values computed to test the respective coefficients against the overall intercept term rather than against zero. That is, the t-values are computed by dividing the difference of the dummy coefficient of the firm concerned, β_i, from the overall constant term B by the variance of their difference, viz., $(\beta_i - B)/\sqrt{\text{var}(\beta_i - B)}$, and for twice the degrees of freedom in this case.

The sum of coefficients is tested against unity. It is a one-tailed test carried out to test whether the sum of coefficients is significantly greater than unity. In the present case, the $t = [(\alpha_1 + \alpha_2) - 1]/\sqrt{\text{var}(\alpha_1) + \text{var}(\alpha_2) + 2\,\text{cov}(\alpha_1\alpha_2)}$. The critical values of t for the one-tailed test for ten, five, and one per cent points are 1.295, 1.670, and 1.999, respectively, for 62 degrees of freedom of the coefficients computed immediately above.

[b] The coefficients of multiple determination. The five and one per cent points with 17 and 31 degrees of freedom of the R^2 in regressions (1) and (3) are .515 and .588, respectively. With 20 and 50 degrees of freedom, the R^2's in regression (2) are .419 and .464, respectively, and with 19 and 37 degrees of freedom of the R^2's in regression (4) are .487 and .552, respectively.

[c] $\bar{R}^2$ is the coefficient of multiple determination adjusted for degrees of freedom lost.

[d] These numbers are the geometric means in millions of dollars converted to 1954 prices.

Sources: The major sources of data are the Security and Exchange Commission statistics as reported in Moody's *Industrial Manual* for all the four sulfur firms and all the five potassium firms included in these regressions. For details, see footnotes to table 1.

while they are not confirmed in the potassium industry.

4) Looking at the individual coefficients of labor and capital in the four regressions of Table 2, the first impression one gets is that the coefficients of labor are a little too low. This appears to be the case especially in sulfur where the share of output attributable to labor comes to only 20 to 23 per cent. The above impression is (partly) corrected, however, when we compare the relative output elasticities computed from these regressions with the observed (market) shares. For instance, the proportion of payrolls to value-added (net of rents for land and depletable assets) was approximately 37 per cent in 1939 and 42 per cent in 1954 in potassium, and approximately 16 per cent in 1939 and 18 per cent in 1954 in sulfur.[14] These proportions are not significantly different from the relative output elasticities obtained from the regression coefficients, viz., approximately 36 per cent during 1936–1947 and 48 per cent during 1947–1960 in potassium, and approximately 20 per cent during 1936–1947 and 23 per cent during 1947–1960 in sulfur.

The estimated marginal products of labor and capital in sulfur are presented in Table 3. They are $2.38 and $3.60 per man-hour for labor and $0.188 and $0.195 per year per dollar of invested capital for the two sub-periods, respectively. They may be compared with the other information on the economic conditions and economic history of this industry, in particular the market prices of inputs. For this purpose, the approximate prices of inputs are also given in the same table. In order to make the market prices and marginal products comparable, however, certain corrections have to be made. For instance, in this industry, one would expect the marginal products of labor and capital to be approximately 27 per cent above their marginal costs during 1936–1947 and approximately 12 per cent above their marginal costs during 1947–1960, given the previous finding of economies of scale of about

these orders during the respective periods.[15] In order to make this adjustment, the marginal products are deflated by scale economies, item (3b). Secondly, the market prices are adjusted to include taxes, in particular the rate of return on invested capital is computed gross of corporation tax.

Due to the prevailing oligopolistic conditions, the strict equality of the value of the marginal product and factor prices is not likely to hold. However, given the plausible assumption of the absence of monopsony, or an even degree of monopsony, in the purchase of labor and capital by the sulfur industry, the tendency towards the proportionality of marginal products to factor prices would still be expected to prevail in the long run. The proportionality condition does not seem to have been violated. For instance, as can be seen from item (4) of Table 3, the ratios of the marginal products of labor and capital to their prices were 1.31 (=$2.27/$1.73) and 1.23 (=14.80%/12.00%), respectively, during 1936–1947, and 1.22 (=$3.22/$2.64) and 1.19 (=17.37%/14.6%), respectively, during 1947–1960, which is not inconsistent with the prevailing degrees of monopoly, in the respective periods, of about the same orders. The proportions are relatively closer in the second period as compared with the first period, which indicates that a small degree of disequilibrium that existed in the first period (possibly due to war) was being corrected in the second period—the oligopolists, too, economize.

THE PRODUCTIVITY SERIES AND ITS COMPONENTS

The prevalence of scale economies and the oligopolistic market structure in the fertilizer mineral industries under study render the factor shares approach to productivity measurement entirely inapplicable. While the covariance matrix method used in this

[14] The observed values were calculated from the census data.

[15] To the extent that economies of scale have been indicated, a margin of marginal product over factor cost is understandable. The adding-up theorem will not hold, because if factors are paid their marginal products, the available product would be over-exhausted.

TABLE 3 Estimated Aggregate Marginal Products, Input Prices, and the Proportionality Relations, Sulfur Industry, United States, 1936–1960[a]

| Item (1) | 1936–1947 | | 1947–1960 | |
	Labor (2)	Capital (3)	Labor (4)	Capital (5)
1) Returns to factors in sulfur				
a) Net of taxes (w)	1.73[b]	24.7[c]	2.64[b]	25.8[c]
b) Gross of taxes $(w*)$[d]	1.73	33.1	2.64	34.5
2) Market prices of factors[e]				
a) Net of taxes (p)	1.47	6.6	2.00	8.0
b) Gross of taxes $(p*)$[d]	1.47	12.0	2.00	14.6
3) Mean value marginal products[f]				
a) Undeflated (MP)	2.38	18.80	3.60	19.45
	(10.9)	(5.8)	(7.7)	(4.2)
b) Deflated by scale economies $(MP*)$	2.27	14.80	3.22	17.37
4) Ratio of marginal product to factor price: (3b)/(2b) for capital (MP_K^*/p_K^*), and (3b)/(1b) for labor	2.27	14.80	3.22	17.37
(MP_L^*/p_L^*)	1.73	12.00	2.64	14.60

[a] The units are, dollars per man-hour for labor and percentage per year for capital.

[b] Calculated from United States Department of Commerce, Bureau of the Census, *Census of Manufactures*, 1947, 1954, and 1958 and checked against the corresponding figures for bituminous coal mining reported in United States Department of Labor, Bureau of Labor Statistics, *Employment and Earnings Statistics for the United States, 1909–1962*, Bulletin No. 1312–1 (1963), 4.

The figures refer to "production-worker average hourly earnings" (in 1954 prices) whereas the man-hours used in the production function are for "all employees." However, the difference between the average hourly earnings of production workers and all employees, if any, is not expected to be large.

[c] These figures denote the actual rate of return on invested capital as reported in the balance sheets.

[d] The taxes included are mainly the corporation income tax payments the entire incidence of which, for the purpose of these calculations, is assumed to be on capital. The average rate of tax on the return to capital comes to about 45 per cent during this period. See Arnold C. Harberger, "The Corporation Income Tax: An Empirical Appraisal," (unpublished paper, Department of Economics, University of Chicago, 1962).

[e] The figures for labor in this item refer to mining as a whole. No further use is made of these figures as the relevant ones, for the current problem, are those for the actual wage rate paid in the industries under study, i.e., the figures of item 1. The figures for capital

study separates the effects of pure technological change from some of the other changes in the overall output, it does not directly yield a composite series of total productivity or output-per-unit-of-input series. However, these estimates can be obtained by minor manipulations of the coefficients of the production function estimated above. In particular, the following three series can easily be computed: (a) the series of percentage changes in output due to intrafirm technical change; (b) the series of percentage changes in output due to interfirm productivity change resulting from the interfirm shifts of resources; and (c) the series of economies of scale.

In addition, rough estimates of non-neutral technical change between the two sub-periods can also be made.

Empirical Relationships for Computing Various Components of Productivity Growth

For this purpose, treating all factors and parameters of (2b) as variables, taking its total differential, i.e., a linear approximation, and interpreting all differentials as discrete changes, we get,

$$\frac{\Delta Q_{it}}{Q_{it}} = \alpha_1 \frac{\Delta L_{it}}{L_{it}} + \alpha_2 \frac{\Delta K_{it}}{K_{it}} + \ln L_{it}\, \Delta\alpha_1$$
$$+ \ln K_{it}\, \Delta\alpha_2 + \beta_i \Delta D_i + \gamma_t \Delta D_t$$
$$+ D_i \Delta\beta_i + D_t \Delta\gamma_t. \quad (3)$$

refer to the average rate of return on capital in manufacturing as a whole, and are taken from Stigler, *op. cit.*, Tables A-59 and A-35.

[f] The marginal products of inputs were obtained by the relation, $\alpha_j(\hat{Q}/\bar{X}_j)$, where $\hat{Q}$ is the level of output estimated by holding each input at its geometric mean, and $\bar{X}$ is the geometric mean of the input to which the coefficient α corresponds.

The numbers in parentheses are the computed t values of the respective coefficients. The variance of the marginal product of the inputs was computed by multiplying the variance of the input coefficient computed in Table 2 by the square of the respective output-input ratio as computed above, viz.,

$$(\hat{Q}/\bar{X}_j)^2 \text{ var } (\alpha_j).$$

For further discussion of this test, see Earl O. Heady and John L. Dillon, *Agricultural Production Functions* (Ames, Iowa: Iowa University Press, 1961), 231.

As was noted earlier, all values of the dummies but the ith are, by definition, always zero in this model. Therefore, all terms but the ith among the dummy variables of (2b) drop out in this differential. Also, since the ith dummy is always unity in this model, the $\Delta D_i \equiv 0$. Accordingly, (3) reduces to,

$$\frac{\Delta Q_{it}}{Q_{it}} = \alpha_1 \frac{\Delta L_{it}}{L_{it}} + \alpha_2 \frac{\Delta K_{it}}{K_{it}} + \ln L_{it}\Delta\alpha_1$$
$$+ \ln K_{it}\Delta\alpha_2 + \Delta\beta_i + \Delta\gamma_t. \quad (4)$$

An implicit assumption of this model is that the β_i's are constant for all years, the γ_t's are constant for all firms, and the α's are constant for all firms and all years for which a regression is run. Accordingly, since the base from which the β_i's are measured is the general constant term B, and the base from which the γ_t's are measured is zero, the $\Delta\beta_i$ and the $\Delta\gamma_t$ are to be interpreted as $\Delta\beta_i = (\beta_i - B)$, and $\Delta\gamma_t = (\gamma_t - 0)$, respectively. With these preliminaries, (4) may be used to get the following four empirical relations:

1) Percentage change in output of the overall industry due to intrafirm (neutral) technical change is given directly by the last term in (4), viz.,

$$\gamma_t = \gamma\text{-series.} \quad (4a)$$

2) Percentage change in output of the overall industry due to interfirm productivity changes resulting from interfirm shifts of resources will be equal to the sum of the efficiency coefficients of the firms weighted by their respective relative gains or losses of resources, i.e.,

$$\sum_{i=1}^{I} \frac{\beta_i}{B}\left[\alpha_1\left(\frac{\Delta L_{it}}{L_{it}} - \frac{\Delta L_t}{L_t}\right) + \alpha_2\left(\frac{\Delta K_{it}}{K_{it}}\right.\right.$$
$$\left.\left. - \frac{\Delta K_t}{K_t}\right)\right] = \beta\text{-series} \quad (4b)$$

which will change only when the terms between the brackets are non-zero, i.e., when there are unequal relative gains or losses of inputs by different firms of the industry.

For example, if the relatively more efficient firms, i.e., firms with $\beta > B$, have been expanding relative to the other firms, overall productivity will rise.

3) Percentage change in output of the overall industry due to scale economies/diseconomies can be separated by rewriting the first two terms on the right-hand side of (4) as follows and aggregating the results over the industry:

$$\sum_{i=1}^{I}\left[(\alpha_1 - \alpha_1^*)\frac{\Delta L_{it}}{L_{it}} + (\alpha_2 - \alpha_2^*)\frac{\Delta K_{it}}{K_{it}}\right],$$

or simply,

$$(\alpha_1 - \alpha_1^*)\frac{\Delta L_t}{L_t} + (\alpha_2 - \alpha_2^*)\frac{\Delta K_t}{K_t} = \text{E-series}$$
$$(4c)$$

where $\alpha_1^* = \alpha_1/\alpha_1 + \alpha_2$, and $\alpha_2^* = \alpha_2/(\alpha_1 + \alpha_2)$, i.e., α_1^* and α_2^* would represent the relative shares of labor and capital if there were constant returns to scale. The terms $(\alpha_1 - \alpha_1^*)$ and $(\alpha_2 - \alpha_2^*)$ denote the excess output (in percentage terms) per unit of labor and capital, respectively, of the firms operating in the range of increasing or decreasing returns to scale over the same firms using identical resources had they operated under constant returns to scale.

4) Percentage change in output of the overall industry due to non-neutral technical change is given by the middle two terms on the right-hand side of (4), i.e.,

$$\sum_{i=1}^{I}(\ln L_{it}\Delta\alpha_1 + \ln K_{it}\Delta\alpha_2),$$

or simply,

$$\ln L_t\Delta\alpha_1 + \ln K_t\Delta\alpha_2. \quad (4d)$$

The productivity, or output-per-unit-of-input, index can be obtained by summing up changes from (4a) to (4d).

Results of the Computations

Since the coefficients of the firm-dummy variables are not significantly different from each other, computations in accordance with (4b) are not relevant. Likewise, changes under (4d) do not appear to be important and will be ignored.[16] In the case of potassium, (4c) is also irrelevant as no evidence of scale economies was found in this industry. Therefore, the estimates of the output-per-unit-of-input series for potassium will be the same as the technical change series computed by (4a) i.e., the γ-series.

The γ_t coefficients of the two regressions for the two periods 1936–1947 and 1947–1960 are combined into one series for both of the industries and brought to the base 1936. These two series, along with the corresponding year-to-year changes, are reproduced in Table 4 and Figures 1 and 2. It will be noted that over the period 1936-1960, the percentage increase in output due to intrafirm (neutral) technical change was 89 per cent in potassium and 75 per cent in sulfur. These figures give an annual geometric average rate of technological change of a little over 2.5 per cent in potassium and approximately2.25 per cent in sulfur.

[16] In order to find out whether the period 1936–1960 had any technological sub-periods within which observations with respect to the α's remained homogeneous, regressions were run over the period by slicing off years one by one, first from the bottom up—i.e., for 1936–1960, 1937–1960, 1938–1960, and so on—and then from the top down—i.e., for 1936–1960, 1936–1959, 1936–1958, and so on. An approximation to the method of tolerance limits (as suggested by Allen Wallis in Jerzy Neyman, ed. "Tolerance Intervals for Linear Regression," *Proceedings of the Second Berkeley Symposium on Mathematical Statistics and Probability* (Berkeley: University of California Press, 1951), 43–51, and as used by Murray Brown and Joel Popkin in "A Measure of Technological Change and Returns to Scale," *Review of Economics and Statistics,* XLVI (Nov. 1962), 402–411) gave some indication that the relative shares changed somewhat around the year 1947 in the sulfur industry, indicating a capital-using non-neutral technical change in this industry. This was an additional reason for sub-dividing the period 1936–1960 into two sub-periods, 1936–1947 and 1947–1960. Computations were then carried out in accordance with (4d), using the mean values of the variables in the two sub-periods. The net change came to less than five per cent over the reference period. Therefore, in computing the output-per-unit-of-input series, this change was ignored.

The final series of intrafirm technical advance, interfirm productivity changes (not significant here), scale economies, and the sum of these three series (or output per-unit-of-input series), for sulfur, are summarized in Table 5. The last mentioned series suggests that, over the reference period, output from sources other than the physical inputs of labor and capital increased by 108 per cent in the sulfur industry. (See also Figure 1.) The reciprocal of this series will be an estimate of the reduction of real costs per unit of output of sulfur.

TABLE 4 Estimates of Intrafirm Technical Change for the Potassium and Sulfur Industries, United States, 1936–1960[a]

	Potassium		Sulfur	
Year (1)	Index (2)	Percentage Year-to-Year Changes (3)	Index (4)	Percentage Year-to-Year Changes (5)
1936	100	0	100	0
1937	99	−1	87	−13
1938	100	+1	121	+34
1939	97	−3	107	−14
1940	99	+2	109	+2
1941	99	0	104	−5
1942	98	−1	112	+8
1943	99	+1	103	−9
1944	107	+8	113	+10
1945	108	+1	123	+10
1946	106	−2	125	+2
1947	110	+4	140	+15
1948	116	+6	145	+5
1949	123	+7	148	+3
1950	150	+27	155	+7
1951	113	−37	164	+9
1952	142	+29	149	−15
1953	151	+9	150	+1
1954	152	+1	168	+18
1955	146	−6	158	−10
1956	153	+7	168	+10
1957	176	+23	173	+5
1958	172	−4	185	+12
1959	189	+17	178	−7
1960	189	0	175	−3

[a] The indices of columns (2) and (4) are derived by multiplying the coefficients of year-dummy variables by 100. The year-to-year changes of columns (3) and (5) are simply the differences of the consecutive years' coefficients.

Sources: Table 2.

FIG. 1 Intrafirm technical change (δ-series), scale economies (E-series), and output-per-unit-of-input index, the sulfur industry, United States, 1936–1960 (Source: Table 4)

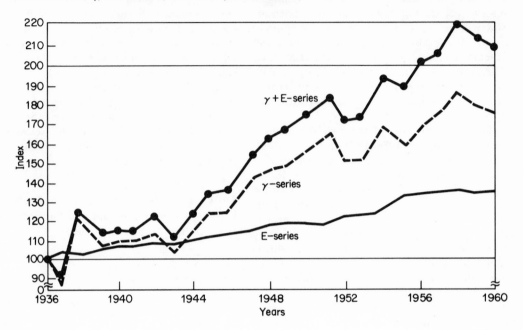

FIG. 2 Percentage change in output resulting from intrafirm technical change. The potassium industry, United States, 1936–1960 (Source: Table 3)

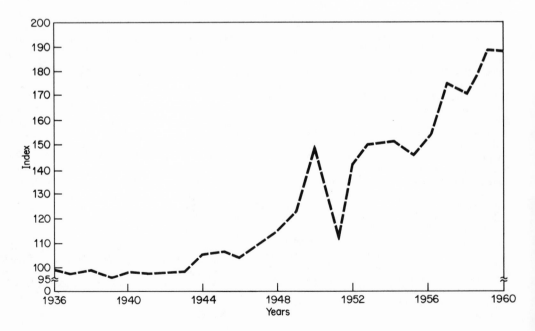

TABLE 5 Output-per-Unit-of-Input Series
and Its Components, for the Sulfur Industry,
United States, 1936–1960

Year (1)	Index of Change in Output as a Result of		
	Intrafirm Technical Change (γ-series) (2)	Scale Economies (E-series) (3)	Output-per-Unit-of-Input [(γ+E-series)–100] (4)
1936	100	100	100
1937	87	103	90
1938	121	102	123
1939	107	106	113
1940	109	107	116
1941	109	107	116
1942	112	109	121
1943	103	108	111
1944	113	109	122
1945	123	111	134
1946	125	112	137
1947	140	114	154
1948	145	117	162
1949	148	119	167
1950	155	119	174
1951	164	119	183
1952	149	121	170
1953	150	122	172
1954	168	123	191
1955	158	131	189
1956	168	132	200
1957	173	132	205
1958	185	135	220
1959	178	133	211
1960	175	133	208

AN ANALYSIS OF INTRAFIRM TECHNICAL CHANGE

In this section, an attempt is made to determine the sources of intrafirm technical change computed in column (2) of Tables 4 and 5. For this purpose, the following hypotheses were formulated and tested. (See Table 6.)

In this study, there are at least three variables, namely, research and exploration outlays, repairs and maintenance outlays, and gross investment in plant and equipment that are likely to have distributed-lag effects. This is a statistically unmanageable problem. For, on the one hand, these three variables cannot, on a priori grounds, be assumed to have the same expected (average) depreciation rate. It is, therefore, unrealistic to assign

the same distribution of lagged effects to each of these variables. If all the three variables are included in the same regression, the interpretation becomes intractable. On the other hand, a partial estimation of the lagged effects using a single independent variable of this nature, and thereby imputing the lagged effects if any to this variable alone where more are clearly involved, must also result in biased estimates due to mis-specification of the function. No easy solution to this problem of distributed lag models has as yet been suggested in econometric literature. In view of this, numerous iterations were carried out and several alternative relations were tried. The variables with coefficients significantly different from zero were then inserted, in appropriately cumulated forms, back into the original production function (2b). The final results are summarized below.

The bulk of the intrafirm technical change in the United States sulfur and potassium industries during the period 1936–1960 can be explained by improvements in factor qualities. Of the 75 per cent progress in intrafirm technology in sulfur and 89 per cent in potassium during the reference period, approximately 40 per cent and 32 per cent, respectively, are explained by technical change embodied in human labor of the sulfur and the potassium industries. Approximately one-half of this human-embodied technical change is attributable to schooling and the other half to on-the-job learning within the fertilizer-mineral industries. From 16 per cent to 22 per cent of technical change in sulfur and from 20 per cent to 30 per cent in potassium is the result of learning-by-doing acquired in the United States capital-goods-producing industries and embodied in new fixed-capital goods purchased and used by the industries under study. An increase of approximately five per cent of interfirm (not intrafirm) productivity growth in sulfur and about seven per cent in potassium due to the decline in the degree of monopoly over the reference period is also indicated. Some of these results are depicted in Figure 3.

The output effectiveness of processing innovations and new discoveries of mineral resources could not be determined as repre-

TABLE 6 Hypotheses Purported to Explain the Sources of Intrafirm Technical Change in the United States Fertilizer-Mineral Industries

Hypothesis	Proxy Variable Used to Test the Hypothesis	Representative Existing Study Using or Suggesting the Hypothesis
1) Technical advance is partly the result of improvements in the quality of labor input, due to a rise in the level of schooling.	Index of the level of schooling of the dominant occupations of the industry concerned.	T. W. Schultz, "Education and Economic Growth," *Social Forces Influencing American Education* (Chicago: University of Chicago Press, 1961); and E. F. Denison, *The Sources of Economic Growth in the U.S. and the Alternatives before Us* (New York: CED, 1962).
2) Technical change is partly the result of on-the-job learning by human labor.	Cumulated gross output per man-hour of recent years.	E. Lundberg, *Produkivitet och rantabilitet* (Stockholm: Norstedt and Soner, 1961) who has named this phenomenon as "Horndal effect"; and P. J. Verdoorn, "Complementarity and Long-Range Projections," *Econometrica*, XXIV, No. 4 (1956), 429–450.
3) Technical progress is partly the result of improvements in the quality of new physical capital.	Gross investment in plant and equipment with distributed lags.[a]	The "vintage approach" of R. M. Solow, "Investment and Technical Progress," in K. J. Arrow, *et al.* (eds.) *Stanford Symposium on Mathematical Methods in Social Sciences* (Stanford: Stanford University Press, 1960), 89–104 and the learning-by-doing model of Arrow, "The Economic Implications of Learning by Doing," *Review of Economic Studies*, XXIX, No. 80 (1962), 155–174.
4) Technical change is, in part, embodied in inherited fixed capital.	Minor renovation and repairs and maintenance outlays, with distributed lag effects.	Ingvar Svennilson, "Economic Growth and Technical Progress: An Essay in Sequence Analysis," paper presented at the OECD conference (Paris, May 20–22, 1963).
5) Technical progress is, in part, the result of improvements in methods of production and processing innovations (including new discoveries of mineral deposits).	Research and development outlays, with distributed lag effects.[b]	W. E. G. Salter, *Productivity and Technical Change* (Cambridge: Cambridge University Press, 1960).
6) An increase in competition may, in part, explain changes in output not accounted for by changes in the quantities and qualities of inputs.	The degree of monopoly as measured by the Herfindahl index and the excess rate of return on invested capital.	Jora R. Minasian, "The Economics of Research and Development," *The Rate and Direction of Inventive Activity: Economic and Social Factors* (Princeton: Princeton University Press, 1962), 93–143.
7) Technical change is, in part, merely trend effect.	The serial number of years in time-series study.	Jan Tinbergen, "On the Theory of Trend Movements," L. H. Klaassen, L. M. Koyck, and H. J. Witteveen, eds. in *Collected Papers*, (Amsterdam: North-Holland, 1959).

[a] A better indicator of capital-embodied technical change would perhaps be the ratio of machinery and equipment to plant and structure (rather than the overall gross investment), or the ratio of professional personnel to production workers. Separate data for the two components of capital and labor could not, however, be obtained. Hence overall gross investment was used as the proxy variable for this purpose.

[b] The research and exploration data could be compiled only for the individual firms of the sulfur and the potassium industries. Large outlays on exploration understood to have been incurred by the oil companies and the federal government in search of oil, and which have been responsible for the discoveries of several sulfur and potassium domes during the past decades, are not available. These outlays may be completely uncorrelated to the fertilizer mineral industries' own outlays on research and exploration. This seems to be the main reason why the coefficient of this variable, as noted in the succeeding pages of the text, could not acquire a positive sign in all types of regressions.

FIG. 3 Determinants of computed intrafirm technical progress, fertilizer mineral industries, United States, 1936–1960[a]

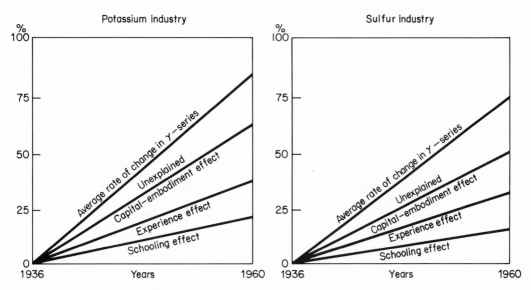

[a] 1) Variables with significant coefficients: Noted in the figure.
2) Variables omitted due to lack of data: Research and exploration.
3) Variables the coefficients of which are not significantly different from zero: (a) Repairs and maintainance, (b) Trend, and (c) Degree of monopoly.

sentative data on the research and exploration outlays presumed to be the source of this component of technical change are not available (see Footnote b to Table 6). The coefficient of the repairs and maintenance variable is not significantly different from zero even at the 20 per cent level. Hypothesis 4, i.e., technical change being embodied in inherited capital cannot, therefore, be accepted. Finally, the trend variable could not survive when entered in the regressions along with the experience variable (with which it is highly intercorrelated). Hence, Hypothesis 7, i.e., the pure trend effectis also rejected.

In all, about two-thirds of the computed intrafirm technical change in sulfur and

about three-fourths in potassium have been explained. Specification errors introduced as a result of the omission of the research and exploration variable (due to the unavailability of representative data) may account for at least part of the short fall in explaining the measured intrafirm technical change and certain other discrepancies that may be read into these results. Because of this unavoidable omission and the shortcomings of the balance sheet data, in general, as well as certain methodological handicaps, the above results should be regarded as no more than broad indicators rather than as the precise magnitudes. Nevertheless, it appears to me that these results are indicative of more general conclusions.

8

A Study of Production and Factor Shares in the

Halibut Fishing Industry

SALVATORE COMITINI AND DAVID S. HUANG*

I. INTRODUCTION

A large number of empirical studies in the area of production functions in recent years have used aggregative time-series data. As a result, the inferences drawn from such studies with respect to the functional forms and the nature of technical progress have not been duly convincing because of the aggregation and related problems. In the present study, we utilize a panel of thirty-two halibut fishing boats representing data that cover seven years of the boats' fishing operations.

Halibut fishing in the North Pacific is regulated by the International Pacific Halibut Commission, and the regulations are provided for by a convention between the United States and Canada. The regulatory measures, which are based on biological

From Journal of Political Economy (1967), *pp. 366–377, by Salvatore Comitini and David S. Huang; publisher, The University of Chicago Press. Reprinted with permission of authors and publisher.*

* [Salvatore Comitini teaches at The Ohio State University, and David S. Huang at Southern Methodist University.] The authors wish to express their sincere appreciation to the following individuals for making available the basic data: Mr. Harold E. Lokken, manager, Fishing Vessel Owners' Association; Mr. F. Howard Bell, director of investigations, International Pacific Halibut Commission; Mr. Gordon J. Peltonen, biologist, International Pacific Halibut Commission; and Mr. W. W. Holroyd, boat surveyor, Seattle, Washington. The authors are also indebted to John Kmenta, Michael McCarthy, Finis Welch, and the referees for helpful comments, and to Scott Turner for computational assistance. Only the authors are responsible for any shortcomings of the paper. Part of the present research was supported by The National Science Foundation under GS-944. This article was completed while the first author held a research fellowship at the Mershon Center for Education in National Security at The Ohio State University.

studies, aim at providing a maximum sustainable yield of halibut to the enterprises comprising the fishery. To analyze the economic effects of such regulations, Crutchfield and Zellner (1963) conducted two surveys during 1957 and 1959, one on the operations and incomes of the Seattle halibut fleet and another on the incomes of the halibut fishermen. In the boat survey, a sample of fifty boats was taken and information on revenues, operating expenses, and physical characteristics of the boats collected. These data, representing information for the years 1953 through 1957, were used for an analysis of rates of return on invested capital and of earnings of boat captains and fishermen (see Crutchfield and Zellner, 1963, pp. 82–94). However, an analysis of the underlying production processes was not performed. We have recently made a similar survey of thirty-two Seattle halibut boats for the years 1958 through 1964. In this second survey, we collected information on more variables than did the first survey.[1]

For each boat for *most* of the years under analysis, we have collected, from income tax records contained in the files of the Fishing Vessel Owners' Association and from the official files of the International Pacific Halibut Commission, information on the following: catch landed; fixed and operating boat expenses; fair market value of each boat at the end of 1964; number of men aboard the vessel; number of days spent

[1] Due to a decline in the size of the Seattle halibut fleet, this represented approximately 37 per cent of the then operating fleet. As it turned out, this second survey did not constitute a complete panel, since seven of the thirty-two boats did not fish for halibut in every year during the 1958–64 period. This does not, however, seriously hinder the analysis.

fishing; standardized units of gear fished,[2] and physical characteristics of the vessels, such as year built, tonnage, engine horsepower, and the existence of electronic and refrigeration equipment on board. We shall analyze this body of data to determine the nature of returns to scale in production, the relative shares of the productive factors, and the degree of technical progress for the sample period. In particular, we shall demonstrate that the underlying production function of the industry is of the usual Cobb-Douglas type, that there are boat differences in the productivity of operations, and that such boat differences are in large part due to the managerial skills of the boat captains.

The plan of this paper is as follows. In Section II we consider the specification of the production relations, while in Section III we discuss the results of our calculations. In the latter, we also test the "good captain" hypothesis as implied by the results preceding it. Some concluding remarks are given in Section IV.

II. SOME BASIC PRODUCTION RELATIONS

A. Types of Functions to Be Used

There are two considerations that must be dealt with before specifying production possibilities functions for the purpose of the present study. They are: (1) Each boat is usually manned with a crew which would

[2] A unit of gear in the Pacific halibut fishery is commonly called a "skate" which consists of short branch lines to which hooks are attached and which are spaced about 13 feet apart as they extend out from a heavy ground-line. Originally, a skate was an amount of gear of size and weight which could be conveniently handled by one man. This, however, will vary over time and from vessel to vessel so that the Halibut Commission has used a "skate correction factor" to standardize the gear among vessels and over time as to character and effectiveness. The implications for our analysis is that this tends to standardize the technique as among vessels and over the time period studied as structural variations in gear (for example, the number of hooks per unit used or different types of bait that may be used) are corrected for by this index.

yield the catch reaching the hold capacity of the boat regardless of whether the capacity catch is achieved; and (2) density of fish population differs from area to area so that the density serves as a shift factor in the production function. Because of the uncertainties inherent in fishing, it is possible that for some levels of output a given boat-crew combination will not be an optimal one. Further, as we move from boat to boat in a cross-section of boats there may be some degree of factor substitution, although for any given boat (that is, in any given year) capital and labor are nearly perfect complements. We shall assume that the elasticity of substitution is constant in a cross-section of boats and that labor and capital are exogenous. The exogeneity assumption is at least approximately satisfied because of the rigidities involved in the planning and execution of fishing.

We shall first utilize the usual constant elasticity of substitution type function for analysis. Mainly because of our ignorance on the nature of returns to scale and on the degree of capital-labor substitution in the industry, we shall first attempt to estimate, using cross-section data, the general form of the constant elasticity of substitution (CES) function

$$q = \theta[\delta K^{-\rho} + (1 - \delta)L^{-\rho}]^{-\nu/\rho}, \qquad (1)$$

where q is output; K and L are capital and labor inputs; and θ, δ, ρ, and ν are, respectively, the efficiency, distribution, substitution, and homogeneity parameters. For future reference, we note that the Cobb-Douglas (CD) function we shall use is of the form:

$$q = AK^{\alpha}L^{\beta}, \qquad (2)$$

where A is a constant, and α and β are parameters.

B. Data and Specification of the Basic Equations

For the measure of capital input in this study, we use an index of the extent of utilization of the boat imputed from its market

TABLE 1 Estimates of Parameters in Kmenta's Approximation of CES Function

Year		Estimates of			R^2
	α_0	α_1	α_2	α_3	
1958	$-.816$	.158	.769	$-.129$	.747
	(.0499)	(.347)	(.382)	(.330)	
1959	-1.162	.242	.560	$-.383$	.810
	(.0477)	(.353)	(.402)	(.350)	
1960	.227	.186	.686	.142	.686
	(.0445)	(.326)	(.362)	(.332)	
1961	-1.341	.602	.333	$-.261$	.819
	(.0514)	(.390)	(.443)	(.398)	
1962	.291	.199	.402	$-.00774$	.769
	(.0453)	(.319)	(.354)	(3.47)	
1963	-1.086	.427	.413	$-.292$	.763
	(.0543)	(.415)	(.499)	(.414)	
1964	-2.771	.806	.325	$-.777$	.858
	(.6732)	(.505)	(.509)	(.519)	

value. Specifically, we divide the market value by fifty and multiply the result by the number of days the boat is out halibut fishing during a year to arrive at an observed value of K for that year.[3] As for labor input, we merely multiply the number of fishermen aboard by the number of days fished for halibut to arrive at the value of L for any given year. Besides capital and labor inputs, one other factor which significantly affects the level of output independently of the L and K is the density of the fish population existing at the points where the boat happens to be fishing. Thus, in an effort to measure the contributions to output by L and K free of this density effect we include the "catch per skate" variable (C) in our production functions.

This last consideration leads us to adapt the usual CD function as follows:

$$q = AK^\alpha L^\beta C^\gamma e^u. \quad (3)$$

As for the CES function, we shall use Kmenta's approximation[4] to function (1) with an additive $\ln C$ term as follows:

[3] As is known, the "returns to scale" parameter in the CES function is invariant with respect to the units of measurement of L and K, but the distribution parameter is not. The main reason for using fifty as the divisor was to bring the level of K to figures that represented rates of utilization of capital stock at something like 4 per cent per year.

[4] See Kmenta (1967) for the details regarding

$$\ln q = \alpha_0 + \alpha_1 \ln K + \alpha_2 \ln L$$
$$+ \alpha_3 \left(\ln \frac{K}{L}\right)^2 + \alpha_4 \ln C + v. \quad (4)$$

The direct least-squares estimates of the coefficients in (4) will be used to derive the CES parameter estimates in the following way:

$$\nu = \alpha_1 + \alpha_2,$$
$$\delta = \alpha_1/(\alpha_1 + \alpha_2), \quad (5)$$
$$\rho = -2\alpha_3(\alpha_1 + \alpha_2)/(\alpha_1\alpha_2).$$

The estimating equation for (3) will be

$$\ln q = A' + \alpha \ln K + \beta \ln L$$
$$+ \gamma \ln C + u, \quad (6)$$

to which the usual direct least-squares procedure is applicable.

III. ESTIMATION AND FURTHER ANALYSIS

A. Results of CES Estimation

The CES equation for each year is estimated from the year's cross-section of sample boats. The results of the variant of Kmenta's

statistical properties of the CES parameter estimators considered here.

approximate estimation (4), are shown in Table 1, while the CES parameter estimates derived from the estimates provided in Table 1 are given in Table 2. One of the points

TABLE 2 Estimates of the CES Parameters Using Annual Cross-Sections

| Year | Estimates of | | | Imputed Labor Share |
	v	δ	ρ	
1958	.926	.170	1.44	.835
1959	.803	.302	4.51	.763
1960	.872	.214	1.93	.799
1961	.935	.644	2.44	.398
1962	.602	.332	8.89	.762
1963	.840	.508	2.78	.518
1964	1.131	.712	6.70	.367

worthy of note in Table 2 is that the homogeneity parameter estimates are consistently close to one. Thus, it is probably reasonable to assume that the industry operates on constant returns to scale. This is about the most significant finding in this section, as the other parameter estimates appear rather unstable. For instance, the estimates of α_1 and α_2, as seen in Table 1, vary over a wide range for the years, causing the estimates of the distribution parameter, δ, to differ considerably from year to year. This is not particularly satisfactory and is probably due to high collinearity existing between K and L. The point estimates of ρ are all greater than zero. However, most of these estimates are statistically insignificant and imply that elasticity of substitution may be close to one.

In the last column of Table 2 we have shown labor's relative share computed on the assumption that labor is paid its marginal product (taking the point estimate of ρ at face value), these relative-share figures have a tendency to decline over the sample period, and it might be suspected that possible improvement in the quality of the labor input tends to cause this decline. That is, given that a boat is fixed in capacity, maximum output of the boat might be maintained with a smaller crew. We shall consider this point in more detail in the remaining sections.

B. Results of CD Estimation

The results of the CES estimation bring out two basic points: (1) the industry under study probably operates under constant returns to scale, and (2) the elasticity of substitution is probably equal to one. Since these are attributes of the CD function, we fitted equation (6), using the entire sample of seven cross-sections with 209 observations, and found the following:

$$\ln q = -1.301 + .120 \ln K$$
$$(.338) \quad (.0704)$$
$$+ .809 \ln L + .498 \ln C;$$
$$(.0873) \quad (.0691)$$
$$R^2 = .643. \qquad (7)$$

The capital and labor production elasticities are, respectively, .120 and .809, indicating that constant returns to scale prevails in the industry. However, the relative labor and capital shares are .87 and .13, respectively.

To probe further the nature of the production processes beyond the above estimated relations, we note the unsatisfactory way in which the K variable was "observed." It is recalled that the market value of the boat at the end of 1964 was used as the base to calculate the extent of capital utilization for each of the years 1958–64. This means that as we go back in time there exists a larger and larger error of observation in K, thus causing its estimated coefficient to be biased toward zero. One way to remedy this is to introduce a time variable (t) into the CD equation in its original form in the following way:

$$q = \mu e^{\lambda t} K^\alpha L^\beta C^\gamma e^u. \qquad (8)$$

Then, the estimate of λ obtained for (8) will be in part reflecting the persistently increasing error of measurement over time of capital and in part reflecting the extent of both embodied and disembodied technical change taking place over the years studied. By taking the logarithm of (8), we can obtain the least-squares estimates of the parameters there. Thus,

$$\ln q = .525 + .0111t + .214 \ln K$$
$$\quad\quad (.300) \quad (.0100) \quad\; (.0620)$$
$$+ .621 \ln L + .576 \ln C;$$
$$\;\;(.0770) \quad\quad (.0610)$$
$$R^2 = .759. \tag{9}$$

As expected, the estimate of the time coefficient, λ, is positive, while the relative sizes of the capital and labor production elasticity estimates change in favor of capital. On the basis of (9), we estimate the long-run competitive equilibrium shares of labor and capital to be .75 and .25, respectively. This comes very close to the then existing system of .78 versus .22. The meaning of the λ estimate is still not very clear. To the extent that it represents some sort of technical progress, it becomes desirable to learn if the technical progress is embodied or disembodied. Unfortunately, this problem cannot be handled in unambiguous terms, since we allow t to reflect at least two effects (error of measurement and over-all technical progress). Furthermore, it is generally recognized that in the CD function, technical progress as represented in the time variable cannot be identified as embodied or otherwise. In what follows, however, we attempt to find some indication as to the nature of the technical progress that might exist in this industry.

C. The Nature of Technical Progress

Because of the way in which t enters the relation (9), its estimated coefficient may be subjected to the influence of differences in the boats in addition to the two effects indicated immediately below equation (8). Thus, within the sample information available, we picked a seven-year panel of ten boats with almost identical physical characteristics and of relatively recent vintage, but allowed the t coefficients for these boats to be different in the following way:

$$\ln q = \ln \mu + \lambda_1 t_1 + \lambda_2 t_2 + \lambda_3 t_3$$
$$+ \lambda_4 t_4 + \lambda_5 t_5 + \lambda_6 t_6 + \lambda_7 t_7$$

$$+ \lambda_8 t_8 + \lambda_9 t_9 + \lambda_{10} t_{10} + \alpha \ln K$$
$$+ \beta \ln L + \gamma \ln C + w. \tag{10}$$

If the ten boats are homogeneous with respect to capital, then the estimated λ_i's will reflect the boat differences in the improvement of productivity that is noncapital. With this reasoning, we can estimate the parameters in (10) by taking the seven observations for each of the ten boats and using seventy observations all at once for least-squares estimation. The result of this estimation is:

$$\ln q = .212 + .0151t_1 + .0574t_2$$
$$\quad\;\; (.0157) \quad (.0145) \quad\;\; (.0174)$$
$$+ .0959t_3 + .0661t_4 - .0261t_5$$
$$\;\;(.0219) \quad\;\; (.0141) \quad\;\; (.0179)$$
$$+ .0447t_6 + .0166t_7 + .0292t_8$$
$$\;\;(.0168) \quad\;\; (.0142) \quad\;\; (.0147)$$
$$+ .0217t_9 + .0311t_{10} + .543 \ln K$$
$$\;\;(.0144) \quad\;\; (.0134) \quad\;\; (.143)$$
$$+ .416 \ln L + .331 \ln C;$$
$$\;\;(.149) \quad\quad (.0754)$$
$$R^2 = .910. \tag{11}$$

Assuming that the sample boats did not appreciably alter in their physical characteristics over the years studied, we can conclude from (11) that there had been significant improvement in the efficiency of non-capital input factors. It is possible, however, that some boats selected in the sample could have made improvement on the equipment aboard, but in general one can assume that such changes were usually minor. (Apparently the fifth boat in the sample did not enjoy any technical progress over the sample period.)

The results in (11), coupled with the relative constancy of the boats' equipment, would seem to imply that the possible technical progress was primarily due to improvement in the quality of labor. Casual observation of the industry, however, quickly dislodges this implication, as the fishermen of the industry are known to be relatively old in their age composition, and any improvement in the fishing skill would have been relatively minor in nature. Also, it should be noted that there has been little change in gear and technique in this industry in the past thirty or thirty-five years, except in auxiliary gears, such as communication and navigational instruments. Thus, the explanation for the possible technical progress reflected in the data is probably to be sought in factors other than quality of labor or efficiency of capital.

D. The Good Captain Hypothesis

Further inquiry of the industry's condition reveals that boats with "good" captains tend to do better than the average boats of the industry. Given the factors previously alluded to, any improvement in the catch over time would tend to be a result of gear modification, or more effective bait, or particular grounds fished—factors whose changes are basically a reflection of managerial decision making. Thus, it would seem that the technical change was in the form of improvement in managerial technique and capacity. Also, since there was no evidence of reduction in the size of crew associated with the boats analyzed, one might conclude that the technical progress was largely neutral in nature.

To carry out a test of the good captain hypothesis, we utilize a further set of data supplied by Harold Lokken of Seattle, who has been with the halibut industry for many years and is thoroughly familiar with the boats and their captains. Lokken has given his subjective evaluation of the managerial skills of the boat captains and ranked these as excellent, good, and average for the period of our analysis (this information is held strictly confidential). We thus posit the following relation:

$$\ln q = \lambda t + \alpha \ln K + \beta \ln L + \theta_1 M_1$$
$$+ \theta_2 M_2 + \theta_3 M_3 + \gamma \ln C + u,$$
$$(12)$$

where $M_i = 1$ if the captain is excellent and $= 0$ otherwise, $M_2 = 1$ if the captain is good and $= 0$ otherwise, and $M_3 = 1$ if the captain is average and $= 0$ otherwise.

By using the entire panel of 209 observations, we find the estimate of (12) to be

$$\ln q = .00595t + .121 \ln K$$
$$ (.00986) \quad (.0670)$$
$$+ .702 \ln L + .993\, M_1$$
$$ (.0790) \quad\quad (.321)$$
$$+ .897\, M_2 + .773\, M_3$$
$$ (.314) \quad\quad (.300)$$
$$+ .495 \ln C;$$
$$ (.0659)$$
$$R^2 = .781. \qquad (13)$$

Indeed the sizes of the estimated coefficients of M_1, M_2, and M_3, respectively, are seen to be in a descending order, providing support to our earlier reasoning about the importance of the managerial ability in the fishing operations. Note that the coefficient of t has become virtually zero, implying that the boat differences in managerial skills account for most of the differences (and the significance) of the t_i coefficients in (11).

IV. CONCLUDING REMARKS

The evidence seems to show that constant returns to scale are probably the rule in the Pacific halibut industry. This justifies, among other things, the straight-line "cost-of-effort" function used in geometrical exposition of fisheries. The results of the analysis of the CES-type functions employing individual cross-sections data seem to indicate that the CD function is appropriate for the industry. Some evidence of technical progress during the sample period that was slightly apparent in the analysis of the CD and CES functions prompted a test of the good captain hypothesis. It was found that good captains made differences in the boats' productivity and that the seeming presence of technical progress in the data was largely accountable by the managerial skills of the captains.

Under the fixed-share system,[5] the re-

---

[5] Actual arrangements setting forth the factors' shares in the value of the catch are specified in the "set line agreement" between the Fishing Vessel Owners' Association and the Deep Sea Fishermen's

turns to boat owners are a proportion of the gross profits from fishing operations; our estimation of the long-run equilibrium shares of the productive factors do fall in line with the existing arrangement. This evidence is testimony to the relatively low returns to boat-owner captains and in part accounts for their gradual departure from the halibut fishery for other fisheries where higher boat shares are the rule. Therefore, remaining

in the industry means a commitment to improved productivity through exercise of managerial skills within the confine of the industry's relatively constant technology.

REFERENCES

CRUTCHFIELD, J. A., AND ZELLNER, A. *Economic Aspects of the Pacific Halibut Fishery* (Fishery Industrial Research, Vol. I, No. 1). Washington: Government Printing Office, 1963.

KMENTA, J. "On Estimation of the CES Production Function," *Internat. Econ. Rev.*, Vol. VIII (in press, 1967).

Union of the Pacific. For instance, the set line agreement signed in 1959 provided that the boat-owners' gross share of the catch was to be 22 per cent, leaving 78 per cent as the gross crew share.

9

Diminishing Returns and the Cost Function: A Reconsideration

SVEN DANØ

I.

The neoclassical theory of the firm, and hence also the supply side of traditional short-run price theory, is dominated by the U-shaped marginal cost curve. Observations of diminishing returns in agriculture led to the formulation of the specific law of variable proportions (the *Ertragsgesetz*), which came to be regarded as a law of nature, a principle of universal application to production processes in industry as well as agriculture, and from which the neoclassical cost function was deduced.

The situation with which a firm is confronted in the short run is characterized by

From Weltwirtschaftliches Archiv (*Heft 2, 1966*), *pp. 97–107. Reprinted with permission of author and publisher (only Parts I, II, and III reproduced here).*

one or more factors of production—land or capital equipment—being fixed; output per period can be expanded only by increasing the input of labour and other variable factors. Variations of this kind are assumed to lead to a production curve of the type illustrated by $OPAB$ in Figure 1, where the variable factor's marginal productivity $\delta x/\delta v$, average productivity x/v, and total output x reach their maxima in the order mentioned.

Assuming that the price of the variable factor is constant, the curve of total variable cost —$OPAB$ in Figure 2—will have the inverse shape of the production curve, and marginal cost is represented by a U-shaped curve.

The curves of Figure 1 have meaning only when the variable factor v represents a single input (such as labour) or a homogeneous complex of inputs assumed to vary propor-

FIG. 1

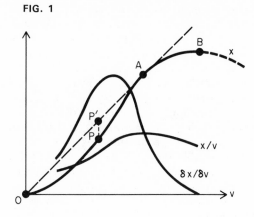

FIG. 2

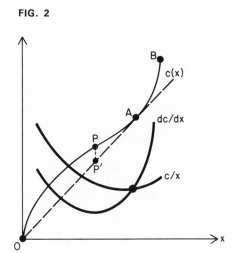

This type of cost curve has shown great persistence in economic literature—it is found in nearly every textbook—though it came to be recognized that the technology of some production processes is characterized by limitational inputs with constant coefficients of production so that total variable cost is proportional to output. The latter model is usually associated with name of Walras, though his assumption of fixed coefficients was largely a provisional simplification from which he proceeded to develop the marginal productivity theory, whereas Pareto and Jantzen explicitly justified the linear model with reference to engineering practice, citing chemical and mechanical processes respectively in support of the linear model of production.[2]

In the thirties and the early forties a number of attempts were made to verify the hypothesis of the U-shaped cost curve by statistical cost studies.[3] Although the results can scarcely be regarded as absolutely conclusive, these empirical studies generally suggested a linear shape of the firm's cost function (constant marginal cost) within a fairly wide interval of output variation, while for lack of empirical data they had little to say about cost behaviour for small output rates or in the neighbourhood of maximum capacity.[4]

tionately. In the case of several variable inputs which can be substituted for one another the expansion of the firm's output will follow a path—determined by cost minimization for parametric level of output —which cannot be expected to be linear, so that the production function cannot be illustrated by a two-dimensional diagram such as Figure 1. However, to the extent that the expansion path in factor space is approximately linear, or at least is a monotonically increasing curve, the essential features of the resulting cost curve are likely to be the same as in Figure 2[1] and the marginal cost curve remains U-shaped.

[1] Cf. Erich Schneider, *Theorie der Produktion*, Vienna, 1934, p. 18.

[2] Cf. Léon Walras, *Élements d'économie politique pure, ou théorie de la richesse sociale*, Éd. définitive, rev. et augmentée, Paris, 1926; Vilfredo Pareto, *Cours d'économie politique*, Vol. II, Lausanne, 1897, p. 102. Ivar Jantzen, "Voxende Udbytte i Industrien," *National-økonomisk Tidsskrift*, Bd. LXII, Copenhagen, 1924, pp. 1 ff. (English translation in: *Idem, Basic Principles of Business Economics and National Calculation: Selected Contributions to Methods of Quantitative Analysis*, Copenhagen, 1939, pp. 1 ff.)

It is perhaps significant that these three economists were all trained as engineers.

[3] For a survey of the more important empirical cost studies see Joel Dean, *Managerial Economics*, New York, 1951, pp. 281ff., and H. v. Natzmer, "Traditionelle und moderne Kostenkurven," *Zeitschrift für Nationalökonomie*, Bd. XXI, Vienna, 1961, pp. 61ff.

[4] Only Ehrke's and Schneider's cost functions for a cement works pointed to increasing marginal cost from a certain rate of output. Cf. Schneider, *op. cit.*, p. 51., and Kurt Ehrke and Erich Schneider, "Versuch einer statistischen Ermittlung von individuellen statischen Kostenkurven," in Kurt Ehrke, *Die Übererzeugung*

These findings would have been in perfect agreement with current theory if the technology underlying the cost function has been characterized by constant coefficients of production, but this was not generally understood to be the case (to the extent that the production model was at all touched upon). Most of the statistical cost studies have been subjected to severe criticism, but the fact remains that the available empirical evidence, such as it is, cannot be said to bear out the neoclassical hypothesis of the U-shaped marginal cost curve.

It is the purpose of the present paper to show how this discrepancy can be overcome by modifying the basic assumption of neoclassical cost analysis, that the "fixed" factor is constant or fixed in an absolute sense as output is expanded within a given plant. Once it is granted that the "fixed" factor which represents land or capital equipment is divisible up to capacity, it follows that the initial phase of decreasing average cost will have to be replaced by a linear phase where average and marginal cost are constant.

II.

It has long been recognized that, although the amount of land or fixed capital equipment available to the firm is given and constant in the short run, the *utilization* of the fixed factor is usually subject to variation, not only in the sense (accepted by the neoclassical economists) that the fixed factor may cooperate with varying amounts of labour and other variable inputs, but also in the sense that there is such a thing as idle capacity. Not all of the land available may be in cultivation, or the services of the firm's capital equipment may not be utilized to the full during the period considered.

This was implicit in, for example, Jantzen's cost model,[5] which assumed that variable cost in an industrial firm or process is proportional to output (as long as the factor

prices remain constant). Jantzen did not explicitly specify the underlying production model in terms of inputs and output, but it is quite clear from his writings that the kind of variation on which his cost function was based was a proportionate expansion of all inputs including capital services (measured in machine hours used per period), the technology being characterized by constant coefficients of production for labour and other variable inputs as well as for machine hours. Maximum output is attained when the plant is employed all available time; up to this capacity point the utilization of the fixed factor is divisible.

The assumption of the fixed factor's indivisibility is equally vulnerable in the context of the neoclassical production model, where the inputs are not limitational but can be substituted for one another. In 1921, Knight had pointed out that points such as P in Figure 1 are inefficient, the fixed factor's marginal productivity being negative.[6] Sraffa,[7] insisting that the factor "land" is always divisible downward, pursued this line of thought to its logical conclusion: point P is ruled out in favour of P', where a greater amount of output is obtained (with the same amount of the variable factor v) by decreasing the acreage in cultivation until the point where the marginal productivity of land is zero and the variable factor's average productivity is at a maximum. This will be so everywhere on the straight line segment OA in Figure 1. In other words, the economic expansion path will be $OP'AB$ rather than the partial production curve $OPAB$, and the initial phase of increasing average returns to the variable input will be replaced by a linear phase of constant returns representing proportionate expansion of both factors.

The same discovery was later made independently by the Danish economist Gloer-

---

in der Zementindustrie von 1858–1913, Beiträge zur Erforschung der wirtschaftlichen Wechsellagen Aufschwung, Krise, Stockung, H. 6, Jena, 1933, pp. 275 ff.

[5] Cf. Jantzen, *op. cit.*

[6] Cf. Frank H. Knight, *Risk, Uncertainty and Profit*, Boston and New York, 1921, pp. 100 ff.

[7] Cf. Piero Sraffa, "Sulle relazioni fra costo e quantità prodotta," *Annali di Economia*, Vol. II, Milan, 1925, pp. 277ff. See also Oskar Morgenstern, "Offene Probleme der Kosten- und Ertragstheorie," *Zeitschrift für Nationalökonomie*, Bd. II, 1931, pp. 498 ff.

felt-Tarp,[8] but it still remained to be shown that the cost function resulting from this modified version of the law of diminishing returns must have an initial phase of constant marginal and average cost so that the cost curve $OPAB$ in Figure 2 would have to be replaced by $OP'AB$, a type of cost function which is consistent with most of the empirical results of statistical cost studies.[9]

In 1933 Winding Pedersen[10] took up the question of capacity utilization in relation to the shape of the cost function. Assuming a production function of neoclassical type he showed that a linear cost function (such as the phase $OP'A$ in Figure 2) will result from variations in the "extensive" dimension of capacity utilization—i.e., proportionate variation of all inputs, including machine hours per period—whereas the traditional cost picture characterized by a U-shaped marginal cost curve ($OPAB$ in Figure 2) corresponds to variations in the "intensive" dimension, where the fixed factor is really fixed (e.g., because the machine is operated all available time) so that output can be increased only by changing the proportion of man-hours to machine hours. According as the current rate of output is small or great, a producer trying to minimize cost will react to output fluctuations by varying the utilization of the plant's capacity in the extensive and the intensive dimension respectively.

This idea was further elaborated by Schneider,[11] which led v. Stackelberg[12] to the

conclusion that the cost curve, as defined by cost minimization for any given level of output, will have the shape $OP'AB$ in Figure 2 above. The same discovery was made independently by Dean[13]—one of the pioneers of statistical cost studies—who also pointed out that physical divisibility of the plant (e.g., a plant composed of several identical machines) will have a similar effect on the cost function as divisibility in time, the other "extensive" dimension.

III.

We shall now proceed to show explicitly how this kind of cost function can be derived from an expansion path determined in the familiar way by cost minimization for parametric level of output.

Let us first assume that there are only two factors of production, v_1 and v_2, representing the services of the fixed factor (e.g., machine hours per period) and a homogeneous complex of variable inputs (labour, raw material, etc., measured in man-hours per period).[14] The two factors are assumed to be substitutable for each other—i.e., the proportion of labour to machine services can be varied at least within limits—as expressed in a continuous and differentiable *production function*

$$x = x(v_1, v_2) \qquad (1)$$

which will be further assumed to be homogeneous of degree one. The latter assumption—plausible enough for our purpose, and usually accepted in neoclassical analy-

---

[8] Cf. B. Gloerfelt-Tarp, "Den φkonomisk definerede Produktionsfunktion og den heterogene Fremstillingsproces," *Nordisk Tidsskrift for Teknisk Økonomi*, Aarg. III, Oslo, Copenhagen, and Stockholm, 1937, pp. 225 ff. Precisely the same argument is found in John Chipman, "Linear Programming," *The Review of Economics and Statistics*, Vol. XXXV, Cambridge, Mass., 1953, p. 106.

[9] The cost function $OP'AB$ is not only linear within a wide interval of output variation but also has a phase of increasing marginal cost, corresponding to some of the findings of Ehrke and Schneider (cf. above).

[10] Cf. H. Winding Pedersen, "Omkring Kapacitetsudnyttelsesteorien," *Nationalφkonomisk Tidsskrift*, Bd. LXXI, 1933, pp. 141 ff.

[11] Cf. Erich Schneider, "Kapacitetsudnyttelsesproblemets to Dimensioner," *Nordisk Tidsskrift for Teknisk Økonomi*, Aarg. III, 1937, pp. 47 ff. *Idem*, "Über den

Einfluß von Leistung und Beschäftigung auf Kosten und Erfolg einer Unternehmung mit homogener Massenfabrikation," *Archiv für mathematische Wirtschafts- und Sozialforschung*, Bd. VI, Stuttgart and Berlin, 1940, pp. 105 ff.

[12] Cf. Heinrich v. Stackelberg, "Stundenleistung und Tagesleistung," *Archiv für mathematische Wirtschafts- und Sozialforschung*, Bd. VII, 1941, pp. 34 ff.

[13] Cf. Joel Dean, *The Relation of Cost to Output for a Leather Belt Shop*, National Bureau of Economic Research, New York, 1941.

[14] The price per unit of the variable factor then becomes the hourly wage rate *plus* the cost of the quantities of material, etc., to be used with a man-hour.

sis—merely implies that half-day operation of the plant will produce half the amount of output that can be produced in a full day, using the same relative factor combination (i.e., the same number of machine operators). Whereas the neoclassical theory of the firm traditionally assumes that the fixed factor is indivisible so that it can be represented by a *parameter* $v_1 = \bar{v}_1$ in the production function (or can be left out entirely, being represented only by the shape of the production function expressing output x in terms of the only variable factor, v_2), we shall treat it as a *variable* v_1 in the production function (1) in order to allow for divisibility, only we must then introduce an explicit *capacity restriction*

$$v_1 \leq \bar{v}_1. \qquad (2)$$

The interpretation of (2) is that the number of hours of effective operation within a period cannot exceed, but may well fall short of, the number of available machine hours per period.

The production function (1) can be illustrated by an isoquant map (factor diagram) as shown in Figure 3. Because of the assumed homogeneity the region of substitution (the efficient region) where the marginal productivities $x_1' = \delta x/\delta v_1$ and $x_2' = \delta x/\delta v_2$ are non-negative is bounded by straight lines passing through the origin (OA and

OB, where $x_1' = 0$ and $x_2' = 0$ respectively).[15] The feasible region is bounded in the v_1 direction by the capacity line $v_1 = \bar{v}_1$. Alternatively, the production function could have been illustrated geometrically by a family of partial production curves showing x as a function of v_2 for given parametric v_1; the shape of each of these curves will be assumed to conform to the law of diminishing returns (Figure 1, with v representing v_2).

Now the expansion path—the locus of least-cost factor combinations—in the factor diagram is determined by minimizing total variable cost

$$c = q_1 v_1 + q_2 v_2 \qquad (3)$$

subject to (1) and (2) for given parametric level of output x, i.e., subject to

$$x(v_1\, v_2) = \bar{x}, \; v_1 \leq \bar{v}_1.$$

Since one of the side conditions is an inequality it would appear that the classical method of constrained maximization or minimization—Lagrange's method of undetermined multipliers—does not apply. However, one can always find a minimum subject to the equality only, provisionally disregarding the inequality constraint; if the solution turns out to respect the inequality, all is well. If it does not, so that the solution is not a feasible one, the problem must be reformulated with the second constraint in equality form.

Applied to the present problem, this means that we ignore (2) and minimize c subject to (1) for $x = \bar{x}$, that is, we minimize the Lagrangeian expression

$$L = c + u \cdot (\bar{x} - x) = q_1 v_1 + q_2 v_2 \\ + u \cdot (\bar{x} - x(v_1, v_2))$$

where u is a Lagrange multiplier, to get the

---

[15] The partial derivatives of a function $v = f(x_1, x_2, \dots, x_n)$ which is homogeneous of the first degree can be written as depending on the $(n-1)$ proportions $x_2/x_1, \dots, x_n/x_1$. Hence each of the equations x_1 = constant and x_2 = constant (e.g., = 0), where $x = x(v_1, v_2)$, determines a constant value of v_2/v_1, independent of x.

FIG. 3

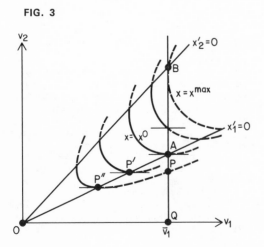

necessary conditions

$$q_i - u \cdot x_i' = 0 \qquad (i = 1,2). \qquad (4)$$

Since x_1' and x_2' depend on the relative factor proportion only, conditions (4) determine v_2/v_1 and u independently of the particular value chosen for x, hence the locus of least-cost points is a straight line through the origin in the factor diagram. For $x = \bar{x}$ the production function determines v_1 and v_2, i.e., a particular least-cost point. The multiplier u can be identified with marginal cost, which is therefore constant (independent of x) along the expansion path.[16]

If q_1 and q_2 are both positive, the expansion path will be in the interior of the region of substitution where x_1' and x_2' are positive. However, the use of the firm's capital equipment can generally be considered a free good: the cost associated with the fixed capital is a historically determined fixed charge, independent of the level of output, so that we can set $q_1 = 0$. Hence the first equation of (4) reduces to $x_1' = 0$ and the expansion path will coincide with one of the boundaries of the region of substitution, that is, OA in Figure 3. Geometrically the expansion path could have been determined as the locus of tangency between the isoquants and the family of isocost lines, which for $q_1 = 0$ become horizontal as shown in Figure 3.

The least-cost points determined in this manner are feasible only as long as the solution for v_1 respects the capacity constraint (2), that is, for $x \le x^0$, $x = x^0$ being the isoquant passing through point A where the linear expansion path intersects the capacity line $v_1 = \bar{v}_1$. For $x > x^0$ the capacity restriction becomes effective and further expansion of output must take place along AB where the capacity is fully utilized ($v_1 = \bar{v}_1$) and where the shape of the cost curve is the inverse of the production curve for $v_1 = \bar{v}_1$,

$$c = q_1 v_1 + q_2 v_2 = q_2 v_2 \text{ where } x = x(\bar{v}_1, v_2)$$

[16] For arbitrary increments dv_i we have

$$dc/dx = (\Sigma q_i dv_i)/(\Sigma x_i dv_i)$$

which for variations along the expansion path as defined by (4) leads to $dc/dx = u$.

so that marginal cost

$$c' = dc/dx = q_2 dv_2/dx = q_2/x_2' \qquad (5)$$

is increasing; as x approaches its maximum at point B where $x_2' = 0$, c' tends to infinity.

In other words, the expansion path is linear up to the point of full capacity utilization, where the path is deflected in the direction of v_2 for constant $v_1 = \bar{v}_1$. The linear phase OA represents proportionate expansion of output and inputs, corresponding to the "extensive" dimension of capacity utilization where the relative factor combination remains the same. The second phase of expansion (AB) represents the "intensive" dimension where output is increased by using more of the variable input with the same (maximal) input of capital service, thus changing the relative factor combination (i.e., full-time operation with variable number of operators per machine).

The corresponding cost function, shown in Figure 4, is pieced together from a linear phase OA ($0 < x \le x^0$) with constant marginal and average variable cost, and a phase of increasing marginal and average cost, AB ($x^0 \le x \le x^{\max}$). At point A, which corresponds to the point of deflexion A in Figure 3, we have $x_1' = 0$, which with Euler's theorem for homogeneous functions

$$x = v_1 x_1' + v_2 x_2'$$

FIG. 4

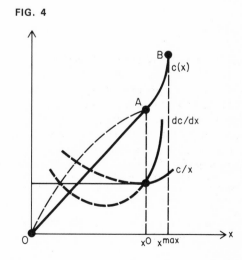

gives

$$x/v_2 = x_2'.$$

This is the condition for maximum average productivity as well as for minimum average cost for variations along $v_1 = \bar{v}_1$ (QAB in Figure 3) so that the point of deflexion corresponds to point A in Figures 1 and 2. Hence the cost function of Figure 4 corresponds to $OP'AB$ in Figure 2. Marginal cost is continuous but kinked at the point of deflexion.[17]

In other words, the initial phase of decreasing average cost that is so characteristic of the neoclassical cost function has been replaced by a phase of constant average and

marginal cost where total cost for given level of output is less than it would have been under neoclassical assumptions. This follows from assuming that the fixed factor, or its services, is divisible up to capacity so that it becomes possible to steer clear of such factor combinations as are characterized by the fixed factor's marginal productivity being negative. In Figure 3, P is such an inefficient point: a greater amount of output can be produced at point P' with less of v_1 and the same amount of v_2 (or the same x with less of both inputs, cf. point P''), and the expansion path along which the cost function is defined switches from QAB to OAB which in its entirety belongs to the region of substitution.

$\cdot \quad \cdot \quad \cdot$

---

[17] The continuity of marginal cost at A also follows from the fact that the left-hand derivative of $c(x)$, as given by the Lagrange multiplier u in (4), and the right-hand derivative—cf. (5)—are both equal to q_2/x_2' at A.

[For a more detailed treatment of plant divisibility applied to a variety of hypothetical production models, see the author's *Industrial Production Models*, Vienna and New York: Springer-Verlag, 1966, ch. VII.]

10

The Firm's Cost Function: A Successful Reconstruction?

JACK HIRSCHLEIFER*

INTRODUCTION AND SUMMARY

One of the difficulties responsible for the seeming lack of relevance of economic theory for business practice concerns the shape of the firm's cost function. Economic theory

From The Journal of Business (*July 1962*), *pp. 235–47; 253–55, by Jack Hirschleifer; publisher, The University of Chicago Press. Reprinted with permission of author and publisher. The author has given permission to omit part III, dealing with questions concerning the long and the short run.*

* The RAND Corporation and the University of California, Los Angeles.

teaches that, at least for a firm with numerous and close competitors, marginal cost at equilibrium must be rising—it becomes increasingly costly to raise output so as to meet successive increments of demand. This teaching is based upon the powerful logic of the law of diminishing returns. On the other hand, businessmen (even in competitive industries) commonly feel that additional units are *not* increasingly costly to produce, except under extreme and exceptional conditions. Certainly, for trades producing to customer order (printing, metalworking, hauling, etc.) it is a practically universal observation that larger orders will be accommodated at falling marginal prices, this being true irrespective of the degree of competition of the various trades. Furthermore, econometric studies, as a general rule, fail to show the rising marginal cost functions called for by theory.

In a recent paper, Professor Armen Alchian has proposed a reformulation of the theoretical cost function that goes far to resolve this contradiction.[1] The key idea is that cost can be regarded as a function of the quantity of "output" in two different dimensions: *rate* of output, and scheduled *volume* of output.[2] The first of these is a flow

measure, and the other a stock; the textbooks ordinarily speak in terms of the flow or rate measure, and ignore the volume or stock measure. Here lies the heart of the confusion, for—according to Alchian—the response of cost to changes in the one dimension is qualitatively different from the response to changes in the other dimension of output. Specifically, Alchian puts forward the hypothesis that marginal cost is *always* (not only in the neighborhood of equilibrium) a *rising function of rate of output*, volume being held constant—and a *falling function of volume of output*, rate being held constant. Granted the hypothesis, we can see how confusion is bound to arise in business parlance, in textbook presentations, and in econometric investigations if assertions that marginal cost is rising or is falling are made—without clearly specifying how each of the two variables, rate and volume of output, is assumed to be behaving.

In what follows I attempt both to review and to develop Alchian's conceptions. The argument for the general shape of the cost functions, as put forward by Alchian, I find to be most compelling for establishments producing to unique customer order (e.g., job printing). It also turns out to be useful here to introduce the concept of "width" as well as "length" (flow and stock measures, respectively, of the individual order). The rate-versus-volume distinction turns out to be very important, too, in industries like transportation and utilities, which produce to *aggregated* rather than individual customer

[1] "Costs and Outputs," in M. Abramovitz and others, *The Allocation of Economic Resources: Essays in Honor of B. F. Haley* (Stanford, Calif.: Stanford University Press, 1959). Unless otherwise specified, page citations refer to this work. An earlier version of Alchian's paper, under the same title, was circulated as RAND Corporation Paper P-1449 (September, 1958).

[2] However "obvious" this point may seem, my rather extensive survey of the literature in both economic theory and in business economics has failed to turn up any significant attention devoted to this topic. The distinction between rate of output and volume of output, insofar as effects on cost are concerned, seems not to have been mentioned in such recent works as J. Johnston, *Statistical Cost Analysis* (New York: McGraw-Hill Book Co., 1960). I have found one earlier statement, however, that does anticipate Alchian's central idea. In listing some of the difficulties of measurement of cost functions, the Committee on Price Determination in 1943 referred to "the difficulty introduced by variation in the size of orders. The output of two periods might be the same, except that in one case it consisted of a large number of small 'runs' which might increase costs. ... It is possible to recognize the influence of this factor by making the size of orders or the rate of change of output explicit determinants of cost along with the level of output itself" (*Cost Behavior and Price Policy* [New York: National Bureau of Economic Research, 1943], p. 84). The committee's suggestion was never followed up, so far as I have been able to discover.

The topic of "economic lot size" discussed in inventory theory (see, e.g., T. M. Whitin, *The Theory of Inventory Management* [2d ed.; Princeton, N.J.: Princeton University Press, 1957], *passim*) would seem to provide a natural starting point for inquiries into the nature of the economies available from larger scheduled production lots. So far as I know, however, in such analyses production costs have always been

handled by some simple assumption—e.g., fixed setup cost per lot and constant variable cost per unit produced—rather than subjected to analysis.

The only substantial earlier discussion I know of that bears upon the effect on cost of volume or size of order centers about the concept of the "learning" (or *progress* or *improvement*) function. A definitive treatment of this topic will be found in Harold Asher, "Cost-Quantity Relationships in the Airframe Industry" (RAND Corporation Report R-291 [July 1, 1956]); Asher's study, for one thing, clearly distinguishes between the effects of rate and of volume of output on cost. (Alchian's ideas on the cost function appear to be derived in large part from the learning-curve discussion, to which he had made earlier contributions.)

orders. Here the neatness with which individual orders bundle themselves into groups that can be satisfied jointly is an independent source of cost variation (e.g., it is expensive to ship to or from a rarely used rail shipment point). But aside from this, common observations and statistical evidence support Alchian's hypothesis: long hauls are less costly than short hauls, base power demand is cheaper to provide than peak demand, etc.

The standard discussion in the textbooks, however, seems to relate to a firm that produces an undifferentiated product, not to order but for the market. The exclusive concentration of the textbook analysis upon the *rate* rather than the *volume* dimension of output can be rationalized in two different ways: the implicit assumption might be that planned volume is always infinite (firms plan to produce at their present rate forever), or alternatively that scheduled volume is finite but moves in strict proportion to changes in rate of output. I adopt the second interpretation: if the length of the "run" is fixed, I argue, volume does move proportionately with rate of output. Furthermore, when this assumption is made explicitly, it is possible to show that the "classical" shape of the marginal-cost curve (for proportionate variation of rate and volume) is consistent with Alchian's hypotheses as to the response of cost to changes of rate or of output in the partial sense.

On my reinterpretation, then, the classical analysis is consistent and correct, though implicitly assuming proportionate variation in rate and volume of output. The separate effect of increasing volume of output, rate being held constant, is bound up (I argue) in the classical distinction between the "short run" and "long run." In particular, the traditional analysis holds that costs are always lower in the long than in the short run; this assertion is here interpreted to mean that, for any rate of output, it is cheaper (per unit) to produce a greater than a smaller volume—precisely Alchian's contention! The longest of all long runs, of course, is where the planned output at the given rate is infinite—this is an ideal rather than a practical category, in which unit cost of production for any rate of output is at an absolute minimum.

This basic analysis is applied herein to a number of theoretical questions: the role of uncertainty in determining the planned length of the production run, the meaning of "fixed" factors of production, the interpretation of the concept of "incurring losses in the short run," and the effects of all these upon the industry supply function. The neglected distinction between the rate and volume dimensions of output is the key to a satisfactory integration of the lessons of theoretical analysis and business practice; the enriched formulation of the cost function should provide a more useful tool for managerial economists and a more tractable subject for econometricians.

In what follows, I shall briefly explain Alchian's basic argument as to the nature of the cost function. Next, I shall first explore the relevance of the new cost function for firms producing to discrete unique orders (for which the conception of "volume" of output raises no difficulties) and then proceed through several intermediate cases to the more classical conception of a firm producing continuously for inventory. Then, I turn to the relation between this generalized cost function and the concept of the long and short run; here I reject Alchian's formulation, and propose another arising more appropriately, in my opinion, out of his reconstructed cost function. In this connection. I should make it clear that Alchian consistently, though implicitly, considers only full-knowledge situations—his firm plans its output pattern with complete confidence about the development of demand over time. As we shall see later in the discussion of the short and long run, certain inconsistencies or apparent errors in the orthodox approach may be explained as attempts to make useful statements about cost in the absence of or with only uncertain knowledge of the future.

I. COST AS A FUNCTION OF OUTPUT

A. Alchian's Basic Propositions

Alchian's propositions of immediate relevance for this section will be summarized below.

First, $C = F(V, X, T, m)$, where C is cost, V is scheduled volume of output, X is rate of output,[3] T is the time at which production begins, and m the length of period in which the output is produced.

We may add here the obvious condition: $C \geq 0$. Alchian bases his analysis on the identity:

$$V = \int_{T}^{T+m} X(t)dt.$$

Hereafter, it will ordinarily be assumed that X is constant over the production period m, and in this section we pass over the possible influence of advances or delays in T; the identity then reduces to the form $V = mX$. Alchian asserts the following about the partial derivatives of cost with respect to the independent variables X and V:

$$\begin{aligned} C_X > 0, \quad C_V > 0 \\ C_{XX} > 0, \quad C_{VV} < 0. \end{aligned} \tag{1}$$

The significance of these assertions may be grasped by comparison of Curves I and III in Figure 1. Curve I shows C_X, marginal cost with respect to changes in the rate of output, holding the volume of output constant; the shape of the curve indicates that it becomes increasingly costly to concentrate the same volume of output V into a shorter and shorter timespan m by increasing X. Curve III shows C_V, marginal cost with respect to changes in volume of output, holding the rate of output constant; the shape of the curve shows that, while marginal cost with respect to volume remains positive, it is always cheaper to produce one more unit than any preceding unit. Here, at the same rate of output X, the larger volume V is scheduled over a longer period m, making possible more effective balancing of inputs and outputs and the use of more durable equipment or materials.[4]

I shall not attempt, for lack of time and space, to formally expound these innovations —their meaning in the logical sense will be almost immediately clear to the reader, and their implications have been explained in Alchian's paper. Rather, the main purpose of this section will be to indicate how the orthodox cost function of the firm stands up against this view of the determinants of cost of production. (I shall generally lean in the direction of rescuing the orthodox cost function, by interpretation or clarification, to maximize its continued relevance for the real-world phenomena it has purported to explain.)

B. Firms Illustrating Alchian's Model: Production to Order

First of all, it will be useful to fix ideas by thinking of particular types of firms that fit more or less well the orthodox model on the one hand, or Alchian's on the other. The standard classical conception seems to be of a firm that produces a steady stream of output for the general market, with a minimum of differentiation to suit individual requirements—a manufacturer of detergent powders may be a suitable example. Since we imagine such a firm as producing essentially continuously, the actual phenome-

FIG. 1   Three marginal cost curves

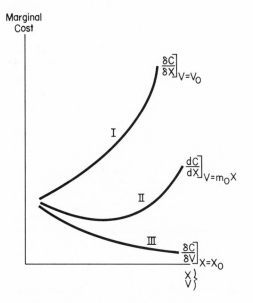

Marginal Cost

$$\left.\frac{\delta C}{\delta X}\right]_{V=V_0}$$

I

$$\left.\frac{dC}{dX}\right]_{V=m_0 X}$$

II

III $$\left.\frac{\delta C}{\delta V}\right]_{X=X_0}$$

$$\left.\begin{array}{c} X \\ V \end{array}\right\}$$

---

[3] Alchian employs the lower-case symbol, x, for rate of output. My reason for diverging from his symbolism here will become apparent shortly.

[4] Curve II in the figure, as will be explained below, is intended to show marginal cost with respect to proportionate changes in X and V (i.e., when m is held constant).

non corresponding to the conception of the planned volume of production in Alchian's sense—the length of the production run—is not immediately obvious. With such firms as models, economists have therefore tended to ignore the dimension of V in theoretical analyses of behavior of firms and of markets and in measurement of statistical cost functions (though, as I shall bring out later, the economists' distinction between the behavior of costs in the "short run" and "long run" can be interpreted as a way of qualitatively representing the influence of V).

On the other hand, to appreciate most clearly the significance of V, consider a firm producing military aircraft to government order. Here each order is obviously unique, and the firm's profitability will be a sensitive function of both the X and the V dimensions of output—an order of two hundred of one model is much less costly to produce than two orders of one hundred, time rate of delivery X remaining the same.[5] Another example that comes immediately to mind is book printing. Each text (that is, each separate composition) is unique and involves heavy setup costs; consequently, we would expect a vast difference in costs incurred by two concerns with the same monthly aggregate output of volumes, if one produced short printings of many different works while the other was able to plan on long printings of just a few. Here V would be the number of copies scheduled to a printing. In a very different line of business, we would similarly expect that a telegraph company would find it much cheaper to transmit a small number of long messages between specified points than a large number of short messages aggregating to the same number of word units.

1. *Source of cost saving as* V *increases.*—Two rather different types of explanation may be given as to why marginal cost with respect to changes of V—C_v—decreases as V rises, with rate of output X held constant. The explanation in terms of "learning" is the more familiar one: as the cumulative number of units manufactured of a specific model rises, both labor and management gradually learn of and incorporate a host of minor improvements into the productive process.[6] Werner Z. Hirsch has explained the improvement phenomenon as representing the introduction of new technological knowledge and thus distinct from the economists' cost function, which holds technology constant.[7] Alchian accepts this explanation, arguing that production of any unit irreversibly increases knowledge and so makes possible cheaper production in the future. This type of improvement will not ordinarily depend upon whether production has cumulated as a single large order or as repeated small orders. However, declining marginal cost due to learning is not our major interest here. According to Alchian, even if we could hold knowledge constant so as to be dealing with a given cost function,[8] marginal cost with respect to V would still be declining.[9]

This second type of cost saving depends on larger volume or production run being *scheduled* in advance. Planning on a larger production run may permit a reduction in capital cost (in the sense of a cost incurred for an entire run rather than for a particular unit) per unit produced, a reduction in operating cost, or a possible exchange of a smaller increment of capital cost per unit for a greater decrement of operating cost. A reduction of capital cost per unit occurs

---

[5] The rule of declining marginal cost with respect to volume of output was first formalized as the "learning curve" for aircraft production (see Asher, *op. cit.*, pp. 1–3).

[6] Asher, *op. cit.*, p. 3. For an early treatment of "learning" as one of the advantages of the division of labor, see Adam Smith, *Wealth of Nations*, chap. i.

[7] See his "Firm Progress Ratios," *Econometrica*, XXIV (April, 1956), 137.

[8] I think it borders on the contradictory to speak of a cost function of X and V, holding technology constant, while at the same time asserting that technology necessarily improves as a function of V. It would be at least verbally superior, in my opinion, to incorporate the predictable learning due to experience within the cost function—relegating to technological change only those improvements outside the normal learning phenomenon. If we do this, we can say that the cost function declines with respect to cumulated V (for reasons of learning) and to scheduled V (for the reasons adduced below).

[9] Pp. 35–36.

as a typical result of lengthening the planned V when there are initial or setup costs necessarily involved in producing to a new order (or terminating an old one): printing provides a very clear example, since each different text must be separately set up in type. Of course, it may be that such capital costs are not exactly halved per unit in doubling the production run—a better quality of type may become necessary for the longer printing, for example—but any such increase is typically only a minor offset to the gain. The airframe industry illustrates very well the saving afforded by the opportunity to introduce machinery to save on operating costs. A single prototype of an aircraft model will be produced largely by hand, while a large order for any one model will justify investing in specialized stamping and pressing machines. Finally, savings in operating cost without corresponding increase of capital cost are typically possible in the form of smoother utilization of existing machinery, more routinizing of labor tasks, greater ability to secure quantity discounts, etc.

2. *Possible cost increases as* V *rises.*—We may also ask at this point whether there are any possible sources of cost saving by *shortening V*—that is, abstracting from uncertainty about the future which might lead us to want to limit our commitments, is there any reason for establishing a V any shorter than the maximum indicated by the quantity demanded on order? If, as Alchian maintains, $C_{VV} < 0$ everywhere, it would always be rational from the cost point of view to maximize V—that is, at a given price and delivery rate X, the firm can only gain by securing a larger rather than smaller order.

However, one can think of causes tending to make C_{VV} positive—a possible illustration is the biological phenomenon of fatigue or its mechanical analogues. We may imagine, for example, a situation in which the only important item of equipment is the human being, and that heavy initial costs are involved in setting up the human being for the work. Reasonably good instances are provided by underground mining and deep-sea

diving, both involving what may be a very long trip to the actual workings. Then an order or production run which can be performed in one cycle by one shift or crew may be cheaper per unit than a somewhat larger run which requires a second shift but cannot fully utilize it. To take a non-biological example, consider the business of chartered air flights on the assumption that the plane's fuel capacity rather than human endurance is limiting. Here, an order for a flight that is just within the fuel capability of the craft is likely to be cheaper per unit of output (taking the output dimension as miles flown) than a somewhat larger order requiring a fuel stop. Both examples, however, illustrate what I regard to be merely a qualification of Alchian's result, because the regions in which C_V rises with V represent only discontinuities. Thus. I would agree that a production schedule requiring two whole shifts or production cycles in succession is cheaper per unit than an order requiring just one; the difficulty arises only for orders requiring, say, one and a half shifts. (The distinguishing characteristic of a "shift" or "production cycle," as the terms are employed here, is the expense involved at the commencement of each such period in setting up the man or machine before productive work starts.)

Another possible rationale for limiting the size of the planned production run is brought out in works on inventory theory. Again abstracting from uncertainty about demand (uncertainty about demand, of course, makes planning for very long production runs very risky, but we are looking for elements of the *cost* function that may tend to limit the size of production runs), inventory theorists sometimes use formulas showing an optimum economic lot size in manufacturing. Such formulas balance declining marginal production cost against rising costs of holding inventories as the lot size rises.[10] The idea seems to be that the average level of (finished-goods) inventories held will be half the lot size, plus whatever safety allowance is normally kept on hand. This calculation involves the rather special assumption, how-

[10] Whitin, *op. cit.,* p. 33.

ever, that sales will be made only at termina-
tions of production periods. The assumption
seems to be that a large lot size may, for
example, imply only monthly sales of products—where a smaller lot size would permit
weekly sales. Given this assumption, the
conclusion certainly follows that inventory
holding costs are an upward force upon
C_V as V rises—increasing lot size from any
given n to $n + 1$ then requires holding all
the previous n units produced longer in
inventory.[11] While the assumption seems
rather peculiar to me, perhaps it is reasonable
for some classes of industrial practice.

3. *"Width" versus "length" of differentiated
orders.*—Centering our attention upon firms
that produce to individually differentiated
orders, it is of some significance to note that
such orders have what I will call a horizontal
"size" (or "width") dimension as well as
serial (or vertical) "length." In the hotel
business, the same aggregate occupancy in the
course of a year may be achieved with greater
or lesser average length of stay, or with greater or smaller average number of units occupied per order. While the size or width
dimension may not be too vital to hotels
(though there may be some cost saving in
renting suites or blocks of rooms to large
groups), it is more important in rental of
office space where it may be much cheaper
to have a few large tenants than many small
ones. In printing there is also a width dimension (length being represented by the number
of copies in the production run) in terms of
number of pages per book (and, also, size
of page). Given rate of output in terms of
pages per month, presumably total costs will
be lower the higher the average number of
pages per book.

It is important to appreciate, however,

that "width" is not V. The latter is the planned length of the production run—a stock
measure. "Size" or "width" of order at a
moment of time is a flow concept; it indicates
how much of the total rate of output X goes
to a specific order. We may denote the
horizontal size of an individual order as x_i
for the ith such order, where $\Sigma x_i = X$.
Nevertheless, it is possible by analogy with
Alchian's main argument to assert some plausible hypotheses here—since some of the same
forces that make long orders economical
are also effective for wide orders. In particular, I shall hypothesize that, given the aggregate rate of output X, costs will be less
the greater the average width of order (the
average of the x_i). To continue with our hotel
example, it will be cheaper to rent the same
aggregate of hotel space in a given time
period to large groups than to individual
order, because of the saving in billing costs
and the like.

4. *Firms producing to aggregated rather than
individual orders.*—We have up to now used,
as situations illustrative of the relevance of
Alchian's type of cost function, only firms
that produce highly differentiated products
in the sense that each customer's order requires unique handling. All such firms, of
which a job machine shop is perhaps the
most perfect example, obviously have cost
functions in which V is a critical variable. It
is not true, however, that the considerations
adduced by Alchian have importance only
where production to such individually differentiated orders takes place. Before considering manufacturers of highly homogeneous
products, it may be helpful to think of businesses illustrating an intermediate degree of
homogeneity. The transportation industries—
specifically, freight, and passenger transport
via road, rail, or air—provide interesting
examples here. While it is still possible to distinguish individual orders for transport (a
particular passenger trip or freight shipment), transportation systems are typically in a position to aggregate orders into
bundles which can be satisfied jointly (for
example, by shipping eighty passengers in
one plane, or by forming hundreds of individual freight shipments into one train).

---

[11] Wagner and Whitin, in fact, anticipate Alchian
in describing a cost function in which rate of output
(Alchian's X) and the time length of the production
run (Alchian's m) are independent arguments. However, they indicate that the average cost curve with
respect to increases in m must be U-shaped (from
which it follows, in contradiction to Alchian, that
$C_{\hat{v}v}$ must eventually become positive). The explanation runs in terms of the increasing cost of holding
inventory, as discussed in the text above (see Whitin,
op. cit., p. 301).

As a result, the "production run" in transport does not depend exclusively upon the characteristics of the individual orders, but also on how well the individual orders sort themselves into packages that can be satisfied jointly. Nevertheless, the characteristics of the individual orders do retain some relevance (there are setup operations for individual orders, like selling tickets for passenger transport and comparable paperwork in freight shipment). In freight shipment particularly, the "horizontal" size of order (quantity shipped) can be clearly distinguished from the "vertical" dimension (length of haul). In fact, the transport industries do make use of statistical measures representing average width and length of orders, as Tables 1 and 2 indicate.

TABLE 1* Total Long-Run Marginal Truck Costs per Revenue Ton Mile, by Length of Haul

Length of Haul (Miles)	Costs (Cents per Revenue Ton Mile)	
	Truck Load	Less than Truck Load
10	34.0	190.0
20	20.0	98.0
30	15.3	64.0
40	13.0	52.5
50	8.80	42.4
100	6.00	23.6
200	4.80	13.7
400	3.85	8.8
600	3.27	7.3
800	3.24	6.5

* J. R. Meyer, M. J. Peck, J. Stenason, and C. Zwick, *The Economics of Competition in the Transportation Industries* (Cambridge, Mass.: Harvard University Press, 1959), p. 94. Data from Interstate Commerce Commission, Bureau of Accounts, Cost Finding, and Valuation, *Cost Study of Class I Carriers of General Freight in the Middlewest Territory, 1953* (Washington, D.C.: Government Printing Office, 1954).

Each of these tables warrants a few remarks, but we cannot here go into an exposition of the meaning of the figures as used in the source. Broadly, however, Table 1 shows high sensitivity of unit trucking costs, in the expected direction, to length of haul. The much higher cost figures for less-than-

TABLE 2* Cost (Cents) per Airline Passenger Mile, by Mileage Blocks

Length of Haul (Miles)	1949 American Airlines Experience†	
	Cost at Actual Load Factors	Cost at 100 Per Cent Load Factor
100	10.0	6.6
200	6.8	4.5
300	5.6	3.8
400	5.0	3.4
500	4.7	3.1
600	4.4	3.0
700	4.3	2.9
800	4.2	2.8
900	4.0	2.7
1,000	4.0	2.6
1,100	3.9	2.5
1,200	3.8	2.5
1,300	3.8	2.5
1,400‡	3.7	2.5

* Meyer *et al., op. cit.,* p. 137. Original source cited as P. W. Cherington, *Airline Price Policy: A Study of Domestic Airline Passenger Fares* (Cambridge, Mass.: Harvard University Press, 1958), pp. 53, 55.
† Based on DC-6 experience.
‡ Meyer *et al.* text has 2,400 miles here, apparently in error.

truckload shipments as compared with truckload shipments suggests similar sensitivity to "width" of order, reflecting imperfect "bunching" of small orders. Table 1, therefore, reveals the influence of both the horizontal and vertical dimensions of orders. The airline figures (Table 2), limited to the vertical dimension ("horizontal" economies would be achievable only by selling tickets to groups rather than individuals) of output, actually show mileage blocks (length of *hop*) rather than length of *trip* for the individual customer. The latter, counting a trip as desired non-stop travel between an initiating and terminating point, is really the appropriate measure of V (or rather, v_i for an individual order); length of hop is undoubtedly highly correlated with length of trip, but divergences will appear in individual cases. Incidentally, Table 2 indicates the uneconomic nature of the so-called "stopover privilege" often granted by airlines: the right of the customer to make one or even several stops along his basic route, thus really taking several different trips, with no extra charge as compared with a through passenger. (While uneconomic in charging the same price for products with differing costs, the privilege may well contribute to profits as a discriminatory form of price cut or improvement in the nature of product offered.)

The distinction between trip and hop which appears here may be of more general importance than first appears. Clearly, because of the eventual need for refueling, we cannot indefinitely increase length of *hop* with declining marginal cost per mile traveled, but it still remains true that it is reasonable to expect declining marginal cost as length of *trip* increases (subject to the discontinuity qualification about the "production cycle" for the aircraft raised earlier). In the generalized sense, length of hop corresponds to the individual working period between stop and start of a unit of productive equipment. The distinction brought out here explains why the existence of an optimal production period for a piece of equipment used to produce jointly to individual orders is not, aside from discontinuities, inconsistent with marginal cost of producing to an individual order diminishing with V.

The electric power production industry reflects a still greater degree of product homogeneity. While even a single consumer will place a bewildering variety of overlapping orders on the system (each separate time a consuming appliance is switched on represents, in principle, a different order) even in a very short period of time, the almost perfect physical homogeneity of the product permits the firm to satisfy all synchronous orders jointly—and thus concern itself in short-run production decisions primarily with the aggregate load rather than the individual orders.[12] As a result, for an elec-

tric power firm, the way in which the individual orders sort themselves into aggregate bundles is much more important than their individual characteristics—for example, if each individual turned on all his appliances simultaneously and only for one hour, this would still not necessitate a short production run provided that the different consuming individuals spaced themselves evenly over the day.

Therefore, while it is still possible to measure the vertical and horizontal dimensions of individual orders for electric power, the characteristics of individual orders have much less significance than in the transport industry. The aggregation of simultaneous individual orders in effect eliminates the horizontal dimension (the way in which a given output for a period is divided among many small or a few large orders). The vertical dimension also loses some of its significance in the case of orders for electric power because of the unpredictability of termination. Under Alchian's postulates, production costs (aside from the learning phenomenon) are only sensitive to V in the sense of *planned* length of the production run; the option of costlessly and instantaneously terminating the order, ordinarily possessed by power customers greatly limits the planning for length of production run that power companies can undertake. (While other public utilities also are usually required to accept customer demands or termination of such demands for service, they need not do so under nearly as stringent time-response conditions as those applicable to the power industry.)

Power companies must, nevertheless, schedule production. They do so typically on the basis of statistical prediction of orders, taking into account trends in growth as well as established patterns of variations in demand over the hours of the day, days of the week and month, and season of the year. Production will, in consequence, be scheduled on a multilayer basis that represents the length of production runs that can be anticipated.

[12] Characteristics of the individual orders may have to be considered for very large consumers, and the product is not perfectly homogeneous (from the producer's point of view) at different delivery points. Also, individual characteristics have to enter into decisions like the type of individual connection to make to the main cable. From the longer run point

of view, the geographical bunching of anticipated orders is crucial in determining the cost of the distribution network.

First there will be the base load, which the company will presumably schedule for an indefinitely long V. Next there will be the longer seasonal plateaus of demand, production for which may be scheduled in months; the work-day (versus week-end) load which may be scheduled for a few days; and the peak demands within the day, for which only brief production will be scheduled. Finally, reserve equipment will be maintained in readiness for handling a possible momentary peak. for which production will not be scheduled in advance. Thus, a power company may at a moment of time be producing to very long and to very short orders (or, rather, bunches of individual orders), as well as a whole series of orders of intermediate length. (We may remark, as an aside, that the short length of production order involved is undoubtedly part of the explanation of the high cost of meeting peak loads.) The upshot of this discussion is that even in rather complex cases of overlapping and aggregated orders, it is possible to distinguish respects in which planned length of production run may have the type of influence on cost asserted by Alchian.

C. Firms Fitting the Classical Model

With these examples in mind, let us turn, finally, to the standard classical model of firm and see if any sense can be made of an effect upon cost of V as well as X. Even a producer of a product perfectly homogeneous with respect to individual orders may be thought of as scheduling his production in terms of some limited anticipation of V. In other words, he will *not* act as if his current rate of output X could be extended to infinity. If, in fact, he did think that V was infinite at the current X, he would buy equipment perfectly specialized to that particular rate of output; he would sign very long-term contracts with his suppliers and his labor; and so forth. To the extent that he does not so act, but reserves flexibility instead, he is implicitly assuming that V is not infinite.[13] That is to say, in purchasing

equipment, signing contracts, and so forth, a certain combination of underlying assumptions about X and V will be implicit.[14] In an uncertain world, there will undoubtedly be a probability distribution for X and V involved rather than single definite numbers.

1. *The relation between* X *and* V.—Now turning to the orthodox theoretical model, two different lines of argument occur to me as ways of defending its exclusive concentration upon X. The first is that the orthodox cost function of the firm might be assumed to represent the cost of producing at rates X into the indefinite future—or, to make it more strict, in perpetuity. Then V is infinite for any positive X and of no particular interest. (I shall argue below that the assumption of an infinite V is, in fact, relevant and appropriate and what we really mean when we speak of *very long-run* cost curves.)

Now, of course, as the future is uncertain no actual firm plans to produce at given rates into perpetuity—but a model of a firm doing so may be a useful representation in many situations, especially for enterprises that produce for the market rather than to order or under contract. The power of compound interest to some extent relieves us of worries about assumptions concerning the far-off future. However, as soon as we enter the range of problems for which variability of future conditions and uncertainty about them become *important*, the question of how long a given rate of output can be maintained cannot be ignored.

---

[13] Such devices of financial planning as the "payout

period" may in part represent crude attempts to prevent expensive investments in overdurable equipment (that is, to prevent planning on too large a V) by imposing an arbitrary sharp cutoff date beyond which no net benefit from the equipment is anticipated. A logically superior method of achieving the same end is to calculate a risk discount on future benefits.

[14] Reducing the decision to these two variables is obviously a major oversimplification. Even with V determined, firms will typically anticipate some cyclical variation of X, although the actual pattern will not be known in advance. And in the choice of V, excessive durability of equipment will threaten less loss to the extent that it is general-purpose rather than highly specialized equipment being purchased, so that different V's may well be appropriate for different elements of the same production line.

Alternatively, ignoring V could be justified even without the assumption of producing at constant rates into infinity, provided that V depended only upon X and did not represent an independent source of variation. The simplest relation would make V proportional to X. Suppose that to meet anticipated market deliveries a given firm plans to produce at the rate $X_0 = 1,000$ units per week. Because of uncertainty as to the future, and especially as to the persistence of demand, the firm's contracts and production schedules are *not* based upon an infinite production period, we will suppose, but upon a period of, say, one year. Then $m = 52$ weeks, and scheduled $V_0 = 52,000$. Now, let the firm suddenly become aware of an increase in demand—the market can currently take 2,000 units per week instead of 1,000. If we assume that the firm can now be, for this or any similar change in current rate of demand, about as confident of the persistence of the new rate X_1 as it was of the old rate X_0—then m remains unchanged at 52 weeks and the new V_1 is 104,000. This same idea can be expressed in a number of ways, among them being the statements that V and X have increased proportionately, that V and X have increased while leaving m unchanged, or that the planning horizon is unchanged but within the horizon our expectations move proportionately to current experience. The proportionality assumption is that implicitly made, I argue, in the orthodox exposition of the firm's cost function.

In Figure 1, the orthodox marginal cost curve embodying the proportionality assumption about changes in demand is Curve II. (It may be helpful to think of Curve I as showing the marginal cost of *accelerations* of demand [changed X with fixed V] and Curve III as showing the marginal cost of *extensions* of demand [changed V with fixed X]. Proportionate changes of X and V might be called *expansions* of demand.) Alchian asserts, quite broadly, that nothing can be derived from his or any other accepted postulate about the shape of the Curve II. If true that would be unfortunate, since we have considerable empirical ground for confidence in the one crucial property of the classical

marginal cost Curve II in Figure 1—that marginal cost eventually begins to rise with proportionate expansion of X and V. Surely we know that, at a given state of technology, if both volume and rate of output expand beyond all bounds we will eventually attain a point where increased units of output can only be purchased at increasing cost. Happily, it can be shown that this property does indeed follow from the Alchian postulates (with a weak addition), so that we can justify the accepted shape of the marginal cost curve in the orthodox theory of the firm within Alchian's model.

2. *Marginal cost rises as X and V increase proportionately.*—I shall not attempt any high degree of mathematical rigor in this demonstration, but I believe that the heuristic argument given below will be convincing. If C were plotted on a vertical axis against the axes X and V in the horizontal plane—the other independent variable, T (date of initiation of production) being held constant throughout this discussion—we would be interested in the shape of the marginal cost function over the ray of slope $V/X = m$ in the horizontal plane. (We are only concerned with the positive quadrant, of course.)

It is immediately possible to assert the following relationships:

$$\frac{dC}{dX}\bigg]_{V=mX} = \frac{\partial C}{\partial X}\bigg]_{V=V_0} + \frac{\partial C}{\partial V}\bigg]_{X=X_0}\frac{dV}{dX}\bigg]_{V=mX},$$

$$\tag{2}$$

or, with a change of notation,

$$\frac{dC}{dX} = C_X + mC_V \tag{3}$$

$$\frac{d^2C}{dX^2} = C_{XX} + 2mC_{XV} + m^2C_{VV}. \tag{4}$$

We wish to show, using inequalities (1) above, that as X and V become proportionately and indefinitely large, the sign of d^2C/dX^2 must beyond some point become positive. In general, the sign is indeterminate because, in equation (4) above, while C_{XX} is positive, C_{VV} is negative and C_{XV} may be negative, m being a positive constant.

But as X and V increase, the positiveness of C_{XX} must eventually dominate over the negativeness of the other two second partial derivatives[15] because the latter are limited by the constraint that the first derivative C_V must remain positive.[16]

More specifically, and assuming that the functions are monotonic rather than irregular cyclic in nature (here is where the argument lacks rigor), if C_V is to remain positive as X and V increase we must have

$$\frac{dC_V}{dX}\bigg]_{V=mX} = \frac{\partial C_V}{\partial X} + m\frac{\partial C_V}{\partial V} \longrightarrow 0, \quad (5)$$

or

$$C_{XV} + mC_{VV} \longrightarrow 0. \quad (6)$$

And, since m is positive, and the two partial derivatives have the same sign, if this sum is to approach zero both C_{XV} and C_{VV} must separately approach zero. Turning back to equation (4), if C_{XV} and C_{VV}, while remaining negative, approach zero, and if C_{XX} remains positive, d^2C/dX^2 must ultimately become positive—subject to a weak restriction on the behavior of C_{XX}. It is sufficient, though stronger than necessary, to postulate that C_{XX} not approach zero. Such a postulate is, of course, eminently reasonable in terms of economics. The condition ruled out would have the marginal cost (with respect to acceleration), C_X, rising but leveling off at some upper asymptote—where we certainly expect the cost of additional acceleration to become steadily greater, or even increasingly greater as the same V is required to be compressed into a shorter and shorter production period.

We may therefore conclude from this demonstration that the orthodox cost func-

---

[15] This argument accepts Alchian's "conjectural" postulate that C_{XV} is negative. The conclusion follows a fortiori if C_{XV} is positive.

[16] For the reader who may have difficulty seeing this purely mathematical point, suppose first a simpler case in which C is only a function of V with the constraints $C_V > 0$ and $C_{VV} < 0$. Then the marginal cost curve is positive but has a negative slope (is falling) throughout. Now, with certain omitted assumptions about smoothness of the curve (regular behavior of the higher derivatives), it is clear that the rate of fall C_{VV} must approach zero as V increases if the marginal cost C_V is to remain positive throughout.

tion of the firm, with its eventually rising marginal cost curve (and consequently, U-shaped average cost curve) is, while a special case, nevertheless an interesting and valid special case (applying when m is constant) of the enriched model of the firm that Alchian develops from his postulates.

. . .

III. IMPLICATIONS AND LIMITATIONS

The fruitfulness of Alchians' reformulation of the cost function of the firm will be indicated, I believe, by the following comments on some of the implications for a number of different branches of economics.

First, and perhaps too obvious to mention, is the contribution to the positive theory of the firm and to its field of application in managerial economics. Surely the orthodox model of the firm fails to provide the essential analytical equipment for an economist to understand or to advise on the operations of a business in which size of the individual order is a crucial variable—a job machine shop, for example. With Alchian's model, the business economist can grasp the essentials of the problem of economies of scale: marginal costs are a rising function of *rate* of production, a declining function of scheduled *volume* of production. He can thus fruitfully separate the problems, hitherto confounded, of responding to accelerations of demand (rate increased, for given volume), extensions of demand (volume increased, for given rate), and expansions of demand (rate and volume increased, in proportion). In addition, the analysis provides the key for the managerial economist to use in advising the businessman to respond in a short-run or long-run manner to a change in demand (i.e., whether fixed factors should or should not be "unfixed"). The answer, as put forward here, is that whether a short-run or long-run response is appropriate depends upon the anticipated volume of production at the new rate of demand—which is, of course, perfectly consistent with common sense.

Another consequence of the analysis, with

possibly important policy implications, is a better understanding of the logical nature of the cost savings that can justify non-discriminatory quantity discounts—that is, discounts not due to the bargaining power of large customers. As an example, we may recall the historic railroad "abuse" of charging more for a short haul than for a long haul. Now, if we accept Alchian's proposition that the marginal cost with respect to length of haul (a "vertical" dimension of orders) is declining, we will be led to a justification of a lower per mile rate for longer hauls but not to a justification of a lower *total charge* for a longer than for a shorter haul. However, if we remember that a railroad characteristically handles freight orders in the aggregate—that is, produces jointly to bundles of individual orders—we may be led to a different conclusion. Thus, a certain long-haul order may represent only a small increase in an already large aggregate tonnage scheduled to be carried between the initial and terminal points. Since marginal cost is also typically declining for increases in size of order as aggregated by the rail-shipment techniques (i.e., marginal cost declines with increases in the "width" of shipments, where the latter may represent a bunching of many separate orders), the increment to total cost may be very small. If the short-haul order, in contrast, involves an initiating or a terminating point not subject to heavy or regular traffic, it will not be possible to aggregate it with many or possibly any other orders. The cost increment due to the short haul may then be quite large compared to that due to the long haul just described.

It follows immediately from the above discussion that there are interesting econometric problems involved in the attempt to measure changes in relevant dimensions of X and V. Sometimes statistics will be available only on characteristics of the individual orders, for example, when it is the characteristics of aggregates rather than individual orders which determine cost. Furthermore, where there are several different dimensions of orders to consider, the problem may be a difficult one. And, finally,

in many situations V (the *planned*, not the actual, production run) is not a directly observable magnitude.

For these reasons, while a review of econometric studies of production and cost functions in an attempt to separate the effects of X and of V might be instructive, the very extensive discussion required could not be undertaken within the limits of this paper. However, from Tables 1 and 2 there is strong reason to believe that V should be considered together with rate of output X for transport cost functions. One statistical cost function, by Ferguson for aircraft fuel consumption, has been explicitly designed to show the effects of a number of different dimensions of output. He does not consider length of haul explicitly but rather number of landings per hour flown—a variable related inversely to length of hop.[17] The influence of number of landings turns out to be very important and in the expected direction.[18] On the other hand, the work by Meyer and associates cited previously in connection with Tables 1 and 2 indicates at one point that train expenses (the line-haul costs of railroad operations) are not affected by length of haul.[19] Station expenses, however, are shown to be extremely sensitive to the relative proportions of carload and less-than-carload freight, indicating the importance of size of shipment.[20] I have not found other studies in which the X, V distinction was considered, but on the basis of the present analysis studies of cost functions in retail trade (to cite only one example) might introduce such dimensions as the number of hours between closing and opening (a vertical measure corresponding, somewhat, to length of hop in air travel) and average size of order (a width dimension).

[17] A. R. Ferguson, "Empirical Determination of a Multidimensional Marginal Cost Function," *Econometrica*, XVIII (July, 1950), 217–35.

[18] *Ibid.*, p. 227.

[19] *Op. cit.*, p. 317. The text indicates only that there was no gross correlation between train expenses (undeflated) and average length of haul. There may or may not have been a partial effect after allowing for other variables such as freight and passenger miles and tonnage.

[20] *Ibid.*, p. 307.

This brings us to the topic of statistical cost functions. Alchian's cost model goes far to explain the great mystery in this realm: Why do statistically measured cost functions generally fail to display rising marginal cost, except possibly very close to the upper extreme of the output data? Many explanations have been offered for this phenomenon, but all have various defects in the face of the surprisingly consistent statistical results.[21] Alchian's model, however, leads to a much weaker expectation of eventually rising marginal cost as usually understood than does the classical model.[22] If the periods observed (for time series studies) of firms or plants observed (for cross-section studies) showing high output reflect both higher X and higher V, as we would generally expect, then the two forces on the measured marginal cost work in opposite directions. This suggests that re-examination of the results of the various attempts to measure cost functions, with the aim of separating the effects of X and V on cost, would be a fruitful line of study.

In conclusion, I believe that the importance of Alchian's fundamental insight—

that scheduled volume of production has an effect on costs which essentially differs from the effect of rate of output—has been sufficiently demonstrated by this review. That the relationships in exactly the form specified by Alchian apply strictly and unfailingly to the real world we have seen some reason to doubt, though I concur with his propositions as broad generalizations. I have tried to develop certain ideas further in distinguishing the effects of separate vertical and horizontal (length and size) dimensions of orders, and in extending the idea of a production run to firms that produce jointly to aggregated rather than individual orders, or even do not produce to order at all. I have attempted, in addition, to defend certain orthodox propositions attacked by Alchian: among them, that marginal costs of proportionate variation of X and V will (eventually) rise; that short run and long run may be usefully distinguished in terms of fixity of certain inputs (although this is not the fundamental basis of the distinction); and that a sensible meaning can be attached (in a world of uncertainty) to the idea of incurring losses in the short run in the expectation of long-run gains. Finally, let me say that this paper will have achieved its prime purpose if it stimulates further discussion and comprehension of Alchian's contribution to our understanding of the fundamental economic concept of cost of production.

[21] For a full discussion, see Johnston, *op. cit.*

[22] Alchian himself has declared that it leads to *no* such expectation (for proportionate expansion of X and V). But we have shown above that, even in Alchian's model, marginal cost should ultimately rise.

11

Multiple Regression Analysis of Cost Behavior

GEORGE J. BENSTON*

Accountants probably have always been concerned with measuring and reporting the relationship between cost and output. The pre-eminence of financial accounting in this century resulted in directing much of our attention towards attaching costs to inventories. However, the recent emphasis on decision making is causing us to consider ways of measuring the variability of cost with output and other decisions variables. In this paper, the application, use, and limitations of multiple regression analysis, a valuable tool for measuring costs, are discussed.[1]

A valid objection to multiple regression analysis in the past has been that its computational difficulty often rendered it too costly. Today, with high speed computers and library programs, this objection is no longer valid: most regression problems ought to cost less than $30 to run. Unfortunately, this new ease and low cost of using regression analysis may prove to be its undoing. Analysts may be tempted to use the technique without adequately realizing its technical data requirements and limitations. The "GI-GO" adage, "garbage in, garbage out," always must be kept in mind. A major pur-

pose of this paper is to state these requirements and limitations explicitly and to indicate how they may be handled.

The general problem of cost measurement is discussed in the first section of this paper. Multiple regression analysis is considered first in relation to other methods of cost analysis. Then its applicability to cost decision problems is delineated. Second, the method of multiple regression is discussed in nonmathematical terms so that its uses can be understood better. The third section represents the "heart" of the paper. Here the technical requirements of multiple regression are outlined, and the implications of these requirements for the recording of cost data in the firm's accounting records are outlined. The functional form of the regression equation is then considered. In the final section, we discuss some applications for multiple regression analysis.

I. THE GENERAL PROBLEM

In his attempts to determine the factors that cause costs to be incurred and the magnitudes of their effects, the accountant is faced with a formidable task. Engineers, foremen, and others who are familiar with the production process being studied usually can provide a list of cost-causing factors, such as the number of different units produced, the lot sizes in which units were made, and so forth. Other factors that affect costs, such as the season of the year, may be important, though they are more subtle than production factors. The accountant must separate and measure the effects of many different causal factors

From The Accounting Review (*October 1966*), *pp. 657–72. Reprinted with permission of author and publisher.*

* George J. Benston is Associate Professor of Accounting at the University of Rochester. This manuscript was awarded first place in the American Accounting Association's 1966 Manuscript Contest, open to members acquiring the doctorate in 1962 or later.

[1] The use of statistical analysis for auditing and control is outside the scope of this paper. Excellent discussions of these uses of statistics may be found in Richard N. Cyert and H. Justin Davidson, *Statistical Sampling for Accounting Information* (Prentice-Hall, 1962), and Herbert Arkin, *Handbook of Sampling for Auditing and Accounting*, Volume I: Methods (McGraw-Hill, 1963).

whose importance may vary in different periods.

Commonly Used Methods of Cost Analysis

Perhaps the most pervasive method of analyzing cost variability is separation of costs into two or three categories: variable, fixed and sometimes semivariable. But this method does not provide a solution to the problem of measuring the costs caused by each of many factors operating simultaneously. In this "direct costing" type of procedure, output is considered to be the sole cause of costs. Another objection to this method is that there is no way to determine whether the accountant's subjective separation of costs into variable and fixed is reasonably accurate. Dividing output during a period into variable cost during that period yields a single number (unit variable cost) whose accuracy cannot be assessed. If the procedure is repeated for several periods, it is likely that different unit variable costs will be computed. But the accountant cannot determine whether the average of these numbers (or some other summary statistic) is a useful number. Another important shortcoming of this method is the assumption of linearity between cost and output. While linearity may be found, it should not be assumed automatically.

A variant of the fixed-variable method is one in which cost and output data for many periods are plotted on a two-dimensional graph. A line is then fitted to the data, the slope being taken as variable cost per unit of output. When the least-squares method of fitting the line is used, the procedure is called simple linear regression. Until the recent advent of computers, simple regression was considered to be quite sophisticated.[2] While it was recognized that its use neglects the effects on cost of factors other than output, it was defended on the then reasonable grounds that multiple regression with more than two or three variables is too difficult computationally to be considered economically feasible.

[2] National Association of Accountants, *Separating and Using Costs as Fixed and Variable*, June, 1960.

Multiple Regression

Multiple regression can allow the accountant to estimate the amount by which the various cost-causing factors affect costs. A very rough description is that it measures the cost of a change in one variable, say output, while holding the effects on cost of other variables, say the season of the year or the size of batches, constant. For example, consider the problem of analyzing the costs incurred by the shipping department of a department store. The manager of the department believes that his costs are primarily a function of the number of orders processed. However, heavier packages are more costly to handle than are lighter ones. He also considers the weather an important factor; rain or extreme cold slows down delivery time. We might want to eliminate the effect of the weather, since it is not controllable. But we would like to know how much each order costs to process and what the cost of heavier against lighter packages is. If we can make these estimates, we can (1) prepare a flexible budget for the shipping department that takes account of changes in operating conditions, (2) make better pricing decisions, and (3) plan for capital budgeting more effectively. A properly specified multiple regression equation can provide the required estimates.

A criticism of multiple regression analysis is that it is complicated, and so would be difficult to "sell" to lower management and supervisory personnel. However, the method allows for a more complete specification of "reality" than do simple regression or the fixed-variable dichotomy. Studies have shown that supervisors tend to disregard data that they believe are "unrealistic," such as those based on the simplification that costs incurred are a function of units of output only.[3] Therefore, multiple regression analysis should prove more acceptable to supervisors than procedures that require gross simplification of reality.

[3] H. A. Simon, H. Guetzkow, G. Kozmetsky, and G. Tyndall, *Centralization versus Decentralization in Organizing the Controllers Department* (New York: The Controllership Foundation, 1954).

The regression technique also can allow the accountant to make probability statements concerning the reliability of the estimates made.[4] For example, he may find that the marginal cost of processing a package of average weight is $.756, when the effects on cost of different weather conditions and other factors are accounted for. If the properties underlying regression analysis (discussed below) are met, the reliability of this cost estimate may be determined from the standard error of the coefficient (say $.032) from which the accountant may assess a probability of .95 that the marginal cost per package is between $.692 and $.820 (.756 ± .064).

Multiple regression analysis, then, is a very powerful tool; however, it is not applicable to all cost situations. To decide the situations for which it is best used, let us first consider the problem of cost estimation in general and then consider the sub-class of problems for which multiple regression analysis is useful.

Types of Cost Decision Problems

In general, cost is a function of many variables, including time. For example, the cost of output may be affected by such conditions as whether production is increasing or decreasing, the lot sizes are large or small, the plant is new or old, the White Sox are losing or winning, and so forth. Since there is *some* change in the environment of different time periods or in the circumstances affecting different decisions, it would seem that the accountant must make an individual cost analysis for every decision considered.

However, the maximization rule of economics also applies to information technology: the marginal cost of the information must not exceed the marginal revenue gained from it. The marginal revenue from cost information is the additional revenue that accrues or the losses that are avoided from not making

mistakes, such as accepting contracts where the marginal costs exceed the marginal revenue from the work, or rejecting contracts where the reverse situation obtains. The marginal cost of information is the cost of gathering and presenting the information, plus the opportunity cost of delay, since measurement and presentation are not instantaneous.[5] Since these costs can be expected to exceed the marginal revenue from information for many decisions, it usually is not economical to estimate different costs for each different decision. Thus, it is desirable to group decision problems into categories that can be served by the same basic cost information. Two such categories are proposed here: (1) recurring problems and (2) one-time problems.

Recurring decision problems are those for which the data required for analysis are used with some regularity. Examples are determining the prices that will be published in a catalogue, preparation of output schedules for expected production, the setting of budgets and production cost standards, and the formulation of forecasts. These decisions require cost data in the form of schedules of expected costs due to various levels of activity over an expected range.

One-time problems are those which occur infrequently, unpredictably, or are of such a magnitude as to require individual cost estimates. Examples of these problems are cost-profit-volume decisions, such as whether the firm should take a one-time special order, make, buy, or lease equipment, develop a new product, or close a plant. These decisions require that cost estimates be made which reflect conditions especially relevant to the problem at hand.

These categories present different requirements for cost estimation. Recurring problems require a schedule of *expected* costs and activity. Since these problems are repetitive, the marginal cost of gathering and presenting data each time usually is expected to be greater than the marginal revenue from the data. Thus, while the marginal cost of

---

[4] This and the following statements are made in the context of a Bayesian analysis, in which the decision maker combines sample information with his prior judgment concerning unknown parameters. In the examples given, a jointly diffuse prior distribution is assumed for all parameters.

[5] These two costs are related since delay can be reduced by expending more resources on the information system.

additional production, for example, will differ depending on such factors as whether overtime is required or excess capacity is available, in general it is more profitable to estimate the amount that the marginal cost of the additional production may be, on the average, rather than to take account of every special factor that may exist in individual circumstances.

In contrast, one-time problems are characterized by the economic desirability of making individual cost estimates. We do not rely on average marginal cost because the more accurate information is worth its cost. This situation may occur when the problem is unique, and average cost data are therefore not applicable. Or the decision may involve a substantial commitment of resources, making the marginal revenue from avoiding wrong decisions quite high.

II. MULTIPLE REGRESSION ANALYSIS

Regression analysis is particularly useful in estimating costs for recurring decisions.[6] The procedure essentially consists of estimating mathematically the *average* relationship between costs (the "dependent" variable) and the factors that cause cost incurrences (the "independent" variables). The analysis provides the accountant with an estimate of the expected marginal cost of a unit change in output, for example, with the effects on total cost of other factors accounted for. These are the data he requires for costing recurring decisions.

The usefulness of multiple regression analysis for recurring decisions of costs can be appreciated best when the essential nature of the technique is understood. It is not necessary that the mathematical proofs of least squares or the methods of inverting matrices be learned since library computer programs do all the work.[7] However, it is necessary that

the assumptions underlying use of multiple regression be fully understood so that this valuable tool is not misused.

Multiple regression analysis presupposes a linear relationship between the contributive factors and costs.[8] The functional relationship between these factors, $x_1, x_2, \ldots, x_n$, and cost, C, is assumed in multiple regression analysis to be of the following form:

$$C_t = \beta_0 x_{0,t} + \beta_1 x_{1,t} + \beta_2 x_{2,t} + \cdots \quad (1)$$
$$+ \beta_n x_{n,t} + \mu_t,$$

where
β_0 is a constant term ($x_0 = 1$ for all observations and time periods),
the β's are fixed coefficients that express the marginal contribution of each x_i to C, and
μ is the sum of unspecified factors, the disturbances, that are assumed to be randomly distributed with a zero mean and constant variance, and
$t = 1, 2, \ldots, m =$ time periods.
The β coefficients are estimated from a sample of C's and x's from time periods 1 through m. For example, assume that the cost recorded in a week is a function of such specified factors as $x_1 =$ units of output, $x_2 =$ number of units in a batch, and $x_3 =$ the ratio of the number of "de luxe" units to total units produced. Then the right hand side of equation (2) is an estimate of the right hand side of equation (1), obtained from a sample of weekly observations, where the b's are estimates of the β's and u is the residual, the estimate of μ, the disturbance term:

$$C_t = b_{0,t} + b_1 x_{1,t} + b_2 x_{2,t} + b_3 x_{3,t} + u_t. \quad (2)$$

If the values estimated for coefficients of the three independent variables, $x_1, x_2,$ and x_3, are $b_0 = 100,$ $b_1 = 30,$ $b_2 = -20,$ and $b_3 = 500,$ the expected cost ($\hat{C}$) for any given week (t) is estimated by:

$$\hat{C} = 100 + 30x_1 - 20x_2 + 500x_3.$$

[6] Indeed, its use requires the assumption that the past costs used for a regressions analysis are a sample from a universe of possible costs generated by a continuing, stationary, normal process.

[7] The mathematics of multiple regression is described in many statistics and econometrics texts.

[8] A curvilinear or exponential relationship also can be expressed as a linear relationship. This technique is discussed below.

Given estimates of the β's, one has, in effect, estimates of the marginal cost associated with each of the determining factors. In the example given above, the marginal cost of producing an additional unit of output, x_1, is estimated to be \$30, with the effects or costs of size of batch (x_2) and the ratio of the number of de luxe to total units (x_3) accounted for. Or, β_2, the marginal reduction in total cost of increasing the batches by 3 units, given fixed values of the number of units and the relative proportions of de luxe units produced, is estimated to be $-\$60$ (\$ $-$ 20/ times 3).

It is tempting to interpret the constant term, b_0, as fixed cost. But this is not correct unless the linear relationship found in the range of observations obtains back to zero output.[9] This can be seen best in the following two-dimensional graph of cost on output.

FIG. 1

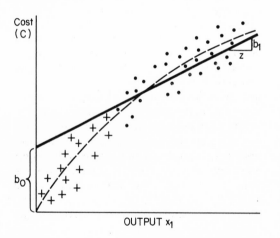

The line was fitted with the equation $C = b_0 + b_1x_1$, where the dots are the observed values of cost and output. The slope of the line is the coefficient, b_1 an estimate of the marginal change in total cost (C) with a unit change (z) in output (x_1). The intercept on the C axis is b_0, the constant term. It would be an estimate of fixed cost if the range of observations included the point

where output were zero, and the relationship between total cost and output were linear. However, if more observations of cost and output (the x's) were available, it might be that the dashed curve would be fitted and b_0 would be zero. Thus the value of the constant term, b_0, is not the costs that would be expected if there were no output; it is only the value that is calculated as a result of the regression line computed from the available data.

The data for the calculations are taken from the accounting and production records of past time periods. The coefficients estimated from these data are averages of past experience. Therefore, the b's calculated are best suited for recurring cost decisions. The fact that the b's are averages of past data must be emphasized, because their use for decisions is based on the assumption that the future will be like an average of past experience.

The mathematical method usually used for estimating the β's is the least-squares technique. It has the properties of providing best, linear, unbiased estimates of the β's. These properties are desirable because they tend "to yield a series of estimates whose average would coincide with the true value being estimated and whose variance about that true value is smaller than that of any other unbiased estimators."[10] While these properties are not always of paramount importance, they are very valuable for making estimates of the expected average costs required for recurring problems.

Another important advantage of the least-squares technique is that when it is combined with the assumptions about the disturbance term (μ_t) that are discussed in Section III-7 below, the reliability of the relations between the explanatory variables and costs can be determined. Two types of reliability estimates may be computed. One, the standard error of estimate, shows how well the equation fits the data. The second, the standard error of the regression coefficients, assesses the probability that the β's estimated are within a range of values. For example,

---

[9] Fixed cost is defined here as avoidable cost related to time periods and not to output variables.

[10] J. Johnston, *Statistical Cost Analysis* (New York: McGraw-Hill, 1960), p. 31.

if a linear cost function is used, the coefficient (b_1) of output (x_1) is the estimated marginal cost of output. With an estimate of the standard error of the coefficient, s_{b_1}, we can say that the true marginal cost, β_1, is within the range $b_1 \pm s_{b_1}$, with a given probability.[11]

III. REQUIREMENTS OF MULTIPLE REGRESSION AND COST RECORDING IMPLICATIONS

Although multiple regression is an excellent tool for estimating recurring costs, it does have several requirements that make its use hazardous without careful planning.[12] Most of the data requirements of multiple regression analysis depend on the way cost-accounting records are maintained. If the data are simply taken from the ordinary cost-accounting records of the company, it is unlikely that the output of the regression model will be meaningful. Therefore, careful planning of the extent to which the initial accounting data are coded and recorded is necessary before regression analysis can be used successfully. This section of the paper is organized into four groupings that include several numbered subsections in which the principal technical requirements are described, after which the implications for the cost system are discussed. In the first group, (1) the length and (2) number of time periods, (3) the range of observations, and (4) the specification of cost-related factors are described, following which their implications for cost recording are outlined. In the second group, (5) errors of measurement and their cost recording implication are considered. The third group deals with (6) correlations among the explanatory variables and the important contribution that accounting analysis can make to this problem. Finally, (7) the requirements for the distribution of the nonspecified factors (disturbances) are given.

[11] The interpretation of the confidence interval is admittedly Bayesian.
[12] Proofs of the requirements described may be found in many econometrics textbooks, such as Arthur S. Goldberger, *Econometric Theory* (Wiley, 1964), and J. Johnston, *Econometric Methods* (McGraw-Hill, 1963).

The implications of these requirements for the functional form of the variables are taken up in Section V.

1. Length of Time Periods

(a) The time periods $(1, 2, 3, \ldots, m)$ chosen should be long enough to allow the bookkeeping procedures to pair output produced in a period with the cost incurred because of that production. For example, if 500 units are produced in a day, but records of supplies used are kept on a weekly basis, an analysis of the cost of supplies used cannot be made with shorter than weekly periods. Lags in recording costs must be corrected or adjusted. Thus, production should not be recorded as occurring in one week while indirect labor is recorded a week later when the pay checks are written.

(b) The time periods chosen should be *short* enough to avoid variations in production within the period. Otherwise, the variations that occur during the period will be averaged out, possibly obscuring the true relationship between cost and output.

2. Number of Time Periods (Observations)

For a time series, each observation covers a time period in which data on costs and output and other explanatory variables are collected for analysis. As a minimum, there must be one more observation than there are independent variables to make regression analysis possible. (The excess number is called "degrees of freedom.") Of course, many more observations must be available before one could have any confidence that the relationship estimated from the sample reflects the "true" underlying relationship. The standard errors, from which one may determine the range within which the true coefficients lie (given some probability of error), are reduced by the square root of the number of observations.

3. Range of Observations

The observations on cost and output should cover as wide a range as possible. If there is very little variation from period to period in cost and output, the functional relationship between the two cannot be estimated effectively by regression analysis.

4. Specification of Cost-Related Factors

All factors that affect cost should be specified and included in the analysis.[13] This is a very important requirement that is often difficult to meet. For example, observations may have been taken over a period when input prices changed. The true relationship between cost and output may be obscured if high output coincided with high input due to price-level effects. If the higher costs related to higher price levels are not accounted for (by inclusion of a price index as an independent variable) or adjusted for (by stating the dependent variable, cost, in constant dollars), the marginal cost of additional output estimated will be meaningful only if changes in input prices are proportional to changes in output and are expected to remain so.

Implications for Cost Recording of 1, 2, 3, and 4

In general, the time period requirements (1a, 1b and 2) call for the recording of production data for periods no longer than one month and preferably as short as one week in length. If longer periods are chosen, it is unlikely that there will be a sufficient number of observations available for analysis because, as a bare minimum, one more period than the number of explanatory variables is needed. Even if it is believed that only one explanatory variable (such as units of output) is needed to specify the cost function in any one period, requirement 4 (that all cost related factors be specified) demands consideration of differences among time periods. Thus, such events as changes in factor prices and production methods, whether production

is increasing or decreasing, and the seasons of the year might have to be specified as explanatory variables.

The necessity of identifying all relevant explanatory variables such as those just mentioned, can be met by having a journal kept in which the values or the behavior of these variables in specific time periods is noted. If such a record is not kept, it will be difficult (if not impossible) to recall unusual events and to identify them with the relevant time periods, especially when short time periods are used. For example, it is necessary to note whether production increased or decreased substantially in each period. Increases in production may be met by overtime. However, decreases may be accompanied by idle time or slower operations. Thus, we would expect the additional costs of increases to be greater than the cost savings from decreases.[14]

Other commonly found factors that affect costs are changes in technology, changes in capacity, periods of adjustment to new processes or types of output, and seasonal differences. The effect of these factors may be accounted for by including variables in the regression equation, by specific adjustment of the data, or by excluding data that are thought to be "contaminated."

The wide range of observations needed for effective analysis also argues against observation periods of longer than one month. With long periods, variations in production would more likely be averaged out than if shorter periods were used (which violates requirement 1b). In addition, if stability of conditions limits the number of explanatory variables other than output that otherwise would reduce the degrees of freedom, this same stability probably would not produce a sufficient range of output to make regression analysis worthwhile. Thus, weekly or monthly data usually are required for multiple regression.

---

[13] Complete specification is not mandatory if requirement 7 (below) is met. However, requirement 7 is not likely to be fulfilled if the specification is seriously incomplete.

[14] A dummy variable can be used to represent qualitative variables, such as $P = 1$ where production increased and $P = 0$ when production decreased. From the coefficient of P, we can estimate the cost effect of differences in the direction of output change and also reduce contamination of the coefficient estimated for output.

5. Errors of Measurement

It is difficult to believe that data from a "real life" production situation will be reported without error. The nature of the errors is important since some kinds will affect the usefulness of regression analysis more than others will. Errors in the dependent variable, cost, are not fatal since they affect the disturbance term, μ.[15] The predictive value of the equation is lessened, but the estimate of marginal cost (β_1) is not affected.

But where there are errors in measuring output or the other independent variables (x's), the disturbance term, μ, will be correlated with the independent variables.[16] If this condition exists, the sample coefficient estimated by the least-squares procedure will be an underestimate of the true marginal cost. Thus, it is very important that the independent variables be measured accurately.

The possibility of measurement errors is intensified by the number of observations requirement. Short reporting periods increase the necessity for careful classification. For example, if a cost caused by production in week 1 is not recorded until week 2, the dependent variable (cost) of both observations will be measured incorrectly. This error is most serious when production fluctuates between observations. However, when production is increasing or decreasing steadily, the measurement error tends to be constant (either in absolute or proportional terms) and hence will affect only the constant term. The regression coefficients estimated, and hence the estimates of average marginal cost, will not be affected.[17]

Another important type of measurement error is the failure to charge the period in which production occurs with future costs caused by that production. For example, overtime pay for production workers may be paid for in the week following their work. This can be adjusted for easily. However, the foreman may not be paid for his overtime directly. Rather, many months after his work he might get a year-end bonus or a raise in pay. These costs cannot easily be associated with the production that caused them but will be charged in another period, thus making both periods' costs incorrect.[18] This type of error is difficult to correct. Usually, all that one can do is eliminate the bonus payment from the data of the period in which it is paid and realize that the estimated coefficient of output will be biased downward. Average marginal costs, then, will be understated.

A somewhat similar situation follows from the high cost of the careful record keeping required to charge such input factors as production supplies to short time periods. In this event, these items of cost should be deducted from the other cost items and not included in the analysis. If these amounts are large enough, specific analysis may be required, or the decision not to account for them carefully may be re-evaluated.

This separation of specific cost items also is desirable where the accountant knows that their allocation to time periods bears no relation to production. For example, such costs as insurance or rent may be allocated to departments on a monthly basis. There is no point in including these costs in the dependent variable because it is known that they do not vary with the independent variables. At best, their inclusion will only increase the constant term. However, if by chance they are correlated with an independent variable, they will bias the estimates made (requirement 7a). This type of error may be built into the accounting system if fixed costs are allocated to time periods on the basis of production. For example, depreciation may be charged on a per unit basis.

---

[15] Let γ stand for the measurement errors in C:

$$C + \gamma = \beta_0 + \beta_1 x_1 + \mu$$
$$C = \beta_0 + \beta_1 x_1 + \mu - \gamma.$$

[16] In this event, where ψ stands for the measurement error in x_1:

$$C = \beta_0 + \beta_1(x_1 + \psi) + \mu$$
$$C = \beta_0 + \beta_1 x_1 + \beta_1 \psi + \mu.$$

The new disturbance term $\beta_1 \psi + \mu$, is not independent of x_1 because of the covariance between these variables.

[17] If the error is proportionally constant (i.e., 10 per cent of production), transformation of the variables (such as to logarithms) is necessary.

[18] Actually, the present value of the future payment should be included as a current period cost.

The variance of this cost, then, may be a function of the accounting method and not of the underlying economic relationships.[19]

6. Correlations Among the Explanatory (Independent) Variables

When the explanatory variables are highly correlated with one another, it is very difficult, and often impossible, to estimate the separate relationships of each to the dependent variable. This condition is called multicollinearity, and it is a severe problem for cost studies. When we compute marginal costs, we usually want to estimate the marginal cost of *each* of the different types of output produced in a multiproduct firm. However, this is not always possible. For example, consider a manufacturer who makes refrigerators, freezers, washing machines, and other major home appliances. If the demand for all home appliances is highly correlated, the number of refrigerators, freezers and washing machines produced will move together, all being high in one week and low in another. In this situation it will be impossible to disentangle the marginal cost of producing refrigerators from the marginal cost of producing freezers and washing machines by means of multiple regression.[20]

Problems similar to that of our manufacturer can be alleviated by disaggregation of total cost into several sub-groups that are independent of each other. Preanalysis and preliminary allocations of cost and output data may accomplish this disaggregation. This is one of the most important contributions the accountant can make to regression analysis.

If the total costs of the entire plant are regressed on outputs of different types, it is likely that the computed coefficients will have very large standard errors and, hence, will not be reliable. This situation may be avoided by first allocating costs to cost centers where a single output is likely to be produced. This allows a set of multiple regressions to be computed, one for each cost center. The procedure (which may be followed anyway for inventory costing) also reduces the number of explanatory variables that need be specified in any one regression.[21] Care must be taken to assure that the allocation of costs to cost centers is not arbitrary or unrelated to output. For example, allocation of electricity or rent on a square footage basis can serve no useful purpose. However, allocation of the salary of the foremen on a time basis is necessary when they spend varying amounts of time per period supervising different cost centers.

A further complication arises if several different types of outputs are produced within the cost centers. For example, the assembly department may work on different models of television sets at the same time. In most instances, it is neither feasible nor desirable to allocate the cost center's costs to each type of output. Cost, then, should be regressed on several output variables, one for the quantity of each type of output. If these independent variables are multicollinear, the standard errors of their regression coefficients will be so large relative to the coefficients as to make the estimates useless. In this event, an index of output may be constructed, in which the different types of output are weighted by a factor (such as labor hours) that serves to describe their relationship to cost. Cost then may be regressed on this weighted index. The regression coefficient computed expresses the average relationship between the "bundle" of outputs and cost and cannot be decomposed to give the relationship between one output element and cost. However, since the outputs were collinear in the past, it is likely that they will be collinear in the future, so that knowledge about the cost of the "bundle" of outputs may be sufficient.

A valid objection to the allocation of costs

---

[19] Depreciation is assumed to be time, not user, depreciation.

[20] However, the computed regression can provide useful predictions of total costs if the past relationships of production among the different outputs are maintained.

[21] The author used this procedure with considerable success in estimating the marginal costs of banking operations. See "Economies of Scale and Marginal Costs in Banking Operations," *National Banking Review*, 1965, pp. 507–549.

to cost centers is that one can never be sure that the allocations are accurate. Nevertheless, some allocations must be made for multicollinearity to be overcome. Therefore, the statistical method cannot be free from the accountant's subjective judgment; in fact, it depends on it.

A limitation of analysis of costs by cost centers also is that cost externalities among cost centers may be ignored. For example, the directly chargeable costs of the milling department may be a function of the level of operations of other departments. The existence and magnitude of operations outside of a particular cost center may be estimated by including an appropriate independent variable in the cost center regression. An over-all index of production, such as total direct labor hours on total sales is one such variable. Or, if a cost element is allocated between two cost centers, the output of one cost center may be included as an independent variable in the other cost center's regressions. The existence and effect of these possible inter-cost center elements may be determined from the standard error of the coefficient and sign of this variable.

Some types of costs that vary with activity cannot be associated with specific cost centers because it is difficult to make meaningful allocations or because of bookkeeping problems (as discussed above). In this event, individual regression analyses of these costs probably will prove valuable. For example, electricity may be difficult to allocate to cost centers although it varies with machine hours.[22] A regression can be computed such as the following:

$$E = b_0 + b_1M + b_2S_1 + b_3S_2 + b_4S_3 \quad (3)$$

where
    E = electricity cost
    M = total machine hours in the plant
    S = seasonal dummy variables

---

[22] Machine hours may not be recorded by cost center although direct labor hours are. If machine hours (M) are believed to be proportional to direct labor hours (L), so that $M_i = k_iL_i$, where k is a constant multiplier that may vary among cost centers, i, k_iL_i is a perfect substitute for M_i.

where
    $S_1 = 1$ for summer, 0 for other seasons
    $S_2 = 1$ for spring, 0 for other seasons
    $S_3 = 1$ for winter, 0 for other seasons
b_0, b_1, b_2, b_3, and b_4 are the computed constants and coefficients.

If the regression is fully specified, with all factors that cause the use of electricity included (such as the season of the year), the regression coefficient of M, b_1, is the estimate of the average marginal cost of electricity per machine hour. This cost can be added to the other costs (such as materials and labor) to estimate the marginal cost of specific outputs.

For some activities, physical units, such as labor hours, can be used as the dependent variable instead of costs. This procedure is desirable where most of the activity's costs are a function of such physical units and where factor prices are expected to vary. Thus, in a shipping department, it may be best to regress hours worked on pounds shipped, percentage of units shipped by truck, the average number of pounds per sale, and other explanatory variables. Then, with the coefficients estimated, the number of labor hours can be estimated for various situations. These hours then can be costed at the current labor rate.

7. Distribution of the Non-Specified Factors (Disturbances)

(a) *Serial correlation of the disturbances.* A very important requirement of least squares that affects the coefficients and the estimates made about their reliability is that the disturbances not be serially correlated. For a time series (in which the observations are taken at successive periods of time), this means that the disturbances that arose in a period t are independent from the disturbances that arose in previous periods, t-1, t-2, etc. The consequences of serial correlation of the disturbances are that (1) the standard errors of the regression coefficients (b's) will be seriously underestimated, (2) the sampling variances of the coefficients will be very large, and (3) predictions of cost made from the regression equation will be more variable than is ordinarily expected from least-squares estimators. Hence, the tests measuring the probability that the true marginal costs and total costs are within a range around the estimates computed from the regression are not valid.

(b) *Independence from explanatory variables.* The disturbances which reflect the factors affecting cost that cannot be specified must be uncorrelated with the explanatory (independent) variables. $(x_1, x_2, \ldots, x_n)$. If the unspecified factors are correlated with the explanatory variables, the coefficients will be biased and inconsistent estimates of the true values. Such correlation often is the result of bookkeeping procedures. For example, repairs to equipment in a machine shop is a cost-causing activity that often is not specified because of quantification difficulties. However, these repairs may be made when output is low because the machines can be taken out of service at these times. Thus, repair costs will be negatively correlated with output. If these costs are not separated from other costs, the estimated coefficient of output will be biased downward, so that the true extent of variableness of cost with output will be masked.

(c) *Variance of the disturbances.* A basic assumption underlying use of least squares is that the variance of the disturbance term is constant; it should not be a function of the level of the dependent or independent variables.[23] If the variance of the disturbance is non-constant, the standard errors of the coefficients estimated are not correct, and the reliability of the coefficients cannot be determined.

When the relationship estimated is between only one independent variable (output) and the dependent variable (cost), the presence of non-constant variance of the disturbances can be detected by plotting the independent against the dependent variable. However, where more than one independent variable is required, such observations cannot be easily made. In this event, the

accountant must attempt to estimate the nature of the variance from other information and then transform the data to a form in which constant variance is achieved. At the least, he should decide whether the disturbances are likely to bear a proportional relationship to the other variables (as is commonly the situation with economic data). If they do, it may be desirable to transform the variables to logarithms. The efficacy of the transformations may be tested by plotting the independent variables against the residuals (the estimates of the disturbances).

(d) *Normal distribution of the disturbances.* For the traditional statistical tests of the regression coefficients and equations to be strictly valid, the disturbances should be normally distributed. Tests of normality can be made by plotting the residuals on normal probability paper, an option available in many library regression programs. While requirement 7 does not have implications for the accounting system, it does determine the form in which the variables are specified. These considerations are discussed in the following section.

IV. FUNCTIONAL FORM OF THE REGRESSION EQUATION

Thus far we have been concerned with correct specification of the regression equation rather than with its functional form. However, the form of the variables must fit the underlying data well and be of such a nature that the residuals are distributed according to requirement 7 above.

The form chosen first should follow the underlying relationship that is thought to exist. Consider, for example, an analysis of the costs (C) of a shipping department. Costs may be a function of pounds shipped (P), percentage of pounds shipped by truck (T), and the average number of pounds per sale (A). If the accountant believes that the change in cost due to a change of each explanatory variable is unaffected by the levels of the other explanatory variables, a linear

---

[23] Constant variance is known as homoscedasticity. Non-constant variance is called heteroscedasticity.

form could be used, as follows:

$$C = a + bP + cT + dA. \qquad (4)$$

In this form, the estimated marginal cost of a unit change in pounds shipped (P) is $\partial C / \partial P$ or b.

However, if the marginal cost of each explanatory variable is thought to be a function of the levels of the other explanatory variables, the following form would be better:

$$C = aP^b T^c A^d. \qquad (5)$$

In this case, a linear form could be achieved by converting the variable to logarithms:

$$\log C = \log a + b \log P \qquad (6)$$
$$+ c \log T + d \log A.$$

Now an approximation to the expected marginal cost of a unit change in pounds shipped (P) is $\partial C / \partial P = baP^{b-1} \bar{T}^c \bar{A}^d$, where the other explanatory variables are held constant at some average values (denoted by bars over the letters). Thus, the estimated marginal cost of P is a function of the levels of the other variables.

The logarithmic form of the variables also allows for estimates of nonlinear relationships between cost and the explanatory variables. The form of the relationships may be approximated by graphing the dependent variable against the independent variable. (The most important independent variable should be chosen where there is more than one, although in this event the simple two-dimensional plotting can only be suggestive.) If the plot indicates that a non-linear rather than a linear form will fit the data best, the effect of using logarithms may be determined by plotting the data on semi-log and log-log ruled paper.

If the data seem curvilinear even in logarithms, or if an additive rather than a multiplicative form describes the underlying relationships best, polynomial forms of the variables may be used. Thus, for an additive relationship between cost (C) and quantity of output (Q), the form fitted may be $C = a$

$+ bQ + cQ^2 + cQ^3$. If a multiplicative relationship is assumed, the form may be log $C = \log a + \log Q + (\log Q)^2$. Either form describes a large family of curves with two bends.

When choosing the form of the variables, attention must always be paid to the effect of the form on the residuals, the estimates of the disturbances. Unless the variance of the residuals is constant, not subject to serial correlation, and approximately normally distributed (requirement 5), inferences about the reliability of the coefficients estimated cannot be made. Graphing is a valuable method for determining whether or not these requirements are met. (The graphs mentioned usually can be produced by the computers.) Three graphs are suggested. First, the residuals should be plotted in time sequence. They should appear to be randomly distributed, with no cycles or trends.[24] Second, the residuals can be plotted against the predicted value of the dependent variable. There should be as many positive or negative residuals scattered evenly about a zero line, with the variance of the residuals about the same at any value of the predicted dependent variable. Finally, the residuals should be plotted on normal probability paper to test for normality.

If the graphs show that the residuals do not meet the requirements of least squares, the data must be transformed. If serial correlation of the residuals is a problem, transformation of the variables may help. A commonly used method is to compute first differences, in which the observation from period t, $t - 1$, $t - 2$, $t - 3$, etc., are replaced with $t - (t - 1)$, $(t - 1) - (t - 2)$, $(t - 2) - (t - 3)$, and so forth. With first difference data, one is regressing the change in cost on the change in output, etc., a procedure which in many instances may be descriptively superior to other methods of stating the data. However, the residuals from

[24] A more formal test for serial correlation is provided by the Durbin-Watson statistic, which is built into many library regression computer programs. (J. Durbin, and G. J. Watson, "Testing for Serial Correlation in Least-Squares Regression," Parts I and II, *Biometrica*, 1950 and 1951.)

first difference data also must be subjected to serial correlation tests, since taking first differences often results in negative serial correlations.[25]

Where non-constant variance of the residuals is a problem, the residuals may increase proportionally to the predicted dependent variables. In this event transformation of the dependent variable to logarithms will be effective in achieving constant variance. If the residuals increase more than proportionately, the square root of the dependent variable may be a better transformation.

V. AN ILLUSTRATION

Assume that a firm manufactures a widget and several other products, in which the services of several departments are used. Analysis of the costs of the assembly department will provide us with an illustration. In this department, widgets and another product, digits, are produced. The widgets are assembled in batches while the larger digits are assembled singly. Weekly observations on cost and output are taken and punched on cards. A graph is prepared, from which it appears that a linear relationship is present. Further, the cost of producing widgets is not believed to be a function of the production of digits or other explanatory variables. Therefore, the following regression is computed:

$$\hat{C} = 110.3 + 8.21N - 7.83B + 12.32D$$
$$\quad (40.8) \quad (.53) \quad (1.69) \quad (2.10)$$
$$\quad + 235S + 523W - 136A$$
$$\quad (100) \quad (204) \quad (154) \qquad (7)$$

where
$\hat{C}$ = expected cost

[25] If there are random measurement errors in the data, observations from period $t - 1$ might be increased by a positive error. Then $t - (t - 1)$ will be lower and $(t - 1) - (t - 2)$ will be higher than if the error were not present. Consequently, $t - (t - 1)$ and $(t - 1) - (t - 2)$ will be negatively serially correlated.

N = number of widgets
B = average number of widgets in a batch
D = number of digits
S = summer dummy variable, where $S = 1$ for summer, 0 for other seasons
W = winter dummy variable, where $W = 1$ for winter, 0 for other seasons
A = autumn dummy variable, where $A = 1$ for autumn, 0 for other seasons
R^2 = .892 (the coefficient of multiple determination)

Standard error of estimate = 420.83, which is 5% of the dependent variable, cost.

Number of observations = 156.

The numbers in parentheses beneath the coefficients are the standard errors of the coefficients. These results may be used for such purposes as price and output decisions, analysis of efficiency, and capital budgeting.

For price and output decisions, we would want to estimate the average marginal cost expected if an additional widget is produced. From the regression we see that the estimated average marginal cost, $\partial C/\partial N$ is 8.21, with the other factors affecting costs accounted for. The standard error of the coefficient, .53, allows us to assess a probability of .67 that the "true" marginal cost is between 7.68 and 8.74 (8.21 $\pm$ .53) and .95 that it is between 7.15 and 9.27 (8.21 $\pm$ 1.06).[26]

The regression also can be used for flexible budgeting and analysis of performance. For example, assume that the following production is reported for a given week:

$$W = 532$$
$$B = 20$$
$$D = 321$$
$$S = \text{summer} = 1$$

Then we expect that, if this week is like an average of the experience for past weeks,

[26] The statements about probability are based on a Bayesian approach, with normality and diffuse prior distributions assumed.

total costs would be:

$$100.3 + 8.21(532) - 7.83(20) + 12.32(321)$$
$$+ 235.3(1) = 8511.14.$$

The actual costs incurred can be compared to this expected amount. Of course, we do not expect the actual amount to equal the predicted amount, if only because we could not specify all of the cost-causing variables in the regression equation. However, we can calculate the probability that the actual cost is within some range around the expected cost. This range can be computed from the standard error of estimate and a rather complicated set of relationships that reflect uncertainty about the height and tilt of the regression plane. These calculations also reflect the difference between the production reported for a given week and the means of the production data from which the regression was computed. The greater the difference between given output and the mean output, the less confidence we have in the prediction of the regression equation. For this example, the adjusted standard error of estimate for the values of the independent variables given is 592.61. Thus, we assess a probability of .67 that the actual costs incurred will be between 7918.53 and 9103.75 (8511.14 $\pm$ 592.61) and probability .95 that they will be between 9696.36 and 7325.92 (8511.14 $\pm$ 2.592.61). With these figures, management can decide how unusual the actual production costs are in the light of past experience.

The regression results may be useful for capital budgeting, if the company is considering replacing the present widget assembly procedure with a new machine. While the cash flow expected from using the new machine must be estimated from engineering analyses, they are compared with the cash flows that would otherwise take place if the present machines were kept. These future expected flows may be estimated by "plugging" the expected output into the regression equation and calculating the expected costs. While these estimates may be statistically unreliable for data beyond the range of those used to calculate the regression, the estimates may still be the best that can be obtained.

VI. CONCLUSION

The assertion has been made throughout this paper that regression analysis is not only a valuable tool but a method made available, inexpensive and easy to use by computers. The reader may be inclined to accept all but the last point, having read through the list of technical and bookkeeping problems. Actually it is the ease of computation that the library computer programs afford which makes it necessary to stress precautions and care: it is all too easy to "crank out" numbers that seem useful but actually render the whole program, if not deceptive, worthless.

But when one considers that costs often are caused by many different factors whose effects are not obvious, one recognizes the great possibilities of regression analysis, limited as it may be. Nevertheless, it is necessary to remember that it is a tool, not a cure-all. The method must not be used in cost situations where there is not an ongoing stationary relationship between cost and the variables upon which cost depend. Where the desired conditions prevail, multiple regression can provide valuable information for solving necessary decision problems, information that can put "life" into the economic models that accountants are now embracing.

12

Linear Programming and Theory of Production

WILLIAM J. BAUMOL

. . .

2. AN ALTERNATIVE LINEAR PROGRAMMING DIAGRAM

In our geometric representation of linear programming we have so far employed exclusively one type of diagram. From our present point of view it can be characterized by the fact that its axes were used to measure *output* quantities rather than *input* quantities. More generally, we might say that it concentrated on ends rather than means. In those diagrams any point represents a combination of outputs (or processes) which is a potential solution to the problem. Inputs only made their appearance in the form of the constraint lines, which show us the extent to which the limited availability of the inputs restricts the magnitude of the outputs.

Partly for easier comparison with the diagrams of standard production theory, it is now appropriate to translate the linear programming problem into a different diagram, one in which input quantities are measured along the axes and outputs are indicated with the aid of production indifference curves. In these new diagrams, then, the input requirements become the focus of the representation.

3. ILLUSTRATIVE EXAMPLE

Since the axes in our diagram will represent input quantities, to avail ourselves of the

From William J. Baumol, Economic Theory and Operations Analysis, *Second Edition, pp. 272–91,* © *1965. Reprinted by permission of Prentice-Hall, Inc., Englewood Cliffs, New Jersey.* All footnotes and Fig. 4 have been omitted.

simplicity of a two-dimensional diagram we will have to take as our illustrative example a two-constraint (two-scarce-input) linear program. We will employ the following case as our illustrative example throughout most of this chapter:

A leather-processing company is engaged, among other operations, in the dyeing of white suede leather. It is limited in its output by the capacity of its dyeing vats and the amount of skilled labor it has available for supervision of its production process. The firm is considering four dyeing processes, or rather, four variants of its basic procedure. Process 1 involves inspection for defects of a sample from each batch before it is put into the dyeing vats. Process 2 involves inspection of every individual hide. Process 3 also calls for examination of a sample as in process 1, but a considerably smaller proportion of the hides is inspected. Finally, process 4 avoids the difficult preinspection process altogether. All hides are dyed and then quickly examined to see if the dye has "taken" satisfactorily.

Let Q_1 be the quantity of dyed leather to be turned out by means of process 1, Q_2 be the amount produced by the second process, 2, etc. Then suppose we have enough data to specify our programming problem as follows:

$$\text{Maximize profits} = 0.9Q_1 + 0.75Q_2$$
$$+ 1.0Q_3 + 1.1Q_4$$

subject to the constraints

$$2Q_1 + 1.5Q_2 + 3.5Q_3 + 7Q_4 \leq 4{,}000$$
$$0.4Q_1 + 0.45Q_2 + 0.35Q_3 + 0.3Q_4 \leq 600$$

and the nonnegativity requirements

$$Q_1 \geq 0, \quad Q_2 \geq 0, \quad Q_3 \geq 0, \quad Q_4 \geq 0.$$

Here 4,000 (gallon-hours per week) is the available vat capacity and 600 (man-hours per week) is the amount of skilled labor the company can use for the production of this dye. Our two limited inputs are thus vat capacity and labor. The first coefficient, 0.9 (dollars) in our profit function, represents the return per square foot of leather treated by means of process number 1, and a similar interpretation holds for the other coefficients in the objective (profit) function. The first number, 2, in our upper constraint indicates the number of gallon-hours of vat capacity which will be taken up by a hide treated by process 1, etc.

4. THE FEASIBLE REGION

We can now proceed to our new diagrammatic representation. The depiction of the feasible region is completely trivial. It is shown in Figure 1. Here there is constructed a rectangle *OABC* bounded by segments *OA* and *OC* of the two axes, the vertical line *AB* above the point which represents 600 labor hours and the horizontal line *CB* to the right of the point which represents 4,000 gallons of vat capacity. Since a maximum of 600 hours of labor time and 4,000 gallon-hours of vat space are available, only this shaded rectangular region represents feasible input combinations. Thus, for example, point *S* outside the shaded region represents the use

of 4,000 gallons of vat space and 800 labor-hours. Since that much labor time of the required skill is not available to the company, point *S* is simply not feasible.

5. REPRESENTATION OF A PROCESS

Next we turn to the geometric representation of a production process. But first we must take care of a matter of definition. For our purposes, a production process is *required* to involve fixed input proportions. For example, in our illustrative model, process number 1 involves the use of 2 gallon-hours of vat capacity and 0.4 hours of labor time per square foot of output. This means that 10 square feet of leather will require 20 gallon-hours and 4 labor-hours, 100 square feet involve the use of 200 vat gallon-hours and 40 labor-hours, etc. In other words, no matter how large the output produced with the aid of process 1, it will employ $2/0.4 = 5$ units of vat time per unit of labor time. This constant ratio of input quantities is, in fact, a property which we use to help define a production process. Thus, given some two processes, *A* and *B*, if procedure *A* involves 6 hours of vat time per unit of labor time, while procedure *B* involves 4 hours of vat time per unit of labor time, *A* and *B* are by definition taken to be different processes.

With the aid of this definition we can now readily represent a process diagrammatically. Since our diagram is constructed to show only inputs, a process must be represented in terms of its input requirements. But any production process requires inputs in fixed proportions, as we just stated. And, as was shown in Section 5 of the previous chapter, *the locus of all points involving unchanging input proportions is always a straight line through the origin.* In Figure 2 the line OP_1 represents process 1. Specifically, we see that point *D* on this line represents the use of 400 hours of labor time and 2,000 vat-gallon hours, so that this point involves the correct input proportions for process 1: two hours of vat capacity for 0.4 hours of labor, and the same is true of any other point on line OP_1. More-

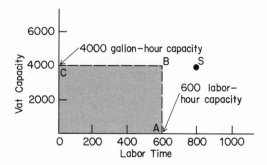

FIG. 2

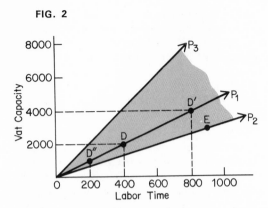

over, a moment of thought indicates that point D must correspond to the production of 1,000 square feet of leather per week (since process 1 requires 0.4 labor hours and 2 vat hours to make 1 foot). Similarly, point D' represents the production of 2,000 square feet of leather. Thus, because it includes all points representing the use of 5 gallon-hours of vat time for every labor hour, every possible output employing process 1 is specified by some point on line OP_1. And, conversely, every point on OP_1 represents an output which can be produced by means of process 1 if sufficient quantities of resources are available. Incidentally, it should be indicated at this point that a "line" such as OP_1, which starts at some definite point, O, but then goes off into space (not stopping at point P_1) is properly called a *ray* not a *line*. This terminology is used in most of the programming literature and it will also be employed here.

In the same way as we found ray OP_1 we now see that ray OP_2 represents process 2. This can be checked by observing that any point on this ray involves the correct input proportions for process 2: for example, point E on this ray represents the use of 3,000 hours of vat time and 900 hours of labor, thus satisfying the 1.5 hours of vat time to 0.45 hours of labor time requirement of process 2.

We end this section by noting that the collection of rays representing such processes constitute a (nonfinite) cone-shaped figure, P_2OP_3 (shaded region). As will be shown in the next section, interior points in the cone

represent the concurrent use of several of these processes. In other words, our cone represents the total set of possible production arrangements involving processes 1, 2, and 3.

6. PRODUCTION INDIFFERENCE CURVES: CONSTRUCTION

Moving one step closer to the diagrams of classical production theory, we can now proceed to construct the production indifference curves of our linear programming model, and in a later section we will use these to derive the profit indifference curves (iso-profit curves) needed for decision making in the profit-maximizing firm. For the moment let us concentrate our attention on just processes 1 and 3. In Figure 3 we see

FIG. 3

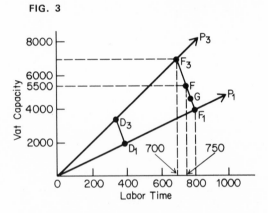

that point D_1 represents 1,000 units of output of process 1, while D_3 represents the same output of process 3. Thus the production indifference curve which involves the production of 1,000 square feet of leather must go through both these points. Similarly, points F_1 and F_3 must both lie on the 2,000-square-foot production indifference curve, etc.

But what about the portion of the 2,000-output indifference curve which lies between points F_1 and F_3? It can be shown that this section of the indifference curve must be the straight line segment which connects points F_1 and F_3.

The meaning of this statement is really not as clear as may at first appear. We know that point F_1 represents some level of operation of process 1 and F_3 refers in a similar manner to process 3. But how can we define an intermediate point such as the midpoint, F, of line F_1F_3? There is no process ray going through point F and so we cannot explain it as a level of operation of any such process.

Instead, we must take such interior points as F and G to represent the simultaneous use of both processes 1 and 3 in some combination. That is, F represents an output of 2,000 square feet of leather, part of which is produced by means of process 1 and part of which is produced by process 3.

More specifically, F, the midpoint of the line F_1F_3, represents 2,000 units of output, produced half by one process, half by the other. Similarly, point G, which is 3/4 of the way along F_1F_3 toward point F_1, represents an output produced 3/4 by process 1 and 1/4 by process 3, i.e., it involves 1,500 square feet produced by process 1 and 500 square feet made by process 3. The reader can readily extend this interpretation to other points on F_1F_3, always remembering that the nearer the point to one of the process lines, the greater the use of that process which it involves.

This interpretation clearly calls for some justification. Let us look more closely at midpoint F. It can be seen to require 750 hours of labor time and 5,500 gallon-hours of vat time. Now it has been stated that F represents a 1,000-unit process 1 output (point D_1) plus a 1,000-unit process 3 output (point D_3). Let us examine the input requirements of these two separate outputs. These figures, which can be read off the diagram or computed from our constraints are summarized in the following table:

Inputs Employed	Labor	Vat Capacity
Point D_1	400	2,000
Point D_3	350	3,500
Total	750	5,500

It will be noted that the total input requirements of D_1 and D_3 together turn out to be exactly equal to the coordinates of point F! That is, *point F represents precisely the total*

input quantities which would be required to operate both processes simultaneously at the 1,000-square-foot output level. And, in the same way, it can be shown that point G represents the inputs needed to produce 1,500 units of output by means of process 1 and 500 units of process 3 output. Since a similar proposition can be proved for every point on line segment F_1F_3, this justifies our interpretation of the line segment, and in particular, shows that F_1F_3 is a segment of our indifference curve.

Having established the basic point that line segment F_1F_3 is part of the production indifference curve connecting points F_1 and F_3, we can now construct the rest of the indifference curve as well as other indifference curves without any difficulty. In Figure 4 we now have included the rays which represent three of our processes 1, 2, and 3. Point F_2 on ray OP_2 represents the output of 2,000 square feet of leather by means of process 2. Therefore line F_1F_2 is also part of the 2,000-unit production indifference curve. In a similar way it can be shown that broken line $E_2E_1E_3$ is (a portion of) the 1,000-square-foot output production indifference curve. Other indifference curves in this map can be constructed similarly.

FIG. 4

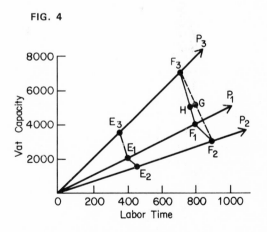

7. SOME PROPERTIES OF THE INDIFFERENCE CURVES

One may well ask why we do not draw the straight line F_2F_3 (broken line) representing the 2,000-unit output combinations of processes 2 and 3 and consider points on this line to constitute a relevant portion of the production indifference curve (or area). The answer is that any point on F_2F_3 (which does indeed represent a 2,000-unit output combination of processes 2 and 3) is necessarily a wasteful arrangement, and it will never occur in an optimal solution. For consider any point, G, on F_2F_3. Corresponding to any such point there will be points on $F_2F_1F_3$, such as point H, which lie below and to the left of G. This means that point H uses less of *both* inputs than does G. But H and G both yield the same outputs. Therefore G clearly represents an inefficient use of resources, is irrelevant for an optimal solution, and can therefore be ignored as far as the 2,000-unit production indifference curve $F_2F_1F_3$ is concerned.

We may now observe the characteristic shape of the production indifference curves of linear programming. They consist of kinked line segments. Their slope is always negative (or at least nonpositive). Their relevant portions are convex to the origin, i.e., they necessarily involve a diminishing (or at least a nonincreasing) marginal rate of substitution.

Thus the production indifference curves of linear programming have the same basic shape as do the corresponding curves of neoclassical production theory except for the fact that the latter are usually taken to be smooth throughout, i.e., they are assumed to contain no kinks or corners. This premise is usually employed in the neoclassical theory to make it easier to apply the differential calculus which breaks down at a kink (corner) point, such as F_1 in Figure 4, since the slope of the curve at that point is not defined.

Linear programming is, then, compatible with the type of diminishing-returns phenomenon represented by a diminishing marginal rate of substitution of one input for another (see the discussion of this term in the preceding two chapters [of the Baumol book]). That is, if labor can be used to save vat time (e.g., by culling out defective pieces of leather which would otherwise waste vat space), increased use of labor for this purpose

(with output remaining unchanged) may yield diminishing returns, i.e., diminishing marginal saving of vat time.

Presently we will see that the ordinary "law" of diminishing returns is also compatible with linear programming, i.e., the marginal yield to increased use of one input may decline, provided the employment of all other inputs remains unchanged. However, linearity does rule out diminishing returns *to scale*. That is, as already stated, it implies that the production function is linear and homogeneous. To see that this is so we recall that such a production function is characterized by indifference curves which are parallel in the sense that they all have the same slope along any straight line from the origin (cf. Section 8 of the previous chapter). But that is precisely what occurs here. In Figure 4 it is readily verified that the slopes of F_1F_3 and of E_1E_3 are equal. For we have

$$\text{slope of } F_1F_3 = \frac{7,000 - 4,000}{700 - 800} = -30$$

and

$$\text{slope of } E_1E_3 = \frac{3,500 - 2,000}{350 - 400} = -30.$$

Similarly, F_2F_1 and E_2E_1 have the same slopes. This illustrates the fact that the production indifference curves have the parallelism property of a linear homogeneous production function: The reader should observe that this property incidentally guarantees that the linear programming indifference curves will never intersect.

8. PROFIT INDIFFERENCE CURVES

The *production* indifference curves in Figure 4 can readily be translated into *profit* indifference curves.

It will be recalled that the four processes are not equally profitable. In fact, from our objective function,

$$\text{Profit} = 0.9Q_1 + 0.75Q_2 + 1.0Q_3 + 1.1Q_4$$

we note that the unit profits of outputs 1, 2, 3, and 4 are, respectively, 90 cents, 75 cents, $1, and $1.10.

In Figure 5 we reproduce production

FIG. 5

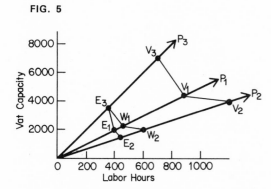

indifference curve $E_2E_1E_3$ from Figure 4. Each of points E_1, E_2, and E_3 represents an output of 1,000 square feet of leather. Let us see what points represent outputs which yield $1,000 in profit.

Since process 3 yields $1 in profit for every square foot of output, point E_3 represents both 1,000 units of product and 1,000 units of profit, i.e., at that point the $1,000 profit and 1,000-unit production indifference curves coincide.

But point E_1 involves considerably less than $1,000 in profit. Specifically, since every unit of process 1 output pays 90 cents, point E_1 represents only $900 in earnings. Thus, to earn $1,000 by means of process 1 we have to manufacture 11.1 per cent more, i.e., 1,111 units must be produced (since 1,111 × .90 = 1,000 approx.). Hence the point W_1 on ray OP_1 which lies on the $1,000 *profit* indifference curve, is 1/9 further from the origin than is E_1. Finally, to find the point of coincidence between this profit indifference curve and ray OP_2, we note that each unit of process 2 output yields only 75 cents, so that it requires 1,333.331/3 units of process 2 output to yield $1,000 in profit. This is represented by point W_2, where length OW_2 is exactly 1.331/3 times as great as length OE_2. [Once again, this is so, because of the linearity of our program which implies that it takes

1/3 more of both inputs to produce 1,333.331/3 units of output via process 2 (600 hours of labor and 2,000 vat gallons) than is required to produce 1,000 units of output by means of this process (450 hours of labor and 1,500 vat gallons—see the coefficients of Q_2 in our constraints).]

For the same reasons as in the production indifference curves, we can again connect points $W_2W_1E_3$ by straight line segments, and the resulting graph will constitute the relevant portion of the $1,000 profit indifference curve. Other profit indifference curves can readily be obtained in the same way.

As in the case of the iso-product curves, the profit indifference curve will have the parallelism feature characteristic of a linear homogeneous production function. A linear program yields constant profit returns to scale, e.g., a tripling of all the operations of our firm will triple its profits. In other words, we can also obtain additional profit indifference curves in Figure 5 directly by just drawing any other "curve" $V_2V_1V_3$ whose segments are equal in slope to the corresponding segments of indifference curve $W_2W_1E_3$.

Observe, finally, that the less profitable a process happens to be, the further out will we shift a point on that ray to transfer it from a given production indifference curve to a specific profit indifference curve. Thus, the move from E_2 to W_2 is (proportionately) greater than the move from E_1 to W_1 in Figure 5 because process 1 yields 90 cents profit per unit while process 2 offers only 75 cents per unit. Suppose, for a moment, that process 1 were very unprofitable. Then curve $W_2W_1E_3$ might even have become concave to the origin.... which means that process 1 is then a totally inefficient profit earner—it is simply not worth considering in comparison with a combination of processes 2 and 3, which can yield the same profits with the use of much smaller quantities of input. In exactly the same way, it may happen that a profit indifference curve acquires a positively sloping segment (see Figure 7b, lines WW' or SS'). This segment can then be ignored because the process at the upper end of the segment (process P in Figure 7b) must be relatively unprofitable—

it takes larger quantities of both inputs to produce the same profits than does the other process, P'.

9. GRAPHIC SOLUTION OF THE PROGRAMMING PROBLEM

We have now obtained a graphic description of both the profit possibilities (Figure 5) and the feasible region as delineated by the availability of labor and vat inputs (Figure 1). It is now a simple matter to combine the two diagrams by superimposing them one upon the other, and then to find the optimal solution of the programming problem. The two diagrams are combined in this way in Figure 6.

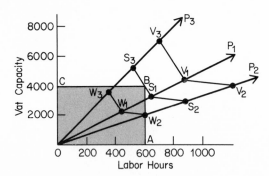

It will be recalled that only points within the shaded rectangle involve input quantities no greater than the amounts available to the company. The object of our calculation is to determine how to earn the largest amount of profit which can be extracted from the available resources. Thus we want to get to the highest possible profit indifference curve which has any point in common with the feasible region.

Since between any two process rays (the OP's) the segments of the indifference curves have the same slopes, we can, given one of these curves, construct as many other indifference curves as we like. In particular, we can construct the curve $S_2S_1S_3$ which just

goes through the upper right-hand corner point, B, of the feasible rectangle. This is the linear programming analogue of the optimal tangency point of classical production theory. Point B, then, represents our optimal solution.

By examining point B we determine the following:

1. Since B lies on line segment S_1S_3, it involves the use of a combination of processes 1 and 3. This illustrates the basic theorem of linear programming—that the solution will usually contain as many nonzero elements as there are constraints in the problem. Where, as in our original linear program, two constraints are involved, there will usually be no more than two production processes employed in an optimal arrangement.

2. Our optimal output involves the use of exactly 600 hours of labor and 4,000 vat-gallon-hours—that is, in this case it involves full use of both limited resources of the firm.

3. Since $S_2S_1S_3$ is a little nearer to W_2W_1 W_3 (the $1,000 curve) than it is to $V_2V_1V_3$ (the $2,000 curve), it yields somewhat less than $1,500 in profit. More specifically, we note that point S_1 on this same indifference curve involves the exclusive use of process 1 and employs about 3,200 units of vat time (and about 640 labor hours). It must produce an output of approximately 1,600 square feet (since process 1 employs 2 units of vat capacity per square foot of leather, then 3,200 vat gallons will suffice to produce 1,600 square feet). At 90 cents per foot this means a profit of about $1,440. In fact, a standard simplex calculation of the optimal solution of our programming problem shows that the total profit will be $1,471.43.

4. Since point B lies approximately 3/5 of the way toward point S_1 on line S_1S_3, the optimal solution involves approximately 3/5 ($1,440) = $864 of profit on process 1 production and 2/5 ($1,440) = $576 of process 3 profits. The precise profit figures yielded by a simplex calculation are $900 on process 1 output and $571.43 on process 3 output.

10. ALTERNATIVE TYPES
OF SOLUTIONS

Figure 7 illustrates several other varieties of solution which sometimes occur in linear programming problems.

Figure 7a represents a rather common situation. Here point B, the upper right-hand corner of the feasible region, lies outside the heavily shaded cone of production possibilities, POP''. In that case, the optimal point is S and not B. The firm's resources will then not be used fully. Specifically, there will be an unused amount of X whose magnitude is indicated by length SB.

Moreover, in this situation just one process, P, will be employed exclusively. Thus one process variable, Q, and one slack variable (the unused output of X) will not be equal to zero, again giving us two nonzero variables in this two-constraint case, as the basic theorem of linear programming requires.

A somewhat similar situation is depicted in Figure 7b where, even though point B lies inside the production possibility cone, process P is highly unprofitable, as is indicated by the positive slope of the profit indifference curves SS' and WW'. That is, point S yields the same profit return as does point S', but since S is above and to the right of

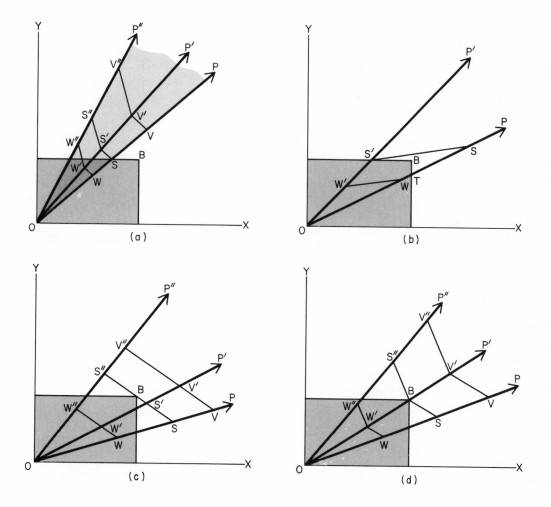

S', it requires more of both inputs than does S' to obtain these same profits. Hence it will pay to use only process P', the more profitable process, and to use it to the full extent permitted by the company's resources. Thus the optimal point, the point on the highest indifference curve in the shaded feasible region, is S'. Like S in Figure 7a, our optimal point S' is a basic solution involving one nonzero level of process operation and one nonzero slack variable (unused X).

Figures 7c and 7d represent rather more freakish cases. In Figure 7c two segments such as VV' and $V'V''$ of the indifference curves happen to form one straight line segment. Since SS' and $S'S''$ together coincide with SS'', there is no disadvantage to using a combination of all three processes, i.e., an optimal solution can be found in which we have simultaneously $Q > 0$, $Q' > 0$, and $Q'' > 0$. However, there is really nothing to be gained by the simultaneous use of all three processes since any three-process solution corresponds to an equivalent two-process solution. For example, point B falls both on SS'' and on $S'S''$, so we can do as well by employing just processes P' and P'' as we would by using all three methods.

Figure 7d is another odd case in which one of the process rays, OP', happens to go through point B, the upper right-hand corner of the feasible region. Here it pays to use only the one process, P'. The basic theorem of linear programming is violated in this case since we have $Q = 0$, $Q' > 0$, $Q'' = 0$, and, since X and Y are both used to capacity, so that both slack variables also take the value zero. Thus, despite the fact that there are two constraints in our problem, its solution involves only one nonzero-valued variable.

Figure 7d represents the phenomenon which is called *degeneracy*. Intuitively it means that one process happens by accident to employ resources in the right proportion to use up the available resources completely (or, in the general case, that this is done by a number of processes smaller than the number of different input resources). Computational experience indicates that such cases are encountered more frequently than might be expected in advance. Degeneracy causes

some computational difficulties but they are not usually very serious.

11. COST CURVES IN LINEAR PROGRAMMING

It is possible to go somewhat further in extending the neoclassical diagrammatic interpretation of linear programming. We will now see how a marginal cost curve can be constructed for our illustrative company. The construction will shed some light on the nature of the solution of a linear programming problem.

Let us recall that the objective function in our leather-processing problem is profit $= 0.9Q_1 + 0.75Q_2 + Q_3 + 1.1Q_4$, so that the unit profits of the four processes are 90 cents, 75 cents, \$1, and \$1.10. Since all four processes produce identical products, white suede leather, they should sell at the same price, say \$2 per square foot, no matter which process is used. In that case we see, by subtraction, that process 1 must incur a unit cost of \$2 − \$0.90 = \$1.10. Similarly, processes 2, 3, and 4 entail average costs of \$1.25, \$1, and 90 cents, respectively.

If the company were to produce only a very small output, one well within the limits of its resources, it would pay to use process 4, the least costly process whose average and marginal costs are 90 cents (line AB in Figure 8). But once an output of approximately 571 units is attained, process 4 will have used completely the 4,000 gallon-hours

FIG. 8

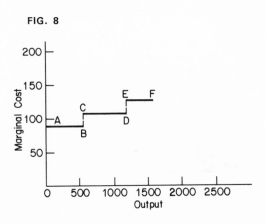

of vat capacity which, our linear program tells us, are available to the firm. For it takes seven vat gallons to turn out a square foot of leather via process 4 (the coefficient of Q_4 in our first constraint is 7), so that the production of 5713/7 square feet, each employing seven vat gallons, requires the full use of the available 4,000-unit vat capacity. Beyond this point, then, larger outputs will require the use of other processes, perhaps in conjunction with process 4.

The second least expensive process is process 3, whose unit production cost is $1, as was indicated previously. Because of the 4,000-unit vat capacity, process 3 can turn out no more than some 1,143 units of output. For that process requires 3.5 units of vat capacity per unit of output; thus 1,143 square feet of leather produced by process 3 requires 3.5 × 1,143 = 4,000 gallon-hours, approximately.

But each additional unit of output produced by means of process 3 requires some curtailment in the use of process 4 in order to release the required vat capacity. For process 3 also requires some vat capacity, and so we can no longer leave all of the 4,000 available vat gallons exclusively to process 4. To supply a unit *net* increase in output, process 3 must then expand more than one unit—it must increase sufficiently to make up for the reduced level of operation of process 4. Because a unit reduction in process 4 releases seven gallons of vat capacity, it permits two units of process 3 operation to be added (since each unit of operation of process 3 requires 3.5 gallons of capacity). Thus we see that by this exchange (a unit reduction in process 4 output and a two-unit increase in process 3 output) we obtain the unit addition to total production which we were seeking.

What has this unit increase cost us? That is, what is the marginal cost of our firm's operation at this level of output? We have added two units of process 3 at a cost of $1 each (=$2), but we have eliminated one unit of process 4 whose cost was 90 cents, making a net cost increase of $2.00 − 0.90 = $1.10. This, then, is the marginal cost of output

increases above 571 units of output. The firm operates at a marginal cost of $1.10 up until an output level of 1,1436/7 units, which is the maximum production level possible with the use of process 3 (line segment CD in Figure 8).

One can produce still larger outputs, but this requires the employment of still another process which is more economical in its use of vat time than is process 3. This time we introduce our third least expensive process, process 1, whose unit costs are $1.10. By a calculation similar to the previous one, ... it can be shown that marginal cost now rises to $1.23, approximately (EF in Figure 8). This marginal cost figure applies until we reach maximum output, 1,571.43 feet, which involves a combination of processes 1 and 3 (as our calculations in Section 9 showed) and which uses up both of the firm's inputs completely. Nothing further can be gained by introducing process 2—we have now attained the company's maximal production level.

The main thing to be noted from all this is the characteristic shape of the marginal cost curve in a linear programming production problem. It involves rising marginal costs, and, indeed, costs which may rise by increasing amounts (DE may exceed BC). But these costs rise in discontinuous jumps, as is illustrated so clearly in Figure 8. Thus, our constant returns to scale do not guarantee constant marginal costs.

The analysis should also give us some intuitive feeling on how processes 1 and 3 happen to be selected as the solution to our programming problem, even though process 4 yields the largest unit profits. The point is that process 4 uses resources most inefficiently, so that while it brings in large returns per unit, it does not permit the production of very many units. More can be earned (and produced) with the aid of somewhat less profitable (per unit of output) processes which are more sparing in their use of the firm's limited input resources.

. . .

13

Internal Economies

ALEC NOVE

This paper is concerned with a phenomenon which is constantly encountered but seldom analysed. An internal economy or diseconomy would be external but for the fact that it occurs within a given firm or organisation. Consideration of this question raises others: the nature of cross-subsidisation, the meaning of organisational economies of scale, the identification of marginal revenue and marginal cost within systems of economic activity, the importance of the institutional setting in identifying costs and benefits, the criteria applicable to the operations of nationalised industries and much else besides. All the problems to be discussed below have been referred to somewhere in modern economic literature. Such words as indivisibilities, complementarities, sub-optimisation, interdependencies, which do raise similar issues, are to be found in many a textbook, but all too often figuratively or literally in footnotes. They are seldom woven into the fabric of analysis. Once mentioned, they are forgotten by author and student, and the analysis, the concept of an optimum, proceeds as if these modifying circumstances did not exist, or could be abstracted without serious loss of theoretical rigour or practical relevance.

Let us begin by identifying an example of an internal economy which simultaneously serves to throw into sharp relief the ambiguity or confusion inherent in the term "cross-subsidisation." To many, the latter is *ipso facto* evidence of resource misallocation. Yet a closer look at the problem shows that

From Economic Journal *(December 1969), pp. 847–55. Reprinted with permission of author and publisher.* Reproduced here are only the first nine pages, which are most closely related to managerial economics.

this view, which we manage to convey to many students, is at best an oversimplification and at worst misleading or even nonsensical.

Suppose an airline flies from A to B, and another airline from B to C, and that some of the passengers change from one to the other, *i.e.*, travel from A to C via B. Suppose further that a given service from A to B is unprofitable, but that its elimination would impose a loss on the company which flies planes from B to C. If this loss exceeds the economy arising from the elimination of the service from A to B, it would clearly be to the advantage of the second airline to pay a sum to the first one so as to persuade it to continue its service.

Similarly, any firm whatsoever whose productive activities impinge, whether favourably or unfavourably, on another might well do a deal with this other firm, thereby taking care of the externality through the market mechanism. If and when such things happen, no economist in his right mind would demur.

However, these are in reality forms of cross-subsidisation, though not recognised as such. If a single airline (private or nationalised, it makes no difference in the present context) or a single firm owned and controlled *both* activities, then it would look as if one were subsidising the other. Therefore many economists would regard such a procedure with great suspicion. What was a straightforward market operation becomes illegitimate in their eyes, though the economic facts are unchanged, save for a change in ownership.

Matters are complicated further by an institutional barrier. The point is that, in nationalised and other large corporations, payment cannot be made by one manager to another manager to cause him to act or to refrain from acting. Thus one region of British Rail cannot offer payment to another to persuade it to run a through train. Consequently, the question cannot be settled at this level, it has to be referred to headquarters. But headquarters are remote, and, save in matters of great importance, the top management there tends to delegate decision-making to the lower echelons of its office staff. These apply rules. Economists can and do influence the drafting of these rules. If they teach "no cross-subsidisation," if they assert that rationality requires that each separate activity be profitable, then it follows that there will be no adjustment for the now internalised externalities, such as might be expected to occur if independent firms divided between themselves the decision-making process. In other words, the internalisation of externalities would occur only in the formal institutional sense, but this would actually lead to a solution farther from the optimum. In fact, *an internality is externalised*.

What, then, is cross-subsidisation? What is its relationship to "internal economies" as here defined?

The belief in the irrationality of cross-subsidisation is based on the apparently elementary principle that a loss-making activity involves resource misallocation, in that, in a market economy, one can increase the national product and welfare by reallocating resources to a profitable use. It is believed that the temptation to subsidise losses out of profits within a corporation or nationalised industry ought therefore to be resisted. Such a temptation may be due to a desire for a quiet life; thus the closing of uneconomic pits might cause questions in Parliament or a protest march by miners.

No one would dispute that irrational forms of cross-subsidisation do occur, or that the *economic* advantages or disadvantages of keeping loss-making pits open should not be confused with social-political externalities. But we are here concerned with *systems* of activities, *i.e.*, with situations in which complementarities and interdependencies are an integral feature of the problem. Some would hold that the very words "cross-subsidisation" are inapplicable to this category of issues. Yet, since these words are so applied, for instance, in the field of transport, one can only reply that the point is not in fact clearly appreciated. It is hardly necessary to devote space to proving the proposition that a transport system contains elements of complementarity and interdependency. Yet many economists still deplore "cross-subsidisation," or urge marginal-cost pricing, on assumptions which would be logical if applied to "widgets." These, let it be recalled, have the quality of suiting text-book analysis: clear definition of "product," no externalities, no economies of scale, no complementarities and so on. We are not here dealing with widgets. Let us examine some examples of what we are dealing with.

There is, first, the *feeder service-complementarity* category. Thus the Manchester United reserve team does not pay, but its existence contributes to the exploits of the first team, which does. A railway branch line may bring passengers to the main line, contributing to its profits, while the revenue accruing to the branch may not cover its costs. Or a municipal docks may lose money on handling a cruise liner whose passengers bring much benefit to the town, and it paid Miami to disburse close on half a million dollars to attract the Republican convention to the city. In all these cases A contributes to the profits of B, and the separate profitability of A is irrelevant, or impossible to attain (in the case of Miami, services are provided at a negative price).

This merges into the issue of the *definition of the product*. A and B could be considered a single product AB. In the real world this is a complex and insufficiently studied problem. Manufacturers of cars, if they are wise, ensure that a spares and after-sales service exists, even if this involves using part of the profits of selling cars to subsidise dealers and garages, because (as Volkswagen showed) this reacts back upon the profits earned in car manufacture. Just as Manchester United reserves, or a branch line, or a docks, should be seen as part of a wider context, so in a very real sense the product "car" *includes* spares and after-sales service. Similarly, a shop or restaurant may find it worth while to operate a car park, or a holiday island boat, even if they make losses as such. This does not cease to be true merely because a separate charge is levied for each of the items referred to above.[1]

Somewhere between the above categories is the case of the railway or turnpike whose construction adds to the value of land. It must be recalled that many a railway made its profits out of land values. It surely cannot be asserted that rationality required them to earn some minimum rate of profit from their railway operations alone. Similarly, if land values are increased by the construction of an eight-lane freeway by more than the cost of building it, so that it would "pay" if no charge were made for road use, it would surely be illogical to assert that *any* price greater than zero could be irrational (even if the turnpike made a loss). The question of whether in fact the additional land values accrue to the builders of the road or railway is, of course, of great practical importance, but does not arise at this stage of the analysis.

Then there is "cross-subsidisation" occasioned by concern for *goodwill* or *reputation*. Here one finds loss leaders, air shuttles ("on the hour, every hour, seats guaranteed"), spare capacity used only at periods of peak demand, the provision of late meals in hotels, the carrying of slow-moving stocks in shops and so on. Reliability has a cost, which benefits those who acquire the reputation for it. In every one of the instances mentioned above there is the probability or cer-

tainty of micro- or marginal losses, which on balance have a positive effect on the profits of the firm. If, for example, there were not spare generating capacity housewives would fear that their electric cookers would fail to function on very cold days, and so extra power stations are needed which do not, of themselves, earn any profits, as they are used only on very cold days. Needless to say, measures can be taken, by differential charging, to try to even out peaks and troughs in demand, but some peaks and troughs there must be.

Within any firm, and particularly a large corporation, whether nationalised or private, decisions have an impact on the profitability of the whole which is not reflected in the profitability of the micro-decision itself. This raises organisational-institutional problems when the corporation is divided for purposes of decision-making into semi-autonomous units. Thus Du Pont (say) has something like twelve divisions and over eighty factories. It would be desirable that the pursuit of profitability by each of these units should be consistent with the profitability of Du Pont. But it is not by any means always so. Profitability is differently perceived at different levels of the corporation. No doubt this is due partly to conflicting interests or time-horizons, but contradictions also arise because the decisions of one sub-unit impinge, positively or adversely, on another unit of the same corporation, to an extent which it cannot perceive. The effect is external to the sub-unit within which the decision is made. The corporation at its headquarters must seek to internalise these externalities. Indeed, this is an important (though not the sole) element of organisational economies of scale. It is one reason why the large corporation is large. But all this, in a superficial sense, involves cross-subsidisation, in so far as division *A*'s loss may be division *B*'s (and the corporation's) gain.

Marginal decisions, then, in a large corporation can best be seen as taking place within a context, or purpose, wider than the rate of return arising out of the marginal decision, wider indeed than the sub-unit within which it is made or to which it refers.

---

[1] This distinction causes some confusion. Naïve economists sometimes argue that everything separately charged for ought to pay its own way, or its provision should depend upon the cost-revenue relationship in each instance. For separate charging is often a matter only of convention. In Glasgow at this moment there are no left-luggage offices because they do not pay, but passengers are provided with handcarts to move their cases about the station. The handcarts are free, and so no one can calculate a profit rate arising directly from their provision. Alas, this can be done with cloakrooms!

So, just as a corporation contains within itself a hierarchy which can be represented in an organisational diagram, so marginal or micro-decisions in the real world form part of multi-dimensional, multi-level classes of relationships and inter-relationships, concerned with units, firms, products or services. It is erroneous, even in elementary or abstract analysis, to present margins as if they had no context. Virtually all decisions affect in some degree other decisions, persons, interests. This is, of course, not an "anti-marginal" argument, just as it is not an argument against devolution of authority within a corporation. One could perhaps envisage microdecision-making on lines of a library classification within a subject: not just two separate though related items A and B, but $A1$ and $A2$, and within them $A2.1$ and $A2.2$ and so on. If A is restaurants, $A2$ is luxury restaurants, $A2.2$ is duck, $A2.2.4$ may be the serving of duck at week-ends, or *à l'orange*, or whatever. This last decision makes sense only within context $A2$, the luxury restaurant. It may be that the ambitiousness of the menu of the $A2$-type restaurant is an integral part of its appeal, and so of its profitability, and so duck might be "on," though most of the profits are made on steak. In this sense margins, the production function indeed, are multi-dimensional. The same duck, even with the same financial results arising directly out of it, might make no sense in a restaurant catering for a different segment of the market.

It is sometimes said that each part even of an inter-related whole ought to pay its way, and that prices should be so adjusted as to ensure this. To such a view there are two objections. The first is the practical one that there may be all kinds of reasons why it ought not to be done: the behaviour of competitors, simplicity (pricing and costing are themselves costly) or impossibility (Manchester United reserves *cannot* pay). But the second objection is more fundamental: reasoning which abstracts from externalities cannot be applied to a situation in which they are present. If a profit gained in activity $B6$ depends on the existence of another activity, let us say $B9$, then calculations of profitability in respect of $B6$ will be misleading

without reference also to $B9$, and pricing policies which isolate each of them cannot be optimal.

Of course, the possibility of considering the profitability of any inter-related class of activities in production or in services depends in considerable degree on the institutional situation. If $B6$ and $B9$ are owned by a single firm B, or by two firms able and prepared to market their externalities, an optimum solution is at least conceivable. If they are jointly owned, and the owners regard "cross-subsidisation" as a sin, or if ownership is so fragmented as to make the marketing of externalities impracticable, or if they are for any reason unmarketable, different decisions would be taken.

It follows that what appears to be an uneconomic or an unprofitable use of resources within a given set of institutional arrangements can appear (and indeed be) both efficient and profitable if the institutional arrangements are altered. One is therefore saddened by the tendency to discuss optima (and Pareto optima at that) in total disassociation from any consideration of structure and on the often implicit assumption of infinite divisibility.

It is worth stressing that the present analysis is confined to the internalisation of *economic* externalities. The writer has read Mishan and is well aware that there are important externalities of other kinds. However, in the present context it may be confusing rather than helpful to bring them into the analysis. Whether within firms, or in the relations of firms with one another or with public authorities, the point is surely to avoid what might be called *vulgarmarginalismus*, an oversimplified one-dimensionalism, because it does *economic* harm. The Swiss keep "loss-making" steamers on their lakes because they are good for the *business* of tourism, not out of a concern for amenity as such. If the Edinburgh Festival (like the Miami Republican convention) is good for the *business* of Edinburgh, then "cross-subsidisation" via the local tax-payer is justified economically, quite apart from the inherent social-cultural virtues of the arts.

Where, it might be asked is then the upper limit of internalisation of externalities? Where does or should one stop?

To find an answer to this question it is useful to take a brief look at the Soviet model. For Stalin long ago claimed that the Soviet planning system is able to substitute national-economic advantage for micro-profitability. Much more recently, the same claim was made by leading Gosplan economists, using a familiar form of words:

> Under socialism, when economies made within every enterprise are at the same time economies for the whole country, and losses are national-economic losses, there is no difference between external economies (or diseconomies) and internal economies (diseconomies). Thereby there exist objective conditions for the implementation of all economic decisions which are profitable from the national-economic point of view.[2]

The U.S.S.R. thus claims to internalise all externalities.

This, however, is a false claim. It is true that state ownership in theory places upon the central planners the duty of seeing all in the context of all. However, the sheer scale of the task, the necessity to organise information flows and decision-making processes, compels the division of the apparently unified and centralised mechanism of planning into units, indeed into hierarchies of units: ministries, departments, territorial administrations, supply organs, trusts, enterprises, banks, etc., etc. For each of these, all matters outside their area of competence and responsibility are external.

It is not only that it is necessary to give some powers of decision to units on the periphery. The logical necessities of centralisation also split the centre. Indeed, it is hard at times to visualise the "central planners" other than as a group of conflicting interests; one must envisage a species of pluralist centralism. The consequences of this for the meaning of the concept "planners' preferences" has been the subject of another article.[3] The relevance of this state of affairs for "internalisation of externalities" is that

total internalisation is impossible, and that externalities are external not primarily because of property relations but because of boundary-lines of responsibility and calculation, which may or may not coincide with boundaries set by ownership, and which exist in some form in all large organisations in any society. A book can readily be filled with examples, taken from Soviet experience, of "localism" and "departmentalism," *i.e.*, of giving priority to the needs and interests of a given region or a particular ministry or department, to the detriment of the interests of some other region, ministry or department, creating situations inconsistent with an ill-defined and sometimes unidentifiable general interest. Were the latter easy to define and identify, appropriate orders could, in principle, be issued; the essence of the problem is that it is not.

Indeed, the experience of British nationalised industries, to which we shall be returning at length, is similar to the Soviet. The co-ordination and reconciliation of decisions made by authorities in charge of gas, electricity, coal and railways is not noticeably simplified by the fact that the State owns all of them. Nor are those in charge of nationalised sectors of industry, in Britain or the Soviet Union, more ready than are private corporations to pay the cost of avoiding social diseconomies such as pollution of rivers and of the atmosphere.

It is because comprehensive internalisation is impossible that reformers in all East European countries are experimenting with various forms of devolution of authority, using "commodity-money" or market relations to determine or influence micro-economic decisions. Some, it is true, assert hopefully that they have or will have "parametric planning," within which "the profitability of every unit shall be consistent with profitability from the standpoint of the whole national economy." Such reformers—Fedorenko and Liberman among others—are seeking to replace Stalin's idea of *centralised* bureaucratic-administrative internalisation with multi-level planning, in which the centre devises criteria by which autonomous pursuit of profit by the periphery leads to the same

[2] A. Efimov, A. Achishkin, in *Mirovaya ekonomika i mezhdunarodnye otnosheniya,* No. 1, 1966, p. 22.

[3] *Economic Journal,* June 1966.

results as *would* have ensued had the centre been all-seeing, all-knowing and all-powerful, *i.e.*, capable of what Wiles called "perfect computation."

The analysis of the present paper serves to cast doubt on the applicability of the above concepts, on theoretical and practical grounds alike. They tend to neglect the sort of internality-externality issues which are bound to distort the micro-profitability indicators. If a corporation is usually unable to reconcile the profitability of its sub-units with that of the whole, it seems inherently unlikely that this can be achieved by U.S.S.R. Ltd.

It follows that there are two dangers: that of not recognising the externality-internality problem (*i.e.*, *vulgarmarginalismus*, the neglect of indivisibilities and complementarities, of organisational economies of scale, of the elements of system in a system of relationships), and secondly, that of imagining that internalisation can be achieved by giving responsibility for this task to one all-pervasive body, such as Gosplan or the Politburo. Internalisation can in fact be costly, in terms of the organisation of information flows, administrative machinery, bureaucratic inflexibilities, delay. It follows that some degree of decentralisation, either to autonomous enterprises or to subunits of corporations or of nationalised industries, is indispensable, even though some potentially internalisable externalities will remain unperceived. This will be rational so long as the cost of internalisation is greater than the benefit. This is a matter of defining, in the given circumstances, the limits of organisational economies of scale. There is a point at which there is a diminishing return to centralisation. No doubt this is taken into account by a corporation making the rules governing the devolution of authority to its various divisions. The degree and pattern of resultant decentralisation must logically vary widely as between sectors. Experience as well as common sense suggests that there will and should be more centralisation, i.e., greater advantage in internalisation, in steel and chemicals than in clothing and vegetables. Consequently, as Soviet, Czech

and Hungarian reformers are finding, variety is essential. In the West it is often worth while to avoid the cost of internalisation by using a mass of sub-contractors, which the principal does not own. A Soviet author noted that the average Soviet enterprise is much larger, in terms of labour used, than its Western counterparts, and particularly so in the engineering industry, where sub-contracting is particularly frequently encountered.

Numbers Engaged in One Enterprise (On Average)

	All Industry.	Machinery and Metal-Working.
U.S.S.R. (1963)	656	2,608
United States (1958)	48	74
West Germany (1963)	83	139

Source: Y. Kvasha, *Voprosy ekonomiki*, No. 5, 1967, p. 26.

The author, after remarking on the small size of many of the sub-contractors ("of the 26,000 suppliers to General Motors, ... 16,000 employed fewer than 50 persons"), made the following relevant comment:

> Small-scale industry in the form of autonomous enterprises fits badly into state ownership because of complexities of administration and control. There is a boundary of scale beyond which the maintenance of administrative, inspecting and auxiliary personnel does not pay. For state enterprises, in our view, this boundary is represented by enterprises employing roughly 50 persons.

Yet many Soviet enterprises are in some respects too big; there is advantage in the flexibility that goes with both smallness and independence in some branches of economic life. He goes on to discuss the desirability of small enterprises in the specialised manufacture of components, and also in the satisfaction of "individual consumer tastes." In the Soviet context, he advocates the recreation of co-operative industry (the remaining co-operative workshops had been "nationalised" in 1961).

Without entering into a discussion of the substance of the case made by this author, or into the precise comparability of his statistics, his ideas can indicate a necessary and useful pattern of thinking: internalisation through ownership and central control can in some circumstances be too expensive and too clumsy. The cost of not internalising, everywhere present, can sometimes be substantially less than the cost of doing so.

.   .   .

part 3

The R & D Submodel
of the Firm

While the research and development effort of the firm, which can lead either to process innovation (resulting in lower production cost) or to the creation of new products, has been retaining the full attention of economists for at least a decade, it has not received full treatment in managerial economics texts. In large segments of industry R & D is absorbing a growing portion of firms' budgets; it is one of the most important functional fields within the enterprise. And, at that, officially reported R & D expenditures are often but a tip of the iceberg: marketing departments, manufacturing and engineering staffs, and financial personnel devote an important part of their time to the analysis of process innovation or new-product proposals. It is therefore timely to examine from an economic perspective the R & D function of the firm.

The first selection (14) uses the by-now familiar production function framework to determine the rate of return on investment in R & D. The second probes the determinants of firms' annual investment expenditures on R & D. The last reading examines the impact of research and development on the firm's export activity and on its expansion into multinational operations.

Minasian's paper (Reading 14) uses the production function approach already discussed in the preceding selections to coax out the contribution of R & D activity to the overall efficiency of the firm. His most important finding is that, in his sample of seventeen chemical firms observed over the period from 1948 through 1957, the rate of return on R & D investment exceeds five times that of the rate of return on capital stock.

Grabowski, in Reading 15, considers two important questions: What are the reasons that make some firms more research-oriented than others? Do large firms tend to be more "research-intensive" than smaller firms? To answer the first question Grabowski builds and tests a model (against data gathered from a sample of firms in the chemical, drug, and petroleum industries over the period from 1959 through 1962) which relates the proportion of sales revenue that a firm spends on R & D to three determining variables: (1) the number of patents received by the firm per technical employee in a prior period (i.e., the firm's past success in R & D effort); (2) an index of the firm's product diversification; and (3) the firm's cash flow. The reader will judge the success of this model in explaining the R & D intensity of the sample firms. In common with several other researchers, Grabowski finds that the answer to the second question is no: giants do not necessarily spend a larger proportion of their sales revenue on R & D than medium-sized firms spend.

Reading 16 (by Gruber, Mehta, and Vernon) attempts to explain the export success of certain U.S. industries. Its chief finding suggests that the most R & D intensive among U.S. industries fare best in competition for world markets. It is probable that such industries (as office equipment and aircraft), by dint of their R & D effort, continuously generate new products and thus keep an edge over competition from other industrially advanced states. Flag then follows trade, as the export leaders invest in facilities abroad to service what they sell and, ultimately, to manufacture locally what they first started to produce back home. The student of managerial economics will find a secondary, methodological, interest in this reading. This is the extensive use of standard industrial classification (SIC) data and their thorough critical examination; such data are the daily bread of the practicing managerial economist.

14

Research and Development, Production Functions, and Rates of Return

JORA R. MINASIAN*

Almost a decade ago I argued that research and development activity represented efforts made towards achieving efficiency, and showed that the rate of growth in productivity of the firms was positively correlated with their research and development expenditures.[1]

This paper reports the results of a study of "rate of return" to research and development expenditures in a production function setting.[2] Although the tenuous nature of the Cobb-Douglas type of production function was originally indicated by two independent studies in the early 1960's[3] because of its predominance in use, the estimates are obtained by both a covariance model and by the use of a production function of the Cobb-Douglas type.

THE MODEL

The production function of a firm may be expressed by equation (1)

From American Economic Review (May 1969), pp. 81–85. Reprinted with permission of author and publisher.

* Jora R. Minasian teaches at the University of Southern California.

[1] Jora R. Minasian, "The Economics of Research and Development," *The Rate and Direction of Inventive Activity: Social and Economic Factors,* A Conference of the Universities-National Bureau Research (Princeton Univ. Press, 1962), pp. 93–143.

[2] For a summary of partial results of a study using the covariance analysis, see my "Technical Change and Production Function," *RAND P-2430,* pp. 1–14, presented at the meeting of the Econometric Society, 1961, and printed in the Proceedings of *Econometrica,* Apr., 1962.

[3] Jora R. Minasian, "Elasticity of Substitution and Constant-Output Demand Curves for Labor," *J.P.E.,* June, 1961. Also K. Arrow, H. B. Chenery, B. S. Minas, and R. M. Solow, "Capital-Labor Substitution and Economic Efficiency," *Rev. of Econ. and Statis.,* 1961.

$$V_{ft} = f(L_{ft}, K_{ft}, T_{ft}) \qquad (1)$$

where V_{ft} L_{ft}, K_{ft}, and T_{ft} represent, respectively, value added, labor, capital, and technology of the firm in time, t. The firm's technology in time, t, is a positive function of the existing stock of knowledge. We postulate that the research and development expenditures are related in additions made to the stock of knowledge. That is,

$$T_t = g(N_t) \qquad (2)$$

and

$$N_t = h\left(\sum_{t=0}^{t=t} R\right) \qquad (3)$$

where N and R stand for stock of knowledge and research and development expenditures. Substituting (2) and (3) in equation (1) we obtain the production function of the firm expressing the value added as function of labor, capital, and accumulated research and development expenditures of the firm in time, t. That is,

$$V_{ft} = k\left(L_{ft}, K_{ft}, \sum_{t=0}^{t=t} R_{ft}\right) \qquad (4)$$

THE STATISTICAL METHOD OF ANALYSIS

Observations on the value added, capital, and labor during 1948–57 for seventeen firms in the chemical industry constitute the sample. We first visualize a production function relating value added to labor and capital but allowing for differences in the firms' technologies. This may be done by constant terms for each firm in the context of covariance analysis. These firm constants summarize the differences among firms. Therefore, we can pool cross-section and time series data of the firms to estimate the constants and the regression coefficients which are freed from the differences in the firms.

A postulated reason for such differences is the firms' research and development expenditures. Therefore, one implication is that if these firm constants were statistically significant when the production function omitted the research and development, they should tend to lose their significance in the presence of the research and development in the function.

In general, firms may differ for reasons not incorporated in research and development variables. It is preferable for this reason to use a function which allows a constant term for each firm. Further, it is not necessary that the firm constants become insignificant as there is no a priori reason to believe that all potential differences among firms are perfectly correlated with research and development expenditures.

It should, therefore, be noted that the primary purpose of adding variables to the function is not to achieve higher multiple coefficients of determination; rather it is to distribute the pie, as it were, more appropriately and thus obtain a more accurate set of partial regression coefficients.

Thus, the methodology will be to employ a multiple regression technique to test an alternative hypothesis involving the inclusion of the variables in the regression equation and to shed light on the nature of the explanation provided by the variables.

Both capital and research and development are gross stock variables. The alternative of assuming that there is a constant relationship between service flows and the stock of capital and research and development was preferred to an attempt to correct the service flows by some arbitrary percentage representing presumably obsolescence, breakdowns, uselessness of knowledge, etc. It was felt that the errors involved in the former would be less than those present in the latter procedure.

Finally, note that the model specifies research and development undertaken by the firm alone. The benefits derived from knowledge generated by the industry and the economy are not explicitly incorporated in the model. The effect of the excluded variable will be captured by the constant term in the regression equation, if the excluded variable is not correlated with the firm's research and development. The returns to research and development will be overestimated in the case of a positive correlation between the excluded variable and the firm's research and development expenditures.

THE EMPIRICAL RESULTS

For each set of variables two types of production functions (linear in the logs) were estimated. In one there is a general constant and seventeen specific constants—one for each firm, and alternatively ten time constants, one for each year. We shall call this Type I formulation. In the other there is only one general constant term. We shall call this Type II formulation. Of course, both use combined cross-section and time series data.

The regression results of Type I formulation are given in Table 1, and those for Type II formulation appear in Table 2. To conserve space, firm and time constants are not given in Table 1. Instead a dagger is used to show which of the constants were estimated in a particular regression.

First, evaluation of time and firm constants. The independent variables explain the variation in the value added not explained by the constants. For example, adding K and L to the equation that contains only the constants, yields an F-value of 2.20 which is highly significant; 1 percent level of significance requires an F-value of 350. Time constants are significant in regressions 2 and 3 but not in regressions 4 and 5. The F-values are, respectively, 4.0, 4.6, 1.12, and 1.72.

Firm constants are highly significant in all the regressions: 6, 7, 8, and 9; the F-values are 27, 17, 36, and 24, respectively.

In all of the cases, the unexplained variations in value added are reduced by a greater amount by firm than by time constants. The combined time and firm constants explain most when the regression equation includes T, but least when R is included in the regression equation. Finally, although statistically significant, the firm constants lose their explanatory power more with R than with other variables included in the regression equation. Adding R to the regression equation reduces the explanatory power of firm constants by 38 percent. In summary, then, time constants are substitutes for T; compare the regression coefficients for L and K in regressions 2 and 3 with those in regressions 4 and 5, respectively, Table 1. Both are inferior to firm constant and R in explaining variation in value added.

Second, the results of the regression coefficients. Once firm constants are introduced, the regression coefficients of L and K are stable, whether R or T or both are included in the regression equation; see regressions 7, 8, and 9, Table 1. This constancy is not achieved with the Type II formulation, Table 2. Moreover, the coefficients of L and K add up to close to 1, suggesting no economies of scale.

Regression equations 7 and 8, Table 1, produce similar results for L and K and also for R and T. But, when both R and T are introduced together in the regression equation 9, Table 1, neither regression coefficients are significant at the 5 percent two-tail level with 148 degrees of freedom. However, the performance of research and development is far better than that of time and, it seems, the success of the time variable is essentially due to its summary of the research and development variable. But when both are present, their intercorrelation reduces the level of significance of both, much more drastically in the case of time than research and development. The credibility of this interpretation of the role of T is enhanced by noting the erratic performance of T in other regressions, 4 and 5, Table 1, and regression 4, Table 2. It seems plausible, therefore, that the firm constants and the research and development variable summarize the variables that are hoped to be captured by the conventional inclusion of T as a separate variable in the regression analysis of production functions.

Having analyzed the regression results, and on the basis of the above conclusion, regression 7 will be used to calculate marginal products of capital and research and development expenditures.

The elasticity of capital and research and development are respectively 0.16 and 0.11. The average real value added per firm per year was $171.8 million, the average real gross capital per firm per year was $407.6 million, while average real accumulated research and development expenditures per firm per year was $35.2 million. An estimate of marginal product for capital is given by $0.16 \times 171.8/407.6 = \$0.09$ and that for research and development expenditures by $0.11 \times 171.8/35.2 = \$0.54$. That is, if the stock of capital increases by $1.00 permanently, the value added increases by $0.09 per year indefinitely. Similarly, $0.54 worth of value added can be created per year indefinitely if the stock of research and development is increased by $1.00 and the new level maintained permanently. This means that gross return on investment in research and development is 54 percent as compared with 9 percent for capital.

Without being overconfident in the accuracy of the estimates, which for one thing are affected by the particular form of the production function used, the estimating procedure employed here has a few merits that may be pointed out briefly. First, in contrast to the tendency to find return to successful projects, a procedure which is on par with estimating returns to the acting profession by looking at the earnings of movie idols, my estimate reflects both successes and failures of research and development projects, which is as it should be. The value added increases due to successes, and research and development expenditures include both the cost of the projects that failed and those that bore fruits.

Second, the estimate is obtained by a joint estimation of the independent variables, in contrast to residual approach where what

TABLE 1 Type I Formulation—Multiple Regressions of the Value Added (V) on Labor (L), Capital (K), Research and Development (R), Time (T), Chemical Firms 1948–57

$$\log V_{ft} = \log b_0 + \log B_f + \log B_t + b_1 \log L_{ft} + b_2 \log K_{ft} + b_3 \log R_{ft} + b_4 \log T_{ft}$$

V_{ft}	b_0	B_f	B_t	L	K	R	T	R^2
1	− .119			.582 (.042) .734	.456 (.039) .678			.970
2	− .069		†	.621 (.040) .771	.418 (.038) .661			.974
3	.282		†	.382 (.042) .583	.357 (.032) .669	.258 (.029) .580		.983
4	.553		†	.621 (.040) .744	.418 (.037) .661		−.950* (2.988) .033	.975
5	.185		†	.382 (.043) .583	.357 (.032) .669	.259 (.029) .580	.150* (2.485) .001	.983
6	−1.173	†		.596 (.083) .505	.645 (.059) .667			.992
7	− .019	†		.820 (.076) .659	.156 (.081) .156	.113 (.015) .531		.995
8	.037	†		.825 (.077) .658	.212 (.076) .221		.124 (.016) .525	.994
9	.007	†		.823 (.076) .659	.167 (.084) .160	.084* (.068) .099	.033* (.075) .036	.995

See Appendix for definition of the variables.

In each regression, the partial regression coefficient is given in the first row, its standard error (in parentheses) in the second row, and the partial coefficients of determination in the third row. Partial regression coefficients that are not significantly different from zero at the 5 percent two-tail level are marked by *. Finally, † indicates the type of constant estimated but is not given in the table for economy of space.

TABLE 2 Type II Formulation—Multiple Regressions of the Value Added (V) on Labor (L), Capital (K), Research and Development (R), Time (T), Chemical Firms 1948–57

$$\log V_{ft} = \log a_0 + a_1 \log L_{ft} + a_2 \log K_{ft} + a_3 \log R_{ft} + a_4 \log T_{ft}$$

V_{ft}	a_0	L_{ft}	K_{ft}	R_{ft}	T_{ft}	R^2
1	−.119	.582 (.042) .734	.459 (.039) .678			.970
2	.129	.522 (.036) .748	.368 (.034) .638	.127 (.015) .540		.990
3	−.130	.621 (.041) .766	.418 (.038) .651		.094 (.021) .326	.973
4	.386	.393 (.043) .577	.356 (.033) .649	.249 (.029) .550	−.172 (.036) .347	.982

See notes at the bottom of Table 1.

we cannot explain (the residual) is attributed to technology or research and development activity.

Third, typical returns to research and development are found to be several thousands percent, with the exception of a few studies that report them in the hundreds. Perhaps this fact has served as the basis for some economists to justify their plea for more government subsidized research and development. As there is no entrance problem in conducting research, the persistence of the fantastic difference between returns to alternative investment cast doubt on the economic significance of the available estimates, regardless of their statistical significance. In contrast, the estimate derived in this paper is in the range of plausibility, especially when we note that the return is "social" rather than "private."

To the extent that increased productivity, caused by research and development, is partially passed on to consumers via lower prices for goods, my estimate will tend to reflect social returns. Lower prices will tend to decrease the firm's profits and the rate of return, but will not affect my measure, since real value added incorporates the benefits created but received by consumers through lower prices.

APPENDIX

Construction of the Variables[4]

1. *Value Added.* Since data on raw materials consumed were not available, the value added was estimated as wage bill + profit before taxes (adjusted by other income or expense not related to production; i.e., dividends received or paid) + interest paid + depreciation. The value added was then deflated by the firm's price index; the Bureau of Labor Statistics wholesale price indexes of subcategories of the chemical industries were weighted by the output mix of the

[4] For a more detailed description of the variables, see my "The Economics of Research and Development," *op. cit.*

firms by broad categories of products to obtain the firms' price index.

2. *Labor.* Total wages, salaries, and other compensations such as vacation, sick leave, insurance, retirement funds, etc., of employees were taken as the contribution of labor to production. The total wage bill was deflated by the firm's wage rate which was obtained by weighting the BLS index of average hourly earnings of subclasses in the total chemical industry by the same weights used in the construction of the price indexes.

3. *Capital.*

a) *Real Gross Plant and Equipment.* Data on gross plant and equipment at the beginning of the year, gross investment, and gross retirement are broken down by categories and types and are given in the *Annual Reports-Form 10-K* submitted to the Securities and Exchange Commission by publicly owned firms. These reports date back to 1934. The gross plant and equipment at the beginning of 1934 was deflated by the 1929 GNP implicit price indexes of new construction and durable equipment, respectively. Yearly gross additions to plant and equipment were deflated by the price index of the year and added to the stock of the real plant and equipment of the initial year successively. It was assumed that the retired capital was generally the oldest. Therefore, the 1929 GNP implicit price deflators were used to deflate the retirements of the years 1934–46. Equipment retired in 1947–57 was assumed to have been purchased during 1940–47, so each of the two price indexes of this latter period were weighted by the relevant gross private domestic investment for 1940–47 to obtain the average deflator. This average weighted deflator was then used to deflate retirements of 1947–57.

b) *Other Real Capital.* This category of assets consists of cash, accounts receivable, government securities, and inventories of the firm. This category of capital was deflated by the GNP implicit price deflator. Thus total real capital of the firms was equated to the total of net real plant and equipment and the other real capital.

4. *Research and Development.* The firms'

research and development expenditures, which include depreciation of laboratories and laboratory equipment, were deflated by the GNP implicit price deflator.

Due to unavailability of earlier data for most firms, the accumulation of research and development starts from 1948.

5. *Time.* For each firm time takes the value of 1, 2 . . . 10 for 1948, 1949 . . . 1957, respectively.

15

The Determinants of Industrial Research and Development:

A Study of the Chemical, Drug, and Petroleum Industries

HENRY G. GRABOWSKI*

Economists have recently grown interested in doing research on research —or R & D, as it is called in industrial circles. Several studies have tested Schumpeter's hoary hypothesis that large firms are responsible for most industrial inventive activity.[1] Few of these studies, however, suggest why this hypothesis is apparently valid for some industries and not for others. And statistical studies going beyond this question, to try to relate R & D expenditures to firm profit expectations and the availability of funds as in other investment decisions, are rare (Mansfield, 1964; Mueller, 1967).

This paper reports the results of an em-

From Journal of Political Economy (*March/April 1968*), *pp. 292–306, by Henry G. Grabowski; publisher, The University of Chicago Press. Reprinted with permission of author and publisher.*

* Some of the results of this paper were first presented in my doctoral dissertation submitted to Princeton University in 1966. I am indebted to B. G. Malkiel, O. Morgenstern, F. M. Scherer, and R. E. Quandt for helpful suggestions and criticisms. For making unpublished data available to me on R & D expenditures, I am especially grateful to Dennis C. Mueller. In addition, data collected by McGraw-Hill, Inc., and compiled under the direction of Professor Robert Eisner of Northwestern were very

pirical investigation into the determinants of research expenditures in three industries—drugs, chemicals, and petroleum refining. These industries have three advantages for such a study: (1) they are among the leaders in total R & D expenditures; (2) most activity is concentrated in an appreciable number of large or moderately large firms; and (3) government support of research work is relatively small, so that decisions are more closely analogous to ordinary investment decisions.[2] Data samples were

helpful in the earlier stages of the work. [Professor Grabowski teaches at Yale University.]

[1] Data collected by the National Science Foundation (hereafter "NSF") definitely show that firms below certain threshold sizes perform very little organized R & D. For example, firms with 1,000 employees or less in 1958 accounted for 60 per cent of total industrial employment but performed only 5 per cent of company-financed R & D (NSF, 1964, p. 6). However, the question which has been extensively investigated in recent studies is whether research intensity increases with size among firms clearly larger than the threshold levels. For a survey of these studies and an attempt to reconcile some conflicting results, see Markham (1965).

[2] Of the six NSF industry classifications performing approximately $300 million or more of company-financed R & D in 1963, government supported R &

constructed for the three industries by requesting total R & D expenditure figures, as defined by the NSF standards,[3] from firms in the 1960 *Fortune 500* listing. The response rate in each industry was almost exactly 70 per cent, with R & D data over the period 1959–62 provided by sixteen firms in chemicals, fifteen in petroleum refining, and ten in drugs.

Since the main variation in the data occurs over the cross-section of firms, rather than for each firm over time, the regression models will be primarily explaining interfirm differences in R & D. However, pooled cross-section time-series samples will be used in order to increase the number of available observations in each industry sample. For each equation estimated with these pooled samples, the hypothesis of time-invariant parameters was tested. Because this hypothesis cannot be rejected at the normal confidence intervals, data pooling may be advantageously employed in the present analysis of R & D determinants.

I. THE CHARACTERISTICS OF THE MODEL

When analyzing the R & D behavior of a group of firms in which substantially different scales of operation exist, research intensity, rather than the absolute level of a firm's expenditures, is a more appropriate dependent variable. When absolute figures are used, heteroscedasticity is invariably present, and scale effects tend to dominate the regression equations. In order to avoid these problems, the procedure adopted in this paper is to measure R & D expenditures as well as size-correlated independent variables, relative to the total sales of the firm.[4] Although there are some good a priori reasons for choosing sales as the particular size deflator,[5] the results are substantially unaltered if either total assets or the number of employees is used instead.

The determinants of research intensity to be considered first relate to the returns from R & D activity. Since there is a considerable lag in the payoff to R & D, a firm's estimated set of returns from current projects will likely depend on its past results. While expectations based on past performance may not vary markedly from one budget period to the next for an individual firm, substantial variations should exist across firms due to the cumulated effects of past differences in firm capacities and attitudes toward R & D. The first explanatory variable of research intensity is, therefore, an index of the research productivity of each firm over a prior period.

In order to construct such a proxy variable of research productivity, three possible measures of a firm's research output were considered: new-product sales, the number of patents granted to the firm, and the number of significant inventions made by the firm. Given the strong product orientation of industrial R & D, perhaps the best measure of the three from a conceptual standpoint is new-product sales. Unfortunately, new-product sales are not generally available, and furthermore, substantial differences in definitions and product classification among

---

D was over 25 per cent of total expenditures except in chemicals and allied products and in petroleum refining. In these two industries it amounted to 21 per cent and 6 per cent, respectively.

[3] The NSF definitions of R & D are given in the technical notes of all its published data reviews. These data have definite advantages over company-published figures in that (1) they are based on a common externally devised definition; and (2) firms are assured of confidential treatment, thereby removing any incentives to inflate the figures artificially. While the NSF data are undoubtedly the best available statistics, it must be emphasized there are still many difficult conceptual problems in measuring inventive efforts by dollar outlays. See the discussions in Kuznets (1962) and Sanders (1962).

[4] An alternative approach for dealing with heteroscedasticity is to estimate the equations using logarithmic transformations when the specifications of the models permit one to do so. Both procedures have been extensively used in dealing with samples that are cross-sectional in nature and span a large size spectrum. For a discussion of the problem associated with using the ratio approach, see Kuh and Meyer (1955).

[5] This question has been analyzed by Scherer (1965*b*, pp. 256–61) in a commentary on some results of Hamberg (1964). Among the reasons for choosing sales are: (1) sales is a more neutral size measure, and (2) firms have emphasized the use of sales as a landmark for budget decisions in various interview studies.

firms make the use of these numbers in a cross-section analysis quite hazardous. Of the two other measures of research output, patents is the more attractive, since all patented inventions must pass certain uniform criteria of the U.S. Patent Office, and patent statistics are readily available.[6]

The measure of research outputs used in the model is, therefore, the number of patents granted to a firm in a specified prior period. To form the productivity variable, this output measure is divided by a research-input measure—specifically, the number of scientists and engineers employed by the firm over the approximate period when the patented inventions were conceived.[7] The first hypothesis put forth here is thus that firms with higher patented output per scientific worker in the past will, *ceteris paribus*, be more research-intensive than their rivals.[8] Of course, this variable at best measures only one aspect of the firm's returns from R & D —the technical quality of its research outputs. Another aspect, relating to the applicability of R & D to the firm's operations, will be considered below.

Before discussing the other explanatory variables, however, it should be mentioned that patents have been used elsewhere as a measure of inventive output, and their limitations in this regard have been extensively discussed (Kuznets, 1962; Sanders,

1962). One of the more serious problems incurred in using patent statistics is the possibility that the propensity to patent might be systematically correlated in a positive way with a firm's degree of research intensity. If this were so, a spurious positive relation between research intensity and patent output per worker would result. However, there are no strong a priori arguments why this will be the case, and some data are available to analyze this question for the firms under study. This problem will taken be up in the next section.

The second explanatory variable of research intensity in the present model is an index of each firm's output diversification. It has been postulated in the literature (see Nelson, 1959) that a firm's degree of diversification will positively influence its profit expectations from R & D. This hypothesis follows from the belief that a more diversified firm will be better able to exploit unexpected research outputs than one with a narrower base of operations. While the original formulation was meant to apply to scientific work at the research end of the spectrum rather than to development expenditures, this hypothesis also implies greater expenditures on total R & D unless these two component activities are complete substitutes, which is highly unlikely.

The index of diversification used in the present model is based on the number of separate five-digit SIC product classifications in which a firm produced during a middle year of the sample period.[9] This

---

[6] Attempts at constructing a series of significant inventions made by each firm were beset by serious methodological problems and therefore discarded. For some interesting attempts to measure inventive output in this manner, see Mansfield (1964, pp. 334–37).

[7] Scherer (1965a, p. 1097) has estimated that over a period somewhat coincident with our sample the patent office took an average of three and one-half years to process a patent. Adding several more months as time necessary to draw up a patent application, the "patent lag" is taken somewhat arbitrarily here to be four years in length.

[8] This relationship is likely to operate in a forward as well as backward manner. That is, more research-intensive firms now should realize a higher level of patented outputs in the future. There is ample evidence that firm behavior often follows such recursive patterns. While firms may certainly radically change past modes of operation, R & D in particular is not an activity that lends itself to frequent and marked changes in emphasis.

[9] All the data on diversification come from the 1961 edition of the *Fortune Plant and Product Directory*. For the chemical and petroleum industries, an examination of the various product classes revealed that they are virtually all of sufficient technical character to have at least some potential relevance to the R & D activity. For these two industries, the index will therefore be the total number of separate SIC classifications encompassed by the firm's product mix. For the drug industry, however, product mixes of highly diversified drug firms indicate a tendency for them to expand into products only tangentially related to the manufacture of drugs proper (that is, adhesives, brushes, glass bottles, toilet preparations, plastic products, and so forth). These product lines offer little opportunity for the applicability of research outputs. It was therefore decided that a more appropriate index of diversifica-

variable, like the index of past research productivity, is designed to capture interfirm differences in expected returns from R & D. It therefore varies only over the cross-section of firms and not over time. Over a four-year interval, the size of the firm's product mix does not change significantly, and the construction of the index as "timeless" during this period is a satisfactory approximation.

Aside from expected returns, financial factors form another basic set of considerations relevant to industrial R & D expenditures. The relationships between financial variables and investment have been extensively explored in the literature on the determinants of fixed capital expenditures (for a bibliography, see Eisner and Strotz, 1963). There is considerable evidence from these studies that retained earnings and other internally generated funds have an especially significant effect on investment expenditures. This has been attributed to the general reluctance of firms to raise funds externally because of the added risks and transaction costs entailed in this type of financing. If this is so, it would seem applicable with some qualifications to investment in R & D.

In the short run, R & D expenditures can be expected to be much less sensitive to changes in cash flow, especially in the downturn. This is true because of the higher fixed cost component in R & D activity. Research workers, whose salaries constitute a sizable percentage of total expenditures, are not perfectly elastic in supply and cannot be alternately fired and rehired in accordance with temporary changes in business conditions.[10] In the long run, however, a significant positive relationship between R & D

and cash flow should be evident if firms behave as many previous investment studies suggest. Since the data samples investigated here are basically cross-sectional and span four years of reasonably stable growth for the firms involved, a long-run effect should be observed in the present case. The third explanatory variable in our model, is, therefore, a measure of the firm's internally generated funds deflated by sales. The specific internal funds variable that will be used is the sum of the firm's after-tax profits plus depreciation and depletion charges, lagged one period.

The above three variables reflect some of the main technological, marketing, and financial factors that one would expect to influence the R & D expenditure decision. Some previous interview studies of R & D suggest some other relevant considerations (see NSF, 1956). One strong trend of thought running through these studies is that firm decisions on R & D are strongly influenced by the behavior of competitors, and, in particular that a great deal of imitation exists among firms with respect to R & D allocations. Since most R & D is performed by firms operating in oligopolistic market structures and it is an activity presumably involving greater uncertainty than other undertakings, firms may imitate each other as a conservative strategy for minimizing risks. Because of the multitude of forms which such imitation may take, however, it is difficult to deal with this phenomenon in the framework of the present empirical analysis.

One particularly simple type of imitation discussed in these interview studies and frequently mentioned in the trade literature is the adherence by firms to a general industry R & D to sales ratio. If this kind of imitative behavior is present to any significant degree in the present industrial samples, it should be evident from the empirical analysis. Since research intensity as measured by the R & D to sales ratio is the dependent variable, imitation by firms of an "industry" ratio would imply less variability in the dependent variable and cause the intercept of the regression equation to become statistically significant relative to the explanatory variables postulated above. The sign and statistical

---

tion for the drug industry would be obtained by counting only the number of SIC classifications that are concerned directly with the manufacture of drugs proper.

[10] That is, there will likely be significant downward rigidities in this relationship due to the technological necessity of maintaining a reasonably stable staff of researchers. Also, the increasing cost associated with rapid expansion will act to constrain this relationship in upturns in the short run as well. While material costs are more flexible, they account for a smaller percentage of total expenditures (for representative cost figures, see the NSF data reviews.)

significance of the intercept term in the regression model therefore provide a first level test of this proposition. However, more subtle and complex forms of imitation are best analyzed in a more disaggregative context than the data permit here.

The present discussion leaves us essentially with three explanatory variables of firm research intensity—a research-productivity variable consisting of the level of patented output realized by the firm relative to its input of scientific personnel over a prior period, an index of firm product diversification, and a variable dealing with the financial resources of the firm which is equal to the level of internally generated funds of the firm as a percentage of its total sales. The model may be expressed formally as

$$\frac{R_{i,t}}{S_{i,t}} = b_0 + b_1 P_i + b_2 D_i + b_3 \frac{I_{i,t-1}}{S_{i,t}}, \quad (1)$$

where $R_{i,t}$ is the level of R & D expenditures of the ith firm in the tth period, $S_{i,t}$ is the level of sales of the ith firm in the tth period, $I_{i,t-1}$ is the sum of after-tax profits plus depreciation and depletion expenses of the ith firm in the $t-1$ period, P_i is the number of patents received per scientist and engineer employed by the ith firm in a prior four-year period (1955–59), and D_i is the index of diversification of the ith firm (the number of the separate five-digit SIC product classification in which it produces).

The hypotheses discussed above suggest that coefficients b_1, b_2, and b_3 will all be positive. In addition, the intercept term, b_0, of this equation serves in a sense as a possible fourth explanatory variable since it shows the influence of sales on research expenditures and in particular provides a test of the proposition that firms adhere to an industry-wide R & D to sales ratio. The results of including some additional variables in equation (1) are also given in the section which follows.

II. THE EMPIRICAL RESULTS

Using the data samples described above, least-squares estimates of the coefficients

of equation (1) were obtained. The results are presented in Table 1. All of the regression coefficients are of the postulated sign and are significant at the 1 per cent level except for the diversification variable coefficient in the petroleum industry, which is positive but statistically insignificant. The over-all explanatory power of our model is quite good in the case of the chemical and drug industries, given the nature of the samples under study, ($R^2 = .63$ and .86, respectively), but is low for the petroleum industry ($R^2 = .29$). An examination of the results in Table 1 also shows that the estimates of the intercept terms of equation (1) are such as to cast considerable doubt on the proposition that firms in this sample adhere to an industry-wide R & D to sales ratio. The only statistically significant intercept is negative (the drug industry), and the positive coefficients for the other two industries were negligible in value.[11]

The above regression results indicate that interfirm differences in technology, diversification, and the availability of funds all are important in explaining differences in research intensity with no single factor having a dominant influence. Table 1 also shows that the size of the regression coefficient associated with each of these variables increases with the research orientation of the industry involved—being the lowest in the petroleum industry and the highest in the drug industry in every case. Thus, as research looms more important as a competitive strategy to the firms of an industry, each of our independent variables exerts a correspondingly greater effect on the level of research that a firm performs.

The much poorer performance of the model in explaining research intensity in petroleum refining can be traced in part to certain structural factors that distinguish it from chemicals and drugs. Among these

[11] All of the results presented in Table 1 are substantially unchanged when the profit component of the available funds variable is measured by the firm's retained earnings rather than its total after-tax profits. The results on the significance of the variables are the same, and the fit of the regression becomes slightly better for chemicals ($R^2 = .67$) and slightly poorer for drugs ($R^2 = .80$).

TABLE 1 Estimation of Regression Equation $R_{i,t}/S_{i,t} = b_0 + b_1 P_i + b_2 D_i + b_3(I_{i,t-1}/S_{i,t})$, for the Chemical, Drug, and Petroleum Industries for the Period 1959–62

Industry	b_0	b_1	b_2	b_3	R^2	F	N
Chemicals . . .	0.006	0.12*	0.019*	0.078*	.63	29.76	60
	(0.004)	(0.02)	(0.004)	(0.023)			
Drugs	−0.03*	0.54*	0.41*	0.26*	.86	73.71	40
	(0.01)	(0.12)	(0.07)	(0.05)			
Petroleum . . .	0.002	0.016*	0.0049	0.020*	.29	5.46	55
	(0.002)	(0.005)	(0.0071)	(0.006)			

* Significant at .01 level.

Note.—Numbers below coefficient estimates are estimates of the standard errors; technological and diversification variables (P_i and D_i) have been multiplied by scale factors in order to present results more conveniently.

factors are: (1) R & D is much more process oriented in petroleum refining;[12] (2) the degree of integration within this industry is very uniform, and the amount of outward diversification is slight; and (3) R & D is more of a peripheral activity, consuming a portion of the budget which is at least an order of magnitude smaller than in the other two industries. In an industry where research is process oriented, patents will likely be a poorer measure of technological output because firms will often wish to keep knowledge of such inventive activity concealed from their competitors. Furthermore, where R & D is a competitive strategy of lesser importance, as in petroleum refining, allocations to it tend to be more vulnerable to fluctuations in other uses of scarce funds. While there is no way to quantify the effects of the above three structural factors, together they probably explain a substantial part of the poorer performance of the model in this industry.

The positive relation observed between patented output per research input and the research intensity of a firm has been interpreted above as a measure of the effects of interfirm technology differences in research intensity. If it were true that more research-

intensive firms have a greater propensity to patent than less intensive ones, this interpretation would be open to serious question. To investigate this latter possibility, data on the number of in-house patent attorneys for all the firms in our sample over the period 1955–59 were obtained. This is the most meaningful measure of patent activity available, although it is far from a complete index of it.[13]

Utilizing these data on patent attorneys, the correlation coefficient between a firm's research intensity and the number of in-house attorneys engaged per scientist and engineer was calculated for each of the three industry samples. Since the regression estimates have shown a significant relation between a firm's research intensity and the number of patents granted to it per research employee, one would also expect a significant relation between this variable and the number of in-house patent attorneys per research employee if this relation were merely the result of more research-intensive firms having a greater propensity to patent. The resulting correlation coefficient between these variables, however, is −.2 in chemicals, .1 in drugs, and .3 in petroleum. These correlations, none of which is significantly positive at the 5 per cent level, do not support the

[12] The fifteenth annual McGraw-Hill *Survey of Business* for 1962 indicated that R & D planned by petroleum firms for that year was 42 per cent process oriented and only 6 per cent so in the chemical and allied products industries. In addition, the 1960 survey showed that new-product sales amounted to 16 per cent of total sales in the latter industry, while constituting only 2 per cent of total sales in the petroleum industry.

[13] The crucial factor here is the relation of in-house patent attorneys to those hired from outside the firm. No statistics are available at present on the latter variable. The use of in-house attorneys by the firms in our sample was, however, quite extensive—almost all firms had at least one attorney, and most had several. In addition, the number of patent attorneys was well correlated with the number of patents ($r = .7$).

hypothesis that more research-intensive firms tend to patent a greater proportion of patentable inventions. Although this is admittedly a rather slim reed of evidence, it is all that is currently available. However, since there is no strong a priori case for any kind of correlation, it may be tentatively accepted as support for the position that no systematic relations exist between these variables.

Finally, in order to investigate other possible factors affecting R & D which are omitted from the present model, a few variables that have been used with success in explaining investment in fixed capital were added to equation (1).[14] In particular, the relevance of the traditional accelerator mechanism to R & D was investigated by including the first differences of sales in a given period (deflated by sales) as an additional explanatory variables of research intensity. While the normal rationale underlying the accelerator does not hold directly for R & D, a relation may still exist if expectations about future business conditions are strongly influenced by current changes in sales.[15] However, the results do not indicate that this effect is important for R & D expenditures in the present industrial samples. When the sales difference term is added to equation (1), the estimate of the regression coefficient is quite insignificant and alternates in sign among the three industries. Specification of the accelerator with other time lags also yielded insignificant regression estimates. The fact that R & D is essentially an activity directed to the discovery and development of new products and processes with long periods until payoff may account for this apparent insensitivity to current sales changes.

III. RESEARCH INTENSITY AND FIRM SIZE

All of the independent variables used in the above model—research productivity, the degree of internal liquidity, and diversifica-

tion—have been cited in the literature as firm attributes positively associated with large size. It has been argued, therefore, that the large firms in a given industry will be more research-intensive than their smaller competitors, and vigorous government antitrust activity may have a harmful effect on technological progress. As noted above, there have been several recent investigations of this form of the Schumpeterian hypothesis, but the results have been quite mixed in nature. A study by Mansfield (1964, pp. 333–37), for example, found a significantly positive relation between research intensity and firm size in chemicals, whereas the drug and petroleum industries exhibited significantly negative ones. Since the variables supposedly underlying the Schumpeterian hypothesis yielded very good fits of research intensity in the chemical and drug industries —and yet these two industries apparently exhibit quite different structural relationships between research intensity and firm size— it is worth investigating the potential source of these differences.

First of all, in order to investigate the Schumpeterian hypothesis for the particular industrial samples under study, the following regression is estimated:

$$\frac{R_{i\,t}}{S_{i,t}} = \frac{a_0}{S_{i,t}} + a_1 + a_2 S_{i,t}, \qquad (2)$$

which in non-ratio form is the quadratic:

$$R_{i,t} = a_0 + a_1 S_{i,t} + a_2 S_{i,t}^2. \qquad (3)$$

A quadratic estimated in the above fashion should indicate whether there is any tendency for research intensity to increase or diminish

---

[14] In addition to the accelerator term discussed in the text, some variables relating to external conditions in financial markets and to the financial position of the firm (that is, the interest rate, the size of the firm's external debt, and the debt-equity ratio) were also included, but these all proved to be very insignificant.

[15] There is some question as to the expected sign of this relationship. If firms undertake investments in R & D on the basis of optimistic expectations and vice versa, a positive sign would or could be anticipated. It has been postulated by Hall (1964, p. 9), however, that firms will turn to R & D as a principal strategy for reversing poor sales performance, and a negative sign would then be expected.

TABLE 2[a] A. Estimation of Regression Equation $R_t/S_t = (1/S_t)(a_0 + a_1 S_t + a_2 S_t^2)$ for Pooled Time-Series Cross-Sections of Firms in the Chemical and Drug Industries over the Period 1959–62

Industry	a_0	a_1	a_2	R^2	F
Chemicals . . .	0.04	0.03*	0.9×10^{-5}*	.28	22.22
	(0.03)	(0.02)	(0.2×10^{-5})		
Drugs	−6.21*	0.17*	-0.4×10^{-3}*	.40	19.35
	(1.29)	(0.02)	(0.1×10^{-3})		

B. Estimation of the Regression Equation $R_{i,t}/S_{i,t} = a_0/S_{i,t} + a_1 + a_2 S_{i,t} + a_3(I_{i,t-1}/S_{i,t}) + a_4 D_i$ for Same Samples

Industry	a_0	a_1	a_2	a_3	a_4	R^2	F
Chemicals . . .	0.05	0.009	0.006×10^{-7}	0.09*	0.020*	.50	13.81
	(0.04)	(0.005)	(0.28×10^{-7})	(0.03)	(0.006)		
Drugs	−2.18	0.01	-0.14×10^{-3}	0.45*	0.44*	.72	22.07
	(1.46)	(0.03)	(0.09×10^{-3})	(0.13)	(0.10)		

[a] See footnotes to Table 1.

significantly as size increases through the behavior of the a_2 coefficient. The regression estimates of equation (2) for the chemical and drug industries are presented in the top of Table 2.[16] While a_1 is positive and statistically significant as expected in both cases, the estimate of a_2 is significantly positive for chemicals and significantly negative for drugs.[17] A plot of these estimated relations is given in Figure 1. It indicates that, for the drug industry, research intensity initially increases with firm size but is characterized by a decreasing relation for most of the relevant range. For the chemical industry, the

[16] The petroleum industry could also be included here, but it is omitted because the independent variables of equation (1) explained only one-third of the total variance for that industry. If one repeats the procedures described in this section for it, however, the interpretation of the results are consistent with those presented for chemicals and drugs. For the details, see Grabowski (1966, pp. 75–83).

[17] It may be noted that while the R^2's are quite modest for this regression equation, the standard errors of estimate indicate quite good fits to the data. This, of course, is because, in the ratio form of estimating equation (3), much of the explanatory power now comes from the intercept term a_1 which affects the goodness of fit of equation (2) but not the R^2; that is, the estimates of equation (2) explain a very large portion of the variation in absolute R & D expenditures (due to the high explanatory power of the a_1 term) but only a moderate amount of the variation in the research intensity of firms.

FIG. 1 Estimated quadratic regression equation of R & D on sales for chemical and drug firms. The units of sales have been changed so that firms in the sample cannot be identified. The sales of the largest firms in each sample are represented in the new units by 100, and the smallest firms in each sample are between 1 and 10.

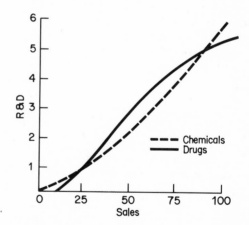

estimated relation indicates that research intensity increases steadily throughout. Thus, the results of testing the Schumpeterian hypothesis on these samples show quite different behavior in the two industries. This is in essential agreement with Mansfield[18] and

[18] Mansfield's estimates (1964, pp. 333–34) were based on a logarithmic model (log R & D regressed on log sales) for pooled time-series cross-sectional data

others investigating this question using different firm samples and time periods.[19]

Given these results, let us now turn to an examination of the relation of size to the three research determinant variables used in equation (1). In Table 3, the simple corre-

TABLE 3

Simple Correlation of Size and Variables P_i, D_i, and $(I_{i,t-1}/S_{i,t})$ for the Chemical and Drug Industries

Industry	P_i	D_i	$(I_{i,t-1}/S_{i,t})$
Chemicals . . .	−0.2	0.8**	0.5**
Drugs	0.3*	0.2	−0.4**

* Significant at .05 level.
** Significant at .01 level.

lations between size as measured by sales and our technological, diversification, and availability of funds variables (P_i, D_i, $[I_{i,t-1}/S_{i,t}]$) are presented. First, it may be noted that, of the three variables, the patent variable is the least size-correlated and varies oppositely to the relationship between firm size and research intensity in the two industries. The absence of a significant correlation in this variable is particularly important for the policy questions at stake here. Of all the arguments put forth by the proponents of corporate bigness, the one maintaining large firms have higher research productivity is potentially the most significant. However, the results of Table 3 clearly do not offer

any real support for this position.[20] With regard to the other two determinants, the internally generated funds and diversification variables are significantly positive in the chemical industry, which exhibited a positive structural relation with size. However, in drugs, where the relation was negative, the internally generated funds variable is significantly negatively correlated with size, and diversification exhibits a positive but insignificant correlation coefficient. Thus, the results suggest that the difference in the observed relation between research intensity and firm size in the two industries is due primarily to the flow of funds variable and, to a lesser extent, the diversification index.

In the current analysis, it has been assumed that the significant relation between research intensity and firm size follows from the size behavior of the underlying independent variables specified in the model. An alternative interpretation is that size is the relevant determinant variable and that the significance of these explanatory variables of the model is spurious, arising from their mutual correlation with size. In order to investigate this alternative hypothesis, a further regression equation was estimated. This involved adding the two significantly size-correlated variables, diversification and the measure of cash flow, to equation (2) and observing the behavior of the previously estimated coefficients between R & D and the size of the firm. As shown in the lower half of Table 2, when these two new variables are present, the a_1 and a_2 coefficients lose their statistical significance in both industries. On the other hand, the estimates associated with the two determinant variables, a_3 and a_4, are significant, as in Table 1. These results are thus consistent with the general interpre-

---

over the period 1945–59. For a review of other recent investigations of this question, see Markham (1965, p. 328–32).

[19] A qualification to the interpretation of the results obtained here and in the studies cited above arises from the fact that total firm sales is used as the independent variable rather than sales only in the particular three-digit industry for which the firm produces its principal products. Now, if it is the case that the nature of firm products in each of these industries varies significantly with size, then the above relationships may be due principally to this phenomenon rather than to any scale effects, such as those postulated above. As indicated earlier (see n. 9 above), the large firms in the drug industry do tend to expand and diversify into non-pharmaceutical areas where the opportunities for R & D applications are low. It is therefore very desirable to estimate equation (2)

using only pharmaceutical sales for each firm. Until the required data are available, however, the present approach must be used in such studies and, accordingly, is quite tentative in nature.

[20] The empirical results here would also be open to question if the propensity to patent were significantly correlated with firm size. By similar procedures to those discussed in the previous section, this was not indicated to be the case. See also discussion of this issue in Scherer (1965a, p. 1110–13).

tation of the regression estimates presented in this paper and not with the alternative hypothesis advanced above.

In summary, the analysis here indicates that there is no basis for the presumption that larger firms will necessarily possess the characteristics that promote a high degree of research intensity. Therefore, it is not surprising that tests of the Schumpeterian hypothesis have yielded such diverse results across industries. While it must be kept in mind that the results here only concern the firms in the *Fortune 500* listings, it is also true that this range of firms is most relevant from the standpoint of antitrust policy.

IV. SUMMARY AND CONCLUSIONS

The main conclusion that emerges from the analysis is that interfirm differences in technology, product diversification, and availability of funds are all significant in explaining firm research intensity. The model presented here fits the two more research-oriented industries, chemicals and drugs, much better than petroleum refining. From a policy standpoint, these results indicate that the level of R & D expenditures will be sensitive to the broad class of government policy devices that affect the financial incentives confronting the firm. In particular, fiscal devices and other policy measures can be expected to influence the level of R & D expenditures through both profitability and flow of funds effects. Government policy actions directed toward stimulating growth should, therefore, be concerned with both of these effects if efficient programs are to be devised.

The major limitations of the present study arise from the substantial conceptual and empirical difficulties in measuring items such as R & D activity and its outputs. Considerable effort was therefore expended to obtain the best set of data that are currently available. While the results must be viewed as tentative, particularly because the total number of firms is small, they are nevertheless internally consistent and in general agreement with some of the past work in this area. They should, therefore, be of interest to economists and policy makers concerned with the economics of R & D.

REFERENCES

EISNER, ROBERT, AND STROTZ, ROBERT H. "Determinants of Business Investment," in Commission on Money and Credit, *Impacts of Monetary Policy*. Englewood Cliffs, N.J.: Prentice-Hall Inc., 1963.

GRABOWSKI, HENRY. "The Determinants and Effects of Industrial Research and Development." Ph.D. dissertation, Princeton Univ., 1967.

HALL, MARSHALL. "The Determinants of Investment Variation in Research and Development," *IEEE Transactions on Engineering Management*, EM-11 (March, 1964), pp. 8–15.

HAMBERG, DANIEL. "Size of Firm, Oligopoly, and Research," *Canadian J. Econ. and Polit. Sci.*, XXX (February, 1964), 62–75.

KUH, EDWIN, AND MEYER, JOHN R. "Correlation and Regression Estimates When Data are Ratios, *Econometrica*, XXIII (October, 1955), 400–416.

KUZNETS, SIMON. "Inventive Activity: Problems of Definition and Measurement," in National Bureau of Economic Research, *The Rate and Direction of Inventive Activity*. Princeton, N.J.: Princeton Univ. Press, 1962.

MANSFIELD, EDWIN. "Industrial Research Expenditures: Determinants, Prospects and Relation to Firm Size and Inventive Output," *J.P.E.*, LXXII (August, 1964), 319–40.

MARKHAM, JESSE W. "Market Structure, Business Conduct and Innovation," *A.E.R.*, LV (May, 1965), 323–32.

MUELLER, DENNIS C. "The Firm Decision Process: An Econometric Investigation," *Q.J.E.*, LXXXI (February, 1967), 58–87.

National Science Foundation. *Science and Engineering in American Industry*. Washington: Nat. Sci. Found., 1956.

———. *Research and Development in Industry, 1961*. Washington: Nat. Sci. Found., 1964.

NELSON, RICHARD R. "The Simple Economics of Basic Scientific Research," *J.P.E.*, LXVII (June, 1959), 297–306.

SANDERS, BARKEV S. "Some Difficulties in Measuring Inventive Activity," in National Bureau of Economic Research, *The Rate and Direction of Inventive Activity*. Princeton, N.J.: Princeton Univ. Press, 1962.

SCHERER, F. M. "Firm Size, Market Structure, Opportunity, and the Output of Patented Inventions," *A.E.R.*, LV (December, 1965), 1097–1125. (*a*)

———. "Size of Firm, Oligopoly, and Research: A Comment," *Canadian J. Econ. and Polit. Sci.*, XXXI (May, 1965) 256–66. (*b*)

16

The R & D Factor in International Trade and International Investment of United States Industries

WILLIAM GRUBER, DILEEP MEHTA, AND RAYMOND VERNON*

In the last ten or fifteen years, the field of international trade theory has been in continuous ferment.[1] The received doctrine drawn from the mainstream of Smith-Ricardo-Mill-Marshall- Heckscher-Ohlin has been re-examined from many different angles. Sometimes, there have been strongly revisionist reactions, such as those encountered in the economic development areas.[2] In other contexts, the emphasis has been mainly on the further testing and refinement of the doctrine of comparative advantage and the role of factor endowments.

Much of the discussion of U.S. trade performance in recent years has taken for granted the main premises of classical and neoclassical theory. A considerable part of the debate over the interpretation of the Leontief paradox and much of the discussion of the implications of other recent empirical work have concentrated on questions of national factor endowments, or the response of national production functions to different

factor prices, or other issues readily compatible with the classical theoretical structure. Leontief, for instance, was inclined to "explain" his familiar paradox by asserting that skilled labor may be relatively cheap in the U.S. economy.

Nonetheless, one can also detect an echo of the discontent voiced so effectively by Williams in 1929, a discontent based on the view that classical doctrine is not structured to deal efficiently with the trade implications of a number of forces that may be of major consequence in any descriptive and analytical work (see Hoffmeyer, 1958; MacDougall, 1957; Linder, 1961; Kindleberger, 1962). For the most part, the literature of dissent seems to have sprung out of efforts to explain the foreign trade patterns of the United States, especially the country's exports of

From Journal of Political Economy (*February 1967*), *pp. 20–37, by William Gruber, Dileep Mehta, and Raymond Vernon; publisher, The University of Chicago Press. Reprinted with permission of author and publisher.*

* [William Gruber teaches at Massachusetts Institute of Technology, Dileep Mehta at Columbia University, and Raymond Vernon at Harvard University.]

Gruber's contribution to this work was financed by a grant from the M.I.T. Center for Space Research funded by NASA, while the work of Mehta and Vernon was financed by a grant from the Ford Foundation to the Harvard Business School for the study of multinational enterprise and nation states. Calculations were done at the M.I.T. Computation Center.

[1] For authoritative summaries, see J. Bhagwati (1964) and J. Chipman (1965*a*, 1965*b*).

[2] This school is epitomized by the writings of Economic Commission for Latin America (see Baer, 1962).

manufactured goods. U.S. labor, it has been observed, is higher priced than labor abroad, to an extent which greatly exceeds any productivity differences (Kreinin, 1965). To be sure, U.S. capital is cheaper and less tightly rationed. But the effective interest rate for major industrial borrowers only differs by a few percentage points among the advanced countries. This difference hardly seems enough to explain the strength and persistence of U.S. exports in manufactured products.

From capital and labor cost considerations, therefore, attention has turned to questions of innovation, of scale, of leads and lags (Posner, 1961; Freeman, 1963, 1965; Hirsch, 1965; Hufbauer, 1965; Wells, 1966). Approaches of this sort have tended to stress the possibility that the United States may base its strength in the export of manufactured goods upon monopoly advantages, stemming in the first instance out of a strong propensity to develop new products or new cost-saving processes. This propensity has usually been credited either to the demand conditions that confront the American entrepreneur or to the scale and structure of enterprise in U.S. markets. In any case, the propensity has given American producers a temporary advantage which has been protected for a time either by patents or by secrecy. Eventually, the monopoly advantage has been eroded; but by that time, the U.S. producers have seized the advantage in other products.

Of late, the tendency has been to search for hypotheses which "explain" not only the apparent strength in U.S. exports of manufactured products but also the apparent propensity of U.S. producers of those very products to set up manufacturing facilities abroad (see, for example, Polk, Meister, and Veit, 1966; Vernon, 1966). This line of speculation takes off from the observation that entrepreneurs in the United States are surrounded by a structure of domestic demand for producer and consumer goods that is in some respects a forerunner of what will later be found in other countries. Labor is costly in relation to its productivity, while capital is comparatively plentiful, facts which influence the nature of the demand for pro-

ducer goods. And per capita incomes are high by international standards, a fact which creates unique consumption patterns. This means that entrepreneurs in the United States are likely to be willing to gamble on the innovation of labor-saving and affluent-consumer products at an earlier point in time than their overseas competitors.

The hypotheses go on to project certain characteristic sequences in the foreign trade of products that have been innovated in the United States. According to the assumption, although the new products that satisfy high-income or labor-substituting wants may have their earliest and largest markets in the United States, some demand for them is generally assumed to exist elsewhere. And in the course of time, that demand will normally grow. For a time, then, the United States will have an oligopoly position in supplying foreign markets. And this oligopoly position will be strongest with respect to the products of those U.S. industries which have been making the largest research and development effort.

According to the hypotheses of this genre, overseas investment eventually comes into the picture partly because the large-scale marketing of technically sophisticated products demands the existence of local facilities and partly because the protection of the oligopoly position of the U.S. producer eventually requires such investment. The threat of competition in foreign markets may come from local sources or from other outside producers, as the original technology-based oligopoly position of the U.S. producer in any given product begins to be eroded. At this point, with profits on exports being threatened, the U.S. company may see a high prospective marginal yield in an investment in local facilities, provided such facilities will help to buttress its existing market position.

A chain of hypotheses as complex as these needs extensive testing before it can gain much in credibility. This brief paper is much less than an adequate test of the chain. But it does contribute modestly to the credibility of the chain for some industries. At the same time, however, the data suggest that simple univariate explanations of the complex causal chain may be dangerous; that while the relevant explanations may involve "research" or "technology" or similar factors in one form or another, the causal role played by such factors may well be rather different from one industry to another.

RESEARCH AND TRADE[3]

All roads lead to a link between export performance and R & D. Whether one accepts the cheap-skilled-labor hypothesis of Leontief or the oligopoly hypotheses in the tradition of Williams, one expects to see a link between exports and research effort. Table 1 provides a simple set of data typical of the evidence which relates research effort by U.S. industry to U.S. trade performance in 1962. The positive correlation between the "research effort" measures, R_1 and R_2, and the "export performance" measures, E_1 and E_2, is evident to the eye. The five industries with the greatest "research effort" are also the five industries with the most favorable trade position.[4] When the five industries with the highest research effort are separated off from the other fourteen industries, it begins to grow clear that the export strength of U.S. industries is centered in the group of five; in fact, the fourteen remaining industries exhibit a net import

rather than a net export balance for the year 1962.

In speaking of "export strength," however, one has to exhibit a certain caution. The phrase may have many different meanings, and a word or two about the measures contained in Table 1 will be helpful to clarify some of the concepts involved.

Measure E_1, a ratio of exports to total sales in each industry, can hardly be thought of as a measure of U.S. comparative advantage for the industry. Such a measure, after all, is not only a function of the competitive position of U.S. industry; it also reflects, *inter alia*, the structure of demand overseas as compared with the United States, as well as the effects of transport and tariff frictions on international trade.

Measure E_2—namely, the excess of exports over imports taken as a percentage of sales— goes a little way in the direction of allowing for the effects of demand differences and trading frictions. We observed earlier that differences in demand, rather than in competitive position, might account for a low level of U.S. exports at an earlier stage in a product's development; but there is a respectable body of opinion for the view that in products for which U.S. demand differs considerably from demand in foreign markets, the risk of heavy imports from abroad is not very great.[5] Where demand differences were holding down exports, therefore, they might also be expected to hold down imports. The same is true of transport frictions; if these were responsible for a poor export showing, it would not be utterly unreasonable to suppose that the same forces might be discouraging imports.

It is slightly reassuring to observe, therefore, that both measures of export performance act in a remarkably parallel fashion, generally reflecting a strong export position for research-oriented industries and a weak export position for industries without large research inputs. To be sure, the parallelism cannot be said to prove too much; the so-called correction provided by the second

---

[3] Attempts to quantify the relationship between research and trade have begun to appear in the literature. The French have coined the term "technological balance of payments," and some quantitative measures of this concept are presented in Freeman and Young (1965, pp. 51–55, 74). The relationship between the employment of scientists and engineers and trade position has been tested by Keesing (1966). Keesing's findings in that paper and in some unpublished work parallel and agree with some of the findings in the first section of this paper.

[4] The Spearman rank coefficient for the association between R_1 and E_1, as those terms are defined in Table 1, is $+0.69$; between R_1 and E_2, is $+0.79$; between R_2 and E_1, $+0.74$; and between R_2 and E_2, $+0.69$. All coefficients are significant at the 1 per cent level. Pearson least-squares coefficients give similar results. In these correlation measures and in others presented hereafter, twenty-two sets of paired observations, rather than nineteen, are used, since each of the three-digit industries shown in Tables 1 and 2 provides the basis for a separate observation.

[5] Characteristic of this view is the case made in Linder (1961).

TABLE 1   Research Effort and World Trade Performance by United States Industries, 1962

Industry Name* and SIC Number	Research Effort		Export Performance	
	Total R & D Expenditures as Percentage of Sales (R_1)	Scientists and Engineers in R & D as a Percentage of Total Employment (R_2)	Exports as Percentage of Sales (E_1)	Excess of Exports over Imports, as Percentage of Sales (E_2)
Transportation (37)	10.0	3.4	5.5	4.1
Aircraft (372)	27.2	6.9	8.4	7.6
Transportation (other than aircraft)	2.8	1.0	4.2	2.6
Electrical machinery (36)	7.3	3.6	4.1	2.9
Instruments (38)	7.1	3.4	6.7	3.2
Chemicals (28)	3.9	4.1	6.2	4.5
Drugs (283)	4.4	6.6	6.0	4.8
Chemicals (other than drugs)	3.8	3.7	6.2	4.4
Machines (non-electrical) (35)	3.2	1.4	13.3	11.4
Rubber and plastic (30)	1.4	0.5	2.0	1.3
Stone, clay, and glass (32)	1.1	†	1.9	− 0.2
Petroleum and coal (29)	0.9	1.8	1.2	− 0.8
Fabricated metal (34)	0.8	0.4	2.1	0.7
Primary metal (33)	0.6	0.5	3.1	− 1.8
Nonferrous metal (333)	0.8	0.5	4.2	− 4.7
Ferrous metal	0.5	0.4	2.5	− 0.2
Leather (31)	0.6	0.1	1.7	− 3.4
Printing and publishing (27)	0.6	0.2	1.7	1.1
Tobacco (21)	0.3	0.2	2.2	2.1
Food (20)	0.2	0.3	0.9	− 1.2
Textile (22)	0.2	0.3	3.4	− 1.1
Furniture and fixtures (25)	0.1	0.2	0.7	†
Lumber and wood (24)	0.1	†	2.0	− 6.2
Paper (26)	0.1	0.3	2.1	− 3.5
Apparel (23)	0.1	†	0.7	− 2.1
All 19 industries:	2.0	1.1	3.2	0.6
5 industries with highest research effort	6.3	3.2	7.2	5.2
14 other industries	0.5	0.4	1.8	− 1.1

* Industries arranged in descending order of research effort, defined by R & D expenditures as a percentage of sales.

† Less than 0.05 per cent.

Source: See Statistical Appendix.

measure need not wipe out all biases of the sort mentioned earlier, if they exist. But we propose to show, as the analysis progresses, that the simple ratio of exports to sales is not wholly misleading as a measure of international competitive strength.

There is still another kind of problem which data of the sort presented in Table 1 may well involve. Each unit of observation in Table 1 is an "industry," arbitrarily defined. Each such "industry" can be proliferated into two or more, by schism. Has the arbitrary grouping used in Table 1 provided an impression of the export importance of the research-oriented industries which distorts the absolute contribution of these industries to the U.S. economy? The data in Table 2 lay that fear to rest. The figures show that the five industries with the strongest research effort accounted for 72.0 per cent of the nation's exports of manufactured goods, though they were responsible for only 39.1 per cent of the nation's total sales of such goods. The same five industries were also

TABLE 2   Distribution of Research Effort, Sales, and Exports Among United States Industries, 1962

Industry Name* and SIC Number	Total R & D Expenditures	Company-financed R & D Expenditures	Scientists and Engineers in R & D	Sales	Exports
	Percentage Distribution				
Transportation (37)	45.6	24.1	25.3	13.5	19.7
Aircraft (372)	36.7	9.3	21.1	3.7	8.9
Transportation (other than aircraft)	9.0	14.7	4.2	9.5	10.8
Electrical machinery (36)	21.1	17.7	27.1	8.5	9.4
Instruments (38)	4.0	4.9	5.9	1.6	3.0
Chemicals (28)	10.5	18.6	16.7	7.9	13.0
Drugs (283)	1.8	3.9	3.5	1.2	1.9
Chemicals (other than drugs)	8.7	14.7	13.2	6.7	11.1
Machines (non-electrical) (35)	8.2	12.9	10.3	7.6	26.9
Rubber and plastic (30)	1.2	2.1	1.0	2.5	1.4
Stone, clay, and glass (32)	1.0	2.0	1.1	2.7	1.4
Petroleum and coal (29)	2.7	5.7	1.7	8.9	2.8
Fabricated metal (34)	1.3	2.4	2.2	5.1	2.9
Primary metal (33)	1.5	3.3	2.5	7.4	6.1
Nonferrous metal (333)	0.6	1.4	1.0	2.5	2.8
Ferrous metal	0.9	1.9	1.6	4.8	3.3
Leather (31)	0.2	0.4	0.2	1.2	0.5
Printing and publishing (27)	0.5	0.9	0.3	2.5	1.1
Tobacco (21)	0.1	0.2	0.1	1.4	0.8
Food (20)	1.1	2.4	2.7	15.5	3.9
Textile (22)	0.2	0.5	1.4	3.8	3.5
Furniture and fixtures (25)	†	0.1	0.3	0.3	0.2
Lumber and wood (24)	†	0.1	†	1.7	0.9
Paper (26)	0.6	1.3	1.0	3.6	2.0
Apparel (23)	†	0.1	0.2	3.4	0.6
All 19 industries:	100.0	100.0	100.0	100.0	100.0
5 industries with highest research effort	89.4	78.2	85.3	39.1	72.0
14 other industries	10.6	21.8	14.7	60.9	28.0

* Industries arranged in descending order of research effort, defined by R & D expenditures as a percentage of sales.

† Less than 0.05 per cent.

Source: See Statistical Appendix.

responsible for 89.4 per cent of the nation's total R & D expenditures and 74.6 per cent of the company-financed R & D expenditures. The five industries concerned, therefore, represent both the heart of U.S. export strength in manufactured products and the heart of its industrial research effort.

In groping for some credible measure of comparative advantage, however, it is not necessary to stop with the measures presented in Tables 1 and 2. Still another set of meas-

ures can be devised which relates U.S. industry export performance to the export performance of the same industry localized in prospective competitor countries. In this case, the "normalizing" variable becomes the total industry exports of all the countries concerned, rather than the total shipments of U.S. industry. Neither normalizer is wholly without latent error as a measure of comparative advantage. But the use of another approach offers an opportunity to expose any lurking anomalies and to generate more information about the underlying forces.

The results of the new approach are presented in Table 3. In general, the figures in the table tend to add a little more credence to the view that the export performance measures used in earlier tables are a function of the international competitive strength of the U.S. industries they represent.

The extreme left-hand column of Spearman coefficients in Table 3 presents measures of correlation between (1) the indicated measures of each U.S. industry's research effort and (2) U.S. exports in each industry taken as a percentage of the exports of the OECD countries in the industry.[6] The resulting relationships are practically indistinguishable from the rank correlations between R & D and export performance calculated from the data in Table 1.

In the next two columns of Table 3, however, almost all these relationships fall apart. In these columns, U.S. exports to the world are "normalized" by calculating them respectively as a ratio to (1) United Kingdom world exports and (2) German world exports. The result is that, suddenly, almost all the statistically significant relationships disappear. What this means, of course, is that the United Kingdom and the German export profiles must be very much like that of the United States. Wherever the United States has a large volume of exports, the United Kingdom and Germany also have a large volume of exports.

Does this mean that all our prior indications of the causes of U.S. export strength were misleading? Not at all. It means rather that the United Kingdom and Germany, also being at the top of the advanced country list with relatively high incomes and a relatively heavy stress on industrial innovation and product development, derive their export strength from roughly the same characteris-

tics as those that govern U.S. export performance. Their export performance differs from that of the other OECD countries in the same general way that U.S. export performance differs from that of the OECD countries.

The extreme right-hand column of Table 3 offers some parallel data for U.S. exports in relation to those of France. These data are more tantalizing than they are revealing. When French exports to the world are used as the normalizer, as the table shows, the significant correlations return; French exports evidently have a profile much more nearly corresponding to the less developed of the OECD countries than to those of the United Kingdom and Germany.

The common view of French industry does paint a picture of an institution that is different in structure, in outlook, and in innovational habits than the industry of the United States, the United Kingdom, and Germany. Table 4 indicates that French industrial research is not on a smaller scale, relatively speaking, than that of Germany. The research tends to be controlled, however, to a greater degree by government institutions which are said to have less concern with industrial applications. Furthermore, French industry's ingenuity, as illustrated by the automobile producers, is said to be devoted to satisfying highly differentiated, highly individual tastes. Up to a point, such innovation might have the same export possibilities as the differentiated products of the United States, the United Kingdom, and Germany. Pushed very far, however, stress on this kind of output has the effect of encouraging an industrial structure which is not highly concentrated, hence a structure which reflects few scale economies in either production or (more importantly, in this context) in research, servicing, or sales. The sale of products for the overseas markets, especially products that have high technical inputs, cannot easily be achieved by an industry of small firms whose innovational stress borders on artistry. The U.S. model of the highly concentrated mass innovator seems more closely to approximate the effective pattern for the successful exporter.

[6] The ratio of U.S. exports to the sum of the exports of a group of nations has been called, "trade competitive power" by Donald Keesing. He found that there was a rank correlation of $+0.60$ between (1) "trade competitive power" and (2) scientists and engineers as a percentage of total employment for a sample of thirty-five non-natural-resource processing industries (Keesing, 1966, p. 256).

TABLE 3 World Exports of U.S. Industries Related to World Exports of OECD Countries, 1962 (Spearman Coefficient of Rank Correlation for Indicated Cell)

Industry Characteristics	U.S. World Exports in 1962 as a Percentage of World Exports of			
	OECD Countries* (1)	United Kingdom (2)	West Germany (3)	France (4)
Total R & D expenditures as a percentage of sales, 1962	+0.68	+0.28†	+0.08†	+0.60
Scientists and engineers in R & D as a percentage of total employment, 1962	+0.64	+0.37	+0.24†	+0.59

   * Although Japan did not join the OECD until after 1962, Japan is included in the data.
   † These coefficients are not significant at the 5 per cent probability level. All other coefficients in the table are significant at that level or at a lower probability level.
Source: See Statistical Appendix.

TABLE 4 Characteristics of R & D Activity in United States, United Kingdom, West Germany, and France, 1962

	United States	United Kingdom	West Germany	France
Number of scientists and engineers in R & D ('000's full-time equivalents)	435.6	50.7	40.1	28.0
R & D personnel as a percentage of working population	1.0	0.6	0.4	0.4
R & D expenditure (billions of U.S. dollars)*	17.5	1.8	1.1	1.1
R & D as a percentage of GNP*	3.1	2.2	1.3	1.5
R & D expenditures performed in the business sector as a percentage of total national R & D expenditures	71.0	63.0	61.0	48.0

   * No adjustment was made for differences in relative factor prices.
Source: Freeman and Young (1965, pp. 71–72).

We now come to another group of measures, slightly different in approach, which appear to offer some added evidence of the sources of U.S. export strength. In Tables 1, 2, and 3, it should be remembered, we were concerned with analyzing and comparing the world exports of each U.S. industry, expressing those exports by various relative measures. Table 5 disaggregates the data into U.S. trade with Europe and U.S. trade with non-Europe. It will be observed that in every case there is a better relationship between research intensity and trade with non-Europe than there is in trade with Europe. In fact, as far as trade with Europe is concerned, there is no significant relationship between (1) R & D as a percentage of sales and (2)

trade advantage as measured by the excess of exports over imports as a percentage of sales.

The U.S. margin of competitive strength in the research-intensive industries is challenged by Europe, therefore, more effectively than by other countries. This is almost self-evident and has already been suggested by the data on the United Kingdom and German trade patterns. We propose shortly to show that part of the result was due, beyond much doubt, to the patterns of U.S. industry's investments in overseas productive facilities. But before we turn to that phase of the analysis, it will be useful to pin down more firmly what is meant by the research-intensive industries.

TABLE 5   Research Effort and Trade Performance with Europe and Non-Europe by United States Industries, 1962 (Spearman Coefficient of Rank Correlation for Indicated Cell)

Industry Characteristics	Trade of U.S. Industries with Europe		Trade of U.S. Industries with Non-Europe	
	Exports as a Percentage of Sales	Excess of Exports over Imports as a Percentage of Sales	Exports as a Percentage of Sales	Excess of Exports over Imports as a Percentage of Sales
Total R & D expenditures as a percentage of sales	+0.63	+0.35*	+0.73	+0.78
Scientists and engineers in R & D as a percentage of total industry employment	+0.65	+0.48	+0.74	+0.67

* Not statistically significant at the .05 level. All other coefficients are significant at that level or lower.

CHARACTERISTICS OF RESEARCH-INTENSIVE INDUSTRIES

So far the presentation has referred to research-intensive and research-oriented industries, as if a research orientation were synonymous with new-product orientation, and as if new-product orientation were the most likely characteristic of those industries to be linked with their export strength. However, a number of different industry characteristics are related to research effort, and some of these characteristics may provide equally plausible explanations of export performance. This proves to be an especially important point because of the message projected by the data in Table 6.

That table begins by reassuring us in one respect. It indicates that the industries with the strongest research effort are also those with the strongest new-product orientation. But the table goes on to demonstrate that a high research and development effort in an industry is closely correlated with various other characteristics. The table demonstrates that industries with a heavy complement of scientists and engineers in research and development also have a heavy complement of scientists and engineers in production, as well as in sales. To a considerable extent, therefore, high technical effort at any stage of the design-production-marketing process is associated with high technical effort at all the other stages.

The measures in Table 6 tell us more,

however. They indicate that the intensity of the research and development effort is greatest in industries in which the degree of employment concentration is high, and in industries in which large firms are particularly dominant.

So far, the statistical picture is familiar enough.[7] Where the statistics begin to break some new ground is in their indication that the large-scale high-concentration pattern is not associated with high capital intensity. To be sure, high indirect labor costs *are* positively correlated with high research effort; and high indirect labor costs could well be consistent with high capital intensity. But the picture of high capital intensity is virtually dispelled by the two final measures in Table 6. Here, two fairly sensitive measures of capital intensity fail to display any systematic relation with high research effort.[8]

These findings, when drawn together, paint a fairly consistent picture. They suggest the existence of national markets in which economies of large scale and barriers to entry stem from the requirements of successful product innovation and successful marketing,

[7] Compare, for instance, the findings in Worley (1962).

[8] This result is consistent with analyses done by George E. Delehanty, in which he finds that the ratio of non-production employment to production employment in U.S. industries is more closely correlated with the degree to which scientists and engineers are in the work force of the industry than with the capital:labor ratio of the industry (see Delehanty, 1962).

TABLE 6 Relationship Between Measures of Intensity of Research Effort and Other Characteristics in United States Industries*

Industry Characteristics	Total R & D Expenditures in Industry as Percentage of Industry Sales, 1962	Company-financed R & D Expenditures as Percentage of Industry Sales, 1962	Scientists and Engineers in R & D as Percentage of Total Industry Employment, 1962	5 Most Research-intensive Industries	14 Other Industries
Research and technology:					
Percentage of companies indicating majority of R & D efforts for new products, 1958	+0.63	+0.64	+0.51	†	†
Scientists and engineers in R & D as percentage of total industry employment, 1962	+0.81	+0.82	+1.00	3.2%	0.4%
Scientists and engineers in production as percentage of total industry employment, 1962	+0.76	+0.79	+0.92	2.1	0.8
Scientists and engineers in sales as percentage of total industry employment, 1962	+0.84	+0.87	+0.86	0.9	0.1
Scale and concentration:					
Index of employment concentration, 1958‡	+0.66	+0.66	+0.59	47.0	21.1
Index of asset scale, 1961§	+0.48	+0.47	+0.60	67.1	46.1
Index of sales scale, 1961‖	+0.58	+0.57	+0.70	35.0	21.1
Cost characteristics:					
Indirect labor costs as percentage of value added, 1957	+0.64	+0.63	+0.68	24.7	17.2
Depreciation expenses as percentage of value added, 1957	−0.11♯	−0.08♯	+0.03♯	4.3	5.3
Net fixed assets as percentage of value added, 1957	−0.09♯	−0.03♯	+0.09♯	31.0	41.0

* The number of industries for which relationships in the table could be calculated was not the same throughout. In some cases data were not available for some industries.

† Not available.

‡ The index, calculated for each SIC 2-digit industry, consists of a ratio whose numerator is employment in constituent SIC 4-digit industries in which the largest 8 firms accounted for 60 per cent or more of 2-digit total employment, and whose denominator was total employment in the 2-digit industry.

§ The index, calculated for each SIC 2-digit industry, consists of a ratio whose numerator is the assets of firms with $50 million or more in assets, and whose denominator is total assets in the industry.

‖ The index, calculated for each SIC 2-digit industry, consists of a ratio whose numerator is sales in firms with one-half billion dollars or more in sales, and whose denominator is total sales in the industry.

♯ These coefficients are not significant at the 5 per cent probability level. All other coefficients in the table are significant at that level or at a lower probability level.

Source: See Statistical Appendix.

rather than from capital intensity.[9] The

[9] This, of course, is hardly a new thought. See Bain (1956). See also C. Freeman's observations about the "reasons for the United States lead" in electronics (Freeman, 1965, p. 51).

forces that determine the propensity to gamble on product innovation are no doubt extraordinarily complex and lend themselves only grudgingly to easy generalization. A firm that can spread its research risks over a large number of efforts will have a more predictable payout in any finite period than one which does not have the resources for a large number of tries, especially if the anticipated yield on any single effort is not systematically different for large firms than for small.

Once the new product has been invented, scale continues to play a part in success. The sale of technically complex producer goods, for instance, requires a detailed understanding of the needs of customers, a continuing sales service, readily accessible spare parts, and a high level of research activity to keep the product competitive. The act of exporting to foreign markets, therefore, represents a marketing investment which one would expect to be associated with significant scale economies.

In sum, one derives a picture of high research effort being correlated with industries that experience substantial trade surpluses. These research-intensive industries, although large and concentrated, are not systematically capital intensive. It is in these industries that the U.S. trade advantage lies.

TRADE AND INVESTMENT IN FOREIGN MANUFACTURING SUBSIDIARIES

Neither the theory of international trade nor the theory of international capital movements has much to offer in explanation of managerial decisions to invest in production facilities abroad. International trade is explained largely in comparative advantage and factor endowment terms; long-term capital movements are seen largely as a reflection of the process of equating the marginal efficiency of capital in different countries. Yet, intuitively, one is aware that the prospective foreign investor, debating whether to invest in a production facility in a foreign market, is engaged in an evaluation process which juggles a number of additional major variables.

One way of looking at the overseas direct investments of U.S. producers of manufactures is that they are the final step in a process which begins with the involvement of such producers in export trade. The export trade of the United States, according to the data presented, is heavily weighted with products that demand large scientific and technical inputs in the selling process. Products of this sort, as we noted earlier, ordinarily demand an apparatus for learning customer needs and for subsequent technical servicing and consulting. Once such an organization has been established for sales purposes, the marginal costs of setting up a facility for production may be sharply reduced; for "marginal cost" in this context should be read not solely as a direct money expenditure but also as a measure of the pain of acquiring information regarding a country, negotiating for entry in a foreign economy, altering the company's organization to accommodate the new element, and tolerating the high subjective risks involved in a novel venture. Once the marginal costs are reduced in this sense, the probability that the venture may appear economical is, of course, enhanced. Whence it follows that industries with comparatively high export sales of products involving scientific and technical aspects in their sales and servicing, *ceteris paribus*, will have a high propensity to invest in manufacturing subsidiaries in the markets they serve.

This hypothesis appears particularly plausible if additional factors are considered. The research-intensive industries tend to be highly concentrated and suggest the existence of strong oligopoly forces. It is in such industries that rule-of-thumb measures of success, such as "maintaining our share of world markets," can be expected to enter most strongly into the investment decisions. In industries with lower concentration characteristics, the individual firm presumably finds share stability a less reliable gauge of its long-run survival or profit-maximizing prospects than in industries in which the principal rivals are few in number. In the oligopoly industries, therefore, individual firms are likely to consider foreign investments as important forestalling tactics to cut off market preemption by others. And they are likely to feel obliged to counter an investment by others with an investment of their own.

TABLE 7 **Plant and Equipment Expenditures, Investment Expenditures, and Sales in the United States and Foreign Countries by United States Industries***†

	4 Research-intensive Industries (Billions of Dollars)	14 Other Industries (Billions of Dollars)	Ratio of 4 Research-intensive Industries to 14 Other Industries (Per Cent)
Plant and equipment expenditures, 1958–64:			
In U.S.	$ 32.7	$ 50.8	64.4%
In Europe, by U.S.-owned subsidiaries	4.3	1.6	266.3
In non-Europe, by U.S.-owned subsidiaries	3.9	3.0	133.4
Direct investment, 1964:‡			
In U.S.	71.7	94.9	75.6
In U.S.-owned subsidiaries in Europe	4.5	2.0	227.5
In U.S.-owned subsidiaries in non-Europe	5.2	4.9	106.0
Sales, 1962:			
In U.S.	143.4	205.7	69.7
By U.S.-owned subsidiaries in Europe	8.4	3.7	227.0
By U.S.-owned subsidiaries in non-Europe	8.7	7.3	119.3

  * Data on the petroleum industry, SIC 29, are not included because not available for all parts of the table.

  † Some of the data on the scientific instruments industry, SIC 38, are not available separately and have to be included in the "14 other industries" totals. This tends to blur slightly the otherwise sharp differences between the research-intensive industries and the other industries.

  ‡ For United States, the figures presented represent total equity interest; for the non-U.S. data, the figures are equity and debt in foreign subsidiaries owned by U.S. parents.

  Source: See Statistical Appendix.

The available figures on foreign direct investment by U.S. enterprise do nothing to undermine the credibility of these hypotheses. The figures in Table 7 indicate in various ways that the propensity for U.S. industry to build facilities or otherwise to invest abroad, when "normalized" by the U.S. investment level, is higher in the research-oriented industries than in other industries The figures on sales by U.S. subsidiaries abroad exhibit the same general characteristics as those for investment; when "normalized" by sales in the United States, sales of U.S. subsidiaries abroad are weighted heavily in favor of the research-oriented groups. The figures in the table have to be interpreted with a certain caution since investments in the non-Europe areas are heavily weighted with resource-oriented activities, such as paper and food processing. But the very limited conclusion suggested above obviously holds.

The figures in Table 8 permit slightly deeper probing of the investment patterns of U.S. industries in foreign countries. In this table, the focus is on the relationship between U.S. exports and the sales of U.S. subsidiaries located abroad. For this purpose, the sales of U.S. subsidiaries have been adjusted to exclude sales to the United States by U.S. subsidiaries abroad. The figures in the table, therefore, begin to approach a comparison between U.S. exports and foreign sales which could conceivably (but need not necessarily) be export substituting from the U.S. viewpoint.

Once again, some familiar patterns emerge. In the European area, the sales of U.S. subsidiaries are more important in relation to U.S. exports than in the non-European areas; if subsidiary sales are a substitute for U.S. exports, then the process would seem to have gone further in Europe than elsewhere. The tendency for Europe to have a higher ratio of subsidiary sales to exports than non-Europe is true both for the research-intensive and the other industries, but the research-intensive industries exhibit the tendency to a somewhat more marked degree. All this is consistent with expectations. Where scale

TABLE 8 U.S. Exports and Foreign Subsidiary Sales to Elsewhere than U.S. by U. S. Manufacturing Industries in 1962*

Industry Name† and SIC Number	U.S. Exports (in Millions of Dollars)			Sales by Foreign Subsidiaries‡ (in Millions of Dollars)			Foreign Subsidiary Sales Related to Exports (Per Cent)		
	Total	Europe	Non-Europe	Total	Europe	Non-Europe	Total	Europe	Non-Europe
Transportation (37)	$ 2,819	$ 315	$ 2,504	$ 6,590	$ 3,235	$ 3,355	233.8	1027.0	134.0
Electrical machinery (36)	1,344	273	1,071	2,553	1,210	1,343	190.0	443.2	125.4
Chemicals (28)	1,866	627	1,239	4,280	1,745	2,535	229.4	278.3	204.6
Machinery (non-electrical) (35)	3,846	1,070	2,776	3,263	2,045	1,218	84.8	191.1	43.9
Rubber and plastic (30)	193	43	150	1,322	455	867	685.0	1058.1	578.0
Primary and fabricated metal (33, 34)	1,286	367	919	1,946	710	1,236	151.3	193.5	134.5
Food (20)	553	187	366	3,287	1,180	2,107	594.4	631.0	575.7
Paper (26)	289	88	201	755	80	675	261.2	90.9	335.8
Other§	1,721	408	1,313	2,777	1,225	1,552	161.4	300.1	118.2
All 18 industries:	13,917	3,378	10,539	26,773	11,885	14,888	192.4	351.8	141.3
4 most research intensive	9,875	2,285	7,590	16,686	8,235	8,451	169.0	395.0	111.3
14 other industries	4,042	1,093	2,949	10,087	3,650	6,437	249.6	333.9	218.3

* Data on the petroleum industry, SIC 29, are excluded because figures for foreign direct investment and foreign subsidiary sales are not available.

† Industries arranged in descending order of research effort.

‡ Sales to the United States have been deleted from the total sales of foreign subsidiaries leaving only sales to local markets and to other countries by such subsidiaries.

§ Data on the scientific instruments industry, SIC 38, are not available separately and have to be included with the "14 other industries." This tends to blur slightly the otherwise sharp differences between the research-intensive industries and the other industries.

Source: See Statistical Appendix.

factors are important, large markets are more likely to stimulate the ultimate commitment of a production facility than small markets.

The one new morsel of information which the table affords is an indication of the extent to which the "other" industries of the United States have moved their overseas operations from the sphere of exports to that of sales through overseas subsidiaries. In these industries, as we have repeatedly observed, neither exports nor overseas investment have much prominence, at least when "normalized" by the level of activities of those industries in the United States. However, of the two externally directed activities, exports and foreign subsidiary sales, the export position appears even less prominent than the subsidiary sales position. In terms of Table 8, the ratio of subsidiary sales to exports is fairly high.

There are at least two observations worth making concerning the high ratios of subsidiary sales to exports in these "other industries." One fits well enough into the theme of this article; the other opens wholly new avenues of inquiry.

The observation that fits fairly well has to do with the present export position of these "other" industries. Time was, some decades ago, when the United States was a heavy exporter of most of the materials included in "other industries"—paper, food, rubber, and metal products, in particular. In the course of time, the initial trade advantage of U.S. industries in these products was eroded. In partial response, these industries set up overseas subsidiaries to service their erstwhile export markets. The subsidiaries did not always do precisely what their parents had done by way of exports; while the subsidiaries of the rubber companies may have taken over the tire markets once serviced by their parents' exports, the subsidiaries of the food companies no doubt engaged in many new activities which could not have been supported by way of exports. In any event, in the end, subsidiary sales were a means by which contact with foreign markets was maintained.

But there is obviously another phenomenon involved. U.S. firms, such as those in food distribution and food processing, are commonly found investing in foreign markets for reasons which have little to do with salvaging an export position. Some of these firms, in effect, are seeking to sell a technique of production, finance, marketing, or general organization; this is certainly the interpretation to be placed on most of the investments of the U.S. food-processing and food-distributing industry in Europe. It is not sufficient, therefore, to explain U.S. overseas investment with a simple set of hypotheses based on the protection of markets previously acquired.

As a more complete explanation is developed of the forces behind U.S. overseas investment, the issue of market defense and market protection will no doubt play a part. But the strengths that derive from research and from the capacity to organize and maintain large complex organizations will surely figure in some independent sense as well .

Further research on the functioning of research and development in the creation of new products, new processes, and new systems, and on the forces that lead to industrial concentration and large-scale operations will be particularly fruitful in shedding more light on the problems that have been only partially answered in this paper.

MAJOR LIMITATIONS OF THE DATA

The following weaknesses of the data should be considered when the findings presented in the paper are evaluated: (1) the conversion of activity from SITC to SIC is only approximate in some cases; (2) the definition of R & D as used by companies in Na-

tional Science Foundation reports differs between firms and industries; (3) the SIC two-digit level aggregates dissimilar industries; (4) research and development data is gathered at the company level, and this distorts the inputs by industry for diversified firms; (5) there is often not a complete matching of industry classification for various measures of activity (for example, scale data are by company while employment data are by establishment); (6) some goods should not be expected to move in international activity (for example, newspapers), and this lowers the ratio of trade performance to sales; (7) trade with Canada may not be a result of the forces under examination, but may result from the partial integration of the two economies; (8) activities related to natural resources have, in general, not been eliminated; (9) other forces, such as the differential impact of the "Buy American" provision of U.S. foreign aid have not been considered; (10) indirect exports have not been evaluated (for example, shipments of instrumentation from SIC 36 that enter into air-planes that are exported by SIC 37).

Fortunately, none of these limitations would affect the ordinal division of manufacturing activity into the five most research-intensive industries and the fourteen less research-intensive industries. There still would be a substantial gap between the fifth and sixth industries in order of research intensity.

These weaknesses, together with the arbitrary definition of the industries and the differences in the size of industries, have led us to use the methodology of dividing manufacturing activity into five research-intensive and fourteen less research-intensive industries. The summation of manufacturing activity into two classes of activity helps to make manifest the differences that exist between the research-intensive and the less research-intensive industries. This measure is less subject to the enumerated statistical weaknesses and is in harmony with the measures of Spearman rank correlation that were given. But it does not permit a disregard for the very substantial limitations that are inherent in the data.

STATISTICAL APPENDIX

Tables 1 and 2[10]

1. Research and development: Industry research and development expenditures in 1962 from NSF 66-15, page 83 for total research and development, and NSF 65-18, page 105 for company-financed research and development. The National Science Foundation divides these figures by the sales of the responding firms that do research and development in order to get a ratio of research and development expenditures as a percentage of sales. This seemed to be inadequate for our purpose of developing an index of research intensity for an industry as it omitted the sales of the firms that do not do research and development. We divided by total industrial sales as measured by the *FTC-SEC Quarterly Financial Reports*. NSF lumped some industries together [22 + 23;   24 + 25;   21, 27 + 31]. We estimated industry inputs by disaggregating the NSF data by the ratios of scientists and engineers in these industries as reported in U.S. Bureau of the Census (1962, Table 2). It is unlikely that errors resulting from this method of estimation would affect the findings because of the very small amounts of research and development to be allocated in these seven industries. In this case, a little bit more or less of a very small amount will cause insignificant errors.

2. Scientists and engineers in research and development in 1962 from B.L.S. Bulletin No. 1418 (1964, p. 35). Employment by industry taken from B.L.S. (1965).

3. Exports and imports from OECD (1963, nos. 1, 5).

Tables 3 and 5

1. World exports of U.S. and all OECD countries (OECD, 1963, nos. 1–6). Japan was not included in the OECD until after 1962, and her world exports [were] taken

[10] Where data are used again in subsequent tables, they are not referenced. For example, scientists and engineers as a percentage of total employment is a variable used in Tables 3 and 5 as well as in Tables 1 and 2.

from the U.N. Department of Economic and Social Affairs (1962). In order to be able to perform parametric tests, a range of values from 0.2 to 5.0 was set. For example, a positive value divided by zero would give a measure of absolute advantage equal to 5.0. Similarly, a zero divided by a positive number would be given a value of absolute disadvantage of 0.2. The conversion from SITC to SIC was done according to the accompanying tabulation.

Table 6

1. The percentage of companies indicating majority of research and development efforts for new products from the 1958 McGraw-Hill *Survey of Capital Spending*.

2. Scientists and engineers in production and in sales as a percentage of total industry employment in 1962 from B.L.S. Bulletin No. 1418 (1964, p. 35).

3. Index of employment concentration: *The Conference Board Record* (1964, p. 52).

4. Index of asset scale, 1961, and index of sales scale, 1961: U.S. Treasury Department Internal Revenue Service (1964, Table 2).

5. Cost characteristics: U.S. Bureau of the Census (1961, Table 3).

Table 7

1. Plant and equipment expenditures from 1958 to 1964 in the United States: U.S. Department of Commerce (July, 1961, p. 29; and September 1965, p. 6). Plant and equipment expenditures of U.S. corporations in Europe and non-Europe: U.S. Department of Commerce (October, 1960, p. 20; September, 1961, p. 21; and September, 1965, p. 29).

2. Direct investment in the United States in 1964: FTC-SEC (1965). For U.S.-owned subsidiaries in Europe and non-Europe: U.S. Department of Commerce (September, 1965, Table 5, p. 27).

3. For sales in the United States in 1964: FTC-SEC (1965). For sales of U.S.-owned subsidiaries in Europe and non-Europe: U.S. Department of Commerce (November, 1965, p. 19).

Table 8

See sources for Table 7.

	SIC	SITC
Food and kindred products	20	013, 023, 024, 032, 046, 047, 048, 053, 055, 061, 062, 091, 099, 111, 112
Tobacco products	21	122
Textile mill products	22	65
Apparel and related products	23	84
Lumber and wood products	24	63, 243
Furniture and fixtures	25	82
Paper and allied products	26	64
Printing and publishing	27	892
Chemicals and allied products	28	5
Drugs	283	541
Chemicals (other than drugs)	...	5 minus 541
Petroleum and coal products	29	332
Rubber and plastic products, n.e.c.	30	62, 893
Leather and leather products	31	611, 612, 613, 83, 85
Stone, clay, and glass products	32	661, 662, 663, 664, 665, 666
Primary metal	33	67, 68
Nonferrous metal	333	68
Ferrous metal	...	67
Fabricated metal products	34	69
Machinery except electrical	35	71
Electrical machinery	36	72
Transportation equipment	37	73
Aircraft and parts	372	734
Transport (other than aircraft)	...	73 minus 734
Instruments and related products	38	86

REFERENCES

BAER, WERNER. "The Economics of Prebisch and ECLA," Part 1, *Econ. Development and Cultural Change*, X, No. 2, Part I (January, 1962), 169–82.

BAIN, JOE S. *Barriers to New Competition*. Cambridge, Mass.: Harvard Univ. Press, 1956.

BHAGWATI, J. "The Pure Theory of International Trade: A Survey," *Econ. J.*, LXXIV, No. 293 (March, 1964), 1–84.

CHIPMAN, JOHN. "A Survey of the Theory of International Trade," Part 1, *Econometrica*, XXXIII, No. 3 (July, 1965), 477–519. (*a*)

———. "A Survey of the Theory of International Trade," Part 2, *ibid.*, No. 4 (October, 1965), pp. 685–760. (*b*)

DELEHANTY, GEORGE E. "An Analysis of the Changing Proportion of Non-Production Workers in U.S. Manufacturing Industries," unpublished doctoral thesis, M.I.T., 1962.

FTC-SEC. *Quarterly Financial Reports*, 1st Quarter, 1965. Washington: Government Printing Office, 1965.

FREEMAN, C. "The Plastics Industry: A Comparative Study of Research and Innovation," *Nat. Inst. Econ. Rev.*, No. 26 (November, 1963), pp. 22–62.

———. "Research and Development in Electronic Capital Goods," *ibid.*, No. 34 (November, 1965), pp. 40–91.

FREEMAN, C., AND YOUNG, A. *The Research and Development Effort in Western Europe, North America and the Soviet Union*. Paris: OECD, 1965.

HIRSCH, S. "Location of Industry and International Competitiveness," unpublished doctoral thesis, Harvard Bus. School, 1965 (to be published by Oxford Univ. Press).

HOFFMEYER, ERIK. *Dollar-Shortage*. Amsterdam: North-Holland Publishing, 1958.

HUFBAUER, G. C. *Synthetic Materials and the Theory of International Trade*. London: Duckworth, 1965.

KEESING, DONALD B. "Labor Skills and Comparative Advantage," *A.E.R. Proc.*, Vol. LVI, No. 2 (May, 1966).

KINDLEBERGER, C. P. *Foreign Trade and the National Economy*. New Haven, Conn.: Yale Univ. Press, 1962.

KREININ, MORDECHAI. "The Leontief Scarce-Factor Paradox," *A.E.R.*, LV, No. 1 (March, 1965), 131–40.

LINDER, S. B. *An Essay in Trade and Transformation*. Uppsala: Almqvist & Wiksells, 1961.

MacDOUGALL, SIR DONALD. *The World Dollar Problem*. London: Macmillan, 1957.

National Industrial Conference Board. *The Conference Board Record*, April, 1964.

National Science Foundation. *Basic Research, Applied Research, and Development in Industry,*

1962, NSF 65–18. Washington: Government Printing Office, 1965.

———. *Basic Research, Applied Research, and Development in Industry, 1963*, NSF 66–15. Washington: Government Printing Office, 1966.

OECD. *OECD Statistical Bulletins. Foreign Trade Series B, Analytical Abstracts Jan.-Dec. 1962.* Paris: OECD, 1963.

POLK, JUDD, MEISTER, I. W., AND VEIT, L. A. *U.S. Production Abroad and the Balance of Payments.* New York: National Industries Conference Board, 1966.

POSNER, M. V. "International Trade and Technical Change," *Oxford Econ. Papers*, XIII, No. 3 (October, 1961), 323–41.

United Nations Department of Economic and Social Affairs. *Trade Statistics, according to SITC*, Series D, Vol. XII, Nos. 1–20. New York: United Nations, January–December, 1962.

U.S. Bureau of the Census. *Census of Manufactures, 1958*, Vol. I, *Summary Statistics*. Washington: Government Printing Office, 1961.

———. *U.S. Census of Population: 1960 Subject Reports Occupation by Industry*, Final Report PC (2)-7C. Washington: Government Printing Office, 1962.

U.S. Bureau of Labor Statistics. *Employment of Scientific and Technical Personnel in Industry, 1962*, Bull. No. 1418. Washington: Government Printing Office, 1964.

———. *Employment and Earnings Statistics for the United States, 1909–64.* Washington: Government Printing Office, 1965.

U.S. Department of Commerce. *Survey of Current Business.* Washington: Government Printing Office, various dates.

U.S. Treasury Department, Internal Revenue Service. *Statistics of Income 1961–62. Corporation Income Tax Returns.* Washington: Government Printing Office, 1964.

VERNON, RAYMOND. "International Investment and International Trade in the Product Cycle," *Q.J.E.*, May, 1966.

WELLS, L. T. "Product Innovation and Directions of International Trade," unpublished doctoral thesis, Harvard Bus. School, 1966.

WILLIAMS, J. H. "The Theory of International Trade Reconsidered," *Econ. J.*, XXXIX (June, 1929), 195–209.

WORLEY, J. S. "The Changing Direction of Research and Development Employment among Firms," in Universities-National Bureau Committee for Economic Research, *The Rate and Direction of Inventive Activity.* Princeton, N.J.: Princeton Univ. Press, 1962.

part 4

The
Marketing Submodel
of the Firm

One of the more general ways of writing the objective function of the firm which is to be optimized is

$$\pi = pf(p, s, x) - qc(q, x) - s$$
$$c = c(q, x)$$
$$q = f(p, s, x)$$

where

q = unit sales per time period
p = price of product
c = average cost of production
s = promotional and personal selling effort outlay per period
x = index of product quality
π = profit for period

Given this formulation, it is clear that the marketing manager is directly responsible for setting the levels of price, of promotional and personal selling effort outlays, and at least in part for determining the index of product quality—in other words, for the marketing mix. This is pretty much an all-embracing task, and it shows the important place the marketing function holds in the enterprise.

Economists have not always given full attention to the nonprice variables which influence q, the unit sales of the firm. An example of an exclusive concentration upon price as demand determinant is the article by Carlin and Park (Reading 17). It must be admitted that in the particular problem these authors cope with, such exclusive—one might say traditional—concentration is fully justified. The problem is how to distribute more effectively hourly aircraft landings and takeoffs at New York's LaGuardia Airport, and thus to minimize delay, or congestion, costs imposed upon customers, while at the same time possibly raising the operating revenues of the airport. This is an issue that has been extensively discussed in public utilities pricing, and the usual solution is found in marginal cost pricing. Carlin and Park suggest a method called *proportional* marginal cost pricing and distinguish their contribution by going exhaustively into the practical consequences of their proposal. The reader might ponder the fact that public authorities have as difficult pricing problems as private enterprise and that they are usually asked to reconcile the public interest (here delay costs mutually inflicted by individual users upon one another) with profitable performance.

The next selection, by Kotler, takes the full spectrum of marketing mix issues as its subject for analysis, but at the cost of using an imaginary, rather than an actual, situation. Price, advertising, and personal selling outlays are considered at various levels; expected values (a probabilistic concept) of sales are forecast; break-even calculations made (this is the only selection included which deals explicitly with this traditional topic of managerial economics); risk preferences of management are taken into account; and, finally, capital budgeting issues are raised.

An econometric study of the filter and nonfilter cigarette market by Bass (Reading 19) illustrates how truly difficult it is to estimate actual demand facing a firm which manipulates but two marketing variables—price and advertising—and is confronted by active rivals. This is an investigation of a *group* of firms; the implications, however, to managements of individual enterprises are not hard to deduce. The leading thought of this article is that everything depends, *simultaneously*, on everything else:

Sales of filters on	filter advertising
	nonfilter advertising
	disposable income
	nonfilter price
Sales of nonfilters on	filter advertising
	nonfilter advertising
	disposable income
	nonfilter price
Advertising of filters on	sales of filters
	sales of nonfilters
Advertising of nonfilters on	sales of nonfilters
	sales of filters

A simultaneous solution of this system of equations yields then, among other things, a comparison of actual and optimal (given the premises of the model) advertising expenditures. They are in close accord. Managements of the cigarette companies are thus seen as optimizing, on the basis of their insight, their advertising outlays in this market. With the benefit of this model they can formalize their judgment and scrutinize more efficiently the outcome of their actions.

The excerpt from Palda's book (Reading 20) summarizes a much longer article. Main attention is given to the *investment*, or long-term, aspects of marketing action, here advertising. Advertising capital, or accumulated goodwill, is just as important an asset—albeit intangible—to the firm as the firm's investment in plant or distribution facilities. The estimating procedure, which is able to distinguish between short-and long-run advertising effects, is based upon the method of distributed lags, employed by other studies in this volume.

17

Marginal Cost Pricing of Airport Runway Capacity

ALAN CARLIN AND R. E. PARK*

In an increasing number of U.S. cities the rapidly growing demand for use of airport runways experienced in the last decade has exceeded the available capacity, resulting in intolerably long delays to aircraft attempting to use them. Although the problem has been most acute and has received the most publicity in New York, similar problems have already arisen in Chicago and Washington and are likely to arise elsewhere in the years to come as the demand for air travel increases.

When faced with such a problem, most economists are likely to consider first the possibility of imposing marginal cost pricing or congestion tolls as a means to optimize the use of the given transportation facilities.[1] It is primarily this approach

From American Economic Review (*June 1970*), pp. 310–19. Reprinted with permission of authors and publisher.

* The authors, economists at The RAND Corporation, are indebted to the referee for helpful suggestions. This paper is largely based on research undertaken for the Port of New York Authority, and reported more fully in our RAND memorandum. Any views expressed in this paper are those of the authors. They should not be interpreted as reflecting the views of The RAND Corporation or the official opinion or policy of any of its research sponsors.

[1] See, for example, M. Beckmann, C. B. McGuire, and C. B. Winsten, R. H. Strotz, and W. Vickrey. For a simple model that emphasizes some features of air transport, see Park. The rationale for congestion tolls is simple: A marginal user imposes congestion costs on other users, but considers only those costs that he bears himself in deciding to use a facility. A charge equal to the marginal congestion cost would internalize the external cost, so that individual decisions would lead to a socially efficient balance between use and congestion. This is clearly a partial argument. To the extent that there are offsetting external benefits from use of the facility, or that alternatives to use also involve external costs, the argument for a congestion toll is weakened. Indeed, any uncorrected departure from

that we will explore here. Although other short-term solutions to the congestion problem are both feasible and interesting, they will be only briefly considered.

Throughout the paper our primary example will be New York's LaGuardia Airport during the period April 1967 through March 1968.[2] This is the most recent period for which data were available at the time the research was carried out.

The paper is divided into two sections. The first develops marginal delay or congestion costs for LaGuardia. The second explores the possible use of congestion tolls as a solution to the short-term congestion problem.

I. MARGINAL DELAY COSTS

What are the congestion costs that an additional user would impose on others? Equivalently, what would the savings to others be if one fewer plane were to use LaGuardia? In order to answer these questions, it is necessary to realize that during a period when an airport is continuously busy, each user imposes some delay on all following users until the end of the busy period. That is, an additional user shoves those following him

optimal conditions elsewhere in the economy makes it unlikely that a partially optimal congestion toll will result in a global second-best allocation. But these considerations do not rob the notion of a congestion toll of its merit. In many real cases, such as the one examined in this paper, it may be possible to say with considerable confidence that use of the facility with a congestion toll, although not globally optimal, would be more efficient than use without the toll.

[2] A similar analysis for Kennedy International Airport in New York is reported in Carlin and Park.

one space back in the queue, and the effect persists until the queue dissipates.

The Model

We seek the delay costs, C_i, imposed by a user of type i on other users at a time t when the remaining busy period equals B minutes. A type of use is defined by the type of plane and by specification as to whether it is a landing or takeoff. Thus $i = 1$ may be a large jet landing, $i = 4$ a light plane takeoff, and so on. Say there are m different types of use. Then if we knew the absolute service times, S_i, the number of operations of each type, N_i, that would occur from time t until the end of the busy period, and the costs per minute of delay to each type of operation, c_i, it would be easy to calculate the marginal delay costs due to an additional operation of type i as

$$C_i = S_i \sum_{i=1}^{m} N_i c_i \qquad (1)$$

The operation delays each of the $N = \sum_{i=1}^{m} N_i$ operations for the length of time it takes to service it, S_i, at a cost to each of c_i per minute. But the N_i and the S_i are awkward to estimate. It is somewhat easier to estimate relative service times $s_i = S_i/S_1$, and proportions of various types of operations $n_i = N_i/N$. So we shall transform the relationship into a more usable form by introducing a second relationship. The length of the remaining busy period must just equal the sum of the time necessary to service each of the airplanes that lands or takes off before its ends:

$$B = \sum_{i=1}^{m} N_i S_i \qquad (2)$$

Dividing (1) by (2), we obtain

$$\frac{C_i}{B} = \frac{S_i \sum_{i=1}^{m} N_i c_i}{\sum_{i=1}^{m} N_i S_i} \qquad (3)$$

If we divide both the numerator and

denominator of the right-hand expression in (3) by $S_1 N$, we obtain

$$\frac{C_i}{B} = s_i \cdot \frac{\sum_{i=1}^{m} n_i c_i}{\sum_{i=1}^{m} n_i s_i}, \qquad (4)$$

which conveniently expresses marginal cost per minute of the remaining busy period in terms of use proportions, relative service times, and individual costs per minute of delay.

At LaGuardia, which always operates with either a single or an intersecting runway configuration, arrivals and departures may be considered to be interdependent. In this case, we can approximate reality reasonably closely by distinguishing among four kinds of operations:

1. air carrier landings,
2. air carrier takeoffs,
3. general aviation landings, and
4. general aviation takeoffs.[3]

Since $s_1 = 1$, the formula for the marginal delay cost C_1 due to an air carrier landing at time t is

$$C_1 = \frac{n_1 c_1 + n_2 c_2 + n_3 c_3 + n_4 c_4}{n_1 + n_2 s_2 + n_3 s_3 + n_4 s_4} \cdot B(t) \qquad (5)$$

and the costs C_i due to other types of operations are $s_i C_1$.

Empirical Estimates

The values of the n's vary throughout the day; hourly average general aviation as a percentage of total traffic on duty runways at LaGuardia varied from under 30 to over 40 percent during the busy afternoon hours.[4] So, of course, do those of the s's, in response to changing traffic mixes and runway configurations. And so, finally, do those of the c's, primarily as result of changing load

---

[3] General aviation, consisting primarily of relatively small aircraft, is a category that includes air taxis, business and private planes.

[4] From an analysis of Federal Aviation Administration Runway Use Logs for 23 random sample days in 1967.

TABLE 1 Parameter Estimates for LaGuardia

	Air Carrier Landings $i = 1$	Air Carrier Takeoffs $i = 2$	General Aviation Landings $i = 3$	General Aviation Takeoffs $i = 4$
1. Proportion of total traffic on duty runways, n_i	.32	.32	.18	.18
2. Service time relative to air carrier landings, s_i	1.00	.86	.54	.46
3a. Cost to aircraft owners (dollars per minute)	6.50	2.60	1.00	.50
3b. Passengers per operation	46.8	46.8	1.8	1.8
3c. Cost of passenger time (dollars per minute)	4.68	4.68	.36	.36
3d. Marginal cost of delays (dollars per minute), c_i	11.18	7.28	1.36	.86
4. Marginal cost of delays per minute of remaining busy period (dollars), $C_i/B(t)$	8.15	7.01	4.40	3.75

Notes on line:
1. From Carlin and Park (Table 5.1).
2. From Carlin and Park (Appendix Table C.3).
3a. From Carlin and Park (Appendix Table D.1), which also gives some cost figures for other airlines.
3b. Based on information supplied by Aviation Department, Port of New York Authority. General aviation and air carrier data are for 1965 and 1967, respectively.
3c. Assumes costs of $6 and $12 for air carrier and general aviation passenger time, respectively.
3d. Sum of lines 3a and 3c.
4. Computed using equation (5) and lines 1, 2, and 3d.

factors throughout the day. However, to deal explicitly with all of these complexities would not, we feel, add enough precision to our estimates to be worth the large increase in computation that would be required. We thus limit our task in the next paragraphs to obtaining estimates of yearly *average* values for the quantities, other than $B(t)$, that enter expression (5) for marginal delay costs. Average values of $B(t)$ are estimated for each hour of the day.

Traffic proportions, n_i: Estimates of the n's are easily obtained from aggregate traffic statistics available for 1967, corrected to eliminate that fraction of general aviation traffic that used non-duty runways. These estimates are shown in line 1 of Table 1.[5]

Relative service times, s_i. By using the airport capacity manual prepared by Airborne Instruments Laboratory (*AIL*), it is possible to derive approximate ratios of the service times required by different classes of aircraft at LaGuardia.[6] Line 2 of Table 1 summarizes our estimates of relative service times.

Cost of delay to airplane owners and passengers, c_i. Line 3 shows our estimates of (or assump-

tions about) average cost of one minute delay to different kinds of operations, including both costs to the airplane owners and costs of passenger time. The estimates of air carrier costs are based on American Airlines figures for the types of planes that they operate at LaGuardia. In addition to direct variable costs of fuel, oil, and crew time, they include some allowance for indirect variable costs such as maintenance and incremental capital costs.[7] The fairly high general aviation costs reflect the fact that the average general aviation plane operating at LaGuardia is quite sophisticated. We assume $6 per hour as an average value for airline passenger time, and $12 per hour for presumably more affluent general aviation passengers.[8]

Marginal delay costs per minute of remaining busy period, $C_i/B(t)$: When the traffic proportions, the relative service times, and the delay costs per minute shown in lines 1 through 3 of Table 1 are substituted in ex-

[5] For details, see Carlin and Park (p.91).
[6] For details, see Carlin and Park (pp. 197–201). J. V. Yance performed a similar analysis for Washington National.

[7] For further details, see Carlin and Park (pp. 202–206). This also shows costs (one higher and one lower) reported by two other airlines.
[8] For comparison, one study finds a value of $2.82 per hour for commuting motorists by a study of their behavior. See T. C. Thomas. Estimated marginal costs are sensitive to this assumption. Estimates for higher and lower values of passenger time are given in fn 10.

pression (5) for marginal delay costs, the results are as shown in line 4 of that Table. These are estimates of the marginal delay costs per minute of remaining busy period that incremental operations of different types impose on other users.

Average remaining busy period, $B(t)$: To complete our estimates of marginal delay costs, we need information on the average length of remaining busy period by time of day, $B(t)$. As far as we know, this is the first time that an attempt has been made to estimate remaining busy periods. The method that we used is in principle a simple one. The basic data, kindly provided by American Airlines and United Air Lines, relate to delays experienced by individual flights. These data can be used to block out periods during which the airport was busy. For example, if an airplane that took off at 1615 was delayed for 15 minutes, this would ordinarily be an indication that the airport was busy between 1600 and 1615 on that day.[9] After busy periods were blocked

out, the length of busy period remaining was tabulated at 10 minute intervals from 0700 to 2400 for each of 14 sample days and during 6 critical afternoon hours for each of 14 additional sample days. These values were averaged over all sample days to estimate expected busy period remaining by time of day. The estimates, together with standard errors, are shown in an appendix to this article which the authors will provide upon request. Hourly averages of the every-ten-minute estimates are shown in column 1 of Table 2.

Full marginal delay costs: It now remains only to multiply the costs per minute of remaining busy period shown in line 4 of Table 1 by the busy period estimates presented in column 1 of Table 2. The resulting figures, shown in columns 2 through 5, are average values of the delay costs imposed on other users by incremental operations at any time of day. Some of these costs are very high. For example, it appears that an additional carrier arrival between 1500 and 1600 will, on the average, impose delay costs of over $1,000 on other users. Conversely, one less arrival during this period could be expected to reduce delay to others by the same amount. Marginal delay costs for general aviation operations during the same hour are in excess of $500.[10]

---

[9] In practice, there were a number of complications. In the first place, we had to use a number of different methods to calculate the delays experienced by individual flights. For some American arrivals, we had pilot reports of delays enroute and in the New York terminal area, both of which can in large part be attributed to airplane congestion at LaGuardia. For such flights we used the pilot reports as the delay measure. For some American arrivals, pilot reports were missing. In such cases, we based the delay estimate on the excess of actual over planned flight time, a measure that reflects other influences, such as enroute wind and weather forecast errors, in addition to terminal area delays. A random sample of about 50 flights for which both pilot-reported delays (*PRD*) and excess of actual over planned flight time (*EFT*) were recorded showed the following regression relationship:

$$PRD = .05 + .92EFT, \quad R^2 = .90,$$
$$(.04)$$

which we used to estimate delays when pilot reports were missing. For a few American flights, and all United flights, neither *PRD* nor *EFT* were available; there are no satisfactory delay measures in such cases. For all departures, both American and United, we calculated delays as the actual time elapsed between gate departure and takeoff, less a standard taxi time from the terminal building to the takeoff runway in use.

A second complication is that the data were occasionally contradictory. For example, one flight took off at 1615 after a calculated delay of 15 minutes, while another took off at 1610 on the same day with no delay. Much more frequently, there were gaps in the observations on individual flights. Although the observations were dense enough during some times of day to show several planes waiting for takeoff or for landing all at the same time, at other times there were periods during which no American or United flights were either waiting or operating undelayed. To resolve contradictions and fill in gaps, we made use of Federal Aviation Administration Runway Use Logs, which record the time of landing or takeoff of all planes using LaGuardia to the nearest minute, and thus provide a rough indication of whether the airport was busy or not at any particular time.

[10] If carrier and general aviation passenger time were valued at $3 and $6 per hour, respectively, the costs shown in Table 2 would be reduced by 25 percent. For $12 and $24 per hour, the costs would be increased by 49 percent.

TABLE 2 Average Remaining Busy Period and Full Marginal Delay Costs by Hour of Day

Hour of Day	Remaining Busy Period (minutes)	Full Marginal Delay Costs ($ per incremental operation)[a]			
		Air Carrier		General Aviation	
		Arrivals	Departures	Arrivals	Departures
	(1)	(2)	(3)	(4)	(5)
0000–0700	0.0[b]	0[b]	0[b]	0[b]	0[b]
0700–0800	7.4	60	52	32	28
0800–0900	33.1	270	232	146	124
0900–1000	33.2	271	233	146	125
1000–1100	19.9	162	140	88	75
1100–1200	11.4	93	80	50	43
1200–1300	30.1	245	211	132	113
1300–1400	72.9	594	511	321	173
1400–1500	85.2	694	597	375	319
1500–1600	133.7	1090	937	588	501
1600–1700	118.2	963	829	520	443
1700–1800	96.4	786	676	424	361
1800–1900	74.5	607	522	328	279
1900–2000	44.6	364	313	196	167
2000–2100	19.5	159	137	86	73
2100–2200	7.2	59	50	32	27
2200–2300	1.7	14	12	8	7
2300–2400	.4	3	3	2	2

Notes:
[a] Computed using line 4, Table 1 and column 1, this Table.
[b] Assumed to be zero.

There are apparently substantial savings to be realized by some reduction in low-value traffic at LaGuardia. Some approaches to achieving a reduction are discussed in the next section.

II. POLICY ALTERNATIVES

No Change in Policy

During the study year, flight fees at LaGuardia were based on airplane weight, with a $5 minimum for each takeoff and no charge for landing. Most general aviation pays the minimum fee. Fees for carriers range from about $50 to $150, depending on the weight of the plane. Similar value-of-service fees are used at almost all major airports.

This fee structure leads to two related inefficiencies. First, there is an inefficiently large amount of general aviation traffic. As shown in Table 1, 36 percent of all duty runway traffic at LaGuardia during 1967 was general aviation. Since most paid only

$5 per landing and takeoff, and marginal congestion costs run up to on the order of 200 times that amount, one must conclude that many general aviation operations are of very low value relative to the congestion costs they impose on others.

It should be pointed out that on August 1, 1968, the Port of New York Authority raised the minimum fee to $25 for flights that land or take off between 0800 and 1000 Monday through Friday, and between 1500 and 2000 every day. This pioneering but limited step in the direction of marginal congestion cost pricing appears to have reduced significantly the amount of general aviation traffic at LaGuardia. The limited information available suggests that general aviation may have been reduced as much as 40 percent at LaGuardia during the hours when the $25 minimum applies.

Second, airline passenger loads are inefficiently low. At LaGuardia, airline load factors averaged 59.4 percent during 1967.[11]

[11] Aviation Division, Port of New York Authority.

In the airline industry, competition is primarily on the basis of service rather than price.[12] One very important part of this service competition is competitive scheduling. With the present level of fares, costs are covered at fairly low load factors. The airlines tend to add flights to the same destination at roughly the same time until load factors are forced down toward these break-even levels. Although the higher frequency of service that results is not without value, it seems certain that less frequent service at higher load factors would be more efficient.

In the remainder of this section we shall discuss two pricing approaches to increasing the efficiency with which the runways are used.

Full Marginal Cost Pricing

One of the difficulties in making estimates of marginal costs with the intention of using them as prices is to allow for the effects that the prices themselves will have on runway use. Use of the costs shown in Table 2, for example, would not represent equilibrium conditions because their use would reduce the number of airplanes using the airport, thereby reducing marginal costs and hence the prices that should be charged. If instituted immediately such a pricing system would be less than optimally efficient by overly reducing traffic. It might even be dynamically unstable, in the sense that costs recomputed in succeeding periods and used as prices might not converge to an equilibrium level. This would be the case if, after Table 2 prices were imposed, traffic decreased so much that marginal costs fell below the level of current flight fees. Using these lower costs as prices during the following period would result in traffic above current levels, and undamped oscillations in prices and traffic would ensue.

Using Table 2 costs as prices without adjustment would clearly be unwise. On the other hand, to determine analytically a set of equilibrium prices would be an impos-

sible task. To do so, we would need to know with some confidence and precision what the pattern of traffic would be under different sets of prices. We do not. One way to implement equilibrium marginal cost prices in light of these difficulties would be to charge an increasing percentage of the full marginal costs as recomputed after each successive increase.

Efficiency: Equilibrium marginal cost prices would result in very efficient runway use. They would obviously exclude low-value general aviation traffic. They would also increase carrier load factors to a more efficient level.[13]

Practicality: Equilibrium marginal cost pricing does not appear to be a practical policy at LaGuardia. At least in the short run, airlines would be hurt by higher flight fees. The formula for calculating present airline flight fees is embodied in lease agreements between the Port Authority and the individual airlines. The airlines would therefore be able to block any move by the Port to impose higher fees.

In the longer run, there may be some offsetting considerations. For one thing, the higher flight fees would be (in principle, completely) offset by reduced operating costs as schedules were reduced and load factors increased. However, given existing airline fleet sizes and commitments for additional airplanes, it would take a long time for this adjustment to work itself out. For another thing, the increased flight fee revenues might be used by the Port Authority for capacity expansion, as Herbert Mohring suggests. However, the constraints on capacity expansion are primarily political, not financial; additional Port Authority revenue would do little or nothing to promote it.

These possible benefits are remote or uncertain enough so that short-run considerations would surely dominate. Airline opposition to full marginal cost pricing would keep it from being a practical alternative.

---

[12] For an extended discussion, see R. E. Caves (pp. 331–55).

[13] For a theoretical treatment of this latter point, see Park.

TABLE 3 Proportional Marginal Cost Prices for LaGuardia Yielding Current Port Authority Airline Revenue (dollars per operation)

Hour of Day	Air Carrier		General Aviation		Post-August 1968[a] Actual Minimums	
	Arrivals	Departures	Arrivals	Departures	Departures	Either[b]
0000–0700	0[c]	0[c]	0[c]	0[c]	5	
0700–0800	7	6	4	3	5	
0800–0900	30	26	16	14		25[d]
0900–1000	31	26	17	14		25[d]
1000–1100	18	16	10	9	5	
1100–1200	11	9	6	5	5	
1200–1300	28	24	15	13	5	
1300–1400	67	58	36	31	5	
1400–1500	78	67	42	36	5	
1500–1600	123	106	66	57		25
1600–1700	109	94	59	51		25
1700–1800	89	76	48	41		25
1800–1900	69	59	37	32		25
1900–2000	41	35	22	19		25
2000–2100	18	15	10	8	5	
2100–2200	7	6	4	3	5	
2200–2300	2	1	1	1	5	
2300–2400	0	0	0	0	5	

Notes:
[a] Prior to August 1968, the minimum was a uniform $5 throughout the day for departures only.
[b] For both arrival and departure if either occurs during the hours shown.
[c] Assumed to be zero.
[d] Monday through Friday only. The $5 minimum departure fee applies on other days.
Source: Table 2.

Proportional Marginal Cost Pricing

A more practical pricing approach is to limit total airline runway use payments to what they would be under the formulas written into the present leases, but attempt to change the basis on which fees are levied so that fees during any hour would be proportional to those that would prevail under full marginal cost pricing. Even if equilibrium marginal cost pricing were to be attempted, this would be the recommended first step toward it.

Using the full marginal costs shown in Table 2 as a basis, it is a simple step to compute what proportional fees would be on the assumption that the airlines as a group are to pay no more than they otherwise would. Using the average of September 1967 and February 1968 airline schedules, hypothetical collections with full marginal cost flight fees were computed. A percentage was then computed by dividing this number into actual airline payments to the Port Authority for

runway use during the period March 1967 through February 1968. When these percentages were used to derive proportional cost fees, the prices shown in Table 3 resulted.

Practicality: Although the factors of proportionality have been chosen to keep payments by airlines as a group constant, particular airlines may pay considerably more or less under such a scheme than under the present weight-based system. Presumably the less individual airline payments exceeded present payments, the easier it would be to obtain airline agreement to such a system.

In order to explore this question, we compared what airline payments would have been using the prices shown in Table 3 and average schedule data for September 1967 and February 1968 with actual payments for the period March 1967 through February 1968. The results, shown as percentages, are presented in Table 4.

With one major exception, the calculations are fairly encouraging for airline acceptance of such a scheme at LaGuardia. The

TABLE 4 Calculated Airline Payments for LaGuardia Runway Use Using Proportional Marginal Cost Pricing as a Percentage of Actual Collections

Trunk carriers	90
American	100
Eastern	66
National	56
Northeast	122
TWA	90
United	88
Local service carriers	230
Allegheny	263
Mohawk	242
Piedmont	142

major exception is the local service airlines, particularly Allegheny and Mohawk. Because they use smaller planes which benefit from the present weight related fees, and have few flights in the early morning hours, they would be particularly affected by proportional cost fees. On the other hand, their higher runway use fees would be at least partially offset by reduced delay costs. Furthermore, airlines as a group would certainly be better off on balance. Since the group is a small one, one might expect informal pressures or side payments to bring about agreement by all airlines to proportional cost fees.

Efficiency: The proportional cost prices in Table 3 would do much to deter low value general aviation traffic during busy hours. The significant effect of a $25 charge for landing and takeoff combined is mentioned above. Proportional cost fees, which range up to almost five times this amount, would probably eliminate almost as much general aviation traffic as would full marginal cost prices. On the other hand, proportional prices by themselves would have little effect on inefficiently low load factors. Flight fees for carrier aircraft using LaGuardia currently range from about $50 to $150 per landing and takeoff combined. If the proportional marginal cost prices of Table 3 were in effect, a carrier plane landing and taking off at peak times would pay as much as about $200. This increase is small enough so that it would probably have little influence on the sched-

ules of the air carriers (with the possible exception of the local service carriers).

Other Alternatives

We have examined in some detail two pricing approaches to increasing the efficiency with which LaGuardia's runways are used. Full marginal cost pricing is the most efficient pricing scheme but it could not be adopted over airline opposition, and airline opposition is likely. Proportional marginal cost pricing is probably the most efficient pricing scheme with a reasonable chance of being implementable, but it does little to correct inefficiently low airline load factors. This suggests that other measures capable of affecting schedules as well as general aviation use would be even more efficient than proportional marginal cost pricing. These other alternatives include purely administrative measures and combination measures involving both pricing and administrative aspects. Although a complete discussion is beyond the scope of this paper, we shall mention a few of the possibilities here.[14]

The most efficient purely administrative measures would restrict both general aviation and air carriers to something less than their current levels of operation. One central problem in the design of an efficient administrative measure is to decide what level each should be restricted to. Another is to formulate the restrictions so as to attempt to exclude the lowest value traffic in each category. On June 1, 1969, the Federal Aviation Administration imposed limits on operations during bad weather at five busy airports, including LaGuardia. Although the limits are higher and allocate a larger share to general aviation than would be efficient, this measure is a small step toward more efficient runway use. However, bargaining among the airlines is a cumbersome way to split up the quota, and there is no guarantee that the schedules will go to the highest-value users.

There are at least two combination measures that are potentially more efficient than

---

[14] For a more detailed discussion, see Carlin and Park (pp. 139–55).

any of the feasible "pure" alternatives. The first of these would consist of the issuance of property rights in schedule slots for particular hours in proportion to current use that could be freely traded among airport users.[15] The number of slots for each hour would be chosen administratively to approximate the efficient number. The free market in slots would then allocate them to the highest-value users. It would, of course, be permissible to subdivide the slots so that, for example, an airline might purchase the right to use a slot on Monday through Friday only. If the slots were issued to airlines in proportion to recent schedules, all would share in the gains from increased efficiency; there should be no airline opposition to overcome in introducing this measure. In theory, one could issue many small fractional slots to nonscheduled users as well, and rely on the market to allocate slots among *all* users. In practice, it would probably be better to rely on some pricing mechanism to control non-scheduled users. As another practical matter, it would be best to issue the property rights in slots on a relatively short-term basis, say one or two years, to make it easier to adjust the number of slots or otherwise to modify the system.

The second combination measure would consist of both proportional marginal cost pricing and administrative limits on airline schedules. The proportional prices would exclude low-value general aviation users, and the schedule limits would increase airline load factors.

III. CONCLUSIONS

Because of the practical problems involved, equilibrium marginal cost pricing does not appear to be a feasible alternative for allocating runway capacity at LaGuardia. The use of proportional marginal cost pricing,

[15] This approach was suggested by Jack Hirshleifer.

however, offers some of the same efficiency advantages without most of the problems. It is certainly preferable on efficiency grounds to the present weight-based, value-of-service pricing used at most airports. Use of administrative limits on schedules would be required in conjunction with proportional marginal cost pricing, however, to increase carrier load factors to more efficient levels.

REFERENCES

Airborne Instruments Laboratory *Airport Capacity*, prepared for Federal Aviation Agency and available from Center for Scientific and Technical Information as PB 181 553, New York, June 1963.

M. BECKMANN, C. B. McGUIRE, and C. B. WINSTEN, *Studies in the Economics of Transportation*. New Haven, 1956, pp. 80–101.

A. CARLIN and R. E. PARK, *The Efficient Use of Airport Runway Capacity in a Time of Scarcity*, RM-5817, The RAND Corporation. Santa Monica, Aug. 1969.

R. E. CAVES, *Air Transport and Its Regulators: An Industry Study*. Cambridge, Mass., 1962.

H. MOHRING, "Urban Highway Investments," in R. Dorfman, ed., *Measuring Benefits of Government Investments*. Washington, 1965, pp. 231–75.

R. E. PARK, "Congestion Tolls for Regulated Common Carriers," P-4153, The RAND Corporation. Santa Monica, Sept. 1969. Also forthcoming in *Econometrica*.

Port of New York Authority, Aviation Department, *Airport Statistics*.

R. H. STROTZ, "Urban Transportation Parables," in Julius Margolis, ed., *The Public Economy of Urban Communities*. Washington, 1965.

T. C. THOMAS, *The Value of Time for Passenger Cars: An Experimental Study of Commuter's Values*, Palo Alto, 1967.

W. VICKREY, "Optimization of Traffic and Facilities," *J. Transp. Econ. Policy*, May 1967, *1*, 123–36.

J. V. YANCE, "Movement Time as a Cost in Airport Operations," *J. Transp. Econ. Policy*, Jan. 1969, *3*, 28–36.

18

Marketing Mix Decisions for New Products

PHILIP KOTLER*

In evaluating a new product idea, it can be misleading to consider only one conception of the product's attributes and marketing program. Different conceptions of the marketing mix will yield different estimates of profit potential. The author shows how the "best" marketing mix can be found under the conditions of limited information. The estimated profit potential of this best mix becomes the basis for judging whether the company should develop the new product.

Companies are increasingly recognizing that new products are basic to their survival and growth. According to one study "it is now commonplace for major companies to have 50% or more of current sales in products new in the past ten years." [1]

At the same time, the development of new products is a costly and risky business undertaking. Some new product ideas turn out to be technically unfeasible after good money has been spent and others turn out to be commercially unsuccessful after still more good money is gone. As many as three out of four new products introduced on the market may fail to attain commercial success.

Thus management finds itself in a dilemma: it must develop new products and yet the odds weigh heavily against their success. The answer lies in making the innovation function a more rational process through

Reprinted from Journal of Marketing Research, *published by the American Marketing Association, "Marketing Mix Decisions for New Products," by Philip Kotler (February, 1964), pp. 43–49. Reprinted with permission of author and publisher.*

* Philip Kotler is a professor of marketing at Northwestern University. The author wishes to acknowledge the helpful comments of the participants in the Ford Research Workshop in Marketing at Berkeley in the summer of 1963.

administrative reforms and improved decision-making procedures. Management is coming to recognize the desirability of centralizing responsibility for overseeing the process in new product committees and departments. Furthermore, it is recognizing the need for better theory and decision procedures at each stage of the new product development process (*search, screening, profit analysis, product development, test marketing,* and *commercialization*). At each stage, a basic decision is called for on whether to abandon the project or continue it. The purpose of this paper is to describe a methodology for improved decision-making at the third stage, that of profit analysis.

THE PROFIT ANALYSIS STAGE

Suppose a new product idea has been screened and found to be compatible with the company's objectives and resources. The next task is to evaluate the profit potential of the product. In practice, this evaluation tends to be conducted in the following manner. On the basis of inspiration or previous research, management develops a particular conception of product attributes and a marketing program for the new product. Based on this specific conception of the marketing mix, management develops two different estimates. One is an estimate of the required sales volume to break even. The other is an estimate of the sales volume which is likely to be stimulated by the marketing mix. If the sales potential estimate comfortably exceeds the break-even volume estimate, the product idea is judged to be profitable. If profits promise to be large in relation to the required investment, the product idea is likely to pass to the fourth stage, that of product development.

Yet a more refined model for the analysis of new product profit potential is both desirable and practical. Instead of considering only one marketing mix and whether break-even volume is likely to be achieved under it, the more refined model provides for a simultaneous evaluation of the profit potential of several marketing mixes. The refined model can be illustrated by the following example:

The ABC Electronics Company is a small manufacturer of transistors and clock radios and is presently engaged in reviewing other electronic products for possible addition to the product line. One of these is a small portable tape recorder. Small novelty tape recorders have appeared recently on the market, and they retail at prices between $20–$50. The company's marketing research department has surveyed the market and found that interest in this type of unit is substantial and growing.

An executive committee is appointed to examine the potential profitability of this product. The production department estimates that $60,000 would have to be invested in specific new equipment and facilities and that this investment would have an estimated life of five years. The accounting department submits that the product would have to absorb $26,000 a year of general overhead to cover the value of supporting facilities, rent, taxes, executive salaries, cost of capital, etc. The marketing department advises that the product be supported initially with an advertising budget of approximately $20,000 and a personal selling budget of approximately $30,000 and furthermore that it should be priced at approximately $18 F.O.B. factory with no quantity discounts. Finally, the various operating departments estimate that the new product would involve a direct material and labor cost of $10 a unit.

In the light of these estimates, should the ABC Electronics Company develop this new product? Is the marketing mix proposed by the marketing department sound?

What Is the Break-Even Volume?

The first step in the business analysis of a new product idea is to estimate how many units would have to be sold in order to cover costs. This break-even volume is found by analyzing how total revenue and total cost vary at different sales volumes.

Total revenue at any particular sales volume is that volume times the unit price adjusted by allowances for early payment, quantity purchases, and freight. The adjustments are fairly straightforward and total revenue as a function of sales volume is generally simple to estimate.

The total cost function is more difficult to estimate. Total costs often bear a non-linear relationship to output. It is difficult enough to establish the shape of the total cost function for existing products because the statistical data are impure; the total cost function for a new product is even more difficult to estimate because the statistical data are non-existent. But as a practical matter, the break-even analyst usually assumes a linear total cost function. This assumption may be faulty for very low and very high levels of output but may be sufficiently accurate for intermediate levels, according to some recent statistical cost studies [3].

The total cost function is composed of variable and fixed cost elements. In the example, variable costs are assumed to be constant at $10 a unit. The following fixed costs are found in the example. The tape recorder requires additional fixed investment of $60,000 with an estimated life of five years. On a straight line basis, this amounts to an annual depreciation cost of $12,000. The new product is also charged $26,000 a year for its share of general overhead. This figure presumably represents a long-run estimate of the opportunity value of the corporate resources required to support this new product. In addition, the company is considering an annual expenditure of $20,000 on advertising and $30,000 on personal selling. Fixed costs therefore add up to $88,000 ($12,000 + $26,000 + $20,000 + $30,000).

The break-even volume can now be estimated. At the break-even volume (Q_B), total revenue (TR) equals total cost (TC). But total revenue is price (P) times the break-even volume, and total cost is fixed cost (F) plus the product of unit variable cost (V) and break-even volume. In symbols:

$$TR = TC$$

$$P \cdot Q_B = F + V \cdot Q_B$$

Combining similar terms, and solving for Q_B, we find that

$$Q_B = \frac{F}{P - V}$$

$P - V$ is the difference between price and unit variable cost and is called the unit contribution to fixed cost. It is \$8 in the example. The company would have to sell 11,000 units (\$88,000 ÷ \$8) to cover fixed costs.

At this point it would be useful to express the break-even volume (Q_B) not as a constant but rather as a function of the elements in the marketing mix. The break-even volume will vary with the product price and the amount of marketing effort devoted to the new product:

$$Q_B = \frac{\$12,000 + \$26,000 + A + S}{P - \$10}$$

$$= \frac{\$38,000 + A + S}{P - \$10}$$

where A = advertising budget

S = sales budget

P = unit selling price to wholesaler

In Table 1, eight alternative marketing programs are listed for this product along with the implied break-even volumes. In the case of mix #5, the company could sell as

TABLE 1 Minimum Volume Requirements as a Function of Marketing Mix

Some Possible Marketing Mixes

	Price	Advertising	Sales Budget	Break-Even Volume Q_B
1.	\$16	\$10,000	\$10,000	9,667
2.	16	10,000	50,000	16,333
3.	16	50,000	10,000	16,333
4.	16	50,000	50,000	23,000
5.	24	10,000	10,000	4,143
6.	24	10,000	50,000	7,000
7.	24	50,000	10,000	7,000
8.	24	50,000	50,000	9,857

few as 4,143 tape recorders to break even; while in the case of mix #4, the company would have to sell as many as 23,000. This high sensitivity of the break-even volume to the marketing mix decision is often over looked in profit analysis.

The eight marketing mixes in Table 1 are a small sample from the very large number of mixes which could be used to market the new tape recorder. They were formed by assuming a high and low level for each of the marketing variables and elaborating all the combinations. Suppose executive opinion held that \$16 is a price on the low side while \$24 is a price on the high side; and that \$10,000 is a low budget for advertising and personal selling respectively, and \$50,000 is a high budget. This yields eight strategy combinations $(2 \cdot 2 \cdot 2 = 2^3)$ and makes the marketing mix problem manageable.

Each mix is a polar case. For example, mix #1 represents the common strategy of setting a low price and spending very little for promotion. This works well when the market is highly price conscious, possesses good information about available brands, and is not easily swayed by psychological appeals. Mix #4 represents a strategy of low price and heavy promotion. The interesting thing about this mix is that it produces a high sales volume but also requires a high sales volume to break even. Mix #5 consists of a high price and low promotion and is used typically in a seller's market where the firm wants to maximize short-run profits. Mix #8 consists of a high price supported by high promotion; this strategy is often used in a market where buyers are sensitive to psychological appeals and to quality. The other mixes (#2, 3, 6, 7) are variations on the same themes, with the additional feature that different assessments are made of the comparative effectiveness of advertising and personal selling. But it should be noted that while the division of a given budget between advertising and personal selling affects the actual sales volume, it does not affect the break-even volume.

Different marketing mixes not only imply different break-even volumes, but also differences in the sensitivity of profits to *devia-*

tions from the break-even volume. For example, the break-even volume is approximately the same for mixes #1 and #8. Yet the high price, high promotion character of #8 promises greater losses or greater profits for deviations from the break-even volume. This is because there are higher fixed costs under mix #8 but once they are covered, additional volume is very profitable because of the high price.

Break-even analysis is necessary, but not sufficient by itself to identify the optimal marketing mix. It indicates what volumes have to be achieved but does not indicate what volumes are likely to be achieved. Missing is an account of how various elements in the marketing mix will affect the actual volume of sales.

Ideally the company requires a demand equation showing sales volume as a function of price, advertising, personal selling, and other important marketing mix elements. Such equations are difficult enough to derive for established products where there are historical data, let alone for new product ideas where there are none. Yet though the product is only an idea at this stage, there are some research procedures which can yield useful information for estimating sales. A survey could be made of the attitudes and interests of various consumers toward alternative product features and prices. It might help to develop some prototypes of the tape recorder in order to get firsthand reactions. The survey may indicate what socio-economic groups constitute major prospects for this product. The approximate number of persons in each prospect group can be estimated from census data. In addition, an analysis can be made of the relative strength of competitors in different segments of the market. Since information is expensive to collect, a Bayesian analysis of the value of specified types of additional information should be performed at each juncture [2].

Through this type of research and analysis, the executives will have a better idea of what sales volumes are likely to be achieved with different marketing mixes. For each particular mix, the executives can develop a subjective probability distribution of pos-

sible sales volumes. The mean of this probability distribution shows the expected sales volume for this marketing mix. Let the expected sales volume be denoted by Q. The fourth column in Table 2 shows an (hypothetical) expected sales volume for each of the eight marketing mixes. It should be noted that sales are expected to move inversely with price and directly with the amounts spent on advertising and personal selling. However, increased promotion is expected to increase sales at a diminishing rate.

What Is the Best Marketing Mix and the Implied Profit Level?

At this point, the expected volume (Q) and the break-even volume (Q_B) can be compared for each mix. The results are shown in column 6 of Table 2. The greatest extra volume $(Q - Q_B)$ is achieved with mix #1. But extra volume is not a sufficient indicator of the best mix. The extra volume must be multiplied by the unit value $(P - V)$. A high price mix delivering a small extra volume may be superior to a low price mix delivering a large extra volume. Therefore $Z = (P - V) \cdot (Q - Q_B)$ has to be calculated for each marketing mix. These results are shown in column 7 of Table 2.

Z is a measure of the absolute profits expected from different marketing mixes. Of the mixes shown in Table 2, mix #5 appears to promise the largest amount of profit. This mix calls for the product to be sold at a high price with little promotional support. This strategy is often used when a company believes its product has been smartly designed and essentially sells itself. But before ABC Electronics can be sure that it has found the best marketing mix, or that the product should be produced at all, it must examine some additional issues.

1. *The profit estimates for the eight marketing mixes may not be equally reliable.* The profit estimates were derived from prior cost and sales estimates. Management may have a varying amount of confidence in these different estimates. Suppose management has

TABLE 2 A Comparison of Expected Volume (Q) and Break-Even Volume (Q$_B$) for Various Marketing Mixes

	(1)	(2)	(3)	(4)	(5)	(6) Volume Above Break-even	(7) Absolute Profits
		Marketing Mix					
	P	A	S	Q	Q$_B$	Q − Q$_B$	Z = (P − V)(Q − Q$_B$)
1.	$16	$10,000	$10,000	12,400	9,667	2,733	$16,398
2.	16	10,000	50,000	18,500	16,333	2,167	13,002
3.	16	50,000	10,000	15,100	16,333	−1,233	−7,398
4.	16	50,000	50,000	22,600	23,000	−400	−2,400
5.	24	10,000	10,000	5,500	4,143	1,357	18,998
6.	24	10,000	50,000	8,200	7,000	1,200	16,800
7.	24	50,000	10,000	6,700	7,000	−300	−4,200
8.	24	50,000	50,000	10,000	9,857	143	2,002

much more confidence in its sales estimate for marketing mix #6 than #5. This greater confidence may arise because the executives have more experience in using strategy #6. The choice they face is between a highly uncertain profit expectation of $18,998 and a more certain profit expectation of $16,800. Most managements have a risk aversion and are willing to accept a strategy with a lower expected profit if the accompanying risk is *sufficiently* less. However the specific amount of trade-off of expected profits for risk reduction will vary among managements.

How can management's taste for risk be measured and introduced into the formal analysis? There are at least two different ways to accomplish this. One is through the preparation of an indifference map in which management expresses its preferences between different combinations of expected profit and risk. Let us recall that in considering each marketing mix, management developed a subjective probability distribution of possible sales outcomes. Only the mean, Q, of the distribution was used. Now assume that the standard deviation of this distribution is used as a measure of risk. A low standard deviation means that management is fairly sure of the sales outcome and a high standard deviation means that management is very unsure. The standard deviation of the profit estimate can be calculated from the standard deviation of the sales estimate.[1] Let us use σ_Z to denote

[1] Expected profit is given by $Z = (P − V)(Q − Q_B)$. Suppose both Q and Q_B are estimated with some

the standard deviation of estimated profit. Let $(Z, \sigma_Z)^*$ represent the expected profit and standard deviation of profit, respectively, of the marketing mix with the highest Z; in our example, this is mix #5 and assume it is ($18,998, $12,000). Then management can be asked to list other (Z, σ_Z) such that it is indifferent between them and $(Z, \sigma_Z)^*$. For example, management may be indifferent to ($18,998, $12,000), ($16,000, $6,800), ($13,000, $4,200), ($10,000, $2,000), and ($7,000, $0). An indifference curve has been fitted through these sample points in Figure 1. The region to the left of this curve consists of inferior profit situations, while the region to the right of this curve consists of superior profit situations. Then the (Z, σ_Z) for the other marketing mixes can be plotted. If these points all plot in the inferior region, then mix #5 remains the best mix, subject to further qualification. If any points plot in the superior region, the foregoing procedure can be repeated to establish a new indifference curve to the right of the

uncertainty. The uncertainty of Q reflects the difficulty of estimating sales; and the uncertainty of Q_B, the break-even volume, reflects the difficulty of estimating costs. Suppose further that the degree of uncertainty in estimating sales is independent of the degree of uncertainty in estimating costs. Let σ_Q and σ_{QB}, the standard deviations, represent the respective degrees of uncertainty. Then σ_Z, the standard deviation of profit, can be derived by applying elementary theorems on variances. Specifically, $\sigma^2_{ax} = a^2\sigma^2_x$ and $\sigma^2_{x+y} = \sigma^2_x + \sigma^2_y$. Applying these theorems to $Z = (P − V)(Q − Q_B)$, $\sigma_Z = (P − V)\sqrt{\sigma_Q^2 + \sigma_{Q_B}^2}$.

FIG. 1 Company indifference curve for expected profit (Z) and risk(σ)

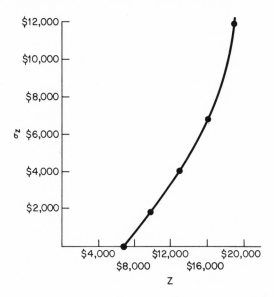

old one and the remaining contending points can be tested again.

If management has difficulty in thinking of risk in terms of standard deviations, an alternative procedure can be used instead. Management can be asked to express its preferences between various gambles where the risks are stated. The preferences become the basis for preparing a corporate utility scale for various money sums. For a management with risk aversion, the chance to earn twice the profit tends to carry *less* than twice the utility. For each marketing mix, the possible profit outcomes are re-stated as utility outcomes. Then the probabilities are used to find the expected utility for that marketing mix. The best marketing mix can be defined as the one with the maximum expected utility [5].

2. *The absolute profit estimates for the eight marketing mixes must be converted into rates of return on investment in order to choose the best marketing mix and to decide whether to develop the new product at all.* For example, management estimates that 5,500 units will be sold in the first year with marketing mix #5 and 8,200 units will be sold with marketing mix #6. But mix #6 will tie up more dollars

than mix #5 because production, inventory, and marketing are carried out on a larger scale. For each mix, Z should be expressed as a ratio to the required investment. Mix #5 is still likely to stand out as the best choice in the example. But now a second question also can be answered: is the expected rate of return greater than the company's target rate of return? The company is not likely to develop a new product whose expected rate of return falls short of the target rate.

3. *The use of expected profits ignores the variability and duration of profits implied by different initial marketing mixes.* At the outset, it should be emphasized that management is *not* trying to determine a permanent marketing mix to be used over the lifetime of this product. Both costs and sales will change over time because of competition, market saturation, business fluctuations, and the like. The company may start with mix #5 and if strong competition enters the market with a reduced price, the ABC Electronics Company may find it expedient to change its mix. It may reduce its price and/or change its promotion. Either reaction is tantamount to adopting a new marketing mix.

By examining different marketing mixes

in the profit analysis stage of new product development, the company is trying to ascertain an initial strategy and its implied initial profit level. Thus $18,998 represents the amount of profits expected in the first year with mix #5. The company is interested in discovering the strategy which will enable it to recover as much cost as possible as soon as possible because of the difficulty of foretelling the fate of the product beyond a few years. Yet it is also a fact that the initial marketing mix can have an important effect on the company's long-run success with this product. A low price, medium promotion mix like #2, in creating a high initial sales volume, tends to bring about an earlier saturation of the market and hence a shorter period of profits. Mix #5, because it employs a high price and brings high profits, is likely to induce an early influx of competition which also tends to shorten the period of good profits. The long-run implications of the initial mixes must be considered. The solution ultimately may lie in simulating on a computer different time sequences of mix decisions under alternative assumptions and events to derive some indication of alternative profit possibilities.

4. *The previous analysis assumes that no marketing mix has been overlooked which might yield a higher expected profit than the eight listed mixes.* The sales estimates (Q) in Table 2 can be viewed as a sample from a larger universe of executive opinion concerning the functional relationship $Q = f(P, A, S)$. It may be possible to find an equation which closely describes these estimates. The equation could then be solved to estimate expected sales, and ultimately profits, for marketing mixes which were not explicitly considered by the executives. For example, a plausible mathematical form for demand functions is the multiple exponential:

$$Q = kP^a A^b S^c$$

where $k =$ a scale factor

$a =$ the price elasticity

$b =$ the advertising elasticity

$c =$ the personal selling elasticity

The multiple exponential equation has provided a useful fit in several demand situations [4]. This form fits quite well the sample values of (Q) in Table 2. This is more by design than by accident. The least squares equation is

$$Q = 100,000 \ P^{-2} A^{1/8} S^{1/4}$$

Price has an elasticity of -2, that is, a one percent reduction in price, other things equal, tends to increase unit sales by 2 percent. Advertising has an elasticity of $1/8$ and the sales budget has an elasticity of $1/4$. The coefficient 100,000 is a scale factor which translates the dollar magnitudes into the appropriate physical volume effects.

Several of the preceding equations can now be drawn together:

profit equation	$Z = (P - 10)(Q - Q_B)$	(1)
demand equation	$Q = 100,000P^{-2}A^{1/8}S^{1/4}$	(2)
break-even volume equation	$Q_B = \dfrac{38,000 + A + S}{P - 10}$	(3)

The best marketing mix was defined initially as the one which maximized Z, that is, profits. Solving equation (1) in terms of (2) and (3), Z can be re-written as:

$$Z = (P - 10)$$
$$\times \left(100,000P^{-2}A^{1/8}S^{1/4} - \frac{38,000 + A + S}{P - 10} \right)$$
$$Z = (P - 10)$$
$$\times (100,000P^{-2}A^{1/8}S^{1/4}) - 38,000 - A - S$$
$$Z = 100,000P^{-1}A^{1/8}S^{1/4} - 1,000,000$$
$$P^{-2}A^{1/8}S^{1/4} - 38,000 - A - S \qquad (4)$$

Thus Z is a function of three marketing variables.

The next step is to find that unique set of values of P, A, and S which maximizes Z in (4). This is a problem in differential calculus. The work is carried out in the appendix where the following values emerge:

$$P = \$20$$

$$A = \$12,947$$

$$S = \$25,894$$

$$Z = \$26,735$$

It is interesting to compare this mix with mix #5 which yielded the highest Z of the eight mixes considered in Table 2. Mix #5 called for a price of $24 and an advertising and sales budget of $10,000 each. The new calculation calls attention to the possibility that a somewhat lower price, a slight increase in advertising expenditure, and a substantial increase in personal selling expenditure might boost profits by several thousand dollars. Thus it may be possible to employ mathematical analysis to overcome the limitations of considering only a small set of marketing mixes. Though we have illustrated this in terms of Z, a more complicated mathematical analysis can be prepared for finding the best marketing mix under conditions of uncertainty, different investment requirements, and more than three marketing variables.[2]

SUMMARY AND CONCLUSIONS

The overall challenge of new product development is to weed out the impracticable ideas as early as possible and to process the remaining ideas as efficiently as possible. The profit analysis stage is where a product idea which has been found to be compatible with the company's objectives and resources must be analyzed for its profit potential.

[2] It possesses a number of plausible properties. First, it provides that the effect of a specific marketing variable depends not only upon its own level but also on the levels of the other marketing variables. Thus a price of $16 will have one demand effect if advertising and selling are each set at $10,000 and another if advertising and selling are each set at $50,000. This interdependency does not exist with linear equations. Second, the exponential equation shows diminishing marginal returns to increases in the advertising and sales budgets and this accords with intuitive expectations. Finally, the exponents represent the respective elasticities of the marketing variables, provided there is no intercorrelation between the independent variables.

It is not sufficient to confine the analysis to one specific conception of how the product will look and be marketed, though this is the typical practice. For the marketing mix will influence both the costs and the sales of the new product, and it is not obvious in advance which mix will maximize expected profits.

The method outlined in this article requires management to develop estimates of likely costs and sales under different marketing mixes on the basis of the best available information. These estimates become the raw data in an analysis which seeks to determine the best marketing mix and whether this mix promises a sufficient level of profits, in the face of uncertainty and the required investment, to justify developing the product. Admittedly there is no way to prove that the suggested analysis does in fact lead to better decisions at the profit analysis stage. Its claim is that it calls attention to the relevant factors and outlines a systematic way to consider them.

APPENDIX

The objective is to find the unique set of price (P), advertising (A), and personal selling (S), which maximize profits (Z) in the equation:

$$Z = 100,000P^{-1}A^{1/8}S^{1/4}$$

$$- 1,000,000P^{-2}A^{1/8}S^{1/4}$$

$$- 38,000 - A - S \qquad (1)$$

First find the first three partial derivatives of Z and set them equal to zero:

$$\frac{\delta Z}{\delta P} = -100,000P^{-2}A^{1/8}S^{1/4} \qquad (2)$$

$$+ 2,000,000P^{-3}A^{1/8}S^{1/4} = 0$$

$$\frac{\delta Z}{\delta A} = 12,500P^{-1}A^{-7/8}S^{1/4} \qquad (3)$$

$$- 125,000P^{-2}A^{-7/8}S^{1/4} - 1 = 0$$

$$\frac{\delta Z}{\delta S} = 25,000P^{-1}A^{1/8}S^{-3/4} \qquad (4)$$

$$- 250,000P^{-2}A^{-1/8}S^{3/4} - 1 = 0$$

Rearrange the terms in (2):

$$\frac{\delta Z}{\delta P} = 100,000P^{-2}A^{1/8}S^{1/4}$$

$$\times (20P^{-1} - 1) = 0 \qquad (2a)$$

Assuming that $P \neq \infty$, $A \neq 0$, and $S \neq 0$, it follows that

$$(20P^{-1} - 1) = 0 \text{ or}$$
$$P = \$20 \qquad (5)$$

Next, rewrite (3) and (4):

$$12,500P^{-1}A^{-7/8}S^{1/4}(1 - 10P^{-1}) = 1 \qquad (3a)$$
$$25,000P^{-1}A^{1/8}S^{-3/4}(1 - 10P^{-1}) = 1 \qquad (4a)$$

Divide (3a) by (4a), term for term:

$$1/2\, A^{-1}S = 1$$
$$S = 2A \qquad (6)$$

Next substitute (5) and (6) in (3a):

$$12,500(20^{-1})(A^{-7/8})(2A)^{1/4}[(1-10)(20^{-1})] = 1$$
$$A = \$12,947 \qquad (7)$$

Substitute (7) in (6):

$$S = 2(12,947) = \$25,894 \qquad (8)$$

The optimal marketing mix (P, A, S) is (\$20, \$12,947, \$25,894). The executives would forecast that this mix would produce a sales volume of:

$$Q = 100,000^{-2}A^{1/8}S^{1/4}$$
$$= 100,000(20^{-2})(12,947^{1/8})(25,894^{1/4})$$
$$= 10,358$$

The break-even volume implied by this mix would be:

$$Q_B = \frac{38,000 + A + S}{P - 10}$$
$$= \frac{38,000 + 12,947 + 25,897}{20 - 10}$$
$$= 7,684$$

Finally, profits (Z) under the optimal mix would be:

$$Z = (P - V)(Q - Q_B)$$
$$= (20 - 10)(10,358 - 7,684)$$
$$= \$26,735$$

REFERENCES

1. Booz, Allen, and Hamilton, *Management of New Products*, third ed., 1960.
2. P. E. Green, "Bayesian Statistics and Product Decisions," *Business Horizons*, 5 (1962), 101–109.
3. J. Johnston, *Statistical Cost Analysis*, New York: McGraw-Hill, 1960.
4. E. Nemmers, *Managerial Economics*, New York: John Wiley and Sons, 1962, 96ff.
5. R. Schlaifer, *Probability and Statistics for Business Decisions*, New York: McGraw-Hill, 1959, Chapter 2.

19

A Simultaneous Equation Regression Study of Advertising and Sales of Cigarettes

FRANK M. BASS*

This article demonstrates the applications of simultaneous equation regression methods in analyzing limited time series data for sales and advertising. In testing a model with sales and advertising relationships for filter and nonfilter cigarette brands, we could not reject a model in which the advertising elasticity for filter brands is substantially greater than that for nonfilter brands.

INTRODUCTION

There is no more difficult, complex, or controversial problem in marketing than measuring the influence of advertising on sales. There is also probably no more interesting or potentially profitable measurement problem than this one. The difficulties involved in measuring the influence of advertising may generally be separated into three major categories:

1. Isolating advertising effects from the many other variables that affect sales
2. Measuring the quantity of advertising, considering that advertising dollar expenditures reflect alternative choices of media, psychological appeals, and copy
3. Identifying the relationship that reflects the

Reprinted from Journal of Marketing Research, *published by the American Marketing Association. "A Simultaneous Equation Regression Study of Advertising and Sales of Cigarettes," by Frank M. Bass, (August 1969), pp. 291–97, 300. Reprinted with permission of author and publisher.*

* Frank M. Bass is professor of industrial administration, Purdue University. The author is indebted to Robert L. Basmann for his advice, criticism, and contribution of ideas. Thomas H. Bruhn, Gordon Constable, and Marvin Margolis provided computational assistance. The author assumes full responsiblity for this article.

influence of sales on advertising, as well as that which reflects advertising's influence on sales—the so-called identification problem.

Quandt [17] has analyzed these and other difficulties at length. Kuehn and Rohloff [12] have argued that because of the severity of these measurement difficulties, greater progress in studying advertising effectiveness can be made by analyzing household or individual consumer behavior than aggregative data. Simple regression studies are particularly susceptible to criticism because of the serial correlation in sales and advertising [5].

There have been several interesting brand-switching studies [7, 9, 10]. However, only a few of these studies have attempted to relate changes in brand-switching activity to marketing decision variables [11, 14, 15, 24]. Furthermore, no known published work deals with the identification problem in advertising. Telser [18, 19], Palda [16], Weinberg [23,] and Vidale and Wolfe [22] have applied single-equation regression models to macro sales and advertising data. Besides failing to solve the identification problem, these single-equation regression studies permit only a weak or ambiguous test of the model.

This article suggests that progress can be made in studying advertising effectiveness by: (a) trying various approaches and models, (b) devising models that must pass an unambiguous test, in a scientific sense, to be found to agree with the data and, (c) publishing enough detail to permit and foster debate and criticism.

The study presented in this article is not without limitations. The scarcity of data not only hinders model formulation but also poses unknown dangers associated with errors in the equations. Because data are only available annually, the number of observations is restricted, and short-term variations are concealed.

This study deals with aggregative sales and advertising data, the form in which data are commonly available to management. The model must pass a severe test to be acceptable. Furthermore, it takes into account the simultaneous nature of the relationship between sales and advertising, a serious omission in previous studies. Not only are sales influenced by advertising, but advertising is also influenced by sales. Advertising decision rules, whether rigid or flexible, certainly account for sales. Therefore, single-equation regression models cannot adequately identify advertising-sales and sales-advertising relationships. The multiple-equation regression model explored here deals explicitly with these simultaneous relationships.

ORGANIZATION

The organization of this study closely follows that suggested by Basmann [3]. The model is formulated in terms of a system of equations including endogenous and exogenous variables—the structural relations. Besides the set of structural equations, the model comprises restrictions on the para-

meters of structural relations which are determined theoretically and provide the basis for testing the model. As indicated by Basmann [3] "... the testing of theoretical premises about an economic parameter is logically prior to its estimation."

The system of structural equations is uniquely related to a set of reduced-form equations in which each endogenous variable is separately related to the exogenous variables. Assumptions that restrict the structural parameters necessarily imply limits on the parameters in the reduced-form equations. Estimates of the reduced-form parameters taken in conjunction with the implied boundaries on these parameters constitute the test of the model.

This model was constructed to explain recent sales levels of groups of competitive cigarette brands for which given initial conditions and background assumptions are met. The initial conditions for this explanatory model are described by sequences of two exogenous variables, disposable personal income and prices. The background conditions imply the absence of external perturbations.

Each structural equation explains a part of the system of relations being studied when that part is isolated from the rest of the system. We shall construct the model by building the parts and then assembling the components to derive the system.

TABLE 1 Endogenous and Exogenous Variables

Year	Y_1	Y_2	Y_3	Y_4	X_1	X_2
1953	2.39851	3.50465	−1.26117	−0.28369	3.41653	−0.60906
1954	2.60060	3.45582	−0.90035	−0.37119	3.41876	−0.60906
1955	2.83890	3.42632	−0.62703	−0.43061	3.44491	−0.60206
1956	2.97883	3.38979	−0.43572	−0.44389	3.46147	−0.60033
1957	3.09065	3.33810	−0.34364	−0.55378	3.46451	−0.59176
1958	3.15067	3.30278	−0.34605	−0.53839	3.46304	−0.59860
1959	3.18361	3.30251	−0.30510	−0.54141	3.47986	−0.57349
1960	3.19626	3.29920	−0.33548	−0.53467	3.48502	−0.57675
1961	3.20779	3.29484	−0.34157	−0.54432	3.49358	−0.57675
1962	3.21945	3.27891	−0.36206	−0.54872	3.50804	−0.57840
1963	3.23843	3.25720	−0.28542	−0.54580	3.51834	−0.56543
1964	3.22329	3.20154	−0.29571	−0.54809	3.54063	−0.55596
1965	3.23099	3.21304	−0.31297	−0.49872	3.56335	−0.53910

Sources: See [1, 2, 20, 21, 26].

SYSTEM AND ASSUMPTIONS

The model consists of two demand equations for two competing groups of cigarette brands and two equations that describe the advertising relations for these groups of brands. The sales of the major filter cigarette brands have been aggregated to give one demand equation for this group. Similarly, there is one demand equation for the major nonfilter brands. The system's two remaining equations describe the behavior of advertising for the two competing groups of cigarette brands. The filter brands are: Winston, Kent, Marlboro, Herbert Tareyton, Viceroy, L&M, and Parliament; the nonfilter brands are: Pall Mall, Camel, Lucky Strike, Chesterfield, Old Gold, and Philip Morris. Sales and advertising data for 1953–1965 were obtained from *Advertising Age* [1, 2].

Since the prices of filter brands are identical as are the prices of nonfilter brands, the aggregation of brand sales in each class is justified theoretically. The Leontieff-Hicks theorem [8, 13, 25] establishes that if the prices of a group of goods change in equal proportion, that group can then be treated as a single commodity. Basmann [4] has shown that this theorem applies when the parameters of the consumer's utility function depend on advertising of competitive commodities. Since the Leontieff-Hicks theorem justifies aggregation in this study, concepts of complementarity, substitutability, price elasticity, income elasticity, etc., apply to the grouped commodities just as the corresponding concepts and measures apply to single goods.

In developing a test of the model we shall require specification of the structural equations as well as hypothesized limits on the values of the structural parameters .... Athough the estimates of parameters are not restricted by the hypotheses, we shall test the hypothesis that the structural parameters lie within certain intervals by making predictions about the reduced-form parameters. We shall therefore give the hypothesized limits on each structural parameter and discuss the reasons for establishing these limits.

DEMAND FOR MAJOR BRANDS OF FILTER AND NONFILTER CIGARETTES

Demand Equation for Filter Brands

For every year i, if the demand for filter brands is considered in isolation from the rest of the system,

$$y_{1t} = \beta_1 y_{3t} + \beta_2 y_{4t} + \gamma_1 x_{1t} + \gamma_2 x_{2t} \quad (1)$$
$$+ \gamma_3 + \mu_{1t},$$

where

y_{1t} is logarithm of sales of filter cigarettes (number of cigarettes) divided by population over age 20

y_{3t} is logarithm of advertising dollars for filter cigarettes divided by population over age 20 divided by advertising price index

y_{4t} is logarithm of advertising dollars for nonfilter cigarettes divided by population over age 20 divided by advertising price index

x_{1t} is logarithm of disposable personal income divided by population over age 20 divided by consumer price index

x_{2t} is logarithm of price per package of nonfilter cigarettes divided by consumer price index

$E(\mu_{1t}) = 0$, and

$$\text{Var } (\mu_{1t}) = E(\mu_{1t}^2) = \omega_{\mu_1}^2.$$

We therefore postulate that the per capita sales of filter cigarettes is a nonlinear function of the ratio of per capita advertising for the two competitive types of cigarettes and the two exogenous variables. Advertising dollars have been deflated by an advertising price index developed by Yang [26]. Although it might have been desirable to include prices of the filter and nonfilter cigarettes as variables, the nonfilter price is available as a component of the consumer price index, but the filter price is not.

Premises About Equation 1 Parameters:

$\beta_1 + \beta_2 = 0$. This premise implies that the ratio of filter advertising to nonfilter advertising governs the influence of advertising on the demand for filter cigarettes. Since Equation 1 is expressed in logarithms of the quantities, it may be written in terms of the original quantities as:

$$Y_{1t} = Y_{3t}^{\beta_1} Y_{4t}^{\beta_2} X_{1t}^{\gamma_1} X_{3t}^{\gamma_2} 10^{\gamma_3 + \mu_1 t}.$$

If $\beta_1 = -\beta_2$, this equation is then:

$$Y_{1t} = (Y_{3t} \mid Y_{4t})^{\beta_1} X_{1t}^{\gamma_1} X_{3t}^{\gamma_2} 10^{\gamma_3 + \mu_1 t}.$$

The premise that $\beta_1 + \beta_2 = 0$ is therefore consistent with the idea that the demand for filter cigarettes is influenced by the ratio of advertising for the two different types of cigarettes. This premise and the others which follow were derived from theory and judgment. Regardless of the origins of the premises, they are explicit and testable.

$.5 \leq \beta_1 \leq .6$. The assumptions that demand elasticity with respect to advertising is inelastic and that advertising has a positive effect on sales imply that β_1 is between zero and one. This range has been substantially narrowed to test rigidly the premises.

$1.0 \leq \gamma_1 < 1.3$. Filter and nonfilter cigarette brands are clearly highly substitutable commodities, the filter brand being favored. The income elasticity of filter brands is assumed to reflect the income effect over the historical period analyzed.

$0 < \gamma_2 \leq .8$. Consistent with the previous premise, it is logical to assume that the cross-elasticity of demand for filter brands with respect to the price of nonfilter brands should be nonnegative and possibly high.

$-1.25 < \gamma_3 \leq -.75$. The intercept term is the most difficult parameter to interpret economically. The restrictions on this parameter have therefore been established resid-

ually, using the other restrictions and typical values of the other variables.

Demand Equation for Nonfilter Brands

For every year t, if the demand for nonfilter brands is considered in isolation from the rest of the system,

$$y_{2t} = \beta_3 y_{3t} + \beta_4 y_{4t} + \gamma_4 x_{1t} + \gamma_5 x_{2t} \quad (2)$$
$$+ \gamma_6 + \mu_{2t},$$

where

y_{2t} is logarithm of sales of nonfilter cigarettes (number of cigarettes) divided by population over age 20

$y_{3t}, y_{4t}, x_{1t}, x_{2t}$ are as defined previously

$E(\mu_{2t}) = 0$,   and

$$\text{Var } (\mu_{2t}) = E(\mu_{2t}^2) = \omega_{\mu_2}^2.$$

Premises About Equation 2 Parameters:

$\beta_3 + \beta_4 = 0$. This premise implies, as in Equation 1, the ratio of the advertising hypothesis.

$.2 \leq \beta_4 \leq .3$. In keeping with the premise that nonfilter cigarettes are inferior, we shall test the hypothesis that the advertising elasticity for this group of brands is approximately one-half that of filter brands.

$0 \leq \gamma_4 \leq .8$. The income elasticity of nonfilter brands is assumed to be less than unity (less than the corresponding elasticity for filter brands) and possibly near zero. This restriction is consistent with the premise that income effects favor differentially filter brands.

$-3.0 \leq \gamma_5 \leq -1.0$. The demand for nonfilter cigarettes is assumed to be price elastic and possibly high. This premise is consistent with the assertion that nonfilters are inferior to filters. An increase in the price of nonfilters therefore induces a more than proportionate decline in demand.

$-1.25 \leq \gamma_6 \leq -.75$. The limits on the intercept term are deduced residually.

ADVERTISING RELATIONSHIPS FOR MAJOR BRANDS OF FILTER AND NONFILTER CIGARETTES

Equation Describing Advertising Behavior of Filter Brands

For every year t, if the advertising of filter cigarettes is considered in isolation from the rest of the system,

$$y_{1t} = \beta_5 y_{2t} + \beta_6 y_{3t} + \gamma_7 + \mu_{3t} \qquad (3)$$

or,

$$y_{3t} = \frac{1}{\beta_6} y_{1t} - \frac{\beta_5}{\beta_6} y_{2t} - \frac{\gamma^7}{\beta_6} - \frac{1}{\beta_6} \mu_{3t}$$

$$E(\mu_{3t}) = 0, \qquad \text{and}$$

$$\text{Var}\ (\mu_{3t}) = E(\mu_{3t}^2) = \omega_{\mu_3}^2.$$

Premises About Equation 3 Parameters:
$.6 \le \beta_6 \le .7.$
$-1.0 \le \beta_5 \le -.9.$ Equation 3 postulates that advertisers consider the sales of both types of cigarettes in determining the advertising budget for filter cigarettes. The restriction on β_5 implies that the advertising of filter cigarettes responds positively to increases in filter cigarette sales. The advertising response is assumed to be more than proportionate to the increase in filter cigarette sales and possibly smaller for nonfilter cigarettes.
$5.0 \le \gamma_7 \le 7.0.$ The limits on the intercept term are deduced residually.

Equation Describing Advertising Behavior of Nonfilter Brands

For every year t, if the advertising of nonfilter cigarettes is considered in isolation from the rest of the system,

$$y_{2t} = \beta_7 y_{1t} + \beta_8 y_{4t} + \gamma_8 + \mu_{4t} \qquad (4)$$

or,

$$y_{4t} = \frac{1}{\beta_8} y_{2t} - \frac{\beta_7}{\beta_8} y_{1t} - \frac{\gamma_8}{\beta_8} - \frac{1}{\beta_8} \mu_{4t}$$

where

$$E(\mu_{4t}) = 0, \qquad \text{and}$$

$$\text{Var}\ (\mu_{4t}) = E(\mu_{4t}^2) = \omega_{\mu_4}^2.$$

Premises About Equation 4 Parameters:
$-1.0 \le \beta_7 \le -1.5.$
$-3.0 \le \beta_8 \le -3.5.$ The advertising of nonfilter cigarettes is assumed to respond negatively to higher levels of sales of both filter and nonfilter cigarettes, but the response is possibly slightly greater to the sales of filter than to nonfilter cigarettes.
$5.0 \le \gamma_8 \le 7.0.$ The limits on the intercept term are deduced residually.

MODEL OF SALES AND ADVERTISING OF FILTER AND NONFILTER CIGARETTES

The model's parts produce the system of structural equations that describe the sales and advertising of the two competing products:

$$-y_{1t} + 0y_{2t} + \beta_1 y_{3t} + \beta_2 y_{4t} + \gamma_1 X_{1t}$$
$$+ \gamma_2 X_{2t} + \gamma_3 + \mu_{1t} = 0$$
$$0y_{1t} - y_{2t} + \beta_3 y_{3t} + \beta_4 y_{4t} + \gamma_4 X_{1t}$$
$$+ \gamma_5 X_{2t} + \gamma_6 + \mu_{2t} = 0$$
$$- y_{1t} + \beta_5 y_{2t} + \beta_6 y_{3t} + 0y_{4t} + 0X_{1t}$$
$$+ 0X_{2t} + \gamma_7 + \mu_{3t} = 0$$
$$\beta_7 y_{1t} - y_{2t} + 0y_{3t} + \beta_8 y_{4t} + 0X_{1t}$$
$$+ 0X_{2t} + \gamma_8 + \mu_{4t} = 0,$$

or

$$\mathbf{B}\, y_t + \mathbf{\Gamma} X_t + u_t = 0.$$

REDUCED-FORM EQUATIONS

The system of structural equations

$$\mathbf{B}y_t + \mathbf{\Gamma}x_t + \mu_t = 0$$

is equivalent to the system of equations

$$y_t = -(\mathbf{B})^{-1}\mathbf{\Gamma}x_t - (\mathbf{B})^{-1}\mu_t$$

if B is nonsingular. The reduced-form equations ... are:

$$y_{1t} = \alpha_1 X_{1t} + \alpha_2 X_{2t} + \alpha_3 + \eta_{1t}$$
$$y_{2t} = \alpha_4 X_{1t} + \alpha_5 X_{2t} + \alpha_6 + \eta_{2t}$$
$$y_{3t} = \alpha_7 X_{1t} + \alpha_8 X_{2t} + \alpha_9 + \eta_{3t}$$
$$y_{4t} = \alpha_{10} X_{1t} + \alpha_{11} X_{2t} + \alpha_{12} + \eta_{4t}.$$

The parameters α_i, $i = 1, 2, \ldots, 12$ and η_{it}, $i = 1, \ldots, 4$ are functions of the structural parameters. Therefore the premises about the structural equations may be used to make predictions about the reduced-form parameters. Unless all the reduced-form parameter estimates lie within the acceptable limits of their predicted values as implied by the structural premises, at least one of the premises is discredited. For this predictive test to be valid, the determinant of B, Δ, must not be zero. Therefore it is necessary to show that the structural premises exclude the possibility of a zero Δ.

No empirical test can prove conclusively that a theory is true, but it can disprove a theory. Under certain circumstances structural parameters may be estimated without testing the model; however, if the structural equations are unidentified or over-identified, estimation procedures are debatable. In any case the predictive test shows whether a theory agrees with the empirical evidence.

TEST OF THE MODEL

To test the model, the implied maximum and minimum values of the reduced-form coefficients were calculated[1] and appear with the estimated values in Table 2.

[1] These calculations were made using the gradient projection method with the computer program Share Distribution #1399 SDGP 90.

A more complete test of the model could have been conducted by making explicit assumptions about the covariance terms of the structural equations and solving for maxi-

TABLE 2 Maxima and Minima of Regression Parameters Admissible Under Structural Premises and Estimates of Regression Parameters

Minimum Value	Coefficient Estimate	Maximum Value
2.30	α_1 (8.75)	39.85
−49.50	α_2 (−7.82)	−0.32
−148.25	α_3 (−31.96)	−7.92
−12.05	α_4 (−2.34)	−0.47
−1.24	α_5 (0.78)	13.50
3.69	α_6 (11.94)	55.75
2.17	α_7 (10.11)	48.34
−62.25	α_8 (−10.90)	−1.19
−215.12	α_9 (−42.01)	−14.13
−15.91	α_{10} (−2.64)	−0.43
0.25	α_{11} (2.77)	20.25
2.83	α_{12} (10.33)	69.87
−1.61	Δ	−0.12

ma and minima of the reduced-form covariance terms. This was not done for this study. The results in Table 2 clearly show that the model satisfies the conditions implied by the structural premises. All 12 reduced-form coefficient estimates lie within the acceptable region. For this test, the model is in good agreement with the data.

IDENTIFIABILITY AND STRUCTURAL PARAMETER ESTIMATION

Since the model satisfies the test conditions associated with the reduced-form equations, we may proceed to structural estimation and further testing, if necessary. ... Since

$$y_t = -(\mathbf{B})^{-1}\mathbf{\Gamma}x_t - (\mathbf{B})^{-1}\mu_t,$$
$$\mathbf{A} + (\mathbf{B})^{-1}\mathbf{\Gamma} = 0 \quad \text{and} \quad \mathbf{BA} + \mathbf{\Gamma} = 0.$$

In this study the structural parameters $\beta_5, \beta_6, \beta_7, \beta_8, \gamma_7,$ and γ_8 are uniquely identified, i.e., estimates of these parameters are implied by estimates of the reduced-form parameters. Estimates of the remaining structural parameters were developed by two-stage least squares regression, but the significance of this estimation was not determined. The unidentified parameters remain unidentified except for the limits of restrictions placed on them. The estimated parameter values are:

$$\hat{\beta}_1 = \quad .594 \qquad \hat{\gamma}_1 = \quad 1.173$$
$$\hat{\beta}_4 = \quad .247 \qquad \hat{\gamma}_2 = \quad .305$$
$$\hat{\beta}_5 = - \ .924 \qquad \hat{\gamma}_3 = - \ .874$$
$$\hat{\beta}_6 = \quad .651 \qquad \hat{\gamma}_4 = \quad .815$$
$$\hat{\beta}_7 = -1.222 \qquad \hat{\gamma}_5 = -2.607$$

$$\hat{\beta}_8 = -3.158 \qquad \hat{\gamma}_6 = -1.027$$
$$\hat{\gamma}_7 = \quad 6.425$$
$$\hat{\gamma}_8 = \quad 5.496$$

Comparisons of the fitted equations with actual observations of sales of both types of cigarette brands are shown in Figure 1.

MANAGERIAL IMPLICATIONS

Having developed a model that satisfies test conditions, we will now explore the model's managerial implications. Because

FIG. 1 Comparison of actual and estimated sales, filter cigarettes and nonfilter cigarettes

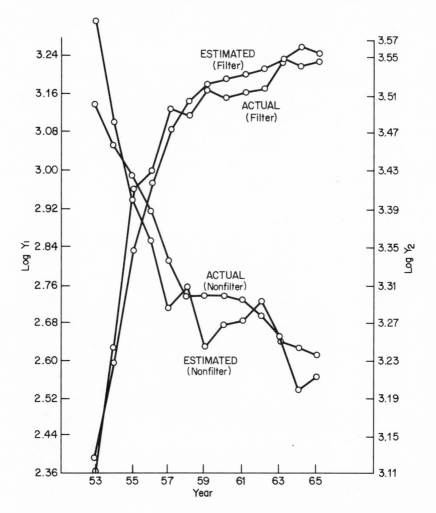

the demand equations in this study aggregate the sales for several brands and no direct information is provided here about the advertising elasticities of individual brands, the following managerial implications are only tentative and suggestive.

We consider a segment of the model in isolation from the system. There are several profit functions which an advertiser might adopt, e.g., game theoretic models, return on investment functions, aspiration level decision rules. The profit function considered here is current annual profit given the values of all variables (including competitive advertising), except the decision variable, advertising.

The profit function is:

$$\pi(A_t) = pq(A_t) - C(q) - A_t,$$

where

p is price
$q(A_t)$ is current sales as a function of current advertising
$C(q)$ is total production cost as a function of the sales volume
A_t is current advertising.

Maximizing, we have:

$$\frac{\partial \pi}{\partial A_t} = \left(p - \frac{\partial C}{\partial q}\right)\frac{dq}{dA_t} - 1 = 0.$$

Defining the advertising elasticity of demand in the usual way,[2] as:

$$\beta_1 = \frac{dq}{dA_t}\frac{A_t}{q},$$

we may write the profit maximization condition as:

$$\left(p - \frac{\partial C}{\partial q}\right)\beta_1 \frac{q}{A_t} = 1, \quad \text{or}$$

$$\frac{A_t}{q} = m\beta_1,$$

if unit production costs are constant, where m is unit gross margin exclusive of advertising costs. The advertising elasticity of demand, β_1, in general is not necessarily constant,

[2] For comparison, see [6].

but is constant in models such as the one developed here in which the logarithm of demand is a linear function of the logarithm of other variables, including advertising.

Using the demand equation developed earlier for filter cigarettes (Equation 1) and assuming that unit production costs are constant, the following profit function applies to filter cigarettes:

$$\pi(A_{1t}) = mq(A_{1t}) - A_{1t} = mP_t\left(\frac{A_{1t}}{C_t}\right)^{\beta_1}\left(\frac{A_{2t}}{C_t}\right)^{-\beta_1}$$

$$(Y_t)^{\gamma_1}(P_t)^{\gamma_2}(10)^{\gamma_3} - A_{1t},$$

where

m is unit gross margin, exclusive of advertising costs
P_t is population at time t over the age of 20
A_{1t} is dollar advertising expenditures for filter brands at time t
A_{2t} is dollar advertising expenditures for nonfilter brands at time t
C_t is P_t times advertising price index at time t
Y_t is disposable personal income divided by P_t times consumer price index at time t
P_t is price of nonfilter cigarettes divided by consumer price index at time t.

Then, $A_{1t}^* = m\beta_1 q(A_{1t}^*)$, and

$$\left(\frac{A_{1t}^*}{C_t}\right) = \left[\frac{m\beta_1 P_t}{C_t}\left(\frac{A_{2t}}{C_t}\right)^{-\beta_1}(Y_t)^{\gamma_1}(P_t)^{\gamma_2}(10)^{\gamma_3}\right]^{1-\beta_1}$$

The logarithm of this quantity has been calculated and measured against the comparable figure for actual advertising expenditures during 1953–1965. Gross margin for cigarettes is between 10 and 15 cents per carton. Calculations have therefore been made for both of these figures and are shown in Figure 2.

The results are perhaps somewhat surprising. Actual expenditures are bracketed by the optimal expenditures calculated at the two different gross margin levels. There is also a startling coincidence of direction and magnitude of change between the optimal and actual advertising expenditures. These

FIG. 2 Comparison of optimal and actual advertising expenditures, filter cigarettes

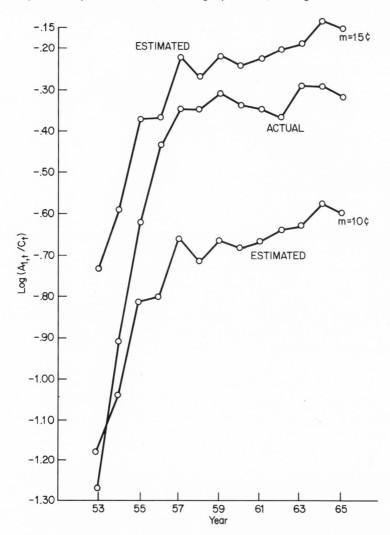

results suggest that the advertising expenditure policy of the average filter brand was nearly optimal according to at least one criterion of optimality. This criterion assumes, among other things, that profit maximization for filter brands is independent of profit maximization for nonfilter brands. However, these results tell little about the optimal advertising strategy for an individual filter brand since the advertising elasticity for an individual brand may differ from that for the group.

Optimal expenditures have also been calc-

ulated using the demand equation and parameter estimates for nonfilter brands and assuming ten cents gross margin per carton. Figure 3 provides a comparison of these calculations with the actual expenditures. The optimal and the actual expenditures follow parallel paths from 1953 until 1958, after which the actual is stable though the optimal continues to decline. It is possible that there was nonoptimal overadvertising of nonfilter brands after 1958 associated with an attempt to maintain minimum market share levels.

FIG. 3 Comparison of optimal and actual advertising expenditures, nonfilter cigarettes

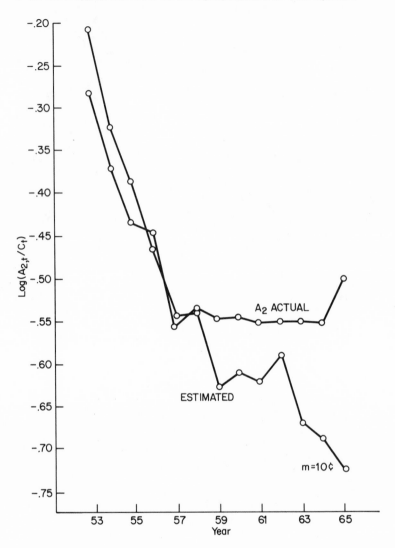

Although this implication about the group's advertising may not apply to every brand, it appears that at least some nonfilter brands were pursuing nonoptimal strategies during the period. The increase of nonfilter advertising in 1965 was associated with the introduction of filter cigarettes under brand names traditionally associated with nonfilters. This product policy has increased and accelerated in the industry since 1965, thus blurring the distinction between the two types of cigarettes and tending to de-

stroy the possible future managerial uses of this study.

SUMMARY AND CONCLUSIONS

Despite its limitations, the simultaneous equation regression model, developed and tested in this article, suggests that it may be successfully applied to advertising problems of this kind and may aid in shaping managerial decisions. Additional data on such variables as media, special sales promotions, distribution, and quality measures of advertising would add greatly to the credibility and rigor of aggregative statistical studies such as this one. However, this information can be obtained within companies. Further study within the framework suggested here may lead to significant managerial benefits.

Although results of this study are tentative with respect to the general applicability to advertising problems of the methodological framework, they suggest the possibility of designing formal, testable models to process the kinds of aggregative information generally available to management. The simultaneous regression model discussed here is the first known published model of its kind. However, a few firms are developing similar models.

· · ·

REFERENCES

1. ADVERTISING PUBLICATIONS, INC, "Costs of Cigarette Advertising: 1952–1959," *Advertising Age*, 31 (September 19, 1960), 126–7.
2. ———, "Costs of Cigarette Advertising: 1957–1965," *Advertising Age*, 37 (July 25, 1966), 56–8.
3. ROBERT L. BASMANN, "On the Application of the Identifiability Test Statistic in Predictive Testing of Explanatory Economic Models," *Econometric Annual, Indian Economic Journal*, 13, No. 3, (1965), 387–423.
4. ———, "A Theory of Demand with Variable Consumer Preferences," *Econometrica*, 24 (January), 1956, 47–58.
5. FRANK M. BASS, "A Dynamic Model of Market Share and Sales Behavior," *Toward Scientific Marketing*, in Stephen A. Greyser, ed., Chicago: American Marketing Association, 1963, 263–76.
6. ROBERT DORFMAN and PETER O. STEINER, "Optimal Advertising and Optimal Quality," *The American Economic Review*, 44 (December 1954), 826–36.
7. RONALD E. FRANK, "Brand Choice as a Probability Process," *Journal of Business*, 35 (January 1962), 43–56.
8. JOHN R. HICKS, *Value and Capital*, Oxford: Clarendon Press, 1946, 312–3.
9. RONALD A. HOWARD, "Stochastic Models of Consumer Behavior," in Frank M. Bass, et al., eds., *Application of the Sciences in Marketing Management*, New York: John Wiley & Sons, Inc., 1967.
10. ALFRED E. KUEHN, "Consumer Brand Choice— A Learning Process?" in Ronald E. Frank, et al., eds., *Quantitative Techniques in Marketing Analysis*, Homewood, Ill.: Richard D. Irwin, 1962.
11. ———, "A Model for Budgeting Advertising," in Frank M. Bass, et al., eds., *Mathematical Models and Methods in Marketing*, Homewood, Ill.: Richard D. Irwin, 1961.
12. ——— and Albert C. Rohloff, "On Methods: Fitting Models to Aggregate Data," *Journal of Advertising Research*, (March 1967), 43–7.
13. WASSILY LEONTIEFF, "Composite Commodities and the Problem of Index Numbers," *Econometrica*, 4 (January 1936), 39–59.
14. RICHARD MAFFEI, "Advertising Effectiveness, Brand Switching and Market Dynamics," *Journal of Industrial Economics*, 9 (April 1961), 119–31.
15. WILLIAM F. MASSY and RONALD E. FRANK, "Short Term Price and Dealing Effects in Selected Market Segments," *Journal of Marketing Research*, 2 (May 1965), 171–85.
16. KRISTIAN S. PALDA, *The Measurement of Cumulative Advertising Effects*, Englewood Cliffs, N.J.: Prentice-Hall, 1964.
17. RICHARD E. QUANDT, "Estimating Advertising Effectiveness: Some Pitfalls in Econometric Methods," *Journal of Marketing Research*, 1 (May 1964), 51–60.
18. LESTER G. TELSER, "The Demand for Branded Goods As Estimated from Consumer Panel Data," *The Review of Economics and Statistics*, 44 (August 1962), 300–24.
19. ———, "Advertising and Cigarettes," *The Journal of Political Economy*, 70 (October 1962), 471–99.
20. U.S. Census Bureau, *Statistical Abstract of United States*, Washington, D.C.: Government Printing Office, 1965, 327; 360–1.
21. U.S. Department of Agriculture, *Agricultural Statistics*, Washington, D.C.: Government Printing Office, 1965, 111–2.
22. M. L. VIDALE and H. B. WOLFE, "An Operation-Research Study of Sales Response to Advertising," *Operations Research*, 5 (June 1957).
23. ROBERT S. WEINBERG, "The Uses and Limitations of Mathematical Models for Market Planning," in Frank M. Bass, et al, eds., *Mathematical Models and Methods in Market-*

ing, Homewood, Ill.: Richard D. Irwin, 1961.

24. DOYLE WEISS, ALFRED A. KUEHN, and T. MCGUIRE, "Measuring the Effectiveness of Advertising," in Ray Haas, ed., *Science, Technology and Marketing*, Chicago: American Marketing Association, 1966.

25. HERMAN WOLD, *Demand Analysis: A Study in Econometrics*, New York: John Wiley & Sons, Inc., 1953, 108–9.

26. CHARLES YANG, "A Theoretical and Empirical Investigation of Advertising Cycles," Unpublished Ph.D. thesis, New York University, 1962.

20

The Measurement and Implications of Long-run Advertising Effects

KRISTIAN S. PALDA

· · ·

2. Long-run supply and, to a limited extent, long-run cooperative advertising effects were considered in the Nerlove–Waugh analysis. The present writer made the existence of long-run advertising effects a keystone of a model to estimate parameters of the demand function facing a single firm, a proprietary drug maker.[1]

The derivation of the basic model was shown in Chapter 4 and some implications were explored at the end of Chapter 5. We shall write the basic relations again with a view to deriving a particularly simple prescription for the optimal advertising appropriation. We shall match the normative model with estimated relationships and inquire to what extent the management of the firm in question behaved optimally, given the framework of the model. *This matching is not an exercise in intellectual curiosity*

From Kristian S. Palda, Economic Analysis for Marketing Decisions, © *1969. Reprinted by permission of Prentice-Hall, Inc., Englewood Cliffs, New Jersey.*

[1] Kristian S. Palda, *The Measurement of Cumulative Advertising Effects* (Englewood Cliffs, N.J.: Prentice-Hall Inc., 1964).

but an example of how marketing management could set about determining whether an optimal advertising appropriation policy is being carried on.

We recall that we postulated that advertising has a lagged effect on sales, of the specific form of convergent geometric series:

$$S_t = k + \alpha A_t + \alpha \lambda A_{t-1} + \alpha \lambda^2 A_{t-2}$$
$$+ \cdots \qquad 0 < \lambda < 1 \qquad (1)$$

This can be reduced to

$$S_t = c + \alpha A_t + \lambda S_{t-1} \qquad (2)$$

and considered for statistical estimation. Let us, for the moment, assume that Equation (2) can be estimated statistically and that we get numerical values for α and λ. The short-run effect of advertising is α. The long-run effect is derived with the help of the equilibrium concept. As the firm approaches its optimal activity level (this optimum level will be, of course, almost always changing; we are interested in the movement of the firm toward it), there is no tendency for sales to move away from an equilibrium level S_e. Then S_e tends to equal S_t and S_{t-1}:

$$S_e = c + \alpha A_t + \lambda S_e \qquad (3)$$

The long-run effect of advertising is then the derivative of sales with respect to advertising:

$$\frac{dS_e}{dA_t} = \frac{\alpha}{1 - \lambda} \qquad (4)$$

(We transposed λS_e to the left and divided through by $1 - \lambda$.) $\alpha/1 - \lambda$ is also the sum to infinity of the convergent geometric series formed by the coefficients of the A's.

Cast in terms of a stock of goodwill, the advertising-sales relationship can be expressed, Nerlove—Arrow-like, as follows:

$$S_t = k + \alpha a_t^* \qquad (5)$$

where a_t^* is advertising capital or goodwill, accumulated over the past. In turn, this capital can be viewed as capital accumulated up to the beginning of the current period, suitably depreciated over this current period and comprising this period's advertising expenditure as well:

$$a_t^* = (1 - p)a_{t-1}^* + A_t \qquad (6)$$

When we now multiply (6) by $1 - p$, lag it one period, and subtract the result from the original equation we get

$$\begin{aligned} S_t = kp &+ (1 - p)S_{t-1} \\ &+ \alpha[a_t^* - (1 - p)a_{t-1}^*] \end{aligned} \qquad (7)$$

Since the expression in the square brackets represents A_t, we have the lagged-effect model in slightly different form, enabling us to see that the rate of depreciation[2]

$$p = 1 - \lambda \qquad (8)$$

[2] Beyond a certain point of time the addition of earlier A_i's has but a slight effect on S_t. To find the length of time required for, say, 95 percent of the total effect to occur, the following procedure is helpful. Remembering that convergent geometric series are dealt with here, write $S_n/S = \geq 0.95$, or $1 - \lambda_n \geq 0.95$, where S is the sum of n (or of an infinite) number of terms of the geometric progression. Solving for n, $n \leq \log 0.05/\log \lambda$. The result indicates the number of periods that will elapse, on the average, before the invested advertising dollar loses 95 percent of its (gross) revenue-generating power.

We now know the short-and long-term sales generating power of advertising. How do we utilize this knowledge to determine the optimal advertising appropriation? We start with the simple prescription that the last dollar spent on advertising should equal the last dollar of revenues, net of all cost, including cost of capital, except advertising costs. We dynamize this statement, in view of the time dimension in our analysis, to say that the present value of the last dollar invested in advertising should be equal to the present value of revenue stimulated by advertising net of all costs, except advertising. We invest now; thus the present value of the advertising dollar is $1. Its effects on sales are postulated to be

$$\alpha A_t + \alpha\lambda A_{t+1} + \alpha\lambda^2 A_{t+2} + \cdots$$

where the A_t's equal $1. We must discount these, naturally. But we must also deduct, from these advertising-generated sales, all other costs except advertising. We can then write

$$\begin{aligned} \$ 1 &= c\alpha + \frac{c\alpha\lambda}{1 + r} + \frac{c\alpha\lambda^2}{(1 + r)^2} + \cdots \\ &= c\alpha\left[1 + \frac{\lambda}{1 + r} + \frac{\lambda^2}{(1 + r)^2} + \cdots\right] \\ &= c\alpha\left[\frac{1}{1 - (\lambda/1 + r)}\right] \quad 0 < c < 1 \end{aligned} \qquad (9)$$

or, in words, the present value of the marginal invested advertising dollar should be equal to the present value of the total revenue generated by it over time, reduced by a coefficient c that is defined to be 1 *minus* all costs, except advertising, as a percentage of sales. The unknown in this equation, which we want to discover, is the marginal rate of return on advertising investment, r. This is the rate that brings to equality the two present values. The formula for it is

$$r = \frac{c\alpha + \lambda - 1}{1 - c\alpha} \qquad (10)$$

The firm, in equilibrium, equalizes the marginal rates of return on the investment possibilities open to it (such as in sales force, product development, manufacturing) *and* the rate at which it can borrow capital. Following Nerlove-Waugh we shall call the latter ρ. The optimal advertising appropriation then yields a rate of return r_A, which is equal to other internal rates of return, $r_1, r_2, \ldots$ and to ρ:

$$r_A = r_1 = r_2 = \ldots = r_n = \rho \qquad (11)$$

Given that advertising returns are in the diminishing-returns stage, this rule implies that advertising expenditures should be increased when $r_A > r_n$ or $r_A > \rho$, and vice versa.

Summarizing, we first assumed a distributed lag model of the geometric progression form representing the impact of advertising outlays on sales over time. We derived a form simple enough for estimation purposes, assumed that the parameters of the model can be estimated, and then showed how to use these estimates to determine the optimal advertising appropriation. As anything done on the demand side, however, the whole attempt was built around the possibility of estimation, and indeed the model was evolved by Koyck, its originator, with this crucial purpose in mind. What are the difficulties of estimation here and how successfully can they be overcome?

In principle, to estimate the net effect of advertising upon sales means to estimate the total demand function facing the firm, in which variables such as prices, income, and other elements play their role besides advertising. To estimate it successfully using the multiple regression approach, the conditions postulated in Chapter 4 must be met. Briefly, the specifications for consistent and efficient least-squares regression estimates require that the *disturbances* follow some, preferably normal, distribution with zero mean and a variance that is finite and independent of particular values of the exogenous variables or of the order of disturbances; that the disturbances be serially uncorrelated; and that, most important, they be independent of the exogenous variables, which are in a

linear relationship with the endogenous variable.

One of the most successful (in terms of fit and prediction) estimating equations of the demand facing the drug firm Lydia Pinkham had the following form:

$$S_t = k + \lambda S_{t-1} + \alpha \log A_t + \beta D$$
$$+ \gamma T + \delta Y_t + u_t - \lambda u_{t-1} \qquad (12)$$

D is a dummy variable that simulates the effect of a qualitative, discrete demand shifter: advertising copy. Over the 53-year period upon which the estimates are based, the copy platform of the firm, under the attack of federal regulatory agencies, underwent one fundamental change in 1925. The dummy takes on a value of 1 from 1908 to 1925, of 0 thereafter. T represents trend, counting 1 to 53 for the years 1908–1960. Y is disposable personal income.

Consider now the disturbance term

$$u_t - \lambda u_{t-1} = v_t \qquad (13)$$

If, and only if, the disturbance terms follow an autoregressive relationship of the form

$$v_i = k u_{t-1} + \epsilon_t \qquad \kappa = \lambda \qquad (14)$$

(where ϵ is a serially independent random term with a finite, constant variance) will (a) the condition of serial independence be fulfilled,

$$v_t = \epsilon_t \qquad (15)$$

and, more important, (b) will v_t be uncorrelated with S_{t-1}. It so happens that in Pinkham's case the assumption (14) of a simple Markov process was a realistic one: There is positive serial correlation in the sales and advertising data—as there often is in economic time series.

Nonlinearity is to be firmly expected in the relationship between advertising expenditure and sales as a consequence of almost certainly present diminishing returns. However, this other potential pitfall in regression analysis is taken care of by the use of the advertising variable in logarithmic form. Indeed, the fact that in the Pinkham investigation advertising in log-linear form gave better results than advertising in terms of the original data tended to strengthen the conviction that diminishing returns are present. There appeared to be no problem of heteroskedasticity: The variance of residuals was not related to the level of advertising activity.

Thus far the discussion of the potential difficulties with the estimation of a demand function facing the firm in which the emphasis is on the advertising relationship—using a specific example, based on time-series data. It had, on the whole, an optimistic tone. For a very *pessimistic* note on the possibilities of econometric estimation the reader is referred to a truly splendid article by Quandt.[3]

And now to the last phase of the Pinkham example. We said we could match the normative model with the estimated relationship to see to what extent the management of the firm pursued optimally their advertising effort. (We can turn the question around, as is frequently done in economics, and ask: Given that it can be assumed that management, on the whole, can be relied upon to know how to maximize profits, do the estimated relationships support the soundness of the normative model?)[4] For this we need to present the numerical estimates of demand equation (15):

$$S_t = 3649 + 0.665 S_{t-1} + 1180 \log A_t$$
$$\qquad\quad (0.063) \qquad (243)$$

$$+ \ 774D + 32T - 2.83Y_t \quad (16)$$
$$\quad (107) \quad (5.9) \quad (0.67)$$

[3] Richard E. Quandt, "Estimating Advertising Effectiveness: Some Pitfalls in Econometric Methods," *Journal of Marketing Research* (May, 1964), pp. 51–60. Quandt deals mainly with problems encountered in *cross-sectional* data analysis, where the chief drawback appears to be the delineation of sales territories and the corresponding assignment of national advertising efforts (and other marketing activities shared jointly by the whole product line of the firm) to those territories.

[4] An attempt to confront a simple normative model of geographical distribution of a given total advertising appropriation with the actual practice of two large

$$R^2 = 0.94, \qquad N = 53, \qquad D - W = 1.59$$

In this equation sales and advertising expenditures are in thousands of dollars, the dummy and the trend are as previously mentioned, and personal disposable income is in billions of dollars—all dollars being current to the year in which they were exchanged. N is sample size and the Durbin-Watson statistic, $D - W$, indicates, at that value, that no serial correlation in the estimated disturbances is suspected. The sizes of the standard errors (in parentheses) are reassuringly small.

The estimated short-term effect of advertising, $\partial S_t / \partial A_t$, is derived by taking the derivative of sales with respect to the decimal-log advertising variable:

$$\frac{\partial S_t}{\partial \log_{10} A_t} = \frac{(0.4343)\hat{a}}{\text{av } A_t} \quad (17)$$

$$\frac{(0.4343)(1180)}{941} = 0.545 = MSE_{ST}$$

(It is the rule in econometric estimation to use the sample mean values in a derivation like this or in the computation of elasticities; the mean value of advertising expenditures over the 53 years was $941,000.) The short-term advertising elasticity is simply

$$\frac{\partial S_t}{\partial \log_{10} A_t} \frac{\text{av } A_t}{\text{av } S_t} = (0.545)\frac{941}{1840} = 0.279 \quad (18)$$

where av S_t is $1,840,000.

The estimated long-term marginal sales effect of advertising is, as was shown previously, $MSE_{ST}/(1 - \hat{\lambda})$. Substituting, we get

$$MSE_{LT} = \frac{\hat{a}(0.4343)/\text{av } A_t}{1 - \hat{\lambda}} \quad (19)$$

$$= \frac{0.545}{1 - 0.665} = 1.63$$

The corresponding long-term elasticity is 0.831.

advertisers is given by Donald C. Marschner, "Theory versus Practice in Allocating Advertising Money," *Journal of Business* (October, 1967), pp. 286–302.

Finally, the estimate for 1961 of

$$r = \frac{c\alpha + \lambda - 1}{1 - c\alpha} \quad (20)$$

$$= \frac{(0.75)(1180)(.4343)/695 + 0.665 - 1}{1 - (0.75)(1180)(.4343)/695}$$

$$= 0.484$$

(where all other costs, except advertising, as a percentage of sales, are 0.25 and 1961 advertising expenditure is \$695,000) furnishes us with the last item that is required to test the normative implications of the results.

1. According to the Dorfman-Steiner theorem, the marginal sales effect of advertising should equal the algebraic value of price elasticity. The short term MSE is less than unity, implying that only the long-term MSE, at 1.63, is relevant. (The firm would not be operating on the inelastic portion of its demand curve, where marginal revenue is negative), Thus advertising does seem to have long-run effects and the firm takes account of these when setting the advertising appropriation.

Since $MSE = -\eta$, it follows that

$$MC = P[1 - (1/MSE)],$$

where MC refers to nonadvertising cost, and that

$$\frac{P}{P - MC} = MSE \quad (21)$$

Pinkham's total expenses, exclusive of advertising and capital costs, averaged 25 percent of sales during the entire period. Imputing capital costs at 10 percent, we have $P - MC$ (in terms of a percentage of the sales dollar) equal to 0.65 and the whole

expression equal to 1.56, not far from the estimated MSE_{LT} at 1.63.

2. The lowest price elasticity—and thus long-term marginal sales effect—above which the firm can conceivably break even is unity. If we set the formula for MSE_{LT} equal to unity and let the advertising expenditure be the unknown, we have, following (19),

$$1 = \frac{\hat{\alpha}(0.4343)/A_t}{1 - \hat{\lambda}} = \frac{(1180)(0.4343)/A_t}{0.335} \quad (22)$$

and

$$A_t = \$1530 \quad \text{(in thousands of dollars)} \quad (23)$$

The upper bound on annual advertising expenditure is thus \$1,530,000. The firm exceeded that amount only five times during the 53 years—and that under very special circumstances.

3. Finally, the estimated contribution of advertising expenditure at the margin to the pretax rate of return on the company's capital, $r = 0.48$, seems plausible for a well-entrenched monopolist that the firm was.[5] An *average* of marginal rates of return on advertising yielded 0.53 pretax. During the whole period taxes took approximately 30 percent of the company's profit, leaving a net rate of return of about 37 percent—again not an implausible figure for a monopolist.[6]

[5] Both positive and negative marginal returns to the advertising dollar of cigarette manufacturers were found by Telser. See Lester G. Telser, "Advertising and Cigarettes," *Journal of Political Economy* (October, 1962), pp. 471–499.

[6] An interesting variant on the just-discussed appropriation model is suggested by Julian Simon in "A Simple Model for Determining Advertising Appropriations," *Journal of Marketing Research* (August, 1965), pp. 285–292. The prospective reader is cautioned against a discrepancy in definitions between sales and net revenue.

part 5
The
Financial Submodel
of the Firm

At the risk of oversimplification it can be said that the marketing manager's principal tasks are to submit to top management a request for such an over-all yearly appropriation as will promise future returns on this type of invest-ment above the cut-off rate of return; and to translate this appropriation into the optimal marketing mix. Similarly for the manager of the R & D function: the total appropriation determined by overall firm considerations must be spent optimally, i.e., on the "best" choice of R & D individual pro-jects. The financial manager's responsibility is currently and almost unani-mously defined as falling under three headings: (1) the examination and approval of the firm's investment of funds (both short-term and long-term), (2) the determination of the proper financial structure of the enterprise (as between equity and borrowed funds), and (3) dividend policy.

Selections in this section fall roughly into this threefold pattern, the major-ity (the first four) being given over to the area in which the managerial econo-mist finds most interest: long-term investment choice. Reading 21 probes the determinants of the *total* level of investment in industrial corporations. The following reading, one of the most influential to appear in capital-budgeting literature, suggests the normative framework within which invest-ments should be selected, given that all are subject to risk. Selection 23 explains briefly and lucidly the principles of a new investment-selection tech-nique, portfolio choice, and demonstrates that the use of this technique need not be restricted to investment funds and financial institutions. The next reading proposes how portfolio selection should be incorporated into the capital-budgeting process of the firm. The last reading throws light on the optimal dividend policy of the enterprise. And now for a more detailed introduction, reading by reading.

In a masterful paper Jorgenson and Siebert (Reading 21) survey and eval-uate the principal economic hypotheses of corporate investment behavior. In order to set the hypotheses up for testing by econometric procedures they first had to do two things: (1) Specify an overall flexible accelerator mechan-ism which translates *changes* in desired capital into actual investment ex-penditures. (2) Add to it a model which would account for gross investment, rather than just its changes. Combining these two features they suggest the model written in Equation (4),

$$I_t = (1 - \lambda)[K_t^* - K_{t-1}] + \delta K_{t-1}$$

where

$$I_t = \text{investment expenditure at time } t$$

$$K_{t-1} = \text{actual level of capital in period } t-1$$

$$K_t^* = \text{desired level of capital in period } t$$

$$\lambda/(1 - \lambda) = \text{average lag of adjustment between the desired} \\ \text{and actual levels of capital}$$

$$\delta = \text{rate of replacement of capital}$$

This model is common to all theories of investment behavior; the point at which the theories differ is in explaining what determines K_t^*, the *desired* level of capital.

Five such theories are exhaustively examined by setting them up into explicit models that are then fitted by data obtained from a sample of fifteen very large U.S. industrial corporations for the period 1949 through 1963. The results for the largest of them, General Motors, are actually presented in detail in Section III.

In the concluding comments the authors make a strong case, based upon this and other studies, for the "narrow" profit-maximizing view of the firm as opposed to those views variously labeled utility maximization, satisficing, etc. Jorgenson and Siebert's findings support those of Lewellen and Huntsman (Reading 2).

The next selection, a paper by Hertz, is generally recognized as a classic in the capital-budgeting field. His Monte Carlo approach to evaluation of risky investments needs no further introduction.

Smith and Schreiner (Reading 23) apply the portfolio selection method to the study of efficient diversification by conglomerates. Theirs being an empirical study of nineteen firms diversified into 67 industries, they first have to come to grips with translating theoretical costructs into testable models. Thus, for instance, they define operationally the term *conglomerate* as a firm which invests capital in several industrial categories and appears to emphasize *external* growth, through mergers and acquisitions, over *internal* growth— a stipulation that excludes such firms as General Electric.

Another interesting feature of this selection is the operational definition of *diversification efficiency*, which is used to compare a sample of mutual funds and conglomerates. Though, unlike conglomerates, funds possess the advantage of almost instant mobility and perfect divisibility of their investment resources, the authors find that among the first ten most efficiently diversified enterprises, six are funds and four are conglomerates.

The next selection (Reading 24) by Mao and Helliwell, while also carrying an empirical part, is rich primarily in theoretical suggestions. It ties into a useful whole various important threads of the economic and financial problems faced by management and proposes a model to solve them. The model incorporates three basic elements:

1. The impact of new capital projects, that the firm wants to undertake, must be evaluated not only in terms of expected rates of return to be yielded by such undertakings, but also in terms of

   a) variances of the new returns
   b) covariances between these returns and returns on existing assets
   c) covariances between the firm's returns and returns from other firms which may attract the firm's shareholders' attention

This is a portfolio formulation of capital budgeting, and it ties in directly with Van Horne's (Reading 1) suggestion that *profit maximization* ought to be defined as the maximization of the market value of the shares of the enterprise.

2. To strengthen the shareholders' stake in the capital-budgeting procedure, *cash flow* is redefined as net of all *financing* charges and thus as "cash flow available for distribution to shareholders." Financing charges are seen as stemming from two sources:

   a) each alternative investment program may have a different pattern of leverage financing
   b) the necessity for dividend stabilization may call for a cushion of liquid resources around an investment project whose yields are volatile

3. All money cash flows are deflated by a general price index. (This aspect is illustrated by Figure 1 in the Mao and Helliwell selection.)

In Reading 25, Schwartz and Aronson address themselves to the question: Is the concept of an optimal financial structure of the firm a valid one? Simple statistical tests of a mass of data produce a resounding yes answer.

Next Brigham and Pappas examine the rates of return on the common stock of 658 industrial and utility firms over the period from 1946 to 1965; they endeavor to attribute these returns to two principal components: paid-out dividends and capital gains. Capital gains are, in turn, traced to growth of earnings and higher price/earnings ratios. As a result we gain much insight into the performance of a firm's stock. The attractiveness to stockholders, of management's decisions as to how much to pay out and how much to retain is reflected in the calculated rate of return, net of general stock market influences (separated through the analysis of changes in the P/E ratio). Incidentally, the raw material used by Brigham and Pappas, the so-called Compustat Tapes (which are computerized financial statements of hundreds of stock exchange listed companies) is one of the most promising sources of data presently available to the managerial economist.

21

A Comparison of Alternative Theories of
Corporate Investment Behavior

DALE W. JORGENSON AND CALVIN D. SIEBERT*

The purpose of this paper is to compare alternative theories of investment behavior with regard to their ability to explain the investment activity of corporations. The theories we consider have already undergone substantial empirical testing and all of them deserve careful consideration as possible explanations of investment behavior. Unfortunately, the evidence already available is not sufficient to provide an adequate comparison of the alternative theories. Given a correct specification of the lag structure underlying the investment process, time series data for industry aggregates do not provide sharp discrimination among alternative explanations of investment behavior.[1] Studies of cross section data on the investment activity of individual firms exhibit little stability over time so that any comparisons based on observations for corporations must first provide a satisfactory explanation of the observations for individual firms over time.[2] In this study we concentrate on time series data for a small but representative sample of firms selected from the Fortune Director [14] of the 500 largest U.S. industrial corporations for 1962. For each individual firm we determine an appropriate specification of the lag between changes in demand for

From American Economic Review (*September 1968*), *pp. 681–712. Reprinted with permission of author and publisher.*

* Dale W. Jorgenson is professor of economics at the University of California, Berkeley; Calvin D. Siebert is associate professor of economics at the University of Iowa. Support for this research was provided by the National Science Foundation.

[1] See, for example, the results of Griliches and Wallace [16].

[2] This point has been emphasized by Kuh [30, esp. Ch. 5, pp. 116–57].

capital and investment expenditures under each of five alternative theories of the demand for capital. We find that the results enable us to discriminate quite sharply among alternative theories of investment.

The point of departure for this study is the flexible accelerator model of investment behavior originated by Chenery [2] and Koyck [29]. In this model attention is focused on the time pattern of investment behavior. The firm is taken to have a desired level of capital, determined by long-run considerations. The precise specification of the desired level of capital has been the subject of a wide variety of alternative theories of investment behavior. The alternative theories do agree, however, on the validity of the fundamental flexible accelerator mechanism for translating changes in desired capital into actual investment expenditures. Denoting the actual level of capital in period t by K_t and the desired level by K_t^*, capital is adjusted toward its desired level by a certain proportion of the discrepancy between desired and actual capital in each period,

$$K_t - K_{t-1} = [1 - \lambda][K_t^* - K_{t-1}]. \quad (1)$$

Alternatively, actual capital may be represented as a weighted average of all past levels of desired capital,

$$K_t = [1 - \lambda] \sum_{\tau=0}^{\infty} \lambda^\tau K_{t-\tau}^*. \quad (2)$$

We refer to the latter form of the flexible accelerator as a distributed lag function with actual capital in period t a function of desired levels of capital. The average lag of adjustment is $\lambda/[1 - \lambda]$. This lag represents the average time required for a change in desired capital that persists indefinitely to be translated into a change in actual capital stock.

The flexible accelerator mechanism can be transformed into a complete theory of investment behavior by adding a model of replacement investment and a specification of the desired level of capital. By accounting definition the change in capital from period to period is equal to gross investment less replacement investment. The flexible accelerator provides an explanation of change in capital, but not of gross investment. The choice of a model of replacement is important since replacement investment predominates in investment expenditures, at least at the aggregate level.[3] A simple model that has been widely adopted for empirical work is that replacement is proportional to actual capital stock. Under this assumption the accounting definition for change in capital may be written,

$$K_t - K_{t-1} = I_t - \delta K_{t-1}, \qquad (3)$$

where δ is the rate of replacement, a fixed constant. This model of replacement investment can be supported on grounds of empirical validity. In repeated tests on the aggregate level[4] and for individual firms[5] this theory has been proved satisfactory as a representation of replacement investment. These empirical results support the validity of the asymptotic approximation that replacement is proportional to capital stock for populations of investment goods whatever the underlying distribution of replacements for individual items.[6] Combining the accounting identity given above with the flexible accelerator mechanism,

$$I_t - \delta K_{t-1} = [1 - \lambda][K_t^* - K_{t-1}],$$

we obtain a model of investment expenditures,

$$I_t = [1 - \lambda][K_t^* - K_{t-1}] + \delta K_{t-1}. \quad (4)$$

To complete the theory of investment behavior it is necessary to add to the flexible accelerator mechanism and the model of replacement investment a specification of the desired level of capital stock. At this point alternative theories of investment behavior diverge. In the empirical studies of Chenery and Koyck the level of desired capital was assumed to be proportional to output. The corresponding theory of investment is often referred to as the capacity utilization theory since high levels of investment expenditure are associated with high ratios of output to capital and low levels of investment with low ratios of output to capital. An alternative theory of investment is that desired capital is proportional to profit. Two alternative rationalizations of this theory have been offered. First, Tinbergen argues that realized profits measure expected profits and that "it is almost a tautology to say that investment is governed by profits expectations."[7] Secondly, the rate of investment may be constrained by the supply of funds. In the strong version of this theory the financial constraint operates at all times; the cost of funds schedule becomes highly inelastic where internal funds are exhausted. In a weaker version of the theory the financial constraint operates at low rates of capacity utilization while extreme pressure on capacity may result in the use of outside sources of finance.[8] Both the capacity utilization and profits theories of investment were originally propounded as alternatives to the rigid accelerator theory. In this theory investment is simply proportional to changes in output. The rigid accelerator was rejected in tests by Kuznets [32], Tinbergen [50], Chenery [2], Koyck [29], and Hickman [20].

---

[3] See Kuznets [31, Table 8, pp. 92–93]; capital consumption has dominated gross capital formation for the economy as a whole since 1919.
[4] See Jorgenson [23, p. 254] and Jorgenson and Stephenson [25, pp. 192–212.].
[5] See Meyer and Kuh [37, pp. 91–94].
[6] See Feller [13, pp. 286–93].

[7] Tinbergen [51, p. 34].
[8] The liquidity theory is discussed by Meyer and Kuh [37, esp. Ch. 13, pp. 190–208], Anderson [1], Meyer and Glauber [36], and Kuh [30]. A theoretical analysis of the liquidity approach is presented by Duesenberry [7, esp. Ch. 5].

Much effort has been devoted to comparison of profits and capacity utilization theories of investment behavior. The culmination of this work is Kuh's intensive study of some 30 different equation forms for the two theories and for combinations of both. Kuh found negative results for nearly all tests of intertemporal homogeneity of cross sections and homogeneity across firms for time series.[9] He emphasizes the results from time series, concluding, "Since the major objective is to improve understanding of dynamic, time series behavior, it should be pointed out that no matter how the contrasts are drawn from time series, the acceleration sales model is superior to the internal fund flow, profit model."[10] An alternative attack on the use of current profits has been made by Grunfeld. He incorporates profits into a flexible accelerator model and finds that the partial correlation of profits and investment, given capital stock, is insignificant. "Our results do not confirm the hypothesis that profits are a good measure of those expected profits that will tend to induce investment expenditures. The observed simple correlation between investment and profits seems to be due to the fact that profits are just another measure of the capital stock of the firm and one that is in most cases inferior to the measure that we have constructed."[11] Grunfeld suggests that discounted future earnings less the costs of future additions to capital provides a better measure of expected profits than current realized profits. In Grunfeld's theory desired capital is proportional to the market value of the firm in the securities markets. Combining Koyck's specification of distributed lags with Tinbergen's profits model, Grunfeld was able to show that realized profits are not an adequate measure of expected profits. An implication of Grunfeld's results is that previous empirical tests of the determinants of investment expenditures should be re-evaluated in the light of Koyck's superior treatment of the time structure of investment behavior.

At the outset of econometric studies of investment behavior in Tinbergen's monograph, *Statistical Testing of Business Cycle Theories*, the neoclassical theory of optimal capital accumulation was considered a serious alternative to the rigid accelerator as an explanation of investment. Explanations based on the neoclassical theory were tested by Tinbergen, subsequently by Roos [45], [46], and by Klein [27], [28]. In these studies the theory of optimal capital accumulation was employed primarily as a source of possible explanatory variables—interest rates, relative prices, and so on. Tinbergen found a significant effect for interest rates in only one of five sets of data he examined.[12] Negative results were also reported by Klein.[13] In these tests of the neoclassical theory little attention was paid to the measurement of the cost of capital, the tax treatment of business income, or to the way that the cost of capital, the tax structure, and the price of capital goods enter the demand for capital services. Perhaps most important, none of these tests was based on a proper specification of the lag structure from changes in desired capital to investment expenditures. A re-evaluation of the neoclassical theory of optimal capital accumulation as an explanation of investment behavior has been undertaken by Jorgenson and Stephenson [25].[14] Their results suggest that the neoclassical theory of investment merits consideration as an alternative to the capacity utilization and profits theories.

Given that profit expectations determine investment behavior, the empirical results of Grunfeld and Kuh suggest that profit expectations cannot be adequately represented by current realized profits. Kuh points out that, " . . . the expectational hypothesis for profits cannot, and perhaps should not, be distinguished from the sales level or capacity accelerator hypothesis. The main candidate variable for the expectational hypothesis is simply net income after tax, a secondary candidate being gross operating

---

[9] Kuh [30, Ch. 6, pp. 158–88].
[10] Kuh [30, p. 213].
[11] Grunfeld [17, p. 219]. See also, Eisner [8–10].

[12] Tinbergen [51].
[13] See Klein [27] [28].
[14] See also Jorgenson [22] [23] and Jorgenson and Stephenson [26].

profit. Both variables will have strong correlations with the level of sales."[15] In this study we retain the profits model as a possible specification of the desired level of capital; however, we choose as our measure of profits the flow of internal funds available for investment. The basic premise of the corresponding theory of investment behavior is that the supply of funds schedule rises sharply at the point where internal funds are exhausted. We call this the Liquidity theory of investment. In view of the strong empirical support for the capacity utilization theory from the results of Kuh and from those of Eisner [8–12] and Hickman [21], we take desired capital to be proportional to output as a possible explanation of investment expenditures. We call this the Accelerator theory of investment. Finally, Grunfeld's results suggest that profit expectations can best be measured by the market value of the firm, so that desired capital is proportional to market value. We call this the Expected Profits theory of investment. All three theories will be included in our comparison of alternative explanations of investment behavior.

The neoclassical theory of investment behavior is based on an optimal time path for capital accumulation. It also implies a theory of the cost of capital. This theory has been developed by Modigliani and Miller [38-43]. In the Modigliani-Miller theory the cost of capital is shown to be independent of the financial structure of the firm or of dividend policy; this view contrasts sharply with the theory of the cost of capital underlying the liquidity theory of investment behavior. In the liquidity theory the supply schedule is horizontal up to the point at which internal funds are exhausted and vertical at that point. If interest payments are deductible for tax purposes, the Modigliani-Miller view must be qualified.[16] The appropriate cost of capital for investment decisions is still a weighted average of the expected return to equity and the return to debt. Return to equity can be measured in a number of

alternative ways. In this study we consider two possibilities: first, capital gains on assets held by the firm may be regarded as transitory so that return to equity and the price of capital services should be measured excluding capital gains; secondly, capital gains on assets may be regarded as part of the return to investment so that return to equity and the price of capital services should include capital gains. We refer to the theory of investment behavior incorporating capital gains as Neoclassical I and the theory excluding capital gains as Neoclassical II. These two theories of investment behavior, differing in their treatment of the cost of capital but based on optimal capital accumulation, complete the list of five alternative explanations of investment behavior to be included in our comparison.

To summarize: We compare the following alternative theories of investment behavior: Neoclassical, Accelerator, Expected Profits, and Liquidity. These theories have been tested on widely varying bodies of data for different time periods and for different specifications of the time structure of investment behavior. Koyck has demonstrated the importance of the lag structure between changes in desired capital and the actual level of capital stock. To evaluate alternative theories of investment behavior it is essential to choose a lag structure that is appropriate for each theory and to compare the resulting explanations of investment expenditures. We take the flexible accelerator model as a point of departure for our study; we assume that replacement is proportional to capital stock. The alternative theories of investment behavior differ in specification of the desired level of capital. Given a proper specification of the lag structure for each theory, we are able to discriminate among the alternative specifications of desired capital and thereby among alternative theories of investment behavior.

In the following section we describe the basic flexible accelerator model in more detail and generalize it to permit a wider range of alternative lag structures. In section II we describe the measurement of variables that enter into the Accelerator, Liquidity,

[15] Kuh [30, p. 208; see also, pp. 12–22] and Eisner [9, p. 8].
[16] See Modigliani and Miller [39].

Expected Profits, and Neoclassical theories of investment behavior. We then turn to the empirical results. Explanations of investment behavior based on each of the alternative theories are compared for each of the corporations included in our sample. The relative performance of the alternative explanations is assessed. We conclude with the implications of our study for the theory of investment and, more generally, for the theory of the firm.

I. FRAMEWORK OF THE STUDY

The studies of Accelerator, Expected Profits, and Liquidity theories of investment behavior by Grunfeld and Kuh are based on the flexible accelerator mechanism. While this mechanism represents a considerable generalization of the rigid accelerator, the resulting empirical characterization of the time structure of investment behavior is implausible. Kuh finds that the average lag between changes in desired capital and actual expenditures ranges from five to ten years or more.[17] Similar results were obtained by Grunfeld[18] and Koyck.[19] These results conflict sharply with survey results for new manufacturing plants obtained by Mayer [35]. Mayer finds that the average time required from the decision to undertake investment to the completion of construction is less than two years.[20] Using a generalization of Koyck's distributed lag function. Jorgenson and Stephenson [26] have corroborated Mayer's survey results. For manufacturing and its subindustries they obtain average lags between changes in desired capital and actual expenditures ranging from a year and a half to three years.[21] These results suggest that a generalization of the flexible accelerator mechanism is required for a valid comparison among alternative theories of investment behavior.

In the original flexible accelerator model (2) actual capital may be represented as a

[17] Kuh [30, pp. 293–302].
[18] See Grunfeld [17].
[19] Koyck [29, pp. 74–110].
[20] See Mayer [35].
[21] Jorgenson and Stephenson [26, Table 2, pp. 21–22].

weighted average of all past levels of desired capital with geometrically declining weights. To generalize this assumption we let μ_τ be the weight of desired capital of period $t - \tau$ in determining the level of actual capital in period t, obtaining the distributed lag function,

$$K_t = \sum_{\tau=0}^{\infty} \mu_\tau K_{t-\tau}^*. \qquad (5)$$

In this version of the distributed lag function the weights are nonnegative and sum to unity,

$$\mu_\tau \geqq 0, \qquad (\tau = 0, 1 \ldots),$$

$$\sum_{\tau=0}^{\infty} \mu_\tau = 1.$$

The weights appropriate for the original flexible accelerator decline geometrically,

$$\mu_\tau = (1 - \lambda)\lambda^\tau, \qquad (\tau = 0, 1 \ldots).$$

To generalize the flexible accelerator mechanism we first difference both sides of the distributed lag function (5),

$$K_t - K_{t-1} = \sum_{\tau=0}^{\infty} \mu_\tau [K_{t-\tau}^* - K_{t-\tau-1}^*],$$

and add the model of replacement (3),

$$I_t - \delta K_{t-1} = \sum_{\tau=0}^{\infty} \mu_\tau [K_{t-\tau}^* - K_{t-\tau-1}^*],$$

so that,

$$I_t = \sum_{\tau=0}^{\infty} \mu_\tau [K_{t-\tau}^* - K_{t-\tau-1}^*] + \delta K_{t-1}. \qquad (6)$$

To complete the theory of investment behavior we must adopt a specification of the desired level of capital; we combine the generalized accelerator mechanism with each of the five alternative specifications of the desired level of capital described in the preceding section.

To estimate the parameters of a theory of investment behavior based on the generalized accelerator mechanism (6) the sequence of weights $\{\mu_\tau\}$ must be approximated by a sequence generated by a finite number of parameters. In the Chenery-Koyck model the weights decline geometrically; Solow [48] has proposed that the weights be taken to correspond to the Pascal probability distribution. Jorgenson [24] has proposed a class of distributed lag functions based on the general Pascal probability distribution. This class of distributed lag functions includes those of Koyck and Solow as special cases; an arbitrary distributed lag function may be approximated to any desired degree of accuracy by a member of this class.[22] To compare alternative theories of investment behavior we must discriminate among alternative specifications of desired capital. Misspecification of the lag distribution for a given theory of investment behavior may bias the results of our comparison. Accordingly, we choose the best lag distribution for each alternative specification of desired capital from among the class of general Pascal distributed lag functions. Differences in the resulting explanations of investment behavior may then be attributed to the specification of the desired level of capital rather than to the specification of the lag distribution.

In the final form[23] of the general Pascal distributed lag function, gross investment is a function of changes in desired capital, lagged values of net investment and the level of capital stock. As an example, suppose that the best lag distribution requires current and lagged changes in desired capital and lagged net investment; the final form of the distributed lag function may be written,

$$I_t = \gamma_0[K_t^* - K_{t-1}^*] + \gamma_1[K_{t-1}^* - K_{t-2}^*] - \omega_1[I_{t-1} - \delta K_{t-2}] + \delta K_{t-1}.$$

Under the Accelerator theory of investment behavior desired capital is proportional to output,

[22] Jorgenson [24, pp. 137–42].
[23] In the final form of a general Pascal distributed lag function, the function is written with a finite number of lags in both dependent and independent variables. For further details, see Jorgenson [24, p. 138].

$$K_t^* = \alpha Q_t,$$

where α is the desired capital-output ratio. For the lag specification we have given, the complete Accelerator theory of investment behavior may be written,

$$I_t = \alpha\gamma_0[Q_t - Q_{t-1}] + \alpha\gamma_1[Q_{t-1} - Q_{t-2}] - \omega_1[I_{t-1} - \delta K_{t-2}] + \delta K_{t-1},$$

where the parameters—α, γ_0, γ_1, ω_1, δ—are estimated from data on output, capital stock, and investment expenditures. Since the weights in the distributed lag function must sum to unity, the coefficients of this function must satisfy,[24]

$$\gamma_0 + \gamma_1 = 1 + \omega_1.$$

This restriction enables us to estimate the parameters—α, γ_0, γ_1, ω_1—from estimates of $\alpha\gamma_0$, $\alpha\gamma_1$ and ω_1. The rate of replacement may be estimated directly in calculating capital stock; as a check on the results, the rate of replacement may also be estimated as the coefficient of capital stock.

To estimate the parameters of the distributed lag function for each theory of investment behavior, an error term must be added to the final form of the distributed lag function as given above. We adopt the specification that the error term is distributed independently on successive observations with zero mean and constant variance. This specification has been employed by Chenery, Grunfeld, Jorgenson and Stephenson, and Kuh in studies based on the flexible accelerator mechanism and its generalization. Letting $\{\epsilon_t\}$ denote the sequence of random errors, we assume that:

$$E(\epsilon_t) = 0, \quad V(\epsilon_t) = \sigma^2, \quad (t = 1 \cdots n)$$

where σ^2 is a constant, and:

$$C(\epsilon_t, \epsilon_{t-\tau}) = 0,$$
$$(t, t - \tau = 1 \cdots n; \tau \neq 0)$$

Gross investment has considerable serial

[24] Jorgenson [24, p. 147].

correlation due to the continuity of investment programs internal to the firm, the effects of the business cycle, and the possibility of trends in investment expenditures. It might be argued that the "true" disturbances in the explanation of investment behavior are also serially correlated. This view is deficient for the following reasons. First, all variables are deflated in order to remove the influence of common price trends; secondly, the investment series is in the main a first difference series so that trends in the underlying capital stock data are largely eliminated; finally, any remaining trend in the observations on investment may be explained by rising replacement requirements as represented by the capital stock variable. The distributed lag function itself fully accounts for serial correlation in the dependent variable since investment is represented as a weighted average of past changes in desired capital. Errors in the explanation may be accounted for by random variations in forces that are independent of the process translating changes in desired capital into actual investment expenditures.

Given a correct specification of the lag structure between changes in desired capital and actual investment expenditures, time series data for industry aggregates do not provide sharp discrimination among alternative explanations of investment behavior. Griliches and Wallace [16] have compared models similar to our Expected Profits and Neoclassical II models using quarterly time series for all of manufacturing. While the Neoclassical model is superior to the Expected Profits model on the basis of their empirical results, both models perform well.[25] On the basis of data for individual firms Grunfeld and Kuh were able to discriminate between the Liquidity model and the Expected Profits and Accelerator models. Accordingly, we employ data on the investment behavior of individual firms as the basis for our comparison of alternative theories. Data on individual firms have been analyzed through both time series and cross section models. The study of Meyer and Kuh [37] relied primarily on cross sections. Kuh has

shown that cross sections for successive years do not provide a stable explanation of investment behavior. The intercepts for cross sections exhibit a strong pattern of cyclical variation, suggesting that the dynamic specification of the models used for cross sections is incorrect.[26] Kuh also rejects the hypothesis that the parameters of successive cross sections are the same.[27] In order to specify the lag structure correctly we concentrate on time series data for individual firms. We do not assume that parameters for all firms are the same for cross sections at a given point in time. Our results are thus free of biases that could result from inappropriate assumptions about the homogeneity of investment behavior across firms in cross sections. We do not assume that the parameters are the same for different firms. The framework of our study is similar in this respect to that of Grunfeld. Our results are free of biases that could result from aggregation across firms in time series for industry groups. In a subsequent paper we will study possible sources of aggregation bias in distributed lag functions estimated from data on industry groups.

To summarize: In order to provide better discrimination among alternative theories of investment behavior our comparison is based on observations for individual firms rather than for industry aggregates. We determine an appropriate lag specification for each firm under each alternative specification of the desired level of capital stock. Each theory of investment behavior is based on a generalized accelerator mechanism and on the assumption that replacement investment is proportional to capital stock. Alternative theories differ in the specification of desired levels of capital stock. To compare alternative theories we first select the best lag distribution for each firm under each specification of desired capital among the class of general Pascal distributed lag functions. Our results are free of biases that could result from misspecification of the lag distribution or from inappropriate assumptions about the homogeneity of investment behavior across firms.

[25] Griliches and Wallace [16, esp. p. 325].

[26] Kuh [30, p. 330].
[27] See Kuh [30, esp. Ch. 5, pp. 116–57].

II. MEASUREMENT

The purpose of this section is to describe the accounting measurements that underlie our empirical evaluation of alternative theories of investment behavior. To provide a valid comparison among alternative explanations of investment expenditures the variables that enter each of the competing theories must be measured with as much precision as accounting data permit. For each firm the data must be available on a consistent basis over a substantial period of time. All firms whose stock is traded publicly have had to file annual reports with the Securities and Exchange Commission since 1934. These annual reports, consisting of complete income and balance sheet statements, are published in *Moody's Industrial Manual* [44] for the larger corporations. It was impossible to include firms in our sample that lost their identity through mergers during the period since 1934. Firms that shifted fiscal accounting years or changed their practices in the consolidations of accounting reports also failed to satisfy the criteria for inclusion in our sample. Limitations in the availability of detailed accounting data resulted in concentration on larger firms. A second justification for concentration on larger firms is the importance of their activity. At least two of the firms in our sample have investment programs that rival those of entire industry groups as reported in the Office of Business Economics (OBE) and Securities and Exchange Commission (SEC) Quarterly Investment Survey [54]. In any case primary interest is in the investment activity of the individual corporation. Stochastic elements in the empirical investment functions are to be attributed to variations in the behavior of individual firms rather than to sampling variation.

In order to provide a wide range of industrial activity, we chose a sample of fifteen firms from the *Fortune* Directory of the 500 largest classification of the OBE-SEC Investment Survey in the selection of individual firms. The firms are selected from 14 different OBE-SEC industry groups. The only industry group not represented is Textiles. In many cases the largest firm in the OBE-SEC industry group was selected. In some cases appropriate data were not available for the largest firm; we then attempted to compile data for the second largest firm, and so on. Although all the firms included in our sample are large, there is considerable variation among them as to size and rate of growth. The firms included are listed in Table 1; the average amount of investment and the capital stock of each firm are given in the table along with the OBE-SEC industry classification of the firm. The average rate of investment in the postwar period for the firm with the largest level of investment activity, General Motors, was 200 times the rate for the firm with the smallest level, Westinghouse Air Brake. Capital stock for the firm with largest net fixed assets in 1961, Standard Oil of New Jersey, was approximately 160 times the capital stock of Westinghouse Air Brake. IBM, the firm with the most rapid rate of growth, had capital stock in 1961 twelve times larger than its 1937 capital stock. At the other extreme, Anaconda Company's 1961 capital stock declined in size by a third from the 1937 level. While it must be emphasized that our sample of firms should not be considered a probability sample of large United States corporations, the sample provides sufficient heterogeneity to serve as an adequate test of alternative theories of investment behavior. A larger sample would have made it difficult for us to give proper attention to compilation of accurate and consistent data for each individual firm. Of course, considerable care should be taken in extrapolating the results of the present study to small firms or to closely held corporations.

Turning to the measurement of individual variables, we give a brief outline of the procedure followed for deriving each variable from accounting reports for an individual corporation. The dependent variable, gross investment, denoted I_t, is the current value of investment in plant and equipment deflated by the investment goods price index for manufacturing, denoted q_t, to obtain the value of investment in constant dollars of 1954. The gross investment data are obtained

TABLE 1

Firm	Average Amount of Investment[a]	Capital Stock[b]	OBE–SEC Industry
General Motors	.7670	3.1225	Motor Vehicles and Equipment
Goodyear Tire and Rubber	.0554	.3616	Rubber Products
American Can	.0414	.5374	Other Durables
Pittsburgh Plate Glass	.0345	.3128	Stone, Clay, and Glass
United States Steel	.2980	2.9437	Primary Iron and Steel
General Electric	.1190	.7247	Electrical Machinery and Equipment
Reynolds Tobacco	.0127	.1267	Other Non-durables
Dupont	.1540	.9404	Chemicals and Allied Products
Anaconda Company	.0511	.7077	Primary Non-ferrous Metal
Standard Oil, N. J.	.6274	6.3560	Petroleum and Coal Products
International Paper	.0563	.4780	Paper and Allied Products
Westinghouse Air Brake	.0038	.0393	Transportation Equipment, excluding Motor Vehicles
International Business Machines	.1839	.9492	Machinery, except Electrical
Swift and Company	.0266	.2467	Food and Beverage
Westinghouse Electric	.0497	.3841	Electric Machinery and Equipment

[a] Mean annual gross investment for the postwar period, 1946–1963, in billions of 1954 dollars.
[b] End of year net fixed assets for 1961 in billions of 1954 dollars.
Source: Moody's Industrial Manual [44].

from Form 10K reports of companies registered with the Securities and Exchange Commission as reported in *Moody's Industrial Manual*. These data are listed under additions at cost in *Moody's* and, following normal tax accounting procedure, include any additions which have an expected life of more than one year. Comparable data on investment are not available for the firms included in our sample for years earlier than 1934. The investment goods price index is based on the implicit deflators for structures and equipment from *U.S. Income and Output* [55] and *Business Statistics* [53]. Calculation of capital stock by the perpetual inventory method was not feasible. The method we employed was to select an initial and terminal date of net capital stock from each firm's balance sheet reports. These benchmark figures were deflated by the National Industrial Conference Board [4–5] fixed capital stock deflators for the firms' industry group. These deflated stock figures were interpolated by gross investment in constant prices,[28] resulting in capital stock values for each

[28] Further details on this and other measurements are contained in the Statistical Appendix to a more extensive version of this paper available from the authors.

year and an estimate of replacement in constant prices for each year.

The independent variables for alternative specifications of desired capital were measured as follows: The value of output, denoted by $p_t Q_t$, was measured by sales plus the change in inventory stock. Output in constant dollars of 1954, denoted Q_t, was measured by the value of output deflated by the Wholesale Price Index [56] of the firm's industry group, denoted p_t. A more accurate measure of output would be sales plus the change in finished goods inventory. Unfortunately, a breakdown of inventory into finished goods, goods in process, and raw materials was not available for all firms. In the Accelerator theory of investment behavior desired capital is assumed to be proportional to output,

$$\text{Accelerator: } K_t^* = \alpha Q_t,$$

where α is the desired capital-output ratio.

Internal funds available for investment expenditures are measured by profits after taxes plus depreciation less dividends paid. This liquidity measure was converted into constant prices of 1954 by dividing the current value of internal funds by the investment goods price index, q_t. The resulting measure of liquidity, denoted L_t, was suggested as the appropriate measure by Kuh on the grounds that the effects of liquidity can be distinguished from those of output while expected profits as measured by profits after taxes cannot be distinguished from output. Since changes in desired capital are employed to explain investment for changes in capacity with replacement accounted for separately, an alternative liquidity measure would be to subtract replacement in constant prices from the liquidity measure suggested by Kuh. A trial of this measure for several firms gave nearly the same results as those for the liquidity variable suggested by Kuh.[29] In the Liquidity theory of investment behavior, desired capital is proportional to liquidity,

$$\text{Liquidity: } K_t^* = \alpha L_t,$$

where α is the desired ratio of capital to the flow of internal funds available for investment.

The market value of the firm was measured as the market value of stocks outstanding plus the book value of debt including short-term liabilities at the beginning of the period. This measure was reduced to constant prices of 1954 by dividing the current market value of the firm by the implicit deflator for gross national product. The resulting measure, denoted V_t, was suggested by Grunfeld as an approximation to the discounted value of expected future cash flow net of future investment expenditures.[30] Since a large part of a corporation's debt is not publicly traded and no selling prices are quoted on some issues for months at a time, our only recourse was to use the book value of debt. The error introduced by this limitation of

the data is relatively small both because book value and market value of debt are quite close and because debt is a very small fraction of the market value of the firm for the corporations included in our sample. In the Expected Profits theory of investment behavior, desired capital is proportional to the market value of the firm,

$$\text{Expected Profits: } K_t^* = \alpha V_t,$$

where α is the desired ratio of capital to market value of the firm.

In the neoclassical theory of investment behavior desired capital stock is equal to the value of output deflated by the price of capital services, denoted c_t. We have already discussed measurement of the value of output. The price of capital services depends on the price of investment goods, the cost of capital, and the tax structure,

$$c_t = \frac{q_t}{1 - u_t} \times$$
$$\left[(1 - u_t w_t)\delta + r_t - \frac{q_t - q_{t-1}}{q_t} \right],$$

where q_t is the investment goods price index, δ the rate of replacement, r_t the cost of capital, u_t the rate of taxation of corporate income, and w_t the proportion of depreciation at replacement cost deductible from income for tax purposes. The rate of replacement is obtained in the calculation of capital stock. The rate of taxation of corporate income is the ratio of profits before taxes less profits after taxes to profits before taxes. The variable, w_t, describing depreciation deductions is the depreciation for tax purposes to depreciation at current replacement cost.

To measure the rate of return we define gross business income as the sum of profits before taxes, depreciation, and interest. Gross business income is equal to the value of capital services for all classes of assets. From balance sheet data we were able to obtain data on the value of depreciable and depletable assets and the value of inventories and cash plus accounts receivable. We derived an expression for the price of capital services for each of the four classes of assets,

[29] Kuh [30, pp. 63 and 208–9]. A number of *ad hoc* liquidity measures were employed at the experimental stages of this study. In addition, sales was used in place of output. The results were not materially different from those reported here.

[30] Grunfeld [17, pp. 226–27]. The market price of stock was estimated as an average of the high and low prices for the stock for January and December from *The Commercial and Financial Chronicle* [3]. The number of shares outstanding was taken from Standard and Poor's *Standard Corporation Descriptions* [49].

using the formula given above with appropriate specializations; for example, for nondepreciable assets, the rate of replacement, δ, is zero. The price of capital services for each asset class depends on the cost of capital; given the fact that gross business income is the sum of the values of capital services, we were able to solve for the cost of capital. Two formulations were employed: First, the cost of capital was taken to be profits after taxes plus depreciation for tax purposes less depreciation at current replacement cost plus accrued capital gains on depreciable assets, depletable assets, and inventories, all divided by the market value of the firm in current prices. Secondly, the cost of capital was measured excluding all accrued capital gains.

For all firms included in the sample interest payments deducted for tax purposes were negligible so that we excluded them from gross business income in both measures of the cost of capital. Similarly, realized capital gains on assets were essentially zero for depreciable and depletable assets. For a number of firms capital gains on inventories are included in recorded profits. This is especially true for firms pricing ending inventory stock on the FIFO (first-in, first-out) method. For the firms using FIFO methods no adjustment of recorded profits for capital gains was made; this practice was also followed for firms following average-cost pricing of ending inventories. Profits were adjusted for inventory capital gains for firms that employed LIFO (last-in, first-out) inventory pricing.[31] In the first version of the neoclassical theory, capital gains are assumed to be taken into account in investment decisions; desired capital is proportional to the value of output divided by the price of capital services including capital gains,

$$\text{Neoclassical I: } K_t^* = \alpha \frac{p_t Q_t}{c_t},$$

$$c_t = \frac{q_t}{1 - u_t}\left[(1 - u_t w_t)\delta + r_t - \frac{q_t - q_{t-1}}{q_t}\right],$$

where α is the elasticity of output with respect to capital input. In the second version of the neoclassical theory, capital gains are assumed to be transitory; they are ignored in assessing the appropriate cost of capital for investment decisions and in the price of capital services; desired capital stock is again proportional to the value of output divided by the price of capital services,

$$\text{Neoclassical II: } K_t^* = \alpha \frac{p_t Q_t}{c_t},$$

$$c_t = \frac{q_t}{1 - u_t}\left[(1 - u_t w_t)\delta + r_t\right],$$

where, as before, α is the elasticity of output with respect to capital and the price of capital services and cost of capital are measured with capital gains set equal to zero.[32]

III. EMPIRICAL RESULTS

To provide a basis for comparing alternative theories of investment behavior, we first determine an appropriate specification of the lag between changes in desired capital and investment expenditures under each specification of desired capital. We choose the best lag distribution for each firm from among the class of general Pascal distributed lag functions. In each case the appropriate specification of the distributed lag function is selected from those with current and two lagged changes in desired capital and two lagged values of net investment. These limitations are not very restrictive since annual data are employed for each firm. A very large variety of alternative lag distributions can be represented in this way, including the geometric distribution proposed by Koyck. Changes in desired capital and lagged net investment were allowed to enter the distributed lag function so long as they lowered the residual variance around the regression. The final set of values of current and lagged changes in desired capital and lagged

[31] Further details are given in the Statistical Appendix; see footnote 28 above.

[32] Further details are given in the Statistical Appendix; see footnote 28 above.

net investment gives the minimum residual variance subject to the restrictions we have indicated. Given the best specification of the generalized accelerator mechanism for each alternative specification of desired capital, we can compare alternative theories of investment behavior with regard to their ability to explain the investment activity of corporations.[33]

To illustrate the empirical results, we consider the fitted distributed lag functions for General Motors as an example. For the Neoclassical I theory of investment, desired capital stock is proportional to the value of output, $p_t Q_t$, divided by the price of capital services, c_t, including capital gains. For the postwar period the form of the distributed lag function selected for General Motors includes current and lagged changes in desired capital and lagged net investment. The final form of the distributed lag function may be written,

$$I_t = \beta + \alpha\gamma_0\left[\frac{p_t Q_t}{c_t} - \frac{p_{t-1}Q_{t-1}}{c_{t-1}}\right]$$
$$+ \alpha\gamma_1\left[\frac{p_{t-1}Q_{t-1}}{c_{t-1}} - \frac{p_{t-2}Q_{t-2}}{c_{t-2}}\right]$$
$$- \omega_1[I_{t-1} - \delta K_{t-2}] + \delta K_{t-1}.$$

Substituting estimated numerical values for the unknown parameters into the distributed lag function, we obtain:

$$I_t = .2449 + .0160\left[\frac{p_t Q_t}{c_t} - \frac{p_{t-1}Q_{t-1}}{c_{t-1}}\right]$$
$$(.0063)$$
$$+ .0150\left[\frac{p_{t-1}Q_{t-1}}{c_{t-1}} - \frac{p_{t-2}Q_{t-2}}{c_{t-2}}\right]$$
$$(.0066)$$
$$+ .3444[I_{t-1} - \delta K_{t-2}] + .1794 K_{t-1}.$$
$$(.2061) \qquad\qquad (.0540)$$

[33] Distributed lag functions were fitted to data for the postwar period, 1949–63, and to the postwar and prewar period, 1937–41 and 1949–63, combined. For purposes of policy and prediction the explanation of investment behavior under postwar conditions is most relevant and only results for the postwar period are discussed below. The results for the combined period are very similar to those for the postwar period. Detailed results of the regressions for each firm for all alternative theories of investment behavior for both time periods are given in a more extensive version of this paper; see footnote 28 above.

For the Neoclassical II theory of investment, desired capital is analogous to that in Neoclassical I, except that capital gains are set equal to zero for the price of capital services and the cost of capital. For the postwar period the form of the distributed lag function selected for General Motors includes three values of change in desired capital and two lagged values of net investment. The estimated distributed lag function with numerical values substituted for the unknown parameters is:

$$I_t = .1231 + .0411\left[\frac{p_t Q_t}{c_t} - \frac{p_{t-1}Q_{t-1}}{c_{t-1}}\right]$$
$$(.0094)$$
$$+ .0654\left[\frac{p_{t-1}Q_{t-1}}{c_{t-1}} - \frac{p_{t-2}Q_{t-2}}{c_{t-2}}\right]$$
$$(.0105)$$
$$+ .0202\left[\frac{p_{t-2}Q_{t-2}}{c_{t-2}} - \frac{p_{t-3}Q_{t-3}}{c_{t-3}}\right]$$
$$(.0089)$$
$$+ .3732[I_{t-2} - \delta K_{t-3}] + .1826 K_{t-1}.$$
$$(.1311) \qquad\qquad (.0361)$$

In the Accelerator theory of investment, desired capital is proportional to output, Q_t. The best distributed lag function for General Motors includes lagged change in desired capital and lagged net investment. The final form of the distributed lag function may be represented as,

$$I_t = \beta + \alpha\gamma_1[Q_{t-1} - Q_{t-2}]$$
$$- \omega_1[I_{t-1} - \delta K_{t-2}] + \delta K_{t-1}.$$

Substituting the estimated numerical values into the distributed lag function, we have:

$$I_t = .1963 + .0666[Q_{t-1} - Q_{t-2}]$$
$$(.0327)$$
$$+ .4780[I_{t-1} - \delta K_{t-2}] + .1878 K_t.$$
$$(.2115) \qquad\qquad (.0593)$$

Similarly, for the Expected Profits theory of investment, desired capital is proportional to the market value of the firm, V_t. The best distributed lag function for General Motors includes current and lagged changes in desired capital and no lagged values of net investment. The final form of the distributed lag function is:

$$I_t = \beta + \alpha\gamma_0 [V_t - V_{t-1}] + \alpha\gamma_1$$
$$[V_{t-1} - V_{t-2}] + \delta K_{t-1}.$$

Substituting the numerical values, the estimated distributed lag function becomes:

$$I_t = .2793 + .0858[V_t - V_{t-1}]$$
$$\quad\quad\quad (.0267)$$

$$+ .0610[V_{t-1} - V_{t-2}] + .1493 K_{t-1}.$$
$$(.0268) \quad\quad\quad\quad\quad (.0571)$$

For the Liquidity theory of investment behavior the best distributed lag function included current and lagged changes in desired capital and lagged net investment; after appropriate substitutions, we obtain:

$$I_t = .2345 + .3032[L_t - L_{t-1}]$$
$$\quad\quad\quad (.2710)$$

$$+ .4941[L_{t-1} - L_{t-2}]$$
$$(.2743)$$

$$+ .3989[I_{t-1} - \delta K_{t-2}] + .1712 K_{t-1}.$$
$$(.2279) \quad\quad\quad\quad\quad (.0620)$$

We have determined the best specification of the distributed lag between changes in desired capital and investment expenditures for each of 5 alternative theories of investment behavior and for each of 15 corporations included in our sample. We can compare the alternative specifications of desired capital with respect to the explanation of investment behavior for the 15 corporations. The relative performance of the alternative specifications provides our criterion for comparison of alternative theories of investment behavior. Relative performance may be measured in many ways. The best measure of performance is the residual variance for the best fitted distributed lag function corresponding to each theory. The theory of investment behavior that results in the least residual variance provides the best explanation of investment behavior. Performance as measured by residual variance can usefully be supplemented by an analysis of the fitted coefficients. The coefficients associated with changes in desired capital are of particular

interest. Without these terms, the fitted distributed lag functions contain only lagged net investment and capital stock, so that the resulting explanation of investment expenditures cannot be attributed to a theory of investment behavior. Finally, an alternative measure of goodness of fit based on the qualitative characteristics of the fitted distributed lag functions is the number of "right" and "wrong" changes in direction for the fitted values of investment by comparison with the actual values.

First, we consider the number and significance of coefficients of changes in desired capital stock entering each fitted distributed lag function. A summary of the evidence is provided by Table 2. The first half of the table gives the number of coefficients of changes in desired capital that enter the fitted distributed lag functions for all firms. In selecting an appropriate form for the lag distribution, a value of change in desired capital was allowed to enter the regression if it lowered the residual variance around the regression. The column labeled X_2 gives the number of values of current changes in desired capital for all firms, the column X_3 the number of lagged changes in desired capital, and the column X_4 the number of changes in desired capital lagged twice. The second half of the table presents the number of coefficients of changes in desired capital stock whose fitted values are twice their estimated standard errors or more. For example, in the fitted distributed lag functions for the Neoclassical I theory of investment, 13 of a possible 15 coefficients of current changes in desired capital enter the regressions. Of these, 10 have coefficients that are twice their standard errors or more. For this same theory, 12 of a possible 15 coefficients of lagged changes in desired capital enter the regressions; 6 of 15 coefficients of changes in desired capital lagged twice enter these regressions. The total number of coefficients for all lags and all firms is 31, or an average of slightly over two per firm; the total number of these coefficients twice their standard errors or more is 20 or between one and two per firm.

The tabulation of coefficients given in

TABLE 2

Model	1949–1963			
	X_2	X_3	X_4	Total
Number of Desired Capital				
Stock Coefficients				
Neoclassical I	13	12	6	31
Neoclassical II	14	10	4	28
Accelerator	9	9	1	19
Expected Profits	13	7	3	23
Liquidity	4	8	2	14
Number of Coefficients Twice				
Their Standard Errors				
Neoclassical I	10	8	2	20
Neoclassical II	10	7	1	18
Accelerator	5	6	0	11
Expected Profits	9	6	1	16
Liquidity	1	4	1	6

Table 2 supports the following conclusions: First, the Neoclassical I theory of investment, including capital gains in the price of capital services and the cost of capital, has the largest number of coefficients entering the fitted distributed lag functions and the largest number of coefficients twice their standard errors or more. The Neoclassical II theory of investment, excluding capital gains, has the second largest number of coefficients in both groups. The Accelerator and Expected Profits theories of investment stand next in order of the number of coefficients entering the fitted distributed lag functions and the number of coefficients that are twice their standard errors or more. The Expected Profits theory has a large number of coefficients in each category. The Liquidity theory of investment has fewer coefficients entering the fitted distributed lag functions than any other theory and fewer coefficients twice their standard errors or more. Only 14 changes in desired capital enter the fitted regressions or less than one per firm. Only six of these coefficients are twice their standard errors or more.

We turn next to the direct measurement of the relative performance of the alternative theories of investment in the explanation of corporate investment behavior. As a standard for evaluation of the performance of all models, we have fitted a "naive" model to the same data. This naive model is the best autoregressive scheme for investment; as many as three lagged values of investment are allowed to enter so long as they reduce the residual variance around the fitted autoregression. The naive model may be written:

$$I_t = \beta_0 + \beta_1 I_{t-1} + \beta_2 I_{t-2} + \beta_3 I_{t-3}.$$

Goodness of fit statistics for all theories of investment behavior and for the naive model are given for each corporation included in our sample in Table 3. The coefficient of multiple determination, R^2, is given in the first column of this table; the standard error of the regression, s, is given in the second column; and the third column gives the Durbin-Watson ratio, d. The standard error of the regression is corrected for degrees of freedom while the coefficient of multiple determination is not. Accordingly, comparison of the relative performance of the different models is based on the standard error. For comparison of the various models on the basis of standard error the random error for the underlying distributed lag model must be serially independent. To provide some evidence on this assumption, we employ the Durbin-Watson statistic. This statistic is biased toward randomness when lagged values of net investment are included in the fitted distributed lag function.[34] However,

---

[34] See Griliches [15] and Malinvaud [34].

TABLE 3 Goodness of Fit Statistics

Firm and Model	1949–1963		
	R^2	s	d
General Motors			
a. Neoclassical I	.70	.1765	2.03
b. Neoclassical II	.89	.1148	2.32
c. Accelerator	.62	.1920	2.21
d. Expected Profits	.64	.1852	1.36
e. Liquidity Model	.61	.2037	2.29
f. Naive Model	.47	.2072	2.22
Goodyear			
a. Neoclassical I	.73	.0119	2.71
b. Neoclassical II	.66	.0127	2.14
c. Accelerator	.61	.0135	1.61
d. Expected Profits	.71	.0118	2.16
e. Liquidity Model	—*	—	—
f. Naive Model	.38	.0157	2.02
American Can			
a. Neoclassical I	.66	.0087	2.21
b. Neoclassical II	.44	.0101	2.16
c. Accelerator	.39	.0105	1.73
d. Expected Profits	.27	.0110	2.15
e. Liquidity Model	—*	—	—
f. Naive Model	.04	.0121	1.76
Pittsburgh Plate Glass			
a. Neoclassical I	.72	.0089	2.16
b. Neoclassical II	.41	.0129	1.86
c. Accelerator	.51	.01178	2.36
d. Expected Profits	.45	.01180	1.91
e. Liquidity Model	—*	—	—
f. Naive Model	.30	.0127	1.83
U.S. Steel			
a. Neoclassical I	.51	.0801	1.46
b. Neoclassical II	.50	.0854	1.63
c. Accelerator	—*	—	—
d. Expected Profits	.69	.0676	1.42
e. Liquidity Model	.46	.0841	1.57
f. Naive Model	.39	.0818	1.70

Firm and Model	1949–1963		
	R^2	s	d
General Electric			
a. Neoclassical I	.72	.0227	1.80
b. Neoclassical II	.85	.0173	1.37
c. Accelerator	.58	.0276	1.89
d. Expected Profits	.71	.0244	2.27
e. Liquidity Model	.71	.0240	2.58
f. Naive Model	.51	.0272	1.71
Reynolds Tobacco			
a. Neoclassical I	.85	.0040	2.20
b. Neoclassical II	.89	.0034	2.28
c. Accelerator	.92	.0028	1.98
d. Expected Profits	.84	.0039	1.87
e. Liquidity Model	.80	.0043	2.03
f. Naive Model	.76	.0044	1.73
Dupont			
a. Neoclassical I	.60	.0321	1.55
b. Neoclassical II	—*	—	—
c. Accelerator	.63	.0309	1.38
d. Expected Profits	—*	—	—
e. Liquidity Model	—*	—	—
f. Naive Model	.30	.0407	1.42
Anaconda Company			
a. Neoclassical I	.87	.0078	1.06
b. Neoclassical II	.78	.0102	1.65
c. Accelerator	.80	.0098	2.48
d. Expected Profits	.87	.0084	2.83
e. Liquidity Model	.85	.0080	1.98
f. Naive Model	.54	.0128	1.93
Standard Oil, N.J.			
a. Neoclassical I	.86	.0736	2.48
b. Neoclassical II	.86	.0755	2.25
c. Accelerator	.69	.1083	1.79
d. Expected Profits	.75	.1022	2.24
e. Liquidity Model	.55	.1249	1.62
f. Naive Model	.50	.1258	1.67

Firm and Model	1949–1963		
	R^2	s	d
International Paper Company			
a. Neoclassical I	.74	.0105	2.01
b. Neoclassical II	.77	.0100	2.02
c. Accelerator	.66	.0121	1.72
d. Expected Profits	.72	.0109	1.39
e. Liquidity Model	.79	.0096	2.37
f. Naive Model	.14	.0177	1.79
Westinghouse Air Brake Corp.			
a. Neoclassical I	.61	.00135	1.87
b. Neoclassical II	.84	.0009	1.76
c. Accelerator	.55	.0015	1.66
d. Expected Profits	.60	.00137	2.08
e. Liquidity Model	.57	.0016	1.71
f. Naive Model	.19	.0018	2.01
International Business Machines			
a. Neoclassical I	.93	.0271	1.27
b. Neoclassical II	.96	.0208	2.57
c. Accelerator	.95	.0218	2.53
d. Expected Profits	.89	.0313	1.91
e. Liquidity Model	.90	.0306	2.38
f. Naive Model	.89	.0324	1.90
Swift			
a. Neoclassical I	.65	.0049	1.37
b. Neoclassical II	.53	.00543	1.83
c. Accelerator	—*	—	—
d. Expected Profits	.59	.0051	1.60
e. Liquidity Model	.49	.00538	1.59
f. Naive Model	.42	.0055	2.07
Westinghouse Electric			
a. Neoclassical I	.64	.0125	2.06
b. Neoclassical II	.75	.0110	1.56
c. Accelerator	.58	.01289	1.64
d. Expected Profits	.57	.01293	1.70
e. Liquidity Model	—*	—	—
f. Naive Model	.47	.0131	1.78

* No K_t^* variable reduces the standard error of the regression.

this bias affects all the distributed lag functions equally so that values of the Durbin-Watson statistic provide useful information about the relative presence or absence of autocorrelation. Employing the tables of Durbin and Watson the hypothesis of randomness cannot be rejected in favor of either positive or negative autocorrelation for any model for any firm for any time period. This evidence points to lack of substantial serial correlation. The tabulation of goodness of fit statistics given in Table 3 reveals that for nearly every firm the fitted distributed lag functions were superior to the Naive Model on the basis of goodness of fit, except for the Liquidity theory of investment. The Liquidity theory is superior to the Naive Model for only 9 of the 15 firms. We conclude that the fitted distributed lag functions are superior to the naive models although the margin of superiority for the Liquidity theory of investment is rather narrow.

Our comparison of alternative theories of investment behavior is based on the criterion of minimum standard error for the fitted distributed lag functions. All possible two-way comparisons of the alternative theories are presented in Table 4. The numbers listed in each row give the number of firms out of 15 for which the theory listed at the left-hand side of the table has a lower standard error than the theory listed at the top of the table. As an example, the Accelerator theory has a lower standard error than Neoclassical I for 3 out of 15 firms; the Accelerator has a lower standard error than Neoclassical II for 4 out of 15 firms and a lower standard error than the Expected Profits theory for 6 out of 15 firms with 2 ties. Finally, the Accelerator theory has a lower standard error than the Liquidity theory for 10 out of 15 firms.

The tabulation presented in Table 4 supports the following ranking of the alternative theories of investment behavior: The Neoclassical I theory of investment, including capital gains in both the price of capital services and the cost of capital, is slightly superior to Neoclassical II theory, excluding capital gains. It is clearly superior to the Accelerator theory with a lower standard error for 12 of 15 firms. It is also superior to the Expected Profits theory with a lower standard error for 12 of 15 firms. Finally, Neoclassical I is superior to the Liquidity theory for 14 of 15 firms. Continuing the ranking, the Neoclassical II theory of investment behavior is superior to the Accelerator theory for 11 of 15 firms. It is superior to the Expected Profits theory for 9 of 15 firms with one tie. Finally, Neoclassical II is superior to the Liquidity theory for 10 of 15 firms with one tie. The Expected Profits theory is superior to the Accelerator theory for 9 of 15 firms. Expected Profits is superior to the Liquidity theory for 10 of 15 firms with one tie. Finally, the Accelerator theory is superior to the Liquidity theory for 10 of 15 firms with one tie. We conclude that the alternative theories may be ranked as follows: (1) Neoclassical I; (2) Neoclassical II; (3) Expected Profits; (4) Accelerator; and (5) Liquidity.

Our first conclusion is that the Liquidity theory of investment can be dismissed from serious consideration as an explanation of corporate investment behavior. As one might suspect, financial constraints play a very minor role in the explanation of investment behavior for large firms. Our results strongly corroborate the previous findings of Grunfeld and Kuh. For eight corporations for the period 1935–54, Grunfeld found that the

TABLE 4   Model Ranking on Minimum Residual Variance Criterion, 1949–1963

Model \ Model	Neoclassical I	Neoclassical II	Accelerator	Expected Profits	Liquidity Model
Neoclassical I		8	12	12	14
Neoclassical II	7		11	9, tie	10, tie
Accelerator	3	4		6	10
Expected Profits	3	5, tie	9		10, tie
Liquidity Model	1	4, tie	5	4, tie	

partial correlation between profits and investment given capital stock was insignificant for six of the eight corporations.[35] Four of the firms in Grunfeld's sample are included in our sample of fifteen firms so that the results are not completely independent. Nevertheless, the differences between the two studies are sufficiently great that the results can be taken to reinforce each other. Kuh's study is based on 60 corporations in the capital goods industry for the period 1935–56. None of the firms in Kuh's sample is included in our sample; furthermore, his sample is concentrated on firms that are considerably smaller than those we have analyzed. Kuh concludes that the results from time series fail to support the internal funds or profits model.[36]

Our second conclusion is that Expected Profits and Accelerator models perform about equally well. The results slightly favor the Expected Profits model. The goodness of fit comparison of the two theories is reinforced by the enumeration of the number of coefficients that enter the fitted distributed lag functions for each theory, presented in Table 2. Again, the results slightly favor the Expected Profits theory. Our findings reinforce and extend Kuh's identification of expected profits with the capacity utilization theory or accelerator. No doubt information about profit expectations may be obtained from stock market data; however, this same information is adequately represented by levels of output or sales. Just as changes in profits before and after taxes are determined primarily by sales changes, alterations in the market value of the firm are adequately accounted for, so far as the determination of investment behavior is concerned, by alterations in output levels. Expected profits, whether measured by realized profits or the market value of the firm, may be represented by output levels. We conclude that a theory of investment behavior based on profit expectations may be identified with the capacity utilization theory so far as empirical results are concerned.

Our final conclusion is that either of the versions of the neoclassical theory of investment behavior we have examined is clearly superior to capacity utilization or profit expectations theories of investment. The neoclassical theory is far superior to internal funds theories of investment. Our findings thus corroborate the conclusions of Griliches and Wallace,[37] based on an analysis of quarterly time series data for all of manufacturing. Of course, our results provide a much sharper discrimination among alternative theories of investment behavior as our comparison of results from aggregate time series and time series for individual firms led us to expect. Between the two versions of the neoclassical theory of investment our results suggest that a better explanation of corporate investment behavior is provided by the Neoclassical I theory, incorporating capital gains in the price of capital services and the cost of capital. In any case the two theories are remarkably similar in performance. In a subsequent paper we will compare the results for these two theories in greater detail.

An alternative method for assessing the goodness of fit of the distributed lag functions corresponding to each theory of investment behavior is the number of "right" and "wrong" changes in direction for the fitted values of investment by comparison with the actual values. The number of correct changes in direction, the number of incorrect changes, and the number of extra turning points for the fitted values of investment are recorded in Table 5. Results are tabulated separately for peaks and troughs. The direction of change at a peak or trough is correct if the fitted value of investment at time $t + 1$ is less than the fitted value at time t for a peak of actual investment and greater than the value at time t for a trough. Where no changes in desired capital enter a fitted distributed lag function, results from the Naive Model are substituted for those of the distributed lag function.

On the basis of the number of correct turning points, the alternative theories may be ranked as follows: The Naive Model

[35] Grunfeld [17, Table 3, p. 219].
[36] Kuh [30, p. 213]. See also, Eisner [8].

[37] Griliches and Wallace [16, p. 325].

TABLE 5   Prediction of Direction of Change of Investment at Turning Points

Model		Totals	
		P [a]	T [b]
Neoclassical I	R [c]	26	33
	W [d]	13	8
	E [e]	6	2
Neoclassical II	R	26	29
	W	13	12
	E	3	2
Accelerator	R	25	27
	W	14	14
	E	5	3
Expected Profits	R	26	26
	W	13	15
	E	4	4
Liquidity Model	R	16	18
	W	23	23
	E	7	3
Naive Model	R	7	12
	W	32	29
	E	5	1

[a] Peak.
[b] Trough.
[c] Right direction.
[d] Wrong direction.
[e] Extra turning points in regression prediction.

ranks last by a considerable margin on the turning point criterion. The Liquidity theory of investment ranks lowest among the alternative theories of investment behavior. Expected Profits and Accelerator theories have nearly identical performance on turning points. Neoclassical I theory is slightly superior to Neoclassical II and both have a better performance record than the Accelerator or Expected Profits theories. We conclude that the ranking produced by an examination of turning points is substantially the same as that produced by the criterion of minimum residual variance.

To summarize: We have compared alternative theories of investment behavior with regard to their ability to explain corporate investment behavior. Although the relative performance of the alternative theories may be measured in a number of ways, the three measures of relative performance we have used—proportion of correct turning points, standard error of the regression, number of changes in desired capital entering the

fitted distributed lag function—produce an almost identical ordering of alternative theories of investment behavior: (1) Neoclassical I; (2) Neoclassical II; (3) Expected Profits; (4) Accelerator; and (5) Liquidity. Our tests discriminate sharply among the Neoclassical theories and the Expected Profits and Accelerator theories and between these theories and the Liquidity, theory. The discrimination between Neoclassical I and Neoclassical II theories, which differ in their treatment of capital gains realized on assets, is less sharp and deserves further examination.

IV. CONCLUSION

The purpose of our study has been to compare five alternative theories of investment behavior: Neoclassical I, including capital gains on assets; Neoclassical II, excluding capital gains; Accelerator, based on output or capacity utilization; Expected Profits, based on the market value of the firm; and Liquidity or internal funds. The point of departure for our study is the flexible accelerator mechanism originated by Chenery and Koyck; we have generalized this mechanism in order to provide a wider range of possible time patterns for investment behavior. Due to the importance of correct specification of the lag structure underlying investment, we have determined the best distributed lag function for each alternative theory from the class of general Pascal distributed lag functions. To permit sharper discrimination among the alternative theories we have employed data for individual firms; we have selected the best lag distribution for each alternative theory for each of the firms included in our sample. Our results are free of biases that could result from misspecification of the lag structure or from inappropriate assumptions about the homogeneity of investment behavior across firms. To measure the relative performance of the alternative theories of investment behavior we have relied primarily on the criterion of minimum residual variance. This measure of performance has been supplemented by measures of the proportion of correct turning points and the number of changes in desired capital entering the fitted distributed lag functions. The three measures of relative performance produce essentially the same results.

Our principal conclusion is that the neoclassical theory of investment behavior is superior to theories based on capacity utilization or profit expectations and that these theories are superior, in turn, to a theory based on internal funds available for investment. The latter part of our conclusion corroborates the previous results of Grunfeld and Kuh. Both of the versions of the neoclassical theory we have examined—including or excluding capital gains realized on assets from the cost of capital and the price of capital services—provide a better explanation of corporate investment behavior than any of the competing theories. The neoclassical theory including capital gains appears to provide a somewhat better explanation of corporate investment behavior.

Our conclusions bear on broader issues in the theory of the firm. Meyer and Kuh have suggested as a possible basis for the theory of investment behavior the asumption that business firms maximize utility defined more broadly than in the characterization of the objectives of the firm in the neoclassical theory of optimal capital accumulation:

> Partial recognition of institutional changes has led in recent years to shift the theory of the firm, and consequently of plant and equipment investment, from a profit maximization orientation to that of utility maximization. Primarily, this move represents a growing belief that profit maximization is too narrow to encompass the full scope of modern entrepreneurial motives, particularly once the previously assumed objective conditions are released from *ceteris paribus*, and the theory seeks to explain a much wider range of behavior response.[38]

Similar views on the theory of the firm have been expressed by Machlup [33], Simon [47], and many others. Simon argues that: "...I should like to emphasize strongly that neither the classical theory of the firm nor any of the amendments to it or substitutes for it that have been proposed have had any substantial amount of empirical testing. If the classical theory appeals to us, it must be largely because it has a certain face validity... rather than because profit maximizing behavior has been observed."[39] Simon ignores the entire econometric literature on cost and production functions, all of which is based on the neoclassical theory of the firm.[40] The evidence is so largely favorable to the theory that current empirical research emphasizes such technical questions as the appropriate form for the production function and the statistical specification for econometric models of production based on this theory. Simon's characterization of alternatives to the neoclassical theory of the firm is correct; this theory has not been subjected to substantial empirical testing. How-

---

[38] Meyer and Kuh [37, p. 9].

[39] Simon [47, p. 8].

[40] A recent survey of the literature by Walters [52] enumerates 345 references, almost all presenting results of econometric tests of the neoclassical theory which are overwhelmingly favorable to the theory.

ever, his characterization of the empirical evidence on the neoclassical theory is seriously incomplete.

Our results reinforce the evidence on the neoclassical theory of the firm from studies of cost and production functions. We conclude that the objections to the neoclassical theory of the firm as a basis for the theory of investment behavior by Meyer and Kuh are ill-founded. The appeal to a broader view of entrepreneurial objectives is not supported by evidence from econometric studies of cost and production functions or from studies of investment behavior. The neoclassical theory of the firm is more powerful than the broader view suggested by Machlup, Meyer and Kuh, and Simon in that a much narrower range of conceivable behavior is consistent with the neoclassical theory. On the basis of our comparison of alternative theories of investment behavior we conclude that further research can fruitfully incorporate precisely the factors central to the neoclassical theory of the firm. Although these factors played some role in early studies of investment behavior, they were not properly evaluated due to imprecise formulation of the theory of demand for capital services and due to misspecification of the time structure of investment behavior.

Obviously, our theory of corporate investment can be further improved. A more sophisticated analysis of the effects of tax policy on corporate investment behavior can be made.[41] Alternative approximations to the cost of capital for individual corporations are possible.[42] All the variables that enter the neoclassical theory of investment behavior can be measured more accurately.[43] All of these further improvements will require time and effort. Our conclusions suggest that this work is likely to be fruitful and that the

time and effort required will be justified by the results.

REFERENCES

1. W. H. L. ANDERSON, *Corporate Finance and Fixed Investment*. Boston, 1964.
2. H. B. CHENERY, "Overcapacity and the Acceleration Principle," *Econometrica*, Jan. 1952, *20*, 1–28.
3. *The Commercial and Financial Chronicle*, New York, William B. Dana Company, various daily issues.
4. D. CREAMER, *Capital Expansion and Capacity in Postwar Manufacturing*, Nat. Indus. Conf. Board, Stud. in Bus. Econ. no. 72, New York, 1961.
5. ———, *Recent Changes in Manufacturing Capacity*, Nat. Indus. Conf. Board, Stud. in Bus. Econ. no. 79, New York, 1962.
6. D. CREAMER, S. DOBROVOLSKY, and I. BORENSTEIN, *Capital in Manufacturing and Mining: Its Formation and Financing*. Princeton 1960.
7. J. S. DUESENBERRY, *Business Cycles and Economic Growth*. New York, 1958.
8. R. EISNER, "Capital Expenditures, Profits, and the Acceleration Principle," in *Models of Income Determination*, NBER Stud. in Income and Wealth, no. 28, Princeton, 1964, pp. 137–76.
9. ———, "A Distributed Lag Investment Function," *Econometrica*, *28*, Jan. 1960, 1–29.
10. ———, "Expectations, Plans, and Capital Expenditures: A Synthesis of Ex Post and Ex Ante Data," in M. J. Bowman, ed., *Expectations, Uncertainty and Business Behavior*. New York, 1958, pp. 165–88.
11. ———, "Investment: Fact and Fancy," *Am. Econ. Rev.*, May 1963, *53*, 237–46.
12. ———, "A Permanent Income Theory for Investment," *Am. Econ. Rev.*, June 1967, *57*, 363–90.
13. W. FELLER, *An Introduction to Probability Theory and Its Applications*, Vol. 1, 2d ed. New York, 1957.
14. *Fortune*, "Plant and Product Directory (The 500 Largest U.S. Industrial Corporations)," Aug. 1963.
15. Z. GRILICHES, "A Note on Serial Correlation Bias in Estimates of Distributed Lags," *Econometrica*, Jan. 1961, *29*, 65–73.
16. Z. GRILICHES and N. WALLACE, "The Determinants of Investment Revisited," *Internat. Econ. Rev.*, Sept. 1965, *6*, 311–29.
17. Y. GRUNFELD, "The Determinants of Cor-

---

[41] See, for example, Hall and Jorgenson [18] [19]; their analysis has not yet been extended to the level of the individual corporation.

[42] For example, it might be useful to include "growth opportunities" in the measurement of the cost of capital, as recently suggested by Modigliani and Miller [43].

[43] Further suggestions for better measurement are given in the Statistical Appendix; see footnote 28 above.

porate Investment," in A. C. Harberger, ed., *The Demand for Durable Goods*. Chicago, 1960, pp. 211–66.

18. R. E. HALL and D. W. JORGENSON, "Tax Policy and Investment Behavior," *Am. Econ. Rev.*, June 1967, *57*, 391–414.

19. ———, "The Role of Taxation in Stabilizing Private Investment," in V. P. Rock, ed., *Policy Makers and Model Builders*. Amsterdam, forth-coming.

20. B. G. HICKMAN, "Capacity, Capacity Utilization, and the Acceleration Principle," in *Problems of Capital Formation*, NBER Stud. in Income and Wealth no. 19, Princeton, 1957, pp. 419–50.

21. ———, *Investment Demand and U. S. Economic Growth*. Washington, 1965.

22. D. W. JORGENSON, "Anticipations and Investment Behavior," in J. S. Duesenberry, E. Kuh, G. Fromm, and L. R. Klein, ed., *The Brookings Quarterly Econometric Model of the United States*. Chicago, 1965, pp. 35–92.

23. ———, "Capital Theory and Investment Behavior," *Am. Econ. Rev., Proc.*, May 1963, *53*, 247–59.

24. ———, "Rational Distributed Lag Functions," *Econometrica*, Jan. 1966, *34*, 135–49.

25. D. W. JORGENSON and J. A. STEPHENSON, "Investment Behavior in U.S. Manufacturing, 1947–60," *Econometrica*, April 1967, *35*, 169–220.

26. ———, "The Time Structure of Investment Behavior in U.S. Manufacturing, 1947–60," *Rev. Econ. Stat.*, Feb. 1967, *49*, 16–27.

27. L. R. KLEIN, *Economic Fluctuations in the United States, 1921–1941*. New York, 1950.

28. ———, "Studies in Investment Behavior," in *Conference on Business Cycles*. New York, 1951, pp. 233–303.

29. L. M. KOYCK, *Distributed Lags and Investment Analysis*. Amsterdam, 1954.

30. E. KUH, *Capital Stock Growth: A Micro-Econometric Approach*. Amsterdam, 1963.

31. S. KUZNETS, *Capital in the American Economy: Its Formation and Financing*. Princeton, 1961.

32. ———, "Relation between Capital Goods and Finished Products in the Business Cycle," in *Economic Essays in Honor of Wesley Clair Mitchell*. New York, 1935, pp. 211–67.

33. F. MACHLUP, "Theories of the Firm: Marginalist, Behavioral, Managerial," *Am. Econ. Rev.*, March, 1967, *57*, 1–33.

34. E. MALINVAUD, "Estimation et prévision dans les modèles économiques autoregressifs,"

Rev. de l'Inst. Internat. Stat., 1961, *29*, 1–32.

35. T. MAYER, "Plant and Equipment Lead Times," *Jour. Bus.*, Apr. 1960, *33*, 127–32.

36. J. R. MEYER and R. R. GLAUBER, *Investment Decisions, Economic Forecasting and Public Policy*. Boston, 1964.

37. J. R. MEYER and E. KUH, *The Investment Decision*. Cambridge, 1957.

38. M. MILLER and F. MODIGLIANI, "Dividend Policy, Growth and the Valuation of Shares," *Jour. Bus.*, Oct. 1961, *34*, 411–33.

39. F. MODIGLIANI and M. MILLER, "Corporate Income Taxes and the Cost of Capital: A Correction," *Am. Econ. Rev.*, June 1963, *53*, 433–43.

40. ———, "The Cost of Capital, Corporation Finance, and the Theory of Investment," *Am. Econ. Rev.*, June 1958, *48*, 261–97.

41. ———, "The Cost of Capital, Corporation Finance, and the Theory of Investment: Reply," *Am. Econ. Rev.*, Sept. 1959, *49*, 655–69.

42. ———, "The Cost of Capital, Corporation Finance, and the Theory of Investment: Reply," *Am. Econ. Rev.*, June 1965, *55*, 524–27.

43. ———, "Some Estimates of the Cost of Capital to the Electric Utility Industry, 1954–57," *Am. Econ. Rev.*, June 1966, *56*, 333–91.

44. *Moody's Industrial Manual*, New York, various annual issues.

45. C. F. ROOS, "The Demand for Investment Goods," *Am. Econ. Rev.*, May 1958, *38*, 311–20.

46. C. F. ROOS and V. S. VON SZELISKI, "The Demand for Durable Goods," *Econometrica*, April 1943, *11*, 97–122.

47. H. SIMON, "New Developments in the Theory of the Firm," *Am. Econ. Rev.*, May 1962, *52*, 1–15.

48. R. M. SOLOW, "On a Family of Lag Distributions," *Econometrica*, Apr. 1960, *28*, 393–406.

49. *Standard Corporation Descriptions*, Standard and Poor's Corp., New York, various annual issues.

50. J. TINBERGEN, "Statistical Evidence on the Acceleration Principle," *Economica*, May 1938, *5*, 164–76.

51. ———, *Statistical Testing of the Business Cycle Theories: Vol. 1, A Method and Its Application to Investment Activity*. Geneva 1939.

52. A. A. WALTERS, "Production and Cost Functions: An Econometric Survey," *Econometrica*, April 1963, *31*, 1–66.

53. U. S. Dept. of Commerce, Office of Business Economics, *Business Statistics: A Supplement to the Survey of Current Business*, various biennial issues.

54. ———, *Survey of Current Business*, various monthly issues.

55. ———, *U.S. Income and Output: A Supplement to the Survey of Current Business*, 1958.

56. U.S. Dept. of Labor, Bureau of Labor Statistics, *Wholesale Prices and Price Indexes*, various monthly issues.

22

Risk Analysis in Capital Investment

DAVID B. HERTZ

Of all the decisions that business executives must make, none is more challenging—and none has received more attention—than choosing among alternative capital investment opportunities. What makes this kind of decision so demanding, of course, is not the problem of projecting return on investment under any given set of assumptions. The difficulty is in the assumptions and in their impact. Each assumption involves its own degree—often a high degree —of uncertainty; and, taken together, these combined uncertainties can multiply into a total uncertainty of critical proportions. This is where the element of risk enters, and it is in the evaluation of risk that the executive has been able to get little help from currently available tools and techniques.

There is a way to help the executive sharpen his key capital investment decisions by providing him with a realistic measurement of the risks involved. Armed with this measurement, which evaluates for him the risk at each possible level of return, he is then in a position to measure more knowledgeably alternative courses of action against corporate objectives.

NEED FOR NEW CONCEPT

The evaluation of a capital investment project starts with the principle that the productivity of capital is measured by the rate of return we expect to receive over some future period. A dollar received next year is worth less to us than a dollar in hand today. Expenditures three years hence are less costly than expenditures of equal magnitude two years from now. For this reason we cannot calculate the rate of return realistically unless we take into account (a) when the sums involved in an investment are spent and (b) when the returns are received.

Comparing alternative investments is thus complicated by the fact that they usually differ not only in size but also in the length of time over which expenditures will have to be made and benefits returned.

It is these facts of investment life that long ago made apparent the shortcomings of approaches that simply averaged expendi-

From Harvard Business Review (*January-February 1964*), *pp. 95–106. Reprinted by permission of publisher. Copyright © by the President and Fellows of Harvard College.*

tures and benefits, or lumped them, as in the number-of-years-to-pay-out method. These shortcomings stimulated students of decision making to explore more precise methods for determining whether one investment would leave a company better off in the long run than would another course of action.

It is not surprising, then, that much effort has been applied to the development of ways to improve our ability to discriminate among investment alternatives. The focus of all of these investigations has been to sharpen the definition of the value of capital investments to the company. The controversy and furor that once came out in the business press over the most appropriate way of calculating these values has largely been resolved in favor of the discounted cash flow method as a reasonable means of measuring the rate of return that can be expected in the future from an investment made today.

Thus we have methods which, in general, are more or less elaborate mathematical formulas for comparing the outcomes of various investments and the combinations of the variables that will affect the investments.[1] As these techniques have progressed, the mathematics involved has become more and more precise, so that we can now calculate discounted returns to a fraction of a per cent.

But the sophisticated businessman knows that behind these precise calculations are data which are not that precise. At best, the rate-of-return information he is provided with is based on an average of different opinions with varying reliabilities and different ranges of probability. When the expected returns on two investments are close, he is likely to be influenced by "intangibles"—a precarious pursuit at best. Even when the figures for two investments are quite far

[1] See for example, Joel Dean, *Capital Budgeting* (New York, Columbia University Press, 1951); "Return on Capital as a Guide to Managerial Decisions," *National Association of Accounts Research Report*, No. 35, December 1, 1959; and Bruce F. Young, "Overcoming Obstacles to Use of Discounted Cash Flow for Investment Shares," *NAA Bulletin*, March 1963, p. 15.

apart, and the choice seems clear, there lurks in the back of the businessman's mind memories of the Edsel and other ill-fated ventures.

In short, the decision-maker realizes that there is something more he ought to know, something in addition to the expected rate of return. He suspects that what is missing has to do with the nature of the data on which the expected rate of return is calculated, and with the way those data are processed. It has something to do with uncertainty, with possibilities and probabilities extending across a wide range of rewards and risks.

The Achilles Heel

The fatal weakness of past approaches thus has nothing to do with the mathematics of rate-of-return calculation. We have pushed along this path so far that the precision of our calculation is, if anything, somewhat illusory. The fact is that, no matter what mathematics is used, each of the variables entering into the calculation of rate of return is subject to a high level of uncertainty. For example:

> The useful life of a new piece of capital equipment is rarely known in advance with any degree of certainty. It may be affected by variations in obsolescence or deterioration, and relatively small changes in use life can lead to large changes in return. Yet an expected value for the life of the equipment—based on a great deal of data from which a single best possible forecast has been developed—is entered into the rate-of-return calculation. The same is done for the other factors that have a significant bearing on the decision at hand.

Let us look at how this works out in a simple case—one in which the odds appear to be all in favor of a particular decision:

> The executives of a food company must decide whether to launch a new packaged cereal. They have come to the conclusion that five factors are the determining variables: *advertising and promotion expense, total cereal market, share of market for this product, operating costs, and new capital investment*. On the basis of the "most likely" estimate for each of these variables the picture looks very bright—a healthy 30% return. This future, however, depends on each

of the "most likely" estimates coming true in the actual case. If each of these "educated guesses" has, for example, a 60% chance of being correct, there is only an 8% chance that *all five* will be correct (.60 × .60 × .60 × .60 × .60). So the "expected" return is actually dependent on a rather unlikely coincidence. The decision-maker needs to know a great deal more about the *other* values used to make each of the five estimates and about what he stands to gain or lose from various combinations of these values.

This simple example illustrates that the rate of return actually depends on a specific combination of values of a great many different variables. But only the expected levels of ranges (e.g., worst, average, best; or pessimistic, most likely, optimistic) of these variables are used in formal mathematical ways to provide the figures given to management. Thus, predicting a single most likely rate of return gives precise numbers that do not tell the whole story.

The "expected" rate of return represents only a few points on a continuous curve of possible combinations of future happenings. It is a bit like trying to predict the outcome in a dice game by saying that the most likely outcome is a "7." The description is incomplete because it does not tell us about all the other things that could happen. In Figure 1, for instance, we see the odds on throws of only two dice having six sides. Now suppose that each dice has 100 sides and there are eight of them! This is a situation more comparable

to business investment, where the company's market share might become any one of 100 different sizes and where there are eight different factors (pricing, promotion, and so on) that can affect the outcome.

Nor is this the only trouble. Our willingness to bet on a roll of the dice depends not only on the odds but also on the stakes. Since the probability of rolling a "7" is 1 in 6, we might be quite willing to risk a few dollars on that outcome at suitable odds. But would we be equally willing to wager $10,000 or $100,000 at those same odds, or even at better odds? In short, risk is influenced both by the odds on various events occurring and by the magnitude of the rewards or penalties which are involved when they do occur. To illustrate again:

Suppose that a company is considering an investment of $1 million. The "best estimate" of the probable return is $200,000 a year. It could well be that this estimate is the average of three possible returns—a 1-in-3 chance of getting no return at all, a 1-in-3 chance of getting $200,000 per year, a 1-in-3 chance of getting $400,000 per year. Suppose that getting no return at all would put the company out of business. Then, by accepting this proposal, management is taking a 1-in-3 chance of going bankrupt.

If only the "best estimate" analysis is used, management might go ahead, however, unaware that it is taking a big chance. If all of the available information were examined, management might prefer an alternative pro-

FIG. 1 Describing uncertainty—a throw of the dice

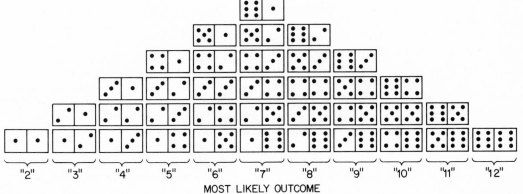

MOST LIKELY OUTCOME

posal with a smaller, but more certain (i.e., less variable), expectation.

Such considerations have led almost all advocates of the use of modern capital-investment-index calculations to plead for a recognition of the element of uncertainty. Perhaps Ross G. Walker sums up current thinking when he speaks of "the almost impenetrable mists of any forecast."[2]

How can the executive penetrate the mists of uncertainty that surround the choices among alternatives?

Limited Improvements

A number of efforts to cope with uncertainty have been successful up to a point, but all seem to fall short of the mark in one way or another:

1. *More accurate forecasts*—Reducing the error in estimates is a worthy objective. But no matter how many estimates of the future go into a capital investment decision, when all is said and done, the future is still the future. Therefore, however well we forecast, we are still left with the certain knowledge that we cannot eliminate all uncertainty.

2. *Empirical adjustments*—Adjusting the factors influencing the outcome of a decision is subject to serious difficulties. We would like to adjust them so as to cut down the likelihood that we will make a "bad" investment, but how can we do that without at the same time spoiling our chances to make a "good" one? And in any case what is the basis for adjustment? We adjust, not for uncertainty, but for bias.

For example, construction estimates are often exceeded. If a company's history of construction costs is that 90% of its estimates have been exceeded by 15% then in a capital estimate there is every justification for increasing the value of this factor by 15 %.This is a matter of improving the accuracy of the estimate.

But suppose that new-product sales esti-

mates have been exceeded by more than 75% in one-fourth of all historical cases, and have not reached 50% of the estimate in one-sixth of all such cases? Penalties for over-estimating are very tangible, and so management is apt to reduce the sales estimate to "cover" the one case in six—thereby reducing the calculated rate of return. In doing so, it is possibly missing some of its best opportunities.

3. *Revising cutoff rates*—Selecting higher cutoff rates for protecting against uncertainty is attempting much the same thing. Management would like to have a possibility of return in proportion to the risk it takes. Where there is much uncertainty involved in the various estimates of sales, costs, prices, and so on, a high calculated return from the investment provides some incentive for taking the risk. This is, in fact, a perfectly sound position. The trouble is that the decision-maker still needs to know explicitly what risks he is taking—and what the odds are on achieving the expected return.

4. *Three-level estimates*—A start at spelling out risks is sometimes made by taking the high, medium, and low values of the estimated factors and calculating rates of return based on various combinations of the pessimistic, average, and optimistic estimates. These calculations give a picture of the range of possible results, but do not tell the executive whether the pessimistic result is more likely than the optimistic one—or, in fact, whether the average result is much more likely to occur than either of the extremes. So, although this is a step in the right direction, it still does not give a clear enough picture for comparing alternatives.

5. *Selected probabilities*—Various methods have been used to include the probabilities of specific factors in the return calculation. L.C. Grant discusses a program for forecasting discounted cash flow rates of return where the service life is subject to obsolescence and deterioration. He calculates the odds that the investment will terminate at any time after it is made, depending on the probability distribution of the service-life factor. After calculating these factors for each year through maximum service life, he then

---

[2] "The Judgement Factor in Investment Decisions," *Harvard Business Review*, March–April 1961, p. 99.

determines an over-all expected rate of return.[3]

Edward G. Bennion suggests the use of game theory to take into account alternative market growth rates as they would determine rate of return for various alternatives. He uses the estimated probabilities that specific growth rates will occur to develop optimum strategies. Bennion points out:

> Forecasting can result in a negative contribution to capital budget decisions unless it goes further than merely providing a single most probable prediction. . . . (With) an estimated probability coefficient for the forecast, plus knowledge of the payoffs for the company's alternative investments and calculation of indifference probabilities . . . the margin of error may be substantially reduced, and the businessman can tell just how far off his forecast may be before it leads him to a wrong decision.[4]

Note that both of these methods yield an expected return, each based on only one uncertain input factor—service life in the first case, market growth in the second. Both are helpful, and both tend to improve the clarity with which the executive can view investment alternatives. But neither sharpens up the range of "risk taken" or "return hoped for" sufficiently to help very much in the complex decisions of capital planning.

SHARPENING THE PICTURE

Since every one of the many factors that enter into the evaluation of a specific decision is subject to some uncertainty, the executive needs a helpful portrayal of the effects that the uncertainty surrounding each of the significant factors has on the returns he is likely to achieve. Therefore, the method we have developed at McKinsey & Company, Inc., combines the variabilities inherent in all the relevant factors. Our objective is to give a clear picture of the relative risk and the probable odds of coming out ahead or behind in the light of uncertain foreknowledge.

A simulation of the way these factors may combine as the future unfolds is the key to extracting the maximum information from the available forecasts. In fact, the approach is very simple, using a computer to do the necessary arithmetic. (Recently, a computer program to do this was suggested by S.W. Hess and H.A. Quigley for chemical process investments.[5])

To carry out the analysis, a company must follow three steps:

1. Estimate the range of values for each of the factors (e.g., range of selling price, sales growth rate, and so on) and within that range the likelihood of occurrence of each value.

2. Select at random from the distribution of values for each factor one particular value. Then combine the values for all of the factors and compute the rate of return (or present value) from that combination. For instance, the lowest in the range of prices might be combined with the highest in the range of growth rate and other factors. (The fact that the factors are dependent should be taken into account, as we shall see later.)

3. Do this over and over again to define and evaluate the odds of the occurrence of each possible rate of return. Since there are literally millions of possible combinations of values, we need to test the likelihood that various specific returns on the investment will occur. This is like finding out by recording the results of a great many throws what per cent of "7"s or other combinations we may expect in tossing dice. The result will be a listing of the rates of return we might achieve, ranging from a loss (if the factors go against us) to whatever maximum gain is possible with the estimates that have been made.

For each of these rates the chances that it may occur are determined. (Note that a specific return can usually be achieved through more than one combination of events. The more combinations for a given rate, the higher the chances of achieving it—as with "7"s in tossing dice.) The average expectation is the average of the values

[3] "Monitoring Capital Investments," *Financial Executive*, April 1963, p. 19.

[4] "Capital Budgeting and Game Theory," *Harvard Business Review*, November–December 1956, p. 123.

[5] "Analysis of Risk in Investments Using Monte Carlo Techniques," *Chemical Engineering Symposium Series 42: Statistics and Numerical Methods in Chemical Engineering* (New York, American Institute of Chemical Engineering, 1963), p. 55.

of all outcomes weighted by the chances of each occurring.

The variability of outcome values from the average is also determined. This is important since, all other factors being equal, management would presumably prefer lower variability for the same return if given the choice. This concept has already been applied to investment portfolios.[6]

When the expected return and variability of each of a series of investments have been determined, the same techniques may be used to examine the effectiveness of various combinations of them in meeting management objectives.

PRACTICAL TEST

To see how this new approach works in practice, let us take the experience of a management that has already analyzed a specific investment proposal by conventional techniques. Taking the same investment schedule and the same expected values actually used, we can find what results the new method would produce and compare them with the results obtained when conventional methods were applied. As we shall see, the new picture of risks and returns is different from the old one. Yet the differences are attributable in no way to changes in the basic data—*only to the increased sensitivity of the method to management's uncertainties about the key factors.*

Investment Proposal

In this case a medium-size industrial chemical producer is considering a $10-million extension to its processing plant. The estimated service life of the facility is 10 years; the engineers expect to be able to utilize 250,000 tons of processed material worth $510 per ton at an average processing

cost of $435 per ton. Is this investment a good bet? In fact, what is the return that the company may expect? What are the risks? We need to make the best and fullest use we can of all the market research and financial analyses that have been developed, so as to give management a clear picture of this project in an uncertain world.

The key input factors management has decided to use are:

1. Market size.
2. Selling prices.
3. Market growth rate.
4. Share of market (which results in physical sales volume).
5. Investment required.
6. Residual value of investment.
7. Operating costs.
8. Fixed costs.
9. Useful life of facilities.

These factors are typical of those in many company projects that must be analyzed and combined to obtain a measure of the attractiveness of a proposed capital facilities investment.

Obtaining Estimates

How do we make the recommended type of analysis of this proposal?

Our aim is to develop for each of the nine factors listed a frequency distribution or probability curve. The information we need includes the possible range of values for each factor, the average, and some ideas as to the likelihood that the various possible values will be reached. It has been our experience that for major capital proposals managements usually make a significant investment in time and funds to pinpoint information about each of the relevant factors. An objective analysis of the values to be assigned to each can, with little additional effort, yield a subjective probability distribution.

Specifically, it is necessary to probe and question each of the experts involved—to find out, for example, whether the estimated cost of production really can be said to be exactly a certain value or whether, as is more likely, it should be estimated to lie within

[6] See Harry Markowitz, *Portfolio Selection, Efficient Diversification of Investments* (New York, John Wiley and Sons, 1959); Donald E. Fararr, *The Investment Decision Under Uncertainty* (Englewood Cliffs, New Jersey, Prentice-Hall, Inc., 1962); William F. Sharpe, "A Simplified Model for Portfolio Analysis," *Management Science*, January 1963, p. 277.

a certain range of values. It is that range which is ignored in the analysis management usually makes. The range is relatively easy to determine; if a guess has to be made—as it often does—it is easier to guess with some accuracy a range rather than a specific single value. We have found from past experience at McKinsey & Company, Inc., that a series of meetings with management personnel to discuss such distributions is most helpful in getting at realistic answers to the a priori questions. (The term "realistic answers" implies all the information management does not have as well as all that it does have.)

The ranges are directly related to the degree of confidence that the estimator has in his estimate. Thus, certain estimates may be known to be quite accurate. They would be represented by probability distributions stating, for instance, that there is only 1 chance in 10 that the actual value will be different from the best estimate by more than 10% Others may have as much as 100% ranges above and below the best estimate.

Thus, we treat the factor of selling price for the finished product by asking executives who are responsible for the original estimates these questions:

1. Given that $510 is the expected sales price, what is the probability that the price will exceed $550?
2. Is there any chance that the price will exceed $650?
3. How likely is it that the price will drop below $475?

Managements must ask similar questions for each of the other factors, until they can construct a curve for each. Experience shows that this is not as difficult as it might sound. Often information on the degree of variation in factors is readily available. For instance, historical information on variations in the price of a commodity is readily available. Similarly, management can estimate the variability of sales from industry sales records. Even for factors that have no history, such as operating costs for a new product, the person who makes the "average" estimate must have some idea of the degree of confidence he has in his prediction, and therefore

he is usually only too glad to express his feelings. Likewise, the less confidence he has in his estimate, the greater will be the range of possible values that the variable will assume.

This last point is likely to trouble businessmen. Does it really make sense to seek estimates of variations? It cannot be emphasized too strongly that the less certainty there is in an "average" estimate, *the more important it is to consider the possible variation in that estimate.*

Further, an estimate of the variation possible in a factor, no matter how judgmental it may be, is always better than a simple "average" estimate, since it includes more information about what is known and what is not known. It is, in fact, this very *lack* of knowledge which may distinguish one investment possibility from another, so that for rational decision making it *must* be taken into account.

This lack of knowledge is in itself important information about the proposed investment. To throw any information away simply because it is highly uncertain is a serious error in analysis which the new approach is designed to correct.

Computer Runs

The next step in the proposed approach is to determine the returns that will result from random combinations of the factors involved. This requires realistic restrictions, such as not allowing the total market to vary more than some reasonable amount from year to year. Of course, any method of rating the return which is suitable to the company may be used at this point; in the actual case management preferred discounted cash flow for the reasons cited earlier, so that method is followed here.

A computer can be used to carry out the trials for the simulation method in very little time and at very little expense. Thus, for one trial actually made in this case, 3,600 discounted cash flow calculations, each based on a selection of the nine input factors, were run in two minutes at a cost of $15 for computer time. The resulting rate-of-return

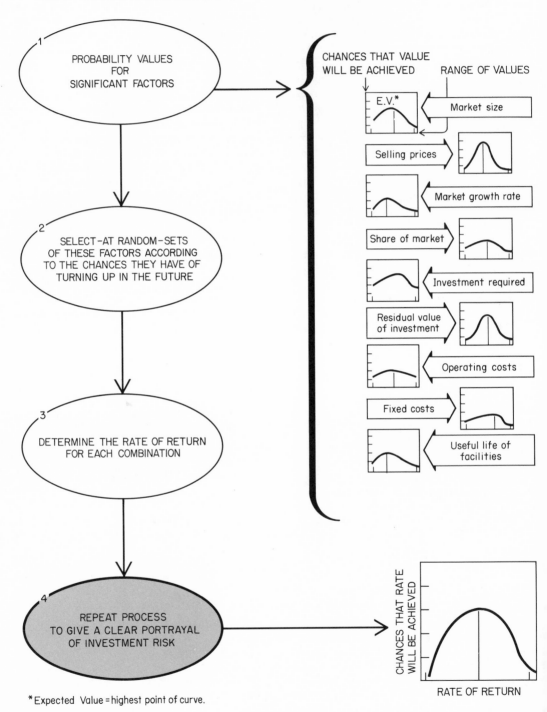

FIG. 2 Simulation for investment planning

*Expected Value = highest point of curve.

probabilities were read out immediately and graphed. The process is shown schematically in Figure 2.

Data Comparisons

The nine input factors described earlier fall into three categories:

1. *Market analyses.* Included are market size, market growth rate, the firm's share of the market, and selling prices. For a given combination of these factors sales revenue may be determined.

2. *Investment cost analyses.* Being tied to the kinds of service-life and operating-cost characteristics expected, these are subject to various kinds of error and uncertainty; for instance,

automation progress makes service life uncertain.

3. *Operating and fixed costs.* These also are subject to uncertainty, but are perhaps the easiest to estimate.

These categories are not independent, and for realistic results our approach allows the various factors to be tied together. Thus, if price determines the total market, we first select from a probability distribution the price for the specific computer run and then use for the total market a probability distribution that is logically related to the price selected.

We are now ready to compare the values obtained under the new approach with the values obtained under the old. This comparison is shown in Table 1.

TABLE 1   Comparison of Expected Values Under Old and New Approaches

	Conventional "Best Estimate" Approach	New Approach
MARKET ANALYSES		
1. *Market size*		
Expected value (in tons)	250,000	250,000
Range	—	100,000–340,000
2. *Selling prices*		
Expected value (in dollars/ton)	$510	$510
Range	—	$385–$575
3. *Market growth rate*		
Expected value	3%	3%
Range	—	0–6%
4. *Eventual share of market*		
Expected value	12%	12%
Range	—	3–17%
INVESTMENT COST ANALYSES		
5. *Total investment required*		
Expected value (in millions)	$9.5	$9.5
Range	—	$7.0–$10.5
6. *Useful life of facilities*		
Expected value (in years)	10	10
Range	—	5–15
7. *Residual value (at 10 years)*		
Expected value (in millions)	$4.5	$4.5
Range	—	$3.5–$5.0
OTHER COSTS		
8. *Operating costs*		
Expected value (in dollars/ton)	$435	$435
Range	—	$370–$545
9. *Fixed Costs*		
Expected value (in thousands)	$300	$300
Range	—	$250–$375

Note: Range figures in right-hand column represent approximately 1% to 99% probabilities. That is, there is only a 1 in a 100 chance that the value actually achieved will be respectively greater or less than the range.

Valuable Results

How do the results under the new and old approaches compare?

In this case, management had been informed, on the basis of the "one best estimate" approach, that the expected return was 25.2% before taxes. When we ran the new set of data through the computer program, however, we got an expected return of only 14.6% before taxes.

This surprising difference not only is due to the fact that under the new approach we use a range of values; it also reflects the fact that we have weighted each value in the range by the chances of its occurrence.

Our new analysis thus may help management to avoid an unwise investment. In fact, the general result of carefully weighing the information and lack of information in the manner I have suggested is to indicate the true nature of otherwise seemingly satisfactory investment proposals. If this practice were followed by managements, much regretted over-capacity might be avoided.

The computer program developed to carry out the simulation allows for easy insertion of new variables. In fact, some programs have previously been suggested that take variability into account.[7] But most programs do not allow for dependence relationships between the various input factors. Further, the program used here permits the choice of a value for price from one distribution, which value determines a particular probability distribution (from among several) that will be used to determine the value for sales volume. To show how this important technique works:

Suppose we have a wheel, as in roulette, with the numbers from 0 to 15 representing one price for the product or material, the numbers 16 to 30 representing a second price, the numbers 31 to 45 a third price, and so on. For each of these segments we would have a different range of expected market volumes; e.g., $150,000–$200,000 for the first, $100,000–$150,000 for the second, $75,000–$100,000 for

[7] See Frederick S. Hillier, "The Derivation of Probabilistic Information for the Evaluation of Risky Investments," *Management Science*, April 1963, p. 443.

the third, and so forth. Now suppose that we spin the wheel and the ball falls in 37. This would mean that we pick a sales volume in the $75,000–$100,000 range. If the ball goes in 11, we have a different price and we turn to the $150,000–$200,000 range for a price.

Most significant, perhaps, is the fact that the program allows management to ascertain the sensitivity of the results to each or all of the input factors. Simply by running the program with changes in the distribution of an input factor, it is possible to determine the effect of added or changed information (or of the lack of information). It may turn out that fairly large changes in some factors do not significantly affect the outcomes. In this case, as a matter of fact, management was particularly concerned about the difficulty in estimating market growth. Running the program with variations in this factor quickly demonstrated to us that for average annual growths from 3% and 5% there was no significant difference in the expected outcome.

In addition, let us see what the implications are of the detailed knowledge the simulation method gives us. Under the method using single expected values, management arrives only at a hoped-for expectation of 25.2% after taxes (which, as we have seen, is wrong unless there is no variability in the various input factors—a highly unlikely event). On the other hand, with the method we propose, the uncertainties are clearly portrayed:

Per Cent Return	Probability of Achieving At Least the Return Shown
0%	96.5%
5	80.6
10	75.2
15	53.8
20	43.0
25	12.6
30	0

This profile is shown in Figure 3. Note the contrast with the profile obtained under the conventional approach. This concept has been used also for evaluation of new-product introductions, acquisitions of new businesses, and plant modernization.

FIG. 3 Anticipated rates of return under old and new approaches

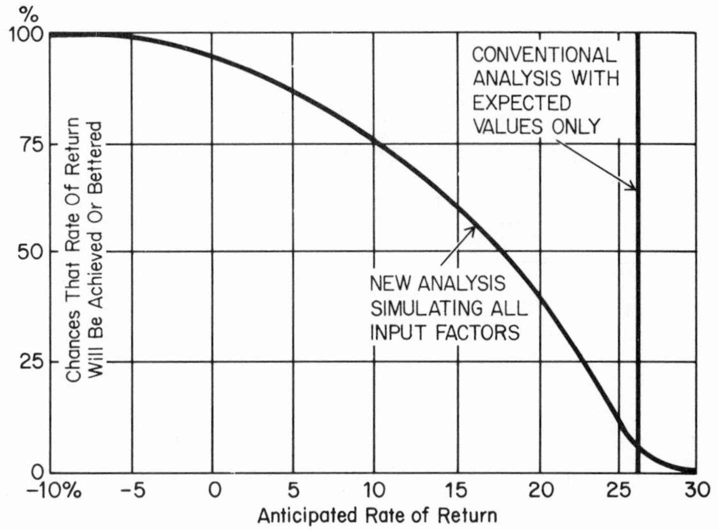

COMPARING OPPORTUNITIES

From a decision-making point of view one of the most significant advantages of the new method of determining rate of return is that it allows management to discriminate between measures of (1) expected return based on weighted probabilities of all possible returns, (2) variability of return, and (3) risks.

To visualize this advantage, let us take an example which is based on another actual case but simplified for purposes of explanation. The example involves two investments under consideration, A and B.

When the investments are analyzed, the data tabulated and plotted in Figure 4 are obtained. We see that:

Investment B has a higher expected return than Investment A.

Investment B also has substantially more variability than Investment A. There is a good chance that Investment B will earn a return which is quite different from the expected return of 6.8%, possibly as high as 15% or as low as a loss of 5%. Investment A is not likely to vary greatly from the expected 5% return.

Investment B involves far more risk than does Investment A. There is virtually no chance of incurring a loss on Investment A. However,

there is 1 chance in 10 of losing money on Investment B. If such a loss occurs, its expected size is approximately $200,000.

Clearly, the new method of evaluating investments provides management with far more information on which to base a decision.

CONCLUSION

The question management faces in selecting capital investments is first and foremost: What information is needed to clarify the key differences among various alternatives? There is agreement as to the basic factors that should be considered—markets, prices, costs, and so on. And the way the future return on the investment should be calculated, if not agreed on, is at least limited to a few methods, any of which can be consistently used in a given company. If the input variables turn out as estimated, any of the methods customarily used to rate investments should provide satisfactory (if not necessarily maximum) returns.

In actual practice, however, the conventional methods do *not* work out satisfactorily. Why? The reason, as we have seen earlier in this article, and as every executive and

FIG. 4 Comparison of two investment opportunities

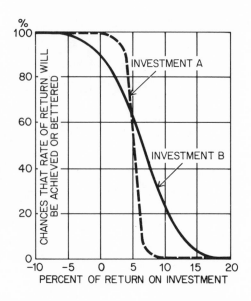

	INVESTMENT A	INVESTMENT B
AMOUNT OF INVESTMENT	$10,000,000	$10,000,000
LIFE OF INVESTMENT (IN YEARS)	10	10
EXPECTED ANNUAL NET CASH INFLOW	$ 1,300,000	$ 1,400,000
VARIABILITY OF CASH INFLOW		
1 Chance in 50 of being <u>Greater</u> than	$ 1,700,000	$ 3,400,000
1 Chance in 50 of being <u>Less</u>* than	S 00,000	($600,000)
EXPECTED RETURN ON INVESTMENT	5.0%	6.8%
VARIABILITY OF RETURN ON INVESTMENT		
1 Chance in 50 of being <u>Greater</u> than	7.0%	15.5%
1 Chance in 50 of being <u>Less</u>* than	3.0%	(4.0%)

RISK OF INVESTMENT
  Chances of a Loss
  Expected Size of Loss
	Negligible	1 in 10
		$200,000

*In the case of negative figures (indicated by parentheses) "less than" means "worse than".

economist knows, is that the estimates used in making the advance calculations are just that—estimates. More accurate estimates would be helpful, but at best the residual uncertainty can easily make a mockery of corporate hopes. Nevertheless, there is a solution. To collect realistic estimates for the key factors means to find out a great deal about them. Hence the kind of uncertainty that is involved in each estimate can be evaluated ahead of time. Using this knowledge of uncertainty, executives can maximize the value of the information for decision making.

The value of computer programs in developing clear portrayals of the uncertainty and risk surrounding alternative investments has been proved. Such programs can produce valuable information about the sensitivity of the possible outcomes to the variability of input factors and to the likelihood of achieving various possible rates of return. This information can be extremely important as a backup to management judgment. To have calculations of the odds on all possible outcomes lends some assurance to the decision-makers that the available information has been used with maximum efficiency.

This simulation approach has the inherent advantage of simplicity. It requires only an extension of the input estimates (to the best of our ability) in terms of probabilities. No projection should be pinpointed unless we are *certain* of it.

The discipline of thinking through the uncertainties of the problem will in itself help to ensure improvement in making investment choices. For to understand uncertainty and risk is to understand the key business problem—and the key business opportunity. Since the new approach can be applied on a continuing basis to each capital alternative as it comes up for consideration and progresses toward fruition, gradual progress may be expected in improving the estimation of the probabilities of variation.

Lastly, the courage to act boldly in the face of apparent uncertainty can be greatly bolstered by the clarity of portrayal of the risks and possible rewards. To achieve these lasting results requires only a slight effort beyond what most companies already exert in studying capital investments.

SUMMARY OF NEW APPROACH

After examining present methods of comparing alternative investments, Mr. Hertz reports on his firm's experience in applying a new approach to the problem. Using this approach, management takes the various levels of possible cash flows, return on investment, and other results of a proposed outlay and gets an estimate of the odds for each potential outcome.

Currently, many facilities decisions are based on discounted cash flow calculations. Management is told, for example, that Investment X has an expected internal rate of return of 9.2%, while for Investment Y a 10.3% return can be expected.

By contrast, the new approach would put in front of the executive a schedule which gives him the most likely return from X, but also tells him that X has 1 chance in 20 of being a total loss, 1 in 10 of earning from 4% to 5%, 2 in 10 of paying from 8% to 10%, and 1 chance in 50 of attaining a 30% rate of return. From another schedule he learns what the most likely rate of return is from Y, but also that Y has 1 chance in 10 of resulting in a total loss, 1 in 10 of earning from 3% to 5% return, 2 in 10 of paying between 9% and 11%, and 1 chance in 100 of 30%. Or portrayed graphically:

FIG. 5

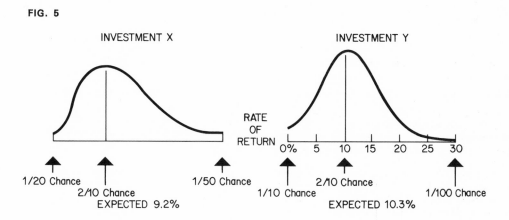

In this instance, the estimates of the rates of return provided by the two approaches would not be substantially different. However, to the decision-maker with the added information, Investment Y no longer looks like the clearly better choice, since with X the chances of substantial gain are higher and the risks of loss lower.

Two things have made this approach appealing to managers who have used it:

1. Certainly in every case it is a more descriptive statement of the two opportunities. And in some cases it might well reverse the decision, in line with particular corporate objectives.

2. This is not a difficult technique to use, since much of the information needed is already available—or readily accessible—and the validity of the principles involved has, for the most part, already been proved in other applications.

23

A Portfolio Analysis of Conglomerate Diversification

KEITH V. SMITH AND JOHN C. SCHREINER*

One of the more remarkable developments within finance during the current decade has been the rapid emergence of the conglomerate type of firm. Viewed internally, the conglomerate phenomenon has proven of great interest to academicians studying economies of scale for both human and non-human resources, while from an external focus, conglomerates represent a new type of investment opportunity.

Although interest in conglomerates has resulted in various theories for explaining or rationalizing conglomerate development, this paper is concerned only with the external view of conglomerates as a means toward

From Journal of Finance (*June 1969*), *pp. 413–27. Reprinted with permission of authors and publisher.*

* The authors are Assistant Professor of Finance and Doctoral Student, respectively, University of California, Los Angeles. Research support was provided by the Bureau of Business and Economic Research, University of California, Los Angeles. The authors are indebted to E. F. Brigham, M. B. Goudzwaard, and D. M. Kaplan for helpful comments.

diversification. Specifically, the purposes of this study are (1) to investigate the relative merits of using a portfolio approach to explain conglomerate diversification, (2) to develop and test a means of measuring the ex ante diversification potential of given conglomerates, and (3) to compare the observed diversification patterns of certain conglomerates with those of mutual funds which presumably are specifically organized for just such a purpose.

Section I summarizes the rapid growth of conglomerate firms during recent years, discusses alternative theories for explaining conglomerate growth, and focuses on the portfolio theory of diversification. It also explains a ranking criterion based on portfolio theory which can be used to measure the effective diversification of a given conglomerate firm. In Section II, the diversification criterion is applied to a sample of 19 conglomerates and also a sample of 8 mutual funds. Results of this empirical test are presented in Section III, and the relationship of a conglomerate's effective diversification is compared to both the age and size of the conglomerate. Finally, Section IV discusses both the implications and limitations of the empirical study.

I. CONGLOMERATE DIVERSIFICATION

One of the most dynamic changes within the private sector in recent years has been the large number of mergers and acquisitions involving firms of all sizes and virtually all industries.[1] The increased emphasis on growth and on investor return has encouraged the combining of smaller business entities. This represents a distinct step in the rapid change of corporate structure within the free enterprise system. Whereas in the past firms have expanded vertically and horizontally, but within a given industrial category, the conglomerate type of firm has grown across numerous, seemingly unrelated activities or product lines.

For purposes of this study a conglomerate is taken to be a company that (1) invests capital in several industrial categories, and (2) appears to emphasize external growth, through mergers and acquisitions, over internal growth. The latter requirement excludes a firm such as General Electric which produces and distributes products in several industrial categories—but whose growth has resulted mainly from internal expansion over many years.[2]

Apart from an explanation of simply growing large, several theories have been expounded for explaining the conglomerate

type of growth. These theories can be categorized as motives having to do with profitability, synergism, or diversification.[3] The profitability motive would suggest that a conglomerate firm should expand into any industrial category provided that the expected rate of return on such an investment exceeds the firm's cost of capital. Conversely, the synergism motive suggests that conglomerates grow in order to achieve ecomonies of scale—either from decreasing costs or from increasing demand—such that the combination of firms is preferable to simply summing over its individual components.[4] Finally, the diversification motive suggests that by engaging in different types of activity, the conglomerate firm is able to reduce its overall exposure to business risk.[5]

Since proper diversification among different investments is the kernel of modern portfolio theory, it would seem appropriate to investigate the value of a portfolio approach as an explanation of conglomerates.[6] Interestingly enough, however, the Markowitz concept of efficient diversification[7]—the forerunner of most portfolio theories—really can include all three of the above motives for conglomerate growth. Efficient

[1] W. T. Grimm and Company in their "1967 Merger Review" reported that the total number of mergers has grown from 1,361 in 1963 to 2,975 in 1967, which is at an annual rate of increase of 16.9 percent. It is estimated that well over 50 percent of the mergers during 1967 were of the conglomerate type.

[2] Paralleling the growth of conglomerates has been an increased anti-trust movement in which the precise definition of a conglomerate has received considerable attention. For an interesting discussion of some of the difficulties encountered in legal circles, see P. Asch, "Conglomerate Mergers and Public Policy," *MSU Business Topics*, 15: 61–67, Winter 1967.

[3] A rigorous and comprehensive theoretical treatment of corporate growth by merger is found in W. S. Alberts, "The Profitability of Growth by Merger," in W. W. Alberts and J. E. Segall (eds.), *The Corporate Merger* (Chicago: University of Chicago Press, 1966), pp. 235–287.

[4] The term "synergism" was first defined as a "two-plus-two-equals-five" effect and applied to mergers in J. Fred Weston, *Managerial Finance* (New York: Holt, Rinehart, and Winston, first edition, 1962), pp. 524–549.

[5] For further discussion of the diversification motive, see M. Gort, "Diversification, Mergers, and Profits," in Alberts and Segall, *op. cit.*, pp. 31–43.

[6] A portfolio approach to conglomerate merger decisions was suggested in G. A. Christy, "Does Today's Investor Appreciate the Diversified Firm's Significance?", *The Commercial and Financial Chronicle*, April 7, 1966, pp. 1–20. Another suggestion that an outsider might take a portfolio approach in order to assess the investment desirability of a conglomerate appeared in B. S. Kopp, "Conglomerates in Portfolio," *Financial Analysts Journal*, 24: 145–148, March-April 1968.

[7] H. M. Markowitz, *Portfolio Selection: Efficient Diversification of Investments* (New York: John Wiley and Sons, 1959).

diversification is concerned not only with the diversification necessary to minimize an investor's exposure to risk, but also to maximize his expectations for profitability.

The efficient approach to diversification is an ex ante model, built upon the random variable portfolio return, which focuses specifically on (1) expected portfolio return E as a measure of profitability, and (2) the standard deviation S of portfolio return as a measure of riskiness. These characteristics are refined by the equations:

$$E = \sum_{j=1}^{m} X_j E_j \qquad (1)$$

$$S = \left[\sum_{i=1}^{m} \sum_{j=1}^{m} X_i X_j S_i S_j C_{ij} \right]^{1/2} \qquad (2)$$

where E_j is the expected return from investment j, S_j is the standard deviation of the return from investment j, X_j is the relative proportion of the entire portfolio investment which is made in investment j, C_{ij} is the correlation coefficient between the returns from investments i and j, and m is the total number of investments under consideration.[8]

Markowitz formulated the problem of portfolio selection as one of minimizing S subject to given levels of E, and where the X_j are the relevant decision variables. Solution of this formulation is the familiar efficient frontier, such as the heavy curve in Figure 1, where all possible combinations of investments are shown as the shaded area. The efficient frontier has the property of simultaneously minimizing risk for a given return and maximizing return for a given risk.

It has been shown that, if the investor can lend at some risk-free rate, such as at point P^o in Figure 1, the optimal portfolio

of risky investments will occur at P^*, which lies at the tangency of the efficient frontier and a straight-line segment from P^o.[9] The reason for this is that by judiciously dividing his investment capital among the portfolios at P^o and P^*, the investor can effectively generate any portfolio along the straight-line segment between them. A similar allocation can also be made between P^o and any portfolio in the closed area—such as the portfolio at P'.[10]

A useful property of the optimal portfolio at P^* is that the angle θ^*, between the straight-line segment from P^o to P^* and the expected return axis, is smaller than the corresponding angle to any other portfolio P' in the shaded area of Figure 1. That is, if θ' represents the angle from the horizontal axis to the portfolio at P', then $\theta' \geqq \theta^*$ for all P' in the shaded area of possible portfolios. A useful measure of the efficiency of diversification of a given portfolio P', therefore, is simply to measure the cotangent of its associated angle θ'. Specifically, diversification D' of the portfolio at P' would be calculated by the expression which measures the cotangent of the angle θ' as follows:

$$D' = \frac{E(P') - E(P^o)}{S(P')} \qquad (3)$$

since $S(P^o)$ is zero by definition of a risk-free investment. Increasingly efficient diversification of a portfolio P' is indicated as θ' decreases, or as $D' = \cot \theta'$ increases. The limiting case, of course, is at P^* where

$$D^* = \frac{E(P^*) - E(P^o)}{S(P^*)} \qquad (4)$$

---

[8] If the portfolio consists of only two investments, the risk measure becomes

$$S = [X_1^2 S_1^2 + X_2^2 S_2^2 + 2X_1 X_2 S_1 S_2 C_{12}]^{1/2} \qquad (2a)$$

The correlation coefficient C_{12} can range from plus one (positive correlation) to zero (independence) to minus one (negative correlation), depending upon how the two investment returns are expected to move together. Moreover, as C_{12} decreases, the standard deviation of the portfolio decreases.

[9] Whereas the Markowitz efficient frontier gives an entire family of optimal portfolios, it does not present a unique solution to portfolio selection. For a complete development of how the addition of lending and borrowing opportunities leads to a unique solution—such as point P^* in Figure 1—see J. Lintner, "Security Prices, Risk, and Maximal Gains from Diversification," *Journal of Finance*, 20: 587–615, December 1965.

[10] A fortunate by-product of introducing lending and borrowing opportunities is that inter-portfolio comparisons can be made without saying anything about the investor's return-risk preferences—other than that he desires return and averts risk.

FIG. 1 The efficient frontier of investments and a suggested measure of diversification

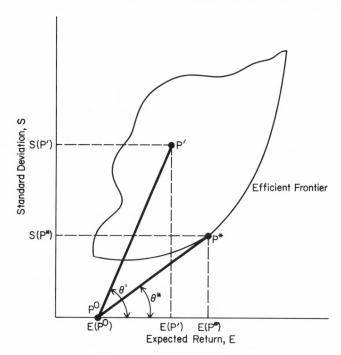

Finally, if two portfolios lie along the same straight-line segment from P^o, their diversification measure is the same.

Admittedly, no firm (or portfolio) is likely to achieve optimal diversification in the Markowitz sense. Nevertheless, the measure D' would appear to be useful in investigating the extent of effective diversification by a conglomerate firm. It summarizes in a single number the expectations of the firm for future profitability as well as the riskiness of such expectations. The diversification measure is an ex ante concept. It clearly does not purport to measure conglomerates on an ex post basis.[11]

II. TESTING FOR DIVERSIFICATION

In order to apply the suggested portfolio approach, it is necessary to think of a con-

glomerate firm as investing in a number of distinct activities—just as an investor would consider investing in various securities. It is well to mention at the outset, however, certain shortcomings of such an analogy. First of all, the conglomerate invests both capital and management resources while the investor allocates only his dollar resources. Secondly, the investor can vary the extent of each investment, but the conglomerate either acquires the other firm or does not. This precludes a temporary stock interest in the pursued firm—a practice which occasionally precedes the full acquisition by a conglomerate firm. And third, the investor can change his mind a day or week later but for the conglomerate, the process is virtually irreversible.[12]

---

[11] For an ex post study of all types of mergers, see J. Kitching, "Why Do Mergers Miscarry?", *Harvard Business Review*, 45: 84–101, November-December 1967. One of his more interesting findings was that the largest synergistic payoffs in mergers appear to be financial rather than marketing or production.

[12] To a limited extent, a conglomerate firm can prune its portfolio of investments. For example, Ling-Temco-Vought, one of the older and more active conglomerates, sold at least eight companies between

Another important limiting factor in treating a conglomerate like a portfolio is that each acquisition or investment of every conglomerate is distinctly unique, whereas General Motors stock (for example) would be the same in any portfolio. The lack of investment homogeneity across all conglomerate companies is clearly a substantial obstacle to applying the portfolio approach. In order to circumvent this difficulty somewhat, industrial categories were treated as securities in which conglomerates could invest. Thus, if a certain conglomerate was found to have shoe manufacturing in its investment portfolio, it was assumed that the conglomerate had simply invested in the shoe industry. Admittedly, this is a strong assertion—but it serves to restore homogeneity and provides a common denominator for making comparisons among many conglomerates.[13]

The first step, therefore, was to select a group of industrial categories to comprise a population of possible portfolio investments. The popular classification scheme of the Standard and Poor's Corporation was chosen because of its detailed breakdown into 88 industries. Of these, there was selected a population of 67 industrial categories in which conglomerates were likely to invest or in which certain conglomerates were known to have invested (Table 1). For example, auto parts, electronics, and business machines were natural choices. Railroads were necessarily included because one of the major conglomerates companies is a rail operator. Seven of the 67 industries listed in Table 1 represent a convenient combination

of two or three Standard and Poor's categories.

The study is based on the Standard and Poor's indexes of the aggregate market value for the sample of common stocks in each industrial category.[14] End-of-year values for these indexes were obtained for the 15-year period 1953–1967. These were then converted into 14 performance relatives (for 1954–1967) by dividing the value of each index in a given year by its value in the prior year.[15] The average value and standard deviation of this performance relative for each industrial category, over the 1953–1967 period, are also included in Table 1. Because cash dividends are not included in the Standard and Poor indexes, the performance relatives are somewhat understated.

Next, the optimal diversification of a conglomerate into business ventures, represented by the 67 industrial categories, was obtained by computing a Markowitz efficient set.[16] The analysis was made as of the end of 1967 and the resulting efficient frontier—as plotted by the solid curve in the return-risk space of Figure 2—represents expectations for the next year. These expectations were thus based on a single-year extrapolation of the market performance of each industry over the past 15 years.[17] The tangent

[14] These data are published annually (as well as monthly and weekly) in *Standard and Poor's Trade and Securities Statistics: Security Price Index Record* (Standard and Poor's Corporation). Data are weighted by the market value of outstanding shares in each component firm.

[15] For one industry (cosmetics), data for the earliest four years were not available. In this instance, the missing data were simulated so as to preserve both the average return and variance of the available data over the entire data horizon. The 15 year horizon was selected to roughly coincide with the age of the "oldest" conglomerate firm.

[16] The actual portfolio selection model which was used is explained in W. F. Sharpe, "A Simplified Model for Portfolio Analysis," *Management Science*, 9: 277–293, January 1963. This model generates the necessary covariance inputs by relating each security to an overall index of market activity. In this study, the Standard and Poor's Composite Stock Price Index was used.

[17] It should be clearly noted that ex post data were used as a means of forming ex ante expectations. Although such a procedure was criticized in Friend

1960–1967. For an anatomy of this conglomerate, see "Corporations: Where the Game is Growth," *Business Week*, September 26, 1968, pp. 99–120.

[13] This choice was not without precedent, however. In one study of investment performance, common stock portfolios of mutual funds were classified into 27 industrial groups, and each group was treated as a single investment. See I. Friend and D. Vickers, "Portfolio Selection and Investment Performance," *Journal of Finance*, 20: 391–415, September 1965. Another industry classification using factor analysis was used in D. E. Farrar, *The Investment Decision Under Uncertainty* (Englewood Cliffs, N.J.: Prentice-Hall, 1962).

TABLE 1 Characteristics of Industrial Categories Used in Portfolio Analysis

Industrial Category	Ave. Return	St. Dev.	Industrial Category	Ave. Return	St. Dev.
1. Aerospace	.180	.388	35. Machinery—Construction and Mat. Handling	.213	.315
2. Airlines	.211	.408	36. Machinery—Industrial	.127	.257
3. Aluminum	.125	.331	37. Machinery—Oil Well	.171	.333
4. Automobile Manufacturing	.111	.337	38. Machinery—Specialty	.141	.285
5. Auto Parts and Accessories	.110	.235	39. Metal Fabricating	.180	.285
6. Banking	.062	.173	40. Metals	.170	.266
7. Beverages—Brewing	.025	.190	41. Motion Pictures	.183	.299
8. Beverages—Distilling	.088	.192	42. Office and Business Equipment	.266	.329
9. Beverages—Soft Drinks	.159	.182	43. Oil	.110	.178
10. Building Materials—Cement	.070	.355	44. Paper	.084	.246
11. Building Materials—Heating, Air Cond., Plumb.	.095	.322	45. Publishing	.205	.226
12. Building Materials—Roofing and Wallboard	.090	.243	46. Radio and TV Broadcasting	.202	.283
13. Building Materials—Other	.091	.261	47. Radio and TV Manufacturing	.240	.490
14. Chemicals	.075	.155	48. Railroads	.083	.247
15. Coal	.182	.280	49. Railroad Equipment Manufacturing	.103	.240
16. Containers—Metal and Glass	.072	.166	50. Retail—Department Stores	.125	.212
17. Containers—Paper	.089	.235	51. Retail—Food Chain Stores	.056	.227
18. Copper	.105	.266	52. Retail—Mail Order and General Chains	.156	.270
19. Cosmetics	.282	.352	53. Retail—Variety Chains	.095	.270
20. Drugs	.183	.184	54. Shipbuilding	.133	.292
21. Electrical Appliances	.119	.235	55. Shoes	.101	.242
22. Electrical Equipment	.187	.250	56. Soaps	.141	.214
23. Electronics	.302	.382	57. Steel	.111	.332
24. Finance Companies	.069	.220	58. Sugar	.105	.204
25. Fire and Casualty Insurance	.079	.186	59. Textile—Apparel Manufacturing	.146	.255
26. Foods—Canned	.147	.254	60. Textile—Products	.142	.295
27. Foods—Dairy Products	.069	.143	61. Textile—Synthetics	.134	.325
28. Foods—Meat Packing	.101	.240	62. Tire and Rubber Goods	.140	.257
29. Foods—Packages	.138	.204	63. Tobacco	.126	.256
30. Foods—Other	.096	.170	64. Truck Manufacturing	.184	.347
31. Lead and Zinc	.065	.273	65. Utilities—Electric Power	.077	.118
32. Life Insurance	.141	.354	66. Utilities—Natural Gas Pipelines	.057	.147
33. Machine Tool Building	.156	.336	67. Utilities—Telephone and Telegraph	.137	.169
34. Machinery—Agricultural	.099	.231			

Note: Average return and standard deviation for each industrial category were based on price relatives using Standard and Poor's industrial indexes for the period 1953–1967.

FIG. 2 Ex ante diversification of conglomerates and mutual funds. Note: identification numbers for conglomerates and mutual funds refer to the listing in Table 3

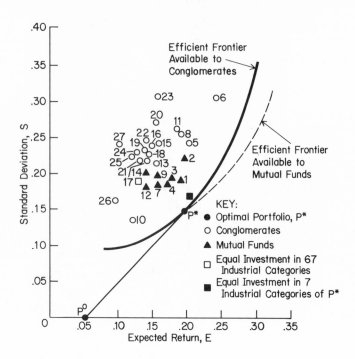

portfolio P^* along this efficient frontier, for a five percent risk-free investment [i.e., when $E(P^o) = .05$], included only seven industrial categories—beverages (soft drinks), cosmetics, drugs, electronics, publishing, radio and TV broadcasting, and utilities (telephone and telegraph). The optimal portfolio at P^* had an expected return of 19.8 percent, a standard deviation of .150, and a diversification measure of .987 using Equation (3) or (4). It is optimal only if one is willing to base future expectations for various industries on how such industries have performed in the past.

A central ingredient of the Markowitz approach is the determination of security combinations which reduce overall portfolio variance (risk). This usually means that a security will be an attractive candidate for an efficient portfolio, if in addition to having a high expected return, it has a low (or even negative) correlation with other securities. Space prohibits the inclusion of a complete correlation matrix of size 67, but the correlation matrix for a sub-population is presented as Table 2. Included are the seven industries in the P^* portfolio, and nine additional industries which have unusually low correlations. The presence of low positive correlations, as well as occasional negative correlations should serve to dispel any thinking that all common stocks are highly correlated. There are, in fact, substantial opportunities for diversification within various industrial categories.[18]

The next step was to select a sample of conglomerates to be evaluated. Any such

and Vickers, *op. cit.*, it has been defended in K. J. Cohen and J. A. Pogue, "An Empirical Evaluation of Alternative Portfolio-Selection Models," *Journal of Business*, 40: 166–193, April 1967. Furthermore, the procedure has been used in numerous empirical studies —mainly because of the difficulty in trying to get an analyst to generate expectations retrospectively.

[18] For example, beverages—brewing offers diversification potential even though it has the lowest average return of all industrial categories included in Table 1.

TABLE 2 Correlation Coefficient Matrix for Selected Industrial Categories

Industrial Category	1	3	7	9	15	19	20	23	25	37	45	46	54	55	57	67
1. Aerospace	1.00															
3. Aluminum	.58	1.00														
7. Beverage—Brewing	-.06	-.01	1.00													
9. Bev.—Soft Drink*	.02	.12	.82	1.00												
15. Coal	.51	.65	-.02	.12	1.00											
19. Cosmetics*	.45	.14	.46	.50	.36	1.00										
20. Drugs*	.23	.48	.52	.48	.32	.62	1.00									
23. Electronics*	.55	.66	.43	.45	.44	.68	.78	1.00								
25. Fire and Casualty	.40	.43	.33	.41	.30	.60	.58	.62	1.00							
37. Mach.—Oil Well	.81	.52	-.03	-.05	.78	.40	.23	.39	.17	1.00						
45. Publishing*	.54	.42	.50	.51	.14	.53	.65	.73	.40	.38	1.00					
46. Radio and TV Broad.*	.50	.60	.02	.04	.53	.20	.30	.60	.57	.40	.34	1.00				
54. Shipbuilding	.72	.35	.26	.25	.57	.64	.31	.44	.15	.82	.41	.10	1.00			
55. Shoes	.33	.22	.50	.49	.44	.42	.34	.43	-.08	.46	.29	-.04	.68	1.00		
57. Steel	.22	.27	.53	.49	.13	.53	.60	.43	.87	.10	.36	.27	.21	-.06	1.00	
67. Util.—Tel and Tel*	.12	.43	.57	.60	.28	.26	.64	.54	.65	.03	.52	.52	-.04	.11	.57	1.00

* Industrial categories included in the optimal efficient portfolio at P*.

229

sample is necessarily arbitrary because of the aforementioned difficulties in defining conglomerates. Moreover, every public list of conglomerates seems to be different. For the Value Line Survey. Of these, three were omitted because of their extremely small size. Then, an additional seven firms which have been active in conglomerate-type mergers were added. The sample of 19 conglomerate firms is identified in Table 3.

An effort was then made through mailed questionnaires to determine the different industries in which each conglomerate conducted operations and in what proportions (X_j). Letters were mailed to the chief financial officers of the conglomerate firms, re-

this study, an initial selection was provided by the 15 firms classified as conglomerates by questing an indication of the percentage of the firm's assets employed in particular industries.[19] Whereas 14 (74 percent) of the questionnaires were returned, the responses were incomplete and inconsistent in certain cases, and the X_j values could not be obtained directly. For these cases, the industries and their relative proportions were estimated from annual reports and other published information. In two cases where reasonable

[19] In order to analyze a conglomerate using a portfolio approach, it was necessary to determine the X_j proportions which are needed in Equations (1) and (2). Ideally, the market value of each conglomerate investment would be used to determine the X_j, but such data are seldom available. Alternative measures for approximating the X_j include sales, earnings, or assets. It was felt that the last would give the most reasonable approximation.

TABLE 3 Comparison of Diversification Measures for Conglomerates and Mutual Funds

Conglomerate or Mutual Fund	Diversification D'	Sensitivity ΔD	Size $W**$	Age $A***$
1. M.I.T. Growth (18)*	.749	−26.6%		
2. Fletcher (11)	.664	−12.9%		
3. Putnam (29)	.659	−14.6%		
4. One William Street (12)	.654	−20.5%		
5. International Tel. & Tel. (11)	.634	−11.5%	$2761	7
6. Teledyne (3)	.632	−9.8%	451	5
7. M.I.T. (23)	.590	−26.9%		
8. Automatic Sprinkler (5)	.552	−0.4%	242	3
9. Enterprise (11)	.545	−2.0%		
10. Foremost-McKesson (4)	.530	−24.7%	1500	1
11. Litton (4)	.521	1.9%	1562	14
12. Loomis-Sayles (21)	.497	−3.4%		
13. Gulf and Western (8)	.492	−9.6%	657	11
14. Dreyfus (38)	.458	−4.1%		
15. Whittaker (7)	.456	−0.2%	225	10
16. Ogden (3)	.425	−7.1%	704	15
17. Eagle Picher Industries (6)	.422	−7.8%	179	16
18. Ling-Temco-Vought (6)	.415	43.1%	1833	9
19. Studebaker-Worthington (2)	.394	21.1%	725	9
20. Textron (4)	.388	0.3%	1466	12
21. Lehigh Valley Industries (4)	.385	n.a.	53	11
22. Bell Intercontinental (5)	.370	5.9%	120	8
23. North American Rockwell (3)	.357	3.6%	2300	1
24. Bangor Punta (6)	.346	−10.7%	143	6
25. Glen Alden (5)	.311	n.a.	538	13
26. Tenneco (10)	.274	46.0%	1778	3
27. A. J. Industries (5)	.223	2.2%	60	12

n.a.—The sensitivity measure was not applicable for this case because X_j values could not be estimated, and were assumed to be equal.

* Figures in parentheses indicate the number of industrial categories of Table 1 in which the conglomerate or mutual fund had investments as of the end of 1967.

** Size W is approximate sales for 1967 in millions of dollars.

*** Age A is number of years since the firm's first conglomerate-type merger.

estimates could be made of the industries but not of the approximate proportions, equal proportions were assumed for the participating industries. The relative effect of this assumption will be investigated in the next section. Also included in Table 3 is the number of industrial categories in which each conglomerate had invested as of the end of 1967.

A secondary objective of this study was to compare the diversification of conglomerates to that of mutual funds. To that end, a small non-random sample of eight mutual funds was selected. Included were two growth funds, two growth-income funds, two balanced funds, as well as the two "best" performers for 1967.[20] The sample of mutual funds is also indicated in Table 3, as well as the number of industrial categories in which each mutual fund held shares.[21]

One interesting methodological accommodation was required in order to handle the comparison with mutual funds. The Standard and Poor's data include five industries with and without a dominant firm.[22] For the purposes of conglomerates, data were used excluding the dominant firm, under the assumption that a conglomerate's operations in one of these industries would most likely perform closer to the group excluding the dominant firm. In short, a conglomerate would be hard-pressed to buy a company

with the strong operating characteristics of an IBM or a General Motors. On the other hand, a mutual fund is able to buy shares in the dominant firm, and it is indeed likely to do so if this leading firm also leads in performance. When evaluating the diversification of the eight mutual funds, it was assumed that they had invested in the industrial category including the dominant firm. Accordingly, the efficient curve available to mutual funds is shown as the dashed curve in Figure 2. Hence, the mutual funds, by virtue of being able to invest in dominant firms, expected slightly higher returns for a given level of portfolio risk.

Finally, in order to measure the effective diversification of a given conglomerate or mutual fund, the procedure was to compute its expected return and risk characteristics using Equations (1) and (2), locate the conglomerate or mutual fund in a return-risk space (Figure 2), and then compute its efficient diversification using Equation (3).

III. EMPIRICAL RESULTS

Results of the portfolio analysis of conglomerate diversification are presented both in Figure 2 and Table 3. Findings relate to the effective, ex ante diversification of both conglomerates and mutual funds, as of the end of 1967, where expectations are based on extrapolations of the past fifteen years of performance for each of the industrial categories. Furthermore, results are based on the difficult homogeneity assumption which does not allow for uniqueness within an industrial category.

Looking first at Figure 2, it is seen that, with few exceptions, the mutual funds have attained more efficient diversification than the conglomerates. And they have done so at a relatively lower level of risk as measured by the standard deviation of portfolio return. One would hope that this would be the case because of their comparative advantage in investment flexibility, divisible investments, and their ability to invest in the dominant firms excluded from the security populations of conglomerates. And, of course, mutual funds are generally organized for just such

---

[20] The mutual fund sample was selected from *Investment Companies 1967* (Arthur Wiesenberger and Company, 1967). The growth funds were Dreyfus and M.I.T. Growth; the growth-income funds were M.I.T. and One William Street; the two balanced funds were Loomis-Sayles and Putnam. The two "best" performers for the year 1967 were Enterprise and Fletcher.

[21] The X_j values for the mutual fund sample were derived from lists of common stocks held as of the end of 1967 as given in *Moody's Industrial Manual* and *Moody's Bank and Finance Manual* (Moody's Investors Service, Inc., 1968). Investments by mutual funds in bonds and preferred stocks were not considered. It is interesting to note that the average number of investment categories for the small sample of mutual funds was 20.4, while only 5.3 for the conglomerate type firms.

[22] These five industries and their respective dominant firms are: automobile manufacturing (General Motors), chemicals (du Pont), office and business equipment (IBM), steel (U.S. Steel), and utilities— telephone and telegraph (AT&T).

a purpose—namely, to provide economies of scale in diversification not attainable by individual investors.

Conversely, some of the conglomerates appear to have done a commendable job of selecting unrelated industries so as to take advantage of low correlations. For example, a straight-line segment to the portfolio, representing either International Telephone and Telegraph or Teledyne, is quite close to the segment extending to M.I.T. Growth—which is the "best"diversifier in that it comes closest to the optimal portfolio at $P*$. Both I.T.T. and Teledyne achieve their diversification, however, with a higher return, higher risk mix of investments than any of the mutual funds. Teledyne achieves its efficient diversification even though it invests in only three of the industrial categories. It has already been demonstrated, by observing the holdings of $P*$ (seven categories), that a high number of categories is not prerequisite to effective diversification. It is interesting to note that within the sample of mutual funds, the best performers for this particular period of time (Enterprise and Fletcher) had the fewest number of industrial categories represented within their portfolios.

More precise comparisons appear in Table 3. Here the total sample of 27 conglomerates and mutual funds are ranked, in decreasing order, by the diversification measure D' which was defined earlier. The measures range from a high of .749 for M.I.T. Growth Fund down to .223 for A. J. Industries. Although all the mutual funds are among the leaders in this measure of effective diversification, four of the top ten are conglomerates.

If portfolio-type diversification is an appropriate motive for conglomerate growth, several conglomerate firms appear to have done an excellent job of diversifying—vis-à-vis some of the leading mutual funds. At the same time, one should not conclude that the managements of other conglomerates, which do not fare as well in this analysis, are doing an ineffective job. They may, in fact, have objectives other than diversification, their expectations may be quite different from those inferred in this study, and finally, certain of

their investments in certain industrial categories may be quite unlike the "average" investments inferred by the Standard and Poor's indices.

One of the difficulties, alluded to in the previous section, was in determining the appropriate X_j values for a given conglomerate. When not specified by management in their response to the questionnaire, the X_j proportion had to be estimated from available financial statements. Because this could not be done in two cases (Lehigh Valley and Glen Alden), equal investments were assumed for the industrial categories in which they have invested. To investigate the relative sensitivity of the empirical results to such an estimating process, a second measure of diversification D_{eq} was calculated for each conglomerate and mutual fund—but assuming equal investments in each case.[23] Table 3 also includes, as a measure of sensitivity, the percentage change ΔD in the suggested diversification measure according to

$$\Delta D = \frac{D_{eq} - D'}{D'} \qquad (5)$$

Both conglomerates and mutual funds can control in some degree, although certainly much less so for conglomerates, the proportion of investments in particular industries. Hence, one would expect the sensitivity measure ΔD to be negative in a majority of cases—thus indicating a degradation of diversification when equal investments are assumed. As seen in Table 3, ΔD is negative for all of the eight mutual funds, but is negative for only nine of the 19 conglomerates. Surprisingly enough, ΔD is negative for eight of the nine best diversified conglomerates. The three large exceptions to the findings to this sensitivity analysis are Tenneco (+46.0%), Ling-Temco-Vought (+43.1%), and Studebaker-Worthington (+21.1%), Tenneco can probably be explained by its large investment in the persistently poor performer, agricultural

[23] That is, if the conglomerate or mutual fund were known to have invested in m industrial categories, then $X_j = 1/m$ for all j investments in the portfolio.

machinery, while the sensitivity index of Ling-Temco-Vought is likely explained by its merger into the meat-packing industry—which is typically a poorly performing industrial category.

Results of this sensitivity analysis serve to emphasize an important aspect of the Markowitz portfolio selection model. Although the model answers the two basic questions of "which securities" and "what size investment," the first question is usually far more important. That is, if the appropriate securities (industrial categories) are chosen, based on both expected return and covariance relationships between all pairs of securities, an equal investment strategy may still result in an efficiently diversified portfolio. For example, if one were to invest equally in the seven industrial categories participating in P^*, a ranking of .941 would result, and also a sensitivity measure of $\Delta D = -4.7\%$. By contrast, if a conglomerate were (hypothetically) to invest equally in all 67 industrial categories, a diversification measure of .424 would result. This naive, but impractical, strategy would still produce more effective diversification than eleven of the conglomerates investigated.

A final comparison, made only for the conglomerate sample, was to see if there was any correlation between the size or age of the conglomerate and the effective diversification which it achieved. Accordingly, size W in sales and age A in years of being active as a conglomerate are included in Table 3.[24] Although one might expect that a larger conglomerate might have the resources and flexibility to achieve "better" diversification, the data do not support such a contention. And, in fact, the correlation between diversification D and size W was slightly negative (-0.187). Similarly, diversification D and age A were only slightly positively correlated ($+0.074$)—thus dispelling any notion that older conglomerates have had longer to construct a well-diversified portfolio of investments.[25]

IV. CONCLUSIONS

There can be little doubt that the conglomerate type of growth is an extremely complex process involving many highly interrelated factors and requiring the best of management skills and imagination. Because of their high growth potential, it is also probable that the common stocks of conglomerate firms will continue to be actively traded in the securities markets. Unfortunately, conglomerates are a relatively new phenomenon and thus any ex post evaluation of conglomerates as investments must, at best, be considered tentative.

The ex ante portfolio analysis of conglomerate diversification presented in this paper is intended only to measure one dimension of conglomerate activity—the ability of the conglomerate to invest in an appropriate group of industrial categories. The suggested methodology does not consider the important variable of management, nor does it consider potential economies of scale other than those reflected in the measure of effective diversification which is developed. In addition, it was necessary to base the empirical test of effective diversificatio non a population of 67 industrial categories—rather than considering the individual merits of each investment made. And finally, the expectational inputs needed for the portfolio selection model were based entirely on historical data.

Despite these obvious shortcomings, which pertain to the sample of mutual funds as well, it appears that certain of the conglomerates have succeeded remarkably well in their diversification objective. Moreover, it would

---

[24] Data for both size and age found in Moody's *op. cit.* Age was determined by consulting the firm's financial history and noting the year in which the first conglomerate-type merger or acquisition took place.

[25] The author of a recent study also failed to find a significant correlation between conglomerate diversification, as measured by the number of industrial categories, and the growth in earnings per share of the conglomerate. See T. O'Hanlon, "The Odd News About Conglomerates," *Fortune*, 75: 175–177, June 1967.

seem that an ex ante measure of diversification, which includes both expected returns and a measure of risk, should prove useful as an additional tool for conglomerate management. That is, the portfolio approach to conglomerate diversification is not intended to replace the complex decision-making process of a conglomerate manager, but rather to assist him in evaluating alternative investments.

24

Investment Decision under Uncertainty: Theory and Practice

JAMES C. T. MAO AND JOHN F. HELLIWELL*

I. INTRODUCTION

This paper is based on the thesis that by studying financial theory and financial practice in relation to one another, we may find ways in which both can be improved. The paper will first present a theory of investment decision under uncertainty which incorporates the following ideas: (1) a firm should choose portfolios rather than projects, (2) investment and financing decisions must be made simultaneously if the optimal program is to be chosen, (3) the risk attributable to an investment should be measured by its contribution to the total risk of a firm viewed in a market context, (4) a firm should trade off risk and return at the market-established rate of substitution, and (5) investors view security returns in real terms rather than in monetary terms. The paper will then present the results of three case studies investigating the actual making of investment decisions. We shall examine the disparity

From Journal of Finance (*May 1969*), *pp. 323–38.*
Reprinted with permission of authors and publisher.
* James C. T. Mao is Professor of Finance at The University of British Columbia. John F. Helliwell is Associate Professor of Economics at The University of British Columbia.

between the theory and practice of investment decisions, and suggest some reasons why the sophisticated techniques developed by theorists are not fully implemented in practice. Finally, the paper will indicate some of the lines along which future research should be directed.

II. UNDERLYING CONCEPTS OF THE MODEL

In this section, we shall present the theoretical considerations underlying our views on four basic issues. These issues are: first, the definition of investment risk in a market context; second, the definition of cash flow in a market context; third, the measurement of risk and return in real rather than money terms; and fourth, the estimation of the market price of risk-bearing.

Definition of Risk in a Market Context

Our model will adopt a definition of the risk of real investment that recognizes the presence of large institutional investors in the capital market and measures their effect.

Harry M. Markowitz's model of (security) portfolio selection [12] has contributed greatly to our understanding of how risk-averse investors can gain through diversification. Although Markowitz was concerned primarily with security investment, there is clearly much similarity between the essentials of financial and real investment decisions. The observation of this similarity has led to the construction of capital budgeting models in which investment risk is measured by the sum of the variance of the returns on new projects and the covariances between these returns and the returns on existing assets. However, although this definition of risk takes account of the covariance within the firm, it neglects the possible impact of new investments on the correlation between the returns of the firm and the returns of other firms. In a capital market where investors have sufficient resources to diversify their security holdings, this traditional definition of investment risk may result in significant over- or under-estimation of the true risk. To measure risk more accurately, our definition of risk will include both the covariances within a firm and between firms.[1]

Our definition of investment risk extends the principles outlined in John Lintner's article "Security Prices, Risk, and Maximal Gains from Diversification," *Journal of Finance* (1965).[2] In that paper, Lintner stressed the importance of defining the risk of a security as the sum of its "own variance" and its covariances with other securities. This definition of risk has clear implications for capital budgeting decisions and our model may be regarded as a logical development of Lintner's basic contribution.

[1] This definition assumes, as does the definition usually employed in valuation studies, that the variability of returns is a source of disutility, while common sense suggests that it should instead be unpredictability which makes a return stream less valuable. Predictable variability, if it can be identified and suitably offset, should be removed from the variance of a return before risk evaluation takes place.

[2] This definition of risk was also adopted by Alexander A. Robichek and Stewart C. Myers [13] in their model of security valuation, and by Donald L. Tuttle and Robert H. Litzenberger [17] in their model of capital budgeting.

Definition of Cash Flow in a Market Context

In defining cash flow, our objective is to devise a framework such that the management of a firm would look at investment in much the same way as potential shareholders look at the returns from shares. Only in this way is it possible to make fully operational our earlier suggestion that financial management evaluate investment risk using the share market's rate of substitution between risk and return.

The usual way of defining the returns stream from a set of investment projects is in terms of the cash flows net of all operating expenses, but before financing transactions. If uncertainty is to be explicitly taken into account, the cash flow in any particular time period is described by a probability distribution rather than as a constant. This definition of cash flow, however, does not provide the management with a clear basis for comparing investment programs with different risk characteristics. The reason is that investment risks are comprised of operating risk *and* financial risk, and the usual definition of cash flow takes account only of the former. We suggest, therefore, that each alternative investment program be given its own pattern of leverage financing initially, and that cash flow be defined as net of all financing transactions. With this adjustment, the cash flow from an investment refers to the cash flow available for distribution to common stockholders. There is still another adjustment that must be made. If firms generally follow a policy of dividend stabilization, the cash flow available for distribution is likely to be more volatile than the cash flow actually paid out. We suggest, therefore, that each investment program includes an investment in liquid assets to act as a buffer between earnings and dividends, thus enabling cash flow distributions to refer to the dividend expectations of the shareholders.

These two adjustments distinguish our definition of cash flow from the usual definition. In any case, the probability distributions of cash flow should be defined in as much detail as the share market is likely to consider important. The minimum amount of detail consistent with our basic model would be the mean value, a measure of dispersion, and a measure of the covariance between this cash flow and those from other shares in the capital market. If the distributions are markedly skewed in either direction, then a measure of skewness may also be necessary.

We can see even at this stage how higher yield is likely to be associated with higher risk. A given probability distribution of returns from a set of investment projects can be converted to a probability distribution of dividends with a smaller degree of dispersion by increasing the size of the buffer stock of liquid assets (or unused borrowing power). Since liquid assets usually carry a financial yield much lower than that available on real assets, the stabilization of dividends is achieved at the cost of a reduction in average yield on total equity investment.

Real vs. Money Returns

The distinction between real and monetary returns is an important one as long as the general price level varies over time in a manner not easily forecast. If wealthholders are primarily interested in the real values of their assets and the income therefrom, it is reasonable that share prices will depend on the level and stability of their real rather than money returns. Portfolio theory, with some exceptions,[3] has generally ignored this issue, and the riskless asset has usually been defined as one whose capital value and income were certain in monetary terms.

While we recognize that no price index can fully indicate the goods and services to which the wealthholder is anxious to have relatively sure access, the use of almost any price index is to be preferred to the assumption that risk is absent when money returns are certain. Therefore, we propose that all money cash flow streams be deflated by a general price index. If the rate of inflation

is variable, this deflation has the effect of making all investments risky, except an investment in the basket of goods whose characteristics are used to define the price level. Since there are limitations on the use of any single measure of prices to reflect the heterogeneous present and future consumption plans of all asset-holders, we prefer to assume that there is in general no riskless asset.[4]

Aside from removing some of the theoretical simplifications provided by the "separation theorem,"[5] our assumptions have an

[3] See, for example, Tobin [16].

[4] As several studies have shown (Arrow [1], Debreu [3], Hirshleifer [7], Diamond [4]), no single basket of goods, or portfolio of securities, can be regarded as riskless unless there are available as many assets (whether real assets or securities) with independent returns as there are distinct states of the world which the decision-maker regards as having a finite probability of coming to pass. There are not likely to be enough independent securities to provide a riskless portfolio for any single asset-holder, let alone for each asset-holder in the market. And even if there *were* "riskless" portfolios available for each, they wouldn't be the same portfolios for all. Hence we are reluctant to assume that there is any asset or portfolio considered as riskless by the market as a whole. This also explains our hesitation about using a single price index as a means of deflating money returns.

No doubt because of the vagueness of our discussion of the process of converting probability distributions of money returns into the corresponding distributions of real returns, our discussant Professor Jen concluded that the "real" distribution would be obtained from the "money" distribution by deflating the latter by the expected value of a price index. As he noted in his comments, this would be an unsatisfactory procedure. In fact, the probability distribution of the real returns is the distribution of (MR/P), where the money return MR and the price index P are both random variables. For example, if both MR and P are lognormally distributed, then the distribution of log (MR/P) will have variance equal to Var (log MR) + Var (log P) − 2 Cov (log MR, log P). As can be inferred from Figure 1, the dispersion of the distribution of MR/P may be less (in the case of shares) or greater (in the case of bonds) than that of MR, depending on the variability and covariability of MR and P.

[5] Suppose a risk-averse investor is faced with the problem of allocating a sum of money between a riskless asset (cash) and various possible portfolios of risk assets (stocks). The separation theorem states that the optimal composition of the stock portfolio is independent of the percentage division of the total funds between cash and stocks. For alternative proofs of this theorem, see Tobin [15] and Lintner [9].

important implication for the empirical estimation of the market price of risk bearing. Since some financial assets have returns fixed in money terms (e.g., bonds) and others have returns which are more certain in real terms (e.g., stocks), defining returns in money terms will distort the observed relationship between risk and return. Thus, if investors are generally averse toward risk measured in real terms, some stocks may have lower ex ante risk *and* return than those available on some bonds Graphically, this means that on an upward-sloping line joining securities of the same market value (but differing in risk and return) there should be bonds and shares interspersed. (Figure la). But if those same assets had their risks and returns measured in money terms, the bond would become the least risky asset, since its return is fixed in dollars, while the diversified share would become more risky, since its return is more closely related to the price level. Thus, we might find a relationship between monetary return and monetary risk such as that indicated by the crosses where there is no longer a uniformly positive relationship between ex ante return and risk. (Figure 1b).

Estimating the Market Price of Risk

We stated earlier that investment programs ought to be assessed by finding the present values of their risk-adjusted cash flows. We now contend that share market data can be used to provide data relevant to this process of risk-adjustment. Nevertheless, there are a number of complications.

We do not think that a cross-sectional regression of dividend yields or some measure(s) of the ex post variability of each firm's dividends will provide a measure suitable for use in risk-adjusting the ex ante probability distribution of dividends expected to flow from an investment program. In the first place, there are cross-sectional differences in the expected growth rates of dividends, differences which are not simply based on past experience, and which may well vary again in the future. In addition, since dividends are kept fairly stable, cross-sectional differences in ex post variability of dividends are not likely to provide adequate evidence about the ex ante probability distributions in the minds of shareholders. Even though the probability of a reduced or postponed dividend may be two or three times as high for one firm as another, actual dividend reductions or postponements may be rare enough for both firms so as not to occur during the time periods whose ex post data are used as evidence. Thus, it may be necessary for cross-sectional regressions to include other factors which provide evidence to shareholders about the likelihood that stable dividend growth will be achieved. Such

FIG. 1   Money illusion in the measurement of risk and return

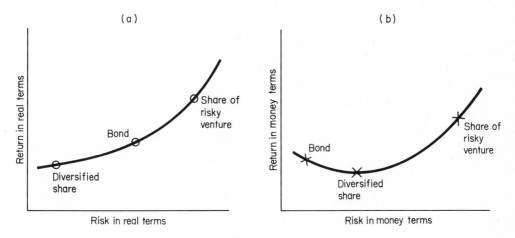

measures might include the variability of profits and the average dividend pay-out ratio. Some measure of the expected rate and duration of dividend growth is also an essential element in any equation, as is some measure of the covariability between different dividend streams. If proxy variables (such as the variability of profits) turn out to be effective supplements to ex post dividend variability in explaining dividend yields, then the derived coefficients should presumably be used when risk-standardizing the cash flows from different investment programs.

III. THE MODEL: ITS FORMULATION, SOLUTION AND IMPLICATIONS

We shall now present a model of investment decision which incorporates the key concepts discussed above.

Mathematical Formulation of the Model

Let R_i $(i = 1, 2, \ldots, n)$ denote the perpetual yearly cash return (deflated) generated by firm i. To simplify the analysis, our formulation will adopt the assumption of William F. Sharpe's diagonal model [14], namely, that the returns from various securities are correlated *only* through some common underlying factor. More specifically,

$$R_i = a_i + b_i I + u_i \quad (i = 1, 2, \ldots, n) \quad (1)$$

where a_i and b_i are constants. I is a random variable representing an external index (e.g., GNP), with $E(I) = I$ and $V(I) = \sigma_I^2$. The u_i's, which denote independent random disturbances in the corresponding R_i's, have means of zero, variances of $\sigma_{u_i}^2$, and covariances of zero. That is, $E(u_i) = 0$, $V(u_i) = \sigma_{u_i}^2$, Cov $(u_i, u_j) = 0$ for $i \neq j$, and Cov $(u_i, I) = 0$ for $i = 1, 2, \ldots, n$.

Next suppose firm k is faced with the problem of choosing an investment program from a list of m new projects. (An investment program here refers to a set of projects, employ-ing a particular pattern of financing and dividend policy.) Let X_j $(j = 1, 2, \ldots, m)$ denote the perpetual[6] annual cash returns generated by project j. It is reasonable to extend the assumption of one common factor in security analysis to projects as well. Accordingly,

$$X_j = \alpha_j + \beta_j I + v_j \quad (j = 1, 2, \ldots, m) \quad (2)$$

where

$$E(v_j) = 0$$

$$V(v_j) = \sigma_{v_j}^2$$

$$\text{Cov}(v_j, v_i) = 0 \quad (j \neq i)$$

$$\text{Cov}(v_j, I) = 0 \quad (j = 1, 2, \ldots, m)$$

$$\text{Cov}(u_i, v_j) = 0$$

$$(i = 1, 2, \ldots, n; j = 1, 2, \ldots, m)$$

Equation (2) says that the random fluctuations in the returns of any project can be viewed as the sum of two components: (i) that part which is correlated with the common factor I, and (ii) that part which is uncorrelated. Thus, the returns from projects are correlated only through some common underlying factor, such as deflated GNP or aggregate corporate profits.[7] Now, if we let $t_j = 1$ if project j is undertaken and $t_j = 0$ if project is not undertaken, then

$$R_k(t_1, t_2, \ldots, t_m) = R_k + \sum_{\substack{j=1 \\ t_j=1}}^{m} X_j \quad (3)$$

[6] For ease of exposition, we have assumed that all investment projects have permanent economic lives. If projects either have finite lives or otherwise have unequal cash flows over time, then there will be separate probability distributions for each time period within the investment time horizon, and presumably distinct discount rates linking each pair of future periods.

[7] This assumption is clearly an oversimplification, since firms often search for projects whose returns vary inversely (either seasonally or cyclically) with those from existing projects. The object of this kind of diversification is to achieve full utilization of the firm's "fixed resources," and hence the best way of taking account of it in the model is to consider investments in sets. Thus, if the activity levels of two projects are negatively covariant, their combined expected cash flow will be higher than the sum of cash flows from the projects treated separately.

represents the dollar return of firm k after it has adopted those projects for which t_j equals one.

The objective of the firm is to choose that investment program which maximizes the value of the firm. This statement can be put in symbolic form if we denote by $M_k(t_1, t_2, \ldots, t_m)$ the market value of the firm's equity after undertaking those projects for which $t_j = 1$. The objective then is to pick t_j^* $(j = 1, 2, \ldots, m)$ such that:

$$M_k(t_1^*, t_2^*, \ldots, t_m^*) \qquad (4)$$
$$= \underset{t_j = 0 \text{ or } 1}{\text{Max}} M_k(t_1, t_2, \ldots, t_m)$$

Analytical Solution

The solution of the problem above will make use of a method of valuation which is best described as the risk-standardization approach. Under this approach, the present value of any random cash flow is calculated by discounting its risk-adjusted equivalent at some standard discount rate. The purpose of this risk-adjustment is to convert cash flows with different risks into cash flows with standard risks so that a standard discount rate can be applied. This standard discount rate must compensate for both the time value of money and the standard risk present in the cash flows.

The following valuation formula calculates the value of a firm in accordance with the risk-standardization approach:

$$(5)$$
$$M_k = \frac{E(R_k) - \gamma[V(R_k) + \sum_{k \neq i} \text{Cov}(R_k, R_i) - V^*]}{r^*}$$

where $E(R_k)$ is the expected cash flow to stockholders, $V(R_k) + \sum_{k \neq i} \text{Cov}(R_k, R_i)$ is the total risk of the firm, V^* is the "standard risk" against which total risk is compared, γ is the constant market price of risk, and r^* is the rate for discounting risk-standardized cash flows. To understand how standard risk V^* is determined, let us envisage each stock as represented by a point whose coordinates are the expected value (E) and variance

plus covariance (V) of its ex ante dividend distributions.[8] Given a set of stock prices, there is a "constant-discount-rate line" passing through all securities whose cash flows are capitalized by the market at the rate r^*. There is also an "equal-market-valuation line" joining all securities with a particular market value. In Figure 2, we assume that these lines can be approximated by the linear functions $E = a + \rho V$ and $E = b + \gamma V$ respectively. Now suppose that the firm has return E_1 and risk V_1, and we wish to find its risk-adjusted equivalent (E_1^*, V_1^*) with the property that r^* is the appropriate discount rate. If (E_1, V_1) is a point on the equal-valuation line $E = b + \gamma V$, then (E_1^*, V_1^*) must be at the intersection of $E = b + \gamma V$ with the equal-discount rate line $E = a + \rho V$. Hence,

$$V^* = \frac{E_1 - \gamma V_1 - a}{\rho - \gamma}$$

where a is the vertical intercept and ρ is the slope of the equal-discount-rate line.[9]

[8] Since we wish to use a constant discount rate, risk-equivalence in this paper is defined in terms of a constant discount rate. This definition of risk-equivalence differs from that adopted in Chapter 1 of Helliwell [5], where the effects of risk and size of an investment program were kept separate by defining "standard risk" independent of the discount rate. Although our present treatment does take account of the effects of both risk and size on the discount rate, we still have not taken account of variations in the discount rate over time, or the relation between the discount rate and the rate of expansion of the firm. Expectations of changes over time in the discount rate can be easily built into the model as long as each time period is considered separately. The effects of the rate of expansion are hard to specify theoretically, and even more difficult to measure empirically.

[9] Since (E_1^*, V_1^*) must be at the intersection of the equal-discount-rate line and the equal-market-valuation line, we have:

$$E^* = a + \rho V^* \qquad (1)$$
$$E^* = b + \gamma V^* \qquad (2)$$

We also know:

$$E_1 = b + \gamma V_1 \qquad (3)$$

By adding (1) and (3), and subtracting (2), we obtain:

$$E_1 = a + (\rho - \gamma)V^* - \gamma V_1$$

which yields the formula for V^* given in the text.

FIG. 2 Determining the risk standardized equivalent of $E_1 V_1$

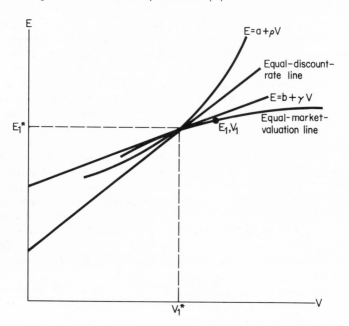

Risk in our model is measured by variances and covariances and the earlier assumption of one common factor greatly simplifies the computation of these figures.[10] It can be readily shown that:

$$V(R_i) = b_i^2 \sigma_i^2 + \sigma_{u_i}^2 \qquad (i = 1, 2, \ldots, n)$$

$$V(X_j) = \beta_j^2 \sigma_I^2 + \sigma_{v_j}^2 \qquad (j = 1, 2, \ldots, m)$$

$$\mathrm{Cov}(R_i, R_j) = b_i b_j \sigma_I^2 \qquad (i \neq j)$$

$$\mathrm{Cov}(X_i, X_j) = \beta_i \beta_j \sigma_I^2 \qquad (i \neq j)$$

These relationships will be needed for further analysis of the model. For this purpose, we also introduce the notation Σ for $\sum_{\substack{j=1 \\ t_i=1}}^{m}$. That is, Σ means to sum only over those j's for which $t_j = 1$. Using this notation, we get

$$R_k(t_1, t_2, \ldots, t_m) = (a_k + \Sigma \alpha_j) \qquad (6)$$

$$+ (b_k \Sigma \beta_j) I + (u + \Sigma v_j)$$

That is, the returns from a particular investment program are equal to the returns from

existing assets plus the returns from the newly accepted projects. Invoking the assumptions of the model, we obtain corresponding formulas for the expected value, variance, and covariances of $R_k(t_1, t_2, \ldots, t_m)$:

$$E[R_k(t_1, t_2, t_3, \ldots, t_m)] \qquad (7)$$

$$= (a_k + \Sigma \alpha_j) + (b_j + \Sigma \beta_j) \bar{I}$$

$$V[R_k(t_1, t_2, t_3, \ldots, t_m)]$$

$$= (b_k + \Sigma \beta_j)^2 \sigma_I^2 + \sigma_{u_n}^2 + \Sigma \sigma_{v_j}^2$$

$$\mathrm{Co\,v}[R_i, R_k(t_1, t_2, \ldots, t_m)]$$

$$= b_i(b_k + \Sigma \beta_j) \sigma_I^2 \qquad i \neq k$$

Substituting these formulas into (5), we get the following value for the equity of the firm *with* the new investments:

$$M_k(t_1, t_2, \ldots, t_m) \qquad (8)$$

$$= \frac{(a_k + \Sigma \alpha_j) + (b_k + \Sigma \beta_j) \bar{I}}{r^*}$$

$$\left[(b_k + \Sigma \beta_j)^2 \sigma_I^2 + \sigma_{u_k}^2 \Sigma \sigma_{v_j}^2 \right.$$

$$\left. + 2 \sum_{\substack{i=1 \\ i \neq k}}^{n} b_i(b_k + \Sigma \beta_j) \sigma_I^2 - V^* \right]$$

$$- \frac{}{r^*}$$

[10] For a description of the contradictions which can arise if variance and covariances are used as a sufficient measure of the risk of a portfolio, see Borch [2, Chapter 4]. Realistically, we expect that a sufficient description of the probability distributions would have to include at least the third moment, and possibly higher ones.

The corresponding value *without* the new investments is given by the formula:

$$(9)$$

$$M_k = \frac{a_k + b_k \bar{I} - \gamma \left[b_k^2 \sigma_I^2 + \sigma_{u_k}^2 + 2 \sum_{\substack{i=1 \\ i \neq k}}^{n} b_i b_k \sigma_I^2 - V^{*\prime} \right]}{r^*}$$

Consequently, the change in value resulting from the new investments is given by the expression:

$$\Delta M = M_k(t_1, t_2, \ldots, t_m) - M_k$$

$$= \frac{\Sigma \alpha_j + \Sigma \beta_j I - \gamma \left[2 b_k (\Sigma \beta_j) \sigma_I^2 + (\Sigma \beta_j)^2 \sigma_I^2 + \Sigma \sigma_{v_j}^2 + 2(\Sigma \beta_j) \left(\sum_{\substack{i=1 \\ i \neq k}}^{n} b_i \right) \cdot \sigma_I^2 \right] + \gamma(V^* - V^{*\prime})}{r^*}$$

$$= \frac{\Sigma \alpha_j + \Sigma \beta_j \bar{I} - \gamma \sigma_I^2 \left[2(\Sigma \beta_j) \left(\sum_{i=1}^{n} b_i \right) + (\Sigma \beta_j)^2 \right] - \gamma \Sigma \sigma_{v_j}^2 + \gamma(V^* - V^{*\prime})}{r^*}$$

Since there are m projects, there is a total of 2^m possible combinations. The firm should calculate for each of these 2^m combinations the resulting increase in the market value of

the firm's equity:

$$\Delta M = \tag{10}$$

$$= \frac{\alpha + \beta I - \lambda \left[2\beta \sum_{i=1}^{n} b_i \sigma_I^2 + \beta^2 \sigma_I^2 + \sigma^2 \right] + \gamma(V^* - V^{*\prime})}{r^*}$$

where $\alpha = \Sigma \alpha_j$, $\beta = \Sigma \beta_j$, $\sigma^2 = \Sigma \sigma_{v_j}^2$ and $\Sigma = \sum_{\substack{i=1 \\ t_j=1}}^{m}$. The optimal investment program is the one that maximizes this value. It should be noted that $\alpha + \beta I$ is the expected return from the new investments and the expression in the square bracket is the risk associated with these investments. This risk can be decomposed as follows. (See Figure 3). The expression $\beta^2 \sigma_I^2 + \sigma^2$ stands for the variance of the return from the new investments, and $2\beta\, b_k \sigma_I^2$ stands for twice the covariance between the return from the new investments and the return from the firm's existing assets. Together these two terms measure the increase in the variance of the return accruing to the shareholders of firm k. The expression $2\beta \sum_{\substack{i=1 \\ i \neq k}}^{n} b_i \sigma_I^2$ is equal to twice the sum of the covariances between the returns from new investments and the returns of all other firms in the capital market, which in turn is equal to twice the sum of the increases in covariance between the returns of firm k and the returns of all other firms. Hence, the expression in the square bracket is simply the increase in the

FIG. 3 The risk effects of accepting a set of new investments

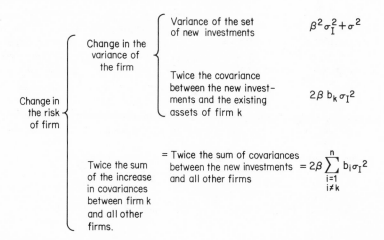

risk of firm k. The term $\gamma(V^* - V^{*\prime})$ represents the adjustment in return to offset the change in standard risk. In other words, equation (10) states simply that the firm should choose that investment program which maximizes the difference between the expected value of investment return and the resulting increase in the firm's risk, multiplied by the price of risk.

Effects of Shifts in Parameters

Given this criterion of optimal investment policy, there are some observations we can make about the effects of shifts in the parameters α, β, σ^2 on the value of an investment program. For simplification, our discussion will be restricted to the special case in which $(V^* - V^{*\prime})$ is sufficiently small that it can be safely ignored. It is quite clear that (1) if β and σ^2, and hence risk, are kept constant, an increase in α increases returns and hence augments the value of the investment program, and (2) if α and β, and hence expected return, are kept constant, an increase in σ^2 (risk) will reduce the value of the investment program. The more interesting question is what happens to value when β changes. Lintner [9] distinguishes between the income effect and the risk effect of a change in β. Since the expected return of the investment program is equal to $\alpha + \beta I$, an increase in β, other things being equal, results in an increase in expected return. This is designated as the income effect. Of course, the income effect can be eliminated if we permit α to change in an offsetting way. When the income effect is thus removed, the remaining impact is designated as risk effect of a change in β.

To analyze risk effect of a change in β, we view $\alpha + \beta I$ as a constant in equation (10). Differentiating (10) with respect to β, we get:

$$\frac{d\Delta M}{d\beta} = -\gamma\sigma_I^2\left[2\sum_{i=1}^n b_i + 2\beta\right]\bigg/r^*$$

Setting $d\Delta M/d\beta$ equal to zero and solving, we obtain:

$$\beta^* = -\sum_{i=1}^n b_i$$

which is the value of β that maximizes ΔM. Thus where $\sum_{i=1}^n b_i > 0$, an investment program is especially valuable if it is negatively correlated with the common factor. This conclusion is valid even if the firm undertaking the investment is itself negatively correlated with the common factor. It should be noted also that $\beta = \beta^*$ does not necessarily imply that the investment program is profitable. β^* maximizes ΔM, but whether this maximal value of ΔM is positive also depends on the values of other parameters in the problem.

Next, to analyze the total (risk plus income) effect of a change in β, we treat α as a constant in equation (10). Differentiating (10) with respect to β, we get:

$$\frac{d\Delta M}{d\beta} = \frac{I - \gamma\sigma_I^2\left[2\sum_{i=1}^n b_i + 2\beta\right]}{r^*}$$

$$\frac{d\Delta M}{d\beta} = 0 \text{ implies:}$$

$$\beta^{**} = -\sum_{i=1}^n b_i + \frac{I}{2\gamma\sigma_I^2}$$

where β^{**} is the value of β that maximizes ΔM when α is treated as a constant. It is interesting to observe that whether $\sum_{i=1}^n b_1$ is positive or negative, β^{**} is algebraically always greater than β^*. (See Figure 4.)

IV. INVESTMENT DECISIONS IN PRACTICE

The final part of this paper will discuss the results of recent personal interviews with the operating and financial management of three companies in the Canadian forest products industry.[11] These three companies account for a significant per cent of industry sales, and they all have made substantial investments in the last ten years. Although the interviews were intensive, ranging from ten to fifteen hours in each company, it is obvious that a sample of three, all within a single

---

[11] These field interviews were carried out by Mao during the second half of 1968. Interested readers may also wish to consult the earlier case studies of Helliwell reported fully in [6] and summarized in Chapter 3 of [5].

FIG. 4 The effects of a change in β

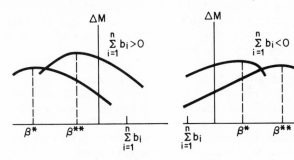

industry, does not provide a basis for making conclusive statements and much additional data remain to be collected in further case studies. Since our focus is on risk analysis, the following material will be organized under the three general headings of administrative procedure, quantification of risk and return, and criteria of investment selection.

Administrative Procedures

A knowledge of the administrative procedures is necessary not only to locate the decision-makers in the organization, but also to determine their different roles in the final selection of investments. The administrative process in all three firms is basically the same. Consider, for example, a plant expansion proposal in the wood products division. The controller of that division will collect the necessary cost and revenue data from the operating managements and prepare a project justification which is then reviewed and modified by the financial vice president from the viewpoint of the company as a whole. This modified proposal is forwarded to the senior executive committee for acceptance, rejection, or postponement. In arriving at its decision, this committee makes use of a 5-year operating and capital expenditures budget, designed to bring out the profitability and financing requirements of the proposed investment program.

This administrative procedure has two implications for our case studies. First, since the investment data originate with the production and marketing personnel, they must be interviewed along with the financial executives in order that investment decisions may be fully understood. Second, since the executive committee evaluates all projects, they are in a good position to employ the portfolio approach. In fact, because all of the firms had more acceptable projects than their budgets could incorporate, capital rationing alone would force them to adopt it. Moreover, they are aware of the risk implications of the portfolio approach. Thus one executive stressed the importance of the firm's investments being diversified so as to present the proper "risk profile" to the company's shareholders. Their concept of risk and attitudes toward it will become clear as we discuss their method of measuring and evaluating investment returns.

Quantification of Risk and Return

Although the executive committee employs the portfolio approach, neither the kind of data they receive nor their concept of risk allows them to understand fully the benefits of diversification. Moreover, their aversion to risk tends to exclude from consideration all but the relatively safe investment prospects.

All three firms use the internal rate of return criterion for project evaluation. Suppose that the pulp and paper division wishes to expand its capacity for producing newsprint. The marketing and production staff will be asked to make three forcasts (optimistic, most likely, and pessimistic) of the incremental effects on cost and revenue over the project's economic life. The optimistic and pessimistic estimates convey a picture of the range of possibilities. The "most-likely" estimate, however, has a rather special meaning. In all three companies, the most-likely estimate is a number lower than any of the usual measures of central tendency of the probability distribution of the random variable being estimated. The amount by which the most-likely estimate is smaller than an ordinary measure of central tendency depends on the probability of unfavorable outcomes, especially those associated with accounting losses. This suggests that the most-likely estimate is a measure of the central tendency of a new subjective probability distribution, which is derived from the official's best guesses of the actual distribution of outcomes by attaching more likelihood to the less favorable outcomes.

Once the forecasts are made, the divisional controller uses the most-likely data to prepare the annual *pro-forma* income statements for the project, from which cash flow figures are derived for the computation of the internal rate of return in the usual way. In one company, cash flow is defined as the flow to common stockholders after interest and preferred dividends have been deducted with the same degree of financial leverage as in the firm's existing capital structure being assumed. The executive committee receives these analyses, accompanied by a discussion of those factors which may cause the actual return to deviate from the most-likely figure. Since these project analyses are submitted by separate divisions, and project by project, no allowance is made in the risk assessment for the covariance between projects. In other words, the proposals top management receive do not contain the figures necessary for evaluating project risks formally on a portfolio basis.

This raises the question of what top management considers as investment risk and whether they take into account the correlation between projects in the measurement of such risks. In all three companies risk is understood as the variability of investment returns, but the emphasis of the decision-makers falls heavily on the probability of loss. Any investment with a significant chance of loss is rejected outright and excluded from further consideration. For an investment to be initially acceptable, it must pass a hurdle rate which varies with the risk category to which the investment belongs. However, even a project which passes this test may be rejected if there is a significant chance of not attaining the hurdle rate of return.

In addition, there is evidence that while the executives may not understand the formal theory of diversification they know that diversification reduces risk. When questioned about their risk-return trade-off, several executives mentioned, as noted above, the importance of selecting a portfolio with the most suitable combination of risk and return. For them, risk is averaged in the same way as returns are averaged, through diversification. What they do not understand is that, unlike return, the risk of a portfolio is not a linear function of the individual risks of the components making up the portfolio. Since none of the firms made quantitative estimates of the dispersion of the cash flow distributions of individual projects, it was not possible to tell how they made their assessments of the riskiness of the whole investment program. All of them recognized the benefits of "stabilizing investments" and cited as an example that while the cyclical patterns of paper and lumber operations had previously balanced each other, they were now seeking other investments to achieve even greater stability. This suggests that they are aware that negatively correlated projects will reduce the variability of the overall return. If it is common for firms to consider chiefly the covariance between the returns of large projects, and pay less attention to either pure diversification or to correlation with a single common factor, then it would be necessary for any realistic theoretical model to drop the simplifying assumption of one common factor.

Criteria of Investment Selection

Once risk and return have been measured, a criterion is needed to decide which investments are most desirable. All three firms appraise the merits of an investment by comparing its internal rate of return with a minimal risk-adjusted discount rate. Since these companies operate under conditions of capital rationing, their hurdle rates are much higher than the cost of capital, which they regard as "purely academic." Since these firms do not seriously consider new equity financing, it is perhaps natural that the managers should not make any explicit use of share market valuations when considering investment alternatives of differing riskiness.

Why do these companies act as if their capital is rationed when they have ready access to the capital market? Since bond indentures limit debt to about one-third of its capital structure, as long as the company refuses to issue new common stock, the rate of expansion is limited by the growth of retained earnings. This explains why their capital is rationed but raises the question why the companies do not expand their equity base through external means. A possible explanation is the personal conservatism of the top management. By holding back the rate of expansion they create a situation in which a high hurdle rate can be justified by the shortage of capital. By requiring a very high expected rate of return on every investment, they reduce the likelihood of a negative rate of return on any particular project, or on the program as a whole. Their strong aversion to risk substantiates this opinion.

V. RECOMMENDATIONS

In making these case studies, we have focused on the major points of disparity between the theory and practice of investment decisions. The evidence suggests that there are a number of ways in which both theory and practice can be improved.

At the theoretical level, our three recommendations are intended to make theory more empirically relevant. First, it is recognized that much more research must be done on the market rate of substitution between risk and return before companies could use this concept in their decisions. It may yet turn out that the risk characteristics of equity shares cannot be measured in such a way as to derive any useful estimate of the price of risk-bearing. Second, clearly a better definition of risk at the conceptual level is

necessary. While most theorists think of risk in terms of dispersions, our case studies show that management is concerned with the skewness as well as the variance of returns. It will no doubt be necessary to deal with intertemporal as well as inter-project and interprogram covariances of cash flow distributions. Third, the theory of optimal capital structure must be made more specific and some quantification made of the consequences of alternative financing patterns if businessmen are to analyze investment and financing as interdependent decisions.

At the practical level, our four recommendations are intended to substitute analysis for intuition in investment decisions. First, these three companies operate under self-imposed conditions of capital rationing. They might be encouraged, in the interests of their shareholders, to consider equity financing more seriously wherever ex ante rates of return on rejected projects appear to exceed substantially the marginal cost of equity capital. Second, it is likely that management could be more explicit about the risks of particular projects, and could develop measures of project risk which would dovetail together to provide an index of the overall riskiness of each alternative investment program. Third, if it is possible to get meaningful measures of program risk, then management could benefit their shareholders by trading-off risk and yield at the market-established rate of substitution, assuming that it becomes possible to identify and estimate the price of risk-bearing. Finally, if management turns out to be systematically more risk-averse than their shareholders would like them to be (as might be indicated by share market data), then some attempt should be made to communicate this fact to the managers in such a way as to alter their investment and financing decisions.

REFERENCES

1. K. J. ARROW. "The Role of Securities in the Optimal Allocation of Risk-Bearing" Cowles Commission Papers, New Series, No. 77 (Chicago: The University of Chicago, 1953).

2. K. H. Borch. *The Economics of Uncertainty* (Princeton, N.J.: Princeton University Press, 1968).

3. G. Debreu. *Theory of Value* (New York: John Wiley & Sons, 1959).

4. P. A. Diamond. "The Role of a Stock Market in a General Equilibrium Model with Technological Uncertainty," *American Economic Review* 57 (September, 1967) pp. 759–775.

5. John F. Helliwell. *Public Policies and Private Investment* (Oxford: Clarendon Press, 1968).

6. John F. Helliwell. *Taxation and Investment: A Study of Capital Expenditure Decisions in Large Corporations*, Study Number 3 of the Royal Commission on Taxation (Ottawa: Queen's Printer, 1967).

7. J. Hirshleifer. "Investment Decision Under Uncertainty: Applications of the State Preference Approach," *Quarterly Journal of Economics* 80 (May, 1966), pp. 252–277.

8. John Lintner. "The Valuation of Risk Assets and the Selection of Risky Investments in Stock Portfolios and Capital Budgets," *Review of Economics and Statistics* 47 (February, 1965), pp. 13–37.

9. John Lintner. "Security Prices, Risk, and Maximal Gains from Diversification," *Journal of Finance* 20 (December, 1965), pp. 587–615.

10. James C. T. Mao. *Quantitative Analysis of Financial Decisions* (New York: Macmillan Company, 1969).

11. James C. T. Mao. "The Cost of Capital Controversy," *Papers and Proceedings of the Michigan Academy of Science, Arts and Letters* LIII (1968), pp. 191–200.

12. Harry M. Markowitz. *Portfolio Selection* (New York: John Wiley & Sons, Inc., 1950).

13. Alexander A. Robichek and Stewart C. Myers. "Valuation of the Firm: Effects of Uncertainty in a Market Context," *Journal of Finance* 21 (May, 1966), pp. 215–227.

14. William F. Sharpe. "A Simplified Model for Portfolio Analysis," *Management Science* (January, 1963), p. 277–293.

15. James Tobin. "Liquidity Preference as Behavior Toward Risk, *Review of Economic Studies* 25 (February, 1958), pp. 65–86.

16. ———. "The Theory of Portfolio Selection," in Hahn and Brechling (eds.) *The Theory of Interest Rates* (London: Macmillan Company, 1965).

17. Donald L. Tuttle and Robert H. Litzenberger. "Leverage, Diversification and Capital Market Effects in a Risk-Adjusted Capital Budgeting Framework," *Journal of Finance* 23 (June, 1968), pp. 427–443.

25

Some Surrogate Evidence in Support of the Concept of Optimal Financial Structure*

ELI SCHWARTZ AND J. RICHARD ARONSON

In the dispute as to whether or not there is an "optimal" corporate financial structure (or put in inverse terms, whether or not an optimal financial mix can reduce the cost of capital to the firm), Ezra Solomon has summed one argument as follows:

From Journal of Finance (*1967*), *pp. 10–18. Reprinted with permission of authors and publisher.*

* [Eli Schwartz is Professor of Finance at Lehigh University, and J. Richard Aronson is Assistant Professor of Economics at Lehigh University.] The authors wish to acknowledge the financial support provided by the Lehigh University Institute of Research. We are also indebted to the referee for his helpful comments and suggestions.

One kind of evidence in favor of the traditional position is that companies in the various industry groups appear to use leverage as if there is some optimum range appropriate to each group. While significant intercompany differences in debt ratios exist within each industry, the average usage of leverage by broad industrial groups tends to follow a consistent pattern over time.[1]

The object of this note is to quantify this evidence by presenting some simple statistics on the typical financial structures of broadly classified groups of firms. This evidence does not refute the basic Modigliani-Miller argument that in a *world of frictionless capital markets*, there would be no optimal financial structure.[2] Our data, however, represent some surrogate evidence that in a capital market where sources of funds may be somewhat segregated, the various classes of firms have developed typical financial structures that are optimal for their operational risks and asset structures. Presumably, if optimal financial structures did not exist for the different industry classifications, then theoretically there should be no recognizable, patterns, and financial structures for different classes of firms should vary randomly.

This study is divided into two parts. In part I, the financial structures of the different industries are examined at two points in time. The statistical tests indicate that firms belonging to the same industry classification generally have similar financial structures whereas firms from different industry classes generally display different financial structures. In part II, financial structures of the different classes of firms are presented for a time period of about 40 years. Although some changes in financial structures within given industries can be identified, the general picture is one of relative stability in spite of changes in the level of taxes and in the structure of the economy. But most important for our purpose is the persistent difference in financial structures of the industry classes

over time in spite of structural changes in the economy and changes in the level of taxes.

I. FINANCIAL STRUCTURES AT GIVEN POINTS IN TIME (1961 AND 1928)

We wished to test the hypothesis that the differences in the financial structures of firms belonging to the same broad industry class are not statistically significant whereas the differences between the financial structures of firms belonging to *different* industry classes are significant.

To show the historical persistence of industry class differences, data on firm financial structures were taken for 1928 and 1961. Firms were divided into four broad classes: railroads, electric and gas utilities, mining, and industrials. Three random samples of each class were then taken for both 1961 and 1928. Each sample consists of eight firms for each class.[3] Financial structures (broken down into short-term debt, long-term debt, preferred stock and common stock plus other capital accounts) were then calculated on a percentage basis.[4] The problem of showing similarities or differences in financial structures was simplified by concentrating on the common stock equity percentage of the total financing. Since common equity is the residual risk carrying class of financing, the ratio of common equity financing to total financing is a strategic variable. All the other classes of financing (current debt, long-term debt, and preferred stock) have some prior claims and have a considerable degree of substitutability for each other; they therefore might be broadly included in the debt portion of the debt-equity division.

[1] Ezra Solomon, *The Theory of Financial Management* (Columbia University Press, 1963) p. 98.

[2] F. Modigliani and M. Miller, "The Cost of Capital, Corporation Finance and the Theory of Investment," *American Economic Review*, Vol. XLVIII, No. 3, June 1958.

[3] Subsidiary firms, non-publicly held firms, and investment companies were eliminated from the sample. To help assure randomness in our sample the equivalent of a table of random numbers was used. A list of sample firms will be furnished on request.

[4] Throughout this study a firm's financial structure is defined as including short-term debt. The financial structure, therefore, differs from the usual definition of the capital structure which generally excludes short-term debt. We feel that our broader concept is the more relevant measure of financial risk because of the high degree of substitutability between long and short-term debt.

TABLE 1 Inter-Industry and Intra-Industry Test of Variation in Common Equity Financing*

	Column 1 SAMPLE #1 Mean Common Equity (Proportion of Total Financing)	Column 2 Standard Deviation	Column 3 SAMPLE #2 Mean Common Equity (Proportion of Total Financing)	Column 4 Standard Deviation	Column 5 SAMPLE #3 Mean Common Equity (Proportion of Total Financing)	Column 6 Standard Deviation	Column 7 OVER-ALL MEAN	Column 8 F (Intra-Industry)
1961								
1. Railroads	.497	.087	.531	.187	.511	.115	.513	0.013
2. Utilities (Electric & Gas)	.349	.046	.333	.063	.294	.068	.325	2.057
3. Mining	.710	.159	.822	.103	.785	.131	.772	1.492
4. Industrials	.700	.087	.588	.189	.668	.146	.652	1.265
5. Over-all Mean (all industries)	.564		.569		.564			
6. F (Inter-Industry)	22.65		15.21		25.59			
1928								
7. Railroads	.385	.136	.473	.128	.433	.170	.430	0.714
8. Utilities (Electric & Gas)	.380	.289	.442	.206	.435	.201	.419	0.172
9. Mining	.738	.212	.798	.187	.727	.249	.754	0.254
10. Industrials	.620	.223	.562	.142	.683	.255	.622	0.658
11. Over-all Mean (all industries)	.531		.569		.570			
12. F (Inter-Industry)	5.15		7.09		4.04			

* *Source:* Unadjusted data taken from *Moody's Investment Manuals.*

Thus differences in the proportions of short-term debt, long-term debt, or even preferred stock within the prior-claim sector of the financial structure may not be significant. If, however, types of firms differ significantly in the per cent of common equity, presumably they differ in a crucial variable.

The results of the F ratio test of statistical significance are presented in Table 1.[5] Thus, for the three railroad samples taken for 1961 the average common equity ratio for the eight rails in sample #1 was 49.7 per cent of their total assets; the average common equity ratio for rail sample #2 was 53.1 per cent; and the average common equity ratio for rail sample #3 was 51.1 per cent. The F ratio distribution was used to test the null-hypothesis that these sample means are statistically equivalent. To accept the null-hypothesis at the 95 per cent confidence level, F must be less than 3.47. (The F test results for all the intra-industry samples appear in column 8 of Table 1.) For the rails for 1961, F is .013, indicating that the means for the railroad samples are statistically equivalent. As shown in column 8 of Table 1, all intra-industry comparisons for both 1928 and 1961 indicated an F-ratio of less than 3.47. The test, therefore, showed no significant statistical differences in the financial structures of a given class of firms either in 1928 or 1961.

Rows 6 and 12 of Table 1 present tests for differences in inter-industry financial structures; that is, between the rails, the utilities, the mining companies, and the industrials. For example, in sample #1 for 1961 the railroads financed 49.7 per cent of their total assets with common equity; the utilities used 34.9 per cent of common equity; mining 71.0 per cent; and industrials 70.0 per cent. In this case, if F is greater than 2.99, the null-hypothesis (that the divergence in the means is merely random) may be rejected at the 95 per cent confidence level. For sample

#1 in 1961, F is calculated at 22.65, a rejection of the null-hypothesis.[6] A reading of the inter-industry F rows (6 and 12) in Table 1 shows that F is greater than 2.99 for all three samples for both 1961 and 1928. Thus, the differences in the financial structure of intra-industry samples may be ascribed to random variability, but the financial structures of firms in different industry classes are significantly different.[7]

II. FINANCIAL STRUCTURES OVER TIME (1923–1962)

Table 2 carries data on the financial structures of four classes of firms over the forty year period 1923–1962. The financial structure was broken down into four basic components: short-term debt, long-term debt, preferred stock, and common stock plus surplus accounts. The figures, shown in percentage terms, are averages for eight randomly selected independent firms in each class. The percentages of the basic components of the financial structure are presented both on a simple mean basis (i.e., a simple unweighted average of the percentages of the individual firms) and weighted mean basis. Although the samples are relatively small, their reliability is buttressed by the fact that the equity ratios for the years 1928 and 1961 bear a close resemblance to the equity ratios of the three dif-

---

[5] The F ratio is a test for small samples to show whether the difference between the sample means is statistically significant or can be reasonably attributed to chance. See: J. E. Freund and F. J. Williams, *Modern Business Statistics* (Prentice-Hall, Englewood Cliffs, N.J., 1958) pp. 261–267.

[6] A rejection of the null-hypothesis indicates that at least two of the four financial structures differ significantly; it does not necessarily indicate that the financial structures of all classes of firms differ significantly from the financial structures of all other classes of firms. It may, therefore, be true that the financial structure of mining companies does not differ significantly from those of the industrials. Since mining companies, however, are generally considered a subclass of the industrial group, this may not be very important.

[7] It may be noted that the inter-industry F value of the three samples is higher in 1961 than in 1928. In 1961 the financial structure of the railroads differed considerably from that of the utilities, whereas in 1928 they were quite similar. Also the deviations within the individual samples were somewhat lower in 1961 than in 1928. This evidence does suggest that there has been some sharpening of inter-industry differences in financial structures over time.

TABLE 2 Financial Structures Over Time, 1921–1962 (Railroads, Utilities, Mining, Industrials)*

	Independent Railroads				
	Current Liabilities	Long-term Debt	Preferred Stock	Common Stock Equity	Total Financing of Sample
	(%)	(%)	(%)	(%)	(billions)
1923	5.8	53.3	7.3	33.6	5.1
	(5.3)	(54.4)	(6.9)	(33.4)	
1928	3.4	49.0	11.1	36.5	2.8
	(3.3)	(50.3)	(10.7)	(35.7)	
1933	3.3	53.9	3.2	39.6	2.6
	(2.5)	(44.0)	(5.3)	(48.2)	
1938	4.8	43.3	2.7	49.2	3.4
	(2.8)	(38.1)	(.8)	(58.3)	
1943	9.8	42.1	6.1	42.0	2.9
	(9.6)	(41.0)	(4.2)	(45.2)	
1948	7.4	41.4	5.5	45.7	4.5
	(7.6)	(40.2)	(4.1)	(48.1)	
1953	6.2	32.3	12.9	48.6	1.7
	(7.1)	(36.3)	(10.6)	(46.0)	
1957	7.3	35.4	2.2	55.1	3.0
	(6.5)	(33.4)	(2.6)	(57.5)	
1962	7.0	42.0	1.0	50.0	4.4
	(6.5)	(28.2)	(2.3)	(63.0)	

	Independent Utilities				
	(%)	(%)	(%)	(%)	(billions)
1923	6.6	49.2	10.0	34.2	.7
	(6.4)	(49.7)	(7.9)	(36.0)	
1928	3.6	46.8	18.5	31.0	2.6
	(3.8)	(43.0)	(18.7)	(34.5)	
1933	4.3	46.0	22.0	27.7	4.1
	(3.5)	(51.1)	(22.7)	(22.7)	
1938	4.5	47.4	16.3	31.8	3.2
	(4.0)	(45.0)	(12.8)	(38.2)	
1943	5.8	46.0	9.1	39.1	1.8
	(4.1)	(33.2)	(14.9)	(47.8)	
1948	8.2	44.7	9.4	37.7	2.0
	(7.7)	(42.6)	(8.1)	(41.6)	
1953	8.7	45.6	15.0	30.7	1.5
	(9.1)	(44.5)	(15.3)	(31.1)	
1957	7.4	46.4	10.9	35.3	2.8
	(7.5)	(48.1)	(8.2)	(36.2)	
1962	7.1	47.8	11.1	34.0	3.4
	(6.3)	(47.8)	(12.3)	(33.6)	

* Data in parenthesis are weighted averages for each eight from sample. Data not in parenthesis are simple means for each eight from sample.
Source: Moody's Investment Manuals

ferent samples presented in Table 1. Table 3 contains additional data on financial structure on an aggregate basis taken from other sources. Although the time spans do not correspond exactly to that covered by the data in Table 2, the general similarity of the series buttresses the reliability of the sample results.

Within the context of this paper, the main purpose of presenting data on financial structures over time is to show the persistence of

TABLE 2 (Continued)

	Mining				
	Current Liabilities	Long-term Debt	Preferred Stock	Common Stock Equity	Total Financing of Sample
	(%)	(%)	(%)	(%)	(billions)
1921	5.9	18.6	4.2	71.3	.9
	(5.0)	(19.3)	(6.6)	(69.1)	
1928	6.1	10.1	5.7	78.1	.4
	(5.1)	(11.5)	(10.3)	(73.1)	
1933	5.2	18.9	5.6	70.3	1.1
	(8.5)	(7.5)	(1.5)	(82.5)	
1938	8.0	6.8	17.3	67.9	1.0
	(8.0)	(5.5)	(20.3)	(66.2)	
1943	14.5	2.5	8.7	74.3	1.6
	(12.3)	(2.1)	(7.2)	(78.4)	
1948	13.4	9.6	5.0	72.0	.5
	(18.8)	(4.2)	(3.6)	(73.4)	
1953	13.0	9.9	11.6	65.5	.7
	(10.7)	(8.1)	(8.6)	(72.6)	
1957	12.0	10.9	5.2	71.9	1.5
	(13.4)	(22.4)	(8.5)	(55.7)	
1962	13.1	11.5	3.4	72.0	1.4
	(7.1)	(5.0)	(2.5)	(85.4)	

	Industrials				
	(%)	(%)	(%)	(%)	(billions)
1921	9.8	7.6	17.6	65.0	.8
	(10.1)	(8.2)	(18.8)	(62.9)	
1928	10.2	9.6	14.1	66.1	2.0
	(7.9)	(12.0)	(12.6)	(67.5)	
1933	5.1	12.9	17.4	64.6	.4
	(5.9)	(16.1)	(15.4)	(62.6)	
1938	7.6	11.2	20.1	61.1	1.6
	(6.1)	(14.0)	(17.9)	(62.0)	
1943	16.7	15.4	9.3	58.6	2.0
	(26.2)	(10.3)	(4.5)	(59.0)	
1948	20.2	12.9	8.7	58.2	1.6
	(19.5)	(14.2)	(7.0)	(59.3)	
1953	17.5	18.6	10.2	53.7	2.3
	(17.7)	(21.7)	(11.3)	(49.3)	
1957	15.5	8.5	2.7	73.3	5.6
	(20.3)	(7.5)	(6.9)	(65.3)	
1962	16.5	16.0	2.6	64.9	2.1
	(14.8)	(16.8)	(1.2)	(67.1)	

differences in typical financial structures. On the whole, the data also show a remarkable stability in these structural differences. However, identifiable systematic changes over time indicate some adjustments to easily explainable outside forces. It should be noted that the changes that did occur *have sharpened* rather than blurred the differences among the classes.

In the case of the rails there is a distinct decrease in the per cent of long-term debt and of preferred stock and an increase in common equity. This movement toward a more conservative financial structure is an understandable consequence of increased competition from other forms of transportation and the increased vulnerability of the rails to economic cycles. In the early 1920's,

TABLE 3 Financial Structures Over Time (Some Evidence from Aggregate Data) (Railroads, Electric Utilities, All Manufacturing) *

	Current Liabilities	Long-term Debt	Preferred Stock	Common Stock Equity	Total Financing
(All Class I Railways)					
	(%)	(%)	(%)	(%)	(billions)
1921	6.6	53.8	6.9	32.7	$ 23.2
1928	4.9	48.1	8.1	38.9	23.2
1933	5.4	52.0	8.0	34.6	22.9
1938	10.2	52.5	8.5	28.8	21.9
1943	12.4	53.7	7.5	26.4	23.6
1948	7.9	39.1	7.4	45.6	25.4
1953	7.5	37.4	6.1	49.0	29.0
1957	5.5	37.2	3.7	53.6	31.5
1962	7.8	33.0	3.7	55.5	30.0
(All Manufacturing)					
1945	22.5	7.0	6.6	63.9	$ 91.8
1948	21.2	9.7	5.6	63.5	122.8
1953	19.0	11.5	3.8	65.7	178.5
1957	22.0	12.9	2.8	62.3	226.2
(All Electric Utilities)					
1943	6.3	43.2	13.8	36.7	$ 15.6
1948	7.8	45.5	12.6	34.1	17.3
1953	8.3	45.9	11.5	34.3	26.7
1957	7.7	47.5	10.3	34.5	36.5
1962	6.7	50.7	9.2	33.4	49.2

* *Source:* (a) Railroad data: "Statistics of Railways in the United States," 1921–1953, and "Transport Statistics in the United States," 1954–1962; both *ICC Reports.* (b) Electric Utility data: "Statistics of Electric Utilities in the United States," *Federal Power Commission.* (c) David Meiselman and Eli Shapiro, *The Measurement of Corporate Sources and Uses of Funds* (National Bureau of Economic Research, 1964), pp. 220–241.

the rails' equity position was not significantly different from that of the utilities. By the 1960's the equity position of the rails was intermediate between the utilities and the industrials. If the trend continues, the rails would probably still be distinguishable from the industrials because of their relatively lower percentage of short-term debt. In any case, the main trend of the railroads' financial adjustment is to a less leveraged financial mix, more consistent with their changed economic environment.

The financial structure of the utilities shows remarkable stability. There were a few cyclical changes. Thus the common equity percentage dropped in the depth of the depression of the 1930's due mainly to dividends paid in excess of current earnings. Subsequently,

there was growth in the percentage of equity during the war years, but this was offset rather rapidly in the post-war expansion which was financed mainly by debt. It would appear that a financial structure containing about 33-1/3 per cent common equity is one that the utilities (electric and gas companies) will return to rapidly if temporary developments push them away from this position.

Mining companies also exhibit relatively little change in their financial structures over time. The data, however, do seem to show a minor shift in favor of short-term debt at the expense of long-term debt. The change is most probably due to the appearance of accrued taxes on post-war balance sheets.

The major shift in the financial structure

of industrials appears to be the movement out of preferred stock into long-term debt. This shift, which can be explained by tax factors, is in harmony with the financing patterns recently uncovered by Creamer, Dobrovolsky and Borenstein.[8] There also appears to have been some increase in short-term debt. This again is probably explained by an increase in tax accruals.

SUMMARY AND CONCLUSIONS

The data of Tables 2 and 3 and the statistical tests presented in Table 1 indicate that the typical financial structure of a firm within a given broad classification differs significantly from the financial structure of a firm belonging to another class. These statistics provide surrogate evidence for the hypothesis that the various classes of industries have developed optimum financial structures conditioned by the intensity of their operational risks and by the characteristic of the industry asset structure.[9] The alternative explanation for the consistency of financial structures is to ascribe them to the traditions and customs prevailing among corporate treasurers and the suppliers of capital. This hypothesis is not untenable, but it is not one that would hold much appeal for most economists. The usual explanation for persistent customs and operational rules-of-thumb is that they have developed as reasonable approximations to a theoretically ideal solution.

The data on financial structures over time in Tables 2 and 3 show but two systematic identifiable changes. The first is the railroads' shift to a more conservative structure, and the second is the industrials' shift from preferred stock to debt. Nevertheless, the most striking revelation of the data is the remarkable over-all stability in the financial structures over time. This tends to confirm the results of Merton Miller's recent study for the CMC:

> The data on aggregate corporate capital structures thus tend to confirm our earlier finding that except for preferred stock, there has been little basic structural change in corporate financial policies in recent years. The debt ratio is currently somewhat higher than in the 1920's, but the increase in the proportion of debt in the capital structures has been only about as large as the decline in the proportion of preferred. Common stock equity, now, as then, by far the largest component in corporate capital structures, has held its own.[10]

In a recent article, Arnold Sametz argues that Miller may be mistaken. Sametz argues that there has been a relative shift from external sources of equity (stock issues) to internal sources of equity (retained earnings) and a relative increase in short-term financing although there has been little alteration in the total debt/total equity ration.[11]

---

[8] D. Creamer, S. Dobrovolsky, and I. Borenstein, *Capital in Manufacturing and Mining: Its Formation and Financing* (National Bureau of Economic Research, Princeton University Press, 1960). In this volume the authors conclude that "In general, manufacturing and mining corporations have not relied heavily on debt financing—especially the long-term type. However, total debt outstanding expanded considerably over the past half century." They report that for manufacturing companies "The ratio of total debt to total assets increased from 23 per cent in 1923 to 36 per cent in 1952" (Creamer, *ibid.*, pp. 189–190). Similarly our data for industrials show that the ratio of total debt to total assets increased from 17.4 per cent in 1921 to 36.1 per cent in 1953.

[9] E. Schwartz, "Theory of the Capital Structure of the Firm," *Journal of Finance*, March 1959.

[10] Merton H. Miller, "The Corporation Income Tax and Corporate Financial Policies," *Stabilization Policies*, CMC Supporting Papers (Prentice-Hall, Englewood Cliffs, N.J., 1963) p. 426.

[11] Arnold W. Sametz, "Trends in the Volume and Composition of Equity Finance," *The Journal of Finance*, Sept. 1964. Much of the analysis in Sametz's article is based on data reported in recent National Bureau of Economic Research volumes. See: Creamer, Dobrovolsky, and Borenstein, *ibid.*; M. J. Ulmer, *Capital in Transportation, Communications, and Public Utilities: Its Formation and Financing*, (NBER, Princeton University Press, Princeton, N.J., 1960); and S. Kuznets, *Capital in the American Economy: Its Formation and Financing*, (NBER, Princeton University Press, Princeton, N.J., 1961). Ulmer concludes that the two outstanding changes in financing patterns from 1870–1950 among regulated industries were the ". . . gradual, steady, and pronounced shift from external to internal financing" and the "shift in the form of external financing from stocks to bonds" (Ulmer, *ibid.*, p. 188).

Professors Shapiro and White question whether the shifts observed by Professor Sametz represents a "structural change."[12] Part of the problem depends on what is meant by a structural change and part on the selection of the "normal" base period from which a change is to be measured. Our data do seem to indicate some increase in the cur-

rent liabilities of industrial and manufacturing firms. It is quite likely, however, that a large part of this can be explained by the increase in accrued taxes. In any case, (except for the railroads), our data support Miller's conclusion that the basic leverage structure— i.e., the total debt percentage—has remained quite stable.

Kuznets concludes that "For corporations, the ratio of internal financing shows a slight upward trend"; that "for all nonfinancial corporations, the share of net stock issues in total external financing declined, although not consistently" (this is also true in the subclasses of mining and manufacturing); and that "For all nonfinancial corporations, the ratio of short-term debt financing to all external financing rose." (Kuznets, *ibid.*, pp. 413, 418, 419). Both the Ulmer and Kuznets studies are mostly concerned with the division of new funds between external and internal sources and in the changes in the composition of external sources between equity and debt capital. Our study,

however, is mainly concerned with the pattern of total debt and equity financing, and so, for our purposes some of the changes shown by Ulmer and Kuznets are irrelevant. We should expect that a shift toward more internal financing would reduce the proportion of new share issues in external financing since internal finance (an equity source) is a substitute for share issues. From the viewpoint then of the over-all division between risk and debt capital, changes in financing patterns are not marked.

[12] E. Shapiro and W. L. White, "Patterns of Business Financing: Some Comments," *Journal of Finance*, Vol. XX, No. 4, Dec. 1965, pp. 693–707.

26

Rates of Return on Common Stock

EUGENE F. BRIGHAM AND JAMES L. PAPPAS*

Although the recent works of Fisher, Lorie, Herzog, and others have contributed greatly to our knowledge about rates of return on common stock, many important questions

remain unanswered:[1] What percentage of the total return is attributable to dividends, and what percentage to capital gains? How

From Journal of Business (*July, 1969*), *pp. 302–16, by Eugene F. Brigham and James L. Pappas; publisher, The University of Chicago Press. Reprinted with permission of authors and publisher.*

* Graduate School of Business Administration, University of Wisconsin. The authors gratefully acknowledge the support of the Bureau of Business and Economic Research, UCLA; Western Data Processing Center; and Standard Statistics Co., Inc., which supplied the Compustat Data Tapes to UCLA. J. P. Shelton and T. A. Andersen made helpful comments on an earlier draft of the paper, and the reviewers of this *Journal* were especially helpful in making suggestions for improving the final draft.

[1] L. Fisher and J. H. Lorie, "Rates of Return on Investment and Common Stocks," *The Journal of Business*, 37 (January 1964): 1–21. John P. Herzog, "Investor Experience in Corporate Securities: A

much of the capital gains results from higher earnings, and how much from higher price/earnings ratios? Are relationships stable over time, among industries, or among firms in a given industry? Providing tentative answers to these questions is the purpose of this paper.

The study examines 658 industrial and utility firms during the period 1946 through 1965.[2] The first section concentrates on aggregate returns for the entire sample. It defines "rate of return"; shows how different weighting schemes, income taxes, and assumptions about reinvestment opportunities affect the realized rate of return; and presents average rates of return for the entire twenty-year period. The second section separates total returns into three components—one attributable to dividends, one to growth in earnings, and one to changes in P/E ratios. The assumptions used in making this separation, including the stock valuation model implicit in our calculations, are described in the appendix. The third section examines inter- and intra-industry variations and shows how these variations differ during different periods of time.

I. AGGREGATE RATES OF RETURN: 1946–65

Internal Rates of Return

The typical method of computing rates of return—the internal rate of return calculation—involves solving for k in the equation

$$P_o = \sum_{t=1}^{n} \frac{D_t(1 - T_p)}{(1 + k)^t} + \frac{P_n - (P_n - P_o)(T_c)}{(1 + k)^n}.$$

Here P_o is the initial price and P_n the terminal price of the stock; D_t is the cash dividend in each year t; T_p is the personal income tax rate; T_c is the capital gains rate; n is length of the holding period; and k is the internal rate of return. Solving the equation with T_p and T_c equal to zero gives the before-tax rate of return. Table 1 gives the before-tax rate of return for the 658 industrial and utility stocks for each year in the period 1946–65.[3] To use the table, one first decides on the holding period he wishes to examine—for example, the period 1949 through 1956. The left column identifies the year in which the purchase was made, while the top row indicates the year in which the security was sold. Looking across the appropriate row and down the correct column, one locates the average rate of return for the period—the before-tax rate of return from 1949 to 1956, for example, is seen to be 20.4 percent.

The figures along the diagonal, which represent one-year holding periods, fluctuate considerably from year to year. For example, had one bought the portfolio in 1960 and sold it in 1961, he would have had a return of 19.3 percent. However, had he bought in 1961 and sold in 1962, his return would have been −4.5 percent. Returns stabilize as longer and longer periods are examined; averaging good years with bad accounts for the tendency toward stability.

Yields are relatively high for all periods greater than six years—they range from 8.4

New Technique for Measurement," *Journal of Finance,* 19 (March 1964): 46–62.

[2] The sample consisted of all those companies listed on the Compustat Tapes for which 1946 data were available; this included 602 of the 895 industrial companies covered by Compustat in 1966, and 56 of the 102 utility companies. An alternative procedure would have been to add companies as data on them became available—generally when they went public, were created in a merger, or were spun off from a public utility holding company. The former procedure is used because it permits us to examine the returns available to a *constant* sample of companies over different periods of time. Had the

alternative procedure been adopted, it would have been impossible to determine whether changes in yields resulted from changes in the firms or from changes in the composition of the sample. One effect of restricting the sample in this way is to virtually exclude certain businesses that have developed since World War II, most notably the electronics industry. The results, probably, are that returns are biased downward and variability is reduced. A further study examining returns and variability by age of firms is in progress.

[3] The values found in Table 1 were obtained by solving equation (1) with stock prices set equal to the average of the high and the low for the year in question.

percent to over 18 percent per annum. These returns are, incidentally, similar to those obtained by Herzog and by Fisher and Lorie for the years when this study overlaps theirs. For example, the rate of return given here for the period 1950–60, 15.4 percent, lies between Herzog's 16.5 and Fisher and Lorie's 15.0 percent.

Dividend Reinvestment

Although the rate of return calculation described above is the one used most frequently, it does have a serious weakness. The mathematics of the internal rate of return calculation implicitly assumes that cash flows (dividends) can be reinvested at the computed internal rate of return.[4] If the internal rate is very high, this may involve an overstatement. Accordingly, rates of return are computed here on the assumption that each dividend is reinvested in the stock of the firm at the average market price prevailing during the year in which the dividend is paid.[5]

Returns calculated on the reinvestment basis for the 658 industrial and utility firms are presented in Table 2. It was somewhat surprising to find that the dividend reinvestment procedure gave results that generally agreed very closely with those obtained by the standard internal rate of return calculation. In most years the two methods yielded virtually identical results; the greatest differential—for the period 1949–63—was only 1.1 percentage points. On reflection, the reason for finding only small differences is obvious. When internal rates of returns are computed, dividends of stocks with exceptionally high returns are assumed to be rein-

[4] This is demonstrated in J. Fred Weston and Eugene F. Brigham, *Managerial Finance*, 2d ed. (New York: Holt, Rinehart & Winston, 1966), appendix to chap. 7, "The Interest Factor in Financial Decisions," pp. 176–78.

[5] It has recently been shown that this method is equivalent to finding the geometric average rate of return on the investment, and that the geometric average rate of return is free of any arbitrary assumptions about reinvestment rates. See Haim Ben-Shahar and Marshall Sarnat, "Reinvestment and the Rate of Return on Common Stocks," *Journal of Finance*, 21 (December 1966): 737–42.

vested at these same exceptionally high rates of return (this involves a perhaps overly optimistic assumption). However, the dividends of stocks with exceptionally low returns are assumed to be reinvested at these same unrealistically low yields—an overly pessimistic assumption. In the aggregate, these two types of unrealistic assumptions tend to cancel one another out, and the aggregate rate of return computed under the internal rate of return method is approximately equal to the return found by the more realistic dividend reinvestment assumption.

Even though it does not particularly matter which method is used when calculating *aggregate* rates of return, the choice of methods does make a difference when one is studying returns in different industries and especially when one is examining the returns on a given company's stock. Since the dividend reinvestment procedure is conceptually superior, this method is used throughout the remainder of the paper.

Weighting Systems

The rates of return given in Tables 1 and 2 are weighted averages of all companies in the sample. The averaging process used assumes that each of the 658 stocks is purchased in proportion to its market value in the initial year. For example, if we are examining the period 1946 through 1965, the stocks are assumed to be bought in proportion to their 1946 market values. If we are examining the period 1953 through 1959, the market values during 1953 would set the weights. In other words, suppose that the total market value of the 658 companies came to $10 billion at the end of 1946. If the market value of Company ABC was $100 million, its rate of return would be given a weight of 1.0 percent when computing the weighted average. If its market value had been $1 billion, its rate of return would have been weighted at 10 percent when calculating the average rate of return.

Other weighting systems could have been used. One alternative would have been to assume that an equal dollar amount was invested in each stock at the beginning of the

TABLE 1 Average Before-Tax Rate of Return for Total Sample, Internal Rate of Return Method

Year Purchased	Year Securities Sold																		
	1947	1948	1949	1950	1951	1952	1953	1954	1955	1956	1957	1958	1959	1960	1961	1962	1963	1964	1965
1946	−0.047	0.001	0.015	0.071	0.101	0.101	0.095	0.112	0.130	0.130	0.119	0.121	0.128	0.122	0.125	0.117	0.119	0.122	0.122
1947		0.066	0.058	0.123	0.151	0.143	0.130	0.145	0.163	0.161	0.146	0.145	0.152	0.144	0.146	0.136	0.137	0.139	0.139
1948			0.056	0.162	0.191	0.172	0.149	0.165	0.184	0.180	0.161	0.158	0.164	0.154	0.155	0.145	0.146	0.148	0.147
1949				0.297	0.276	0.222	0.180	0.195	0.213	0.204	0.180	0.175	0.181	0.168	0.169	0.157	0.157	0.159	0.158
1950					0.271	0.191	0.144	0.172	0.200	0.191	0.164	0.160	0.168	0.154	0.156	0.142	0.144	0.146	0.146
1951						0.124	0.085	0.142	0.186	0.179	0.148	0.145	0.155	0.139	0.142	0.128	0.130	0.134	0.134
1952							0.053	0.157	0.213	0.198	0.157	0.150	0.161	0.142	0.145	0.129	0.132	0.136	0.136
1953								0.291	0.316	0.261	0.192	0.178	0.187	0.163	0.163	0.143	0.145	0.149	0.147
1954									0.363	0.260	0.167	0.155	0.170	0.144	0.146	0.124	0.129	0.133	0.133
1955										0.177	0.082	0.092	0.126	0.101	0.109	0.089	0.097	0.106	0.108
1956											0.002	0.054	0.011	0.082	0.095	0.072	0.084	0.095	0.098
1957												0.125	0.181	0.119	0.127	0.093	0.104	0.114	0.115
1958													0.262	0.132	0.143	0.094	0.106	0.117	0.117
1959														0.031	0.096	0.045	0.069	0.090	0.094
1960															0.193	0.062	0.089	0.109	0.111
1961																−0.045	0.045	0.086	0.093
1962																	0.164	0.172	0.153
1963																		0.196	0.159
1964																			0.133

TABLE 2 Average Before-Tax Rate of Return for Total Sample, Reinvestment Method

Year Pur-chased	Year Securities Sold																		
	1947	1948	1949	1950	1951	1952	1953	1954	1955	1956	1957	1958	1959	1960	1961	1962	1963	1964	1965
1946	−0.047	0.003	0.017	0.078	0.110	0.108	0.100	0.119	0.141	0.140	0.125	0.125	0.135	0.126	0.129	0.118	0.120	0.124	0.125
1947		0.066	0.057	0.128	0.157	0.147	0.130	0.148	0.169	0.165	0.146	0.144	0.153	0.142	0.144	0.131	0.133	0.136	0.136
1948			0.056	0.166	0.195	0.174	0.147	0.166	0.188	0.182	0.158	0.155	0.163	0.149	0.151	0.137	0.138	0.142	0.141
1949				0.297	0.275	0.217	0.173	0.191	0.212	0.202	0.172	0.167	0.175	0.159	0.161	0.144	0.146	0.149	0.147
1950					0.271	0.189	0.140	0.171	0.203	0.192	0.160	0.156	0.166	0.149	0.151	0.134	0.137	0.140	0.140
1951						0.124	0.084	0.144	0.191	0.182	0.147	0.143	0.155	0.137	0.140	0.123	0.126	0.131	0.131
1952							0.053	0.160	0.217	0.201	0.155	0.148	0.160	0.139	0.142	0.123	0.128	0.133	0.133
1953								0.291	0.317	0.259	0.186	0.172	0.183	0.156	0.157	0.134	0.138	0.142	0.141
1954									0.363	0.257	0.162	0.151	0.168	0.139	0.142	0.118	0.124	0.130	0.129
1955										0.177	0.080	0.091	0.127	0.100	0.109	0.087	0.097	0.107	0.109
1956											0.002	0.055	0.114	0.083	0.096	0.072	0.085	0.098	0.100
1957												0.125	0.182	0.117	0.127	0.091	0.103	0.115	0.115
1958													0.262	0.130	0.142	0.092	0.105	0.118	0.118
1959														0.031	0.098	0.045	0.071	0.092	0.096
1960															0.193	0.060	0.089	0.110	0.112
1961																−0.045	0.046	0.088	0.095
1962																	0.164	0.172	0.153
1963																		0.196	0.158
1964																			0.133

258

holding period. This particular system was examined and for longer holding periods was found to produce results very similar to the weighting system used in the tables shown here. However, as the period became shorter, the results of the two methods diverged. Generally, the equal market value system gave higher rates of return because smaller, more rapidly growing companies were given heavier weights.

Still another weighting system that was examined used an average rate of return based on the market values of each security at the end of the holding period. The result of this procedure was to give substantially more weight to those companies having the fastest growth. This weighting system produced significantly higher average rates of return than either of the other two.

It is apparent that the weighting system used plays a major role in determining the average rates of return. The method used here—which amounts to simply "buying the market and reinvesting dividends in the stocks which paid the dividends"—seems for our purposes to be the most reasonable of the several feasible alternatives.

After-Tax Returns

For all taxpayers who received dividends, Jolivet found an average marginal tax rate of approximately 40 percent during the period 1955–65.[6] Using this value and assuming that dividends are used to buy stocks in the payee firms, Table 3 gives the after-tax returns corresponding to the before-tax returns in Table 2. The after-tax figures are, naturally, lower than those on a before-tax basis (except in loss years), but the exact amount of the differential varies considerably from year to year depending on whether the bulk of the total return came from dividends or from capital gains. For example, the 26.2 percent before-tax return on the one-year holding period 1958–59 is almost entirely attributable to capital gains, and it

falls only slightly—to 20.2 percent—on an after-tax basis. On the other hand, the 5.6 percent before-tax return from 1948–49 is entirely attributable to dividends, which are taxed at a higher rate, and it falls substantially—to 3.2 percent—on an after-tax basis. The relative declines were 23 percent versus 43 percent for 1958–59 and 1948–49, respectively.

These tax effects become even more significant when the sample is disaggregated into industries and individual firms. This has important implications for the breakdown of the total return into dividend and capital gain components, which are considered in the following section.

II. RETURNS FROM DIVIDENDS AND FROM CAPITAL GAINS

Stockholders' returns are derived from dividends and from capital gains; capital gains (or losses) result from growth in earnings and from changes in P/E ratios.[7] Table 4 shows the derivation of total rates of return, before and after taxes, for three time periods selected to represent (1) the entire period, (2) a market peak-to-trough, and (3) a market trough-to-peak.[8]

Dividends Versus Capital Gains: Before Taxes

1946–65.—Over the entire postwar period, 1946–65, dividends accounted for approximately 38 percent of the before-tax returns on the 658 stocks, and capital gains for 62 percent. Surprisingly, the dividend percentage was slightly higher for industrials than for utility companies—38 percent versus 37 percent. Dividends were most important in the period 1946–49 (not shown separately), when the market was declining and capital losses were prevalent.

It is also interesting to note that most of

[6] Vincent Jolivet, "The Weighted Average Marginal Tax Rate on Dividends Received by Individuals in the U.S.," *American Economic Review*, 56 (June 1966): 473–77.

[7] The manner in which capital gains are split between earnings growth and P/E ratio changes is described in the Appendix.

[8] These figures were also computed for over 100 industry groups (SIC 4-digit industrial groupings) and for each of the 658 firms.

TABLE 3 Average Rate of Return for Total Sample after a 40 Percent Tax Reinvestment Method

Year Purchased	Year Securities Sold																		
	1947	1948	1949	1950	1951	1952	1953	1954	1955	1956	1957	1958	1959	1960	1961	1962	1963	1964	1965
1946	−0.047	−0.008	0.003	0.051	0.077	0.077	0.070	0.087	0.106	0.106	0.094	0.095	0.104	0.097	0.100	0.090	0.093	0.097	0.098
1947		0.041	0.034	0.090	0.115	0.108	0.095	0.111	0.130	0.129	0.113	0.112	0.120	0.111	0.113	0.102	0.104	0.108	0.108
1948			0.032	0.119	0.145	0.130	0.109	0.126	0.146	0.143	0.123	0.121	0.128	0.117	0.120	0.107	0.110	0.113	0.108
1949				0.221	0.209	0.166	0.130	0.147	0.167	0.160	0.136	0.132	0.140	0.127	0.129	0.115	0.117	0.120	0.113
1950					0.204	0.141	0.103	0.130	0.158	0.151	0.125	0.122	0.132	0.118	0.120	0.106	0.108	0.112	0.110
1951						0.088	0.057	0.107	0.147	0.142	0.114	0.111	0.122	0.107	0.110	0.096	0.099	0.104	0.112
1952							0.032	0.118	0.168	0.157	0.120	0.115	0.126	0.109	0.112	0.096	0.100	0.106	0.104
1953								0.222	0.249	0.206	0.146	0.135	0.146	0.123	0.125	0.106	0.109	0.114	0.106
1954									0.280	0.201	0.125	0.116	0.132	0.108	0.112	0.092	0.097	0.103	0.113
1955										0.133	0.057	0.066	0.097	0.075	0.083	0.065	0.074	0.082	0.103
1956											−0.006	0.037	0.085	0.061	0.073	0.053	0.064	0.074	0.084
1957												0.092	0.140	0.090	0.099	0.069	0.079	0.089	0.077
1958													0.202	0.099	0.110	0.069	0.080	0.091	0.090
1959														0.018	0.073	0.031	0.052	0.069	0.092
1960															0.148	0.043	0.066	0.084	0.073
1961																−0.042	0.032	0.066	0.086
1962																	0.124	0.133	0.119
1963																		0.150	0.122
1964																			0.100

the capital gains resulted from increased earnings, not from higher P/E ratios. In fact, P/E ratio increases were responsible for only about 6 percent of the total rate of return.

1949–55.—Capital gains produced the bulk of the very high returns during the 1949–55 bull market—74 percent versus 26 percent for dividends for the entire sample. The capital gains contribution for the utilities was somewhat lower than for the industrials during this period. Increases in P/E ratios provided about 54 percent of the capital gains (40 percent of the total return), and increases in earnings per share about 46 percent; this relationship might be expected during a strong bull market.

1956–62.—Returns were lower during the period 1956–62; only 7.2 percent versus 21.2 percent during the 1949–55 bull market. Over half of the return was from dividends both in the aggregate sample and for the industrial firms, but the utilities derived an even larger share of their total return from capital gains than they did during the 1949–55 period. Utilities were recognized as "growth" stocks during the late 1950's, and their "defensive" characteristics also gave them favor with investors during the recessions of 1958 and 1960. Utility earnings also continued to grow, while industrial-firm earnings were rather stagnant. This points out very clearly the fact that the various groups perform differently during different periods of time.

Dividends Versus Capital Gains: After Taxes

When returns are computed after taxes, the lower capital gains tax rate causes a significant increase in the percentage of the total return attributable to capital gains. For example, dividends accounted for 38 percent of the before-tax return in the total portfolio from 1946 through 1965, but this falls to 30 percent when returns are computed after a 40 percent personal tax rate. (At a higher tax rate the decline would have been even more pronounced, and conversely for a lower rate.)

III. VARIABILITY OF THE RETURNS

The average rates of return presented above are by no means uniform for all firms in the samples. On the contrary, a great deal of variation is found both between and within industries. This section examines the variability (1) between the industrial and utility sectors, (2) among two groups within the industrial sector, and (3) among the individual firms in the paper industry.

Industrial Versus Utility Stocks

Individual industrial firms vary around their sample mean considerably more than utility firms. The coefficients of variation presented in Table 5 show industrials to be about twice as variable as utilities in the 1946–65 and 1949–55 periods, and over seven times as variable from 1956 to 1962. Given the great diversity of "industrial" firms (with wide differences in growth opportunities and inherent risks), combined with the regulated nature of the utilities, this finding is not at all surprising.

Industrial Stocks: Beverages (Soft Drinks) Versus Paper

Tabulations similar to Tables 4 and 5 were constructed for each of the 103 SIC classifications in the industrial sample. Space limitations preclude presenting all of this data, but Table 6 gives some comparative statistics on two rather typical industries— soft drinks (seven firms) and paper (fourteen firms). Over the entire period, the paper stocks had a considerably higher average before-tax return than soft drink stocks (14.0 percent versus 9.2 percent) and a higher percentage of the total paper returns came from dividends. Much greater inter-industry variation appears when the sub-periods are examined. In the period 1949–55, average before-tax returns in the paper industry amounted to a huge 35.8 percent compound rate versus only 3.6 percent in the soft drink industry. Most of the returns

TABLE 4 Distribution of Total Return into Dividends and Capital Gains

	1964–65				1949–55				1956–62			
	Rate of Return (%)	Percent Attributable to			Rate of Return (%)	Percent Attributable to			Rate of Return (%)	Percent Attributable to		
		Divi- dends	Earn- ings Growth	Change in P/E		Divi- dends	Earn- ings Growth	Change in P/E		Divi- dends	Earn- ings Growth	Change in P/E
I. Before-tax returns:												
Industrials	12.5	37.7	56.0	6.3	21.7	25.9	33.4	40.8	6.8	63.1	7.5	29.4
Utilities	11.8	36.6	49.6	13.8	15.3	37.2	35.7	27.1	14.3	30.7	38.0	31.3
Total	12.5	37.6	55.8	6.6	21.2	26.6	33.6	40.2	7.2	60.9	9.4	29.7
II. After-tax returns:												
Industrials	9.8	30.3	62.7	7.0	17.2	20.9	35.6	43.5	4.9	55.8	9.0	35.3
Utilities	9.0	29.9	54.9	15.3	11.5	31.0	39.2	29.8	11.0	24.9	41.2	33.9
Total	9.8	30.3	62.4	7.3	16.8	21.2	35.9	43.0	5.3	53.5	11.2	35.3

TABLE 5 Variability of Returns

	1946–65			1949–55			1956–62		
	Rate of Return (%)	Standard Devia- tion	Coeffi- cient of Variation	Rate of Return (%)	Standard Devia- tion	Coeffi- cient of Variation	Rate of Return (%)	Standard Devia- tion	Coeffi- cient of Variation
I. Before-tax returns:									
Industrials	12.5	5.5	0.44	21.7	11.6	0.53	6.8	12.6	1.85
Utilities	11.8	2.9	0.25	15.3	4.3	0.28	14.3	3.6	0.25
Total	12.5	5.3	0.42	21.2	11.3	0.53	7.2	12.2	1.69

TABLE 6 Distribution of Total Return into Dividends and Capital Gains (Beverages and Papers)

	1946–65				1949–55				1956–62			
	Rate of Return (%)	Percent Attributable to			Rate of Return (%)	Percent Attributable to			Rate of Return (%)	Percent Attributable to		
		Divi- dends	Earnings Growth	Change in P/E		Divi- dends	Earnings Growth	Change in P/E		Divi- dends	Earnings Growth	Change in P/E
I. Before-tax returns												
Beverages (soft drinks)	9.2	24.9	73.9	1.2	3.6	*	*	*	18.0	22.1	41.7	36.3
Paper	14.0	41.4	38.3	20.3	35.8	17.3	17.7	65.0	2.2	*	*	*
II. After-tax returns												
Beverages (soft drinks)	7.0	20.3	78.4	1.3	2.1	*	*	*	14.2	17.6	44.0	38.3
Paper	11.2	33.3	43.6	23.1	29.7	13.6	18.5	67.9	1.2	*	*	*

* The split between dividends and capital gains is omitted when the return from capital gains is negative (i.e., when dividends account for more than 100 percent of the return).

in the paper industry during this period came from capital gains, but dividends accounted for over 100 percent of the soft drink firms' returns. The last period studied—the relatively weak market from 1956 through 1962—showed a reversal in industry performance. Beverage companies had an 18.0 percent before-tax return versus only 2.2 percent for the paper firms.

The very obvious implication of these

comparisons is that different industries are subject to varying conditions during different time periods; thus, an aggregate rate of return is by no means representative of all industries in the sample.[9]

Variations Within the Paper Industry

Even firms in a given industry vary considerably among themselves (this is illustrated by the paper industry, as shown in Table 7). The fourteen firms all yielded reasonably high returns over the full twenty-year period, but the range was from S. D. Warren's 20.4 percent to Great Northern's 6.7 percent. Capital gains were the dominant contributor to the returns in most cases, with growth in earnings, not changes in P/E ratios, playing the major role.

Although earnings after the war had continued to grow, paper stocks in 1949 were selling at only five times earnings. A combination of factors, but most importantly the Korean war and the reduced fear of a postwar recession, boosted both earnings and investors' confidence, resulting in a striking 35.8 percent average return for the period 1949–55. During these years all of the paper stocks performed quite well; the lowest rate of return in the group was 21 percent. Capital gains, most of which resulted from higher P/E ratios, accounted for nearly all (83 percent) of the total return.

The period 1956–62 produced a remarkable shift within the paper industry. St. Regis Paper Company, whose 39.6 percent return for 1949–55 was the fourth highest, was one of only four stocks to have a negative return in the bearish 1956–62 market. S. D. Warren Company, on the other hand, moved up from tenth to first place with a relatively outstanding 16.6 percent return. Because of the falling stock prices and negative capital gains, dividends accounted for more than 100 percent of the return in most cases. It is interesting to note that a drop in earnings, not declining P/E ratios, produced the negative capital gains.

A further examination of the data revealed that the volatility found in the paper industry is not atypical. Even in the relatively stable, two-firm telephone industry, the companies reversed their positions between the two subperiods. From 1949–55, General Telephone yielded a 26.0 percent before-tax return, as compared with only 9.5 percent for AT&T. However, from 1956 to 1962 General Telephone's yield declined to 12.8 percent, while AT&T's rose to 16.5 percent.

IV. CONCLUSIONS

The major findings of the study may be summarized as follows. First, investors in common stocks received relatively high returns during the postwar period. On holding periods of six or more years, before-tax returns ranged from 7.2 to 21.2 percent and averaged about 15 percent. After a marginal personal income tax rate of 40 percent, returns were scaled down to a range of 5.3 percent to 16.7 percent, and averaged about 12 percent.

The return on common stock is derived from both dividend income and capital gains. Although different percentages of the total return came from these two sources in various years, over the entire period 1946–65 dividends accounted for about 38 percent of the total before-tax return versus 62 percent for capital gains. On an after-tax basis, the dividend percentage declined to only 30 percent, while capital gains rose to 70 percent.

The capital gain was split into components attributable to growth in earnings and to changes in P/E ratios. Over the entire postwar period, about 11 percent of the capital gains could be attributed to higher

---

[9] An interesting extension of this type of analysis would be to calculate the period rates of return for the firms in each industry, obtain the time series standard deviations for each firm as a measure of the ex post riskiness of the firm, then aggregate the firms in the industries to obtain a measure of industry risk. If ex post and ex ante risk are closely related, we would expect to find a positive correlation between rates of return and the standard deviation of one-period returns in a cross-sectional sample of industries. We did not conduct this experiment.

TABLE 7 Distribution of the Total Return into Dividends and Capital Gains, Paper Industry, Before Taxes (14 Companies)

	1946–65				1949–55				1956–62*			
		Percent Attributable to				Percent Attributable to				Percent Attributable to		
	Rate of Return	Dividends	Earnings Growth	Change in P/E	Rate of Return	Dividends	Earnings Growth	Change in P/E	Rate of Return	Dividends	Earnings Growth	Change in P/E
Champion Papers Inc.	0.143	0.414	0.280	0.306	0.358	0.180	0.167	0.652	–0.000	0.000	1.704	–0.704
Crown Zellerbach	0.143	0.399	0.192	0.409	0.409	0.148	0.117	0.735	0.016	1.000	0.000	0.000
Great Northern Paper	0.067	0.584	0.538	–0.122	0.210	0.264	–0.059	0.794	–0.093	0.000	0.870	0.130
Hammermill Paper Co.	0.148	0.342	0.623	0.036	0.349	0.233	0.590	0.177	0.025	1.000	0.000	0.000
International Paper Co.	0.163	0.391	0.327	0.282	0.377	0.160	0.185	0.655	0.002	1.000	0.000	0.000
Kimberly-Clark Corp.	0.128	0.435	0.425	0.141	0.349	0.179	0.041	0.780	0.081	0.409	0.372	0.220
Mead Corporation	0.150	0.429	0.281	0.290	0.422	0.161	0.328	0.511	0.069	0.647	–0.279	0.633
Oxford Paper Co.	0.155	0.389	0.212	0.399	0.560	0.142	0.313	0.546	0.009	1.000	0.000	0.000
Riegel Paper Corp.	0.118	0.396	0.470	0.134	0.271	0.193	0.430	0.377	0.009	1.000	0.000	0.000
St. Regis Paper Co.	0.116	0.509	0.402	0.089	0.396	0.172	0.642	0.185	–0.031	0.000	1.423	–0.423
Scott Paper Co.	0.157	0.263	0.746	–0.010	0.341	0.128	0.272	0.600	0.102	0.264	0.500	0.236
Union Camp Corp.	0.139	0.472	0.336	0.192	0.323	0.231	0.255	0.513	0.033	1.000	0.000	0.000
Warren, S. D., Co.	0.204	0.236	0.497	0.267	0.328	0.211	0.259	0.530	0.166	0.186	0.077	0.738
West Virginia Pulp & Paper Co.	0.130	0.398	0.485	0.117	0.317	0.181	0.117	0.702	–0.031	0.000	1.842	–0.842
Industry Averages	0.140	0.414	0.383	0.203	0.358	0.173	0.177	0.650	0.022	1.000	0.000	0.000
S.D. rate of return	0.030				0.080				0.064			

SUMMARY

	1946–65		1949–55		1956–62*	
Average earnings per share	$1.030	$2.660	$1.470	$2.240	$2.398	$1.944
Average share price	8.12	38.55	7.04	31.38	39.25	36.91
Average P/E Ratio	8.96	14.88	5.19	14.65	16.97	19.33

* The computer program is constrained to assign a zero value to dividends if the rate of return is *negative* (none of the negative returns could arise directly from dividends), but 100 percent to dividends if the total return is positive but the capital gains is negative (i.e. capital losses were incurred).

P/E ratios and 89 percent to growth in earnings.

These relationships were by no means stable over time, among different industries, or even within given industries. This instability holds for total rates of return and for the distribution of the return among dividends, capital gains resulting from higher earnings, and capital gains resulting from higher P/E ratios. In particular, differences appear when the periods being compared include market peaks-to-troughs and market troughs-to-peaks.

In the course of the study we were frequently tempted to deviate from our goal of *describing* returns to attempt the much more difficult task of *explaining* differences. We resisted the temptation in this paper, but the next step in our research program is to investigate the relationships between rates of return and such factors as dividend payout, incremental returns on investment within the firm, leverage, and the like. The Compustat Tapes contain the raw materials for this, and using actual historical returns in a regression analysis should prove to be a useful supplement to the type of analysis already carried out by Gordon, Benishay, Modigliani-Miller, and others.

It is appropriate to conclude with a caveat: In this study, as in any other which attempts to measure investment returns in the aggregate, a number of assumptions are required. One must first decide on the reinvestment procedure to follow—this is mandatory for calculating any rate of return. Next, an averaging technique is required, and different weighting systems produce different results. Third, to split total returns into dividend and capital gains components one must decide how to treat the reinvestment returns on dividends. At this third stage it is necessary to specify a stock valuation model, and different valuation models would result in different allocations of the total return among dividends and capital gains. We considered the problems carefully and made what seemed to us to be reasonable assumptions. However, one must be aware of the fact that the results given are vitally dependent upon the assumptions employed.

APPENDIX: METHOD OF SPLITTING RATES OF RETURN INTO DIVIDEND AND CAPITAL GAINS COMPONENTS

The rate of return realized on common stocks consists partly of dividends and partly of capital gains. The capital gains, in turn, are derived partly from the growth resulting from earnings reinvestment and partly from changes in market capitalization rates. Unfortunately, the total rate of return does not consist of the sums of the components; it is, rather, a *product*, and this makes splitting the total into the components a rather arbitrary process much akin to the joint cost problem faced by accountants and economists.

We recognize both the problem and the fact that any solution to it involves making assumptions that can be attacked. If there are N investors operating in the market, there are at least N different possible ways of formulating decision rules, hence at least N different ways of measuring total returns and of splitting these returns into component parts. We examined several different approaches and selected the ones that have the greatest intuitive appeal. This appendix sets forth our reasoning in making the choices.

Capital Gains Versus Dividends

The capital gains and dividends on the initial investment are easily separated. Dividends received, however, are reinvested in the firm's stock, and these incremental shares receive, in turn, capital appreciation as well as dividends.

Our method of handling this is simply to have the computer keep track of each dividend and the resulting dividends and capital gains from reinvestment. That is, we allocate all the dividends received on the incremental shares to the dividend component and all the capital appreciation on these shares to the capital gains component.[10] For example,

---

[10] This method lies between the possible extremes of assuming no return from dividends (i.e., dividends are spent or reinvested at a 0 percent rate of return)

suppose we examine an investment over a five-year period, during which the stock has a constant price/earnings ratio of 15, initial earnings of $1.67, a growth rate sufficient to make the capital appreciation each year equal retained earnings,[11] and a constant dividend payout rate of 40 percent. Our investment would be $25.00, the initial price (P_o). In the first year we would receive one dividend on this initial share ($0.69) and with it would purchase 0.027 shares:[12]

$$\text{shares purchased} = \frac{D_1}{P_1} = \frac{0.69}{26.01} = 0.027.$$

In the second year there would be two dividends received: first, we would receive $0.72 on the original share (both D and P would rise proportionately, keeping shares bought constant); then, there would be an $0.18 dividend on the share purchased in the first year which would buy an additional 0.0007 shares. In the third year there are four dividend and stock purchase transactions; the dividend on the original share ($0.75) would buy 0.027 shares; the shares purchased in the first period would receive a $0.20 dividend, again buying 0.0007 shares; the 0.027 shares purchased in the second period would also receive a $0.20 dividend, buying 0.0007 shares; and the 0.0007 shares purchased in the second period would receive dividends of $0.00053, buying 0.00002 shares. It can be seen that the number of dividend transactions per period is increasing geometrically; therefore, in the fourth year, eight transactions would occur, in the fifth year sixteen transactions, and so on.[13] For purposes of

and of crediting all additional returns, whether in the form of dividends or capital gains, to the dividend component.

[11] This growth rate is equal to Gordon's br, where b is equal to 1 minus the payout ratio and r, the rate of return on retained earnings, is assumed to be equal to earning/price. Cf. M. J. Gordon, *The Investment, Financing, and Valuation of the Corporation* (Homewood, Ill.: Irwin, 1962). As will be shown below, these assumptions are necessary only to simplify our example, not for our method of analysis.

[12] Assuming a 0 tax rate and no brokerage fees.

[13] While it is difficult to extend an example very far manually, it should be noted that the computer handles the calculations quite easily.

continuing the illustration, let us note that the sum of all the dividends received during the five years is $3.97, and this, plus the sum of all the capital gains on the incremental as well as the original shares ($5.73) would be the total return on the investment. Discounting this gain over the five years, we find that the investment has a rate of return of 6.8 percent, and that dividends have accounted for 40 percent and capital gains for 60 percent of the return.

The example was worked out under a special set of assumptions purely for expository simplicity. These assumptions are by no means necessary in the computer program, and the program makes the split between dividends and capital gains for any set of dividends and stock price changes. There is, however, a stock valuation model implicit in our formulations. This model will be made explicit following our discussion of the partitioning of capital gains into components attributable to earnings growth versus changes in the P/E ratio.

Capital Gains from Earnings Growth and P/E Changes

Suppose a stock is bought for $25.00, held for ten years during which time no dividends are paid, then sold for $75.00. The internal rate of return on the stock is 11.8 percent. Suppose the initial price was based on $2.50 earnings per share and a P/E ratio of 10 times, while the ending price was based on $5.00 earnings and a 15 times P/E ratio. Had the P/E ratio remained constant while the earnings were increasing, the ending price would have been $50.00 (10 × $5.00); therefore, $25.00 of the total increase is directly attributable to the higher earnings. On the other hand, if the earnings had remained constant while the P/E ratio was increasing, the ending price would have been $37.50 (15 × $2.50); therefore, $12.50 of the total increase is directly attributable to the higher P/E ratio. The two direct components of the total gain sum to $37.50; however, the total gain is $50.00, leaving $12.50 to be accounted for as the joint product of the two factors—earnings growth and the higher

FIG. 1 Diagram of capital gains from earnings growth and P/E ratio changes (Total area represents $75)

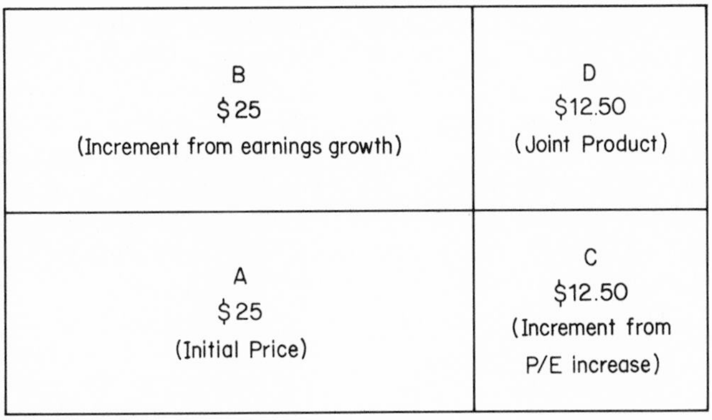

B $25 (Increment from earnings growth)	D $12.50 (Joint Product)
A $25 (Initial Price)	C $12.50 (Increment from P/E increase)

P/E ratio. These relationships are graphed in Figure 1.

The joint product is next allocated to higher earnings and to the higher P/E ratio on the basis of their direct contributions to the total gain. Accordingly, 2/3 of the $12.50, or $8.33, is allocated to earnings growth and 1/3, or $4.17, is allocated to the change in the P/E ratio.[14]

The Implicit Stock Valuation Model

There is, however, a stock valuation model implicit in our formulations. Specifically, it is the basic Gordon model used as a starting point for most recent theoretical and empirical research on the cost of corporate capital.[15] Gordon shows that, under a particular set of assumptions, the value of a share of stock (P) is equal to

$$P = \frac{D}{k-g} \qquad (1)$$

[14] One could argue that the change in the P/E ratio resulted from the earnings growth, invalidating our procedure. We recognize this problem but ignore it on the grounds that it produces an indeterminacy at this level of analysis. We feel that the tentative split we reach under our assumptions is better than nothing. This question is considered in the following section.

[15] For a discussion of the use of this model in the recent literature, see Eugene F. Brigham and Myron J. Gordon, "Leverage, Dividend Policy, and the Cost of Capital," *Journal of Finance*, 23 (March 1968): 85–103. See Gordon, *op. cit.*, for an explanation of the derivation of the basic model.

where D is the current dividend, k is the rate of return required by investors, and g is the rate of growth in dividends. Gordon goes on to show that equation (1) can be transformed into

$$P = \frac{Y(1-b)}{k-br} \qquad (2)$$

where Y is current earnings per share, b is the retention rate, and r is the rate of return earned on retained earnings. Rearranging terms in equation (2), we see that the price/earnings ratio is a function of the retention rate, the rate of return on retained earnings, and the required rate of return, or

$$\frac{P}{Y} = \frac{1-b}{k-br}. \qquad (3)$$

The discretionary or management variable is b, while k and r are determined (in our view) jointly by management and market forces.

A change in the price/earnings ratio might be the result of a change in dividend payout policy, the capitalization rate, or the rate of return on retained earnings. Further, there could well be an interdependency among these variables, and any or all of them might be related to such additional factors as leverage.

For our empirical results, we have not attempted to sort out the separate effects of the fundamental determinants on the ex post rate of return. Rather, we stop one step earlier, breaking total returns down into percentages attributable to dividends paid out, earnings growth (which in turn could be attributable to earnings retention, higher rates of return on both new and old assets, increased use of financial leverage, etc.), and changes in the price/earnings ratio (which could be attributable to any number of factors, including the market-determined required rate of return).

It is apparent that a particular stock valuation model is implicit in our method of partitioning the total rate of return, and it is also apparent that different models would cause the partition to be different. We plan, in the future, to pursue this line of attack. Some preliminary sensitivity tests suggest that our present results will not be altered dramatically by changes in the implicit valuation model, but our work has not progressed far enough to permit a stronger statement.

part **6**

The
Overall Model
of the Firm

The building and parameter estimation of comprehensive, overall models of the firm is of comparatively recent origin.[1] Ideally, we should wish for a model dealing with the most general case which could perhaps be described by the following conditions:

1. The firm sells several products whose cost and demand functions are interrelated.
2. It sells in perfectly and/or imperfectly competitive markets, and it buys its inputs in markets which may be either perfectly or imperfectly competitive, or both.
3. It faces competitors whose actions must be taken into account.
4. It optimizes over several periods in conditions of uncertainty.
5. Finally, the model should be so specified as to be of direct assistance to decisions at the operational levels of the firm, i.e., in the production, R & D, marketing, and finance functions; and it should account for their simultaneous and mutual impact upon each other.

We are some distance yet from having such a model which approaches the complex reality of the modern enterprise. As usual, it is the econometricians who—having to come to grips with "reality"—open up the frontiers of our knowledge. Thus the pride of place is given, in this group of readings, to the contribution of three econometricians: Mueller and the Tsurumi brothers.

Mueller's investigation (Reading 27) addresses itself primarily to the fifth point outlined above—the necessarily simultaneous nature of the firm's major decisions—and that in a multiperiod context (see point 4).[2] It views the firm's top management as deciding how to allocate the funds generated by the firm's past and present sales among the four major "claimants" for

---

[1] The grand, solitary exception is Hans Brems' *Product Equilibrium under Monopolistic Competition* (Cambridge, Mass.: Harvard University Press, 1951), which, however, is a purely theoretical contribution.

[2] The only selections partly meeting requirement No. 1 are Grabowski (No. 15), who uses an index of product diversification as one of the determinants of the R & D investment model, and Tsurumi and Tsurumi (No. 28). The Bass article (No. 19) and, again, Tsurumi and Tsurumi, deal specifically with requirement No. 3. Requirement No. 4 is the primary concern of the capital budgeting group of selections and of several others, such as Palda (No. 20).

them: capital investments (plant, machinery, buildings, other acquisitions), R & D investments, advertising investments, and dividend payments.

The level of *each* of these four variables (one might think of them as "decisions") is assumed to be determined by the level of two *groups* of variables—the simultaneously determined three other "competitors," or "claimants", called in econometric language *endogenous variables*, and other, exogenous, variables predetermined from "outside" the immediate system. (These are listed in Table 1.)

Mueller gives his theoretical justification for each of the four equations of his system and examines at length the results contained in Table 2. The reader will notice that only the R & D equations are specified to include the three other endogenous variables. The explanation is merely statistical—variables which did not "perform" well were dropped. Table 3 shows results from regressions in which each firm policy variable is written as a function of all the *predetermined* variables.

Mueller's estimates are based on a sample of 67 firms from all walks of U.S. industry. Had the sample encompassed a less heterogeneous group, say, one industry alone,[3] one would have more confidence in the conclusions. For clearly the importance of advertising decisions may vary widely between a detergent maker and an aircraft manufacturer.

Another possibility is a case investigation of a single firm, which is precisely what the Tsurumi brothers undertook (Reading 28). Theirs is a model of the firm which comes closest to the ideal requirements set out under points 1 through 5 in our list. The reading, however, does not do full justice to the data gathered from a Japanese drug firm. To accomplish this the authors will have to write at least one monograph; a paper, long though it may be, can only trace out the theoretical framework and assumptions underlying the estimates. But while the reader may find explanations all too brief and footnotes all too curt, this paper points the way to the future of the work on the problems of the firm seen as a whole. The Tsurumi model looks simultaneously at environmental influences (industry demand functions, labor supply, tax structure), competitive struggles within the industry, and the firm's internal decision rules (investment, advertising and others).

For the concluding selection the editor has chosen a brief article on the merger of two large Western European concerns, which appeared in the world's foremost economic weekly, *The Economist* (London). With its help, the reader is invited to judge to what extent the various models of the firm presented in this book can aspire to cope with the complexity of an actual modern business situation.

---

[3] Mueller has looked at samples of firms in individual industries in an extension of his researches. His results have not, however, been published in time for inclusion here.

27

The Firm Decision Process: an Econometric Investigation*

DENNIS C. MUELLER

This article adds to an already long list of econometric studies of firm behavior. Its emphasis is upon the complexity of this behavior, and upon the eventual need for attempting to explain this behavior with models of corresponding complexity. It differs from much of the previous work on firm behavior in that it stresses the inherent simultaneity of many of the firm's decisions, and asserts that a complete understanding of this decision process can be obtained only by explicitly accounting for the numerous interactions which are a result of this simultaneity. Similarly, in formulating policy recommendations one must be aware of these interactions, not only in order to avoid undesirable side effects which might stem from a given policy, but also to be certain that these interactions do not actually result in a negation of a policy's primary goal.

The more forces a model takes into account, the more difficult full comprehension of the mechanisms depicted in the model becomes, and the more arduous is the task of estimation. Still, it is felt that these are costs which at some time must be incurred,

for there are limits to the amount of information which can be obtained about a subject through the use of simple approximations. What is more important, no information about the location of these limits can be obtained unless we occasionally are able to penetrate deep enough to glimpse the entire structure we wish to understand.

I. A GENERAL FORMULATION OF THE MODEL

A. The Direct Statement of the Model

The allocation of the flow-of-funds to a firm may be viewed as a stepwise process in which some uses receive very high priority and others are determined almost as a residual. Expenditures which tend to meet a given set of firm objectives and are to some extent substitutes for one another will be given equal priority and will be determined by weighing one against the others.

An econometric model which sought to explain decisions having equal claim to a firm's funds might be formulated as follows: Letting $n_1, n_2, \ldots n_r$ represent the endogenous variables and $x_1, x_2 \ldots x_s$, the set of predetermined variables, then

$$n_1 = f_1(n_2, n_3, \cdots n_r, X_1) + \mu_1,$$
$$n_2 = f_2(n_1, n_3, \cdots n_r, X_2) + \mu_2,$$
$$\cdots \cdots \cdots \cdots \cdots \quad (1)$$
$$n_r = f_r(n_1, n_2 \cdots n_{r-1}, X_r) + \mu_r$$

is the stochastic representation of the model, where the X_j are subsets of the set of all x_j. That is, each dependent variable at a given level of priority is a function of *all* other decision variables at that level and *some* of

From The Quarterly Journal of Economics (*February 1967*), pp. 58–87. Reprinted with permission of author and publisher. Copyright © by the President and Fellows of Harvard College.
* [Professor Mueller teaches at Cornell University.] The work on this paper was supported in part by the Ford Foundation grant to the Inter-University Program on the Micro-Economics of Technological Change and Economic Growth. The paper has benefited from comments on earlier drafts by my dissertation advisors, Professors Jesse Markham and Stephen Goldfeld. Professor John Meyer has provided a number of additional suggestions which have improved greatly the content of the paper. The estimates of the model were made using a computer program written by Mr. Edward Pearsall.

the predetermined variables. The set of predetermined variables may include decision variables of higher priority, lagged dependent variables at this level of priority, or variables completely exogenous to the system. If one is willing to make a number of assumptions regarding the form of the functional relationships, the process which generates the error terms, etc., in (1), the model can be estimated using one of a number of statistical techniques. Preferably direct-least-squares will not be employed, for this procedure ignores the simultaneity we wish to emphasize. Instead one of the methods of estimation which explicitly allows for this simultaneity should be employed.[1]

B. An Optimization Model

In writing each equation the researcher makes explicit assumptions only regarding the variables the entrepreneur considers relevant for each decision and not about the motives behind these decisions. One's preconceptions regarding the goals of the firm are often implicitly introduced via the selection of the predetermined variables to be included in each question. Still, some equations will be consistent with a variety of assumptions about the goals of entrepreneurs. By stressing decision variables rather than motives, the approach is general in the sense that a model may be reconcilable with a number of hypotheses regarding the goals of the firm.

One might prefer to introduce assumptions concerning entrepreneurial goals explicitly by defining an objective function. Corresponding to (1) there would then be an objective function O, such that

$$O = O(n_1, n_2, \cdots n_r, x_1, x_2, \cdots x_s)$$

If O is maximized with respect to the n_j, a set of r equations is obtained which can be solved for each of the r dependent variables. Unless a rather complex functional relationship is hypothesized for O, each dependent variable will be a function of

[1] J. Johnston, *Econometric Methods* (New York: McGraw-Hill, 1960), Chap. 9.

all predetermined variables and none of the other dependent variables. If a linear relationship is assumed the system (2) results. Making the usual

$$n_1 = a_1 x_1 + b_1 x_2 + \cdots w_1 x_5 + v_1,$$
$$\cdots \cdots \cdots \cdots \cdots \cdots$$
$$n_r = a_r x_1 + b_r x_2 + \cdots w_r x_5 + v_r \quad (2)$$

assumptions concerning the error terms and the x_j, the direct-least-squares estimates of this system will be maximum likelihood estimates. Formulating the problem explicitly as one of maximization has apparently eased the computational burden. While with (1) a sophisticated simultaneous estimating technique was required, with (2) it appears direct-least-squares will suffice.

The simplification of the computational task has not been without some cost. The decisions, over which predetermined variables should be included in each of the equations of (1), will have been made on the basis of a priori knowledge of firm behavior. The performance of (1) can be evaluated both on the basis of the usual statistical tests, and upon the amount of agreement between the estimated and predicted values of the structural coefficients. With (2) the latter test is not possible. The coefficient of a predetermined variable in (2) is a measure of the net impact of this variable upon the equation's dependent variable, after account has been taken of all the interactions of the system of equations. This is a direct result of having derived the system (2), by first solving algebraically the set of equations which resulted from the optimization of O. For small systems one may able to make predictions concerning the signs and magnitudes of the coefficients of (2). For complex models this procedure is hazardous.

That (2) makes less use of one's a priori knowledge of firm behavior than (1) is not surprising, for (2) is the reduced form equivalent of (1). Indeed, a possible method for estimating (1) is first to estimate (2) using direct-least-squares and use the resulting estimates to solve for the coefficients of (1). But here again one's predictions about various coefficients could not be confirmed until after such a substitution had taken place. This procedure for estimating (1) has the least to recommend it of all the simultaneous equation techniques, and in fact, only results in unambiguous estimates of the coefficients of (1), when each of the equations in that system is exactly identified. We conclude that the results from empirical work can be best employed as a check upon the reasonableness of one's preconceptions regarding firm behavior, and as a means of making further inferences about this behavior, if one concentrates upon a model analogous to (1).[2]

II. THE CHOICE OF DEPENDENT VARIABLES

Later sections of this article present the results for a model which focuses upon four decisions of the firm: capital investment, research and development (R & D), advertising, and dividend payments. The firm's decision concerning any one of these variables is assumed to be made while it considers the other three.

In what follows we assume the firm acts implicitly so as to maximize the present net worth of its stockholders. It may use its funds to pay out dividends, or employ them in some combination of the three competitive strategies included in the model. The trade-off between dividend payments and the strategy variables will depend upon: (1) the time-preference schedule of the firm's stockholders, (2) the extent to which the market reflects increases in expenditure on the strategies in increases in the value of equity shares, and

(3) the expected returns from the three strategies. For example, a particularly attractive R & D opportunity should lead to: an increase in R & D, a reduction in dividend payments, the anticipation of a future rise in dividends, and an increase in the current value of a firm's stock.

Capital investment, R & D, and advertising are often alternative means to a similar end. When deciding between a marginal increase in capital investment and an increase in R & D, the firm may be weighing a change to a known but as yet unadopted process against trying to develop a process superior to anything currently available. Similarly, when it determines its R & D and advertising budgets, the firm may compare the opportunities for creating a new image for an old product with those of inventing an entirely new product.

Over a period of years, the firm can rely upon three sources of funds to finance these outlays, profits, depreciation, and equity issues. Since the third of these has been a limited source of funds for firms, in recent years[3] we feel justified in concentrating on the two flows, profits and depreciation. Profits are returns from past expenditures on one of the three competitive strategies: investment, R & D, or advertising. They may be re-employed in these same activities, or distributed to stockholders in the form of dividend payments. Depreciation is a rebate upon specific past expenditure decisions, investments in capital equipment. It can be reinvested in capital equipment, used to finance

[2] W. H. Locke Anderson maximizes an objective function subject to a balance-sheet constraint which equates the sources and uses of funds for the firm. It should be noted that whether one chooses to think of the firm as operating within a balance-sheet constraint or not in no way affects the arguments in favor of estimating (1) as opposed to (2). The system of equations (1) easily can be modified to take into account such an identity by replacing one of the equations in the system by the identity. See *Corporate Finance and Fixed Investment* (Boston: Graduate School of Business Administration, Harvard University, 1964), Chaps. 3 and 4.

A balance-sheet constraint only seems appropriate for decisions of the lowest priority and, therefore, will be ignored in the model presented below.

[3] *Ibid.*, p. 25. An additional reason for not including equity issues in the model is because of the problem of determining the direction of causality. This is also the problem with using long-term debt as a predetermined variable as Anderson does. That is, equity and debt are better treated as dependent variables in a model which focuses on lower priority decisions than as independent variables in our model. This is consistent with Anderson's work in Chap. 4. In Chap. 5 Anderson argues from aggregate time series data that increasing risk has a negative effect upon investment. His results conflict with those of John R. Meyer and Robert R. Glauber, *Investment Decisions, Economic Forecasting, and Public Policy* (Boston: Harvard Graduate School of Business Administration, Harvard University, 1964), pp. 88–91. Our sample resembles more closely that of Meyer and Glauber than that of Anderson and we have not tested, therefore, this particular hypothesis.

TABLE 1   Variable Definitions

RD	Firm R & D outlays	G	Ten-year change in sales
I	Gross capital investment	TRD	Total R & D undertaken during a previous one-year period
A	Advertising	IRD	Industry R & D/industry sales
D	Cash dividend payments	IAS	Industry assets/industry sales
S	Sales	IA	Industry advertising/industry sales
P	Profits before taxes	dS	One-year change in sales
DP	Depreciation plus depletion		

R & D and advertising, or paid out as dividends. In short, the firm is envisaged as acting in a completely fluid manner, receiving funds as profits and depreciation, employing them either by investing in one of the three competitive strategies examined here, or paying them out as dividends. Its decisions are motivated by the desire to maximize stockholder net worth and are made by simultaneously weighing the effects of one choice versus those of the others.

In order to conserve space we shall not present a priori justifications for the inclusion of each predetermined variable in the four equations. Each dependent variable is assumed to be a function of the other three dependent variables and a group of the predetermined variables. While predictions were made concerning the signs of the predetermined variables in each equation, no attempt was made to penetrate the maze of interactions in the model and predict the signs of the right-hand-side dependent variables. Their inclusion in an equation will be justified on statistical grounds alone. Despite the absence of any small-sample theoretical support for such an action, the t, R, and F statistics will be calculated and interpreted in a manner similar to that usually followed using their direct-least-squares analogues. Partial justification for this can be obtained from John Cragg's work with Monte Carlo experiments.[4]

Table I lists the codetermined and predetermined variables employed in the model. In order to avoid the problem of heteroscedasticity, all variables, except the industry index variables, will be deflated by sales.

This procedure was justified using a test of homoscedasticity recently developed by Goldfeld and Quandt.[5] Using their nonparametric test one cannot reject the hypothesis that the four equations in their deflated forms have homogeneous residuals for 1960. The intercepts of the equations will be interpreted as the coefficients of the sales variable.[6]

The sample consists of observations on 67 firms for the four years 1957–60.[7] The model was estimated for each of the four years using the direct-least-squares, two-stage-least-squares, unbiased K-class, and limited-information procedures.[8] The estimates from the three consistent K-class procedures were bunched rather closely and often showed sharp differences in contrast to the estimates from direct-least-squares. Unfortunately, it does not appear that this result alone can be relied upon as evidence that these estimates are closer to the true values than the direct-least-squares estimates. Cragg's work indicates that this same type of bunching occurs, even when the direct-

[4] J. G. Cragg, "Small-Sample Properties of Various Simultaneous-Equation Estimators: The Results of Some Monte-Carlo Experiments," Princeton Econometric Research Program, Research Memorandum No. 68, Oct. 1964, pp. 81–94 and 183–84.

[5] Stephan M. Goldfeld and Richard E. Quandt, "Some Tests for Homoscedasticity," *Journal of the American Statistical Association*, LX (June 1965).

[6] Ideally, an index of interindustry differences which is not already deflated by sales should be employed, e.g., in the R & D equation, average firm R & D. This would allow us to employ the Goldfeld and Quandt test to both the ratio and the nonratio forms of the equations. Not possessing such a variable we have chosen industry R & D as a percentage of sales as a substitute. The use of variables of this form precludes the formation of nonratio models by multiplying each variable by sales in the deflated investment, R & D, and advertising equations. When their test was applied to the deflated and undeflated forms of the dividends equation, the latter was heteroscedastic at the 1 per cent level of significance and the former was not (8 versus 4 residual peaks). For a complete discussion of these variables see Table 1, and the Appendix.

[7] The sample is discussed fully in the Appendix.

[8] Johnston, *op. cit.*, Chap. 9.

TABLE 2 Regression Analysis Results

Year Method	I =	RD	A	TRD	IAS	dS	P_{t-1}	DP_{t-1}	F	R
1960 DLS		−.404	−.290	.294	.489	.110	.071	1.221	75.54	.95
		1.22	1.77	1.31	3.69	2.66	1.01	6.98		
1960 TSLS		−.905	−.421	.566	.500	.101	.136	1.180	70.64	.95
		.61	.72	.76	2.62	1.45	.83	6.17		
1959 TSLS		−1.648	−.062	.756	.302	−.021	.257	1.271	57.11	.93
		2.00	.18	2.19	1.73	.53	1.87	6.77		
1958 TSLS		−1.045	−.121	.407	.613	.042	.212	.631	57.92	.93
		1.73	.46	1.84	3.90	1.64	2.16	3.66		
1957 TSLS		−1.912	−.508	.723	.689	.142	.225	1.329	69.34	.95
		2.26	1.52	3.02	3.61	2.65	1.74	5.63		

Year Method	RD =	I	A	D	IRD	G	P_{t-1}	DP_{t-1}	S	F	R
1960 DLS		−.035	.051	−.125	.697	.0021	.138	.127	−.011	11.08	.75
		.63	.63	1.02	5.76	.94	3.02	1.15	1.99		
1960 TSLS		−.056	.170	−.151	.660	.0023	.149	.180	−.012	10.22	.77
		.55	1.22	1.07	5.21	1.02	2.93	1.16	1.80		
1959 TSLS		−.055	.178	−.258	.581	.0025	.213	.240	−.013	15.02	.79
		.44	1.42	1.87	5.46	1.28	4.09	1.43	2.28		
1958 TSLS		−.161	.021	−.054	.603	.0019	.125	.247	−.0066	10.93	.75
		2.07	.19	.35	5.19	.91	2.26	2.43	1.29		
1957 TSLS		−.041	.098	−.301	.467	.0017	.198	.186	−.0095	10.21	.76
		.73	.99	2.32	4.67	.96	4.17	1.73	1.98		

Year Method	A =	I	D	G	IA	S	F	R
1960 DLS		.028	−.272	−.0013	.669	.0089	10.21	.63
		.49	2.33	.45	5.71	1.54		
1960 TSLS		.099	−.383	−.0014	.753	.0059	9.55	.65
		1.23	2.81	.47	5.68	.89		
1959 TSLS		.048	−.293	−.0011	.666	.0084	10.04	.61
		.52	1.97	.38	5.05	1.38		
1958 TSLS		.087	−.367	−.0013	.716	.0081	8.66	.59
		.87	2.29	.39	5.48	1.11		
1957 TSLS		.083	−.410	−.0027	.773	.0090	8.88	.64
		1.10	2.52	.82	5.64	1.32		

Year Method	D =	RD	P	D_{t-1}	F	R
1960 DLS		.072	.042	.837	1702.28	.99
		2.45	3.63	26.48		
1960 TSLS		.075	.041	.836	1702.04	.99
		2.23	3.57	26.28		
1959 TSLS		.076	.033	1.007	507.69	.98
		.89	1.20	13.64		
1958 TSLS		−.067	.106	.731	1225.55	.99
		1.23	5.55	18.90		
1957 TSLS		.072	.030	.973	732.85	.99
		.80	.86	12.27		

Notes: TSLS = Two-stage-least-squares. DLS = Direct-least-squares. Values below regression coefficients are *t* values. Coefficients for sales variables are intercepts of ratio equations.

least-squares estimates possess the smaller bias.[9] Our emphasis upon the estimates obtained from the consistent *K*-class techniques will be justified, therefore, by their superior statistical properties and their generally superior performance in Monte Carlo studies.[10] Because of the closeness of the three consistent *K*-class estimates only the results obtained using the two-stage technique will be presented (Table 2). These

[9] *Op. cit.,* Appendix D, Table C–1.

[10] *Ibid.,* and Johnston, *op. cit.,* Chap. 10.

results may be compared for 1960 with those obtained using direct-least-squares, which are presented in the same table. Hereafter, all references are to the two-stage estimates.

III. THE CAPITAL INVESTMENT EQUATION

A. Some Preliminary Considerations

Of the four outlays examined in the model, capital investment has received by far the most attention in the literature. Indeed, an adequate review of past effort in this area does not seem feasible within the confines of this study.[11] In place of such a review, we shall justify our equation by first sketching the firm investment process as we see it, and secondly by rejecting two alternative formulations often employed.

A firm may invest in new capital equipment for the purpose of adopting presently known production processes, which it previously did not employ (these may be the result of past R & D), or it may reinvest in the same processes it has utilized in the past. A newly adopted process may produce an entirely new product, or it may produce at a lower cost a product currently marketed by the firm. A large portion of a firm's capital expenditure is to replace wornout plant and equipment, and is necessary for the firm's very survival. To some extent this fraction of a firm's investment differs from its expenditures on R & D and advertising, in that it is more of a necessity and involves less uncertainty. This point should not be overemphasized, however. Capital investment also involves uncertainty, and R & D and advertising expenditures are in part necessary in order for a firm to maintain its market position.

Our use of cross-section data requires that we interpret the estimated regression coeffi-

cients as long-run elasticities.[12] The firm is envisaged as relying upon the flows of profits and depreciation, in the long run, in order to finance its investment. These variables each serve a dual role in the equation. Profits represent both a flow-of-funds and a possible indication of future returns. To the extent the firm relates present profits to past capital expenditures, it may use them as a measure of future returns from similar investments. Depreciation is both a flow-of-funds and an index of replacement needs. Whether the firm decides to reinvest these funds in capital equipment will depend upon the comparative advantage this strategy has over the others. In periods of peak demand this advantage is likely to be great and the firm will reinvest in the same processes in an effort to meet current orders. In periods of low demand it may prefer to divert some of these funds into increasing present and future demand through advertising and R & D.

Zvi Griliches has argued that any equation which is used to explain investment should have as one of its explanatory variables a present or past value of the firm's capital stock.[13] This type of hypothesis envisages the firm as seeking a desired capital stock (K^*), and a negative coefficient is predicted for the present stock of capital variable. The higher this present stock is, the smaller the investment needed to reach the desired level, K^*. In a cross-section model, the present stock of capital will act as an index of the capital-intensiveness of the firm relative to the other firms in the sample and not as a measure of its present level of capital relative to some ideal quantity. The coefficient of this variable will not be negative as predicted, and therefore, it does not seem justifiable to include present capital stock as an independent variable in cross-section models. In our model, depreciation acts as an index of the capital-intensiveness of the firm and the predicted sign for its coefficient is positive.

[11] Robert Eisner and Robert H. Strotz have tackled the job in "Determinants of Business Investment," in Commission on Money and Credit, *Impacts of Monetary Policy* (Englewood Cliffs, N. J.: Prentice-Hall, 1963).

[12] Edwin Kuh, *Capital Stock Growth: A Micro-Econometric Approach* (Amsterdam: North Holland, 1963), p. 182.

[13] "Capital Stock in Investment Functions: Some Problems of Concept and Measurement," in Carl F. Christ and others, *Measurement in Economics* (Stanford: Stanford University, 1963).

The stock adjustment model also can be used to justify including lagged investment in the equation. More generally one can follow Koyck and assume that

$$I_t = aS_t + \sum_{i=1}^{n} \lambda^i S_{t-i} \cong aS_t + \lambda I_{t-1}, \quad (3)$$

because

$$\lambda I_{t-1} \cong \sum_{i=1}^{n} \lambda^i S_{t-i}.^{14} \quad (4)$$

Alternatively, one can assume that a given investment flow is desired. If I_t^* is current desired investment, and b the one-period reaction coefficient, then one might hypothesize a function of the form

$$I_t - I_{t-1} = b(I_t^* - I_{t-1}). \quad (5)$$

If I_t^* is dependent upon S_t, an equation analogous to (3) results.

Similar demonstrations would justify the inclusion of lagged dependent variables in all of the equations of the model. In a cross-section model (particularly with a sample which is as heterogeneous as ours is), the performance of a lagged dependent variable will approach the spectacular. This performance may be out of proportion with that of the theory which it represents, for the variable may act as a surrogate for a number of separate influences upon firm behavior. This characteristic of lagged dependent variables introduces a number of problems in interpretation. The distributed lag variable conceivably might be any one of the variables in the equation which has a positive coefficient, it may be a combination of these variables, or even an excluded variable. The same problems of interpretation are present when one attempts to specify the determinants of I^*. When deciding whether or not to include a lagged dependent variable in an equation, the analyst is faced, therefore, with a dilemma. To include the variable is to risk misinterpreting the results, usually in favor of whatever hypothesis is being tested. If the variable is not included, the equation may be misspecified and the estimated regres-

sion coefficients are likely to be biased.[15] The choice should rest upon the analyst's confidence regarding the theory which justifies including the lagged variable. If he is certain about his theory and believes the parameter estimates can be interpreted without ambiguity, then the lagged variable approach is appropriate. In situations where some doubt exists regarding the true underlying structural relations, it is felt a little bias should be incurred in an effort to avoid misinterpreting the results. Using these criteria, we have rejected the lagged dependent variable approach for all but the dividends equation.[16]

In place of an investment equation which includes lagged investment as a predetermined variable, we have chosen one which has depreciation as its most important explanatory variable. Our use of depreciation should not be thought of as part of a rigid stock adjustment model, however. Depreciation is thought of as a measure of the flow-of-funds over time the firm *could* reinvest without implying that they will be so employed. If depreciation were also an accurate measure of the annual deterioration in plant and equipment, one would expect that in years of normal business activity this entire flow would be reinvested, i.e., a regression coefficient for depreciation of about one. In years of greater or less activity coefficients which were correspondingly greater or smaller would be anticipated. In years of expansion the increased incentives to invest should be proportional to the firm's capital stock and therefore to depreciation. In recession years, one expects that other expenditure outlets will have a comparative advantage over investment. This should result in a shifting of depreciation funds out of investment and into these other activities. Depreciation is not, of course, a perfect index of capital deterioration. On the other hand, it is not entirely unrelated to the size and

[14] Leendert Marinus Koyck, *Distributed Lags and Investment Analysis* (Amsterdam: North Holland, 1954).

[15] Yehuda Grunfeld, "The Interpretation of Cross-Section Estimates in a Dynamic Model," *Econometrica*, Vol. 29 (July 1961).

[16] Meyer and Glauber seem to find that lagged investment represents variables other than those they hypothesized, *op. cit.*, p. 134.

durability of a firm's capital stock. This suggests that we can still look for a cyclical variation in the magnitude of the depreciation coefficient, as described above, but that its expected value in normal years may not be one.

B. The Empirical Results

In Table 2, we find that the depreciation variable has positive and significant coefficients for all four of the sample years. The coefficients exceed one for every year except 1958. In years when the pressure from demand is weak, depreciation funds appear to be channeled into activities promising higher returns than current investment. A glance at the results for the R & D equation suggests a possible recipient of these funds. The coefficient of depreciation in that equation has its highest and most significant value in 1958. These findings are in agreement with the dual interpretation given the depreciation variable above. The extent to which a firm chooses to use the available flow-of-funds from depreciation to restore the previous period's capital stock depends upon the comparative advantage this alternative has over others at the firm's disposal. The results for the investment and R & D equations viewed together stress the flexibility the firm has in allocating the funds at its disposal among their many potential uses. The coefficients of the profits variable are positive for all four years and of relatively close magnitudes. This consistent behavior argues in favor of its retention as an explanatory variable in the equation. Of the four coefficients the one for the recession year, 1958, has the highest *t* value. This is consistent with the Meyer and Kuh findings[17] and suggests, in accordance with their theory, that the liquidity component of the profits variable may be more important in explaining investment than are firm expectations.

The results for the change in sales variable are extremely interesting. Its coefficients are positive for all years except 1959. Meyer and

Glauber interpret this variable as a surrogate for capacity utilization.[18] They anticipate a positive relationship between this variable and investment in years of high business activity. The most expansionary years in our sample are 1957 and 1959, and the change in sales variable receives respectively its highest and lowest coefficients for these two years, the latter being of the wrong sign. These results suggest that the variable should be interpreted in some way other than as a measure of capacity utilization in our model. For the years under examination here, a change in sales variable constitutes a poor measure of utilized capacity. The year 1957 followed two years of very high economic activity. Firms having high increases in sales in 1957 are likely to be closer to (further above) full capacity than are firms experiencing relatively high increases in 1959, a year following a recession. The same argument may be applied to explain the high coefficient for 1960. The change in sales variable would seem to be better interpreted as a measure of expectations than as an index of capacity. Firms which continue to experience relatively strong sales growth in nonpeak years may be very optimistic about the future. Conversely, firms experiencing high sales growth in years of greater than average economic expansion may realize that this is a transitory phenomenon and not base their expectations upon this increase in sales. We conclude that, in our model, the change in sales variable acts chiefly as a measure of expectations, not capacity, and that it measures expectations most accurately in years of normal economic expansion.[19]

[18] *Op. cit.*, p. 95.
[19] Meyer and Glauber also suggest that change in sales may measure expectations, but are not able to distinguish this variable from their index of capacity statistically. They therefore lump the expectational and capacity elements of these variables into a single accelerator hypothesis. The difference in the composition of the two samples and in the years covered may explain most of the contrast in performance for the change in sales variable in our model and the Meyer and Glauber study. In this respect, it is interesting to note the agreement between our results and the findings and inferences of the Meyer and Kuh study, *op. cit.*, pp. 121–22.

[17] John R. Meyer and Edwin Kuh, *The Investment Decision* (Cambridge: Harvard University Press, 1957), pp. 117–20.

R & D is expected to induce future investment, both by making current production processes obsolete and by creating a need for new techniques to produce new products. The coefficient for lagged total R & D is positive for all four sample years, and significant for two. Its magnitudes seem extremely large, e.g., in the 1960 equation the coefficient indicates that for every dollar spent on total R & D in 1956, 57 cents in investment is induced in 1960. Even assuming some of this apparent causal relationship is spurious and attributable to interfirm differences not accounted for by the industry index variable, our results suggest that R & D can be highly influential in inducing future investment.

The industry index variables have high coefficients and t values for all four years, indicating, not surprisingly, that significant interindustry differences exist to account for interfirm differences in capital investment.

The equations as presented do not contain intercepts. When intercepts are included, they are small and insignificant. Since in our ratio model the intercept represents the coefficient of sales, this result indicates that sales do not play an important part in explaining investment in our equation. Sales are interpreted usually as a measure of a firm's expectations. Both change in sales and profits have been interpreted as measures of expectations in our model. The fact that these variables consistently possess the anticipated sign may explain why the sales variable does not. While these findings disagree with those of others,[20] they do seem more in accordance with what our theory predicts. Both profits and change in sales reflect more accurately a firm's goal of maximizing stockholder income than do current sales.

Of the three codetermined variables, only the original performance of the dividends variable was such as to warrant an assumption of a zero coefficient. Hence the equation was re-estimated omitting this variable.

IV. THE R & D EQUATION

Investments in R & D have as their objectives new products or processes. Schumpeter viewed this competitive strategy as the most lethal of those at the firm's disposal.[21] Of the three considered here, its returns are the most uncertain and distant, and in this respect its appeal as a strategy is reduced.

In the R & D equation, depreciation's coeficient is positive for all years, but significant only for the year 1958, in which its t value exceeds even that for the profits variable. The increased strength of its impact upon R & D in the recession year, coupled with its low coefficient for that year in the investment equation, indicates that a shifting of resources from investment to R & D occurs in years when the returns on the former activity are low. The returns from R & D can be expected to increase relative to those from investment in recession years; first, because they are more distant and uncertain and less subject to cyclical phenomena and, second, because it is a more continuous process requiring gradual changes in personnel in order to achieve optimal performance.

The Meyer and Kuh thesis, that liquidity has its strongest impact upon firm expenditures in recession years, is supported by the behavior of both depreciation in the R & D equation and profits in the investment equation. If we accept their theory, on the basis of these two instances of support, then profits in the R & D equation must be regarded chiefly as a measure of expectations. The ranking of the magnitudes of the four positive coefficients corresponds identically

---

An attempt was made to include a capacity variable similar to that employed in the Meyer and Kuh and Meyer and Glauber studies (Meyer and Glauber, *op. cit.*, pp. 39–42), but without success. Their capacity measure has the undesirable property, in light of our view of the firm, of incorporating the concept of a fixed optimal capital/output ratio.

[20] Kuh finds, for example, that sales are superior to profits as an explanatory variable in his investment equations, *op. cit.*, pp. 208–20. He observes, also, that the profits formulation of the model is aided when this variable is lagged and the equation deflated, *ibid.* The particular formulation of the model employed here is, therefore, perhaps conducive to the finding of a positive coefficient for profits.

[21] Joseph A. Schumpeter, *Capitalism, Socialism, and Democracy*, (3d ed.; New York: Harper and Row, 1950), Chap. 7.

to the ranking of the percentage changes in GNP for the four years. It appears that in peak years when expectations are most buoyant, high returns, to the extent they are attributed to past R & D, have their strongest impact upon firm decision-making. The increased importance of profits as an explanatory variable in years of high economic activity suggests both, that past R & D outlays are reinforced by present profits, and that firms expect future returns to be similarly affected.[22]

The importance of R & D as a competitive strategy must rest in large part upon the technological foundation and opportunities available to the firm. These vary greatly from one industry to another, and it is not surprising to find the industry index of R & D intensity the most important explanatory variable in the equation. In part, the strongly positive coefficient for this variable, and its analogue in the advertising equation, may measure a firm's response to similar outlays by its competitors. In this respect the industry index variables assume dual roles: (1) as measures of interindustry technological differences, and (2) as measures of intraindustry competition using identical strategies.[23]

Somewhat surprisingly the sales coefficient (intercept) is negative for all four years. One expects that larger firms will undertake more

R & D: (1) because they can command more resources and possess more confidence over their future and are for these reasons in a better position to assume the uncertainties which accompany this activity,[24] and (2) because they have a greater economic incentive to do so, a given expenditure resulting in a greater gain for the large firm than for the small.[25] Simple correlation coefficients between undeflated firm R & D outlays and sales are positive. The negative intercepts are a result, therefore, of having included in the equation other positively correlated variables which offer a better explanation of the variance in firm R & D than sales. In the long run, firms can be expected to be extremely reluctant to finance uncertain R & D by borrowing. Sales, while possibly a good measure of a firm's capacity to raise funds from outside sources, are obviously inferior to both profits and depreciation as a measure of its command over internal funds. Similarly, profits, in their role as a measure of expectations, can better test a demand-pull hypothesis than sales. We conclude that the negative coefficients for sales should be interpreted not as refutation of the importance of uncertainty and demand-pull factors upon R & D, but merely as indicative of the inferiority of sales relative to other variables in the equation as a test of these hypotheses. The intercepts can be interpreted, also, as inconsistent with the assertion that size alone is necessary to induce R & D.[26] Indeed, weight is added to the arguments presented by skeptics of this thesis.[27]

The faster a firm's sales are increasing, the

[22] Jora R. Minasian's work with time series data argues in favor of an expectational role for the profits variable, also. He found a causal chain running from R & D to productivity, and from productivity to profits. He rejected a hypothesis assigning a liquidity role to profits. "The Economics of Research and Development," in National Bureau of Economic Research, *The Rate and Direction of Inventive Activity* (Princeton: Princeton University, 1962).

[23] The inclusion of these variables is an attempt to remove some of the heterogeneity inherent in the sample without appealing to the costly (in terms of degrees of freedom) dummy variable procedure. Two studies which employ the latter technique also have found that interindustry differences explain a large fraction of the variance in firm R & D activity. See, Frederic M. Scherer, "Firm Size, Market Structure, Opportunity, and the Output of Patented Inventions," *American Economic Review*, LV (Dec. 1965); and Marshall Hall, "The Determinants of Investment Variation in Research and Development," *IEEE Transactions on Engineering Management*, Vol. EM-11 (March 1964).

[24] D. E. Lilienthal, *Big Business: A New Era* (New York: Harper, 1952), Chap. 6; Henry H. Villard, "Competition, Oligopoly, and Research," *Journal of Political Economy*, LXVI (Dec. 1958).

[25] See Jacob Schmookler's papers with Oswald Brownlee, "Determinants of Inventive Activity," *American Economic Review*, LII (May 1962), and Zvi Griliches, "Inventing and Maximizing," *American Economic Review*, LIII (Sept 1963); and for a recent test of the demand-pull hypothesis using sales, Scherer's paper, *op. cit.*

[26] Lilienthal, *op. cit.*

[27] Jacob Schmookler, "Bigness, Fewness and Research," *Journal of Political Economy*, LXVII (Dec. 1959).

more confidence it will have about its ability to secure the benefits from uncertain R & D projects, and the more patience it can afford to show in waiting for these benefits. The faster a firm's sales are growing, the greater the economic advantage it receives from a given cost-reducing invention. The ten-year growth variable may be expected, therefore, to have a positive coefficient in the R & D equation, on the basis of both uncertainty and demand-pull hypotheses. It also may contribute to the poor behavior of sales as a test of these hypotheses in the equation. If present growth is a result of past R & D,[28] then the positive coefficient for growth may indicate merely a positive correlation between present and past R & D. If this is the case, the variable may serve as a measure of a firm's expectations. Firms continue to invest in R & D in the same relative proportions as they did in the past, because their previous R & D outlays have been reinforced by the growth in their sales.

The reader should note, also, the R & D equation's sensitivity to cyclical conditions. Six of the eight regression coefficients achieve an extreme value in the recession year, 1958.

Investment and dividends appear to have negative coefficients in the equation, and advertising the reverse.

V. THE ADVERTISING EQUATION

Advertising is a strategy for shifting the demand schedule of a product without changing its physical characteristics. Its impact is more rapid than R & D and for this reason probably involves less uncertainty. Like R & D it can be a strategy for achieving dominance over a market. Unlike R & D, this domination is liable to be temporary and is more susceptible to counterattacks by competitors.[29] In general, advertising probably involves more uncertainty and quicker payoffs than capital investment, although this may vary among industries.

Neither profits nor depreciation exhibited any influence upon firm advertising outlays. This suggests that firms regard advertising more as a necessary business expense than as an investment. The lack of any positive relationship between profits and advertising leads us to reject a causal chain running from past advertising to present profits, and in turn from these profits to present advertising.

The equation is dominated by the industry index variable. As with R & D, this variable may be thought of as serving two purposes: (1) measuring interindustry differences which are a direct result of the characteristics of the products sold, and (2) measuring firm responses to changes in advertising by other firms in the industry. In light of the absence of any positive relationship between the two flow-of-funds variables and advertising, the latter purpose takes on added importance. For, to the extent the industry index measures the second phenomenon, the results suggest that firms consider advertising a business expense, the amount of which is dependent partly upon the advertising of their competitors.

The intercepts were positive for all four years. It was not surprising to find that firms which sell more, advertise more. Indeed, what was surprising was not to find analogous relationships in the previous two equations. The reason given for not observing the positive relationship in those two equations was the presence of the profits and depreciation variables in each equation. These variables exhibit no influence upon advertising, and we are left with a scale effect which is captured by sales.[30]

---

[28] It is doubtful whether the immediate postwar growth is a result of previous R & D. Some of the growth later in the ten-year period may be, however.

[29] The toothpaste industry, since the advent of Crest, provides an interesting case study of the moves and countermoves of oligopolists using the advertising strategy, "Colgate's 3-Month, $3,751,000 Campaign Hikes Share 1.5%," *Advertising Age,* XXXIV (Aug.

26, 1963); "Toothpaste Tempest," *Chemical Week,* XCV (Aug. 22, 1964); "Look Ma, No Cavities," *Barron's,* XLV (Jan. 4, 1965).

[30] Lester G. Telser has recently discussed the pros and cons of expecting increasing returns to scale from advertising, "Advertising and Competition," *Journal of Political Economy,* LXXII (Dec. 1964), 537–62.

There is one difficulty with including sales in the advertising equation which is not present with the other equations. Advertising's impact upon sales may be rapid enough to result in a feedback effect. It is felt,

A positive coefficient was predicted for the ten-year growth variable in the R & D equation, by arguing that a rapidly expanding firm is in a better position to wait for R & D's distant and uncertain payoffs. Turning the argument around, the slowly expanding firm, feeling much more concerned about the future, may place heavier reliance on advertising with its more rapid and predictable returns. The four negative coefficients for the ten-year growth variable support this interpretation. The variable will be retained in the equation, because of this consistent agreement between the observed and predicted signs for the coefficients, and despite the fact that none of them is significant.

The investment and dividends variables possessed coefficients of the same sign for all four years and were retained in the equation. The R & D variable's coefficients were erratic in sign for the four years and it was excluded from the equation. The reader is reminded that it is because of the simultaneous nature of our model that no predictions, and hence no discussion, for these variables are given and their inclusion in an equation is justified on statistical criteria alone.

VI. THE DIVIDENDS EQUATION

In Section III two justifications for including a lagged dependent variable in an equation were presented. An analogue to equation (5) is Lintner's dividend behavior hypothesis.[31] For the purposes of our model Lintner's equation will be modified by including the three codetermined strategies and deflating all variables by sales.[32]

A lagged dependent variable formulation of the equation has been employed for two reasons. First, the equation as hypothesized by Lintner is entirely consistent with a model which assumed that firms finance investment and similar competing outlays out of retained earnings.[33] Secondly, the chance of misinterpreting the actual behavior represented by the empirical results is much smaller than for the other equations in the model. We join with Kuh in believing that Lintner's hypothesis "stand(s) among the more thoroughly founded behavioral hypotheses in the area of business behavior."[34]

The results for the four years are completely dominated by the lagged dividends variable. A positive relationship is evident between the magnitude of its coefficient and the level of overall economic activity. This produces the rather disturbing result, that the reaction coefficients are about zero for both the years 1959 and 1957. It should be noted that this poor theoretical performance of the equation in these years is matched by a comparatively poor statistical performance. On the basis of both the t values of the lagged dividends variable and the F values of the equation, the estimates obtained for the years 1959 and 1957 are inferior to those for the other two years. The results for these latter years will be used, therefore, in a comparison with those of Lintner and Kuh.

Lintner, using time series data from 1918 to 1941, obtained values for b, the reaction coefficient, ranging from .21 to .30, and for a, the payout ratio, from .37 to .25.[35] Kuh

---

however, that the overriding causal flow is from right to left and that any feedback will not introduce serious bias into the estimates.

[31] John Lintner, "Distribution of Incomes of Corporations Among Dividends, Retained Earnings and Taxes," *American Economic Review*, XLVI (May 1956).

[32] A word is in order concerning the use of lagged and unlagged predetermined variables. In the investment and R & D equations lagged profits and depreciation were employed because of their superior statistical performance in comparison with the unlagged variables and in order to avoid biases which would accompany the use of the unlagged variables (e.g., since R & D

can be expensed, a negative bias is introduced when profits are included in this equation). Others have observed the statistical superiority of the lagged variables, also, e.g., Meyer and Glauber, *op. cit.*, p. 80; and Kuh, *op. cit.*, p. 211.

The use of current profits in the dividends equation was justified on theoretical grounds and by the superior statistical properties it exhibited.

[33] Kuh, *op. cit.* pp. 16–26.

[34] *Ibid.*, p. 17. If one prefers to think in terms of a distributed lag model, the possibility of misinterpretation is still small, the most probable choice of a distributed lag variable being profits.

[35] *Op. cit.*, p. 109. Both Lintner's and Kuh's coefficients for the profits variables have been divided by 2 to make their work using after-tax profits comparable to ours using the before-tax figures.

obtained estimates of .50 and .22, respectively.[36] Our figures yield reaction coefficients (*b*) of .16 and .27, and payout ratios (*a*) of .26 and .39 for the years 1960 and 1958 respectively. Our results resemble those of Lintner more closely than those of Kuh. It is difficult to discern why this is so. Perhaps the answer lies in the fact that our sample, like Lintner's, is representative of the entire population of manufacturing firms, while Kuh's estimates are actually the median values of a group of individual industry estimates.

Lintner's hypothesis is an attempt to explain dividend behavior in the long run. Because we regard the coefficients obtained using cross-section data as estimates of long-run structural parameters, it is encouraging to see how closely our estimates correspond to Lintner's. While it is obvious that great care must be taken to assure that estimates are chosen which are truly representative of firm behavior, it appears that given a sufficient number of years of observations (and this number certainly exceeds 4), accurate representations of firm behavior can be obtained using cross-section data.

The only strategy whose performance warranted its inclusion in the equation was R & D. Its coefficients for 1957, 1959, and 1960 were remarkably close together. There is a reversal of signs in 1958, which is consistent with the peculiar cyclical behavior of R & D already noted in the discussion of that equation.

Because of this rather weak performance by the strategy variables in the dividends equation, it has been suggested that a recursive formulation of the model might be superior to the one employed here, i.e., that dividends have prior claim to a firm's funds over investment, R & D, and advertising. While the writer does believe that few firm decisions have identical claims on a firm's funds, he still feels justified in including dividends as a variable that is codetermined with investment, R & D, and advertising because: (1) The extreme heterogeneity in the sample results in the domination of the equation by the lagged dividends variable; with a

more homogeneous sample of firms, more of the variation in dividend payments probably would be explained by the other codetermined variables. (2) To deny dividends a place in this model would be equivalent to arguing that dividends are never adjusted in light of the profitability of alternative expenditure opportunities. The writer finds this argument intuitively objectionable, particularly with regard to R & D—the only codetermined variable whose statistical performance appeared to warrant its retention in the equation.

The equation was estimated without an intercept. This assumes, ignoring the impact of the codetermined variables, that $D_t = D_{t-1}$, if $D_t^* = D_{t-1}$. When the equation was estimated with intercepts their t values ranged from -2.59 to 0.09.

VII. AN APPRAISAL OF THE MODEL

Of the four decisions examined in the study, advertising has proved the most enigmatic. The coefficients of multiple correlation for its equation are the lowest of any equation in the model. The absence of any correlation between advertising and either of the liquidity variables, profits and depreciation, leads us to conclude that firms regard advertising chiefly as a necessary business expense determined by the nature of their products, the advertising of their competitors, and the size of their operations.

In contrast with advertising, the dividends equation, borrowed from Lintner, is quite successful. Not only are all of the R's high but the estimates of the reaction coefficients are close to those obtained by Lintner. It is apparent, however, that observations for a number of years would be required in order to select the appropriate set of estimates for a prediction model.

In addition to the fact that some of our results support those of the Meyer and Kuh and Meyer and Glauber studies, we feel our entire approach is in the same "eclectic" spirit[37] of these earlier studies. For this reason

---

[36] *Op. cit.*, p. 310.

[37] Meyer and Glauber, *op. cit.*, pp. 3–7.

some comparisons between our work and theirs will be made in the discussion of the investment and R & D equations.

Throughout the paper, the dual roles played by some of the predetermined variables have been emphasized. This interpretation was given originally to the profits and depreciation variables. When the investment and R & D equations are viewed together, however, there is evidence that one component of a variable often dominates the other. In the R & D equation, depreciation can act only as a measure of a liquidity flow. The increased importance of this variable as an explanation of R & D in 1958, as evidenced by its high t value for that year, agrees with the Meyer and Kuh thesis that liquidity flows play their most important role in determining firm expenditure decisions during periods of recession. If one continues to think in terms of the Meyer and Kuh theory, then profits appear to represent mainly a flow of liquidity in the investment equation, for here also the t value for the variable's coefficient it highest in 1958. In the R & D equation, on the other hand, the variable's behavior is reversed. The coefficients of profits in the R & D equation vary directly with the level of overall business activity. If liquidity considerations are most important in recession years, then profits must measure something besides liquidity in the R & D equation. We regard this cyclical behavior of the profits' coefficients as consistent with an interpretation of the variable as a measure of expectations. In years of strong economic activity, firms are encouraged to spend heavily upon R & D as a result of present profit levels, which they probably attribute largely to past R & D expenditures.

In contrast with the findings of the Meyer and Kuh and Meyer and Glauber studies, the liquidity component of depreciation is not dominant in the investment equation. The variable exhibits its smallest amount of explanatory power in this equation for 1958, where both its regression coefficient and t value are roughly half of their respective magnitudes for other years. The Meyer and Kuh and Meyer and Glauber samples do

not contain as much interfirm variation in capital stock as the sample employed in this study; hence, they feel justified in regarding depreciation as a measure of a cash flow. It is obvious that for our sample the variable measures both capital deterioration and liquidity.

The results for the profits and depreciation variables alone make evident the need for examining more than one facet of a firm's behavior at a time, in order to gain an understanding of this behavior. The performance of these two variables in the R & D and investment equations distinctly argues for a theory of the firm, based on the profits maximization assumption, which stresses the importance of internal funds. In years of economic expansion, the marginal returns on investment are high and firms reinvest their entire depreciation allowances. They spend on R & D during these years to the extent that returns therefrom are comparable with those from investment. Firms, which experience high profits from past R & D probably allocate proportionally larger amounts to this activity, on the assumption that these outlays will continue to prove profitable. In years of recession, the returns on investment are lower than normal, and depreciation funds, which ordinarily are reinvested, are diverted into R & D, from which returns increase relative to investment returns during these years.

Mayer and Glauber prefer to use a "residual cash throw-off" variable equal to profits plus depreciation less dividend payments, rather than consider the separate effects of these three variables.[38] Their decision not to separate profits from depreciation is made because of the marked reduction in the explanatory power of the latter, once lagged investment is introduced into the equation. That lagged investment detracts from, and surpasses, the explanatory power of depreciation is not surprising. Depreciation measures but two forces upon firm investment decisions. A high correlation can be expected between the forces which determined last year's investment and the ones which deter-

[38] *Ibid.*, pp. 109–17.

mine this year's. Lagged investment will measure, therefore, roughly the same forces which are included in depreciation *plus all others* which affect current investment. The problem with lagged investment, as mentioned above, is to identify these additional forces and determine their relative importance in explaining this year's investment. In short, while lagged investment has more *statistical* explanatory power, depreciation has more *behavioral* explanatory power. We feel more understanding of firm behavior is gained by omitting lagged investment, separating the effects of profits and depreciation, and trying to explain rather than assume dividend payment policy.

More emphasis has been placed upon expectations here than in the Meyer and Kuh and Meyer and Glauber studies. The interpretation of the one-year change in sales variable as a measure of capacity has been rejected, due largely to its negative coefficient in the boom year 1959, and it along with profits and the ten-year change in sales variable have been assumed to reflect, in part, the operations of expectations upon firm decisions. Greater than average increases in sales during years of normal or below normal economic activity appear to encourage firms to increase their capital investment in anticipation of future growth in sales. Here again it should be noted that the contrast between the results reported here and those in the Meyer and Glauber study may be due to differences in sample composition.

We are forced to reject the hypothesis that sales have a positive influence on either investment or R & D. Indeed, the variable is retained in the latter equation because it consistently and once significantly exhibits the opposite impact, suggesting that, *ceteris paribus*, size acts as a deterrent to inventive activity. Once again the findings for this variable are best explained after viewing the entire model. Profits and depreciation measure the same phenomena sales are often thought to represent, i.e., expectations and command over economic resources. In the investment and R & D equations they consistently have positive and often highly significant coefficients. By including them

in these equations along with sales, we have effectively usurped the power of sales to affect R & D and investment positively. Consistent with these findings, in the advertising equation, where profits and depreciation exhibit no correlation with the dependent variable, the sales variable has a positive coefficient for all four years. The superiority of profits and depreciation over sales in the R & D and investment equations is consistent with both our emphasis on the importance of internal funds for these decisions and our view of the firm as a profits-maximizer.

To summarize the comparison of our work with that of Meyer and Kuh and Meyer and Glauber, we find ourselves in agreement with the general approach of these works, differing only with regard to some of the particulars of the structural model which "best" explains firm behavior. In part these differences can be attributed to the greater heterogeneity of the present sample and the differences in the time periods investigated.

The model has explained its four decision variables with mixed success. The coefficients of multiple correlation range from around 0.63 for the advertising equation to near perfect figures of 0.99 for the dividends equation. An additional point in the model's favor, however, is its performance when viewed over the entire four-year period. We were able to obtain insights to firm decision-making by examining the behavior of the four equations over the cycle, which could not have been inferred from the results for any one equation.

It should be noted that it was more important for our conclusions that the equations be viewed simultaneously than that they be estimated using a technique which eliminates Haavelmo bias. The conclusions for the profits, depreciation, and change in sales variables, for example, are the same regardless of whether direct-least-squares or a consistent K-class technique is used.[39] Indeed, these conclusions are unchanged when each dependent variable is simply

---

[39] For years other than 1960, the differences between the direct-least-squares and consistent K-class estimates were sometimes more pronounced than those appearing in Table 2.

regressed on its respective set of predetermined variables. Hence virtually all of our most interesting observations are unchanged by a more recursive formulation of the model. The simultaneous equation approach has been stressed, because it is the most appealing intuitively and has been supported by the results. The consistent K-class estimating techniques have been emphasized because of their statistical superiority given the underlying structure of the hypothesized model.

VIII. POLICY IMPLICATIONS OF THE RESULTS

A. Problems Raised by the Dual Variables

Table 3 presents the coefficients of the reduced form equivalent of the model, which were obtained from Table 2 using the esti-

able in the same proportions as measure their impact upon a dependent variable, the former's coefficient will not represent the marginal effect upon the latter of a change in the policy. The seriousness of this problem for the policymaker naturally depends upon: (1) the relative importance of each component of the variable, and (2) the asymmetry of a given policy's effects upon the components of a variable. Regarding the first, most analysts glean from their results enough confidence to assert that a given variable represents a flow-of-funds, expectations or some other single phenomenon. Our results also suggest that a particular component of a variable may be more important in one equation than in others. It is doubted, however, that in most instances the estimated parameters measure a single force upon the regressor. The second point varies in importance for each variable. For example, a change in the tax code regarding deprecia-

TABLE 3 Reduced Form Coefficients for 1960

S	TRD	IAS	IA	G	dS	P_t	P_{t-1}	DP_{t-1}	D_{t-1}	IRD
					Investment					
.0465	.2086	.4377	.4628	−.0002	.1191	.0120	.0915	1.1181	.2431	.1936
					R & D					
−.0190	.0152	.0318	−.0938	.0025	.0087	.0044	.1544	.2603	.0886	.6700
					Advertising					
.0548	−.0212	−.0444	.7098	−.0015	−.0121	.0145	−.0135	−.1185	.2934	−.0384
					Dividends					
.0014	−.0011	−.0024	.0070	−.0002	−.0006	.0410	−.0116	−.0195	.8298	−.0501

mates for 1960. It was felt that 1960 was the year for which the results might be best characterized as "normal." Each dependent variable is written as a function of all the predetermined variables in the model. The net marginal effect of a change in one of the predetermined variables upon each of the four dependent variables can be observed by moving down the column representing the predetermined variable.

Unfortunately, the effects of different policies on the predetermined variables are not always easy to predict. This is due partly to the dual interpretation given to many of these variables. Unless a policy affects all of the components of a predetermined vari-

tion will alter the relationship between the actual deterioration in plant and equipment and the figure reported by firms. The coefficient of depreciation in the investment equation, but not the R & D equation, therefore, is not independent of changes in the tax statutes. Because of these difficulties, the following policy discussion should be regarded as suggestive rather than demonstrative.

B. Some Policy Implications

Consider the effects of an expansionary cut in the personal income tax rate. Both the expectations and liquidity components of the predetermined variables should be affected by this policy. The coefficients of current profits indicate an initial increase in all four outlays. Dividend payments receive the largest increase and R & D the smallest. The coefficients for lagged profits imply that later adjustments by the firms result in substantial increases in R & D and capital investment, an actual reduction in advertising (probably in response to the increased profitability of the competing R & D activity), and another slight increase in dividend payments.[40] The increase in expectations measured by the one-year change in sales variable will result in increases in R & D and investment and decreases in advertising and dividends The coefficients for lagged depreciation imply a future expansion in investment and R & D in response to the increase in capital replacement needs and flow of depreciation funds induced by increases in current investment. Advertising and dividends will be cut in response to these needs (the latter only trivially). Finally, the coefficients of TRD, our measure of past R & D, imply a substantial stimulus to future investment as a result of present increases in R & D.

The implications of other policy changes can be derived from Table 3 in a similar manner. Some particularly interesting observations can be obtained from a closer examination of the coefficients of the industry R & D and advertising variables. R & D and advertising resemble one another in that the successful use of either can result in a firm's domination of a market. If the market structure warrants heavy expenditures for the promotion of a firm's current line of products, it also probably will warrant a heavy investment in the improvement of these products. Similarly, the invention of a new product usually will be followed by an increase in advertising to promote this product. Hence, it is not surprising to find

a positive correlation between R & D and advertising in the long run.[41]

In the short run R & D and advertising are in direct competition for the flow-of-funds available to the firm. Hence, one might expect a temporary cutback in one in response to an increase in a predetermined variable which stimulated the other. This is what is observed when one examines the coefficients for the industry R & D and advertising variables. In part, the coefficients of these variables measure firm's response to an increase in expenditures by its competitors. An increase in R & D by a firm's competitors results in an increase in its own R & D and a reduction in its advertising. Analogously, if industry advertising goes up the firm increases its advertising and cuts its R & D. These are very interesting findings. They indicate that while long-run competitive pressures result in a high allocation of funds to R & D and advertising, the short-run response of a firm to an intensification of a specific form of competition—say advertising—is a withdrawal of funds from the competing strategy—R & D.[42]

These findings have most provocative policy implications. Assume the government initiates a matching grant policy to encourage industrial R & D. Assuming the policy does result in some increase in R & D expenditures, there will be two incentives for a firm to increase its R & D; the lure of the matching grant, and the impetus of increased R & D outlays by some of its competitors. Some of the funds used to finance the increase in R & D would come from advertising budgets. A doubly reinforcing way to finance this grant program even might be to levy a tax on advertising.

---

[40] In order to calculate the *net* impact of lagged profits on dividend payments, its coefficient must be added to the product of the lagged dividends' and current profits' coefficients. The reader should recall, also, that to get the after-tax coefficients of profits all figures should be multiplied roughly by a factor of 2.

[41] We interpret cross-section correlations as "long-run correlations," In 1960 the simple correlation between firm R & D and advertising was 0.13 and between industry R & D and advertising 0.44. For further evidence of a positive correlation between R & D and advertising, see National Science Foundation, *Industrial R & D Funds in Relation to Other Economic Variables* (NSF 64–25; Washington, 1964), pp. 41–43.

[42] The implications of these two industry index variables are the same for all four years.

IX. CONCLUSION

We have attempted to place sufficient emphasis upon the important findings of the study so that no detailed review is necessary. We have had three major goals in this undertaking: (1) to outline a general econometric approach to the analysis of firm behavior which takes explicit account of the complex interactions which characterize this behavior, (2) to illustrate this approach by estimating a model which explains a specific set of firm decisions, and (3) to demonstrate the possible usefulness of such models to both students of firm behavior and those interested in policy issues.

APPENDIX

The sample consists of 67 firms selected on a cross-section basis from a population which corresponded roughly to all manufacturing firms. It is part of a larger sample of 150 firms which responded to a request for R & D data in the form of a questionnaire resembling closely those used by the National Science Foundation.[43] The definitions appropriate for our R & D variables are, therefore, those of the NSF.[44] Much has been said of the difficulties inherent in defining inventive activity,[45] and a review of this controversy would take up too much space to be appropriately included here. Let us only say in defense of our use of figures reported according to NSF definitions that: (1) these definitions have been employed virtually without change by the NSF since 1956, resulting in concepts which are as consistent over time as any possible alternatives; (2) the NSF's employment of 100 per cent sampling procedures among large firms of each industry assures the researcher that these

figures have been recorded annually using the desired set of definitions, by all firms in the sample; (3) the fact that these figures were reported initially in response to a government survey which promised not to reveal the identity of any individual firm should result in figures compiled as conscientiously as one can hope for, and minimize any "status bias" appearing in the figures reported to stockholders; and (4) the use of expenditure input figures seems more appropriate in a model which also attempts to explain investment, advertising, and dividend payments, than the alternatives of R & D employment, significant inventions, patents, etc. The R & D figure used as a dependent variable in the model was that reported by the firm as having been conducted in their own laboratories and financed by themselves. The figure used as a predetermined variable in the investment equation was the total amount of R & D undertaken by the firm regardless of the financial source. Almost all of the noncompany financed R & D was government contract work. If the figure for 1956 was not available that for 1957 was substituted. The sample was somewhat biased against heavy government contract work both by the initial sampling selection process and by eliminating any firms for which more than 50 per cent of their R & D was financed by outside sources. It was hoped that this would make our conclusions more applicable to nondefense than to defense oriented R & D. In order to take advantage of the NSF's 100 per cent sampling practice among large firms an additional large firm bias was introduced into the original sampling list. Otherwise it was felt that a reasonably good cross-sectional representation of manufacturing firms was obtained with no pronounced biases in favor of firms which undertake a large amount of R & D, advertising, etc. Table 4 groups the firms according to NSF industry definitions.

Advertising expenditure figures refer to outlays for advertising within the major media as reported in *Printer's Ink*.[46] The few

---

[43] National Science Foundation, *Funds for Research and Development in Industry, 1959* (Washington, 1962), pp. 93–96.

[44] *Ibid.*, p. 97.

[45] S. Kuznets, "Inventive Activity: Problems of Definition and Measurement," and comment by Jacob Schmookler, also B. S. Sanders, "Some Difficulties in Measuring Inventive Activity," both in National Bureau of Economic Research, *The Rate and Direction of Inventive Activity, op. cit.*

[46] *Printer's Ink Advertiser's Guide to Marketing 1961*, pp. 345–70.

TABLE 4 Distribution of Sample Among NSF Industries According to Firm R & D

Industry Number	Industry Name	Number of Firms
1.	Atomic Energy Devices	0
2.	Food and Kindred Products	6
3.	Industrial Inorganic and Organic Chemicals	9
4.	Plastics Materials, Synthetic Resins, Rubber, etc.	5
5.	Drugs	7
6.	Agricultural Chemicals	0
7.	All Other Chemicals	3
8.	Petroleum Refining and Extraction	9
9.	Rubber and Miscellaneous Plastics Products	4
10.	Stone, Clay, and Glass Products	4
11.	Primary Ferrous Products	3
12.	Primary and Secondary Nonferrous Metals	0
13.	Fabricated Metal Products	2
14.	Engines and Turbines	1
15.	Farm Machinery and Equipment	3
16.	Constructions, Mining, and Materials Handling Machinery	3
17.	Metalworking Machinery and Equipment	2
18.	Office, Computing, and Accounting Machinery	2
19.	Other Machinery, Except Electrical	5
20.	Electric Transmission and Distribution Equipment	0
21.	Electrical Industrial Apparatus	0
22.	Electronic Components and Accessories, etc.	6
23.	Other Electrical Machinery Equipment and Supplies	1
24.	Guided Missiles	1
25.	Aircraft and Parts	1
26.	Motor Vehicles and Equipment	5
27.	Other Transportation Equipment	0
28.	Professional and Scientific Equipment, etc.	0
29.	Optical, Surgical, and Photographic Instruments, etc.	0
30.	Other Ordnance, Except Guided Missiles	1
31.	Other	10

Source: Industries defined in National Science Foundation, *Funds for Research and Development in Industry 1959* (Washington, 1962), p. 99.

Note: Firms were assumed to be in an industry if at least 25 per cent of their R & D for any of the four sample years was reported in that industry.

firms which did not undertake a sufficient amount of advertising to be included in this survey were given expenditure figures of $500,000.

All other figures referring to individual firm variables were taken either from *Moody's, Standard and Poor's Industry Surveys* or directly from company reports. Investment figures refer to gross capital investment. Depreciation equals depreciation plus depletion. Profits are operating income before taxes. While this variable is less appropriate for a flow-of-funds hypothesis than the after-tax variable, it is thought to be more so for an expectations hypothesis. The correlation between the two is high enough to produce only a trivial statistical difference regardless of which is used. Dividends are cash dividend payments to common stockholders.

So little variation in the industry index variables was present that they were not changed from year to year. The index in the investment equation is gross depreciable assets divided by business receipts.[47] The R & D industry index is company-financed R & D as a percentage of sales for 1959 using NSF industry definition.[48] The industry

[47] Industry definitions conform to SIC two-digit industry definitions. See, U.S. Internal Revenue Service, *Statistics of Income, 1959–60.*

[48] *Funds for Research and Development in Industry, 1959, op. cit.,* Table A–22, p. 74.

index for the advertising equation is advertising as a percentage of industry sales.[49]

The 150 firms responding to the R & D questionnaire were the starting point of the sample. The firms were asked to report their R & D figures for 1956–63. All 150 did so for 1963, and only 40 for 1956, with a gradually diminishing number of firms reporting figures for each year in between. In order to have a homogeneous sample, only firms which reported figures for 1957 and the three subsequent years were included in the sample. This greatly reduced the number

[49] *Advertising Age*, XXX (Aug. 27, 1962), 201–2.

of usable observations. The *Printer's Ink* figures on advertising are available only through 1960; hence observations for the three most recent years had to be ignored. In general firms were excluded from the analysis because of: (1) failure to report all necessary data for any one year, (2) ten-year growth in sales in excess of 500 per cent (it should be noted that the same growth period 1947–56 was used for all four years to avoid the vagaries brought about by business cycle phenomena), (3) noncompany-financed R & D in excess of 50 per cent, and (4) mergers for which no data adjustments were possible.

28

An Econometric Model of a Japanese Pharmaceutical Company*

HIROKI TSURUMI AND YOSHI TSURUMI

I. INTRODUCTION

We present here a comprehensive econometric model of a single company within the Japanese pharmaceutical industry. Earlier, the first author built an oligopolistic model of American automobile firms [31], demonstrating the possibility of econometric model building at the firm level. In the present

* *This research is partly financed by the Seagram Business Faculty Award of the Samuel Bronfman Foundation of Canada and a grant from Canada Council. The authors wish to thank Mr. Yuji Naito, president of the Eisai Company, Tokyo, who made available confidential data on the Japanese pharmaceutical industry and his company.*

The authors are, respectively, associate professors, Department of Economics and School of Business, Queen's University, Kingston, Canada.

paper, this possibility is again demonstrated and further refined on the basis of more detailed corporate data made available to the authors by the Eisai Company, the sixth largest of Japan's major pharmaceutical firms.

The major objective of this company model is to analyze the simultaneous determination of such variables as market share, advertising, factor demand, and price and wage determination under dynamic conditions. Obviously the relationship among these variables depends upon the industrial market structure as well as upon the goal of the firm, and thus it is essential that the model should be formulated so as to grasp the behavior of the decision makers, i.e., consumers and firms, within the industry concerned. Given the industrial framework, imperfect competitors within the industry would share many behavioral characteristics. The model could therefore be applied to other firms within the industry, if adjustments were made for those behaviors particular to each firm. In addition, although the model is limited to a particular firm and industry, the theoretical formulations and estimation procedures may be usefully applied to other cases in other industries.

The model, expressed in a system of simultaneous equations, may explain some of the reasons for the rapid growth of the Eisai Company, and it may be used, by forecast exercises, to examine the likely outcome of corporate strategy under a certain set of assumptions on the exogenous variables.

Section II of this paper appraises the competitive environment of the pharmaceutical industry of Japan, and Section III presents the model. Section IV discusses the behavioral hypotheses and estimated results of the behavioral equations in the model. In Section V, some examples of forecast exercises are presented to demonstrate the use of the model for corporate planning.

II. THE PHARMACEUTICAL INDUSTRY OF JAPAN

The Japanese pharmaceutical industry has grown in output 4.8 times in the ten years between 1959 and 1968. It is one of the fastest growing industries in Japan. The demand for ethical (prescription) drugs and over-the-counter drugs including medicated cosmetics has increased steadily with the rise in disposable income among consumers, and more importantly, with the growth of national and municipal medicare systems which cover also the cost of drugs.

Although there are estimated to be approximately 2,300 firms manufacturing drugs in Japan, eleven of these firms produce 60 percent of the nation's pharmaceutical products. These eleven firms control 80 percent of the market share in sales of ethical drugs alone, which represent 60 percent of all drugs produced. In research and develop-

ment, as well as in marketing penetration into hospitals, clinics, and pharmacies, the top eleven firms set the industrial climate. The remaining firms survive on processing and packaging standard drugs for limited local markets.

Table 1 summarizes the net sales and the

TABLE 1 Net Sales and Growth Rates of Top Nine Companies

Company	Net Sales of the Second Six-Month Period, 1968 (100 million yen)	Growth Rate of Net Sales (1968/1964)
Group I		
Takeda	780	45.5%
Group II		
Sankyo	240	43.0
Shionogi	220	33.5
Tanabe	206	29.5
Group III		
Fujisawa	145	75.1
Eisai	130	111.0
Yamanouchi	127	81.0
Banyu	120	119.3
Daiichi	112	36.9

Source: Nihon Keizai Shinbun, June 20, 1969

growth rate of the top nine companies during the second 1968 fiscal period. It is still customary for Japanese firms to maintain a six-month fiscal period; the first period runs from April to September, and the second period runs from October to March. Table 1 presents the nine firms in three groups according to their sales for the six-month period from October 1968 to March 1969. The first group is the Takeda Company alone whose sales are more than three times as large as those of Sankyo, the second largest company. The second group consists of three companies whose net sales range between 20 and 24 billion yen for the six months, and the third group consists of five companies whose net sales are from 11 to 14.5 billion yen for the six months. The Eisai Company, whose case the authors are analyzing, belongs to the third group and has registered the second largest growth rate over the four years between 1964 and 1968.

Net sales growth is currently the overriding concern of all Japanese companies, and pharmaceutical firms are no exception. This is partly because during the last 25 years, the government and financial institutions have consciously encouraged this emphasis. In determining export licenses and import quotas or approving new investment plans, the government has had a tendency to use the size of a firm measured in terms of its market share as the working rule of allocation. Similarly financial institutions, when making decisions on loans, favor companies whose market shares are growing. Furthermore, Japan is committed to the practice of lifetime employment, and over the years, management has resorted to a net sales growth strategy as an easy solution to the problem of providing lifelong job security for a growing labor force.

Among the pharmaceutical companies, emphasis on net sales growth has set in firmly as a necessary strategy to keep up with the competition. For example, the larger the number of drugs a company manufactures, the more likely it is that some will be approved by the government medicare agency as drugs eligible to be paid for by medical insurance. The larger the market share of a firm, the easier it becomes to gain additional favor among the general public and the medical professions.

The pharmaceutical market is customarily divided into *ethical drugs* (prescription drugs) and *over-the-counter drugs* and medicated cosmetics. The prices of ethical drugs are set by the government medicare agency. Thus, lacking the possibility of open price competition, detail salesmen's personal contacts with physicians and pharmacists seem to be the only effective marketing strategy for ethical drugs.[1]

The general public who buy over-the-counter drugs and medicated cosmetics tend to be influenced by mass media adver-

tising and by drug store attendants' recommendations. In general, physicians, pharmacists, and the general public are all prone to identify their confidence in a pharmaceutical product with the size and growth of the manufacturing firm. This tendency on the part of the consumers reinforces the emphasis of the pharmaceutical firms on net sales growth goals.

The rapid growth of the industry has been possible in part because many Japanese companies have obtained licenses or know-how for manufacturing new products from foreign companies. This fact is illustrated in Table 2 which presents the leading nine companies again, showing research and development (R & D) expenditure, the number of "star" products (those with a gross sales value of over 100 million yen per month) which each company manufactures, and the number of "star" products which are foreign license-based.

Except for the Eisai Company, all other companies have fairly high proportions of foreign licensed products among their "star" products. In order to compensate for this lack of foreign products, the Eisai Company has had to spend proportionately higher amounts on research and development.

The stimulant of foreign licensing is expected to dwindle rapidly in the near future. With the expected "liberalization of capital" (as unrestricted foreign ownership is called in Japan), many foreign companies are already "landing" in Japan either to open their own subsidiaries or to buy up existing Japanese firms, rather than continuing the past strategy of selling know-how to Japanese companies. If the Japanese companies are to survive or to compete with foreign subsidaries, they will have to develop their own products. Consequently, research and development expenditure may become a key factor in determining the future of any firm.

Exports of the Japanese pharmaceutical industry have been negligible, partly because the firms have been occupied with meeting the rapidly growing demand of the domestic market and partly because foreign licensing agreements often prohibit the Japanese licensees from exporting license-related

[1] This does not mean that there is no "price cutting." This effectively does happen, behind the scenes and by personal agreement between the detail salesman and the physician or pharmacist, usually in the form of adding a bonus supply of drugs to the amount purchased at the official rate. Expense account entertaining is also a common sales promotion practice. Recently, the Japanese government banned the practice of adding a bonus supply.

TABLE 2 Research and Development (R & D) Expenditure and Star Products of the Top Nine Companies

Firm	R & D Expenditure (100 million yen) (1)	R & D Expenditure/ Sales Ratio (%) (2)	Star Products Selling 100 million yen per month (3)	Star Products under Foreign Licence (4)	(4)/(3) ×100 (%) (5)
Takeda	37.0	5.2	27	8	29.6
Sankyo	17.5	7.7	10	2	20.0
Shionogi	15.9	7.9	11	8	72.7
Tanabe	15.5	7.8	11	4	36.3
Fujisawa	12.7	9.3	10	7	70.0
Eisai	15.1	12.2	4	0	0.0
Yamanouchi	9.0	7.7	5	3	60.0
Banyu	2.3	2.0	6	4	66.7
Daiichi	9.7	9.3	8	3	37.5

Source: Nihon Keizai Shinbun, June 26, 1969

products. However, the recent infiltration of foreign companies into Japan has begun to force Japanese firms to explore export markets. However acute the need may be, it will take a long and cumulative investment of time and money to reap any profit from the export market.

As foreign companies study the practices of marketing in Japan, the Japanese firms' advantage in this area will tend to decline. The public is already prepared to accept foreign drugs as quality products because Japanese firms have in the past deliberately emphasized in their advertising the prestige of manufacturing and selling foreign, say, American or German products.

Foreign competition will increase. The past remarkable growth rate of the Japanese economy will eventually slow down as the economy reaches its maturity. The problem of pollution will continue to grow into a tense social issue. In this changing economic and social environment of the 1970's, a firm will need carefully made medium- and long-term plans. For this effort, a comprehensive econometric model such as ours may be a useful planning tool.

III. THE ESTIMATED MODEL

On the basis of semi-annual data for twenty-one observations from the second half of 1959 and to the second half of 1969,[2]

[2] This does not include the lagged observations necessary for the estimation of the distributed lags.

the behavioral equations are estimated by such methods as two-stage least squares (2SLS), Marquart's nonlinear least squares (NLLS) of [18], the nonlinear two-stage least squares (NL2SLS) given in [30], the scanning method (SCAN) of [5], and the modified Sargan's two-stage least squares (MS2SLS) given in [1]. $\bar{R}^2$ denotes the coefficient of determination adjusted for degrees of freedom, and DW indicates the Durbin-Watson test statistic. The figure just below a coefficient is the estimated standard error of the coefficient. $1/G$, or $1/Z$ in front of each gamma distributed lag is to make the sum of the lag coefficients equal to unity, e.g., $G = \sum e^{-ak}$, and $Z = \sum k^{s-1} e^{-k}$.

The List of Variables

The variables are given in alphabetical order and endogenous variables in the system are indicated by an asterisk in the upper left-hand corner.

$*AE_t$ = net stock of effects of current and past advertising expenditure, or *goodwill*, of Eisai at time t, millions of 1965 yen.

AO_t = net stock of effects of current and past advertising expenditure, or *goodwill*, of ten companies excluding Eisai at time t, millions of 1965 yen. These ten companies are, in alphabetical order, Banyu, Chugai, Dai-Nippon, Daiichi, Fujisawa, Takeda,

Tanabe, Sankyo, Shionogi, and Yamanouchi.

$*BLD_t$ = depreciation allowances of buildings at time t, millions of 1965 yen.

$*CP_t$ = production costs of Eisai at time t, millions of current yen.

DET_t = outstanding debts at time t, millions of current yen.

DIV_t = dividend payments at time t, millions of current yen.

$\bar{E}_{BC,t}$ = Eisai's sales of chemotherapeutics and antibiotics at time t, millions of current yen.

$*E_{CR,t}$ = Eisai's sales of cardiovascular agents and agents affecting respiratory organs at time t, millions of 1965 yen.

$*E_{D,t}$ = Eisai's sales of agents affecting digestive organs and agents for uro-genital and anal organs at time t, millions of 1965 yen.

$*E_{DER,t}$ = Eisai's sales of dermatological agents at time t, millions of 1965 yen.

$*E_{NS,t}$ = Eisai's sales of agents affecting the nervous system and sensory organs at time t, millions of 1965 yen.

$*E_{NU,t}$ = Eisai's sales of nutrients and tonics at time t, millions of 1965 yen.

$\bar{E}_{OT,t}$ = Eisai's sales of miscellaneous products at time t, millions of current yen.

$*E_{V,t}$ = Eisai's sales of vitamin preparations at time t, millions of 1965 yen.

$*EX_t$ = real net sales of Eisai at time t, millions of 1965 yen.

$EXRM_t$ = remunerations to the executives at time t, millions of current yen.

FRP_t = the proportion of female workers to the total production force at time t.

FRS_t = the proportion of female workers to the total sales force at time t.

$*GIBL_t$ = gross investment in buildings at time t, millions of 1965 yen.

$*ID_t$ = payments of interest on debts at time t, millions of current yen.

$\Delta INCOM_t$ = change in inventories of office and distribution materials at time t, millions of current yen.

$\Delta INPR_t$ = change in inventories of production materials at time t, millions of current yen.

$*L_{p,t}$ = the number of production workers at time t.

$*L_{RD,t}$ = the number of research and development employees at time t.

$*L_{s,t}$ = the number of sales employees at time t.

$*MED_t$ = depreciation allowances of machinery and equipment at time t, millions of 1965 yen.

N_t = total population at time t, thousands of persons.

$*NIBL_t$ = net investment in buildings at time t, millions of 1965 yen.

$*NIME_t$ = net investment in machinery and equipment at time t, millions of 1965 yen.

$*NKBL_t$ = net capital stock of buildings at time t, millions of 1965 yen.

$*NKME_t$ = net capital stock of machinery and equipment at time t, millions of 1965 yen.

$*OAC_t$ = other administrative costs at time t, millions of current yen.

$*OPRC_t$ = other production costs at time t, millions of current yen.

$*OREV_t$ = other revenues at time t, millions of current yen.

$OTEX_t$ = other miscellaneous expenses not related to sales activities at time t, millions of current yen.

$P_{d,t}$ = price index of consumer expenditure at time t, 1965 = 100.

$P_{i,t}$ = industrial price level of pharmaceutical product i at time t, 1965 = 100.0, $i = NS, CR, D, V, NU, DER, BC,$ and OT.

$*PE_{i,t}$ = the price index of Eisai's i-th product at time t, 1965 = 100.0, $i = NS, CR, D, V, NU,$ and DER.

$P_{k,t}$ = the price index of capital goods at time t, 1965 = 100.0.

$P_{M,t}$ = the price index of raw materials at time t, 1965 = 100.0.

$P_{NU,t}$ = industrial price index of nutrients and tonics at time t, 1965 = 100.0.

$*PRE_t$ = Eisai's advertising expenditure at time t, millions of 1965 yen.

$\phi_{i,t}$ = the coefficient to determine the price index of the i-th product of Eisai at time t.

$*\pi_{A,t}$ = profits after taxes at time t, millions of current yen.

$*\pi_{B,t}$ = profits before national corporate income taxes at time t, millions of current yen.

$*\pi_{G,t}$ = sales profits and other revenues at time t, millions of current yen.

$*\pi_{GS,t}$ = gross sales profits at time t, millions of current yen.

$*\pi_{NS,t}$ = profits out of net sales at time t, millions of current yen.

$*RD_t$ = research and development expenditure at time t, millions of current yen.

$*RE_t$ = retained earnings at time t, millions of current yen.

$*TC_t$ = national corporate income taxes at time t, millions of current yen.

$*TL_t$ = prefecture and local taxes at time t, millions of current yen.

$*V_t$ = net sales of Eisai at time t, millions of current yen.

$w_{o,t}$ = the wage, salary, and bonus rate of the employees of other companies at time t, millions of current yen.

$*w_{p,t}$ = the wage, salary, and bonus rate of Eisai production employees at time t, millions of current yen.

$*w_{RD,t}$ = the wage, salary, and bonus rate of Eisai research and development employees at time t, millions of current yen.

$*w_{s,t}$ = the wage, salary, and bonus rate of Eisai sales employees at time t, millions of current yen.

$*x_{BC,t}$ = per capita industrial production of antibiotics and chemotherapeutics at time t, thousands of 1965 yen.

$*x_{CR,t}$ = per capita industrial production of cardiovascular agents and agents affecting respiratory organs at time t, thousands of 1965 yen.

$*x_{D,t}$ = per capita industrial production of agents affecting digestive organs and agents for urogenital and anal organs at time t, thousands of 1965 yen.

$*x_{DER,t}$ = per capita industrial production of dermatological agents at time t, thousands of 1965 yen.

$*x_{NS,t}$ = per capita industrial production of agents affecting the nervous system and sensory organs at time t, thousands of 1965 yen.

$*x_{NU,t}$ = per capita industrial production of nutrients and tonics at time t, thousands of 1965 yen.

$*x_{OT,t}$ = per capita industrial production of miscellaneous pharmaceutical products at time t, thousands of 1965 yen.

$*x_{V,t}$ = per capita industrial production of vitamin preparations at time t, thousands of 1965 yen.

$*X_{i,t}$ = industrial production of the i-th product at time t, millions of 1965 yen, $i = NS, CR, D, V, NU, DER, BC,$ and OT.

y_t = per capita real personal consumption and medicare expenditure at time t, millions of 1965 yen.

(I) Industrial Demand Block

$$(3\text{-}1) \quad \ln x_{NS,t} = \underset{(.0592)}{1.5036} \frac{1}{G} \sum_{k=1}^{6} e^{-ak}\left(\ln y_{t-k+1} - .687 \ln \frac{P_{NS,t-k+1}}{P_{d,t-k+1}}\right)$$

$$-15.6587 \qquad \bar{R}^2 = .972$$
$$a = 2.0927 \qquad (.5299) \qquad \text{DW} = 1.16$$
$$(.7082) \qquad\qquad\qquad \text{NLLS}$$

$$(3\text{-}2) \quad \ln x_{CR,t} = \underset{(.0759)}{2.0148} \frac{1}{Z} \sum_{k=1}^{15} k^{s-1}e^{-k}\left(\ln y_{t-k+1} - .687 \ln \frac{P_{CR,t-k+1}}{P_{d,t-k+1}}\right)$$

$$-20.6476 \qquad \bar{R}^2 = .991$$
$$s = 7.1389 \qquad (.5180) \qquad \text{DW} = 1.72$$
$$(1.1370) \qquad\qquad\qquad \text{NLLS}$$

(3-3) $\ln x_{DU,t} = \underset{(.0438)}{1.3918} \frac{1}{G} \sum_{k=1}^{14} e^{-ak}\left(\ln y_{t-k+1} - .687 \ln \frac{P_{DU,t-k+1}}{P_{d,t-k+1}}\right)$

$$\begin{array}{ccc} & -15.1490 & \bar{R}^2 = .983 \\ a = .6635 & (.3805) & \mathrm{DW} = 1.50 \\ (.5768) & & \mathrm{NLLS} \end{array}$$

(3-4) $\ln x_{V,t} = \underset{(.2210)}{1.1814} \frac{1}{G} \sum_{k=1}^{3} e^{-ak}\left(\ln y_{t-k+1} - .687 \ln \frac{P_{V,t-k+1}}{P_{d,t-k+1}}\right)$

$$\begin{array}{ccc} & -12.5928 & \bar{R}^2 = .887 \\ a = 15.0290 & (.0118) & \mathrm{DW} = .221 \\ (.1145) & & \mathrm{NLLS} \end{array}$$

(3-5) $\ln x_{NU,t} = \underset{(.1044)}{1.6688} \frac{1}{G} \sum_{k=1}^{3} e^{-ak}\left(\ln y_{t-k+1} - .687 \ln \frac{P_{NU,t-k+1}}{P_{d,t-k+1}}\right)$

$$\begin{array}{ccc} & -17.5674 & \bar{R}^2 = .987 \\ a = 14.4689 & (.0059) & \mathrm{DW} = .482 \\ (.0883) & & \mathrm{NLLS} \end{array}$$

(3-6) $\ln x_{DER,t} = \underset{(.0658)}{.4815} \frac{1}{G} \sum_{k=1}^{3} e^{-ak}\left(\ln y_{t-k+1} - .687 \ln \frac{P_{DER,t-k+1}}{P_{d,t-k+1}}\right)$

$$\begin{array}{ccc} & -6.5739 & \bar{R}^2 = .881 \\ a = 13.0273 & (.0025) & \mathrm{DW} = .582 \\ (.0058) & & \mathrm{NLLS} \end{array}$$

(3-7) $\ln x_{BC,t} = \underset{(.0357)}{1.2775} \frac{1}{G} \sum_{k=1}^{6} e^{-ak}\left(\ln y_{t-k+1} - .687 \ln \frac{P_{BC,t-k+1}}{P_{d,t-k+1}}\right)$

$$\begin{array}{ccc} & -13.4777 & \bar{R}^2 = .988 \\ a = 2.0750 & (.3035) & \mathrm{DW} = 1.19 \\ (.8883) & & \mathrm{NLLS} \end{array}$$

(3-8) $\ln x_{OT,t} = \underset{(.1326)}{.5011} \frac{1}{Z} \sum_{k=1}^{12} k^{s-1} e^{-k}\left(\ln y_{t-k+1} - .687 \ln \frac{P_{OT,t-k+1}}{P_{d,t-k+1}}\right)$

$$\begin{array}{ccc} & -6.8940 & \bar{R}^2 = .472 \\ s = 2.0757 & (1.1057) & \mathrm{DW} = .472 \\ (.7757) & & \mathrm{NLLS} \end{array}$$

(II) Eisai's Market Share Equations

(3-9) $\ln E_{NS,t} = \underset{(.0795)}{.7717} \frac{1}{G} \sum_{k=1}^{6} e^{-ak} \ln\left(\frac{AE_{t-k+1}}{AO_{t-k+1}} X_{NS,t-k+1}\right)$

$$\begin{array}{ccc} & +1.1036 & \bar{R}^2 = .927 \\ a = 2.0474 & (.5860) & \mathrm{DW} = 1.91 \\ (1.0766) & & \mathrm{NL2SLS} \end{array}$$

(3-10) $\ln E_{CR,t} = \underset{(.2453)}{.6584} \frac{1}{G} \sum_{k=1}^{3} e^{-ak} \ln\left(\frac{AE_{t-k+1}}{AO_{t-k+1}} X_{CR,t-k+1}\right)$

$$\begin{array}{ccc} & +2.3852 & \bar{R}^2 = .771 \\ a = 7.8000 & (.0222) & \mathrm{DW} = .31 \\ (.0684) & & \mathrm{NL2SLS} \end{array}$$

$$(3\text{-}11) \quad \ln E_{D,t} = \underset{(.2731)}{.4426} \; \frac{1}{Z} \sum_{k=1}^{7} k^{s-1} e^{-k} \ln \left(\frac{AE_{t-k+1}}{AO_{t-k+1}} X_{DU,t-k+1} \right)$$

$$+ \underset{(.6463)}{4.3522} \qquad \bar{R}^2 = .590$$

$$s = 3.9282 \qquad\qquad DW = .69$$
$$(1.6574) \qquad\qquad\qquad NL2SLS$$

$$(3\text{-}12) \quad \ln E_{V,t} = \underset{(.1282)}{1.4743} \; \frac{1}{G} \sum_{k=1}^{7} e^{-ak} \ln \left(\frac{AE_{t-k+1}}{AO_{t-k+1}} X_{V,t-k+1} \right)$$

$$- \underset{(1.1929)}{4.7774} \qquad \bar{R}^2 = .918$$

$$a = .7715 \qquad\qquad DW = 1.31$$
$$(.4652) \qquad\qquad\qquad NL2SLS$$

$$(3\text{-}13) \quad \ln E_{NU,t} = \underset{(.2109)}{1.5202} \; \frac{1}{Z} \sum_{k=1}^{7} k^{s-1} e^{-k} \ln \left(\frac{AE_{t-k+1}}{AO_{t-k+1}} X_{NU,t-k+1} \right)$$

$$- \underset{(3.2992)}{5.2426} \qquad \bar{R}^2 = .803$$

$$s = 3.6219 \qquad\qquad DW = .52$$
$$(1.8833) \qquad\qquad\qquad NL2SLS$$

$$(3\text{-}14) \quad \ln E_{DER,t} = \underset{(.3833)}{1.5510} \; \frac{1}{Z} \sum_{k=1}^{7} k^{s-1} \, e^{-k} \ln \left(\frac{AE_{t-k+1}}{AO_{t-k+1}} X_{DER,t-k+1} \right)$$

$$- \underset{(2.4934)}{4.7287} \qquad \bar{R}^2 = .548$$

$$s = 3.4408 \qquad\qquad DW = 2.95$$
$$(1.1056) \qquad\qquad\qquad NL2SLS$$

(III) Advertising Expenditure

$$(3\text{-}15) \quad PRE_t = \underset{(.1557)}{.5902} \; \frac{1}{Z} \sum_{k=1}^{7} k^{s-1} e^{-k} (V_{t-k+1} - V_{t-k}) + \underset{(.0328)}{.4494} \, AE_{t-1}$$

$$\bar{R}^2 = .988$$

$$s = 2.7009 \qquad\qquad DW = 2.01$$
$$(1.4683) \qquad\qquad\qquad NL2SLS$$

(IV) Price and Wage Determination

$$(3\text{-}16) \quad PE_t - .5254 PE_{t-1} = \underset{(11.4112)}{38.8120} \left[\frac{V_t - \Pi NS_t}{EX_t} - .5254 \frac{V_{t-1} \Pi NS_{t-1}}{EX_{t-1}} \right]$$

$$+ \underset{(4.3762)}{31.6575} \qquad \bar{R}^2 = .649$$

$$DW = 1.021$$
$$MS2SLS$$

$$(3\text{-}17) \quad PE_{i,t} = \phi_{i,t} PE_t, \; i = NS, CR, D, V, NU \text{ and } DER$$

$$(3\text{-}18) \quad w_{s,t} - .5753 \, w_{s,t-1} = 1.4136 \, [w_{o,t} - .5753 w_{o,t-1}]$$
$$(.1647)$$

$$- \underset{(.7402)}{1.4431} \, [FRS_t - .5753 FRS_{t-1}] + \underset{(.083)}{.1128}$$

$$\bar{R}^2 = .966$$
$$DW = 1.940$$
$$SCAN$$

(3-19) $\quad w_{p,t} = .8118\, w_{s,t} - .3012\, FRP_t + .2606$
$\qquad\qquad\quad (.2137)\qquad (.5031)\qquad\quad (.3140)$

$$\bar{R}^2 = .921$$
$$\text{DW} = 1.916$$
$$\text{2SLS}$$

(3-20) $\quad w_{RD,t} = .7005\, w_{s,t} + .1171$
$\qquad\qquad\quad (.0722)\qquad (.0241)$

$$\bar{R}^2 = .870$$
$$\text{DW} = 1.656$$
$$\text{2SLS}$$

(V) Labor Demand

(3-21) $\quad L_{s,t} - .5897 L_{s,t-1} = .0397\,[EX_t - .5897 EX_{t-1}] + 210.9635$
$\qquad\qquad\qquad\qquad\qquad (.0119)\qquad\qquad\qquad\qquad\qquad (41.8835)$

$$\bar{R}^2 = .848$$
$$\text{DW} = 2.307$$
$$\text{MS2SLS}$$

(3-22) $\quad L_{p,t} = .0339 Ex_t - 311.1904\, \dfrac{w_{p,t-1}}{P_{k,t-1}} + 463.2034$
$\qquad\qquad (.0130)\qquad (482.8105)\qquad\qquad\quad (88.8703)$

$$\bar{R}^2 = .723$$
$$\text{DW} = 1.484$$
$$\text{2SLS}$$

(3-23) $\quad L_{RD,t} = .0103\, EX_t + 111.5623$
$\qquad\qquad\quad (.0017)\qquad\quad (13.4723)$

$$\bar{R}^2 = .725$$
$$\text{DW} = 1.695$$
$$\text{2SLS}$$

(VI) Investment Functions

(3-24) $\quad NIME_t = .0553 \left[\dfrac{1}{G} \sum_{k=1}^{6} k^{s-1} e^{-k} (EX_{t-k+1} - EX_{t-k}) \right]$
$\qquad\qquad\qquad (.0352)$

$\qquad\qquad\quad -.0545 L_{p,t-1} + 44.2853 \qquad \bar{R}^2 = .514$
$\qquad\qquad\qquad (.0542)\qquad\quad (19.4635)\qquad \text{DW} = 1.432$
$\qquad\qquad s = 2.4332 \qquad\qquad\qquad\qquad \text{NL2SLS}$
$\qquad\qquad\quad (1.2252)$

(3-25) $\quad GIBL_t - .6453\, GIBL_{t-1} = .0297 \left\{ \dfrac{1}{G} \sum_{k=1}^{6} k^{s-1} e^{-k} [(EX_{t-k+1} - EX_{t-k}) \right.$
$\qquad\qquad\qquad (.1176)\qquad\qquad\quad (.2066)$

$\qquad\qquad\qquad\qquad\qquad\quad \left. - .6453(EX_{t-k} - EX_{t-k-1})] \right\}$

$\qquad\qquad\qquad\qquad + .0616\,[NKBL_{t-1} - .6453 NKBL_{t-2}] + 71.2103$
$\qquad\qquad\qquad\qquad\quad (.3254)\qquad\qquad\qquad\qquad\qquad\qquad (30.4011)$

$$\bar{R}^2 = .538$$
$\qquad\qquad\qquad s = 2.6500 \qquad\quad \text{DW} = 1.964$
$\qquad\qquad\qquad\quad (1.5205)\qquad\quad \text{NL2SLS}$

(3-26) $\quad NIBL_t = GIBL_t - BLD_t$

$$(3\text{-}27) \quad NKME_t = NIME_t + NKME_{t-1}$$

$$(3\text{-}28) \quad NKBL_t = NIBL_t + NKBL_{t-1}$$

(VII) Research and Development Expenditure

$$(3\text{-}29) \quad RD_t - .7436RD_{t-1} = .0761 \, [V_t - .7436V_{t-1}] - 31.8356$$
$$\qquad\qquad\qquad\quad (.0154) \qquad\qquad\qquad\qquad (36.7710)$$
$$\bar{R}^2 = .980$$
$$\text{DW} = 1.498$$
$$\text{MS2SLS}$$

(VIII) Raw Materials

$$(3\text{-}30) \quad RM_t = .2155 \, EX_t + 179.2333$$
$$\qquad\qquad\quad (.0071) \qquad (52.9826)$$
$$\bar{R}^2 = .985$$
$$\text{DW} = 2.046$$
$$\text{2SLS}$$

(IX) Other Production Costs

$$(3\text{-}31) \quad OPRC_t - .5897OPRC_{t-1} = .0270 \, [V_t - .5897V_{t-1}]$$
$$\qquad\qquad\qquad\qquad\qquad\quad (.0063)$$

$$+11.1628 \qquad \bar{R}^2 = .951$$
$$(19.4592) \quad \text{DW} = 2.225$$
$$\text{2SLS}$$

(X) Other Administrative Costs

$$(3\text{-}32) \quad OAC_t = .0516 \, V_t - 20.0484$$
$$\qquad\qquad\quad (.0035) \qquad (25.2659)$$
$$\bar{R}^2 = .940$$
$$\text{DW} = 2.225$$
$$\text{2SLS}$$

(XI) Interest on Debts

$$(3\text{-}33) \quad ID_t - .4872ID_{t-1} = .0413 \, [DET_t - .4872DET_{t-1}]$$
$$\qquad\qquad\qquad\qquad (.0032)$$
$$\bar{R}^2 = .924$$
$$+42.8960 \qquad \text{DW} = 1.454$$
$$(9.5884) \qquad \text{SCAN}$$

(XII) Depreciation Allowances

$$(3\text{-}34) \quad MED_t = .1753NKME_{t-1} - 11.2101$$
$$\qquad\qquad\quad (.0231) \qquad\qquad (13.8102)$$
$$\bar{R}^2 = .802$$
$$\text{DW} = 1.474$$
$$\text{OLS}$$

(3-35) $BLD_t = .0597\ NKBL_{t-1} - 10.6404$
             $(.0028)$ (3.2204)

$$\bar{R}^2 = .970$$
$$DW = 1.614$$
$$OLS$$

(XIII) Other Revenues

(3-36) $OREV_t = .0076\ V_t + 26.8614$
               $(.0015)$ (11.1441)

$$\bar{R}^2 = .627$$
$$DW = 1.545$$
$$2SLS$$

(XIV) Taxes

(3-37) $TL_t - .3077\,TL_{t-1} = .1164\ [\Pi_{B,t-1} - .3077\Pi_{B,t-2}] + 13.9347$
                          $(.0146)$ (10.5720)
$$\bar{R}^2 = .818$$
$$DW = 1.386$$
$$SCAN$$

(3-38) $TC_t = .3638\Pi_{B,t} + 48.9143$
             $(.0099)$ (11.1187)

$$\bar{R}^2 = .990$$
$$DW = 1.496$$
$$2SLS$$

(XV) Identities

(3-39) $X_{i,t} = x_{i,t}N_t \quad i = NS, CR, DU, V, NU, DER, BC,$ and OT

(3-40) $V_t = \sum_i PE_{i,t}E_{i,t} + \bar{E}_{BC,t} + \bar{E}_{OT,t} \quad i = NS, CR, DU, V, NU,$ and DER

(3-41) $AE_t = \sum_{h=0}^{\eta} (.5506)^h PRE_{t-h}$

(3-42) $EX_t = \dfrac{V_t}{PE_t}$

(3-43) $CP_t = w_{p,t}L_{p,t} + OPRC_t + P_{M,t}RM_t - \Delta INPR_t$

(3-44) $\Pi_{GS,t} = V_t - CP_t - \Delta INCOM_t$

(3-45) $\Pi_{NS,t} = \Pi_{GS,t} - (PRE_t + w_{s,t}L_{s,t} + w_{RD,t}L_{RD,t} + RD_t + TL_t + P_{k,t}MED_t + P_{k,t}BLD_t + OAC_t)$

(3-46) $\Pi_{G,t} = \Pi_{NS,t} + OREV_t$

(3-47) $\Pi_{B,t} = \Pi_{G,t} - ID_t - OTEX_t$

(3-48) $\Pi_{A,t} = \Pi_{B,t} - TC_t$

(3-49) $RE_t = \Pi_{A,t} - DIV_t - EXRM_t$

IV. EVALUATION OF THE BEHAVIORAL EQUATIONS

(4.1) Consumer Demand for Pharmaceutical Products

The demand for pharmaceutical products is based on both additive utility functions and Gompertz curves.

The proposal of additive utility functions by Frisch [9] and Houthakker [15] has been quickly adopted to a number of empirical applications, since one can easily derive explicit consumer demand functions from it. From the maximization of an additive utility function

$$u(x_1, \ldots, x_n) = u_1(x_1) + \cdots + u_n(x_n) \quad (4\text{-}1)$$

subject to budget constraint, Sato [24] derived a system of demand functions of the form

$$d \ln x_i = \eta_i \, d \ln Y/P_a - \sigma \eta_i \, d \ln P_i/P_m, \quad (4\text{-}2)$$
$$i = 1, \ldots, n$$

where
- x_i = the quantity of good i demanded by a consumer
- Y = the money income of the consumer
- P_a = the price index with average share weights, i.e., $d \ln P_a = \sum \theta_i d \ln P_i$, $\theta_i = P_i X_i / Y$
- P_m = the price index with marginal share weights, i.e., $d \ln P_m = \sum \mu_i d \ln P_i$, $\mu_i = P_i (\partial x_i / \partial Y)$
- η_i = the income elasticity of demand for good i
- σ = overall average elasticity of substitution ($1/\sigma$ is equal to the income elasticity of the marginal utility of income).

(4-2) suggests double-log demand functions.[3]

$$\ln x_i = \eta_i \ln Y/P_a - \sigma \eta_i \ln P_i/P_m + \gamma_i, \quad (4\text{-}3)$$
$$i = 1, \ldots, n$$

[3] In order to integrate (4-2) to derive (4-3), one has to assume constant coefficients, and as Sato [23] says this is indeed a stringent assumption, but (4-3) is usually adopted in empirical studies as an approximation.

and we shall use (4-3) in estimating the demand functions for pharmaceutical products.

As we noted in Section II, the Japanese pharmaceutical industry is characterized by fast growth. When industry is growing fast, a major concern is to identify when the pace of fast growth will slow down. A mathematical function to express the life cycle of such growth may take the form of a logistic curve. The usual logistic curve is given by

$$x_i = \frac{x_i^*}{1 + me^{-\alpha t}} \quad (4\text{-}4)$$

while the Gompertz curve is given by

$$x_i = x_i^* a^{b^t}, \quad 0 < b < 1 \quad (4\text{-}5)$$

where x_i^* is the expected demand for commodity i. The differentiation of (4-4) and (4-5) respectively yield

$$\frac{dx_i}{dt} = \alpha x_i \left(1 - \frac{x_i}{x_i^*}\right) \quad (4\text{-}6)$$

$$\frac{d \ln x_i}{dt} = \frac{1}{x_i} \frac{dx_i}{dt} = -\ln b(\ln x_i^* - x_i) \quad (4\text{-}7)$$
$$= \beta(\ln x_i^* - \ln x_i)$$

where $\beta = -\ln b$. This may be called a reaction coefficient.

The usual logistic curve (4-4) has the property of being symmetric around the point of inflection, while the Gompertz curve does not. Which curve should be adopted is an empirical question. After preliminary examination we found that our data tend to support the Gompertz curve.[4] Then following Chow [3] (4-7) may be approximated in

[4] (4-6) and (4-7) may be approximated in discrete form by putting $dx_i = \Delta x_{i,t}$ and $dt = \Delta t$:

$$\frac{\Delta x_{i,t}}{x_{i,t}} = \alpha - \frac{\alpha}{x^*} x_{i,t-1} \quad (4\text{-}6)'$$

and (4-7)' $\Delta \ln x_{i,t} = \beta_i \ln x_{i,t}^* - \beta_i \ln x_{i,t-1}$
Then given data we may plot $\Delta x_{i,t}/x_{i,t}$ against $x_{i,t-1}$ and $\Delta \ln x_{i,t}$ against $\ln x_{i,t-1}$ and see which may fit better into a linear function. Our data suggest the choice of the Gompertz curve over the logistic curve.

discrete form

$$\ln x_{i,t} - \ln x_{i,t-1} \qquad (4\text{-}8)$$
$$= \beta_i(\ln x_{i,t}^* - \ln x_{i,t-1})$$

or

$$\ln x_{i,t} = \beta_i \sum_{k=0}^{m_i-1} (1 - \beta_i)^k \ln x_{i,t-k}^* \quad (4\text{-}8)'$$
$$+ (1 - \beta_i)^{m_i} \ln x_{i,t-m_i}$$
$$= \beta_i \sum_{k=0}^{m_i-1} (1 - \beta_i)^k L^k \ln x_{i,t}^*$$
$$+ (1 - \beta_i)^{m_i} \ln x^{i,t-m_i}$$

where $x_{i,t-m_i}$ is the initial value of x_i, and L is the distributed lag operator (or the backward shift operator)[5] and as $m_i \rightarrow \infty$, we will have

$$\ln x_{i,t} = \frac{\beta_i}{1 - (1 - \beta_i)L} \ln x_{i,t}^* \qquad (4\text{-}9)$$
$$= \frac{\Phi(L)}{\Psi(L)} \ln x_{i,t}^* = B(L) \ln x_{i,t}^*$$

provided that $|\beta_i| < 1$ and $|(1 - \beta_i)L| < 1$, and $\Phi(L) = \beta_i$, $\Psi(L) = 1 - (1 - \beta_i)L$.
The transform function $B(L)$ in (4-9) is the Koyck lag with the moving average operator $\Phi(L) = \beta_i$, and the autoregressive operator $\Psi(L) = 1 - (l - \beta_i)L$. In many empirical studies the Koyck lag is estimated by premultiplying (4-9) by the autoregressive operator $\Psi(L)$ and then rearranging terms. However, it is well known that this transformation generates an autocorrelated disturbance term and the ordinary least squares (or for that matter any simultaneous estimation procedure which does not take care of autocorrelated error terms) estimates will generally be inconsistent.

[5] The word *distributed lag operator* is the term used in econometrics, whereas *backward shift operator* is used in electrical engineering and statistical time series analysis. This operator forms an algebraic space of a linear operator and in the frequency domain (i.e., Fourier transform) we have $L = \exp(-i2\pi f\Delta)$, where Δ is the time interval. An interested reader should consult [2] or [4]. $B(L)$ in (2-9) is called the transfer function or, in its Fourier transform, generalized frequency function.

Faced with this problem, we may directly estimate $B(L)$ from (4-8)'. If m_i is sufficiently large, the last term of (4-8)' may be treated as constant. Then our basic demand function to be estimated is given by

$$\ln x_{i,t} = B(L) \ln x_{i,t}^* + \gamma_{o,t} + u_{i,t} \quad (4\text{-}10)$$

where $B(L) = \sum_{k=0}^{m_i-1} \beta_{i,k} L^k$, with $\beta_{i,k} = \beta_i(1-\beta_i)^k$, $\gamma_{o,i} = (1 - \beta_i)^{m_i} \ln x_{i,t-m_i}$, and $u_{i,t}$ is the disturbance term.

The coefficients of L^k in the polynomial $B(L)$ in (4-10), $\beta_{i,k}$, will be geometrically declining as the power k increases. One empirical question one might ask is whether the given data will indeed imply the Koyck lag. To answer this question $B(L)$ in (4-10) is represented in more general form by the gamma distributed lags proposed in [29], $\{\beta_{i,k} = k^{s_i-1} e^{-k}\}$, where s_i is an unknown parameter to be estimated, and for this purpose we use the nonlinear least squares estimation technique [18].[6]

If preliminary investigation indicates that the coefficient of L^k indeed declines as the Koyck lag indicates, then the gamma distributed lags, $\{k^{s_i-1} e^{-k}\}$ are replaced by $\{e^{-a_i k}\}$, which can be shown to be the Koyck lag, and the equation is re-estimated with this particular form of the gamma distributed lag.

The Gompertz curve formulation (4-8) may be interpreted as the usual adaptive adjustment process in log-linear form, and we may represent the expected demand, $x_{i,t}^*$ by (4-3). Then from (4-3) and (4-10) we will obtain

$$\ln x_{i,t} = \eta_i B(L)(\ln Y_t/P_{a,t} \qquad (4\text{-}10)'$$
$$- \sigma \ln P_{i,t}/P_{m,t}) + \gamma_{i,o}' + u_{i,t}$$

where $\gamma_{i,o}'$ is the new constant term. Since the price index with marginal weighting, P_m, is virtually impossible to obtain, we will represent P_m by the price index with average

[6] The consistency of the nonlinear least squares estimator under certain regularity conditions is proven by Hartley and Booker [14]. To estimate the gamma distributed lags it is necessary to give a priori the value of m_i, i.e., the length of lags. We allowed as great a number of lags as possible with our data.

weighting, P_a. Rather than estimating the over-all average elasticity of substitution σ from (4-10)', we will use the estimate of the Japanese Economic Planning Agency given in Sato [23], which is $\hat{\sigma} = .687$.[7]

The demand equation (4-10)' is estimated for the following eight product groups on a per capita basis: (i) agents affecting the nervous system and sensory organs; (ii) cardiovascular agents and agents affecting respiratory organs; (iii) agents affecting digestive organs and agents for uro-genital and anal organs; (iv) vitamin preparations; (v) nutrients and tonics; (vi) dermatological agents; (vii) chemotherapeutics and antibiotic preparations, and (viii) miscellaneous pharmaceutical products. This classification conforms to the practice in the industry. For the income variable, $Y_t/P_{a,t}$, we shall use per capita real personal consumption and medicare expenditure. P_a is represented by the price index of consumer expenditure.

As shown in the preceding paragraphs, consumer demand for pharmaceutical products is estimated on the basis of the additive utility function and the Gompertz curve. From this, interesting empirical results arise. They are (i) income elasticities, η_i; (ii) price elasticities $\sigma\eta_i$;[8] and (iii) the time response form of distributed lags. These results are included in the estimated equations from (3-1) to (3-8) and are summarized in Tables 3 and 4.

Table 3 indicates that except for dermatological agents, x_{DER}, and miscellaneous products, x_{OT}, the estimated income elasticities, $\hat{\eta}_i$, range from 1.18 to 2.01, i.e., the estimated income elasticities are above unity.[9]

The estimated income elasticity of dermatological agents, $\hat{\eta}_{DER}$, is .48. This may be the result of changes in the standard of living as the Japanese economy has expanded: for example, frost bite used to be a common phenomenon during the winter, but as diet and heating facilities improved it has become rare except in some rural villages.

On examining Table 4 to see whether the Koyck lags as indicated by (4-10) are valid or not, we find that in seven out of eight groups the Koyck lags indeed are appropriate.[10] The exception is group II, cardiovascular agents and agents affecting respiratory organs, whose time response is well distributed over long periods: the sum of the coefficients after eight periods amounts to .7283. On the other hand, the following three products have a spontaneous time response: (i) vitamin preparations; (ii) nutrients and tonics; and (iii) dermatological agents.

To estimate the gamma distributed lags one needs to specify the length of lags m in $\{\sum_{k=1}^{m} k^{s-1}e^{-k}\}$. In this study we first used the maximum length of lags which were available from our data. When the estimated length of lags was shorter than the maximum length of lags, we cut the length shorter at the point where the lag coefficients were in the neighborhood of zero and we reestimated the equation.[11] The maximum length of

---

[7] σ can be estimated directly from (4-10)'. However, our data indicate a strong multicollinearity between $Y_t/P_{a,t}$ and $P_{i,t}/P_{a,t}$, thus making the estimation difficult. This multicollinearity is due to the fact that while the real expenditure of the consumer has grown steadily, the price index of pharmaceutical product i, $P_{i,t}$, relative to the price index of consumer expenditure, $P_{a,t}$ has tended to decline.

[8] Sato [23] calls $\sigma\eta_i$ "own-price" elasticities of demand.

[9] One might wish to compare these estimated income elasticities of pharmaceutical products with income elasticities of other consumer goods in Japan. The only source we have at hand is Tsujimura's work [28] reported in [24]. His income elasticity estimates for

1960 are for more aggregated expenditure categories. Among the 16 categories he studied, only five register income elasticities above unity, and they are cereals, rent, furniture and household equipment, recreation and entertainment, and education and miscellaneous expenses. The estimated income elasticity of the last item, under which pharmaceutical products are classified, is 1.07.

[10] In the case of miscellaneous products the coefficients decline as a Koyck type lag indicates. However, the Koyck lag formulation with $\{e^{-ak}\}$ yielded much poorer results than with $\{k^{s-1}e^{-k}\}$, judged by such rough measures as estimated standard errors and the coefficient of determination. Hence, the latter form was retained.

[11] The strategy of choosing m in $\{k^{s-1}e^{-k}\}$ is discussed in [29]. There it is suggested that one may choose m such that the estimated variance of the equation is minimized. This strategy tends to be costly because it requires examination of the range of m, and furthermore the experiment in [29] indicates that the estimated coefficients do not vary much over the different

TABLE 3 Estimates of Income Elasticities ($\hat{\eta}_i$) and "Own-price" Elasticities ($\hat{\sigma}\hat{\eta}_i$) of Japanese Pharmaceutical Products

Per Capita Demand Product Groups	Income Elasticities ($\hat{\eta}_i$)	"Own-price" Elasticities ($\hat{\sigma}\hat{\eta}_i$) with $\hat{\sigma}$ = .687
1. Agents affecting the nervous system and sensory organs, x_{NS}	1.50	−1.03
2. Cardiovascular agents and agents affecting respiratory organs, x_{CR}	2.01	−1.38
3. Agents affecting digestive organs and agents for uro-genital and anal organs, x_{DU}	1.39	−.95
4. Vitamin preparations, x_V	1.18	−.81
5. Nutrients and tonics, x_{NU}	1.67	−1.15
6. Dermatological agents, x_{DER}	.48	−.33
7. Chemotherapeutics and antibiotic preparations, x_{BC}	1.28	−.88
8. Miscellaneous products, x_{OT}	.50	−.34

TABLE 4 Time Response Form of Distributed Lags in Industrial Demand Equations

Time Lags	x_{NS} $\{e^{-ak}\}$ a = 2.0927	x_{CR} $\{k^{s-1}e^{-k}\}$ s = 7.1389	x_{DU} $\{e^{-ak}\}$ a = .6635	x_V $\{e^{-ak}\}$ a = 15.029	x_{NU} $\{e^{-ak}\}$ a = 14.4689	x_{DER} $\{e^{-ak}\}$ a = 13.0273	x_{BC} $\{e^{-ak}\}$ a = 2.075	x_{OT} $\{k^{s-1}e^{-k}\}$ s = 2.0757
0	.8766	.0004	.4850	1.0	1.0	1.0	.8744	.3814
1	.1082	.0102	.2498	0	0	0	.1098	.2957
2	.0134	.0452	.1287				.0139	.1683
3	.0016	.0973	.0663				.0017	.0844
4	.0002	.1408	.0341				.0002	.0395
5	0	.1586	.0176				0	.0177
6		.1503	.0091					.0077
7		.1255	.0047					.0033
Sum of coefficients above	1.0	.7283	.9953	1.0	1.0	1.0	1.0	.9980

lags available from our data for the industrial demand equations was 15.

(4.2) Market Share Determination

Whether a firm tries to expand its market share or not depends upon the firm's behavioral goal. As noted earlier, the main objective of the Eisai Company (and of many Japanese firms) is the maximization of present valued sales, subject to a target level of the present value of profit.

If the demand for the industry as a whole

is given then sales maximization may be interpreted as maximization of the market share, provided that the firm is a price taker. Such is the case with the Japanese drug companies as discussed in Section II. Consequently, the variables which the company controls in order to increase its market share are advertising expenditure and research and development (R & D) expenditure. The relationship between the R & D expenditure and the development of new products is now receiving more attention, and so it should. As much as we would like to explore this further, the available data on R & D activities of the firm we investigated are too rough to enable thorough analysis. Thus, we will focus here on the relationship between market share and advertising expenditure. For this purpose, we formulate

---

values of m. Hence in this study we followed the method explained above. For (3-4), (3-5), and (3-6), however, we retained the lags up to the second period although the estimated Koyck type lag coefficients, a, were around 13.03 to 15.03, indicating instantaneous reactions.

a simple hypothesis

$$E_{i,t}^e = \left(\frac{AE_t}{AO_t}X_{i,t}\right)^{\mu_i}{}^{12} \qquad (4\text{-}11)$$

$$\ln E_{i,t} - \ln E_{i,t-1} \qquad (4\text{-}12)$$
$$= \theta_i(\ln E_{i,t}^e - \ln E_{i,t-1})^{13}$$

where

$X_{i,t}$ = industrial demand for the i-th product at time t

$E_{i,t}^e$ = expected demand for the i-th product of Eisai at time t

$E_{i,t}$ = actual demand for the i-th product of Eisai at time t

AE_t = net stock of effects of current and past advertising expenditure, or *goodwill*, of Eisai at time t

AO_t = net stock of effects of current and past advertising expenditure, or *goodwill*, of companies other than Eisai at time t.

From (4-11) and (4-12) we will obtain

$$\ln E_{i,t} = \theta_i \sum_{k=0}^{n_i-1}(1-\theta_i)^k \ln \frac{AE_{t-k}}{AO_{t-k}}X_{i,t-k} \quad (4\text{-}13)$$
$$+ (1-\theta_i)^{n_i} \ln E_{i,t-n_i} + \gamma_i$$

where γ_i is a constant term containing $(1-\theta_i)$ and μ_i. If n_i is sufficiently large, or if $(1-\theta_i)$ is sufficiently small, then treating the term $(1-\theta_i)^{n_i} \ln E_{i,t-n_i}$ as zero may not incur much error. (4-13) indicates again the Koyck lag. Here, however, we will examine whether the

---

[12] One may wonder whether the two variables, AE_t and AO_t in (4-11) should be replaced by the advertising expenditure for a particular product i, $AE_{i,t}$ and $AO_{i\ t}$. We have information on $AE_{i,t}$ but not on $AO_{i\ t}$. However, the way advertising expenditure is divided into product categories tends to be more for accounting convenience than for actual functional classification. Furthermore, advertising expenditure by the firm tends to have a spill-over effect in the sense that even if the advertisement is on product i, it may serve to promote any other product of the company.
[13] (4-12) may imply the Gompertz curve formulation as in (4-8). The reason we chose the logarithmic adjustment process is that (4-11) implies constant elasticity of demand with respect to advertising expenditure, and constant elasticity is assumed in deriving the optimal advertising policy.

Koyck lag coefficients are indeed valid or not by adopting the same procedure as we discussed in the estimation of the industrial demand functions; thus, the equation to be estimated becomes

$$\ln E_{i,t} = C(L) \ln \frac{AE_t}{AO_t}X_{i,t} + \gamma_i + e_{it} \quad (4\text{-}13)'$$

where e_{it} is the disturbance term, and the transform function $C(L)$ is given by the gamma distributed lags:

$$C(L) = \sum_{k=1}^{n_i+1} k^{s_i-1}e^{-k}L^{k-1}$$

or

$$C(L) = \sum_{k=1}^{n_i+1} e^{-\alpha_i k}L^{k-1}$$

(4-13)' will be estimated for the following six product groups: (i) agents affecting the nervous system and sensory organs; (ii) cardiovascular agents and agents affecting respiratory organs; (iii) agents affecting digestive organs and agents for uro-genital and anal organs; (iv) vitamin preparations; (v) nutrients and tonics; and (vi) dermatological agents. We will treat the two remaining product groups as exogenous variables, since the Eisai Company just began producing chemotherapeutics and antibiotics (group vii) in the second half of 1967, and since miscellaneous products (group viii) represent at most 3 percent of the total sales of the company. For the estimation of (4-13)' we will use the nonlinear two-stage least squares used in [30].

(4.3) Advertising Expenditure

The goal of the Eisai Company is to maximize the present value of sales, subject to a target level of the present valued profit. Under this proposition let us derive an optimal advertising policy as follows. First we start with the following three assumptions.

(1) The firm's net stock of effects of current and past advertising expenditure, *good-*

will, obeys the formula

$$\dot{A} + \delta A = a, \text{ or} \qquad (4\text{-}14)$$

$$g = \dot{A} + \delta A - a = 0$$

where $\dot{A} = \dfrac{dA}{dt}$, a is current advertising

expenditure and δ is the depreciation rate of *goodwill*.

(2) The firm's market share function is given by

$$m = m(A, z) \qquad (4\text{-}15)$$

where z is any other variable (it can be a vector) which the firm does not control, e.g., AO. The industrial demand, Q, is given by the consumer's choice:

$$Q = Q(Y_d/P_a, \ P/P_a) \qquad (4\text{-}16)$$

where Y_d/P_a, is per capita real income and P_a is the price index of consumer expenditure. Then the firm's demand, q, is

$$q = mQ = q(A, P, z_1) \qquad (4\text{-}17)$$

where z_1 is again a variable exogenous to the firm and includes P_a.

(3) Given the cost function

$$C = C(q) \qquad (4\text{-}18)$$

the profit, Π, is given by

$$\Pi = Pq - C(q) - a = Pq(A, z_1)$$
$$- C(q) - a = R(P, A, z_1) - a$$

where P is the price of q. Then the minimum level of the present valued profit to be maintained, Π^*, may be given by

$$\Pi^* = \int_0^\infty e^{-rt}\{P \cdot q(A, P, z_1) \qquad (4\text{-}19)$$
$$- C(q) - a\} \, dt = \int_0^\infty \Psi \, dt$$

where r is the discount rate.

Our problem is now stated in the following Lemma.

Lemma 1: Under the assumptions (1), (2), and (3) above and given the initial value $A(O) = A_o$, the time path of A which maximizes

$$\int_0^\infty e^{-rt} P \cdot q(A, P, z_1) \, dt = \int_0^\infty \Phi \, dt \qquad (4\text{-}20)$$

subject to the constraints (4-14) and (4-19) is given by

$$A = \frac{\omega}{(\xi - 1)(\delta + r)} C'q$$

where

$$\xi = \frac{\partial q}{\partial P}\frac{P}{q}; \ \ \omega = \frac{\partial q}{\partial A}\frac{A}{q}; \text{ and } C' = \frac{\partial C}{\partial q}.$$

Proof: This is an isoperimetric problem, let

$$H(A, P, \mu, \lambda) = \int_0^\infty \{\Phi - \mu\Psi - \lambda(t)g\} \, dt$$

$$= \int_0^\infty F \, dt$$

then the necessary conditions for a maximum are given by the following Euler equations

$$F_A - \frac{d}{dt}F_{\dot{A}} = 0 \qquad (4\text{-}20)'$$

$$F_a - \frac{d}{dt}F_{\dot{a}} = 0 \qquad (4\text{-}21)$$

$$F_p - \frac{d}{dt}F_{\dot{p}} = 0 \qquad (4\text{-}22)$$

(4-20), (4-21), and (4-22) become

$$F_A - \frac{d}{dt}F_{\dot{A}} = e^{-rt}p\frac{\partial q}{\partial A} \qquad (4\text{-}23)$$

$$- \mu e^{-rt}\left(P - \frac{\partial C}{\partial q}\right)\frac{\partial q}{\partial A}$$

$$- \delta\lambda(t) + \frac{d}{dt}\lambda(t) = 0$$

$$F_a - \frac{d}{dt}F_a = -\mu e^{-rt} + \lambda(t) \qquad (4\text{-}24)$$

$$= 0$$

$$F_p - \frac{d}{dt}F_p = e^{-rt}\left\{ q + P\frac{\partial q}{\partial P} - \mu \right. \qquad (4\text{-}25)$$

$$\times \left. \left(q + P\frac{\partial q}{\partial P} - \frac{\partial C}{\partial q}\frac{\partial q}{\partial P} \right) \right\} = 0$$

From (4-24) we obtain

$$\lambda(t) = \mu e^{-rt}, \text{ and } \frac{d}{dt}\lambda(t) \qquad (4\text{-}26)$$

$$= -r\mu e^{-rt}$$

Substituting (4-26) into (4-23) and rearranging the terms we have

$$P\frac{\partial q}{\partial A} - \mu\left(P - \frac{\partial C}{\partial q} \right)\frac{\partial q}{\partial A} - \delta\mu + r\mu = 0$$

or

$$\mu = \frac{P\dfrac{\partial q}{\partial A}}{(P - C')\dfrac{\partial q}{\partial A} - (\delta + r)} \qquad (4\text{-}27)$$

where $C' = \dfrac{\partial C}{\partial q}$. On the other hand, from (4-25) we obtain

$$\mu = \frac{q(1 + \xi)}{q(1 + \xi) - C'\dfrac{\partial q}{\partial P}} \qquad (4\text{-}28)$$

where $\xi = \dfrac{\partial q}{\partial P}\dfrac{P}{q}$. Equating (4-27) to (4-28) and rearranging the terms we get

$$A = \frac{\omega}{(\xi - 1)(\delta + r)}C'q = k_1 C'q \qquad (4\text{-}29)$$

where $\omega = \dfrac{\partial q}{\partial A}\dfrac{A}{q}$, and $k_1 = \dfrac{\omega}{(\xi - 1)(\delta + r)}$

(4-29) gives the optimal advertising policy. Whether or not the proportional factor k_1 stays constant will depend on whether ω, ξ, δ, and r are constant. Our demand function (4-2) implies a constant price elasticity

($\xi = -\sigma\eta_i$), and we have formulated (4-11) and (4-12) to conform to the constant elasticity with respect to *goodwill*, ω.

In actuality the optimal condition (4-29) may only be attained with some adjustment over time, and thus we apply Jorgenson's investment function [16] as follows. (4-24) indicates that current advertising expenditure, a, consists of net *goodwill* investment, A, and replacement, δA. Now suppose the net *goodwill* investment in a discrete time period, NA_t, is given by

$$NA_t = \tau(L)(A_t^* - A_{t-1}^*) \qquad (4\text{-}30)$$

where $\tau(L)$ is the transform function and A_t^* is the expected *goodwill* at time t. Then the current advertising expenditure, PRE_t, will be given by

$$PRE_t = NA_t + \delta AE_{t-1} \qquad (4\text{-}31)$$

$$= \tau(L)(A_t^* - A_{t-1}^*) + \delta AE_{t-1}$$

and if we treat (4-29) as representing the expected net stock of *goodwill*, then (4-31) now becomes

$$PRE_t = k_1\tau(L)(C_t'q_t - C_{t-1}'q_{t-1}) \qquad (4\text{-}32)$$

$$+ \delta AE_{t-1}.$$

We do not have the marginal cost estimate, C_t', so let us represent $C_t'q_t$ by the net sales value, V_t. This is equal to the assumption that the marginal cost is proportional to the price. AE_{t-1} in (4-32) is the net stock of *goodwill*, and given the identity

$$AE_t = NA_t + \delta AE_{t-1}$$

and (4-31), we will obtain

$$AE_t = PRE_t + (1 - \delta)AE_{t-1} \qquad (4\text{-}33)$$

$$= \sum_{\kappa=0}^{l}(1 - \delta)^\kappa PRE_{t-k}$$

$$+ (1 - \delta)^l AE_{t-l}.$$

If δ is sufficiently large or if l is large, we may treat the second term as zero. Substituting (4-33) into (4-32) and adding the disturbance term, ϵ_t, we obtain

$$PRE_t = k_1\tau(L)(V_t - V_{t-1}) \qquad (4\text{-}34)$$
$$+ \delta\left(\sum_{k=0}^{l}(1-\delta)^k PRE_{t-k-1}\right).$$

It is better to have a large integer value for l on the summation sign of the second term above, but this is constrained by the availability of data, and in our empirical estimation we have to set l equal to 7. As in the demand and market share equations given earlier, let us represent the coefficients of L^k in the transform function, $\tau(L)$, by the gamma distributed lag coefficients, $\{k^{s-1}e^{-k}\}$. For estimating the market share equations (4-13) and advertising expenditure (4-34) we used nonlinear two-stage least squares.[14]

The nonlinear estimation allows us to estimate δ, which enters in the equation as the 8th order polynomial. The estimated $\hat{\delta}$ is given in (3-15) as .4494. This indicates that approximately 45 percent of *goodwill* depreciates in one period (i.e., half a year), indicating a high rate of depreciation.

We used this estimate of the depreciation rate to derive the *goodwill* of competitors, AO_t, and hence it is given as

$$AO_t = \sum_{k=0}^{7}(.5506)^k PRO_{t-k}$$

where PRO_t is competitors' advertising expenditure at time t. To obtain some measure of real advertising expenditure, we deflated the current advertising expenditure by the price index of consumer services. This price index is chosen because it reflects the range of advertising activities of the pharmaceutical industry, i.e., from advertising in the mass media to expense account entertaining.

(4.4) Price Determination

Over the years the wholesale prices of pharmaceutical products in Japan have been decreasing, whereas the general wholesale price index and especially the consumer

price index has been rising. Table 5 demonstrates this trend.

TABLE 5 Price Index Movement, 1967–1969 (1967 = 100)

Year	Wholesale Price of Pharmaceutical Products	General Wholesale Price	General Consumer Price
1967	100.0	100.0	100.0
1968	99.3	100.2	102.5
1969	98.3	101.7	105.7

Source: Bank of Japan, *Economic Statistics Annual*, 1969, pp. 255–258.

In addition to this general decrease in wholesale prices, the "effective price" (or the price per unit allowing for the bonus supply practice) tends to be reduced by 20 to 50 percent in three years, the rate of reduction depending on each product and the competition it faces.[15] To prevent this price reduction, a pharmaceutical firm frequently changes some characteristics of the product such as packaging design, form of dosage (e.g., tablets or capsules, or composition of ingredients of the product), and the firm sells it as a "new" product. This is a conscious effort by the firm to prevent a product from following the general trend of price decline.

In view of this, most of the price index formulae currently used in Japan and elsewhere may tend to overestimate the price reduction of pharmaceutical products, since the index formulae follow the weights given by a fixed bundle of commodities. If the characteristics of the product can be easily identified in terms of quantitative information or dummies, one may construct a price index following the works of Griliches [13], Dhrymes [7], and Kravis [17]. However, unlike cars or refrigerators, characteristics of drugs cannot be easily identified. If one tries to

---

[11] The statistical properties of this procedure such as consistency are not yet known.

[15] The "effective price" level allowing for discounts resulting from price-cutting, rebate, and bonus supply of quantity should be computed rather than the medicare agency price level which we used in our model merely for a lack of more appropriate data. Then, the effective price can be properly analyzed in its relation to sales promotion expenditure.

identify them then one is risking a distortion (or, an over-or under-estimation) of the price movement.

A solution one finds may be simple but time consuming: to change the basket of commodities frequently to cope with the changes in the characteristics of the products.[16] We constructed the price indices of Eisai products, $PE_{i,t}$, by changing the bundle of commodities for the weights whenever substantial changes in the characteristics of the commodities occurred. This method compared to a Laspeyres type price index, which keeps the same bundle of commodities, tended to lessen the price reduction of the pharmaceutical products.

The prices of ethical drugs in Japan are determined by the medicare points each product can get from the Medicare Agency. Medicare points are based on equivalent products which are competing in the market. The prices of pharmaceutical products sold over the counter are influenced by the prices of their counterparts in ethical drugs and their competitors. In view of this practice, the prices of Eisai products may as well be treated exogenously. However, just as an illustration to check the mark-up hypothesis, we made the general price level of Eisai products a function of total unit cost. Once the general level is determined as a mark-up guideline, the price of each product may be determined by the sales strategy of the company which has to take into account the strategies of its rivals.

(4.5) Wage Determination

The Japanese employment and wage system is characterized by life-time employment and uniform pay scale according to seniority, age, and sex. The wage rate is determined by the average wage rate of other companies. The employees union, on the other hand, uses the highest rate in the industry as the target of its salary increase demands. Thus, there exists a strong pattern setting and

pattern following as far as wage determination goes.[17] We may formulate the wage rate equation as

$$w_{s,t} = b_1 + b_1 w_{o,t} + b_3 FRS_t$$

where

$w_{s,t}$ = the average annual wage rate of the sales employees of Eisai at time t

$w_{o,t}$ = the average annual wage rate of pharmaceutical companies except Eisai, at time t

FRS_t = the ratio of female to the total sales employees at time t.

In the model the wage rate of sales employees, $w_{o,t}$, is treated as the basis to determine the wage rates of production employees and research employees, $w_{p,t}$ and $w_{RD,t}$, respectively. In determining the wage rate of production workers, $w_{p,t}$, the ratio of female to the total production workers, FRS_t, is used since there is a wage differential between male and female workers.

(4.6) Labor Demand

The demand for sales employees, $L_{s,t}$, is made a function of output, EX_t. It is not clear whether there exists a clear-cut substitution between sales employees and capital. In some cases office machines and the increasing use of cars for sales activities may contribute to the substitution of capital for labor in the sense that the sales area per sales promoter may be widened by the use of a car. However, in the face of the rapid expansion of the company, this phenomenon, if any, is hard to put into a quantitative relationship, and the management policy on employment has not yet been too conscious of the substitution.

The production workers, $L_{p,t}$, on the other hand, will be more susceptible to the substitution of capital for labor, and for this reason the lagged relative price variable, $w_{p,t-1}/P_{k,t-1}$, is put into the equation. The estimated standard error of this variable is not significant, but the sign of the coefficient was cor-

---

[16] The Price Statistics Review Committee of the NBER, New York, presents this approach as a recommendation. See *The Price Statistics of the Federal Government* (New York: NBER, 1961), pp. 48–39.

[17] Tsurumi, Y., [32].

rect, indicating the substitution of capital for labor at work. The demand for employees in research and development, $L_{RD,t}$, is determined in the model by the output, EX_t. This category of employment will be least subject to the substitution of capital for labor. And this demand is strategically determined by the policy of the firm. The independent variable, EX_t, indicates the ability of the firm to sustain the required level of R & D activity.

(4.7) Investment Functions

Capital goods in the model are divided into two categories—machinery and equipment, ME_t, and buildings, BLD_t. The investment function follows the Jorgenson type formulation [16]. Instead of Jorgenson's Cobb-Douglas production function, however, we use a fixed coefficient production process. Investment and capital figures are taken from the balance sheet statement, and thus they suffer from the usual difficulties of measuring "capital stock" such as the problem of whether the figures reflect real capital equipment in use.

It will be better to estimate net investment rather than gross investment, and this we have done in estimation of investment of machinery and equipment. However, in the case of buildings, gross investment, $GIBL_t$, is estimated. This is due to the fact that the net investment figures were derived as the difference between gross investment and depreciation allowances. Depreciation allowances often vary because the firm can "accelerate" or "decelerate" the depreciation process within the boundary of tax laws. The net investment for construction and buildings was sometimes negative due to the fact that in some periods depreciation allowances were large compared to gross investment. Capital goods such as buildings have a long life span, and the depreciation policy, that is, the decision of when to replace an old facility may be altered or postponed depending upon business conditions, and the policy of the firm which may "window dress" depreciation to make its income statement look neat. Hence, new investment as

defined above may be subject to unduly irregular factors. For this reason the gross investment of construction and buildings was estimated rather than the net investment, and in turn the latter was defined to be the difference between the former and depreciation allowances.

Investment in machinery and equipment will reflect substitution of capital for production workers, and hence, the one period-lagged production employment, L_p, is included in the equation.

(4.8) Research and Development Expenditure and Other Equations

Here, we will discuss the rest of the behavioral equations in the model. Research and development expenditure, RD_t, is becoming more and more important in the Japanese pharmaceutical industry.

In the estimated model, R & D expenditure is made a function of net sales. In the simulation exercises, however, R & D expenditure may be treated as a policy variable. At more micro levels than our model, one should examine the relationship between R & D expenditure and the development and marketing of a new product. In particular, the marketing spill-over that the new product provides for standard products of the firm will make an interesting study.

Other equations are self-explanatory. For example, interest on debts are made a function of the level of debts. How one manages the level of debts is a matter of corporate financing, and with a proper mix of internal and external financing, one may make an effort to obtain some optimal cost of capital for the firm. If this is the case, interest on debts may be made a policy variable.

State and local taxes, TL_t, are levied on profits before taxes, but they can be claimed as a tax deductible expense in the next period. Hence, they are made a function of profits before taxes of the previous period.

Dividend payments, DIV_t, are exogenous to the model, since in the Japanese practice of dividend payments a fixed percentage (generally 20 percent) of the par value of a common share is paid out as dividends.

TABLE 6   A Set of Some of the Exogenous Variables Used for the Forecasting Exercises

	1970.I	1970.II	1971.I	1971.II	1972.I	1972.II	1973.I	1973.II	1974.I
N	103488	104006	104524	105041	105559	106077	106594	107112	107630
CE	27076	27891	28706	29521	30336	31151	31966	32781	33596
MED	1192	1247	1302	1357	1412	1467	1522	1577	1632
PRO	45086	46529	48018	49554	51140	52776	54465	56208	58007
W_o	.5467	.5659	.5851	.6043	.6235	.6427	.6619	.6811	.7003
P_k	110.2	111.1	112.0	112.8	113.7	114.5	115.4	116.3	117.1
$\Delta INPR$	502	530	559	587	616	643	672	701	729
$OTEX$	77.4	79.6	81.9	84.2	86.5	88.8	91.1	93.4	95.7

Assumptions
1. Population, N, grows according to the time trend of 1959.I–1968.II.
2. Consumer expenditure in billions of 1965 yen, CE, grows according to the time trend of 1959.I–1968.II.
3. Medicare expenditure, MED, grows according to the time trend of 1959.I–1968.II.
4. Competitors' advertising expenditure, PRO, grows at 3.2 percent per half a year (average of 1959.I–1968.II growth rates).
5. The relative prices, P_i/P_d, in the industrial demand equations (3-1)–(3-8) stay at the same level as in 1969.II.
6. The prices of Eisai Products, PE_t, stay at the same level as in 1969.II.
7. The rate of growth of sales of chemotherapeutics and antibiotics of the Eisai Company is the same as that of the industry.
8. The sale of miscellaneous products of the Eisai Company stays at the same level as in 1969.II.
9. The wage level of other companies, W_0, follows the time trend of the period from 1959.I to 1968.II. So do a change of inventories of production materials, $\Delta INPR$, and other miscellaneous expenses, $OTEX$.
10. For the simulation period we set dividend payments, $DIV = 180$; the remuneration to the executives, $EXRM = 10$; change in inventories of office and distribution materials, $\Delta INCOM = 100$; the ratio of female sales employees to all sales employees, $FRS = .2769$; the ratio of female production workers to all production workers, $FRP = .4556$.

Hence, they are independent of the level of profits.

V. SIMULATION EXPERIMENTS: COMPETITORS' REACTION TO THE FIRM'S ADVERTISING POLICY

The model given in Section III was solved by a modified Siedel method. First, a sample period simulation was made to check whether the model explains the actual values of the endogenous variables, and for this purpose the actual values of the exogenous variables were used. The computed values of endogenous variables were reasonably close to the actual values, judged by the Theil inequality coefficients which ranged in our case from .003 to .09. Since there are no well-developed significance tests for the coefficients or for any other measure of sample period simulation within the framework of finite sample distributions, the Theil inequality coefficients are regarded as a rough test of the workability of the model.

After the sample period simulation was

done, two forecasting exercises were completed for the four and one-half years between 1970.I and 1974.I to examine how a possible competitors' reaction to the Eisai Company's advertising policy would influence the various activities of the firm. In the first forecasting simulation we assumed that the competitors' advertising activity does not respond to that of the Eisai Company. In the second forecasting simulation, we relax this assumption by introducing a "reaction function" which expresses the competitors' advertising expenditure as a function of Eisai's advertising expenditure.

First, we start with a basic forecast based on the set of exogenous variables given in Table 6. In Table 6 most of the key exogenous variables such as population, consumption, and medicare expenditure are based on the time trend of the period from 1959.I to 1968.II. The assumptions which gave rise to the exogenous variables are given under Table 6. If any other reasonable forecasts of national economy are available, one may use them instead of the time trend values.

The time trend estimate of consumption

expenditure, CE_t, gives an average growth rate of approximately 2.76 percent per half a year (or 5.6 percent per annum). The consumption expenditure has grown at an average rate of 4.1 percent per half a year (or 8.4 percent per annum) in the five years between October 1964 and September 1969. In view of this past performance of the Japanese economy, 2.76 percent per half a year may be a conservative estimate, if one supposes that the high growth rate of the late sixties is to be continued.

From the exogenous variables we have obtained the forecast values of the endogenous variables. Forecasts of industrial demand for pharmaceutical products are given in Table 7. Table 8 presents forecasts of the Eisai Company's activities and its market shares. The predicted values of other endogenous variables are summarized in Table 9.

Table 8 indicates that given the exogenous variables of Table 6, the Eisai Company will double the value of net sales in four years from 170.64 billion yen in 1970.I to 371.5 billion yen in 1974.I, indicating a rate of growth of 117.7 percent. As indicated in Table 1 in Section II, the Eisai Company grew 111 percent in the four years between 1964 and 1968. Table 8 indicates that the company can expect to grow in similar fashion in the coming four years.

However, can the company expect to maintain such a high rate of growth? In the past the company was sufficiently small and thus competitors have not been sensitive to the expansion of the Eisai Company. If the company maintains its high rate of growth by cutting into the competitors' market shares, the latter will feel it necessary to react to Eisai's sales activities.

The fact that in the past Eisai's competitors did not react much to its advertising activity may be indicated in the following regression over the sample period, 1959.II– 1969.II.

$$\Delta PRO_t = 7.2746 \ \frac{1}{G} \sum_{k=1}^{7} e^{-ak} \quad (5\text{--}1)$$
$$(5.0017)$$
$$\Delta PRE_{t-k+1} + 327.0957$$
$$(981.3894)$$

$$\bar{R}^2 = .292$$
$$a = 1.4952 \qquad \text{DW} = 1.18$$
$$(1.8401) \qquad \text{NLLS}$$

where

ΔPRO_t = increment in competitors' advertising expenditure at time t

ΔPRE_t = increment in Eisai's advertising expenditure at time t.

TABLE 7 Forecasts of Industrial Demand Based on the Set of Exogenous Variables Given in Table 8

	1970.I	1970.II	1971.I	1971.II	1972.I	1972.II	1973.I	1973.II	1974.I
x_{NS}	1.0649	1.1123	1.1626	1.2138	1.2658	1.3185	1.3719	1.4261	1.4809
x_{CR}	.6023	.6829	.7749	.8755	.9799	1.0838	1.1846	1.2814	1.3749
x_{DU}	.4737	.4997	.5239	.5473	.5703	.5932	.6162	.6393	.6626
x_V	.7159	.7420	.7683	.7946	.8212	.8478	.8746	.9015	.9285
x_{NU}	.7622	.8018	.8421	.8833	.9252	.9679	1.0114	1.0556	1.1006
x_{DER}	.2024	.2054	.2083	.2112	.2140	.2169	.2196	.2223	.2250
x_{BC}	.8074	.8379	.8699	.9024	.9351	.9681	1.0013	1.0348	1.0686
x_{OT}	.1544	.1576	.1603	.1629	.1653	.1676	.1700	.1722	.1745
X_{NS}	110206	115690	121515	127498	133615	139863	146240	152750	159389
X_{CR}	62329	71023	80999	91962	103438	114968	126271	137256	147980
X_{DU}	49019	51971	54764	57489	60201	62927	65683	68479	71317
X_V	74089	77175	80302	83471	86681	89934	93227	96562	99938
X_{NU}	78883	83391	88024	92781	97664	102671	107805	113066	118455
X_{DER}	20947	21362	21774	22185	22595	23003	23410	23816	24221
X_{BC}	83558	87146	90927	94786	98708	102694	106738	110843	115008
X_{OT}	15975	16388	16757	17107	17447	17783	18117	18449	18779
X	495006	524144	555062	587277	620349	653843	687489	721220	755087

TABLE 8 Forecasts of Eisai Activities: Net Sales and Market Shares

	1970.I	1970.II	1971.I	1971.II	1972.I	1972.II	1973.I	1973.II	1974.I
E_{NS}	4086	4359	4675	5041	5435	5865	6332	6841	7396
E_{CR}	3531	3942	4420	4968	5551	6163	6796	7453	8140
E_{DU}	2480	2593	2708	2826	2946	3070	3197	3330	3469
E_V	3965	4435	4983	5643	6408	7297	8324	9513	10891
E_{NU}	1943	2277	2640	3042	3505	4048	4678	5430	6315
E_{DER}	796	852	914	990	1083	1192	1318	1464	1631
PRE	4864	5252	5674	6165	6706	7311	7980	8728	9566
V	17064	18641	20438	22537	24848	27431	30302	33526	37151
AE	7518	8139	8798	9553	10379	11300	12322	13460	14734
Market Shares									
E_{NS}	.0371	.0377	.0385	.0395	.0407	.0419	.0433	.0448	.0464
E_{CR}	.0566	.0555	.0546	.0540	.0537	.0536	.0538	.0543	.0550
E_{DU}	.0506	.0499	.0495	.0492	.0489	.0488	.0487	.0486	.0486
E_V	.0535	.0575	.0621	.0676	.0739	.0811	.0893	.0985	.1090
E_{NU}	.0246	.0273	.0300	.0328	.0359	.0394	.0434	.0480	.0533
E_{DER}	.0380	.0399	.0420	.0446	.0479	.0518	.0563	.0615	.0674

TABLE 9 Forecast of Eisai Activities: Some Endogenous Variables in the Model

	1970.I	1970.II	1971.I	1971.II	1972.I	1972.II	1973.I	1973.II	1974.I
Raw materials, and profits (millions of current yen)									
RM	3951	4335	4811	5286	5850	6431	7137	7858	8768
IIA	1721	1755	2076	2461	2718	3120	3599	3951	4668
Wages and number of employees									
w_s	.6327	.6625	.6911	.7191	.7467	.7741	.8014	.8287	.8559
L_s	1132	1193	1275	1350	1462	1568	1697	1829	1996
L_p	761	815	884	954	1038	1125	1232	1341	1480
L_{RD}	267	285	308	331	358	385	419	454	497
L	2160	2293	2467	2645	2858	3078	3348	3624	3973
Depreciation allowances (millions of 1965 yen)									
MED	216	461	491	524	558	597	638	684	732
BLD	133	289	293	295	297	300	303	306	310
Capital formation (millions of 1965 yen)									
$NIME$	83	85	93	99	110	118	130	138	156
$GIBL$	358	355	351	351	355	361	369	377	390
$NKME$	1379	1465	1558	1657	1767	1885	2014	2152	2308
$NKBL$	2599	2628	2650	2669	2690	2714	2743	2777	2820

The estimated coefficients and the coefficient of determination adjusted for degrees of freedom are hardly significant.

However, the competitors may now tend to react strongly against Eisai's advertising activity. As an exercise, suppose that from 1970.I the competitors' advertising activity begins to react as given in (5-1). Then what will happen to Eisai's net sales and market shares? Table 10 presents the result.

From Table 10 we notice that Eisai's net sales, V, will increase by 58.9 percent in

four years from 168.1 billion yen in 1970.I to 267.0 billion yen in 1974.I, and this is a marked decline from the rate of growth of 117.7 percent as shown in Table 8. If the Eisai Company is to maintain its past high rate of growth in the face of the competitors' reaction, the company will have to increase its advertising activities. Also it will have to direct expenditure into research and development in a search for new quality products and more efficient manufacturing processes.

TABLE 10   Forecasts of Eisai ActivitiesWhen the Competitors' Advertising Expenditure Reacts to that of Eisai as Given in (5–1)

	1970.I	1970.II	1971.I	1971.II	1972.I	1972.II	1973.I	1973.II	1974.I
E_{NS}	3980	4129	4322	4507	4709	4906	5110	5317	5527
E_{CR}	3441	3750	4122	4496	4893	5268	5634	5983	6318
E_{DU}	2477	2577	2670	2754	2832	2905	2974	3042	3109
E_V	3844	4110	4417	4725	5066	5413	5777	6159	6558
E_{NU}	1931	2215	2491	2750	3019	3296	3584	3903	4343
E_{DER}	790	826	857	887	922	957	994	1034	1074
PRE	4838	5109	5415	5683	5982	6261	6543	6832	7126
V	16807	17831	19109	20240	21551	22769	24046	25360	26699
AE	7498	7965	8489	8924	9413	9863	10322	10788	11262
Market Shares									
E_{NS}	.0361	.0357	.0356	.0353	.0352	.0351	.0349	.0348	.0347
E_{CR}	.0552	.0528	.0509	.0489	.0473	.0458	.0446	.0436	.0427
E_{DU}	.0505	.0496	.0488	.0479	.0470	.0462	.0453	.0444	.0436
E_V	.0519	.0533	.0550	.0566	.0584	.0602	.0620	.0638	.0656
E_{NU}	.0245	.0266	.0283	.0296	.0309	.0321	.0332	.0345	.0358
E_{DER}	.0377	.0387	.0394	.0400	.0408	.0416	.0425	.0434	.0443

VI. CONCLUSION

Since this model (and any other existing econometric model) is built to reflect a given institutional environment, it should be revised from time to time as new information on changes in that environment becomes available.

For example, ethical and over-the-counter drugs are now aggregated in the model. If, however, the consumer behavior of the general public who purchase over-the-counter drugs becomes significantly different from the behavior of the physicians and pharmacists who buy ethical drugs, the model will have to be revised to reflect this difference. Furthermore, the overseas marketing activities and net export sales of the firm can be incorporated into the model if they become significant. In addition, as it was noted in the text, research and development expenditures should be disaggregated to reflect individual products, when more relevant data become available. The impact of these expenditures could be related to individual product sales and profits and to the overall market position of the firm.

However, for the time being, the model may be adequate for conducting strategic simulation exercises related to the present goals of the Eisai Company within the present institutional environment.

The forecast exercises presented in Section V may illustrate how a model such as ours may be used in short-, medium-, or long-range corporate planning. As shown in the exercises, the forecasted values depend largely on what kinds of exogenous variables are built into the exercise. By testing the sensitivity of endogenous target variables, such as net sales, market share, profit, manpower requirements, to assumed exogenous variables, the decision makers within a firm have a much clearer understanding of the impact of their decisions.

An exercise such as ours is not a substitute for decision makers' wisdom. Rather, it is an effective tool which can force the decision makers to become more keenly aware of the economic and social environment in which the firm is operating. By constantly examining changes taking place in the national economy and in the industry in relation to changes within the firm, the decision makers will increase their capacity for reasoned analysis in corporate planning.

REFERENCES

1. AMEMIYA, T., "Specification Analysis in the Estimation of Parameters of a Simultaneous Equation Model with Autoregressive Residuals," *Econometrica*, April 1966, pp. 283–306.

2. BOX, GEORGE E., and JENKINS, G. M., *Time Series Analysis, Forecasting and Control* (San Francisco: Holden-Day), 1970.

3. CHOW, G. C., "Technological Change and the Demand for Computers," *American Economic Review*, Vol. 57, December 1967, 1117–1130.

4. DHRYMES, P. J., *Distributed Lags* (San Francisco: Holden-Day), 1970.

5. ——, "Efficient Estimation of Distributed Lags with Autocorrelated Errors," *International Economic Review*, February 1969, pp. 47–67.

6. ——, "On Optimal Advertising Capital and Research Expenditures under Dynamic Conditions," *Economica*, August 1962, pp. 275–279.

7. ——, "On the Measurement of Price and Quality Changes in Some Consumer Capital Goods," Discussion Paper No. 67, University of Pennsylvania, 1967.

8. EISENPRESS, H., and GREENSTADT, J., "The Estimation of Nonlinear Econometric Systems," *Econometrica*, Vol. 34, October 1966, 851–861.

9. FRISCH, R., "A Complete Scheme for Computing All Direct and Cross Demand Elasticities in a Model with Many Sectors," *Econometrica*, Vol. 27, April 1959, 177–196.

10. GELFAND, I. M., and FOMIN, S. V., *Calculus of Variations* (Englewood Cliffs, N.J.; Prentice-Hall, Inc.), 1963.

11. GOLDFELD, S. M., and QUANDT, R. E., "Nonlinear Simultaneous Equations: Estimation and Prediction," *International Economic Review*, Vol. 9, February 1968, 113–136.

12. GOLDMAN, S. M., and UZAWA, H., "A Note on Separability in Demand Analysis," *Econometrica*, July 1964, pp. 387–398.

13. GRILICHES, Z., "Hedonistic Price Indexes for Automobiles: An Econometric Analysis of Quality Change," *The Price Statistics of the Federal Government*, National Bureau of Economic Research, 1961, pp. 173–196.

14. HARTLEY, H. O., and BOOKER, A., "Nonlinear Least Squares Estimation," *Annals of Mathematical Statistics*, Vol. 36, 1965, 638–650.

15. HOUTHAKKER, H. S., "Additive Preferences," *Econometrica*, Vol. 28, April 1960, 244–257.

16. JORGENSON, D. W., "Anticipations and Investment Behavior," *The Brookings Quarterly Econometric Model of the United States* (Chicago: Rand McNally & Co.), 1965, pp. 35–92.

17. KRAVIS, I. B., and LIPSEY, R. E., "International Price Comparisons by Regression Methods," *International Economic Review*, June 1969, pp. 233–246.

18. MARQUARDT, D. W., "An Algorithm for Least-Squares Estimation of Nonlinear Parameters," SIAM, *Applied Mathematics*, Vol. 11, 1963, 431–441.

19. NERLOVE, M., and ARROW, K. J., "Optimal Advertising Policy Under Dynamic Conditions," *Economica*, Vol. 39, May 1962, 129–142.

20. NERLOVE, M., and WAUGH, F. V., "Advertising Without Supply Control: Some Implications of a Study of the Advertising of Oranges," *Journal of Farm Economics*, Vol. 43, November 1961, 813–837.

21. PALDA, K. S., "The Measurement of Cumulative Advertising Effects," *Journal of Business*, Vol. 38, April 1965, 162–179.

22. SAGE, ANDREW P., *Optimal Systems Control* (Englewood Cliffs, N.J.: Prentice-Hall, Inc.), 1968.

23. SATO, KAZUO, "Additive Utility Functions with Double-Log Consumer Functions," Mimeograph, September 1969.

24. ——, "On Japan's Household Utility Function and Consumer Demand," *Keizai Kenkyu*, Vol. 21, February 1970, 10–20.

25. STROTZ, R. H., "The Utility Tree—A Correction and Further Appraisal," *Econometrica*, July 1959, pp. 482–488.

26. TELSER, L. G., "Advertising and Cigarettes," *Journal of Political Economy*, Vol. 70, October 1962, 471–499.

27. THEIL, H., *Economic Policy and Forecasts*, (Amsterdam: North-Holland), 1961.

28. TSUJIMURA, K., *Shohi Kozo to Bukka* (Consumption Structure and Prices), Tokyo, 1968.

29. TSURUMI, H., "A Note on Gamma Distributed Lags," *International Economic Review*, Vol. 12, June 1971, 317–324.

30. ——, "Nonlinear Two-Stage Least Squares Estimation of CES Production Functions Applied to the Canadian Manufacturing Industries, 1926–39, 46–67," *Review of Economics and Statistics*, Vol. 52, May 1970, 200–207.

31. ——, "An Econometric Study of Oligopolistic Competition Among American Automobile Firms, Together with a Forecast Exercise," L. R. Klein, ed., *Essays in Industrial Econometrics*, Vol. I (Philadelphia; University of Pennsylvania, 1969), pp. 29–92.

32. Tsurumi, Y., *Industrial Relations System in Japan*, Graduate School of Business Administration, Harvard University, April 1966, ICH Catalogue No. 11G 1.

33. Wald, A., "Notes on the Consistency of the Maximum Likelihood Estimate," *Annals of Mathematical Statistics*, Vol. 20, 1949, 595–601.

29

Agfa-Gevaert: Merger or Partnership?

THE ECONOMIST

Dunlop-Pirelli is not the first European cross-frontier merger. . . . Shell and Unilever are the classic examples. But they were conceived not so much in European terms but rather as mergers between global companies whose headquarters happened to be in Britain and the Netherlands. There are only two parallel precedents for a cross-frontier merger intended to create a European-scale organisation. One happened only last year. This was the deal between the Dutch aircraft company, Fokker, and the German Vereinigte Flugtechnische Werke (VFW). The other is a more instructive case study: the 1964 merger between Agfa and Gevaert.

Nobody disputes the urgent need for European mergers across frontiers. The urgency is provided by the threat of American business, or, more precisely, American business in Europe. American business is ahead on technology and management. And it is bigger. Therefore if European industry is to hold its own in technologically advanced industries its industrial units must be big too. Yet to have, say, one big German producer, one big French one and so on in each industry would only mean muted competi-

From The Economist (*March 7, 1970*), *pp. 52–53.*
Reprinted with permission of the publisher.

tion within the EEC itself—because of non-tariff barriers within the area, like preferential buying by national governments. Even then the units might not be big enough. Hence the inescapable need for mergers to take place across internal European frontiers.

Unfortunately a cross-frontier European merger entails a host of legal, fiscal and psychological complications. To circumvent these in the early days of the EEC the idea of the "European company" was mooted, a new sort of company incorporated under a special section of company law applying equally in all common market countries. But nothing has been done to implement the 1966 proposals of the group of legal experts headed by the Dutchman, Professor Pieter Sanders.

There are some weighty problems to be solved first. Any European company statute would inevitably be either more or less attractive than the law governing companies in individual countries. If it is more attractive, firms will flock to become "Europeanised," so the question will arise of who should be eligible for European company status. If it is worse, firms will not opt for it, so the whole object of the exercise will be lost. As long as tax systems are not har-

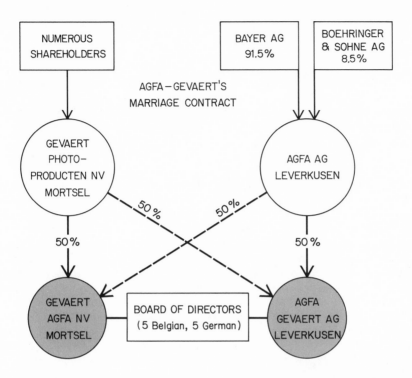

AGFA – GEVAERT'S
MARRIAGE CONTRACT

monised, how should supranational companies be taxed?

The rationale behind the Agfa-Gevaert deal was not pan-European ideology, but straight economics. The German company Agfa, 90% owned by the vast chemicals group Bayer, is known mainly for its amateur photographic products. Gevaert, the Belgian partner, specialises in technical photographic products for industrial and business use. Both were operating in a world market dominated 55% to 60% by the American Kodak. Although both were number two in their respective fields, with very much higher market shares than their worldwide average in some European countries, neither of them could hope to compete with the vast sums Kodak could afford to spend on research and development—a prerequisite for survival in the fast-moving technology game. Both companies were already co-operating in the field of office copying where they had independently made similar discoveries in the early 1950s. The merger would give them a joint world market share of 10% to 12%, with a combined research budget which, after cutting out duplication, could put up a more useful showing against Kodak. And there would obviously be economies from the streamlining of overseas distribution.

Once the basic decision for a merger had been made, the organisational details had to be sorted out. For a merger in the legal sense either one or the other of the two companies would have had to transfer its registered offices to the other country. Under both West German and Belgian laws, this is only possible by liquidating the company in the country of origin and reconstituting it in the country of destination—a procedure both inconvenient and expensive in terms of legal fees, and tax bills upon liquidation and re-registration. For Gevaert there was the added complication that under Belgian law a company can only move outside the country with the unanimous approval of all the shareholders. As the Gevaert holdings are split up among thousands of small shareholders, the prospects for getting consent for a move from every one of them were very dim.

PSYCHOLOGICAL FACTORS

Legal and fiscal problems aside, a takeover by either company would have been psychologically unacceptable to the other side. Both firms were household names in their respective countries; the disappearance of either through absorption by a firm of another nationality would have been bitterly resented.

After close study of the Shell and Unilever precedents, the partners-to-be decided on a cross-holding structure, with the two parents becoming holding companies with a 50% stake in each of the two newly set up operating companies, Agfa-Gevaert AG in Germany and Gevaert-Agfa NV in Belgium, and an identical board of directors made up of equal numbers of each nationality. The new set-up did require a rough premerger parity of size between the two companies. Agfa, the smaller of the two, solved this problem by absorbing several smaller German photographic companies (Perutz, Mimosa and Leonar).

Within the present European legal company framework, this double holding company system is the nearest anyone can get to a transnational merger. Even under this arrangement, Agfa-Gevaert was nominally laying itself open to a prosecution under article 85 of the Treaty of Rome which deals with cartel agreements between companies. But this was a calculated risk. In any case in 1964, at the time of the merger, a European company statute looked much more imminent than it has turned out to be, and Agfa-Gevaert expected to be able to switch out of its dual set-up within a very few years. For ingenious as the cross-over structure may be, it is also clumsy and must slow up the process of decision-making.

One very big point in favour of the merger was the degree to which products of the two companies were complementary. Agfa had been specialising in the amateur photo-

graphic field, Gevaert in the technical and industrial sector. Each of them had 70% or 80% of its turnover from its respective speciality. The postmerger policy adopted was to push this product specialisation as far as it would go. As a result of the main reorganisation—which was kept deliberately brief, to a maximum of two years—the percentage of speciality production for both companies went up to 95%, after a fairly ruthless pruning of the product ranges. This compartmentalisation has made it possible to run each company very much as an independent unit, with a minimum of contact and personnel integration between the two.

Cutting out duplication has saved money. But it has also lost sales where customers refused to switch to the alternative offered after their usual product had been discontinued. The new policy was to retain the Agfa name for all amateur products in order to capitalise on the goodwill built up and the past expenditure on consumer advertising; and to keep the Gevaert label for X-ray films, office copying equipment, microfilm and other technical and industrial products. Even so, integration meant a welter of small problems, such as redesigning packages, where Agfa's orange colour was gradually changed to Gevaert's red over a period of two years so no one would notice the difference. And there were the larger problems of dovetailing overseas operations; together, the two companies had been operating in 144 countries, with a fair amount of duplication. This is one area where the merger has produced some striking savings. The companies' combined cost of operations outside Benelux and Germany (principally selling and distribution costs) is now some 10% lower than at the time of the merger, at the price of some 400 redundancies.

But at home, just how well has the merger worked? Has it produced enough of the economies and benefits to justify the disruption it caused? The consolidated balance sheet of the two companies shows no staggering increases in turnover, even after an initial adjustment period of two or three years. Sales in the last few years have risen by around 5% a year, while profits have been drooping, both because of a reduction in gross profit and a hefty rise in depreciation.

But the merger can hardly be blamed for this. The group exports about two-thirds of its production outside Germany and the Benelux countries. So it is highly sensitive to changes in exchange rates. Last year's German revaluation is reckoned to cost about £1mn in a full year, or virtually as much as last year's profit. And the recent silver crisis added an extra £3 mn or so to costs in 1967–68. The results for the current year, expected this month, should be brighter than for the last few years, partly because the silver

situation has calmed down and partly because most customer countries have lately enjoyed economic boom conditions which have helped sales. Agfa-Gevaert's market share vis-à-vis Kodak has failed to expand. But then it could be argued that the merger was a defensive move without which Agfa-Gevaert's share would have contracted.

PROBLEMS AHEAD?

At the moment both the Belgian and the German halves of the group seem enthusiastic about the success of the combination.

FIG. 2

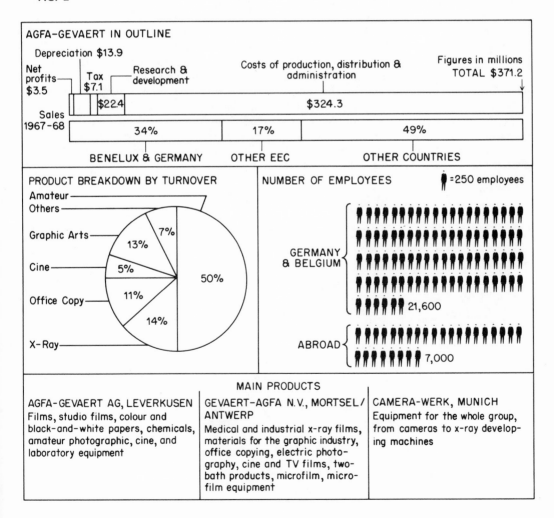

But there could be problems ahead. Under the 50-50 set-up profits are pooled and then divided equally between the two halves. This is fine as long as the two halves contribute a roughly equal amount, but it could become a source of friction once they don't. Already the burden of corporate taxation weighs a lot more heavily on the German than on the Belgian partner, at about 65% of gross profits as opposed to about 40%. And neat though the division of the two halves by product groups may look at the moment, this too could become a future source of trouble. For while the amateur photographic market is now saturated and will continue to grow only slowly, technical and industrial products will expand in leaps and bounds over the next few years. If the strict division is to be maintained, this could in the long run lead to imbalances between the two operating companies. And it has not been possible to integrate the still largely distinct management structures of the two operating companies, except in the finely balanced boardroom, and overseas. In some ways Agfa-Gevaert still resembles a co-operation deal between two independent firms, for product specialisation and merging overseas operations. Agfa-Gevaert executives express surprise that other companies have not followed their transnational example. But observers—the common market commission for one, which has a more than academic interest in the matter—can think of a number of reasons. Given the present legal framework, this sort of merger needs a fairly special set of circumstances, and not many companies fit the bill, textbook fashion, as Agfa and Gevaert did. Once Agfa had absorbed the smaller German photographic interests, both companies were roughly equal in size; they were already working together; their products complemented each other to an unusual degree; and they were geographically close enough to make frequent consultation in person possible.

Dunlop–Pirelli does not fit the bill nearly so neatly. For this reason the progress of its merger will be a more instructive pointer to the scope for cross-frontier mergers within Europe. If full integration proves difficult it will confirm the current view, that, by and large, until a suitable legal and organisational framework for international mergers has been developed and tax harmonisation has gone a great deal further, the few companies with a genuinely multi-national base will remain much-quoted examples—but special cases.